Social Interaction

READINGS IN SOCIOLOGY

SECOND EDITION

Social Interaction

READINGS IN SOCIOLOGY

SECOND EDITION

Edited by **HOWARD ROBBOY**
Trenton State College
CANDACE CLARK
Fairleigh Dickinson University,
Rutherford

St. Martin's Press   New York

To Our Parents

For information, write St. Martin's Press, Inc.,
175 Fifth Avenue, New York, New York 10010

book design: Judith Woracek

ISBN: 0-312-73299-6

Acknowledgments

Lynn Atwater: "Women and Marriage: Adding an Extramarital Role" was written for the first edition of *Social Interaction.*

Gary L. Albrecht: "Defusing Technological Change in Juvenile Courts: The Probation Officer's Struggle for Professional Autonomy," *Sociology of Work and Occupations*, Vol. 6, No. 3, pp. 259–282 (with deletions). Reprinted by permission of Sage Publications, Inc. and the author.

Roy L. Askins, Timothy J. Carter, and Michael Wood: "Rule Enforcement in a Public Setting: The Case of Basketball Officiating," *Qualitative Sociology*, Vol. 4, No. 2 (Summer 1981), pp. 87–101 (with deletions). Copyright © 1981 by Human Sciences Press, 72 Fifth Avenue, New York, N. Y. 10011. Reprinted by permission of the publisher and the authors.

Howard S. Becker and Blanche Geer: "The Fate of Idealism in Medical School," *American Sociological Review*, Vol. 23 (February 1958), pp. 50–56. Reprinted by permission of the American Sociological Association and the authors.

Acknowledgments and copyrights continue at the back of the book on pages 591–593, which constitute an extension of the copyright page.

Contents

Part VIII. Interaction in Institutional Contexts

Part IX. Social and Cultural Change

Correlation Chart For Social Interaction and Standard Sociology Texts

Part (part #)	Babbie 2/e (1980)	Babbie (1982)	Broom & Selznick 7/e (1981)	DeFleur, D'Antonio, DeFleur 3/e (1981)	Federico 2/e (1979)	Grenblat 4/e (1981)	Hess, Markson, and Stein (1982)	Horton & Hunt 5/e (1980)	Landis 4/e (1980)	Light & Keller 3/e (1982)	McGee 2/e (1980)	Popenoe 4/e (1980)	Ritzer, Kammeyer, Yetman 2/e (1982)	Robertson 2/e (1981)	Rose, Glazer, and Glazer 2/e (1982)	Shepard (1981)	Smelser (1981)	Smith & Preston 2/e (1982)	Spencer 3/e (1982)	Stewart 2/e (1981)	Turner 2/e (1981)	Van der Zanden 4/e (1979)	Westhues (1982)
INTRODUCTION (I)	1, 2, 3	1, 2	1, 2	1, 2	1	1, 2	1, 2	1, 2	1, 12	1, 2	1, 2	1, 2	1	1, 2	1, 2	1, 2	1	1, 2	1, 2	1, 2	1, 2, 3	1	1, 2
CULTURE (II)	4	3	3	4	2	3	3	3, 4	3	3	3, 19	5	2	3	2, 3	3	8	3	3	3	5	2	
TRANSMISSION OF CULTURE: SOCIALIZATION (III)	5	4	4	6	3	5	5	5	2	5	4	6	5	5	5, 7	5	2	4	5	4	8	3	4
INTERACTION IN EVERYDAY LIFE (IV)				3							5	3		6	4		3		4		6	4	4
SOCIAL ORGANIZATION: FROM PRIMARY GROUP TO SOCIETY (V)	7, 8, 16	5, 12	5, 6, 17	3, 5, 13	4, 17	4, 7, 15, 16	4, 16	6, 9, 19	4, 8	4, 7, 8, 16	6, 10	4, 10, 17	3, 8, 11	7, 20		4, 6, 15	5, 6, 7, 18	5, 6, 7, 18	7, 17	5, 17	7, 10, 11, 22	5, 16	3

Topic																							
INEQUALITIES (VI)	5	8, 9, 10	13, 14, 15, 16, 20	6, 7, 8, 14	6, 9, 10, 11	8, 9, 10, 14	9, 10, 11, 12, 17	8, 9, 10, 13	9, 10, 11	10, 11, 12, 13	6, 9, 12, 17	7, 8, 11, 12, 16	7, 8, 14	6, 10, 11, 12	5, 6	7, 15, 16, 17	7, 8, 9, 10, 13	8, 9, 10	7, 16	8, 9, 10, 18	8, 9, 10, 11, 16	8, 9	9, 10, 11, 14
DEVIANCE, CONFORMITY, AND SOCIAL CONTROL (VII)	10	6	9	9	8	15	4	7	14	8	7	9	16	9	11	8	6, 17	6	8	7, 18	7, 15	10	6
INTERACTION IN INSTITUTIONAL CONTEXTS: FAMILY (VIIIA)	8	12	17	11	12	11	13	11	8	14	13	13	11	13	7	11	11	11	12	15	12	6	12
INTERACTION IN INSTITUTIONAL CONTEXTS: EDUCATION (VIIIB)	9	15	21	12	14	13	14	12	9	15	14	14	12	14		13	14	13	14	17	13	7	
INTERACTION IN INSTITUTIONAL CONTEXTS: WORK AND ECONOMICS (VIIIC)	6	14	19	16		16	16		6, 9	18	15	15	15				12	14	15				
INTERACTION IN INSTITUTIONAL CONTEXTS: RELIGION (VIIID)	7	13	18	13	13, 15	12	15	14	9	16	16	15	13	15	12	12	15	12	13	16	14	7	13
SOCIAL AND CULTURAL CHANGE (IX)		6	23, 24	10, 19	19, 20	19, 20	19, 20	17	15	22, 23	4	18, 19, 20	17, 18	18, 19	9, 10	18, 20, 21	19, 20	17, 18	18	11, 12, 14	19	11, 13	18, 19

Preface

THIS SECOND EDITION OF *SOCIAL INTERACTION* IS A MUCH REVISED VERSION OF THE first edition published in 1979. Half of the articles in this volume are new to this edition, and many of those retained have been edited to make them more accessible and readable. Also, we have reorganized the sections to provide a more logical sequence of topics and to reflect more clearly the major substantive issues within the discipline of sociology. Finally, we have added review questions at the end of each article.

The revision of *Social Interaction* has been a labor of love. In some ways we feel like disc jockeys playing their favorite recordings on the air. Some of the articles here are ones we read when we were beginning sociologists, articles that led us to reexamine our taken-for-granted perspectives on the social world. Although these "oldies but goodies" may have been written decades ago, the sociological principles they illustrate are timeless. The streetcorner boys studied by William Foote Whyte in the 1930's may be grandfathers by now, and the newer generation may not join athletic clubs and "hang out" in same-sex groups on the street, but the group processes discovered in this setting continue to operate everywhere around us.

The new articles will, we hope, become favorites as well. We have tried to uncover new material that is more than mere journalistic illustration of the concepts introduced in the standard texts—material that is illustrative but that also adds something conceptually and theoretically on its own. We hope the result is a collection that will prove interesting for the professor as well as for the student.

The intellectual roots of this volume are, broadly speaking, in the symbolic interactionist tradition of George Herbert Mead. Our theme is perhaps best summarized in Herbert Blumer's words: "Society is symbolic interaction." The pieces include works by those closely allied with the symbolic-interactionist school—for example, Gregory P. Stone, Erving Goffman, Donald Roy, Howard S. Becker, John Lofland, Julius Roth, and others. We have also incorporated pieces that illustrate symbolic interactionism in a wider context. G. William Domhoff's research into the summer retreats of the wealthy and powerful, Rosabeth Moss Kanter's research on the importance of sex-role definitions in the organization of modern corporations, and Candace Clark's review essay on the process and consequences of the expansion of medical models as explanations of human behavior—all of these aim to link symbols and social interaction to macro-level processes and events.

Women, both as subjects of research and as authors, are integrated throughout the various parts of the volume, rather than being relegated to a single section. If women hold up more than half the sky, as the Chinese saying goes, they deserve more than a tiny proportion of the attention of sociologists. The women authors included here are Lynn Atwater, Sandra Bem, Candace Clark, Rose Laub Coser, Blanche Geer, Rosabeth Moss Kanter, Janet Lever, Kristine Rosenthal, Lucinda SanGiovanni, Pepper Schwartz, Carol Stack, and Diane Vaughan.

Many people have been helpful in guiding the development of this book. We appreciate the assistance of Ellen Boshko in selecting and editing articles and devising review questions. Colleagues especially helpful include Lynn Atwater, Regina Kenen, and Robert J. Anderson. We also appreciate the editorial help of Carol Ewig at St. Martin's Press. Her calm, disciplined presence smoothed the way for us. Walter Kossmann proved to be an ideal editor, helpful at all stages yet allowing us great freedom. We also wish to thank Bob Woodbury, whose efforts laid the groundwork for this edition. Finally, the suggestions of the following critics aided us in the process of finding new articles, eliminating some old ones, and strengthening the introductory materials: G. Thomas Behler, Jr., Moravian College; Jerry G. Bode, Ball State University; Maria E. Carrion, Boston University; Robert E. Davidson, University of Texas—San Antonio; V. Aileen Hall, Ohio University; Jill H. Kasen, California State College—San Bernardino; Judith A. Levy, University of Illinois—School of Public Health; Earl C. Nance, Rockford College; John H. Strength, Jr., San Antonio College; Andrew C. Twaddle, University of Missouri; Shirley Varmette, Southern Connecticut State College; and Alan Woolfolk, Southern Methodist University.

Since the publication of the first edition of *Social Interaction*, Erving Goffman, Gregory P. Stone, Donald F. Roy, and Werner J. Cahnman have died. Although their work remains with us, we shall miss them.

Howard Robboy
Candace Clark

Social Interaction

READINGS IN
SOCIOLOGY

SECOND EDITION

Part I. Introduction

As PARTICIPANTS IN THE WORLD OF HUMAN INTERACTION, WE TAKE MUCH OF OUR social experience for granted. We move from group to group—family, friends, strangers; in classrooms, in stores, in the workplace—unconcerned with the amazing complexity of human activity. We pay as little attention to what goes on beneath the surface of social activity as we do to the inner workings of the telephone or the automobile.

But the electronics technician and the automobile mechanic know that inside the telephone or under the hood of the car lies intricate machinery. In much the same way, the student of sociology learns to peer beneath the veneer of conventional understanding to take a systematic look at the patterns and processes of our daily lives. Sociology is, then, a unique way of viewing the human world that enables us to achieve an awareness of the complex interaction of society.

In this volume we have collected readings from articles and books that we, and especially our students, have found to be exciting and challenging explorations beneath the surface of social life. The readings analyze human relationships taking place in small groups and huge bureaucracies; report on investigations set in private homes, public offices, and street-corner shops; and consider important social processes—cooperation, conflict, socialization, and social change.

In the first selection, Peter Berger welcomes us to the sociological perspective. He examines the special meanings to sociology of the terms "society" and "social." *Society*, according to Berger, can be defined as "a large complex of human relationships," "a system of interaction." A society is not necessarily comprised of large numbers of interacting people; rather, a society is any relatively self-contained, autonomous system. The term *social* is used by sociologists to refer to actions which are oriented toward others. Thus, social interaction refers to those aspects of all types of human behavior which involve an awareness of other human beings.

Further, Berger delineates four major sociological themes, or motifs. When used together, these motifs allow us to view the world through sociological "lenses," thereby gaining increased insight into the workings of the social world. The first theme is that of *debunking* many myths that societal members hold. Social scientists cannot be so naive as to accept at face value the common explanations of how things work; they must question these very explanations and gather evidence to determine their accuracy or inaccuracy.

1

The second motif which Berger describes is that of paying attention to aspects of the social world that would be considered *unrespectable* by many middle-class members of society. Only by looking at criminals, the poor, minorities, and the like, can we gain a complete picture of our world. "Respectable" citizens often describe the world in ways which protect and justify their own behavior. Also, their experiences with the system are not the same as the experiences of the "unrespectable." We need both viewpoints. For instance, a presidential commission studying the causes of widespread rioting in the mid-1960s included testimony of city officials *and* interviews with the residents of poor neighborhoods where rioting occurred. Their conclusion was that, contrary to the officials' views, societal racism (in which the officials themselves played a part) was responsible for the conditions which sparked the violence. In another vein, sociologists who have attempted to understand the failure of our prison system to rehabilitate criminals have paid as much attention to the prisoners' descriptions of prison life and how it affects them as to the statements of guards and wardens.

Third, sociologists must always keep in mind the *relativity* of social values and beliefs. By this is meant that standards of "right" and "wrong," as well as opinions and even "knowledge," can be understood fully only within the context of a given society at a given time. What is considered appropriate behavior, or truth, or evil in one society at one historical moment, may be considered inappropriate behavior, or falsehood, or good in another. Values are, therefore, *relative* to the society under study, rather than being absolute or universal. The sociologist will not be able to understand what a value or belief *means to those who hold it* unless he or she maintains awareness of the principle of relativity.

Fourth, Berger discusses the *cosmopolitan* motif in sociological thought. Rather than being oriented strictly toward local issues and concerns, sociologists have generally been oriented toward other lands, other peoples, other ways of life and world views.

Of course, these four motifs are interrelated and mutually reinforcing; they are the essence of the "sociological imagination." As you read Berger's explanations of them, and the articles that follow, you too will start to view human interaction from the sociological perspective. Berger also notes that the sociologist works by making "inquisitive intrusions" beyond the facades of social life. Above all, sociology is an *empirical* study of human interaction, which means that it rests on *research* and *observation* of the social world rather than on prior assumptions or hunches about how society works. Research takes many forms for sociologists, but all forms involve searching for evidence that will help us discover the abstract patterns operating behind the facades. These forms include the *survey*, in which a series of predetermined questions is put to a large sample of people in order to get the same kinds of information about all of them in a relatively short period of time. A survey can be very short and focused—as with Gallup polls of voters' intentions—or longer and more encompassing—as with studies of life styles, aspirations, attitudes, and the like.

Participant observation is another commonly used method of getting information about social behavior. The researcher actually becomes involved as a member of the group or situation under study, in order to gain clearer insights into the meanings that people give to their behavior and to absorb more of the flavor of the lives of those under study.

With *intensive interviews*, the sociologist begins with a brief, open-ended interview schedule that allows him or her to delve and probe into the life situations of those chosen for research, while at the same time allowing the respondent to answer in his or her own words and to explain the answers in detail.

The *classical experiment* is seldom used in sociology, because many human characteristics and patterns of behavior cannot be dictated or altered by the researcher. In a true experiment, the researcher must begin with at least two groups—the *experimental* group and the *control* group—which are identical in all ways considered relevant for the purpose at hand. The experimental group must then be manipulated by the experimenter; that is, some "treatment," such as an educational program, a frightening film, or additional income, must be administered to the *experimental group only*. Any changes found within this group are then compared to developments within the control group. *If* the groups were in fact identical to begin with, and if the experimental group changed more than the control group, we then infer that the treatment caused those changes. In reality, it is often difficult to say that the two groups were identical. Furthermore, many of the factors that we might expect to cause differences in people's lives—for instance, being born poor or black—cannot easily or ethically be introduced by the experimenter as treatments. Thus, we rely often on other research methods, such as the survey or participant observation. With these methods, we can look at *existing* differences among people (whether they are poor or well off, for example) to see if these differences are related to other factors (such as whether they can afford to attend college).

Using *unobtrusive measures* involves looking for *traces* of human actions and interactions without having to deal directly with those people under study. For example, one way of getting evidence about drinking patterns without asking people how much they drink is to observe the number of empty bottles thrown away. Researchers have determined which museum exhibits are more popular by counting noseprints that accumulate on the glass enclosures. Documentary evidence of how people feel and act can be found in magazine stories, advertisements, newspaper editorials, telephone directories, and the like.

All of the methods listed here except unobtrusive measures are *reactive*. By this we mean that the researcher must interact with those being studied, and the researcher's mere presence may cause others to *react* in ways that are not typical or completely truthful. Research involving humans is, therefore, necessarily subject to unique problems that chemists and physicists do not face. The research encounter itself is a type of interaction, and that interaction is based on informal, unwritten rules for how to act as, say, an "interviewer" and an "interviewee." Of course, this fact may cause us to question the validity, or accuracy, of research findings. No research method or technique is perfect, and we should be aware of likely flaws of various methods so that we can become critical consumers of information.

The last two articles in Part I alert us to problems of reactivity and other sources of error in survey research and experimental research. Julius Roth, in "Hired Hand Research," shows us the problems that may result when people other than the principal researcher are hired to interview, to observe, to code, and/or to tabulate information. Of course, an argument could also be presented that principal researchers may "find" what they want or expect to find because they are so closely and personally involved with the topics they are studying. Thus, we may trade one source of inaccuracy for another when we do research ourselves instead of hiring helpers.

Martin Orne's widely regarded work on the expectations, or *demand characteristics*, of the experiment demonstrates that informal norms about how to be a "good subject" interfere with the collection of accurate data. In other words, experimental subjects may behave in very different ways while they are "in the laboratory" than when they are in their everyday interactional situations. Findings from such experiments may, therefore, have "validity" only in the "ecological" context of the lab and may *not be generalized* from the laboratory to other situations.

There are several themes introduced in this section that will recur again and again. First, as we noted earlier, societal members are generally unaware of *patterned regularities* and *processes* of beliefs and behavior that exist in their society. Second, when members of a society attempt to make sense of their social world, creating explanations for various events and phenomena, their explanations are often *wrong*. This is so because they do not have the time, the inclination, or the expertise to gather information appropriate for making valid observations and interpretations. Thus, *myths* continue to exist in abundance.

A third theme that you will encounter here many times is the importance of *social interaction* for determining how we define the world, what we think of ourselves, and how we behave. By learning the symbols of our culture from those with whom we interact, we come to share in a common understanding of reality. Despite the fact that we in the United States have learned to think of ourselves as unique individuals who exercise "free will" to determine our own thoughts and behavior, in reality our interactions with others in various settings and situations are constantly constraining both our thoughts and actions. All you need to do to convince yourself of the validity of this point is to imagine what your thoughts, values, opinions, and actions would be if you had been born into a different society—say, in Japan, in Iran, in South America, or in the Italian communities described by Eames and Robboy in Part II of this reader. All of these societies or subsocieties allow for *some* personal discretion in thought and behavior; but at the same time, all have definitions of reality, values, symbolic universes, and mechanisms of social control that shape those who happen to be born there (or who migrate there) at almost every turn. The very alternatives available to us are limited in number. And our "choices" among these alternatives are influenced by others with whom we interact, from parents to teachers to co-workers to police.

SOCIOLOGY AS A FORM OF CONSCIOUSNESS

Peter L. Berger

. . . SOCIOLOGY IS NEITHER A TIMELESS NOR A NECESSARY UNDERTAKING OF THE human mind. If this is conceded, the question logically arises as to the timely factors that made it a necessity to specific men. Perhaps, indeed, no intellectual enterprise is timeless or necessary. But religion, for instance, has been well-nigh universal in provoking intensive mental preoccupation throughout human history, while thoughts designed to solve the economic problems of existence have been a necessity in most human cultures. Certainly this does not mean that theology or economics . . . are universally present phenomena of the mind, but we are at least on safe ground if we say that there always seems to have been human thought directed towards the problems that now constitute the subject matter of these disciplines. Not even this much, however, can be said of sociology. It presents itself rather as a peculiarly modern and Western cogitation. And, as we shall try to argue [here], it is constituted by a peculiarly modern form of consciousness.

The peculiarity of sociological perspective becomes clear with some reflection concerning the meaning of the term "society," a term that refers to the object *par excellence* of the discipline. Like most terms used by sociologists, this one is derived from common usage, where its meaning is imprecise. Sometimes it means a particular band of people (as in "Society for the Prevention of Cruelty to Animals"), sometimes only those people endowed with great prestige or privilege (as in "Boston society ladies"), and on other occasions it is simply used to denote company of any sort (for example, "he greatly suffered in those years for lack of society"). There are other, less frequent meanings as well. The sociologist uses the term in a more precise sense, though, of course, there are differences in usage within the discipline itself. The sociologist thinks of "society" as denoting a large complex of human relationships, or to put it in more technical language, as referring to a system of interaction. The word "large" is difficult to specify quantitatively in this context. The sociologist may speak of a "society" including millions of human beings (say, "American society"), but he may also use the term to refer to a numerically much smaller collectivity (say, "the society of sophomores on this campus"). Two people chatting on a street corner will hardly constitute a "society," but three people stranded on an island certainly will. The applicability of the concept, then, cannot be decided on quantitative

Peter L. Berger, *Invitation to Sociology: A Humanist Perspective*. Garden City, N.Y.: Anchor Books, 1963, pp. 25–53.

grounds alone. It rather applies when a complex of relationships is sufficiently succinct to be analyzed by itself, understood as an autonomous entity, set against others of the same kind.

The adjective "social" must be similarly sharpened for sociological use. In common speech it may denote, once more, a number of different things— the informal quality of a certain gathering ("this is a social meeting—let's not discuss business"), an altruistic attitude on somebody's part ("he had a strong social concern in his job"), or, more generally, anything derived from contact with other people ("a social disease"). The sociologist will use the term more narrowly and more precisely to refer to the quality of interaction, interrelationship, mutuality. Thus two men chatting on a street corner do not constitute a "society," but what transpires between them is certainly "social." "Society" consists of a complex of such "social" events. As to the exact definition of the "social," it is difficult to improve on Max Weber's definition of a "social" situation as one in which people orient their actions towards one another. The web of meanings, expectations and conduct resulting from such mutual orientation is the stuff of sociological analysis.

Yet this refinement of terminology is not enough to show up the distinctiveness of the sociological angle of vision. We may get close by comparing the latter with the perspective of other disciplines concerned with human actions. The economist, for example, is concerned with the analyses of processes that occur in society and that can be described as social. These processes have to do with the basic problem of economic activity—the allocation of scarce goods and services within a society. The economist will be concerned with these processes in terms of the way in which they carry out, or fail to carry out, this function. The sociologist, in looking at the same processes, will naturally have to take into consideration their economic purpose. But his distinctive interest is not necessarily related to this purpose as such. He will be interested in a variety of human relationships and interactions that may occur here and that may be quite irrelevant to the economic goals in question. Thus economic activity involves relationships of power, prestige, prejudice or even play that can be analyzed with only marginal reference to the properly economic function of the activity.

The sociologist finds his subject matter present in all human activities, but not all aspects of these activities constitute this subject matter. Social interaction is not some specialized sector of what men do with each other. It is rather a certain aspect of all these doings. Another way of putting this is by saying that the sociologist carries on a special sort of abstraction. The social, as an object of inquiry, is not a segregated field of human activity. Rather (to borrow a phrase from Lutheran sacramental theology) it is present "in, with and under" many different fields of such activity. The sociologist does not look at phenomena that nobody else is aware of. But he looks at the same phenomena in a different way.

As a further example we could take the perspective of the lawyer. Here we actually find a point of view much broader in scope than that of the economist. Almost any human activity can, at one time or another, fall within the province of the lawyer. This, indeed, is the fascination of the law. Again, we find here a very special procedure of abstraction. From the immense wealth and variety of human deportment the lawyer selects those aspects that are pertinent (or, as he would say, "material") to his very particular frame of reference. As anyone who has ever been involved in a lawsuit well knows, the criteria of what is relevant or irrelevant legally will often greatly surprise the principals in the case in question. This need not concern us here. We would rather observe that the legal frame of reference consists of a number of carefully defined models of human activity. Thus we have clear models of obligation, responsibility or wrongdoing. Definite conditions have to prevail before any empirical act can be subsumed under one of these headings, and these conditions are laid down by statutes or precedent. When these conditions are not met, the act in question is legally irrelevant. The expertise of the lawyer consists of knowing the rules by which these models are constructed. He knows, within his frame of reference, when a business contract is binding, when the driver of an automobile may be held to be negligent, or when rape has taken place.

The sociologist may look at these same phenomena, but his frame of reference will be quite different. Most importantly, his perspective on these phenomena cannot be derived from statutes or precedent. His interest in the human relationships occurring in a business transaction has no bearing on the legal validity of contracts signed, just as sociologically interesting deviance in sexual behavior may not be capable of being subsumed under some particular legal heading. From the lawyer's point of view, the sociologist's inquiry is extraneous to the legal frame of reference. One might say that, with reference to the conceptual edifice of the law, the sociologist's activity is subterranean in character. The lawyer is concerned with what may be called the official conception of the situation. The sociologist often deals with very unofficial conceptions indeed. For the lawyer the essential thing to understand is how the law looks upon a certain type of criminal. For the sociologist it is equally important to see how the criminal looks at the law.

To ask sociological questions, then, presupposes that one is interested in looking some distance beyond the commonly accepted or officially defined goals of human actions. It presupposes a certain awareness that human events have different levels of meaning, some of which are hidden from the consciousness of everyday life. It may even presuppose a measure of suspicion about the way in which human events are officially interpreted by the authorities, be they political, juridical or religious in character. If one is willing to go as far as that, it would seem evident that not all historical circumstances are equally favorable for the development of sociological perspective.

It would appear plausible, in consequence, that sociological thought would have the best chance to develop in historical circumstances marked by severe jolts to the self-conception, especially the official and authoritative and generally accepted self-conception, of a culture. It is only in such circumstances that perceptive men are likely to be motivated to think beyond the assertions of this self-conception and, as a result, question the authorities. . . . It was with the disintegration of [Christendom and feudalism and the emergence of urban, industrial states] that the underlying frame of "society" came into view—that is, a world of motives and forces that could not be understood in terms of the official interpretations of social reality. Sociological perspective can then be understood in terms of such phrases as "seeing through" "looking behind," very much as such phrases would be employed in common speech—"seeing through his game," "looking behind the scenes"—in other words, "being up on all the tricks."

We will not be far off if we see sociological thought as part of what Nietzsche called "the art of mistrust." Now, it would be a gross oversimplification to think that this art has existed only in modern times. "Seeing through" things is probably a pretty general function of intelligence, even in very primitive societies. The American anthropologist Paul Radin has provided us with a vivid description of the skeptic as a human type in primitive culture. We also have evidence from civilizations other than that of the modern West, bearing witness to forms of consciousness that could well be called protosociological. We could point, for instance, to Herodotus or to Ibn-Khaldun. There are even texts from ancient Egypt envincing a profound disenchantment with a political and social order that has acquired the reputation of having been one of the most cohesive in human history. However, with the beginning of the modern era in the West this form of consciousness intensifies, becomes concentrated and systematized, marks the thought of an increasing number of perceptive men. This is not the place to discuss in detail the prehistory of sociological thought. . . . Suffice it to stress once more that sociological thought marks the fruition of a number of intellectual developments that have a very specific location in modern Western history.

Let us return instead to the proposition that sociological perspective involves a process of "seeing through" the facades of social structures. We could think of this in terms of a common experience of people living in large cities. One of the fascinations of a large city is the immense variety of human activities taking place behind the seemingly anonymous and endlessly undifferentiated rows of houses. A person who lives in such a city will time and again experience surprise or even shock as he discovers the strange pursuits that some men engage in quite unobtrusively in houses that, from the outside, look like all the others on a certain street. Having had this experience once or twice, one will repeatedly find oneself walking down a street, perhaps late in the evening, and wondering what may be going on under the bright lights showing through a line of drawn curtains. An ordinary family engaged in pleasant talk with guests? A scene of desperation amid illness or death? Or a scene of debauched pleasures? Perhaps a strange cult or a dangerous conspiracy? The facades of the houses cannot tell us, proclaiming nothing but an architectural conformity to the tastes of some group or class that may not even inhabit the street any longer. The social mysteries lie behind the facades. The wish to penetrate to these mysteries is [analogous] to sociological curiosity. In some cities that are suddenly struck by calamity this wish may be abruptly realized. Those who have experienced wartime bombings know of the sudden encounters with unsuspected (and sometimes unimaginable) fellow tenants in the air-raid shelter of one's apartment building. Or they can recollect the startling morning sight of a house hit by a bomb during the night, neatly sliced in half, the facade torn away and the previously hidden interior mercilessly revealed in the daylight. But in most cities that one may normally live in, the facades must be penetrated by one's own inquisitive intrusions. Similarly, there are historical situations in which the facades of society are violently torn apart and all but the most incurious are forced to see that there was a reality behind the facades all along. Usually this does not happen and the facades continue to confront us with seemingly rocklike permanence. The perception of the reality behind the facades then demands a considerable intellectual effort.

A few examples of the way in which sociology "looks behind" the facades of social structures might serve to make our argument clearer. Take, for instance, the political organization of a community. If one wants to find out how a modern American city is governed, it is very easy to get the official information about this subject. The city will have a charter, operating under the laws of the state. With some advice from informed individuals, one may look up various statutes that define the constitution of the city. Thus one may find out that this particular community has a city-manager form of administration, or that party affiliations do not appear on the ballot in municipal elections, or that the city government participates in a regional water district. In similar fashion, with the help of some newspaper reading, one may find out the officially recognized political problems of the community. One may read that the city plans to annex a certain suburban area, or that there has been a change in the zoning ordinances to facilitate industrial development in another area, or even that one of the members of the city council has been accused of using his office for personal gain. All such matters still occur on the, as it were, visible, official or public level of political life. However, it would be an exceedingly naive person who would believe that this kind of information gives him a rounded picture of the political reality of that community. The sociologist will want to know above all the constituency of the "informal power structure" (as it has been called by Floyd Hunter, an American sociologist interested in such studies), which is a configuration of men and their power that cannot be found in any statutes, and probably cannot be read about in the newspapers. The political scientist or the legal expert might find it very interesting to compare the city charter with the constitutions of other similar communities. The sociologist will be far more concerned with discovering the way in which powerful vested interests influence or even control the actions of officials elected under the charter. These vested interests will not be found in city hall, but rather in executive suites of corporations that may not even be located in that community, in the private mansions of a handful of powerful men, perhaps in the offices of certain labor unions or even, in some instances, in the headquarters of criminal organizations. When the sociologist concerns himself with power, he will "look behind" the official mechanisms that are supposed to regulate power in the community. This does not necessarily mean that he will regard the official mechanisms as totally ineffective or their legal definition as totally illusionary. But at the very least he will insist that there is another level of reality to be investigated in the particular system of power. In some cases he might conclude that to look for real power in the publicly recognized places is quite delusional.

• • •

Or take an example from economic life. The personnel manager of an industrial plant will take delight in preparing brightly colored charts that show the table of organization that is supposed to administer the production process. Every man has his place, every person in the organization knows from whom he receives his orders and to whom he must transmit them, every work team has its assigned role in the great drama of production. In reality things rarely work this way—and every good personnel manager knows this. Superimposed on the official blueprint of the organization is a much subtler, much less visible network of human groups, with their loyalties, prejudices, antipathies and (most important) codes of behavior. Industrial sociology is full of data on the operations of this informal network, which always exists in varying degrees of accommodation and conflict with the official system. Very much the same coexistence of formal and informal organization are to be found wherever large numbers of men work together or live together under a system of discipline—military organizations, prisons, hospitals, schools, going back to the mysterious leagues that children form among themselves and that their parents only rarely discern. Once more, the sociologist will seek to penetrate the smoke screen of the official versions of reality (those of the foreman, the officer, the teacher) and try to grasp the signals that come from the "underworld" (those of the worker, the enlisted man, the schoolboy).

Let us take one further example. In Western countries, and especially in America, it is assumed that men and women marry because they are in love. There is a broadly based popular mythology about the character of love as a violent, irresistible emotion that strikes where it will, a mystery that is the goal of most young people and often of the not-so-young as well. As soon as one investigates, however, which people actually marry each other, one finds that the lightning-shaft of Cupid seems to be guided rather strongly within very definite channels of class, income, education, racial and religious background. If one then investigates a little further into the behavior that is engaged in prior to marriage under the rather misleading euphemism of "courtship," one finds channels of interaction that are often rigid to the point of ritual. The suspicion begins to dawn on one that, most of the time, it is not so much the emotion of love that creates a certain kind of relationship, but that carefully predefined and often planned relationships eventually generate the desired emotion. In other words, when certain conditions are met or have been constructed, one allows oneself "to fall in love." The sociologist investigating our patterns of "courtship" and marriage soon discovers a complex web of motives related in many ways to the entire institutional structure within which an individual lives his life—class, career, economic ambition, aspirations of power and prestige. The miracle of love now begins to look somewhat synthetic. Again, this need not mean in any given instance that the sociologist will declare the romantic interpretation to be an illusion. But, once more, he will look beyond the immediately given and publicly approved interpretations. Contemplating a couple that in its turn is contemplating the moon, the sociologist need not feel constrained to deny the emotional impact of the scene thus illuminated. But he will observe the machinery that went into the construction of the scene in its nonlunar aspects—the status index of the automobile from which the contemplation occurs, the canons of taste and tactics that determine the costume of the contemplators, the many ways in which language and demeanor place them socially, thus the social location and intentionality of the entire enterprise.

It may have become clear at this point that the problems that will interest the sociologist are not necessarily what other people may call "problems." The way in which public officials and newspapers (and, alas, some college textbooks in sociology) speak about "social problems" serves to obscure this fact. People commonly speak of a "social problem" when something in society does not work the way it is supposed to according to the official interpretations. They then expect the sociologist to study the "problem" as they have defined it and perhaps even to come up with a "solution" that will take care of the matter to their own satisfaction. It is important, against this sort of expectation, to understand that a sociological problem is something quite different from a "social problem" in this sense. For example, it is naive to concentrate on crime as a "problem" because law-enforcement agencies so define it, or on divorce because that is a "problem" to the moralists of marriage. Even more clearly, the "problem" of the foreman to get his men to work efficiently or of the line officer to get his troops to charge the enemy more enthusiastically need not be problematic at all to the sociologist (leaving out of consideration for the moment the probable fact that the sociologist asked to study such "problems" is employed by the corporation or the army). *The sociological problem is always the understanding of what goes on here in terms of social interaction.* Thus the sociological problem is not so much why some things "go wrong" from the viewpoint of the authorities and the management of the social scene, but *how the whole system works in the first place,* what are its presuppositions and by what means it is held together. The fundamental sociological problem is not crime but the law, not divorce but marriage, not racial discrimination but racially defined stratification, not revolution but government.

This point can be explicated further by an example. Take a settlement house in a lower-class slum district trying to wean away teen-agers from the publicly disapproved activities of a juvenile gang. The frame of reference within which social workers and police officers define the "problems" of this situation is constituted by the world of middle-class, respectable, publicly approved values. It is a "problem" if teen-agers drive around in stolen automobiles, and it is a "solution" if instead they will play group games in the settlement house. But if one changes the frame of reference and looks at the situation from the viewpoint of the leaders of the juvenile gang, the "problems" are defined in reverse order. It is a "problem" for the solidarity of the gang if its members are seduced away from those activities that lend prestige to the gang within its own social world, and it would be a "solution" if the social workers went way the hell back uptown where they came from. What is a "problem" to one social system is the normal routine of things to the other system, and vice versa. Loyalty and disloyalty, solidarity and deviance, are defined in contradictory terms by the representatives of the two systems. Now, the sociologist may, in terms of his own values, regard the world of middle-class respectability as more desirable and therefore want to come to the assistance of the settlement house, which is its missionary outpost *in partibus infidelium*. This, however, does not justify the identification of the director's headaches with what are "problems" sociologically. The "problems" that the sociologist will want to solve concern an understanding of the entire social situation, the values and modes of action in *both* systems, and the way in which two systems coexist in space and time. Indeed, this very ability to look at a situation from the vantage points of competing systems of interpretation is, as we shall see more clearly later on, one of the hallmarks of sociological consciousness.

We would contend, then, that there is a *debunking* motif inherent in sociological consciousness. The sociologist will be driven time and again, by the very logic of his discipline, to debunk [or show that myths are not true regarding] the social systems he is studying. This unmasking tendency need not necessarily be due to the sociologist's temperament or inclinations. Indeed, it may happen that the sociologist, who as an individual may be of a conciliatory disposition and quite disinclined to disturb the comfortable assumptions on which he rests his own social existence, is nevertheless compelled by what he is doing to fly in the face of what those around him take for granted. In other words, we would contend that the roots of the debunking motif in sociology are not psychological but methodological. The sociological frame of reference, with its built-in procedure of looking for levels of reality other than those given in the official interpretations of society, carries with it a logical imperative to *unmask the pretensions* and the propaganda by which men cloak their actions with each other. This unmasking imperative is one of the characteristics of sociology particularly at home in the temper of the modern era.

· · ·

The debunking tendency of sociology is implicit in all sociological theories that emphasize the autonomous character of social processes. For instance, Émile Durkheim, the founder of the most important school in French sociology, emphasized that society was a reality . . . that could not be reduced to psychological or other factors on different levels of analysis. . . . This is perhaps most sharply revealed in his well-known study of suicide, in the work of that title, where individual intentions of those who commit suicide are completely left out of the analysis in favor of statistics concerning various social characteristics of these individuals. In the Durkheimian perspective, to live in society means to exist under the domination of society's logic. Very often men act by this logic without knowing it. To discover this inner dynamic of society, therefore, the sociologist must frequently disregard the answers that the social actors themselves would give to his questions and look for explanations that are hidden from their own awareness. This essentially Durkheimian approach has been carried over into the theoretical approach now called functionalism. In functional analysis society is analyzed in terms of its own workings as a system, workings that are often obscure or opaque to those acting within the system. The contemporary American sociologist Robert Merton has expressed this approach well in his concepts of "manifest" and "latent" functions. The former are the conscious and deliberate functions of social processes, the latter the unconscious and unintended ones. Thus the "manifest" function of antigambling legislation may be to suppress gambling, its "latent" function to create an illegal empire for the gambling syndicates. Or Christian missions in parts of Africa "manifestly" tried to convert Africans to Christianity, "latently" helped to destroy the indigenous tribal cultures and thus provided an important impetus towards rapid social transformation. Or the control of the Communist Party over all sectors of social life in Russia "manifestly" was to assure the continued dominance of the revolutinary ethos, "latently" created a new class of comfortable bureaucrats uncannily bourgeois in its aspirations and increasingly disinclined toward the self-denial of Bolshevik dedication. Or the "manifest" function of many voluntary associations in America is sociability and public service, the "latent" function to attach status [indicators] to those permitted to belong to such associations.

· · ·

It has been suggested above that sociological consciousness is likely to arise when the commonly accepted or authoritatively stated interpretations of society become shaky. As we have already said, there is a good case for thinking of the origins of sociology in France (the mother country of the discipline) in terms of an effort to cope intellectually with the consequences of the French Revolution, not only of the one great cataclysm of 1789 but of what De Tocqueville called the continuing Revolution of the nineteenth century. In the French case it is not difficult to perceive sociology against the background of the rapid transformations of modern society, the collapse of facades, the deflation of old creeds and the upsurge of frightening new forces on the social scene. In Germany, the other European country in which an important sociological movement arose in the nineteenth century, the matter has a rather different appearance. If one may quote Marx . . . , the Germans had a tendency to carry on in professors' studies the revolutions that the French performed on the barricades. At least one of these academic roots of revolution, perhaps the most important one, may be sought in the broadly based movement of thought that came to be called "historicism." This is not the place to go into the full story of this movement. Suffice it to say that it represents an attempt to deal philosophically with the overwhelming sense of the *relativity of all values in history* [The term "relativity of values" refers to the fact that events and objects considered "good" or "bad" in one society may not be valued in the same way in other societies. Values are, thus, relative to the society in question at a given time.] This awareness of relativity was an almost necessary outcome of the immense accumulation of German historical scholarship in every conceivable field. Sociological thought was at least partly grounded in the need to bring order and intelligibility to the impression of chaos that this array of historical knowledge made on some observers. Needless to stress, however, the society of the German sociologist was changing all around him just as was that of his French colleague, as Germany rushed towards industrial power and nationhood in the second half of the nineteenth century. We shall not pursue these questions though. If we turn to America, the country in which sociology came to receive its most widespread acceptance, we find once more a different set of circumstances, though again against a background of rapid and profound social change. In looking at this American development we can detect another motif of sociology, closely related to that of debunking but not identical with it—its fascination with the *unrespectable* view of society.

In at least every Western society it is possible to distinguish between respectable and unrespectable sectors. In that respect American society is not in a unique position. But American respectability has a particularly pervasive quality about it. This may be ascribed in part, perhaps, to the lingering aftereffects of the Puritan way of life. More probably it has to do with the predominant role played by the bourgeoisie [or middle class] in shaping American culture. Be this as it may in terms of historical causation, it is not difficult to look at social phenomena in America and place them readily in one of these two sectors. We can perceive the official, respectable America represented symbolically by the Chamber of Commerce, the churches, the schools and other centers of civic ritual. But facing this world of respectability is an "other America," present in every town of any size, an America that has other symbols and that speaks another language. This language is probably its safest identification tag. It is the language of the poolroom and the poker game, of bars, brothels and army barracks. But it is also the language that breaks out with a sigh of relief between two salesmen having a drink in the parlor car as their train races past clean little Midwestern villages on a Sunday morning, with clean little villagers trooping into the whitewashed sanctuaries. It is the language that is suppressed in the company of ladies and clergymen, owing its life mainly to oral transmission from one generation of Huckleberry Finns to another (though in recent years the language has found literary deposition in some books designed to thrill ladies and clergymen). The "other America" that speaks this language can be found wherever people are excluded, or exclude themselves, from the world of middle-class propriety. We find it in those sections of the working class that have not yet proceeded too far on the road of *embourgeoisement*, in slums, shantytowns, and those parts of cities that urban sociologists have called "areas of transition." We find it expressed powerfully in the world of the American Negro. We also come on it in the subworlds of those who have, for one reason or another, withdrawn voluntarily from Main Street and Madison Avenue—in the worlds of hipsters, homosexuals, hoboes and other "marginal men," those worlds that are kept safely out of sight on the streets where the nice people live, work and amuse themselves. . . .

American sociology, accepted early both in academic circles and by those concerned with welfare activities, was from the beginning associated with the "official America," with the world of policy makers in community and nation. Sociology today retains this respectable affiliation in university, business and government. The appellation hardly induces eyebrows to be raised, except the eyebrows of such Southern racists sufficiently literate to have read the footnotes of the desegregation decision of 1954. However, we would contend that there has been an important undercurrent in American sociology, relating it to that "other America" of dirty language and disenchanted attitudes, that state of mind that refuses to be impressed, moved or befuddled by the official ideologies.

This unrespectable perspective on the American scene can be seen most clearly in the figure of Thorstein Veblen, one of the early important sociologists in America. His biography itself constitutes an exercise in marginality: a difficult, querulous character; born on a Norwegian farm on the Wisconsin frontier; acquiring English as a foreign language; involved all his life with morally and politically suspect individuals; an academic migrant; an inveterate seducer of . . . women. The perspective on America gained from this angle of vision can be found in the unmasking satire that runs like a purple thread through Veblen's work, most famously in his *Theory of the Leisure Class*, that merciless look from the underside at the pretensions of the American [newly rich]. Veblen's view of society can be understood most easily as a series of non-Rotarian insights—his understanding of "conspicuous consumption" as against the middle-class enthusiasm for the "finer things," his analysis of economic processes in terms of manipulation and waste as against the American productivity ethos, his understanding of the machinations of real estate speculation as against the American community ideology, most bitterly his description of academic life (in *The Higher Learning in America*) in terms of fraud and flatulence as against the American cult of education. We are not associating ourselves here with a certain neo-Veblenism that has become fashionable with some younger American sociologists, nor arguing that Veblen was a giant in the development of the field. We are only pointing to his irreverent curiosity and clear-sightedness as marks of a perspective coming from those places in the culture in which one gets up to shave about noon on Sundays. Nor are we arguing that clear-sightedness is a general trait of unrespectability. Stupidity and sluggishness of thought are probably distributed quite fairly throughout the social spectrum. But where there is intelligence and where it manages to free itself from the goggles of respectability, we can expect a clearer view of society than in those cases where the oratorical imagery is taken for real life.

A number of developments in empirical studies in American sociology furnish evidence of this same fascination with the unrespectable view of society. For example, looking back at the powerful development of urban studies undertaken at the University of Chicago in the 1920s we are struck by the apparently irresistible attraction to the seamier sides of city life upon these researchers. The advice to his students of Robert Park, the most important figure in this development, to the effect that they should get their hands dirty with research often enough meant quite literally an intense interest in all the things that North Shore residents would call "dirty." We sense in many of these studies the excitement of discovering the picaresque undersides of the metropolis—studies of slum life, of the melancholy world of rooming houses, of Skid Row, of the worlds of crime and prostitution. One of the offshoots of this so-called "Chicago school" has been the sociological study of occupations, due very largely to the pioneering work of Everett Hughes and his students. Here also we find a fascination with every possible world in which human beings live and make a living, not only with the worlds of respectable occupations, but with those of the taxi dancer, the apartment-house janitor, the professional boxer or the jazz musician. The same tendency can be discovered in the course of American community studies following in the wake of the famous *Middletown* studies of Robert and Helen Lynd. Inevitably these studies had to bypass the official versions of community life, to look at the social reality of the community not only from the perspective of city hall but also from that of the city jail. Such sociological procedure is *ipso facto* a refutation of the respectable presupposition that only certain views of the world are to be taken seriously.

We would not want to give an exaggerated impression of the effect of such investigations on the consciousness of sociologists. We are well aware of the elements of muckraking and romanticism inherent in some of this. We also know that many sociologists participate as fully in the respectable [outlook] as all the other PTA members on their block. Nevertheless, we would maintain that sociological consciousness predisposes one towards an awareness of worlds other than that of middle-class respectability, an awareness which already carries within itself the seeds of intellectual unrespectability. In the second *Middletown* study the Lynds have given a classic analysis of the mind of middle-class America in their series of "of course statements"—that is, statements that represent a consensus so strong that the answer to any question concerning them will habitually be prefaced with the words "of course." "Is our economy one of free enterprise?" "Of course!" "Are all our important decisions arrived at through the democratic process?" "Of course!" "Is monogamy the natural form of marriage?" "Of course!" The sociologist, however conservative and conformist he may be in his private life, knows that there are serious questions to be raised about every one of these "of course statements." In this knowledge alone he is brought to the threshold of unrespectability.

This unrespectable motif of sociological consciousness need not imply a revolutionary attitude. We would even go further than that and express the opinion that sociological understanding is inimical to revolutionary ideologies, not because it has some sort of conservative bias, but because it sees not only through the illusions of the present *status quo* but also through the illusionary expectations concerning possible futures, such expectations being the customary spiritual nourishment of the revolutionary. This nonrevolutionary and moderating soberness of sociology we would value quite highly. More regrettable, from the viewpoint of one's values, is the fact that sociological understanding by itself does not necessarily lead to a greater tolerance with respect to the foibles of mankind. It is possible to view social reality with compassion or with cynicism, both attitudes being compatible with clear-sightedness. But whether he can bring himself to human sympathy with the phenomena he is studying or not, the sociologist will in some measure be detached from the taken-for-granted postures of his society. Unrespectability, whatever its ramifications in the emotions and the will, must remain a constant possibility in the sociologist's mind. It may be segregated from the rest of his life, overlaid by the routine mental states of everyday existence, even denied ideologically. Total respectability of thought, however, will invariably mean the death of sociology. This is one of the reasons why genuine sociology disappears promptly from the scene in totalitarian countries, as is well illustrated in the instance of Nazi Germany. By implication, sociological understanding is always potentially dangerous to the minds of policemen and other guardians of public order, since it will always tend to [question the universality of] the claim to absolute rightness upon which such minds like to rest.

Before concluding this chapter, we would look once more on this phenomenon of *relativization* that we have already touched upon a few times. We would now say explicitly that sociology is so much in tune with the temper of the modern era precisely because it represents the consciousness of a world in which values have been radically relativized. This relativization has become so much part of our everyday imagination that it is difficult for us to grasp fully how closed and absolutely binding the world views of other cultures have been and in some places still are. . . . For the traditional mind one is what one is, where one is, and cannot even imagine how one could be anything different. The modern mind, by contrast, is mobile, participates vicariously in the lives of others differently located from oneself, easily imagines itself changing occupation or residence. Thus [a sociologist working in the contemporary Middle East] found that some of the illiterate respondents to his questionnaires could only respond with laughter to the question as to what they would do if they were in the position of their rulers and would not even consider the question as to the circumstances under which they would be willing to leave their native village. Another way of putting this would be to say that traditional societies assign definite and permanent identities to their members. In modern society identity itself is uncertain and in flux. One does not really know what is expected of one as a ruler, as a parent, as a cultivated person, or as one who is sexually normal. Typically, one then requires various experts to tell one. The book club editor tells us what culture is, the interior designer what taste we ought to have, and the psychoanalyst who we are. To live in modern society means to live at the center of a kaleidoscope of everchanging roles.

Again, we must forego the temptation of enlarging on this point, since it would take us rather far afield from our argument into a general discussion of the social psychology of modern existence. We would rather stress the intellectual aspect of this situation, since it is in that aspect that we would see an important dimension of sociological consciousness. *The unprecedented rate of geographical and social mobility in modern society means that one becomes exposed to an unprecedented variety of ways of looking at the world.* The insights into other cultures that one might gather by travel are brought into one's own living room through the mass media. Someone once defined urbane sophistication as being the capacity to remain quite unperturbed upon seeing in front of one's house a man dressed in a turban and a loincloth, a snake coiled around his neck, beating a tom-tom as he leads a leashed tiger down the street. No doubt there are degrees to such sophistication, but a measure of it is acquired by every child who watches television. No doubt also this sophistication is commonly only superficial and does not extend to any real grappling with alternate ways of life. Nevertheless, the immensely broadened possibility of travel, in person and through the imagination, implies at least potentially the awareness that one's own culture, including its basic values, is relative in space and time. Social mobility, that is, the movement from one social stratum to another, augments this relativizing effect. Wherever industrialization occurs, a new dynamism is injected into the social system. Masses of people begin to change their social position, in groups or as individuals. And usually this change is in an "upward" direction. With this movement an individual's biography often involves a considerable journey not only through a variety of social groups but through the intellectual universes that are, so to speak, attached to these groups. Thus the Baptist mail clerk who used to read the *Reader's Digest* becomes an Episcopalian junior executive who reads *The New Yorker*, or the faculty wife whose husband becomes department chairman may graduate from the best-seller list to Proust or Kafka.

In view of this overall fluidity of world views in modern society it should not surprise us that our age has been characterized as one of conversion. Nor should it be surprising that intellectuals especially have been prone to change their world views radically and with amazing frequency. The intellectual attraction of strongly presented, theoretically closed systems of thought such as Catholicism or Communism has been frequently commented upon. Psychoanalysis, in all its forms, can be understood as an institutionalized mechanism of conversion, in which the individual changes not only his view of himself but of the world in general. The popularity of a multitude of new cults and creeds, presented in different degrees of intellectual refinement depending upon the educational level of their clientele, is another manifestation of this proneness to conversion of our contemporaries. It almost seems as if modern man, and especially modern educated man, is in a perpetual state of doubt about the nature of himself and of the universe in which he lives. In other words, the awareness of relativity, which probably in all ages of history has been the possession of a small group of intellectuals, today appears as a broad cultural fact reaching far down into the lower reaches of the social system.

We do not want to give the impression that this sense of relativity and the resulting proneness to change one's entire [world view] are manifestations of intellectual or emotional immaturity. Certainly one should not take with too much seriousness some representatives of this pattern. Nevertheless, we would contend that an essentially similar pattern becomes almost a destiny in even the most serious intellectual enterprises. It is impossible to exist with full awareness in the modern world without realizing that moral, political and philosophical commitments are relative, that, in Pascal's words, what is truth on one side of the Pyrenees is error on the other. Intensive occupation with the more fully elaborated meaning systems available in our time gives one a truly frightening understanding of the way in which these systems can provide a total interpretation of reality, within which will be included an interpretation of the alternate systems and of the ways of passing from one system to another. Catholicism may have a theory of Communism, but Communism returns the compliment and will produce a theory of Catholicism. To the Catholic thinker the Communist lives in a dark world of materialist delusion about the real meaning of life. To the Communist his Catholic adversary is helplessly caught in the "false consciousness" of a bourgeois mentality. To the psychoanalyst both Catholic and Communist may simply be acting out on the intellectual level the unconscious impulses that really move them. And psychoanalysis may be to the Catholic an escape from the reality of sin and to the Communist an avoidance of the realities of society.

This means that the individual's choice of viewpoint will determine the way in which he looks back upon his own biography. American prisoners of war "brainwashed" by the Chinese Communists completely changed their viewpoints on social and political matters. To those that returned to America this change represented a sort of illness brought on by outward pressure, as a convalescent may look back on a delirious dream. But to their former captors this changed consciousness represents a brief glimmer of true understanding between long periods of ignorance. And to those prisoners who decided not to return, their conversion may still appear as the decisive passage from darkness to light.

Instead of speaking of conversion (a term with religiously charged connotations) we would prefer to use the more neutral term of *"alternation"* to describe this phenomenon. The intellectual situation just described brings with it the possibility that an individual may alternate back and forth between logically contradictory meaning systems. Each time, the meaning system he enters provides him with an interpretation of his existence and of his world, including in this interpretation an explanation of the meaning system he has abandoned. Also, the meaning system provides him with tools to combat his own doubts. Catholic confessional discipline, Communist "autocriticism" and the psychoanalytic techniques of coping with "resistance" all fulfill the same purpose of preventing alternation out of the particular meaning system, allowing the individual to interpret his own doubts in terms derived from the system itself, thus keeping him within it. On lower levels of sophistication there will also be various means employed to cut off questions that might threaten the individual's allegiance to the system, means that one can see at work in the dialectical acrobatics of even such relatively unsophisticated groups as Jehovah's Witnesses or Black Muslims.

If one resists the temptation, however, to accept such [narrow world views], and is willing to face squarely the experience of relativity brought on by the phenomenon of alternation, then one comes into possession of yet another crucial dimension of sociological consciousness—the awareness that not only identities but ideas are relative to specific social locations. . . . Suffice it to say here that this relativizing motif is another of the fundamental driving forces of the sociological enterprise.

In this chapter we have tried to outline the dimensions of sociological consciousness through the analysis of three motifs—those of debunking, unrespectability and relativizing. To these three we would, finally, add a fourth one, much less far-reaching in its implications but useful in rounding out our picture—the *cosmopolitan* motif. Going back to very ancient times, it was in cities that there developed an openness to the world, to other ways of thinking and acting. Whether we think of Athens or Alexandria, of medieval Paris or Renaissance Florence, or of the turbulent urban centers of modern history, we can identify a certain cosmopolitan consciousness that was especially characteristic of city culture. The individual, then, who is not only urban but urbane is one who, however passionately he may be attached to his own city, roams through the whole wide world in his intellectual voyages. His mind, if not his body and his emotions, is at home wherever there are other men who think. We would submit that sociological consciousness is marked by the same kind of cosmopolitanism. This is why a narrow parochialism in its focus of interest is always a danger signal for the sociological venture (a danger signal that, unfortunately, we would hoist over quite a few sociological studies in America today). The sociological perspective is a broad, open, emancipated vista on human life. The sociologist, at his best, is a man with a taste for other lands, inwardly open to the measureless richness of human possibilities, eager for new horizons and new worlds of human meaning. It probably requires no additional elaboration to make the point that this type of man can play a particularly useful part in the course of events today.

Review Questions

1. Briefly summarize the four major sociological themes, or motifs, which Berger sets forth.
   a. debunking
   b. unrespectability
   c. cultural relativism
   d. cosmopolitanism

2. How would the "sociological consciousness" lead you to study the power structure of a city which is a gambling center (e.g., Atlantic City, New Jersey, or Las Vegas, Nevada)? How would your approach differ from the economist's approach or the lawyer's approach?

3. Berger claims that most of us are unaware of the patterned regularities in the phenomenon of love. What are our myths about love? What are some of the patterned regularities that show our myths to be partly or entirely false?

4. Why is it important to understand that a "sociological problem" is quite different from a "social problem"?

HIRED HAND RESEARCH

Julius A. Roth

CASE I

AFTER IT BECAME OBVIOUS HOW TEDIOUS IT WAS TO WRITE DOWN NUMBERS ON PIECES of paper which didn't even fulfill one's own sense of reality and which did not remind one of the goals of the project, we all in little ways started avoiding our work and cheating on the project. It began, for example, when we were supposed to be observing for hour and a half periods, an hour and a half on the ward and then an hour and a half afterwards to write up or dictate what we had observed in terms of the category system which the project was supposed to be testing and in terms of a ward diary. We began cutting corners in time. We would arrive a little bit late and leave a little bit early. It began innocently enough, but soon boomeranged into a full cheating syndrome, where we would fake observations for some time slot which were never observed on the ward. Sam, for example, in one case, came onto the ward while I was still finishing up an assignment on a study patient and told me that he was supposed to observe for an hour and a half but that he wasn't going to stay because he couldn't stand it anymore. He said he wasn't going to tell anyone that he missed an assignment, but that he would simply write up a report on the basis of what he knew already about the ward and the patients. I was somewhat appalled by Sam's chicanery, and in this sense I was the last one to go. It was three or four weeks after this before I actually cheated in the same manner.

It was also frequent for us to miss observation periods, especially the 8 to 9:30 a.m. ones. We all had a long drive for one thing, and we were all chronic over-sleepers for another. For a while we used to make up the times we missed by coming in the next morning at the same time and submitting our reports with the previous day's date. As time went on, however, we didn't bother to make up the times we'd missed. When we were questioned by our supervisor about the missing reports, we would claim that there had been an error in scheduling and that we did not know that those time slots were supposed to be covered.

There were other ways we would cheat, sometimes inadvertently. For example, one can decide that one can't hear enough of a conversation to record it. People need to think fairly highly of themselves, and when you think that you're a cheat and a liar and that you're not doing your job for which you are receiving high wages, you are likely to find little subconscious ways of getting out of having to accuse yourself of these things. One

Julius A. Roth, "Hired Hand Research," *American Sociologist*, 1 (August 1966), 190–196.

of the ways is to not be able to hear well. We had a special category in our coding system, a question mark, which we noted by its symbol on our code sheets whenever we could not hear what was going on between two patients. As the purgatory of writing numbers on pieces of paper lengthened, more and more transcripts were passed in with question marks on them, so that even though we had probably actually heard most of the conversations between patients, we were still actually avoiding the work of transcription by deceiving ourselves into believing that we could not hear what was being said. This became a good way of saving yourself work. If you couldn't hear a conversation, it just got one mark in one column of one code sheet, and if you wrote down an elaborate conversation lasting even ten minutes, it might take you up to an hour to code it; one hour of putting numbers in little blocks. In the long run, all of our data became much skimpier. Conversations were incomplete; their duration was strangely diminishing to two or three minutes in length instead of the half-hour talks the patients usually had with each other. We were all defining our own cutting off points, saying to ourselves, "Well, that's enough of that conversation." According to the coding rules, however, a communication can't be considered as ended until the sequence of interaction has been completed and a certain time lapse of silence has ensued.

In order to ensure the reliability of our coding, the research design called for an "Inter-Rater Reliability Check" once every two months, in which each of the four of us would pair up with every other member of the team and be rated on our ability to code jointly the same interaction in terms of the same categories and dimensions. We learned to loathe these checks; we knew that the coding system was inadequate in terms of reliability and that our choice of categories was optional, subjective, and largely according to our own sense of what an interaction is really about, rather than according to the rigid, stylized, and preconceived design into which we were supposed to make a reality fit. We also knew, however, that our principal investigators insisted on an inter-rater reliability coefficient of .70 in order for the research to proceed. When the time came for another check, we met together to discuss and make certain agreements on how to bring our coding habits into conformity for the sake of achieving reliability. In these meetings we would confess our preferences for coding certain things in certain ways and agree on certain concessions to each other for the duration of the check. Depending on what other individual I was to be paired with, for example, I had a very good idea of how I could code in order to achieve nearly the same transcriptions. We didn't end it there. After each phase of a check, each pair of us would meet again to go over our transcriptions and compare our coding, and if there were any gross discrepancies, we corrected them before sending them to the statisticians for analysis. Needless to say, as soon as the reliability checks were over with, we each returned to a coding rationale which we as individuals required in order to do any coding at all—in order to maintain sanity.

CASE II

There didn't appear to be too much concern with the possibility of inconsistency among the coders. Various coders used various methods to determine the code of an open-end question. Toward the end of the coding process, expediency became the keynote, leading to gross inconsistency. The most expedient method of coding a few of the trickier questions was to simply put down a "4." (This was the middle-of-the-road response on the one question that had the most variation.) If the responses were not clear or comprehensible, the coder had two alternatives: on the one hand, he could puzzle over it and ask for other opinions or, on the other hand, he could assign it an arbitrary number or forget the response entirely.

In the beginning, many of us, when in doubt about a response, would ask the supervisor or his assistant. After a while, I noted that quite often the supervisor's opinion would differ when asked twice about the same response and he would often give two different answers in response to the same question. One way the supervisor and his assistant would determine the correct coding for an answer would be to look at the respondent's previous answers and deduce what they should have answered—thereby coding on *what they thought the respondent should have answered*, not on the basis of what he *did* answer. One example that I distinctly remember is the use of magazines regularly read as reported by the respondent being used as a basis on which to judge and code their political views. This, in my opinion, would be a factor in some of the cases, such as the reading of an extreme leftist or extreme rightist magazine, but to use magazines such as *Time* or *Reader's Digest* to form any conclusions about the type of person and his views, I feel is quite arbitrary. Furthermore, I feel questionnaires should be used to see *if* consistent patterns of views exist among respondents and it is not the coder's job to put them in if the respondents fail to!

Some of the coders expected a fixed pattern of response. I, not being sure of what responses meant in a total political profile, treated each response separately—which I feel is the correct way of coding a questionnaire. Others, as I learned through their incessant jabbering, took what they thought was a more sophisticated method of treating an interview. A few would discuss the respondent's answers as if they took one political or social standpoint as an indicator of what all the responses should be. They would laugh over an inconsistency in the respondent's replies, feeling that one answer did not fit the previous pattern of responses.

The final problem leading to gross inconsistency was the factor of time. The supervisor made it clear that the code sheets had to be in the computation center by Saturday. This meant that on Saturday morning and early afternoon the aim of the coders was to code the questionnaires as quickly as possible, and the crucial factor was speed, even at the expense of accuracy. The underlying thought was that there were so many questionnaires coded already (that we *assumed* to be coded consistently and correctly) that the inconsistencies in the remainder would balance themselves out and be of no great importance. I found myself adapting to this way of thinking, and after spending two or three hours there on Saturday morning, I joined in the game of "let's get these damn things out already." It did indeed become a game, with the shibboleth, for one particularly vague and troublesome question, "Oh, give it a four."

CASE III

One of the questions on the interview schedule asked for five reasons why parents had put their child in an institution. I found most people can't think of five reasons. One or two—sometimes three. At first I tried pumping them for more reasons, but I never got any of them up to five. I didn't want (the director) to think I was goofing off on the probing, so I always filled in all five.

Another tough one was the item about how the child's disability affected the family relationships. We were supposed to probe. Probe what? You get so many different kinds of answers, I was never sure what was worth following up. Sometimes I did if the respondent seemed to have something to say. Otherwise I just put down a short answer and made it look as if that was all I could get out of them. Of course, (the director) *did* list a few areas he wanted covered in the probing. One of them was sex relations of the parents. Most of the time I didn't follow up on that. Once in a while I would get somebody who seemed to be able to talk freely without embarrassment. But most of the time I was afraid to ask, so I made up something to fill that space.

Then there was that wide open question at the end. It's vague. Most people don't know what to say. You've been asking them questions for about an hour already. Usually you get a very short answer. I didn't push them. I'd write up a longer answer later. It's easy to do. You have their answer to a lot of other questions to draw on. You just put parts of some of them together, dress it up a little, and add one or two bits of new information which fits in with the rest.

Any reader with research experience can probably recall one or more cases in which he observed, suspected, or participated in some form of cheating, carelessness, distortion, or cutting of corners in the collection or processing of research data. He probably thought of these instances as exceptions—an unfortunate lapse in ethical behavior or a failure of research directors to maintain proper controls. I would like to put forth the thesis that such behavior on the part of hired data collectors and processors is not abnormal or exceptional, but rather is exactly the kind of behavior we should expect from people with their position in a production unit.

The cases I have presented do not constitute proof, of course. Even if I presented ten or twenty more, my efforts could be dismissed as merely an unusually industrious effort to record professional dirty linen (or I might be accused of making them up!) and not at all representative of the many thousands of cases of hired researching carried out every year. Rather than multiply examples, I would like to take a different tack and examine the model we have been using in thinking about research operations and to suggest another model which I believe is more appropriate.

The ideal we hold of the researcher is that of a well-educated scholar pursuing information and ideas on problems in which he has an intrinsic interest. Frequently this ideal may be approximated when an individual scholar is working on his own problem or several colleagues are collaborating on a problem of mutual interest. Presumably such a researcher will endeavor to carry out his data collection and processing in the most accurate and useful way that his skills and time permit.

When a researcher hires others to do the collecting and processing tasks of his research plan, we often assume that these assistants fit the "dedicated scientist" ideal and will lend their efforts to the successful conduct of the overall study by carrying out their assigned tasks to the best of their ability. As suggested by my examples, I doubt that hired assistants usually behave this way even when they are junior grade scholars themselves. It becomes more doubtful yet when they are even further removed from scholarly tradition and from the direct control of the research directors (e.g., part-time survey interviewers).

TOWARD GREATER ACCURACY

It seems to me that we can develop a more accurate expectation of the contribution of the hired research worker who is required to work according to somebody else's plan by applying another model which has been worked out in some detail by sociologists—namely, the work behavior of the hired hand in a production organization. First, let us look at one of the more thorough of these studies, Donald Roy's report on machine shop operators.[1]

Roy's workers made the job easier by loafing when the piece rate did not pay well. They were careful not to go over their informal "quotas" on piece rate jobs because the rate would be cut and their work would be harder. They faked time sheets so that their actual productive abilities would not be known to management. They cut corners on prescribed job procedures to make the work easier and/or more lucrative even though this sometimes meant that numerous products had to be scrapped. Roy's calculations show that the workers could have produced on the order of twice as much if it had been in their interest to do so.

But it is *not* in their interest to do so. The product the hired hand turns out is not in any sense his. He does not design it, make any of the decisions about producing it or about the conditions under which it will be produced, or what will be done with it after it is produced. The worker is interested in doing just enough to get by. Why should he concern himself about how well the product works or how much time it takes to make it? That is the company's problem. The company is his adversary and fair game for any trickery he can get away with. The worker's aim is to make his job as easy and congenial as the limited resources allow and to make as much money as possible without posing a threat to his fellow workers or to his own future. The company, in turn, is placed in the position of having to establish an inspection system to try to keep the worst of their products from leaving the factory (an effort often unsuccessful—the inspectors are hired hands, too) and of devising some form of supervision to limit the more extreme forms of gold-bricking and careless workmanship.

Almost all the systematic research on "restriction of output" and deviation from assigned duties has been done on factory workers, office clerks, and other low prestige work groups. This is mostly because such work is easier to observe and measure, but also because much of this research has been controlled in part by those in a position of authority who want research done only on their subordinates. However, there is evidence to indicate that work restrictions and deviations in the form of informal group definitions and expectations are probably universal in our society. They can be found among business executives and in the professions, sports, and the creative arts. They are especially likely to crop up when one is working as a hired hand, and almost all productive activities have their hired hand aspects. A professor may work hard on scholarly tasks of his own choosing and perhaps even on teaching a course which he himself has devised, but he becomes notoriously lax when he is assigned to a departmental service course which he does not like—spending little or no time on preparation, avoiding his students as much as possible, turning all the exams over to a graduate assistant, and so on.

"Restriction of production" and deviation from work instructions is no longer regarded by students of the sociology of work as a moral issue or a form of social delinquency. Rather, it is the expected behavior of workers in a production organization. The only problem for an investigator to work practices is discovering the details of cutting corners, falsifying time sheets, defining work quotas, dodging supervision, and ignoring instructions in a given work setting.

There is no reason to believe that a hired hand in the scientific research business will behave any different from those in other areas of productive activity. It is far more reasonable to assume that their behavior will be similar. They want to make as much money as they can and may pad their account or time sheet if they are paid on that basis, but this type of behavior is a minor problem so far as the present discussion is concerned. They also want to avoid difficult, embarrassing, inconvenient, time-consuming situations as well as those activities which make no sense to them. (Thus, they fail to make some assigned observations or to ask some of the interview questions.) At the same time they want to give the right impression to their supervisors—at least right enough so that their material will be accepted and they will be kept on the job. (Thus, they modify or fabricate portions of the reports in order to give the boss what he *seems* to want.) They do not want to "look stupid" by asking too many questions, so they are likely to make a stab at what they think the boss wants—e.g., make a guess at a coding category rather than having it resolved through channels.

Even those who start out with the notion that this is an important piece of work which they must do right will succumb to the hired hand mentality when they realize that their suggestions and criticisms are ignored, that their assignment does not allow for any imagination or creativity, that they will receive no credit for the final product, in short, that they have been hired to do somebody else's dirty work. When this realization has sunk in, they will no longer bother to be careful or accurate or precise. They will cut corners to save time and energy. They will fake parts of their reporting. They will not put themselves out for something in which they have no stake except in so far as extrinsic pressures force them to. Case I is an excerpt from the statement of a research worker who started out with enthusiasm and hard work and ended with sloppy work and cheating when she could no longer escape the fact that she was a mere flunky expected to do her duty whether or not it was meaningful. The coders in Case II soon gave up any effort to resolve the ambiguities of their coding operation and followed the easiest path acceptable to their supervisor. In this case, the supervisor himself made little effort to direct the data processing toward supplying answers to meaningful research issues. We must remember that in many research operations the supervisors and directors themselves are hired hands carrying out the requests of a client or superior as expeditiously as possible.

Many of the actions of hired hand researchers are strikingly analogous to restrictive practices of factory operatives. Interviewers who limit probing and observers who limit interaction recording are behaving like workers applying "quota restriction," and with interacting hired hands informal agreements may be reached on the extent of such restrictions. To fabricate portions of a report is a form of goldbricking. The collusion on the reliability check reported in Case I is strikingly similar to the workers' plot to mislead the time-study department. Such similarities are no accident. The relationship of the hired hand to the product and the process of production is the same in each case. The product is not "his." The production process gives him little or no opportunity to express any intrinsic interest he may have in the product. He will sooner or later fall into a pattern of carrying out his work with a minimum of effort, inconvenience, and embarrassment—doing just enough so that his product will get by. If he is part of a large and complex operation where his immediate superiors are also hired hands with no intrinsic interest in the product and where the final authority may be distant and even amorphous, quality control of the product will be mechanical and the minimal effort that will get by can soon be learned and easily applied. The factory production situation has at least one ultimate limitation on the more extreme deviations of the hired hands: The final product must "work" reasonably well in a substantial proportion of cases. In social science research, on the other hand, the product is usually so ambiguous and the field of study so lacking in standards of performance that it is difficult for anyone to say whether it "works" or not.

What is more important is the effect of the hired hand mentality on the *nature* of the product. Workmen not only turn out less than they could if it were in their interest to maximize production, but often produce shoddy and even dangerous products.[2] In the case of research, the inefficiency of hired hands not only causes a study to take longer or cost more money, but is likely to introduce much dubious data and interpretations into the process of analysis. Our mass production industrial system has opted to sacrifice individual efficiency and product quality for the advantages of a rationalized division of labor. The same approach has been applied to much of our larger scale scientific research and the results, in my opinion, have been much more disastrous than they are in industrial production with little compensating advantages.

When the tasks of a research project are split up into small pieces to be assigned to hired hands, none of these data collectors and processors will ever understand all the complexities and subtleties of the research issues in the same way as the person who conceived of the study. No amount of "training" can take the place of the gradual development of research interests and formulations on the part of the planner. Since the director often cannot be sure what conceptions of the issues the hired hands have as a result of his explanations and "training," he must make dubious guesses about the meaning of much of the data they return to him. If he attempts to deal with this difficulty by narrowly defining the permissible behavior of each hired hand (e.g., demand that all questions on a schedule be asked in a set wording), he merely increases the alienation of the hired hand from his work and thus increases the likelihood of cutting corners and cheating. As he gains in quantity of data, he loses in validity of meaningfulness.[3]

I do not want to give the impression that the hired hand mentality with its attendant difficulties is simply a characteristic of the large-scale ongoing research organization. We may find it at all size levels, including the academic man hiring a single student to do his research chores. The argument may be advanced that assignment of specified tasks by the director of a study is essential to getting the job done in the manner that he wants it done. My answer is that such assignments are often not effectively carried out and it is misleading to assume that they are.

Let me illustrate this point. A researcher wants to do a study of the operation of a given institution. He has some definite notion of what aspects of behavior of the institutional personnel he wants information about and he has some ideas about the manner in which he will go about analysing and interpreting these behaviors. He finds it possible and useful to engage four trained and interested assistants. Let me outline two ways the study might be conducted.

A. Through a series of discussions, general agreement is reached about the nature of the study and the manner in which it might be conducted. Some division of labor is agreed upon in these discussions. However, none of the field workers is held to any particular tasks or foci of interest. Each is allowed to pursue his data collection as he thinks best within the larger framework, although the field workers exchange information frequently and make new agreements so that they can benefit from each other's experience.

B. The director divides up the data collection and processing in a logical manner and assigns a portion to each of the assistants. Each field worker is instructed to obtain information in all the areas assigned to him and to work in a prescribed manner so that his information will be directly comparable to that of the others. The director may use a procedural check such as having each assistant write a report covering given issues or areas at regular intervals.

Which is the preferred approach? Judging from my reading of social science journals, most research directors would say Method B is to be preferred. Method A, they would maintain, produces information on subjects, issues, or events from one field worker which is not directly comparable to that collected by another field worker. They would also object that if each field worker is permitted to follow his own inclinations even in part, the total study will suffer from large gaps. These accusations are quite true—and, I would add, are an inevitable result of dividing a research project among a number of people. What I disagree with, however, is the assumption that Method B would not suffer from these defects (if indeed, they should be regarded as defects.) It is assumed that the assistants in Method B are actually carrying out their assigned tasks in the manner specified. In line with my earlier discussion of the behavior of hired hands, I would consider this highly unlikely. If the information produced by these assistants is indeed closely comparable, it would most likely be because they had reached an agreement on how to restrict production. And, whether the study is carried out by Method A or by Method B, gaps will occur. The difference is that the director of Study A—assuming he had succeeded in making his assistants into collaborating colleagues—would at least know where the gaps are. The director of Study B would have gaps without knowing where they are—or, indeed, that they exist—because they have been covered over by the fabrications of his alienated assistants.

It is ironic that established researchers do not ascribe the same motivating forces to their subordinates as they do to themselves. For many years research scientists have been confronting those who pay their salaries and give them their grants with the argument that a scientist can do good research only when he has the freedom to follow his ideas in whatever way seems best. They have been so successful with this argument that university administrations and research organization directorates rarely attempt to dictate—or even suggest—problems or procedures to a researcher on their staff, and the more prominent granting agencies write contracts with almost no strings attached as to the way in which the study will be conducted. Yet research directors fail to apply this same principle to those they hire to carry out data collection and processing. The hired assistant's desire to participate in the task and the creative contribution he might make is ignored with the result that the assistants' creativity is applied instead to covertly changing the nature of the task.

· · ·

What is a hired hand? So far I have been talking as if I knew and as if the hired hand could readily be distinguished from one who is not. This, of course, is not true. The issue is a complex one and information on it is, by its very nature, not very accessible. It is a crucial question which deserves study in its own right as part of the more general study of the process of "doing research."

Let me attempt a crude characterization of hired hand research, a characterization which hopefully will be greatly refined and perhaps reformulated with further study. *A hired hand is a person who feels that he has no stake in the research that he is working on, that he is simply expected to carry out assigned tasks and turn in results which will "pass inspection."* Of course, a hired assistant may not start out with the hired hand mentality, but may develop it if he finds that his talents for creativity are not called upon and that his suggestions and efforts at active participation are ignored.

From specific examples from the research world and by analogy from research on hired hands in other occupational spheres, I am convinced that research tasks carried out by hired hands are characterized, not rarely or occasionally, but *typically*, by restricted production, failure to carry out portions of the task, avoidance of the more unpleasant or difficult aspects of the research, and outright cheating. The results of research done in part or wholly by hired hands should be viewed as a dubious source for information about specific aspects of our social life or for the raw material for developing broader generalizations.

Of course, this leaves open the question of what constitutes a "stake in the research" and how one avoids or reduces the hired hand mentality. Again, I have no specific answers and hope that issue will receive much more attention than it has up to now. A stake may mean different things in various circumstances. For graduate students, a chance to share in planning and in writing and publication may often be important. For interviewers or field workers, the determination of the details of their procedure may be crucial. In an applied setting, the responsibility for the practical consequences of the research findings may be most important.[4]

It would also be worthwhile to examine the conditions which make for hired hand research. Here again, I have little specific to say and this subject, too, needs much more investigation. However, I will suggest a few factors I consider important.

SIZE: Hired hands can be found in research staffs of all sizes from one on up. However, it is clear that when a very small number of researchers are working together, there is a greater possibility of developing a true colleagueship in which each will be able to formulate some of his own ideas and put them into action. The larger the group, the more difficult this becomes, until the point is probably reached where it is virtually impossible, and the organization must be run on the basis of hierarchical staff relations with the lower echelons almost inevitably becoming hired hands.

SUBORDINATION: If some members of the research group are distinctly subordinate to others in a given organizational hierarchy or in general social status, it will be more difficult to develop a true colleague working relationship than if their status were more closely equal. The subordinate may hesitate to advance his ideas; the super-ordinate might be loath to admit that his lower-level co-worker be entitled to inject his ideas into the plans. Formal super-subordinate relationships can of course be muted and sometimes completely overcome in the course of personal contact, but certainly this is an initial, and sometimes permanent, basis for establishing hired hand status.

ADHERENCE TO RIGID PLANS: If a researcher believes that good research can be done only if a detailed plan of data collection, processing, and analysis is established in advance and adhered to throughout, he has laid the basis for hired hand research if he makes use of assistance from others who have not participated in the original plan. Sticking to a pre-formed plan means that others cannot openly introduce variations which may make the study more meaningful for them. Any creativity they apply will be of a surreptitious nature.

In their research methods texts, our students are told a great deal about the mechanics of research technique and little about the social process of researching. What little is said on the latter score consists largely of Pollyannaish statements about morale, honesty, and "proper motivation." It should be noted that appeals to morality and patriotism never reduced goldbricking and restriction of production in industry, even during the time of a world war. There is no reason to believe that analogous appeals to interviewers, graduate students, research assistants, and others who serve as hired hands will be any more effective. If we want to avoid the hired hand mentality, we must stop using people as hired hands.

Glaser and Strauss state that we regularly "discount" aspects of many, if not most, of all scientific analyses we read because we consider the research design one-sided, believe that it does not fit the social structure to which it was generalized, or that it does not fit in with our observations in an area where we have had considerable experience.[5]

I would like to suggest another area in which we might consistently apply the "discounting process." When reading a research report, we should pay close attention to the description of how the data were collected, processed, analyzed, interpreted, and written up with an eye to determining what part, if any, was played by hired hands. This will often be a difficult and highly tentative judgment, requiring much reading between the lines with the help of our knowledge of how our colleagues and we ourselves often operate. However, we can get hints from such things as the size of the staff, the nature of the relationship of the staff members, the manner in which the research plans were developed and applied, the organizational setting in which the research was done, mention made of assignment of tasks, and so on. If there is good reason to believe that significant parts of the research have been carried out by hired hands, this would, in my opinion, be a reason for discounting much or all of the results of the study.

NOTES

1. Donald Roy, "Quota Restriction and Goldbricking in a Machine Shop," *American Journal of Sociology*, 57 (March 1952), 427–42.

2. I want to emphasize once again that in a business setting, supervisors and executives, as well as production line workmen, participate in aspects of the hired hand mentality. None of them may have an intrinsic interest in the quality of the product. (See, for example, Melvin Dalton, *Men Who Manage* [New York: Wiley, 1959], esp. chaps. 7,8, and 9.) The same is the case in much large-scale research.

3. In this discussion I am assuming there *is* someone (or a small group of colleagues) who has initially formulated the research problem or area of concern because of intrinsic interest and curiosity. In much of our social science research we do not have even this saving grace and the research is formulated and carried out for various "political" reasons. In such cases, we cannot count on having anyone interested enough to try to turn the accumulations of data into a meaningful explanatory statement.

4. The "human relations in industry" movement has given us some useful suggestions about the circumstances which alienate workers and executives, and also ways in which industrial employees may be given a real stake in their jobs. See, for example, Douglas McGregor, *The Human Side of Enterprise* (New York: McGraw-Hill, 1960), Part 2.

5. Barney Glaser and Anselm L. Strauss, "Discovery of Substantive Theory: A Basic Strategy Underlying Qualitative Research," *American Behavioral Scientist*, 8 (February 1965), 5–12.

Review Questions

1. Discuss Roth's comparison of machine-shop operators and hired researchers. Give specific examples from both groups on restriction of output, deviation from work instructions, and the like.

2. How would you design a research project involving hired assistants so as to avoid or reduce the hired hand mentality?

3. By not being aware of the problems of hired hand research which Roth describes, sociologists themselves are guilty of failing to view the research process with a "sociological consciousness." What would Peter Berger have us do to research the research process?

ON THE SOCIAL PSYCHOLOGY OF THE PSYCHOLOGICAL EXPERIMENT: WITH PARTICULAR REFERENCE TO DEMAND CHARACTERISTICS AND THEIR IMPLICATIONS

Martin T. Orne

It is to the highest degree probable that the subject['s] . . . general attitude of mind is that of ready complacency and cheerful willingness to assist the investigator in every possible way by reporting to him those very things which he is most eager to find, and that the very questions of the experimenter . . . suggest the shade of reply expected. . . . Indeed . . . it seems too often as if the subject were now regarded as a stupid automaton. . . .

A. H. PIERCE, 1908[1]

SINCE THE TIME OF GALILEO, SCIENTISTS HAVE EMPLOYED THE LABORATORY EXPERIMENT as a method of understanding natural phenomena. Generically, the experimental method consists of abstracting relevant variables from complex situations in nature and reproducing in the laboratory segments of these situations, varying the parameters involved so as to determine the effect of the experimental variables. This procedure allows generalization from the information obtained in the laboratory situation back to the original situation as it occurs in nature. The physical sciences have made striking advances through the use of this method, but in the behavioral sciences it has often been difficult to meet two necessary requirements for meaningful experimentation: reproducibility and ecological validity.[2] It has long been recognized that certain differences will exist between the types of experiments conducted in the physical sciences and those in the behavioral sciences because the former investigates a universe of inanimate objects and forces, whereas the latter deals with animate organisms, often thinking, conscious subjects. However, recognition of this distinction has not always led to appropriate changes in the traditional experimental model of physics as employed in the behavioral sciences. Rather the experimental model has been

Martin T. Orne, "On the Social Psychology of the Psychological Experiment: With Particular Reference to Demand Characteristics and Their Implications," *American Psychologist*, 17 (November 1962), pp. 776–783. This paper was presented at the Symposium, "On the Social Psychology of the Psychological Experiment," American Psychological Association Convention, New York, 1961. The work reported here was supported in part by a Mental Health Service Research Grant, M-3369, National Institute of Mental Health. I wish to thank my associates Ronald E. Shor, Donald N. O'Connell, Ulric Neisser, Karl E. Scheibe, and Emily F. Carota for their comments and criticisms in the preparation of this paper.

so successful as employed in physics that there has been a tendency in the behavioral sciences to follow precisely a paradigm originated for the study of inanimate objects, i.e., one which proceeds by exposing the subject to various conditions and observing the differences in reaction of the subject under different conditions. However, the use of such a model with animal or human subjects leads to the problem that the subject of the experiment is assumed, at least implicitly, to be a *passive responder* to stimuli—an assumption difficult to justify. Further, in this type of model the experimental stimuli themselves are usually rigorously defined in terms of what *is done* to the subject. In contrast, the purpose of this paper will be to focus on what the human subject *does* in the laboratory: what motivation the subject is likely to have in the experimental situation, how he usually perceives behavioral research, what the nature of the cues is that the subject is likely to pick up, etc. Stated in other terms, what factors are apt to affect the subject's reaction to the well-defined stimuli in the situation? These factors comprise what will be referred to here as the "experimental setting."

Since any experimental manipulation of human subjects takes place within this larger framework or setting, we should propose that the above-mentioned factors must be further elaborated and the parameters of the experimental setting more carefully defined so that adequate controls can be designed to isolate the effects of the experimental setting from the effects of the experimental variables. Later in this paper we shall propose certain possible techniques of control which have been devised in the process of our research on the nature of hypnosis.

Our initial focus here will be on some of the qualities peculiar to psychological experiments. The experimental situation is one which takes place within the context of an explicit agreement of the subject to participate in a special form of social interaction known as "taking part in an experiment." Within the context of our culture the roles of subject and experimenter are well understood and carry with them well-defined mutual role expectations. A particularly striking aspect of the typical experimenter-subject relationship is the extent to which the subject will play his role and place himself under the control of the experimenter. Once a subject has agreed to participate in a psychological experiment, he implicitly agrees to perform a very wide range of actions on request without inquiring as to their purpose, and frequently without inquiring as to their duration.

Furthermore, the subject agrees to tolerate a considerable degree of discomfort, boredom, or actual pain, if required to do so by the experimenter.

For a more extensive discussion of these issues, see the following:

Martin T. Orne, "Demand Characteristics and the Concept of Quasi-Controls," in R. Rosenthal and R. Rosnow, eds., *Artifact in Behavioral Research*, New York: Academic Press, 1969, pp. 143–179.

Martin T. Orne, "Communication by the Total Experimental Situation: Why It is Important, How It is Evaluated, and Its Significance for the Ecological Validity of Findings," in P. Pliner, L. Krames, and T. Alloway, eds., *Communication and Affect*. New York: Academic Press, 1973, pp. 157–191.

Just about any request which could conceivably be asked of the subject by a reputable investigator is legitimized by the quasi-magical phrase, "This is an experiment," and the shared assumption that a legitimate purpose will be served by the subject's behavior. A somewhat trivial example of this legitimization of requests is as follows:

A number of casual acquaintances were asked whether they would do the experimenter a favor; on their acquiescence, they were asked to perform five push-ups. Their response tended to be amazement, incredulity and the question "Why?" Another similar group of individuals were asked whether they would take part in an experiment of brief duration. When they agreed to do so, they too were asked to perform five push-ups. Their typical response was "Where?"

The striking degree of control inherent in the experimental situation can also be illustrated by a set of pilot experiments which were performed in the course of designing an experiment to test whether the degree of control inherent in the *hypnotic* relationship is greater than that in a waking relationship.[3] In order to test this question, we tried to develop a set of tasks which waking subjects would refuse to do, or would do only for a short period of time. The tasks were intended to be psychologically noxious, meaningless, or boring, rather than painful or fatiguing.

For example, one task was to perform serial additions of each adjacent two numbers on sheets filled with rows of random digits. In order to complete just one sheet, the subject would be required to perform 224 additions! A stack of some 2,000 sheets was presented to each subject—clearly an impossible task to complete. After the instructions were given, the subject was deprived of his watch and told, "Continue to work; I will return eventually." Five and one-half hours later, the *experimenter* gave up! In general, subjects tended to continue this type of task for several hours, usually with little decrement in performance. Since we were trying to find a task which would be discontinued spontaneously within a brief period, we tried to create a more frustrating situation as follows:

Subjects were asked to perform the same task described above but were also told that when [they] finished the additions on each sheet, they should pick up a card from a large pile, which would instruct them on what to do next. However, every card in the pile read,

> You are to tear up the sheet of paper which you have just completed into a minimum of thirty-two pieces and go on to the next sheet of paper and continue working as you did before; when you have completed this piece of paper, pick up the next card which will instruct you further. Work as accurately and as rapidly as you can.

Our expectation was that subjects would discontinue the task as soon as they realized that the cards were worded identically, that each finished piece of work had to be destroyed, and that, in short, the task was completely meaningless.

Somewhat to our amazement, subjects tended to persist in the task for several hours with relatively little sign of overt hostility. Removal of the one-way screen did not tend to make much difference. The postexperimental inquiry helped to explain the subjects' behavior. When asked about the tasks, subjects would invariably attribute considerable meaning to their performance, viewing it as an endurance test or the like.

Thus far, we have been singularly unsuccessful in finding an experimental task which would be discontinued, or, indeed, refused by subjects in an experimental setting.[4,5] Not only do subjects continue to perform boring, unrewarding tasks, but they do so with few errors and little decrement in speed. It became apparent that it was extremely difficult to design an experiment to test the degree of social control in hypnosis, in view of the already *very high degree of control in the experimental situation itself.*

The quasi-experimental work reported here is highly informal and based on samples of three or four subjects in each group. It does, however, illustrate the remarkable compliance of the experimental subject. The only other situations where such a wide range of requests are carried out with little or no question are those of complete authority, such as some parent-child relationships or some doctor-patient relationships. This aspect of the experiment as a social situation will not become apparent unless one tests for it; it is, however, present in varying degrees in all experimental contexts. Not only are tasks carried out, but they are performed with care over considerable periods of time.

Our observation that subjects tend to carry out a remarkably wide range of instructions with a surprising degree of diligence reflects only one aspect of the motivation manifested by most subjects in an experimental situation. It is relevant to consider another aspect of motivation that is common to the subjects of most psychological experiments: high regard for the aims of science and experimentation.

A volunteer who participates in a psychological experiment may do so for a wide variety of reasons ranging from the need to fulfill a course requirement, to the need for money, to the unvoiced hope of altering his personal adjustment for the better, etc. Over and above these motives, however, college students tend to share (with the experimenter) the hope and expectation that the study in which they are participating will in some material way contribute to science and perhaps ultimately to human welfare in general. We should expect that many of the characteristics of the experimental situation derive from the peculiar role relationship which exists between subject and experimenter. Both subject and experimenter share the belief that whatever the experimental task is, it is important, and that as such no matter how much effort must be exerted or how much discomfort must be endured, it is justified by the ultimate purpose.

If we assume that much of the motivation of the subject to comply with any and all experimental instructions derives from an identification with the goals of science in general and the success of the experiment in particular,[6] it follows that the subject has a stake in the outcome of the study in which he is participating. For the volunteer subject to feel that he has made a useful contribution, it is necessary for him to assume that the experimenter is competent and that he himself is a "good subject."

The significance to the subject of successfully being a "good subject" is attested to by the frequent questions at the conclusion of an experiment, to the effect of, "Did I ruin the experiment?" What is most commonly meant by this is, "Did I perform well in my role as experimental subject?" or "Did my behavior demonstrate that which the experiment is designed to show?" Admittedly, subjects are concerned about their performance in terms of reinforcing their self-image; nonetheless, they seem even more concerned with the utility of their performances. We might well expect then that as far as the subject is able, he will behave in an experimental context in a manner designed to play the role of a "good subject" or, in other words, *to validate the experimental hypothesis.* Viewed in this way, the student volunteer is *not* merely a passive responder in an experimental situation but rather he has a very real stake in the successful outcome of the experiment. This problem is implicitly recognized in the large number of psychological studies which attempt to conceal the true purpose of the experiment from the subject in the hope of thereby obtaining more reliable data. This maneuver on the part of psychologists is so widely known in the college population that even if a psychologist is honest with the subject, more often than not he will be distrusted. As one subject pithily put it, "Psychologists always lie!" This bit of paranoia has some support in reality.

The subject's performance in an experiment might almost be conceptualized as problem-solving behavior; that is, at some level he sees it as his task to ascertain the true purpose of the experiment and respond in a manner which will support the hypotheses being tested. Viewed in this light, the totality of cues which convey an experimental hypothesis to the subject become significant determinants of subjects' behavior. We have labeled the sum total of such cues as the *"demand characteristics of the experimental situation"* (Orne, 1959a). These cues include the rumors or campus scuttlebutt about the research, the information conveyed during the original solicitation, the person of the experimenter, and the setting of the laboratory, as well as all explicit and implicit communications during the experiment proper. A frequently overlooked, but nonetheless very significant source of cues for the subject lies in the experimental procedure itself, viewed in the light of the subject's previous knowledge and experience. For example, if a test is given twice with some intervening treatment, even the dullest college student is aware that some change is expected, particularly if the test is in some obvious way related to the treatment.

The demand characteristics perceived in any particular experiment will vary with the sophistication, intelligence, and previous experience of each experimental subject. To the extent that the demand characteristics of the experiment are clear-cut, they will be perceived uniformly by most experimental subjects. It is entirely possible to have an experimental situation with clear-cut demand characteristics for psychology undergraduates which, however, does not have the same clear-cut demand characteristics for enlisted army personnel. It is, of course, those demand characteristics which are perceived by the subject that will influence his behavior.

We should like to propose . . . that a subject's behavior in any experimental situation will be determined by two sets of variables: (a) those which are traditionally defined as experimental variables and (b) the perceived demand characteristics of the experimental situation. The extent to which the subject's behavior is related to the demand characteristics, rather than to the experimental variable, will in large measure determine both the extent to which the experiment can be replicated with minor modification (i.e., modified demand characteristics) and the extent to which generalizations can be drawn about the effect of the experimental variables in nonexperimental contexts (the problem of ecological validity [Brunswik, 1947]).

It becomes an empirical issue to study under what circumstances, in what kind of experimental contexts, and with what kind of subject populations, demand characteristics become significant in determining the behavior of subjects in experimental situations. It should be clear that demand characteristics cannot be eliminated from experiments; all experiments will have demand characteristics, and these will always have some effect. It does become possible, however, to study the effect of demand characteristics as opposed to the effect of experimental variables. However, techniques designed to study the effect of demand characteristics need to take into account that these effects result from the subject's *active* attempt to respond appropriately to the *totality* of the experimental situation.

It is perhaps best to think of the perceived demand characteristics as a contextual variable in the experimental situation. We should like to emphasize that, at this stage, little is known about this variable. In our first study which utilized the demand characteristics concept (Orne, 1959b), we found that a particular experimental effect was present only in records of those subjects who were able to verbalize the experimenter's hypothesis. Those subjects who were unable to do so did not show the predicted phenomenon. Indeed we found that whether or not a given subject perceived the experimenter's hypothesis was a more accurate predictor of the subject's actual performance than his statement about what he thought he had done on the experimental task. It became clear from extensive interviews with subjects that response to the demand characteristics is not merely conscious compliance. When we speak of "playing the role of a good experimental subject," we use the concept analogously to the way in which Sarbin (1950) describes role playing in hypnosis: namely, largely on a nonconscious level. The demand characteristics of the situation help define the role of "good experimental subject," and the responses of the subject are a function of the role that is created.

We have a suspicion that the demand characteristics most potent in determining subjects' behavior are those which convey the purpose of the experiment effectively but not obviously. If the purpose of the experiment is not clear, or is highly ambiguous, many different hypotheses may be formed by different subjects, and the demand characteristics will not lead to clear-cut results. If, on the other hand, the demand characteristics are so obvious that the subject becomes fully conscious of the expectations of the experimenter, there is a tendency to lean over backwards to be honest. We are encountering here the effect of another facet of the college student's attitude toward science. While the student wants studies to "work," he feels he must be honest in his report; otherwise, erroneous conclusions will be drawn. Therefore, if the subject becomes acutely aware of the experimenter's expectations, there may be a tendency for biasing in the opposite direction. (This is analogous to the often observed tendency to favor individuals whom we dislike in an effort to be fair.)[7]

Delineation of the situations where demand characteristics may produce an effect ascribed to experimental variables, or where they may obscure such an effect and actually lead to systematic data in the opposite direction, as well as those experimental contexts where they do not play a major role, is an issue for further work. Recognizing the contribution to experimental results which may be made by the demand characteristics of the situation, what are some experimental techniques for the study of demand characteristics?

As we have pointed out, it is futile to imagine an experiment that could be created without demand characteristics. One of the basic characteristics of the human being is that he will ascribe purpose and meaning even in the absence of purpose and meaning. In an experiment where he knows some purpose exists, it is inconceivable for him not to form some hypothesis as to the purpose, based on some cues, no matter how meager; this will then determine the demand characteristics which will be perceived by and operate for a particular subject. Rather than eliminating this variable then, it becomes necessary to take demand characteristics into account, study their effect, and manipulate them if necessary.

One procedure to determine the demand characteristics is the systematic study of each individual subject's perception of the experimental hypothesis. If one can determine what demand characteristics are perceived by each subject, it becomes possible to determine to what extent these, rather than the experimental variables, correlate with the observed behavior. If the subject's behavior correlates better with the demand characteristics than with the experimental variables, it is probable that the demand characteristics are the major determinants of the behavior.

The most obvious technique for determining what demand characteristics are perceived is the use of post-experimental inquiry. In this regard, it is well to point out that considerable self-discipline is necessary for the experimenter to obtain a valid inquiry. A great many experimenters at least implicitly make the demand that the subject not perceive what is really going on. The temptation for the experimenter, in, say, a replication of an Asch group pressure experiment, is to ask the subject afterwards, "You didn't realize that the other fellows were confederates, did you?" Having obtained the required, "No," the experimenter breathes a sigh of relief and neither subject nor experimenter pursues the issue further.[8] However, even if the experimenter makes an effort to elicit the subject's perception of the hypothesis of the experiment, he may have difficulty in obtaining a valid report because the subject as well as he himself has considerable interest in appearing naive.

Most subjects are cognizant that they are not supposed to know any more about an experiment than they have been told and that excessive knowledge will disqualify them from participating, or, in the case of a postexperimental inquiry, [that] such knowledge will invalidate their performance. As we pointed out earlier, subjects have a real stake in viewing their performance as meaningful. For this reason, it is commonplace to find a pact of ignorance resulting from the intertwining motives of both experimenter and subject, neither wishing to create a situation where the particular subject's performance needs to be excluded from the study.

For these reasons, inquiry procedures are required to push the subject for information without, however, providing in themselves cues as to what is expected. The general question which needs to be explored is the subject's perception of the experimental purpose and the specific hypotheses of the experimenter. This can best be done by an open-ended procedure starting with the very general question of "What do you think that the experiment is about?" and only much later asking specific questions. Responses of "I don't know" should be dealt with by encouraging the subject to guess, use his imagination, and in general, by refusing to accept this response. Under these circumstances, the overwhelming majority of students will turn out to have evolved very definite hypotheses. These hypotheses can then be judged, and a correlation between them and experimental performance can be drawn.

Two objections may be made against this type of inquiry: (a) that the subject's perception of the experimenter's hypotheses is based on his own experimental behavior, and therefore a correlation between these two variables may have little to do with the determinants of behavior, and (b) that the inquiry procedure itself is subject to demand characteristics.

A procedure which has been independently advocated by Riecken (1958) and Orne (1959a) is designed to deal with the first of these objections. This consists of an inquiry procedure which is conducted much as though the subject had actually been run in the experiment, without, however, permitting him to be given any experimental data. Instead, the precise procedure of the experiment is explained, the experimental material is shown to the subject, and he is told what he would be required to do; however, he is not permitted to make any responses. He is then given a postexperimental inquiry as though he had been a subject. Thus, one would say, "If I had asked you to do all these things, what do you think that the experiment would be about, what do you think I would be trying to prove, what would my hypothesis be?" etc. This technique, which we have termed the pre-experimental inquiry, can be extended very readily to the giving of pre-experimental tests, followed by the explanation of experimental conditions and tasks, and the administration of post experimental tests. The subject is requested to behave on these tests as though he had been exposed to the experimental treatment that was described to him. This type of procedure is not open to the objection that the subject's own behavior has provided cues for him as to the purpose of the task. It presents him with a straight problem-solving situation and makes explicit what, for the true experimental subject, is implicit. It goes without saying that these subjects who are run on the pre-experimental inquiry conditions must be drawn from the same population as the experimental groups and may, of course, not be run subsequently in the experimental condition. This technique is one of approximation rather than of proof. However, if subjects describe behavior on the pre-inquiry conditions as similar to, or identical with, that actually given by subjects exposed to the experimental conditions, the hypothesis becomes plausible that demand characteristics may be responsible for the behavior.

It is clear that pre- and post-experimental inquiry techniques have their own demand characteristics. For these reasons, it is usually best to have the inquiry conducted by an experimenter who is not acquainted with the actual experimental behavior of the subjects. This will tend to minimize the effect of experimenter bias.

Another technique which we have utilized for approximating the effect of the demand characteristics is to attempt to hold the demand characteristics constant and eliminate the experimental variable. One way of accomplishing this purpose is through the use of simulating subjects. This is a group of subjects who are not exposed to the experimental variable to which the effect has been attributed, but who are instructed to act as if this were the case. In order to control for experimenter bias under these circumstances, it is advisable to utilize more than one experimenter and to have the experimenter who actually runs the subjects "blind" as to which group (simulating or real) any given individual belongs.

Our work in hypnosis (Damaser, Shor, & Orne, 1963; Orne, 1959b; Shor, 1959) is a good example of the use of simulating controls. Subjects unable to enter hypnosis are instructed to simulate entering hypnosis for another experimenter. The experimenter who runs the study sees both highly trained hypnotic subjects and simulators in random order and does not know to which group each subject belongs. Because the subjects are run "blind," the experimenter is more likely to treat the two groups of subjects identically. We have found that simulating subjects are able to perform with great effectiveness, deceiving even well-trained hypnotists. However, the simulating group is not exposed to the experimental condition (in this case, hypnosis) to which the given effect under investigation is often ascribed. Rather, it is a group faced with a problem-solving task: namely to utilize whatever cues are made available by the experimental context and the experimenter's concrete behavior in order to behave as they think that hypnotized subjects might. Therefore, to the extent that simulating subjects are able to behave identically, it is possible that demand characteristics, rather than the altered state of consciousness, could account for the behavior of the experimental group.

The same type of technique can be utilized in other types of studies. For example, in contrast to the placebo control in a drug study, it is equally possible to instruct some subjects not to take the medication at all, but to act as if they had. It must be emphasized that this type of control is different from the placebo control. It represents an approximation. It maximally confronts the simulating subject with a problem-solving task and suggests how much of the total effect could be accounted for by the demand characteristics—assuming that the experimental group had taken full advantage of them, an assumption not necessarily correct.

All of the techniques proposed thus far share the quality that they depend upon the active cooperation of the control subjects, and in some way utilize his thinking process as an intrinsic factor. The subject does *not* just respond in these control situations but, rather, he is required *actively* to solve the problem.

The use of placebo experimental conditions is a way in which this problem can be dealt with in a more classic fashion. Psychopharmacology has used such techniques extensively, but here too they present problems. In the case of placebos and drugs, it is often the case that the physician is "blind" as to whether a drug is placebo or active, but the patient is not, despite precautions to the contrary; i.e., the patient is cognizant that he does not have the side effects which some of his fellow patients on the ward experience. By the same token, in psychological placebo treatments, it is equally important to ascertain whether the subject actually perceived the treatment to be experimental or control. Certainly the subject's perception of himself as a control subject may materially alter the situation.

A recent experiment in our laboratory illustrates this type of investigation (Orne & Scheibe, 1964). We were interested in studying the demand characteristics of sensory deprivation experiments, independent of any actual sensory deprivation. We hypothesized that the overly cautious treatment of subjects, careful screening for mental or physical disorders, awesome release forms, and, above all, the presence of a "panic (release) button" might be more significant in producing the effects reported from sensory deprivation than the actual diminution of sensory input. A pilot study (Stare, Brown, & Orne, 1959), employing pre-inquiry techniques, supported this view. Recently, we designed an experiment to test more rigorously this hypothesis.

This experiment, which we called Meaning Deprivation, had all the *accoutrements* of sensory deprivation, including release forms and a red panic button. However, we carefully refrained from creating any sensory deprivation whatsoever. The experimental task consisted of sitting in a small experimental room which was well lighted, with two comfortable chairs, as well as ice water and a sandwich, and an optional task of adding numbers.

The subject did not have a watch during this time, the room was reasonably quiet, but not soundproof, and the duration of the experiment (of which the subject was ignorant) was four hours. Before the subject was placed in the experimental room, 10 tests previously used in sensory deprivation research were administered. At the completion of the experiment, the same tasks were again administered. A microphone and a one-way screen were present in the room, and the subject was encouraged to verbalize freely.

The control group of 10 subjects was subjected to the identical treatment, except that they were told that they were control subjects for a sensory deprivation experiment. The panic button was eliminated for this group. The formal experimental treatment of these two groups of subjects was the same in terms of the objective stress—four hours of isolation. However, the demand characteristics had been purposively varied for the two groups to study the effect of demand characteristics as opposed to objective stress. Of the 14 measures which could be quantified, 13 were in the predicted direction. . . .

This study suggests that demand characteristics may in part account for some of the findings commonly attributed to sensory deprivation. We have found similar significant effects of demand characteristics in accounting for a great deal of the findings reported in hypnosis. It is highly probable that careful attention to this variable, or group of variables, may resolve some of the current controversies regarding a number of psychological phenomena in motivation, learning, and perception.

In summary, we have suggested that the subject must be recognized as an active participant in any experiment, and that it may be fruitful to view the psychological experiment as a very special form of social interaction. We have proposed that the subject's behavior in an experiment is a function of the totality of the situation, which includes the experimental variables being investigated and at least one other set of variables which we have subsumed under the heading, demand characteristics of the experimental situation. The study and control of demand characteristics are not simply matters of good experimental technique; rather, it is an empirical issue to determine under what circumstances demand characteristics significantly affect subjects' experimental behavior. Several empirical techniques have been proposed for this purpose. It has been suggested that control of these variables in particular may lead to greater reproducibility and ecological validity in psychological experiments. With an increasing understanding of these factors intrinsic to the experimental context, the experimental method in psychology may become a more effective tool in predicting behavior in nonexperimental contexts.

NOTES

1. See reference list (Pierce, 1908).

2. Ecological validity, in the sense that Brunswik (1947) has used the term: appropriate generalization from the laboratory to nonexperimental situations.

3. These pilot studies were performed by Thomas Menaker.

4. Tasks which would involve the use of actual severe physical pain or exhaustion were not considered.

5. This observation is consistent with Frank's (1944) failure to obtain resistance to disagreeable or nonsensical tasks. He accounts for this "primarily by S's unwillingness to break the tacit agreement he had made when he volunteered to take part in the experiment, namely, to do whatever the experiment required of him" (p. 24).

6. This hypothesis is subject to empirical test. We should predict that there would be measurable differences in motivation between subjects who perceive a particular experiment as "significant" and those who perceive the experiment as "unimportant."

7. Rosenthal (1961) in his recent work on experimenter bias, has reported a similar type of phenomenon. Biasing was maximized by ego involvement of the experimenters, but when an attempt was made to increase biasing by paying for "good results," there was a marked reduction of effect. This reversal may be ascribed to the experimenters' becoming too aware of their own wishes in the situation.

8. Asch (1952) himself took great pains to avoid the pitfall.

REFERENCES

Asch, S. E., *Social Psychology* (New York: Prentice-Hall, 1952).

Brunswik, E., *Systematic and Representative Design of Psychological Experiments with Results in Physical and Social Perception* (Berkeley: University of California Press, 1947), Syllabus Series, no. 304.

Damaser, Esther C., Shor, R. E., and Orne, M. T., "Physiological Effects During Hypnotically-Requested Emotions," *Psychosomatic Medicine*, 4 (1963), 334–43.

Frank J. D., "Experimental Studies of Personal Pressure and Resistance: I. Experimental Production of Resistance." *Journal of General Psychology*, 30 (1944), 23–41.

Orne, M.T., "The Demand Characteristics of an Experimental Design and their Implications," paper read at American Psychological Association, Cincinnati, 1959a.

Orne, M. T., "The Nature of Hypnosis: Artifact and Essence," *Journal of Abnormal and Social Psychology*, 58 (1959b), 277–99.

Orne, M. T., and Scheibe, K. E., "The Contribution of Nondeprivation Factors in the Production of Sensory Deprivation Effects: The Psychology of the 'Panic Button,' " *Journal of Abnormal and Social Psychology*, 68 (1964), 3–12.

Pierce, A. H., "The Subconscious Again," *Journal of Philosophy, Psychology, and Scientific Method*, 5 (1908), 264–71.

Riecken, H. W., "A Program for Research on Experiments in Social Psychology," paper read at Behavioral Sciences Conference, University of New Mexico, 1958.

Rosenthal, R., "On the Social Psychology of the Psychological Experiment: With Particular Reference to Experimenter Bias," paper read at American Psychological Association, New York, 1961.

Sarbin, T. R., "Contributions to Role-taking Theory: I. Hypnotic Behavior," *Psychological Review*, 57 (1950), 255–70.

Shor, R. E., "Explorations in Hypnosis: A Theoretical and Experimental Study," unpublished doctoral dissertation, Brandeis University, 1959.

Stare, F., Brown, J., and Orne, M. T., "Demand Characteristics in Sensory Deprivation Studies," unpublished seminar paper, Massachusetts Mental Health Center and Harvard University, 1959.

Review Questions

1. Define the concepts "reproducibility" and "ecological validity." Why are these problems in experimental research?

2. What, according to Orne, are the characteristics of a "good subject" in a social science experiment?

3. How might the problems discussed by Orne with regard to experimental research also exist in survey research?

4. Give examples of how "demand characteristics" of experimental settings might affect the behavior of the subjects. Are these demand characteristics present in the research of physicists and chemists?

Suggested Readings: Introduction

Berger, Peter L. *Invitation to Sociology: A Humanist Perspective.* Garden City,N.Y.: Anchor Books, 1963.

_____, and Hansfried Kellner. *Sociology Reinterpreted: An Essay on Method and Vocation.* Garden City, N.Y.: Anchor Books, 1981.

Mills, C. Wright. *The Sociological Imagination.* New York: Oxford University Press, 1959.

Simmel, Georg. "The Problem of Sociology," trans. Albion W. Small, *The American Journal of Sociology,* 15, 3 (1909), 290–316.

Part II. Culture

A PRIMARY REASON FOR THE COMPLEXITY OF SOCIAL INTERACTION IS THAT OUR species has no instinctive patterns of behavior. While we do have biological drives and needs, we have no instincts that force us to meet these needs in patterned ways. Unlike other species, humans must create and learn their own ways of coping with the environment, which includes their fellow beings. Such strategies for coping and interacting are, to a large extent, shared with others. They make up a way of life, or *culture*. A culture comprises all the objects, ideas, beliefs, norms, and values of a group of people—and the meanings that the group applies to its cultural elements. From the culture, we learn what to define as good and bad, which animals to consider suitable for food and which to consider inedible, and even which smells are pleasant and which are not.

Cultures vary a great deal, according to both time and place. The way people earn their living, rear children, and clean their homes in Bolivia, for instance, is different from the way people in Iceland or even in Mexico carry out these tasks. But all cultures are alike in that they are *ethnocentric* (culture-centered). That is, the members of every society come to believe that their culture is best and natural and that societies which do things differently are inferior. Imagine that you are traveling in the Far East. There you learn that it is a common practice for people to eat dog meat—but because you have learned not to consider the dog as a source of food, you are likely to react very negatively. In India, you might consider it strange that people your own age marry partners selected by their parents. Upon questioning, you discover that the mates hadn't met until the wedding day. Your immediate reaction may be that the American way is superior. But why? Because it is the way that you know. Of course, current American dating practices are seen as strange and unnatural by people from India.

As we go through our daily routines we are usually unaware of the influence that culture has on human behavior. We eat with knives and forks, believe that one type of car is better than another, make assumptions about "human nature," pay bills printed by computers, and fall in love—oblivious of the fact that such behavior is *not* typical of people in every other society.

It is relatively easy to recognize the influence of culture by examining societies other than our own. When we read of the eating of dog meat or arranged marriages, we become aware that people's behavior depends upon the culture in which they are reared. It is more difficult, though, for us to step outside our own society to analyze the elements of American culture and to see their effects on *us*. When we do, however, we reduce the tendency to assume that other cultures are peculiar and wrong, and that ours is normal and good.

In a classic article, "Body Ritual among the Nacirema," the anthropologist Horace Miner helps us to stand apart from our culture and observe it in a more objective light. Miner originally wrote this article as a spoof on ethnocentric American anthropologists; the portion that is reprinted here humorously and imaginatively induces us to view components of our daily bathroom behavior from a new, and quite different, perspective. Miner's description is valuable just because it makes us realize how odd our behavior might seem to someone from another culture. We are so used to doing things in certain ways that we are often unaware of much of our own behavior and fail to consider that alternative behavior patterns (called "functional alternatives") exist.

The second and third selections alert us to the importance of *subcultural* norms, beliefs, and behavior patterns. A subculture is a somewhat, but not totally, unique way of life that exists within a larger culture. That is, members of a subsociety—such as an ethnic, religious, occupational, or even a deviant group, whose members choose and/or are forced to interact largely within that group—are affected both by the larger culture and by their subculture. In addition, subcultural patterns may exert an influence on the larger culture, as happened when the style of dress of 1960s youth spread to the fashion industry as a whole.

Migration from one society to another is a major way in which subcultures come to exist. Often, the way of life of the parent culture is brought with the migrants, surviving for one or more generations in the new environment. But at times, mere interaction within the confines of an immigrant subsociety leads to the creation of new cultural elements which existed neither in the old nor the new culture.

Italians who immigrated to America provide a good example. The adjustment they faced in their daily lives, as they moved from a primarily agricultural existence in southern Italy to an industrial way of life in the large cities of the United States, was severe. As Edwin Eames and Howard Robboy show in "The Sociocultural Context of an Italian-American Dietary Item," a sandwich evolved which allowed Italian factory workers to bring a part of their cultural heritage into the American factory to ease the cultural transition. The sandwich that we know as the submarine, hoagie, hero, poor boy, musalatta, zeppelin, torpedo, garibaldi, grinder, or Italian sandwich never existed in Italy and initially was eaten only by Italian workers in American factories. Soon other workers noticed them and began having them for lunch too. As time went on, the Italians began *assimilating*—becoming more like those in the dominant culture—and the sandwich underwent similar "assimilation." Two distinct processes of change can thus be observed. First, the immigrant group introduced a new food item into the culture. Second, over time, the item underwent modifications to meet the larger needs of the host society.

In the final selection, Mark Zborowski focuses on definitions of and reactions to the biologically based phenomenon of pain among members of several subsocieties—Jews, Italians, and "Old Americans." From his research, we learn that it is a mistake to assume that everyone attaches the same meaning to pain or that everyone deals with pain in the same way. We also see that the social meaning attached to pain is *learned* through *socialization*, rather than being a biological given. (The process of socialization will be examined in more detail in Part III.)

BODY RITUAL AMONG THE NACIREMA

Horace Miner

THE ANTHROPOLOGIST HAS BECOME SO FAMILIAR WITH THE DIVERSITY OF WAYS IN which different peoples behave in similar situations that he is not apt to be surprised by even the most exotic customs. In fact, if all of the logically possible combinations of behavior have not been found somewhere in the world, he is apt to suspect that they must be present in some yet undescribed tribe. This point has, in fact, been expressed with respect to clan organization by Murdock (1949:71). In this light, the magical beliefs and practices of the Nacirema present such unusual aspects that it seems desirable to describe them as an example of the extremes to which human behavior can go.

Professor Linton first brought the ritual of the Nacirema to the attention of anthropologists twenty years ago (1936:326), but the culture of this people is still very poorly understood. They are a North American group living in the territory between the Canadian Cree, the Yaqui and Tarahumare of Mexico, and the Carib and Arawak of the Antilles. Little is known of their origin, although tradition states that they came from the east. According to Nacirema mythology, their nation was originated by a culture hero, Notgnihsaw, who is otherwise known for two great feats of strength—the throwing of a piece of wampum across the river Pa-To-Mac and the chopping down of a cherry tree in which the Spirit of Truth resided.

Nacirema culture is characterized by a highly developed market economy which has evolved in a rich natural habitat. While much of the people's time is devoted to economical pursuits, a large part of the fruits of these labors and a considerable portion of the day are spent in ritual activity. The focus of this activity is the human body, the appearance and health of which loom as a dominant concern in the ethos of the people. While such a concern is certainly not unusual, its ceremonial aspects and associated philosophy are unique.

The fundamental belief underlying the whole system appears to be that the human body is ugly and that its natural tendency is to debility and disease. Incarcerated in such a body, man's only hope is to avert these characteristics through the use of the powerful influences of ritual and ceremony. Every household has one or more shrines devoted to this purpose. The more

Horace Miner, "Body Ritual Among the Nacirema," *American Anthropologist*, 58 (1955), 503–507.

powerful individuals in the society have several shrines in their houses and, in fact, the opulence of a house is often referred to in terms of the number of such ritual centers it possesses. Most houses are of wattle and daub construction, but the shrine rooms of the more wealthy are walled with stone. Poorer families imitate the rich by applying pottery plaques to their shrine walls.

While each family has at least one such shrine, the rituals associated with it are not family ceremonies but are private and secret. The rites are normally only discussed with children, and then only during the period when they are being initiated into these mysteries. I was able, however, to establish sufficient rapport with the natives to examine these shrines and to have the rituals described to me.

The focal point of the shrine is a box or chest which is built into the wall. In this chest are kept the many charms and magical potions without which no native believes he could live. These preparations are secured from a variety of specialized practitioners. The most powerful of these are the medicine men, whose assistance must be rewarded with substantial gifts. However, the medicine men do not provide the curative potions for their clients, but decide what the ingredients should be and then write them down in an ancient and secret language. This writing is understood only by the medicine men and by the herbalists who, for another gift, provide the required charm.

The charm is not disposed of after it has served its purpose, but is placed in the charm-box of the household shrine. As these magical materials are specific for certain ills, and the real or imagined maladies of the people are many, the charm-box is usually full to overflowing. The magical packets are so numerous that people forget what their purposes were and fear to use them again. While the natives are very vague on this point, we can only assume that the idea in retaining all the old magical materials is that their presence in the charm-box, before which the body rituals are conducted, will in some way protect the worshipper.

Beneath the charm-box is a small font. Each day every member of the family, in succession, enters the shrine room, bows his head before the charm-box, mingles different sorts of holy water in the font, and proceeds with a brief rite of ablution. The holy waters are secured from the Water Temple of the community, where the priests conduct elaborate ceremonies to make the liquid ritually pure.

In the hierarchy of magical practitioners, and below the medicine men in prestige, are specialists whose designation is best translated "holy-mouth-men." The Nacirema have an almost pathological horror of and fascination with the mouth, the condition of which is believed to have a supernatural influence on all social relationships. Were is not for the rituals of the mouth, they believe that their teeth would fall out, their gums bleed, their jaws shrink, their friends desert them, and their lovers reject them. They also believe that a strong relationship exists between oral and moral characteristics. For example, there is a ritual ablution of the mouth for children which is supposed to improve their moral fiber.

The daily body ritual performed by everyone includes a mouth-rite. Despite the fact that these people are so punctilious about care of the mouth, this rite involves a practice which strikes the uninitiated stranger as revolting. It was reported to me that the ritual consists of inserting a small bundle of hog hairs into the mouth, along with certain magical powders, and then moving the bundle in a highly formalized series of gestures.

In addition to the private mouth-rite, the people seek out a holy-mouth-man once or twice a year. These practitioners have an impressive set of paraphernalia, consisting of a variety of augers, awls, probes, and prods. The use of these objects in the exorcism of the evils of the mouth involves almost unbelievable ritual torture of the client. The holy-mouth-man opens the client's mouth and, using the above mentioned tools, enlarges any holes which decay may have created in the teeth. Magical materials are put into these holes. If there are no naturally occurring holes in the teeth, large sections of one or more teeth are gouged out so that the supernatural substance can be applied. In the client's view, the purpose of these ministrations is to arrest decay and to draw friends. The extremely sacred and traditional character of the rite is evident in the fact that the natives return to the holy-mouth-men year after year, despite the fact that their teeth continue to decay.

It is to be hoped that, when a thorough study of the Nacirema is made, there will be careful inquiry into the personality structure of these people. One has but to watch the gleam in the eye of a holy-mouth-man, as he jabs an awl into an exposed nerve, to suspect that a certain amount of sadism is involved. If this can be established, a very interesting pattern emerges, for most of the population shows definite masochistic tendencies. It was to these that Professor Linton referred in discussing a distinctive part of the daily body ritual which is performed only by men. This part of the rite involves scraping and lacerating the surface of the face with a sharp instrument. Special women's rites are performed only four times during each lunar month, but what they lack in frequency is made up in barbarity. As part of this ceremony, women bake their heads in small ovens for about an hour. The theoretically interesting point is that what seems to be a preponderantly masochistic people have developed sadistic specialists.

The medicine men have an imposing temple, or *latipso*, in every community of any size. The more elaborate ceremonies required to treat very sick patients can only be performed at this temple. These ceremonies involve not only the thaumaturge [or miracle worker] but a permanent group of vestal maidens who move sedately about the temple chambers in distinctive costume and headdress.

The *latipso* ceremonies are so harsh that it is phenomenal that a fair proportion of the really sick natives who enter the temple ever recover. Small children whose indoctrination is still incomplete have been known to resist attempts to take them to the temple because "that is where you go to die." Despite this fact, sick adults are not only willing but eager to undergo the protracted ritual purification, if they can afford to do so. No matter how ill the supplicant or how grave the emergency, the guardians of many temples will not admit a client if he cannot give a rich gift to the custodian. Even after one has gained admission and survived the ceremonies, the guardians will not permit the neophyte to leave until he makes still another gift.

The supplicant entering the temple is first stripped of all his or her clothes. In everyday life the Nacirema avoids exposure of his body and its natural functions. Bathing and excretory acts are performed only in the secrecy of the household shrine, where they are ritualized as part of the body-rites. Psychological shock results from the fact that body secrecy is suddenly lost upon entry into the *latipso*. A man, whose own wife has never seen him in an excretory act, suddenly finds himself naked and assisted by a vestal maiden while he performs his natural functions into a sacred vessel. This sort of ceremonial treatment is necessitated by the fact that the excreta are used by a diviner to ascertain the course and nature of the client's sickness. Female clients, on the other hand, find their naked bodies are subjected to the scrutiny, manipulation and prodding of the medicine men.

Few supplicants in the temple are well enough to do anything but lie on their hard beds. The daily ceremonies, like the rites of the holy-mouth-men, involve discomfort and torture. With ritual precision, the vestals awaken their miserable charges each dawn and roll them about on their beds of pain while performing ablutions, in the formal movements of which the maidens are highly trained. At other times they insert magic wands in the supplicant's mouth or force him to eat substances which are supposed to be healing. From time to time the medicine men come to their clients and jab magically treated needles into their flesh. The fact that these temple ceremonies may not cure, and may even kill the neophyte, in no way decreases the people's faith in the medicine men.

There remains one other kind of practitioner, known as a "listener." This witch-doctor has the power to exorcise the devils that lodge in the heads of people who have been bewitched. The Nacirema believe that parents bewitch their own children. Mothers are particularly suspected of putting a curse on children while teaching them the secret body rituals. The counter-magic of the witch-doctor is unusual in its lack of ritual. The patient simply tells the "listener" all his troubles and fears, beginning with the earliest difficulties he can remember. The memory displayed by the Nacirema in these exorcism sessions is truly remarkable. It is not uncommon for the patient to bemoan the rejection he felt upon being weaned as a babe, and a few individuals even see their troubles going back to the traumatic effects of their own birth.

In conclusion, mention must be made of certain practices which have their base in native esthetics but which depend upon the pervasive aversion to the natural body and its functions. There are ritual fasts to make fat people thin and ceremonial feasts to make thin people fat. Still other rites are used to make women's breasts larger if they are small, and smaller if they are large. General dissatisfaction with breast shape is symbolized in the fact that the ideal form is virtually outside the range of human variation. A few women afflicted with almost inhuman hypermammary development are so idolized that they make a handsome living by simply going from village to village and permitting the natives to stare at them for a fee.

Reference has already been made to the fact that excretory functions are ritualized, routinized, and relegated to secrecy. Natural reproductive functions are similarly distorted. Intercourse is taboo as a topic and scheduled as an act. Efforts are made to avoid pregnancy by the use of magical materials or by limiting intercourse to certain phases of the moon. Conception is actually very infrequent. When pregnant, women dress so as to hide their condition. Parturition takes place in secret, without friends or relatives to assist, and the majority of women do not nurse their infants.

· · ·

REFERENCES

Linton, Ralph, 1936, The Study of Man. New York, D. Appleton-Century Co.

Malinowski, Bronislaw, 1948, Magic, Science, and Religion. Glencoe, The Free Press.

Murdock, George P., 1949, Social Structure. New York, The Macmillan Co.

Review Questions

1. Using Miner's style of analysis, describe dating and courtship among the Nacirema.

2. Miner's article on the Nacirema was intended to point out the ethnocentrism of American anthropologists and sociologists. How does it do this?

3. Give examples of the sociological concepts *values, beliefs,* and *norms* from Miner's article.

THE SOCIO-CULTURAL CONTEXT OF AN ITALIAN-AMERICAN DIETARY ITEM

Edwin Eames and Howard Robboy

THE STIMULUS FOR THE FOLLOWING DISCUSSION WAS A SET OF OBSERVATIONS MADE IN the Philadelphia area which indicated to the authors that a particular kind of sandwich, most frequently called a hoagie, was extensively consumed by the general population, as well as the selected population of high school and college students.

The hoagie is a sandwich served on a long Italian roll which is generously filled with varieties of Italian meat and cheese, lettuce, tomato, onion, and sprinkled with oregano, red peppers and olive oil. This description does not fit all the sandwiches known by this name, but acts as an ideal type from which the other conglomerations are derived. It is not uncommon at the present time to find sandwiches of this type filled with tuna salad, boiled ham, turkey roll, corned beef, chipped steak and roast beef. The basic characteristics of this sandwich which distinguish it from other types is the roll, the use of fresh vegetables, such as lettuce, tomato and onion, and the use of dressing, such as oil and mayonnaise.

Some questions about the distribution of this item and the terms used for it presented themselves to the authors. Specifically, how extensively are such sandwiches found in the United States, how, where and when were they introduced, and what are the various names used for the item? Finally, we should like to discuss the changing utilization of this dietary item in the nation.

A major reason for viewing this item as more than a sandwich is its integration into the general cultural system. In a society on the move, one which is partially mesmerized by nonparticipatory mass communication media such as television, a society which truncates the time set aside for the consumption of food, this item has positive functions for the maintenance of the socio-cultural system.

Edwin Eames and Howard Robboy, "The Socio-Cultural Context of an Italian-American Dietary Item," *The Cornell Journal of Social Relations* 2 (Fall 1967), 63–75, by permission of the publisher.

METHODOLOGY

An extensive survey of classified advertisements was conducted for one
hundred American cities, selected on a geographic and population basis.
Telephone volumes were then obtained from the Temple University Library, the main branch of the Philadelphia Free Library, and the central
Philadelphia office of the Bell Telephone Company. The years covered were
1964–1966 in this part of the survey. In addition, telephone volumes from
1938–1943, 1945–1946, for Philadelphia were examined. An initial source in
the classified volumes was the listing of pizzerias and restaurants. If no listing for this sandwich appeared under either category, advertisements for
wholesale bakery goods were examined.[1] In those cases where pizzerias or
Italian restaurants were found, the advertisements were carefully examined
to determine if this type of sandwich, the sub, was being sold.

Prior to initiating the library research and continuing throughout the entire study, informants from various cities were utilized to establish an initial
list of terms for this sandwich. Since most of these informants were temporary residents of Philadelphia attending Temple University, they had some
knowledge of the sandwich, locally known as a hoagie, and could give us
the equivalent term used in the area where they had formerly resided.

Figure 1

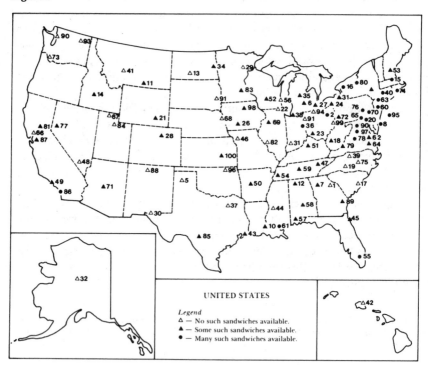

Another source of information was the travels of the authors and their residence in various cities. These visits were primarily centered in the Middle Atlantic, New England, and Southeastern states. Within this limited geographic region most of the terms found throughout the United States appeared.

EXTENT

Out of the one hundred cities investigated, sixty-eight are known or were known to have submarine sandwiches.[2] Converted to simple ratio terms, approximately seven out of ten cities have restaurants where subs are sold.

There are apparently three major geographic zones within the United States in which subs are not found. These three areas are the Northwest (Seattle, Portland, Boise and Helena), the Midwest (Milwaukee, Chicago, St. Louis, Kansas City, Omaha, Tulsa) and a portion of the Southeastern coast (Augusta, Charleston and Charlotte). (See Figure 1.) If a line is extended from the Northwest (Seattle) moving southeast to Fort Worth and then continued in a northerly direction to Bismarck, most of the cities lacking subs would be contained within the circumscribed area. Apparently this is an area in which the diffusion of the item has not taken place. Within the limits of our present knowledge it is not possible to determine the reasons for this particular geographic pattern.

In addition to exploring the existence or lack of existence of the sub, a very rough estimate of its utilization within a city can be made based upon the number of pizzerias and restaurants advertising this item. An intensive analysis of the frequency of advertising in the various cities suggests that the sandwich is extensively found in the Boston–Washington corridor which includes New York, Trenton, Newark, Philadelphia and Baltimore. One of the surprising results of this analysis is that Buffalo has more restaurants selling subs on a per capita basis than any other city.

ORIGINS

There seems to be little doubt that the sandwich was initially introduced into the United States by Italian immigrants. Arriving in the United States they maintained a dietary preference for Italian meat and cheese. This preference, coupled with the need for an inexpensive yet filling lunch, provided the stimulus for the invention of the sub.

Some studies have shown that immigrants of the late nineteenth century usually resided in the city in which their boat docked (Jones, 1960). It is for this reason that New Orleans could have been one center of invention and diffusion for the submarine sandwich. It is probable that people from the same area in southern Italy emigrated to the United States on different ships, and then settled in New Orleans and New York City respectively.

M.A. Jones (1960, p. 118), when speaking of the British and German ship-ping lines, states: "They started services to New York, Boston and New Or-leans from Naples, Genoa, Palermo, Fiume and Trieste. . . ."

When they arrived, they would have developed the need for a sandwich; the results of the interaction between the old and new environments pro-duced the submarine sandwich. That is, they brought with them their die-tary preferences including certain meat and cheese preparations; this coup-led with the need for an inexpensive yet filling sandwich at lunch, provided the setting for the introduction of this item. When the typical Italian mi-grant arrived in the United States, he had to make the adjustment from a peasant society with an agricultural base to a thriving industrial society; he had to shift from peasant to unskilled laborer. In Italy meals were eaten with the family; in the United States lunch had to be consumed on the job with fellow workers.[3] Since wages were low, an inexpensive yet filling meal was needed. The submarine sandwich fulfilled this requirement. It allowed the worker to eat his traditional homeland meats and cheese in a roll which provided adequate protection to the contents during travels from home to factory.

Since its first appearance in the United States (in the late 1880s) (Gehman, 1955) the submarine sandwich has always been popular with the working and/or lower socioeconomic groups, for it provides a large filling sandwich for a relatively low price. A dietician employed by a local hospital has ana-lyzed the contents of a typical sub produced in the Philadelphia area and has made the statement that this sandwich is a perfectly balanced meal.

Widespread acceptance of this item by the non-Italian working class pop-ulation seems to be highly correlated with periods of economic instability. The early twenties and thirties of the present century when the United States encountered economic depressions were times when the item was in great demand. This cannot, however, explain the current popularity since the United States has not faced a major depression since the World War II pe-riod.

The sandwich is usually associated with the Southern Italian since it is this immigrant group which constitutes the majority of the Italian migrants living in the United States today. However, there is no record of this sand-wich ever existing in its present form in Italy.[4] The closet analogy appears in Naples where little round rolls are filled with meat and cheese (Gehman, 1955) and in Rome where the "Pagnottella Imbottila," a large round roll split and stuffed with salami, prosciutto (ham) and cheese was sold in 1907 (Pei, 1955).

The New Orleans claim as the center of origin is based upon the existence of this item when C. O. Baily reported that he purchased this type of sand-wich in 1891 on a round roll for five cents (Baily, 1955). Another individual makes the claim that this sandwich first appeared in New Orleans in 1921 when Clovis and Benjamin Martin, in their French Market Cafe, invented the "Poor Boy." The Martins took the round family sized loaf and reshaped it to a long loaf and filled it with cheese, ham and tomatoes (Gehman, 1955). The discrepancy in dates may reflect a time lag between the original introduction and its popular acceptance.

New York's claim is based on the statement that Ernest Petrucci and the Manganaroas emigrated from Naples in 1885 and began selling the sandwich in a grocery store in Greenwich Village later that year (Gehman, 1955).

Chester, Pennsylvania, claims to be the "Hoagie Capital of the World" (Bagish, 1955). Catherine DiCostanza states that it was in her newly opened grocery store in 1924 that the "Italian Sandwich" was born. She claims that one evening in 1924, a group of men were playing cards next door, when one of the players became hungry and proceeded to split an Italian bread and pile different varieties of meat, cheese and fresh vegetables into the large loaf. A few weeks later, Mrs. DiCostanza made a similar sandwich for a truck driver working in the neighborhood, who, amazed by the size and taste, proceeded to show the sandwich to the other workers in the depot. They began eating the sandwich, and by the summer of 1927, lines two blocks long were formed by people who craved this meal. Mrs. DiCostanza, an excellent informant, is still preparing these sandwiches in the same store. She claims to have been one of the first users of an electric meat slicer for the preparation of the ingredients for these. The great demand for the sandwich led to the use of the electric cutter.

Philadelphia's claim to be the originator of the "Hoagie" is based on an account which states that during the first World War, shipyard workers in South Philadelphia used to eat them for their lunch (*Philadelphia Evening Bulletin*, 1953c).

There is a distinct difference between the roll used in the sandwich first seen in New York in 1885 and the one introduced in New Orleans in 1891. The New York version was identical to that of today, while its New Orleans' counterpart was reported to be served on a round roll similar to the one used in Naples and Rome. The round roll is no longer used in New Orleans, but the date of its transformation to its longer brother is unknown.

Thus there are conflicting statements about the location of the original diffusion center for the submarine sandwich. With the current recognition of the extent of independent invention (Herskovits, 1964), it is possible that this is a case of parallel development: "What the culture needs, people invent." It is unlikely that Philadelphia and Chester can be considered as primary diffusion centers because of chronological factors. The New York and New Orleans claims date back to the 1880s, while the former two cities can only substantiate their claims with evidence from the First World War at best. It is also possible to suggest that the principle of limited possibilities is operative (Goldenweiser, 1913); given the Italian roll, Italian meats and cheese, it is quite possible that a number of different shopkeepers put them together without any knowledge of this item being invented in other places at approximately the same time.

TERMINOLOGICAL VARIATION AND DERIVATION

The term submarine has been used as a general name for this sandwich because it is the one most frequently found (see Table 1). There are ten additional terms which have been found: hoagie,[5] poor boy,[6] grinder, torpedo,
Italian sandwich, hero, rocket, zeppelin, Garibaldi, Musalatta. There may
be additional terms which we have not been able to determine with the data
collecting techniques employed. This is quite probably the case, since David

**Table 1. Terms Used for Submarine Sandwich in One Hundred American
Cities Listed Alphabetically (Numbers Correspond to Map)**

NO.	EXTENT	CITY	TERMS*	NO.	EXTENT	CITY	TERMS*
1	X	Augusta	—	30	X	El Paso	—
2	#	Akron	S, G	31	+	Erie	S, H
3	+	Albany	S	32	X	Evansville	—
4	#	Allentown	H, I. S.	33	X	Fairbanks	—
5	X	Amarillo	—	34	+	Fargo	H
6	+	Ann Arbor	H	35	+	Flint	S
7	+	Atlanta	P. B.	36	#	Fort Wayne	S
8	#	Atlantic C.	S	37	X	Fort Worth	—
9	#	Baltimore	S	38	+	Gary	S-T
10	+	Baton Rouge	P. B.	39	X	Greensboro	—
11	+	Billings	P. B.-S	40	#	Hartford	G
12	+	Birmingham	H	41	X	Helena	—
13	X	Bismarck	—	42	X	Honolulu	—
14	X	Boise	—	43	+	Houston	P. B.
15	#	Boston	S	44	X	Jackson	—
16	#	Buffalo	S, H	45	+	Jacksonville	S
17	X	Charleston, S.C.	—	46	X	Kansas City, Mo.	—
18	+	Charleston, W. Va.	S	47	+	Knoxville	H
19	X	Charlotte	—	48	X	Las Vegas	—
20	#	Chester	H, G	49	+	Los Angeles	S
21	+	Cheyenne	R	50	+	Little Rock	S
22	X	Chicago	—	51	+	Louisville	I. S.
23	+	Cincinnati	H, S, R	52	+	Madison	G
24	+	Cleveland	S, G	53	+	Manchester	T
25	#	Columbus	S	54	+	Memphis	P. B.
26	+	Des Moines	G, S-H	55	#	Miami	S
27	+	Detroit	S	56	X	Milwaukee	—
28	+	Denver	S	57	+	Mobile	P. B.
29	X	Duluth	—	58	+	Montgomery	P. B.
				59	+	Nashville	S

Table 1/continues

Shulman (1959) indicates that restaurant proprietors may call sandwiches by any name they desire. He states:

> A slight change in the preparation of some well known sandwich, for example, may evoke various names, such as "hero sandwich," "French dip," and so on. Every cook or luncheonette owner may change or add names to his menus to suit his own taste or fancy. . . . The question is when are these names accepted by the general population. (Shulman, 1959, p. 26.)

These terms may be grouped into two categories. One category is descriptive of the roll and sandwich; terms such as submarine, torpedo, rocket and

Table 1. Continued

NO.	EXTENT	CITY	TERMS[*]	NO.	EXTENT	CITY	TERMS[*]
60	#	Newark	H, S-H	81	+	Sacramento	P. B.-S
61	#	New Orleans	P. B.	82	X	Saint Louis	—
62	+	Newport		83	+	Saint Paul	S
		News	S	84	X	Salt Lake City	—
63	#	New York City	H	85	+	San Antonio	T
64	+	Norfolk	S	86	#	San Diego	T
65	#	Norristown	Z	87	+	San Francisco	G
66	X	Oakland, Cal.	—				
67	X	Ogden	—	88	X	Santa Fe	—
68	X	Omaha	—	89	+	Savannah	S
69	+	Peoria	P. B.	90	X	Seattle	—
70	#	Philadelphia	H, S, G				
71	+	Phoenix	S	91	X	Sioux Falls	—
72	+	Pittsburgh	H, S	92	X	South Bend	—
				93	X	Spokane	—
73	X	Portland	—	94	+	Toledo	S
74	#	Providence	G, H	95	#	Trenton	H, S
75	X	Raleigh	—	96	X	Tulsa	—
76	#	Reading	I.S., H.-S	97	#	Washington, D.C.	S, H
77	+	Reno	T				
78	#	Richmond	S	98	+	Waterloo	S
79	+	Roanoke	S	99	X	Wheeling	—
80	#	Rochester	S	100	+	Wichita	S

S: SUBMARINE; G: GRINDER; I.S.: ITALIAN SANDWICH; P.B.: POOR BOY; R: ROCKET; H: HERO; T: TORPEDO; Z: ZEPPELIN; G: GARIBALDI; M: MUSALATTA; H: HOAGIE.

X   NO SUBS
+   SOME SUBS
#   MANY SUBS
•   WHERE MORE THAN ONE TERM IS USED, THE FIRST TERM SEPARATED BY A COMMA INDICATES THE TERM MOST COMMONLY LISTED.
IF TWO TERMS ARE APPROXIMATELY EQUAL IN THE LISTINGS THEN THEY ARE CONNECTED BY A HYPHEN.

zeppelin would be subsumed under this type. It is worth noting that submarine and torpedo are terms found extensively in coastal areas where shipping interests are important. The only place in the country where it is called a zeppelin is Norristown, Pennsylvania.

The second major category of terms is descriptive of the consumer; this would include terms such as hero and poor boy. Although both terms describe the sandwich eater, one term, hero, has affirmative characteristics while the other term, poor boy, used primarily in the southern portion of the United States, indicates negative characteristics of the person who is consuming this particular item. The use of this term is additional evidence of the lower class origin and initial consumption of the item.

The term Italian sandwich is descriptive of the originators of the item, rather than the appearance or present consumer. It does not appear to have either positive or negative connotations. A similar term found only in Madison, Wisconsin, is Garibaldi (*Newsweek*, 1967).

In New Orleans, where the common term is poor boy, an alternative Italian term, Musalatta, is found for that type of sandwich which contains Italian meat and cheese, rather than the ham and swiss cheese normally found in the poor boy. The Musalatta is sold in specialty Italian stores, particularly those near the French market. The translation of the term is "wide snout." Therefore, it is possible that this name could fit into either of the two previously suggested categories; it might describe the pig, since snout commonly refers to this animal's facial composition, and it is the common source of the meats used, or it could refer to the consumer, who would have to have a wide mouth to consume the product.

Two terms which present problems for this analysis are grinder and hoagie. M. Gehman (1955) suggests that the term grinder refers to the need to grind the materials contained in the sandwich with one's teeth.

Perhaps the most intriguing term we have discovered is hoagie. In some of the earlier advertisements the terms hoggy and hoggie appear. However, the first use of any of these terms is in the 1943 Philadelphia Telephone Directory. Hoagie may refer to either the meat content of the sandwich which is derived from hogs or to the consumer who would appear to the observer of the consuming process as a hog. Some explanations of this term found in a local Philadelphia newspaper in response to a query are:

1. Pat, the owner of Pat's Steaks, the originator of the Philadelphia steak sandwich and proprietor of a well-known stand in the Philadelphia Italian market, claims the name hoggie is derived from hoggy, which refers to either the fact that the meats used are normally of pork origin or the sandwich resembles a hog's back. From these terms, the currently used hoagie was a simple derivative (*Philadelphia Evening Bulletin*, 1953d).

2. Another reader claims that during World War I, Italian laborers at the Hog Island[7] Shipyard used to congregate in one area at lunch time. Their

lunches consisted of long loaves of Italian bread filled with cold meat and cheese. Other people watching them eat used to shout, "There's enough there to feed a couple of pigs." The retort of the laborers would be, "That's what they are (the sandwiches), Hog Islanders." The term Hog Islanders was shortened to "Hoggies" and then to "Hoagie" (*Philadelphia Evening Bulletin*, 1953c).

3. A third account refers to the legend that in South Philadelphia when Irishmen worked with Italians, the latter would call the former by the nickname, "Hogans." The sandwich was also popular with the Irish laborers who imitated the eating habits of their fellow workers. Thus the sandwich was known as a "Hogan" and later changed to "Hoagie" (*Philadelphia Evening Bulletin*, 1953a).

4. A fourth reader claims, "About 1926, my mother had a grocery store in South Philadelphia near a railroad and hoboes used to buy these large Italian sandwiches. Since all hoboes were known to be "on the hoke," it became known as the hoke sandwich, later as hokie and the name later changed to hoagie" (*Philadelphia Evening Bulletin*, 1953b).

USE OF THE ITEM

Although our primary concern in this paper has been the distribution of the submarine sandwich and the derivation and use of various terms for this item, it might be worth noting some of the changes in its use during the last two decades.

It has previously been stated that subs were initially part of lower class life, particularly life among Italian urban laborers. Acceptance of the sub by other segments of the working class and members of the middle class cannot be adequately documented at that time, although its popularity during the economic depressions of the twenties and thirties has been noted by several older informants. It is apparent, however, that the sandwich has been accepted by middle class segments of the population at the present time.

As an indication of this acceptance, a recent newspaper article stated that the Methodist Church in Philadelphia was using hoagies in a fund raising drive (*Philadelphia Evening Bulletin*, 1967). Significantly, this article appears on the society page. Additional evidence of widespread acceptance by middle-class society can be deduced from an advertisement which is carried by the *New York Times* (*New York Times*, 1967). This advertisement is for a six-foot-long hero sandwich which must be ordered in advance and will be · delivered any place in New York City. Since the advertised cost of this item is $34.50, it certainly falls outside the economic range within which lower class social groups entertain one another. An informant from New York City stated that she and her husband, along with approximately ten additional couples, had recently been entertained with the serving of this somewhat questionable delicacy after midnight.

Another significant shift which has occurred is the addition of the submarine sandwich to a list of foods such as snack dinners and late evening meals. Our informant in Chester, who claims to have been the originator of the sub, stated that she is now selling more subs in the evening than at lunch time. The previously cited *New York Times* advertisement also confirms this change. In a society which is experiencing rapid change, it is not surprising that an integral part of that society's culture, such as the sub, will also show change and adaptation.

It should be noted that the sub is also very popular among high school and college students. Many of the same reasons for the origin of the sandwich among the laboring urban population can be related to the extensive occurrence of the sandwich in cities with large nonindigenous college populations.

The acceptance of this lower-class cultural item by the middle-class population is an interesting example of what might be called the "trickle up" process, or more generally, cultural assimilation. Most studies of culture change have emphasized the opposite process, "trickle down" or the "massification" of relatively elite cultural items. The process of "trickle up" is an interesting contrast of an opposing process called lagging emulation (Friedl, 1964) in which the lower class, rural segments of the population do not "catch up" with the urban elite segment. In this instance, and in other cases such as the acceptance of jazz and items of clothing, it is the middle class borrowing from the lower class.

Since America is a pluralistic society with a synthetic culture based upon the borrowing of cultural traits from a wide range of originating or donor cultures (Linton, 1936) it should not be surprising that in the blending process Italian, Irish, Polish, and other national elements have been borrowed. However, the process which we are presently describing is not just borrowing from an ethnic group; more important, it is borrowing from a lower socioeconomic stratum with an overlay of ethnicity. Not enough attention has been paid to this process in the literature. It is hoped that a paper of the type presented here will help stimulate such studies in the future.

NOTES

1. In the case of Los Angeles no listing appeared under pizzerias or restaurants. However, a wholesale bakery advertised submarine rolls which led to the inclusion of this city in the group having the item. This procedure was followed for all cities which did not have a listing under either of the two common categories. However, only one case was obtained through this method. One additional technique used was to telephone restaurant owners in those cities where a sandwich was advertised under some indeterminate name. In Cheyenne, we found a listing for rockets. After

telephoning the restaurant and obtaining a description of the sandwich we were able to include the city and name in the appropriate places.

2. The term *sub* or *submarine sandwich* will be used as the general term for this item since it is the most extensively used term in the United States.

3. Recent field work in an Italian village by Mr. E. Cohen suggests that peasants do not take sandwiches to the fields for lunch. Personal communication.

4. Mr. Cohen's fieldwork in 1956–1966 confirmed this statement made by Gehman (1955, p. 69). Mr. Cohen has suggested that it is possible that in some remote local area of southern Italy this sandwich might be found. It is possible that such an item did not attain any great popularity in Italy, but when transported to the United States it did receive general acceptance. This is, of course, completely conjectural and would have to be submitted to detailed empirical testing in southern Italy.

5. Also appears as hoggy, hoggie, hoagy.

6. Also appears as po boy.

7. Hog Island is located in South Philadelphia near the present location of the Navy Yard. Its shape on the map is supposed to resemble a hog's snout.

REFERENCES

Bagish, D., Letters to the Editor. *Saturday Evening Post*, 1955, 227, 6.

Bailey, C. Letters to the Editor. *Saturday Evening Post*, 1955, 227, 6.

Friedl, E., Lagging Emulation in Post-Peasant Society, *American Anthropologist*, 1964, 66, 569–86.

Gehman, R., The Noblest Sandwich of Them All. *Saturday Evening Post*, 1955, 16–17.

Goldenweiser, A., The Principle of Limited Possibilities in the Development of Culture. *Journal of American Folk-Lore*, 1913, 26, 259–290.

Herskovits, M., *Cultural Anthropology*. New York: Knopf, 1964.

Jones, M., *American Immigration*. Chicago: University of Chicago Press, 1960.

Linton, R., *The Study of Man*. New York: Appleton-Century-Crofts, 1936.

New York Times, March 18, 1963, 116, 33.

Pei, M., Letters to the Editor. *Saturday Evening Post*, 1955, 227, 6.

Philadelphia Evening Bulletin, September 7, 1953, 106, 29. (a)

Philadelphia Evening Bulletin, September 23, 1953, 106, 59. (b)

Philadelphia Evening Bulletin, October 7, 1953, 106, 59. (c)

Philadelphia Evening Bulletin, October 9, 1953, 106, 63. (d)

Philadelphia Evening Bulletin, March 8, 1967, 120, 33.

Shulman, D., Culinary Americanisms. *American Speech*, 1959, 34, 26–32.

Review Questions

1. How does the history of the submarine sandwich parallel the history of the Italian-American community in the United States?

2. What part did migration and interaction within the Italian subsociety play in the creation of the submarine sandwich?

3. How has the diffusion of the submarine sandwich through the social classes of American society differed from usual patterns of diffusion?

CULTURAL COMPONENTS IN RESPONSES TO PAIN

Mark Zborowski

THIS PAPER REPORTS ON ONE ASPECT OF A LARGER STUDY: THAT CONCERNED WITH discovering the role of cultural patterns in attitudes toward and reactions to pain which is caused by disease and injury—in other words, responses to spontaneous pain.

SOME BASIC DISTINCTIONS

In human societies biological processes vital for man's survival acquire social and cultural significance. Intake of food, sexual intercourse or elimination—physiological phenomena which are universal for the entire living world—become institutions regulated by cultural and social norms, thus fulfilling not only biological functions but social and cultural ones as well. Metabolic and endocrinal changes in the human organism may provoke hunger and sexual desire, but culture and society dictate to man the kind of food he may eat, the social setting for eating or the adequate partner for mating.

Moreover, the role of cultural and social patterns in human physiological activities is so great that they may in specific situations act against the direct biological needs of the individual, even to the point of endangering his survival. Only a human being may prefer starvation to the breaking of a religious dietary law or may abstain from sexual intercourse because of specific incest regulations. Voluntary fasting and celibacy exist only where food and sex fulfill more than strictly physiological functions.

Thus, the understanding of the significance and role of social and cultural patterns in human physiology is necessary to clarify those aspects of human experience which remain puzzling if studied only within the physiological frame of reference.

Pain is basically a physiological phenomenon and as such has been studied by physiologists and neurologists such as Harold Wolff, James Hardy, Helen Goodell, C. S. Lewis, W. K. Livingston and others. By using the most ingenious methods of investigation they have succeeded in clarifying complex problems of the physiology of pain. Many aspects of perception and re-

Mark Zborowski, "Cultural Components in Responses to Pain," *Journal of Social Issues*, 8 (1953), 16–31. .

action to pain were studied in experimental situations involving most careful preparation and complicated equipment. These investigators have come to the conclusion that "from the physiological point of view pain qualifies as a sensation of importance to the self-preservation of the individual."[1] The biological function of pain is to provoke special reactive patterns directed toward avoidance of the noxious stimulus which presents a threat to the individual. In this respect the function of pain is basically the same for man as for the rest of the animal world.

However, the physiology of pain and the understanding of the biological function of pain do not explain other aspects of what Wolff, Hardy and Goodell call the *pain experience,* which includes not only the pain sensation and certain automatic reactive responses but also certain "associated feeling states."[2] It would not explain, for example, the acceptance of intense pain in torture which is part of the initiation rites of many primitive societies, nor will it explain the strong emotional reactions of certain individuals to the slight sting of the hypodermic needle.

In human society pain, like so many other physiological phenomena, acquires specific social and cultural significance, and, accordingly, certain reactions to pain can be understood in the light of this significance. As Drs. Hardy, Wolff and Goodell state in their recent book, ". . . the culture in which a man finds himself becomes the conditioning influence in the formation of the individual reaction patterns to pain . . . A knowledge of group attitudes toward pain is extremely important to an understanding of the individual reaction."[3]

In analyzing pain it is useful to distinguish between *self-inflicted, other-inflicted* and *spontaneous* pain. Self-inflicted pain is defined as deliberately self-inflicted. It is experienced as a result of injuries performed voluntarily upon oneself, e.g., self-mutilation. Usually these injuries have a culturally defined purpose, such as achieving a special status in the society. It can be observed not only in primitive cultures but also in contemporary societies on a higher level of civilization. In Germany, for instance, members of certain student or military organizations would cut their faces with a razor in order to acquire scars which would identify them as members of a distinctive social group. By other-inflicted pain is meant pain inflicted upon the individual in the process of culturally accepted and expected activities (regardless of whether approved or disapproved), such as sports, fights, war, etc. To this category belongs also pain inflicted by the physician in the process of medical treatment. Spontaneous pain usually denotes the pain sensation which results from disease or injury. This term also covers pains of psychogenic nature.

Members of different cultures may assume differing attitudes toward these various types of pain. Two of these attitudes may be described as pain expectancy and pain acceptance. Pain expectancy is anticipation of pain as being unavoidable in a given situation, for instance, in childbirth, in sports activities or in battle. Pain acceptance is characterized by a willingness to experience pain. This attitude is manifested mostly as an inevitable component of culturally accepted experiences, for instance, as part of initiation rites or part of medical treatment. The following example will help to clarify the differences between pain expectancy and pain acceptance: Labor pain is expected as part of childbirth, but while in one culture, such as in the United States, it is not accepted and therefore various means are used to alleviate it, in some other cultures, for instance in Poland, it is not only expected but also accepted, and consequently nothing or little is done to relieve it. Similarly, cultures which emphasize military achievements expect and accept battle wounds, while cultures which emphasize pacificistic values may expect them but will not accept them.

In the process of investigating cultural attitudes toward pain it is also important to distinguish between *pain apprehension* and *pain anxiety*. Pain apprehension reflects the tendency to avoid the pain sensation as such, regardless of whether the pain is spontaneous or inflicted, whether it is accepted or not. Pain anxiety, on the other hand, is a state of anxiety provoked by the pain experience, focused upon various aspects of the causes of pain, the meaning of pain or its significance for the welfare of the individual.

Moreover, members of various cultures may react differently in terms of their manifest behavior toward various pain experiences, and this behavior is often dictated by the culture which provides specific norms according to the age, sex and social position of the individual.

The fact that other elements as well as cultural factors are involved in the response to a spontaneous pain should be taken into consideration. These other factors are the pathological aspect of pain, the specific physiological characteristics of the pain experience, such as the intensity, the duration and the quality of the pain sensation, and, finally, the personality of the individual. Nevertheless, it was felt that in the process of a careful investigation it would be possible to detect the role of the cultural components in the pain experience.

THE RESEARCH SETTING

In setting up the research we were interested not only in the purely theoretical aspects of the findings in terms of possible contribution to the understanding of the pain experience in general; we also had in mind the practical goal of a contribution to the field of medicine. In the relationship between the doctor and his patient the respective attitudes toward pain may play a crucial role, especially when the doctor feels that the patient exaggerates his pain while the patient feels that the doctor minimizes his suffering. The same may be true, for instance, in a hospital where the members of the medical and nursing staff may have attitudes toward pain different from those held by the patient, or when they expect a certain pattern of behavior ac-

cording to their cultural background while the patient may manifest a behavior pattern which is acceptable in his culture. These differences may
play an important part in the evaluation of the individual pain experience,
in dealing with pain at home and in the hospital, in administration of
analgesics, etc. Moreover, we expected that this study of pain would offer
opportunities to gain insight into related attitudes toward health, disease,
medication, hospitalization, medicine in general, etc.

With these aims in mind the project was set up at the Kingsbridge Veterans Hospital, Bronx, New York,[4] where four ethnocultural groups were
selected for an intensive study. These groups included patients of Jewish,
Italian, . . . and "Old American" stock. [Two] groups—Jews [and] Italians
. . .—were selected because they were described by medical people as manifesting striking differences in their reaction to pain. Italians and Jews were
described as tending to "exaggerate" their pain. . . . [T]he "Old Americans"
were chosen because the values and attitudes of this group dominate in the
country and are held by many members of the medical profession and by
many descendants of the immigrants who, in the process of Americanization, tend to adopt American patterns of behavior. The members of this
group can be defined as white, native-born individuals, usually Protestant,
whose grandparents, at least, were born in the United States and who do
not identify themselves with any foreign group, either nationally, socially
or culturally.

The Kingsbridge Veterans Hospital was chosen because its population
represents roughly the ethnic composition of New York City, thus offering
access to a fair sample of the [three] selected groups, and also because various age groups were represented among the hospitalized veterans of World
War I, World War II and the Korean War. In one major respect this hospital
was not adequate, namely, in not offering the opportunity to investigate sex
differences in attitude toward pain. This aspect of research will be carried
out in a hospital with a large female population.

In setting up this project we were mainly interested in discovering certain
regularities in reactions and attitudes toward pain characteristic of the
[three] groups. Therefore, the study has a qualitative character, and the efforts of the researchers were not directed toward a collection of material
suitable for quantitative analysis. The main techniques used in the collection of the material were interviews with patients in the selected groups, observation of their behavior when in pain and discussion of the individual
cases with doctors, nurses and other people directly or indirectly involved
in the pain experience of the individual. In addition to the interviews with
patients, "healthy" members of the respective groups were interviewed on
their attitudes toward pain, because in terms of the original hypothesis
those attitudes and reactions which are displayed by the patients of the
given cultural groups are held by all members of the group regardless of
whether or not they are in pain although [when] in pain these attitudes may
come more sharply into focus. In certain cases the researchers have inter-

viewed a member of the patient's immediate family in order to check the report of the patient on his pain experience and in order to find out what are the attitudes and reactions of the family toward the patient's experience.

These interviews, based on a series of open-ended questions, were focused upon the past and present pain experiences of the interviewee. However, many other areas were considered important for the understanding of this experience. For instance, it was felt that complaints of pain may play an important role in manipulating relationships in the family and the larger social environment. It was also felt that in order to understand the specific reactive patterns in controlling pain it is important to know certain aspects of child-rearing in the culture, relationships between parents and children, the role of infliction of pain in punishment, the attitudes of various members of the family toward specific expected, accepted pain experiences, and so on. The interviews were recorded on wire and transcribed verbatim for an ultimate detailed analysis. The interviews usually lasted for approximately two hours, the time being limited by the condition of the interviewee and by the amount and quality of his answers. When it was considered necessary an interview was repeated. In most of the cases the study of the interviewee was followed by informal conversations and by observation of his behavior in the hospital.

The information gathered from the interviews was discussed with members of the medical staff, especially in the areas related to the medical aspects of the problem, in order to get their evaluation of the pain experience of the patient. Information as to the personality of the patient was checked against results of psychological testing by members of the psychological staff of the hospital when these were available.

The discussion of the material presented in this paper is based on interviews with 103 respondents, including 87 hospital patients in pain and 16 healthy subjects. According to their ethnocultural background the respondents are distributed as follows: "Old Americans," 26; Italians, 24; Jews, 31; and others, 22.[5] In addition there were the collateral interviews and conversations noted above with family members, doctors, nurses and other members of the hospital staff.

With regard to the pathological causes of pain the majority of the interviewees fall into the group of patients suffering from neurological diseases, mainly herniated discs and spinal lesions. The focusing upon a group of patients suffering from a similar pathology offered the opportunity to investigate reactions and attitudes toward spontaneous pain which is symptomatic of one group of diseases. Nevertheless, a number of patients suffering from other diseases were also interviewed.

This paper is based upon the material collected during the first stage of study. The generalizations are to a great extent tentative formulations on a descriptive level. There has been no attempt as yet to integrate the results with the value system and the cultural pattern of the group, though here and there there will be indications to the effect that they are part of the culture pattern. The discussions will be limited to main regularities within three groups, namely, the Italians, the Jews and the "Old Americans." Factors related to variations within each group will be discussed after the main prevailing patterns have been presented.

PAIN AMONG PATIENTS OF JEWISH AND ITALIAN ORIGIN

As already mentioned, the Jews and Italians were selected mainly because interviews with medical experts suggested that they display similar reactions to pain. The investigation of this similarity provided the opportunity to check a rather popular assumption that similar reactions reflect similar attitudes. The differences between the Italian and Jewish culture are great enough to suggest that if the attitudes are related to cultural pattern they will also be different despite the apparent similarity in manifest behavior.

Members of both groups were described as being very emotional in their responses to pain. They were described as tending to exaggerate their pain experience and being very sensitive to pain. Some of the doctors stated that in their opinion Jews and Italians have a lower threshold of pain than members of other ethnic groups, especially members of the so-called Nordic group. This statement seems to indicate a certain conclusion as to the concept of the threshold of pain. According to people who have studied the problem of the threshold of pain, for instance Harold Wolff and his associates, the threshold of pain is more or less the same for all human beings regardless of nationality, sex or age.

In the course of the investigation the general impressions of doctors were confirmed to a great extent by the interview material and by the observation of the patients' behavior. However, even a superficial study of the interviews has revealed that though reactions to pain appear to be similar the underlying attitudes toward pain are different in the two groups. While the Italian patients seemed to be mainly concerned with the immediacy of the pain experience and were disturbed by the actual pain sensation which they experienced in a given situation, the concern of patients of Jewish origin was focused mainly upon the symptomatic meaning of pain and upon the significance of pain in relation to their health, welfare and, eventually, for the welfare of the families. The Italian patient expressed in his behavior and in his complaints the discomfort caused by pain as such, and he manifested his emotions with regard to the effects of this pain experience upon his immediate situations in terms of occupation, economic situation and so on; the Jewish patient expressed primarily his worries and anxieties as to the extent to which the pain indicated a threat to his health. In this connection it is worth mentioning that one of the Jewish words to describe strong pain is *yessurim*, a word which is also used to describe worries and anxieties.

Attitudes of Italian and Jewish patients toward pain-relieving drugs can serve as an indication of their attitude toward pain. When in pain the Italian calls for pain relief and is mainly concerned with the analgesic effects of the drugs which are administered to him. Once the pain is relieved the Italian patient easily forgets his sufferings and manifests a happy and joyful disposition. The Jewish patient, however, often is reluctant to accept the drug, and he explains this reluctance in terms of concern about the effects of the drug upon his health in general. He is apprehensive about the habit-forming aspects of the analgesic. Moreover, he feels that the drug relieves his pain only temporarily and does not cure him of the disease which may cause the pain. Nurses and doctors have reported cases in which patients would hide the pill which was given to them to relieve their pain and would prefer to suffer. These reports were confirmed in the interviews with patients. It was also observed that many Jewish patients after being relieved from pain often continued to display the same depressed and worried behavior because they felt that though the pain was currently absent it may recur as long as the disease was not cured completely. From these observations it appears that when one deals with a Jewish and an Italian patient in pain, in the first case it is more important to relieve the anxieties with regard to the sources of pain, while in the second it is more important to relieve the actual pain.

Another indication as to the significance of pain for Jewish and Italian patients is their respective attitudes toward the doctor. The Italian patient seems to display a most confident attitude toward the doctor which is usually reinforced after the doctor has succeeded in relieving pain, whereas the Jewish patient manifests a skeptical attitude, feeling that the fact that the doctor has relieved his pain by some drug does not mean at all that he is skillful enough to take care of the basic illness. Consequently, even when the pain is relieved, he tends to check the diagnosis and the treatment of one doctor against the opinions of other specialists in the field. Summarizing the difference between the Italian and Jewish attitudes, one can say that the Italian attitude is characterized by a present-oriented apprehension with regard to the actual sensation of pain, and the Jew tends to manifest a future-oriented anxiety as to the symptomatic and general meaning of the pain experience.

It has been stated that the Italians and Jews tend to manifest similar behavior in terms of their reactions to pain. As both cultures allow for free expression of feelings and emotions by words, sounds and gestures, both the Italians and Jews feel free to talk about their pain, complain about it and manifest their sufferings by groaning, moaning, crying, etc. They are not ashamed of this expression. They admit willingly that when they are in pain they do complain a great deal, call for help and expect sympathy and assistance from other members of their immediate social environment, especially from members of their family. When in pain they are reluctant to be alone and prefer the presence and attention of other people. This behavior, which is expected, accepted and approved by the Italian and Jewish cultures often conflicts with the patterns of behavior expected from a patient by American or Americanized medical people. Thus they tend to describe the behavior of the Italian and Jewish patients as exaggerated and overemotional. The material suggests that they do tend to minimize the actual pain experiences of the Italian and Jewish patient regardless of whether they have the objective criteria for evaluating the actual amount of pain which the patient experiences. It seems that the uninhibited display of reaction to pain as manifested by the Jewish and Italian patient provokes distrust in American culture instead of provoking sympathy.

Despite the close similarity between the manifest reactions among Jews and Italians, there seem to be differences in emphasis especially with regard to what the patient achieves by these reactions and as to the specific manifestations of these reactions in the various social settings. For instance, they differ in their behavior at home and in the hospital. The Italian husband, who is aware of his role as an adult male, tends to avoid verbal complaining at home, leaving this type of behavior to the women. In the hospital, where he is less concerned with his role as a male, he tends to [be] more verbal and more emotional. The Jewish patient, on the contrary, seems to be more calm in the hospital than at home. Traditionally the Jewish male does not emphasize his masculinity through such traits as stoicism, and he does not equate verbal complaints with weakness. Moreover, the Jewish culture allows the patient to be demanding and complaining. Therefore, he tends more to use his pain in order to control interpersonal relationships within the family. Though similar use of pain to manipulate the relationships between members of the family may be present also in some other cultures it seems that in the Jewish culture this is not disapproved, while in others it is. In the hospital one can also distinguish variations in the reactive patterns among Jews and Italians. Upon his admission to the hospital and in the presence of the doctor the Jewish patient tends to complain, ask for help, be emotional even to the point of crying. However, as soon as he feels that adequate care is given to him he becomes more restrained. This suggests that the display of pain reaction serves less as an indication of the amount of pain experienced than as a means to create an atmosphere and setting in which the pathological causes of pain will be best taken care of. The Italian patient, on the other hand, seems to be less concerned with setting up a favorable situation for treatment. He takes for granted that adequate care will be given to him, and in the presence of the doctor he seems to be somewhat calmer than the Jewish patient. The mere presence of the doctor reassures the Italian patient, while the skepticism of the Jewish patient limits the reassuring role of the physician.

To summarize the description of the reactive patterns of the Jewish and Italian patients, the material suggests that on a semiconscious level the Jewish patient tends to provoke worry and concern in his social environment as to the state of his health and the symptomatic character of his pain, while the Italian tends to provoke sympathy toward his suffering. In one case the function of the pain reaction will be the mobilization of the efforts of the family and the doctors toward a complete cure, while in the second case the function of the reaction will be focused upon the mobilization of effort toward relieving the pain sensation.

On the basis of the discussion of the Jewish and Italian material two generalizations can be made: *(1) Similar reactions to pain manifested by members of different ethno-cultural groups do not necessarily reflect similar attitudes to pain. (2) Reactive patterns similar in terms of their manifestations may have different functions and serve different purposes in various cultures.*

PAIN AMONG PATIENTS OF "OLD AMERICAN" ORIGIN

There is little emphasis on emotional complaining about pain among "Old American" patients. Their complaints about pain can best be described as reporting on pain. In describing his pain, the "Old American" patient tries to find the most appropriate ways of defining the quality of pain, its localization, duration, etc. When examined by the doctor he gives the impression of trying to assume the detached role of an unemotional observer who gives the most efficient description of his state for a correct diagnosis and treatment. The interviewees repeatedly state that there is no point in complaining and groaning and moaning, etc., because "it won't help anybody." However, they readily admit that when pain is unbearable they may react strongly, even to the point of crying, but they tend to do it when they are alone. Withdrawal from society seems to be a frequent reaction to strong pain.

There seem to be different patterns in reacting to pain depending on the situation. One pattern, manifested in the presence of members of the family, friends, etc., consists of attempts to minimize pain, to avoid complaining and provoking pity; when pain becomes too strong there is a tendency to withdraw and express freely such reactions as groaning, moaning, etc. A different pattern is manifested in the presence of people who, on account of their profession, should know the character of the pain experience because they are expected to make the appropriate diagnosis, advise the proper cure and give the adequate help. The tendency to avoid deviation from certain expected patterns of behavior plays an important role in the reaction to pain. This is also controlled by the desire to seek approval on the part of the social environment, especially in the hospital, where the "Old American" patient tries to avoid being a "nuisance" in the ward. He seems to be, more than any other patient, aware of an ideal pattern of behavior which is identified as "American," and he tends to conform to it. This was characteristically expressed by a patient who answered the question how he reacts to pain by saying, "I react like a good American."

An important element in controlling the pain reaction is the wish of the patient to cooperate with those who are expected to take care of him. The situation is often viewed as a team composed of the patient, the doctor, the nurse, the attendant, etc., and in this team everybody has a function and is supposed to do his share in order to achieve the most successful result. Emotionality is seen as a purposeless and hindering factor in a situation which calls for knowledge, skill, training and efficiency. It is important to note that this behavior is also expected by American or Americanized members of the medical or nursing staff, and the patients who do not fall into this pattern are viewed as deviants, hypochondriacs and neurotics.

As in the case of the Jewish patients, the American attitude toward pain can be best defined as a future-oriented anxiety. The "Old American" patient is also concerned with the symptomatic significance of pain which is correlated with a pronounced health consciousness. It seems that the "Old American" is conscious of various threats to his health which are present in his environment and therefore feels vulnerable and is prone to interpret his pain sensation as a warning signal indicating that something is wrong with his health and therefore must be reported to the physician. With some exceptions, pain is considered bad and unnecessary and therefore must be immediately taken care of. In those situations where pain is expected and accepted, such as in the process of medical treatment or as a result of sports activities, there is less concern with the pain sensation. In general, however, there is a feeling that suffering pain is unnecessary when there are means of relieving it.

Though the attitudes of the Jewish and "Old American" patients can be defined as pain anxiety they differ greatly. The future-oriented anxiety of the Jewish interviewee is characterized by pessimism or, at best, by skepticism, while the "Old American" patient is rather optimistic in his future orientation. This attitude is fostered by the mechanistic approach to the body and its functions and by the confidence in the skill of the expert which are so frequent in the American culture. The body is often viewed as a machine which has to be well taken care of, be periodically checked for dysfunctioning and eventually, when out of order, be taken to an expert who will "fix" the defect. In the case of pain the expert is the medical man who has the "know-how" because of his training and experience and therefore is entitled to full confidence. An important element in the optimistic outlook is faith in the progress of science. Patients with intractable pain often stated that though at the present moment the doctors do not have the "drug" they will eventually discover it, and they will give the examples of sulfa, penicillin, etc.

The anxieties of a pain-experiencing "Old American" patient are greatly relieved when he feels that something is being done about it in terms of specific activities involved in the treatment. It seems that his security and confidence increases in direct proportion to the number of tests, X-rays, examinations, injections, etc. that are given to him. Accordingly, "Old American" patients seem to have a positive attitude toward hospitalization, because the hospital is the adequate institution which is equipped for the necessary treatment. While a Jewish and an Italian patient seem to be disturbed by the impersonal character of the hospital and by the necessity of being treated there instead of at home, the "Old American" patient, on the contrary, prefers the hospital treatment to the home treatment, and neither he nor his family seems to be disturbed by hospitalization.

To summarize the attitude of the "Old American" toward pain, he is disturbed by the symptomatic aspect of pain and is concerned with its incapacitating aspects, but he tends to view the future in rather optimistic colors, having confidence in the science and skill of the professional people who treat his condition.

SOME SOURCES OF INTRA-GROUP VARIATION

In the description of the reactive patterns and attitudes toward pain among patients of Jewish and "Old American" origin certain regularities have been observed for each particular group regardless of individual differences and variations. This does not mean that each individual in each group manifests the same reactions and attitudes. Individual variations are often due to specific aspects of pain experience, to the character of the disease which causes the pain or to elements in the personality of the patient. However, there are also other factors that are instrumental in provoking these differences and which can still be traced back to the cultural backgrounds of the individual patients. Such variables as the degree of Americanization of the patient, his socio-economic background, education and religiosity may play an important role in shaping individual variations in the reactive patterns. For instance, it was found that the patterns described are manifested most consistently among immigrants, while their descendants tend to differ in terms of adopting American forms of behavior and American attitudes toward the role of the medical expert, medical institutions and equipment in controlling pain. It is safe to say that the further the individual is from the immigrant generation the more American is his behavior. This is less true for the attitudes toward pain which seem to persist to a great extent even among members of the third generation and even though the reactive patterns are radically changed. A Jewish or Italian patient born in this country of American-born parents tend to *behave* like an "Old American" but often expresses *attitudes* similar to those which are expressed by the Jewish or Italian people. They try to appear unemotional and efficient in situations where the immigrant would be excited and disturbed. However, in the process of the interview, if a patient is of Jewish origin he is likely to express attitudes of anxiety as to the meaning of his pain, and if he is Italian he is likely to be rather unconcerned about the significance of his pain for his future.

The occupational factor plays an important role when pain affects a specific area of the body. For instance, manual workers with herniated discs are more disturbed by their pain than are professional or business people with a similar disease because of the immediate significance of this particular pain for their respective abilities to earn a living. It was also observed that headaches cause more concern among intellectuals than among manual workers.

The educational background of the patient also plays an important role in his attitude with regard to the symptomatic meaning of a pain sensation. The more educated patients are more health-conscious and more aware of pain as a possible symptom of a dangerous disease. However, this factor plays a less important role than might be expected. The less educated "Old American" or Jewish patient is still more health-conscious than the more educated Italian. On the other hand, the less educated Jew is as much worried about the significance of pain as the more educated one. The education of the patient seems to be an important factor in fostering specific reactive patterns. The more educated patient, who may have more anxiety with regard to illness, may be more reserved in specific reactions to pain than an unsophisticated individual, who feels free to express his feelings and emotions.

THE TRANSMISSION OF CULTURAL ATTITUDES TOWARD PAIN

In interpreting the differences which may be attributed to different socioeconomic and education backgrounds there is enough evidence to conclude that these differences appear mainly on the manifest and behavioral level, whereas attitudinal patterns toward pain tend to be more uniform and to be common to most of the members of the group regardless of their specific backgrounds.

These attitudes toward pain and the expected reactive patterns are acquired by the individual members of the society from the earliest childhood along with other cultural attitudes and values which are learned from the parents, parent-substitutes, siblings, peer groups, etc. Each culture offers to its members an ideal pattern of attitudes and reactions, which may differ for various sub-cultures in a given society, and each individual is expected to conform to this ideal pattern. Here, the role of the family seems to be of primary importance. Directly and indirectly the family environment affects the individuals' ultimate response to pain. In each culture the parents teach the child how to react to pain, and by approval or disapproval they promote specific forms of behavior. This conclusion is amply supported by the interviews. Thus, the Jewish and Italian respondents are unanimous in relating how their parents, especially mothers, manifested overprotective and overconcerned attitudes toward the child's health, participation in sports, games, fights, etc. In these families the child is constantly reminded of the advisability of avoiding colds, injuries, fights and other threatening situations. Crying in complaint is responded to by the parents with sympathy, concern and help. By their overprotective and worried attitude they foster complaining and tears. The child learns to pay attention to each painful experience and to look for help and sympathy which are readily given to him. In Jewish families, where not only a slight sensation of pain but also each deviation from the child's normal behavior is looked upon as a sign of illness, the child is prone to acquire anxieties with regard to the meaning and significance of these manifestations. The Italian parents do not seem to be concerned with the symptomatic meaning of the child's pains and aches, but instead there is a great deal of verbal expression of emotions and feelings of sympathy toward the "poor child" who happens to be in discomfort because of illness or because of an injury in play. In these families a child is praised when he avoids physical injuries and is scolded when he does not pay enough attention to bad weather, to drafts or when he takes part in rough games and fights. The injury and pain are often interpreted to the child as punishment for the wrong behavior, and physical punishment is the usual consequence of misbehavior.

In the "Old American" family the parental attitude is quite different. The child is told not to "run to mother with every little thing." He is told to take pain "like a man," not to be a "sissy," not to cry. The child's participation in physical sports and games is not only approved but is also strongly stimulated. Moreover, the child is taught to expect to be hurt in sports and games and is taught to fight back if he happens to be attacked by other boys. However, it seems that the American parents are conscious of the threats to the child's health, and they teach the child to take immediate care of any injury. When hurt the right thing to do is not to cry and get emotional but to avoid unnecessary pain and prevent unpleasant consequences by applying the proper first aid medicine and by calling a doctor.

Often attitudes and behavior fostered in a family conflict with those patterns which are accepted by the larger social environment. This is especially true in the case of children of immigrants. The Italian or Jewish immigrant parents promote patterns which they consider correct, while the peer groups in the street and in the school criticize this behavior and foster a different one. In consequence, the child may acquire the attitudes which are part of his home life but may also adopt behavior patterns which conform to those of his friends.

The direct promotion of certain behavior described as part of the child-rearing explains only in part the influence of the general family environment and the specific role of the parents in shaping responses to pain. They are also formed indirectly by observing the behavior of other members of the family and by imitating their responses to pain. Moreover, attitudes toward pain are also influenced by various aspects of parent-child relationship in a culture. The material suggests that differences in attitudes toward pain in Jewish, Italian and "Old American" families are closely related to the role and image of the father in the respective cultures in terms of his authority and masculinity. Often the father and mother assume different roles in promoting specific patterns of behavior and specific attitudes. For example, it seems that in the "Old American" family it is chiefly the mother who stimulates the child's ability to resist pain thus emphasizing his masculinity. In the Italian family it seems that the mother is the one who inspires the child's emotionality, while in the Jewish family both parents express attitudes of worry and concern which are transmitted to the children.

Specific deviations from expected reactive and attitudinal patterns can often be understood in terms of a particular structure of the family. This became especially clear from the interviews of two Italian patients and one Jewish patient. All three subjects revealed reactions and attitudes diametrically opposite to those which the investigator would expect on the basis of his experience. In the process of the interview, however, it appeared that one of the Italian patients was adopted into an Italian family, found out about his adoption at the age of fourteen, created a phantasy of being of Anglo-Saxon origin because of his physical appearance and accordingly began to eradicate everything "Italian" in his personality and behavior. For instance, he denied knowledge of the Italian language despite the fact that he always spoke Italian in the family and even learned to abstain from smiling, because he felt that being happy and joyful is an indication of Italian origin. The other Italian patient lost his family at a very early age because of family disorganization and was brought up in an Irish foster home. The Jewish patient consciously adopted a "non-Jewish" pattern of behavior and attitude because of strong sibling rivalry. According to the respondent, his brother, a favored son in the immigrant Jewish family, always manifested "typical" Jewish reactions toward disease, and the patient who strongly disliked the brother and was jealous of him, decided to be "completely different."

NOTES

1. James D. Hardy, Harold G. Wolff, and Helen Goodell, *Pain Sensations and Reactions*, Baltimore: Williams and Wilkins Company, 1952, p. 23.

2. *Ibid.*, p. 204.

3. *Ibid.*, p. 262.

4. I should like to take the opportunity to express my appreciation to Dr. Harold G. Wolff, Professor of Neurology, Cornell University Medical College, Dr. Hiland Flowers, Chief of Neuropsychiatric Service, Dr. Robert Morrow, Chief of Clinical Psychology Section, Dr. Louis Berlin, Chief of Neurology Section, and the Management of the hospital for their cooperation in the setting up of the research at the Kingsbridge Veterans Hospital.

5. Italian respondents are mainly of South Italian origin; the Jewish respondents, with one exception, are all of East European origin. Whenever the Jews are mentioned they are spoken of in terms of the culture they represent and not in terms of their religion.

Review Questions

1. Explain the difference between *reactions to pain* and *attitudes toward pain*. Give examples from Zborowski's study to illustrate the differing reactions and attitudes among the members of the various subsocieties.

2. Distinguish between pain as a biological experience and pain as a culturally shaped experience. Give examples from Zborowski's study to illustrate your points.

3. If the physician understands differences in patients' cultural background, will he or she be better able to understand the individual's response to pain? Explain your answer.

Suggested Readings: Culture

Berger, Peter L., and Thomas Luckmann. *The Social Construction of Reality: A Treatise in the Sociology of Knowledge.* Garden City, N.Y.: Anchor Books, 1967.

Hall, Edward T. *The Silent Language.* Garden City, N.Y.: Anchor Books, 1959.

Kephart, William. *Extraordinary Groups.* 2nd ed. New York: St. Martin's Press, 1982.

Largey, Gale Peter, and David Rodney Watson. "Sociology of Odors," *American Journal of Sociology,* 77 (May 1972), 1021–1034.

Wallace, Samuel E. *Skid Row As A Way of Life.* Totowa, N.J.: Bedminster, 1965.

Part III. Transmission of Culture: Socialization

THE HUMAN INFANT IS NOT BORN KNOWING WHAT TO EAT, WHAT TO VALUE, HOW TO communicate, or what to believe about the social world or its own self. It is born with curiosity and, according to developmental psychologists, a need to "make sense" out of the events and objects it encounters. The infant interacts with others in its social milieu, searching for category systems, meanings, and rules. At the same time, other members of the child's social world attempt to mold, to instruct, to reward and punish, to explain the culture's symbols and ways of classifying experience. This two-way process of learning and teaching culture by and to new members, called *socialization*, enables the child to become a part of its society, to interact relatively smoothly with others, to share in the culture's common stock of symbols, norms, and knowledge.

Moreover, through the socialization process, the child develops a *self concept*. By this term we mean the sum of all cognitions or thoughts one holds about oneself. The self concept is comprised of what are sometimes called "identity elements" that are more or less organized into "subidentities" corresponding to societal statuses or categories. The child must learn the *categories* in which to think about itself—e.g., son, friend, female, driver, consumer, farmer, and so on—as well as learning *how to evaluate* its performance, relative to others, in these roles. Our self concepts are, then, learned by observing others and their reactions to us, as Charles Horton Cooley's term, "looking-glass self," implies.

In turn, our behavior is affected by our self concepts; we often act in ways that are consistent with the images of ourselves which we have developed through interaction in our society. Sociologists say that the individual has *internalized* the culture once the societal categories and standards for evaluation are learned and applied to oneself. In other words, the individual comes to rely less on the input of others and to reward and punish him- or herself—by feeling guilt, pride, or shame—for behaving according to the rules of the culture.

The articles in this section illustrate a number of aspects of the socialization process. One of the most far-reaching categorizations in American culture is the one based on sex. No other social statuses have such an impact on the behavior of societal members. Children are socialized from infancy onward to the *social roles*, or scripts, attached to the statuses "male" and "female." Sandra and Daryl Bem's article, "Training the Woman to Know Her Place: The Power of a Nonconscious Ideology," shows us how thoroughly most of us have internalized our culture's sex-role scripts and how important are our gender subidentities. Although some of our beliefs have changed in recent years, even the most "liberated" among us are still apt to see child care and housework as "women's work" and economic activity as largely "men's work." Furthermore, we often feel that we have chosen these roles from "free will," when in fact they have been learned. Bem and Bem argue that sex roles have come to be problematic in today's society because it has become increasingly clear that they are inconsistent with other important values, such as equality and freedom of choice. If we did not hold these latter values, considerable confusion and tension would be avoided.

In "A Child's Eye View of Work," Bernard Goldstein and Jack Oldham show us how even very young children have been socialized to modern, industrial society's values and norms regarding work, long before they actually enter the world of work. Even first graders understand some of the rudiments of how to get a job, pay differentials, the role of boss, and the like. Seventh graders have developed an even greater comprehension of the economic world. They learn their beliefs and values from family members, from peers, from the mass media, and from schoolbooks and schoolteachers, that is, from *agents of socialization*. As is the case with sex roles, work roles are internalized and become part of the individual's set of standards for judging self and others.

The last article in this section is based on research among medical students. In "The Fate of Idealism in Medical School," Howard S. Becker and Blanche Geer document what is often called "adult socialization." They show that the college graduate who arrives at the doors of the medical school is not the same person as the second- or third-year medical student whose behavior, values, and self concept have been altered by the situation in which he or she has been living. Through "anticipatory socialization" in undergraduate school, the role of the idealistic "premed student" was learned. Further socialization in the medical-school environment creates the cynical "medical student."

As the physician who emerges from the medical-school setting moves through other situations, he or she will be socialized yet again to the new roles of, perhaps, "intern," "resident," "junior partner in a medical group," "senior partner," and "retired physician." As it is with a professional moving through the stages of a career, so all of us moving through other occupations and other life-cycle categories will be socialized repeatedly to the new roles we are to enact. Consider in your own case the process of learning the ins and outs of the role of the "high school student" and then the "college student." Indeed, according to evidence collected by sociologists such as David Sudnow, we may eventually be socialized to the role of "the dying."

TRAINING THE WOMAN TO KNOW HER PLACE: THE POWER OF A NONCONSCIOUS IDEOLOGY

Sandra L. Bem and Daryl J. Bem

IN THE BEGINNING GOD CREATED THE HEAVEN AND THE EARTH. . . . AND GOD SAID, let us make man in our image, after our likeness; and let them have dominion over the fish of the sea, and over the fowl of the air, and over the cattle, and over all the earth. . . . And the rib, which the Lord God had taken from man, made he a woman and brought her unto the man. . . . And the Lord God said unto the woman, What is this that thou has done? And the woman said, The serpent beguiled me, and I did eat. . . . Unto the woman He said, I will greatly multiply thy sorrow and thy conception; in sorrow, thou shalt bring forth children; and thy desire shall be to thy husband, and he shall rule over thee. (Gen. 1, 2, 3)

And lest anyone fail to grasp the moral of this story, Saint Paul provides further clarification:

> For a man . . . is the image and glory of God; but the woman is the glory of man. For the man is not of the woman, but the woman of the man. Neither was the man created for the woman, but the woman for the man. (1 Cor. 11)
> Let the woman learn in silence with all subjection. But I suffer not a woman to teach, nor to usurp authority over the man, but to be in silence. For Adam was first formed, then Eve. And Adam was not deceived, but the woman, being deceived, was in the transgression. Notwithstanding she shall be saved in childbearing, if they continue in faith and charity and holiness with sobriety. (1 Tim. 2)

And lest it be thought that only Christians have this rich heritage of ideology about women, consider the morning prayer of the Orthodox Jew:

> Blessed art Thou, oh Lord our God, King of the Universe, that I was not born a gentile.
> Blessed art Thou, oh Lord our God, King of the Universe, that I was not born a slave.
> Blessed art Thou, oh Lord our God, King of the Universe, that I was not born a woman.

Or the Koran, the sacred text of Islam:

> Men are superior to women on account of the qualities in which God has given them pre-eminence.

Sandra L. Bem and Daryl J. Bem, "Training the Woman to Know Her Place: The Power of a Nonconscious Ideology," in Michele Hoffnung Garskof, ed., *Roles Women Play: Readings Toward Women's Liberation*. Belmont, Calif.: Brooks/Cole, 1971, pp. 84–96.

Because they think they sense a decline in feminine "faith, charity, and holiness with sobriety," many people today jump to the conclusion that the ideology expressed in these passages is a relic of the past. Not so. It has simply been obscured by an equalitarian veneer, and the ideology has now become nonconscious. That is, we remain unaware of it because alternative beliefs and attitudes about women go unimagined. We are like the fish who is unaware that his environment is wet. After all, what else could it be? Such is the nature of all nonconscious ideologies. Such is the nature of America's ideology about women. For even those Americans who agree that a black skin should not uniquely qualify its owner for janitorial or domestic service continue to act as if the possession of a uterus uniquely qualifies *its* owner for precisely that.

Consider, for example, the 1968 student rebellion at Columbia University. Students from the radical left took over some administration buildings in the name of equalitarian principles which they accused the university of flouting. Here were the most militant spokesmen one could hope to find in the cause of equalitarian ideals. But no sooner had they occupied the buildings than the male militants blandly turned to their sisters-in-arms and assigned them the task of preparing the food, while they—the menfolk— would presumably plan further strategy. The reply these males received was the reply they deserved, and the fact that domestic tasks behind the barricades were desegregated across the sex line that day is an everlasting tribute to the class consciousness of the ladies of the left.

But these conscious coeds are not typical, for the nonconscious assumptions about a woman's "natural" talents (or lack of them) are at least as prevalent among women as they are among men. A psychologist named Philip Goldberg (1968) demonstrated this by asking female college students to rate a number of professional articles from each of six fields. The articles were collated into two equal sets of booklets, and the names of the authors were changed so that the identical article was attributed to the male author (e.g., John T. McKay) in one set of booklets and to a female author (e.g., Joan T. McKay) in the other set. Each student was asked to read the articles in her booklet and to rate them for value, competence, persuasiveness, writing style, and so forth.

As he had anticipated, Goldberg found that the identical article received significantly lower ratings when it was attributed to a female author than when it was attributed to a male author. He had predicted this result for articles from professional fields generally considered the province of men, like law and city planning, but to his surprise, these coeds also downgraded articles from the fields of dietetics and elementary school education when they were attributed to female authors. In other words, these students rated the male authors as better at everything, agreeing with Aristotle that "we should regard the female nature as afflicted with a natural defectiveness." We repeated this experiment informally in our own classrooms and discovered that male students show the same implicit prejudice against female authors that Goldberg's female students showed. Such is the nature of a nonconscious ideology!

. . .

INDIVIDUALITY AND SELF-FULFILLMENT

The dominant values of today's students concern personal growth on the one hand, and interpersonal relationships on the other. The first of these emphasizes individuality and self-fulfillment; the second stresses openness, honesty, and equality in all human relationships.

The values of individuality and self-fulfillment imply that each human being, male or female, is to be encouraged to "do his own thing." Men and women are no longer to be stereotyped by society's definitions. If sensitivity, emotionality, and warmth are desirable human characteristics, then they are desirable for men as well as for women. (John Wayne is no longer an idol of the young, but their pop-art satire.) If independence, assertiveness, and serious intellectual commitment are desirable human characteristics, then they are desirable for women as well as for men. The major prescription of this college generation is that each individual should be encouraged to discover and fulfill his own unique potential and identity, unfettered by society's presumptions.

But society's presumptions enter the scene much earlier than most people suspect, for parents begin to raise their children in accord with the popular stereotypes from the very first. Boys are encouraged to be aggressive, competitive, and independent, whereas girls are rewarded for being passive and dependent (Barry, Bacon, & Child, 1957; Sears, Maccoby, & Levin, 1957). In one study, six-month-old infant girls were already being touched and spoken to more by their mothers while they were playing than were infant boys. When they were thirteen months old, these same girls were more reluctant than the boys to leave their mothers; they returned more quickly and more frequently to them; and they remained closer to them throughout the entire play period. When a physical barrier was placed between mother and child, the girls tended to cry and motion for help; the boys made more active attempts to get around the barrier (Goldberg & Lewis, 1969). No one knows to what extent these sex differences at the age of thirteen months can be attributed to the mothers' behavior at the age of six months, but it is hard to believe that the two are unconnected.

As children grow older, more explicit sex-role training is introduced. Boys are encouraged to take more of an interest in mathematics and science. Boys, not girls, are given chemistry sets and microscopes for Christmas. Moreover, all children quickly learn that mommy is proud to be a moron when it comes to mathematics and science, whereas daddy knows all about these things. When a young boy returns from school all excited about biology, he is almost certain to be encouraged to think of becoming a physician. A girl with similar enthusiasm is told that she might want to consider nurse's training later so she can have "an interesting job to fall back upon in case—God forbid—she ever needs to support herself." A very different kind of encouragement. And any girl who doggedly persists in her enthusiasm for science is likely to find her parents as horrified by the prospect of a permanent love affair with physics as they would be by the prospect of an interracial marriage.

These socialization practices quickly take their toll. By nursery school age, for example, boys are already asking more questions about how and why things work (Smith, 1933). In first and second grade, when asked to suggest ways of improving various toys, boys do better on the fire truck and girls do better on the nurse's kit, but by the third grade, boys do better regardless of the toy presented (Torrance, 1962). By the ninth grade, 25% of the boys, but only 3% of the girls, are considering careers in science or engineering (Flanagan, unpublished, cited by Kagan, 1964). When they apply for college, boys and girls are about equal on verbal aptitude tests, but boys score significantly higher on mathematical aptitude tests—about 60 points higher on the College Board examinations, for example (Brown, 1965, p. 162). Moreover, girls improve their mathematical performance if problems are reworded so that they deal with cooking and gardening, even though the abstract reasoning required for their solutions remains the same (Milton, 1958). Clearly, not just ability, but motivation too, has been affected.

But these effects in mathematics and science are only part of the story. A girl's long training in passivity and dependence appears to exact an even higher toll from her overall motivation to achieve, to search for new and independent ways of doing things, and to welcome the challenge of new and unsolved problems. In one study, for example, elementary school girls were more likely to try solving a puzzle by imitating an adult, whereas the boys were more likely to search for a novel solution not provided by the adult (McDavid, 1959). In another puzzle-solving study, young girls asked for help and approval from adults more frequently than the boys; and, when given the opportunity to return to the puzzles a second time, the girls were more likely to rework those they had already solved, whereas the boys were more likely to try puzzles they had been unable to solve previously (Crandall & Rabson, 1960). A girl's sigh of relief is almost audible when she marries and retires from the outside world of novel and unsolved problems. This, of course, is the most conspicuous outcome of all: the majority of American women become full-time homemakers [for some portion of their lives. Even women employed outside the home on a full-time basis continue to do the vast majority of child care and housework]. Such are the consequences of a nonconscious ideology.

But why does this process violate the values of individuality and self-ful-fillment? It is *not* because some people may regard the role of homemakers as inferior to other roles. That is not the point. Rather, the point is that our society is managing to consign a large segment of its population to the role of homemaker solely on the basis of sex just as inexorably as it has in the past consigned the individual with a black skin to the role of janitor or do-mestic. It is not the quality of the role itself which is at issue here, but the fact that in spite of their unique identities, the majority of America's women end up in the *same* role.

Even so, however, several arguments are typically advanced to counter the claim that America's homogenization of its women subverts individual-ity and self-fulfillment. The three most common arguments invoke, respec-tively, (1) free will, (2) biology, and (3) complementarity.

1. The free will argument proposes that a 21-year-old woman is perfectly free to choose some other role if she cares to do so; no one is standing in her way. But this argument conveniently overlooks the fact that the society which has spent twenty years carefully marking the woman's ballot for her has nothing to lose in that twenty-first year by pretending to let her cast it for the alternative of her choice. Society has controlled not her alternatives, but her motivation to choose any but one of those alternatives. The so-called freedom to choose is illusory and cannot be invoked to justify the so-ciety which controls the motivation to choose.

2. The biological argument suggests that there may really be inborn dif-ferences between men and women in, say, independence or mathematical ability. Or that there may be biological factors beyond the fact that women can become pregnant and nurse children which uniquely dictate that they, but not men, should stay home all day and shun serious outside commit-ment. Maybe female hormones really are responsible somehow. One diffi-culty with this argument, of course, is that female hormones would have to be different in the Soviet Union where one-third of the engineers and 75% of the physicians are women. In America, women constitute less than 1% of the engineers and only 7% of the physicians (Dodge, 1966). Female physiol-ogy *is* different, and it may account for some of the psychological differ-ences between the sexes, but America's sex-role ideology still seems primar-ily responsible for the fact that so few women emerge from childhood with the motivation to seek out any role beyond the one that our society dictates.

But even if there really were biological differences between the sexes along these lines, the biological argument would still be irrelevant. The rea-son can best be illustrated with an analogy.

Suppose that every black American boy were to be socialized to become a jazz musician on the assumption that he has a "natural" talent in that direc-tion, or suppose that his parents should subtly discourage him from other pursuits because it is considered "inappropriate" for black men to become physicians or physicists. Most liberal Americans, we submit, would disap-prove. But suppose that it *could* be demonstrated that black Americans, *on the average*, did possess an inborn better sense of rhythm than white Americans. Would *that* justify ignoring the unique characteristics of a *particular* black youngster from the very beginning and specifically socializing him to become a musician? We don't think so. Similarly, as long as a woman's socialization does not nurture her uniqueness, but treats her only as a member of a group on the basis of some assumed *average* characteristic, she will not be prepared to realize her own potential in the way that the values of individuality and self-fulfillment imply she should.

The irony of the biological argument is that it does not take biological differences seriously enough. That is, it fails to recognize the range of biological differences between individuals within the same sex. Thus, recent research has revealed that biological factors help determine many personality traits. Dominance and submissiveness, for example, have been found to have large inheritable components; in other words, biological factors *do* have the potential for partially determining how dominant or submissive an individual, male or female, will turn out to be. But the effects of this biological potential could be detected only in males (Gottesman, 1963). This implies that only the males in our culture are raised with sufficient flexibility, with sufficient latitude given to their biological differences, for their "natural" or biologically determined potential to shine through. Females, on the other hand, are subjected to a socialization which so ignores their unique attributes that even the effects of biology seem to be swamped. In sum, the biological argument for continuing America's homogenization of its women gets hoisted with its own petard.

3. Many people recognize that most women do [spend some or most of their lives as] full-time homemakers because of their socialization and that these women do exemplify the failure of our society to raise girls as unique individuals. But, they point out, the role of the homemaker is not inferior to the role of the professional man: it is complementary but equal.

This argument is usually bolstered by pointing to the joys and importance of taking care of small children. Indeed, mothers *and* fathers find child rearing rewarding, and it is certainly important. But this argument becomes insufficient when one considers that the average American woman now lives to age 74 and has her *last* child at about age 26; thus, by the time the woman is 33 or so, her children all have more important things to do with their daytime hours than to spend them entertaining an adult woman who has nothing to do during the second half of her life span. As for the other "joys" of homemaking, many writers (e.g., Friedan, 1963) have persuasively argued that the role of the homemaker has been glamorized far beyond its intrinsic worth. This charge becomes plausible when one considers that the average American homemaker spends the equivalent of a man's working day, 7.1 hours, in preparing meals, cleaning house, laundering, mending, shopping, and doing other household tasks. In other words, 43% of her waking time is spent in activity that would command an hourly wage on the open market well below the federally-set minimum for menial industrial work.

The point is not how little she would earn if she did these things in someone else's home, but that this use of time is virtually the same for homemakers with college degrees and for those with less than a grade school education, for women married to professional men and for women married to blue-collar workers. Talent, education, ability, interests, motivations: all are irrelevant. In our society, being female uniquely qualifies an individual for domestic work.

It is true, of course, that the American homemaker has, on the average, 5.1 hours of leisure time per day, and it is here, we are told, that each woman can express her unique identity. Thus, politically interested women can join the League of Women Voters; women with humane interests can become part-time Gray Ladies; women who love music can raise money for the symphony. Protestant women play Canasta; Jewish women play Mah-Jongg; brighter women of all denominations and faculty wives play bridge; and so forth.

But politically interested *men* serve in legislatures; *men* with humane interests become physicians or clinical psychologists; *men* who love music play in the symphony; and so forth. In other words, why should a woman's unique identity determine only the periphery of her life rather than its central core?

Again, the important point is not that the role of homemaker is necessarily inferior, but that the woman's unique identity has been rendered irrelevant. Consider the following "predictability test." When a boy is born, it is difficult to predict what he will be doing 25 years later. We cannot say whether he will be an artist, a doctor, or a college professor because he will be permitted to develop and to fulfill his own unique potential, particularly if he is white and middle class. But if the newborn child is a girl, we can usually predict with confidence how she will be spending her time 25 years later. Her individuality doesn't have to be considered; it is irrelevant.

The socialization of the American male has closed off certain options for him too. Men are discouraged from developing certain desirable traits such as tenderness and sensitivity just as surely as women are discouraged from being assertive and, alas, "too bright." Young boys are encouraged to be incompetent at cooking and child care just as surely as young girls are urged to be incompetent at mathematics and science.

Indeed, one of the errors of the early feminist movement in this country was that it assumed that men had all the goodies and that women could attain self-fulfillment merely by being like men. But that is hardly the utopia implied by the values of individuality and self-fulfillment. Rather, these values would require society to raise its children so flexibly and with sufficient respect for the integrity of individual uniqueness that some men might emerge with the motivation, the ability, and the opportunity to stay home and raise children without bearing the stigma of being peculiar. If homemaking is as glamorous as the women's magazines and television commercials portray it, then men, too, should have that option. Even if homemaking isn't all that glamorous, it would probably still be more fulfilling for some men than the jobs in which they now find themselves.

And if biological differences really do exist between men and women in "nurturance," in their inborn motivations to care for children, then this will show up automatically in the final distribution of men and women across the various roles: relatively fewer men will choose to stay at home. The values of individuality and self-fulfillment do not imply that there must be equality of outcome, an equal number of men and women in each role, but that there should be the widest possible variation in outcome consistent with the range of individual differences among people regardless of sex. At the very least, these values imply that society should raise its males so that they could freely engage in activities that might pay less than those being pursued by their wives without feeling that they were "living off their wives." One rarely hears it said of a woman that she is "living off her husband."

Thus, it is true that a man's options are limited by our society's sex-role ideology, but as the "predictability test" reveals, it is still the woman in our society whose identity is rendered irrelevant by America's socialization practices. In 1954, the United States Supreme Court declared that a fraud and hoax lay behind the slogan "separate but equal." It is unlikely that any court will ever do the same for the more subtle motto that successfully keeps the woman in her place: "complementary but equal."

INTERPERSONAL EQUALITY

> Wives, submit yourselves unto your own husbands, as unto the Lord. For the husband is the head of the wife, even as Christ is the head of the church; and he is the savior of the body. Therefore, as the church is subject unto Christ, so let the wives be to their own husbands in everything. (Eph. 5)

As this passage reveals, the ideological rationalization that men and women hold complementary but equal positions is a recent invention of our modern "liberal" society, part of the equalitarian veneer which helps to keep today's version of the ideology nonconscious. Certainly those Americans who value open, honest, and equalitarian relationships generally are quick to reject this traditional view of the male-female relationship; and, an increasing number of young people even plan to enter "utopian" marriages very much like the following hypothetical example:

> Both my wife and I earned Ph.D. degrees in our respective disciplines. I turned down a superior academic post in Oregon and accepted a slightly less desirable position in New York where my wife could obtain a part-time teaching job and do research at one of the several other colleges in the area. Although I would have preferred to live in a suburb, we purchased a home near my wife's college so that she could have an office at home where she would be when the children returned

from school. Because my wife earns a good salary, she can easily afford to pay a maid to do her major household chores. My wife and I share all other tasks around the house equally. For example, she cooks the meals, but I do the laundry for her and help her with many of her other household tasks.

Without questioning the basic happiness of such a marriage or its appropriateness for many couples, we can legitimately ask if such a marriage is, in fact, an instance of interpersonal equality. Have all the hidden assumptions about the woman's "natural" role really been eliminated? Has the traditional ideology really been exorcised? There is a very simple test. If the marriage is truly equalitarian, then its description should retain the same flavor and tone even if the roles of the husband and wife were to be reversed:

> Both my husband and I earned Ph.D. degrees in our respective disciplines. I turned down a superior academic post in Oregon and accepted a slightly less desirable position in New York where my husband could obtain a part-time teaching job and do research at one of the several other colleges in the area. Although I would have preferred to live in a suburb, we purchased a home near my husband's college so that he could have an office at home where he would be when the children returned from school. Because my husband earns a good salary, he can easily afford to pay a maid to do his major household chores. My husband and I share all other tasks around the house equally. For example, he cooks the meals, but I do the laundry for him and help him with many of his other household tasks.

It seems unlikely that many men or women in our society would mistake the marriage *just* described as either equalitarian or desirable, and thus it becomes apparent that the ideology about the woman's "natural" role nonconsciously permeates the entire fabric of such "utopian" marriages. It is true that the wife gains some measure of equality when her career can influence the final place of residence, but why is it the unquestioned assumption that the husband's career solely determines the initial set of alternatives that are to be considered? Why is it the wife who automatically seeks the part-time position? Why is it *her* maid instead of *their* maid? Why *her* laundry? Why *her* household tasks? And so forth throughout the entire relationship.

The important point here is not that such marriages are bad or that their basic assumptions of inequality produce unhappy, frustrated women. Quite the contrary. *It is the very happiness of the wives in such marriages that reveals society's smashing success in socializing its women.* It is a measure of the distance our society must yet traverse toward the goals of self-fulfillment and interpersonal equality that such marriages are widely characterized as utopian and fully equalitarian. It is a mark of how well the woman has been kept in her place that the husband in such a marriage is often idolized by women, including his wife, for "permitting" her to squeeze a career into the interstices of their marriage as long as his own career is not unduly inconvenienced. Thus is the white man blessed for exercising his power benignly while his "natural" right to that power forever remains unquestioned.

Such is the subtlety of a nonconscious ideology!

A truly equalitarian marriage would permit both partners to pursue careers or outside commitments which carry equal weight when all important decisions are to be made. It is here, of course, that the "problem" of children arises. People often assume that the woman who seeks a role beyond home and family would not care to have children. They assume that if she wants a career or serious outside commitment, then children must be unimportant to her. But of course no one makes this assumption about her husband. No one assumes that a father's interest in his career necessarily precludes a deep and abiding affection for his children or a vital interest in their development. Once again America applies a double standard of judgment. Suppose that a father of small children suddenly lost his wife. No matter how much he loved his children, no one would expect him to sacrifice his career in order to stay home with them on a full-time basis—*even if he had an independent source of income*. No one would charge him with selfishness or lack of parental feeling if he sought professional care for his children during the day. An equalitarian marriage simply abolishes this double standard and extends the same freedom to the mother, while also providing the framework for the father to enter more fully into the pleasures and responsibilities of child rearing. In fact, it is the equalitarian marriage which has the most potential for giving children the love and concern of two parents rather than one.

But few women are prepared to make use of this freedom. Even those women who have managed to finesse society's attempt to rob them of their career motivations are likely to find themselves blocked by society's trump card: the feeling that the raising of the children is their unique responsibility and—in time of crisis—ultimately theirs alone. Such is the emotional power of a nonconscious ideology.

In addition to providing this potential for equalized child care, a truly equalitarian marriage embraces a more general division of labor which satisfies what might be called "the roommate test." That is, the labor is divided just as it is when two men or two women room together in college or set up a bachelor apartment together. Errands and domestic chores are assigned by preference, agreement, flipping a coin, given to hired help, or—as is sometimes the case—left undone.

It is significant that today's young people, many of whom live this way prior to marriage, find this kind of arrangement within marriage so foreign to their thinking. Consider an analogy. Suppose that a white male college student decided to room or set up a bachelor apartment with a black male friend. Surely the typical white student would not blithely assume that his black roommate was to handle all the domestic chores. Nor would his conscience allow him to do so even in the unlikely event that his roommate would say: "No, that's okay. I like doing housework. I'd be happy to do it." We suspect that the typical white student would still not be comfortable if he took advantage of this offer, if he took advantage of the fact that his roommate had been socialized to be "happy" with such an arrangement. But change this hypothetical black roommate to a female marriage partner, and somehow the student's conscience goes to sleep. At most it is quickly tranquilized by the thought that "she is happiest when she is ironing for her loved one." Such is the power of a nonconscious ideology.

Of course, it may well be that she *is* happiest when she is ironing for her loved one.

Such, indeed, is the power of a nonconscious ideology!

REFERENCES

Barry, H., III, Bacon, M. K., & Child, I. L. A cross-cultural survey of some sex differences in socialization, *Journal of Abnormal and Social Psychology*, 1957, 55, 327–332.

Brown, R. *Social psychology*. New York: Free Press, 1965.

Crandall, V. J. & Rabson, A. Children's repetition choices in an intellectual achievement situation following success and failure. *Journal of Genetic Psychology*, 1960, 97, 161–168.

Dodge, N. D. *Women in the Soviet economy*. Baltimore: The Johns Hopkins Press, 1966.

Flanagan, J. C. Project talent. Unpublished manuscript.

Friedan, B. *The feminine mystique*. New York: Norton, 1963.

Goldberg, P. Are women prejudiced against women? *Transaction*, April 1968, 5, 28–30.

Goldberg, S. & Lewis, M. Play behavior in the year-old infant: Early sex differences. *Child Development*, 1969, 40, 21–31.

Gottesman, I. I. Heritability of personality: A demonstration. *Psychological Monographs*, 1963, 77 (Whole No. 572).

Kagan, J. Acquisition and significance of sex typing and sex role identity. In M. L. Hoffman & L. W. Hoffman (Eds.), *Review of child development research, Vol. 1*. New York: Russell Sage Foundation, 1964. Pp. 137–167.

McDavid, J. W. Imitative behavior in preschool children. *Psychological Monographs*, 1959, 73 (Whole No. 486).

Milton, G. A. Five studies of the relation between sex role identification and achievement in problem solving. Technical Report No. 3, Department of Industrial Administration, Department of Psychology, Yale University, December, 1958.

Sears, R. R., Maccoby, E. E., & Levin, H. *Patterns of child rearing*. Evanston, Ill.: Row, Peterson, 1957.

Smith, M. E. The influences of age, sex, and situation on the frequency of form and functions of questions asked by preschool children. *Child Development*, 1933, 3, 201–213.

Torrance, E. P. *Guiding creative talent*. Englewood Cliffs, N.J.: Prentice-Hall, 1962.

Review Questions

1. Bem and Bem state that, just as fish are not conscious of the water around them, so too may humans be unaware of the value systems, or ideologies, regarding inequality based on gender. Explain this statement, giving examples. What other value systems do we ignore?

2. What *agents* of socialization are involved in transmitting sex-role ideology in our culture?

3. Discuss the arguments based on (1) free will, (2) biology, and (3) complementarity, which are used in our society to justify the current distribution of the sexes in the occupational world. Then describe Bem and Bem's counterarguments.

4. The woman is effectively "trained to know her place" when she comes to accept traditional gender roles for herself. Explain how this process of *internalization* of norms occurs.

A CHILD'S EYE VIEW OF WORK

Bernard Goldstein and Jack Oldham

"IN MEDIEVAL SOCIETY THE IDEA OF CHILDHOOD DID NOT EXIST . . . AS SOON AS THE child could live without the constant solicitude of his mother, his nanny, or his cradle rocker, he belonged to adult society."[1] In sharp contrast to this description provided by cultural historian Philippe Aries, ours is a very child-oriented society. Childhood is not only a socially distinct age, but one which in the more recent phases of the Industrial Age has clearly been prolonged. The movement for the establishment of child labor laws, for example, signalled the onset of an era in which children have increasingly been regarded as objects to be protected from the harsher aspects of reality.

Insofar as these "harsher" aspects may be presumed to include the social institution of work, we face an interesting sociological problem. On the one hand, educators and public officials have expressed willingness to entrust more of the responsibility for the child's work-related socialization experiences to the school. On the other hand there is little agreement on such issues as when to begin imparting such information, how much may be taken for granted, or the existence of benchmarks in terms of children's readiness to assimilate certain types of information. A society such as our own, which is highly work-oriented yet protective of its offspring insofar as their exposure to work is concerned, inevitably finds it necessary on occasion to monitor the effects of such countervailing tendencies upon its children. Our task in this chapter will be to survey what the children in our sample know about work and a variety of related phenomena.

Work is sufficiently pervasive as to be taken for granted by children. In the words of one seven-year-old: "Work is work. You'd better drop dead if you don't understand what work is." But as numerous studies by political scientists have shown, the fact that children take their knowledge for granted does not necessarily mean their views are accurate or even settled. Our interests here therefore include the recording and interpretation of children's misconceptions as well as the charting of their learning curves with regard to work. The focus in this chapter will be almost exclusively upon matters of cognition. The goal is to establish the existence of "baselines" of information from which children start, as well as any "plateaus" they may reach during childhood.

This paper is a revised version of Bernard Goldstein and Jack Oldham, *Children and Work: A Study of Socialization*. New Brunswick, N.J.: Transaction Books, 1979, pp. 33–34, 49–63, 81–84.

Our discussion of cognitive development will be restricted here to knowledge of selected work-related phenomena.

RESEARCH METHODS

Before proceeding to our findings, it is necessary to say something about the children who answered our questions, and the questions that were asked. This being an exploratory study, the primary research goals were descriptive. The ideal strategy for a developmental study is to follow the subjects over time. Not having the luxury of conducting the ideal study, a cross-sectional design was employed. In keeping with procedures followed in other studies of childhood socialization, pupils in grades one, three, five and seven were sampled at the same point in time.

Respondents attended schools in five communities in north-central New Jersey. The cooperating schools had in common that they were suburban or semirural in location and overwhelmingly white in enrollment. Thus, the sample was comprised largely of white suburban or semirural residents ranging in socioeconomic background from working class to upper-middle class. Generalizations must be limited accordingly, but the findings are thought to be representative of the largely white, public, primary-school population of the state.

While no town is completely homogeneous in socioeconomic composition, the communities from which the pupils in this study were selected can be characterized as working-, middle-, and upper-middle class, respectively. Two are venerable towns whose white frame homes and congenial business districts attest to the prosperity of times gone by. Both are classified for census purposes as "rural centers" but their inhabitants today typically earn their livings as nonfarm industrial, retail, or clerical workers or as shopkeepers. Two other localities are burgeoning middle-class bedroom communities whose occupants are a mixed lot of upwardly-mobile workers: skilled craftsmen and foremen, teachers and lower echelon bureaucrats, and a minority of junior executives and young professionals for whom these towns are "first stops" rather than long-term homes. The fifth area is also a newer bedroom community populated not by "old wealth" but by upwardly-mobile business and professional people, many of whom presumably regard themselves as "having arrived."

Altogether, 905 children were surveyed during the period 1973–75, with boys constituting 55 percent of the sample. Children were surveyed an average of four to seven times during the course of the school site visits. As a general rule, first- and third-grade children either responded in groups to pictorial or simple verbal stimuli or were interviewed individually. Fifth and seventh graders ordinarily responded to questionnaires or other verbal tasks.

It was necessary to develop a series of research instruments of varying formats appropriate for children of different age groups. Following numerous leads in the literature, and after considerable experimentation with instruments of our own design, a battery of ten instruments (some of which had multiple versions) was finally adapted. These ranged in format from straightforward questionnaires about the world of work or parental work roles, to inquiries from a hypothetical "Man from Mars" seeking explanations of everyday work-related phenomena, to picture-stimuli and drawing exercises, to tasks involving the sorting of occupations into categories, to the ranking of occupational value statements.

With the questions of how responses were elicited from the children, and what kind of children were surveyed, out of the way, we can now proceed to the issue of the findings.

CHILDREN'S KNOWLEDGE OF SPECIFIC WORK-RELATED PHENOMENA

[In this paper, we will focus on] children's knowledge of five phenomena related to the world of work: (1) the process of getting a job; (2) their perceptions of pay differentials; (3) knowledge of occupational authority figures; (4) insight into labor disputes; and (5) understanding of welfare payments. Each will be considered in turn.

GETTING A JOB: As anyone with the slightest experience in counseling college seniors can attest, it is often surprising how little prospective graduates know of the finer points of the "job hunting" process. Yet our findings suggest that even young children are aware of the *general* procedures involved in obtaining work. Perhaps we should let our younger respondents speak for themselves in testimony that this is so. The following are representative of the answers given by first and third graders to the question "How do people get jobs?"[2]:

> When someone quits, someone else replaces him. You find out about it by looking on the sign outside the place . . . The boss decides if you're good enough.
>
> > Ellen, age 6

> A counselor tells them what job they have to do . . . You look for one [a job] in the city. You ask someone and they tell you if you can have it.
>
> > Sharon, age 6

> You go to an office and you pick out the job you want. You ask the boss. And you tell him how old you are, and fill out papers to show how smart you are. A computer does it. The boss decides when he looks at your papers.
>
> > Jeremy, age 8

> You graduate and then look for a "help wanted" sign, and ask at the place.
>
> > Tommy, age 8

> You decide in college. You study it. They let you be it if you take a test.
>
> > Rita, age 9

> They look in the papers. And then drive around and see the "job needed" signs. And they go in, and if they want, they take it. The manager looks to see if you do a good job, and if you do, he hires you.
>
> > Keith, age 8

These responses are simplistic in that hiring decisions are rarely so automatic or clearcut as depicted, but they could hardly be called inaccurate. Most first and third graders were able to furnish some level of correct information regarding job hunting. This usually involved an explanation that one learns of the opening by seeing an advertisement in a newspaper or on a sign, then presents oneself in application. Many also elaborated on the criteria involved in the decision to hire. A small minority asserted that such decisions depended primarily on "if they like you or not." More often, pupils recognized that achieved factors play a role, citing needs for education or the passing of tests, or a trial of sorts staged so that the person hiring might decide "if you're good enough." Fifth graders seemed to take much of this for granted, with a slightly greater number (41 percent) answering instead in terms of the fit between one's interests, knowledge, skills, and/or training and the position sought. Among seventh graders,[3] the latter sort of response emerged as the dominant one (47 percent), with a re-emphasis, too, on "other" answers, including recognition of the roles of employment agencies and the like.

There is a clear age-related trend in which answers stressing getting in contact with the hiring source fade in favor of responses which stress introspection and evaluation of the goodness of fit between the job and one's interests, capacities, and qualifications. The general pattern of these results is very much in keeping with that described by Ginzberg et al.[4] in their important study of occupational choice. That is to say, there is definite developmental progress in the direction of increasing "realism," as Ginzberg would call it. But there are also some differences worthy of note. When younger children are asked how one gets a job, their answers are hardly fantasy-based, as Ginzberg presumed their occupational choices to be at ages six to eleven. Rather, they furnish reasonably accurate and objective, if incomplete, accounts of the process of job-hunting. That fifth and seventh graders apparently interpret the question somewhat differently is in itself significant, for it suggests a basic cognitive shift which likely means that many have entered the so-called "tentative period." At this stage they are prone, for the first time, to weigh potential job satisfactions versus that which the individual brings to the job. The older children in our sample were less concerned with how one finds *a* job than with how one finds *the* job he or she is suited for.

· · ·

PAY DIFFERENTIALS: Children at all grade levels tested recognize that most people derive their incomes through work. When we broached the subject of pay with children we found nearly universal recognition of the existence of wage and salary differentials. When asked whether all workers received the same pay, 83 percent of first graders, 95 percent of third graders and 96 percent of fifth graders answered in the negative. Many could give no reasons for the inequities they presumed to exist but, among those who could, there could be found an obvious trend with age in the direction of realism. As Table 1 shows, the older children in the sample are increasingly likely to ascribe pay differentials to the nature of the job rather than to such individual factors as personal diligence or time spent on the job.

. . . [S]uch explanations as "some work harder" and "some work longer hours" are important to children's work schemes, but give signs of crumbling by fifth grade.

It is of interest, too, to examine children's answers in relation to their socioeconomic status. Working-class children are more likely, at all grades tested, to ascribe pay differentials to individual diligence or the number of hours worked. Among working-class children who furnished reasons for the existence of pay differentials, 83 percent attributed these to the above two reasons, compared to 58 percent of the middle-class children who provided reasons. Whether this may be taken as an indicant of greater realism on the part of middle-class pupils is another question, however. One cannot rule out that these children are extrapolating on the basis of different types of experiences. For example, it may be that children of white-collar workers hear little of the concept of "overtime," while working-class children may quite reasonably equate same with increased pay, and generalize accordingly.

THE BOSS: That young children idealize political authority has often been interpreted as the basis of subsequent attachment to the political system.[5] But it has also been demonstrated that positive [feelings toward] political authority fades from third through ninth grade, a fact which casts doubt on the notion that early feelings are simply transferred.[6] The question has not been resolved. Here, our concern is with a parallel question, namely that of children's conceptions of occupational authority figures, i.e. "bosses." Although as it turned out cognition and evaluation are difficult to separate, our primary concern for the present lies with the former. Therefore, we began our inquiry by asking children merely, "What is a boss?"

Table 1. Percentages, Among Children Giving Reasons, of Explanations for Pay Differentials by Grade in School

Why isn't everyone's pay the same?	GRADE IN SCHOOL		
	1st	*3rd*	*5th*
Pay varies with occupation	19.7%	28.4%	49.1%
	(24)	(50)	(85)
Some work more hours	28.7	14.8	8.1
	(35)	(26)	(14)
Some work harder	51.6	56.8	42.8
	(63)	(100)	(74)
Total	100.0%	100.0%	100.0%
	(122)	(176)	(173)

While there were a great many variations in the responses, three conceptual themes figured most prominently in the answers of children in grades one, three, and five. (The responses of seventh graders were somewhat different and will therefore be discussed separately, below.) The dominant first response, which was offered by about two or three children below grade seven, stressed the "instrumental" [or *task-oriented*] role of the boss. Most children conceived of the boss primarily as an instrumental leader whose role involves telling others what to do and how to do it, or controlling employees' use of time. A small minority identified the boss as an *owner* of the work organization. And a handful formulated their answers in terms of the status or *prestige* associated with the role, noting for example that, "He's the most important person," or "He gets paid the most." There were also numerous "other" responses, for the most part entirely reasonable, but few of which recurred with any regularity among children's first answers to this question.

Table 2 portrays the relative distribution of these responses, as well as the "Don't know" answers among children in grades one, three, and five. While the age differences are less apparent here, it is clear that children are familiar with the concept of occupational authority. Only 9.5 percent of first graders and negligible proportions of older children cannot offer an explanation. But there are slight variations with age in the relative distributions of children giving each of the principal answers. After the first grade, not only do the "Don't know" responses disappear, the "Other" responses also drop off in favor of the more prominent ones. By third grade, one child in six identifies the boss as an owner; by fifth grade a few (9 percent) answer in terms of [prestige] differentials which distinguish such authority figures.

Table 2. Distribution of First Responses to the Question "What is a Boss?" by Grade in School

	GRADE IN SCHOOL		
Response:	1st	3rd	5th
Don't know	9.5%	1.0%	0.5%
	(18)	(2)	(1)
Instrumental leader	58.5	69.0	62.4
	(111)	(138)	(123)
Person with prestige	0.5	1.5	9.1
	(1)	(3)	(18)
Owner	6.8	16.5	13.7
	(13)	(33)	(27)
All other responses	24.7	12.0	14.2
	(47)	(24)	(28)
Total	100.0%	100.0%	99.9%
	(190)	(200)	(197)

With age, we see at least the beginnings of a shift from conceptualization of the boss as a social role to an economic one.[7]

This general pattern changed very little when sex, socioeconomic status, and community of residence were taken into account. Boys were in general slightly more apt to provide a [prestige]-related definition than girls (14 percent to 11 percent), but this remained a minority response at all grade levels for both sex groups.

While first responses may be assumed to be most salient in children's thinking, most furnished more than one answer here. When additional responses were taken into account, it was clear that while instrumental conceptions continue to dominate children's definitions, others emerge or disappear with age. Older children, in addition to being more likely to speak of status or ownership, also begin to mention the *responsibility* which falls upon the boss, as did 22.5 percent of third graders, and 20 percent of fifth graders. That a few first graders attend to [emotional] aspects in defining the boss is also clear: 5 percent noted that the boss is one who helps people, while 12 percent defined the role as that of someone who scolded a lot or was disliked or feared. Older children did not employ such referents. The *control* exercised by the boss over the fate of workers also emerged in additional responses, with 12 percent of children mentioning the boss' significance in hiring and firing. There were no age differences in this last matter.

Among seventh graders, who were asked essentially the same question but in a different format,[8] it was obvious that the burdensome responsibilities of the position were more salient. In fact, this category, which had not even been among the prominent first responses of younger children, rose to second place behind instrumental responses here, with 26 percent of all the responses. We also asked what it is like *to be* a boss. The [most common] answer (35 percent) among seventh graders who responded stressed the difficulty of the role, calling it "hard work" or "a lot of trouble."

What then can be concluded from our analysis of children's conceptualizations of occupational authority? In order to answer this, our findings must be considered in relation to those of previous studies. Danziger had explored the concept of the boss in children five to eight years of age;[9] Haire and Morrison had done the same with respondents in grades seven through eleven.[10] The former had found even the youngest children sampled quite conversant with the term, as we have. We are also able to corroborate the general pattern discerned by Danziger of a shift from answers in terms of purely social functions of the boss to those describing economic functions. In our sample, however, this transition was far from complete, as even among seventh graders instrumental role activities dominated children's social definitions. The economic role of the boss as owner and source of wages and the [prestige] and higher salary associated with the role were, to be sure, more prominent among the older children, but not dominant themes. Nor did we find the pronounced differences b[etween social classes] which had characterized the Haire and Morrison study of children in grades seven and up. We did, however, note slight . . . differences in this regard, with middle-class children somewhat more given to the instrumental, responsibility, and status themes, while working-class children were slightly more inclined to view the boss as the source of wages and the one who hires and fires. It would seem that the [social class] differences found by Haire and Morrison come to prominence [sometime after seventh grade].

LABOR DISPUTES: The final two work-related phenomena to be considered present us with a departure from the pattern of gradual but steady cognitive development we have seen thus far. For it is only when we examine children's knowledge of labor disputes and welfare that we find, for the first time, a suggestion of the existence of "threshold effects" in children's work orientations. That is to say, here we encounter evidence which suggests a clear age-related demarcation: a certain age prior to which very few children grasp the concept, but beyond which it is understood by most.

It is crystal clear that for the majority of children sampled, recognition of the nature of labor disputes comes between third and fifth grade. As Table 3 shows, there is a forty percentage-point leap in the correct response rates at that point. This suggests either a dramatic increase in "readiness" to grasp this notion of labor disputes by grade five or some unexplained increase in older children's experiential exposure to the term and consequent understanding of it.

During the elementary years, children progress from virtually no knowledge of strikes in first grade to the opposite extreme, at which nearly all seventh graders can render a reasonable account of the concept. The youngest children were unable to account for the depicted hypothetical situation of men with signs picketing a factory to keep others from entering. About three in five drew blanks. The bulk of the remainder resorted to a variety of explanations, especially that of a disaster of some sort—a fire, an explosion, theft, a leak, a fuel shortage, or even the death of a child within the building—which prevented the plant from operating. Some grasped that such actions as were depicted are often taken in protest, citing noise levels or pollution or attributes of the personal behavior of the boss as the reasons for

Table 3. Children's Recognition of Strikes by Grade in School

	GRADE IN SCHOOL			
Response:	*1st*	*3rd*	*5th*	*7th*
Don't know	59.2%	42.6%	6.0%	0.0%
	(100)	(80)	(13)	(0)
Misconceptions	31.9	18.6	15.2	4.5
	(54)	(35)	(33)	(6)
Identified labor	8.9	38.8	78.8	95.5
dispute	(15)	(73)	(171)	(127)
Total	100.0%	100.0%	100.0%	100.0%
	(169)	(188)	(217)	(133)

same. Fewer than one in ten first graders, however, answered that the men were striking, i.e., that they were refusing to work due to a disagreement with management over wages or conditions. When asked if they had heard the term "strike," over 90 percent indicated they had not, at least not in its present context.

By third grade the term had passed into the recognition vocabularies of a distinct minority of children. The frequency of misconceptions decreased and some children could indeed answer on an informed basis. Nine-year-old Jonathan, while somewhat atypical, is a case in point. He understood picketing as an effort to make management an offer it could not refuse:

> It's a strike. [Why?] They wanted something—more money, a raise, a better place—and the boss wouldn't give it to them. And they wanted it. And they didn't want anyone to get into their place. So the boss could go out of business, or give it to them.

Such an answer was relatively rare among third graders. It was, however, typical among the responses of fifth graders, 70 percent of whom supplied the terms "strike" or "picketing" in their accounts of the depicted situations. Haire and Morrison, who had also explored knowledge of strikes [but] in grades seven through eleven, had noted that seventh and eighth graders tended to personalize labor disputes, "to see issues and rights and wrongs as residing in the persons of the protagonists."[11] In light of the present findings, such an appraisal seems relativistic indeed. We have no doubt that, in comparison with the responses of high school students, the views of seventh and eighth graders did in fact seem simplistic due to personalization. But if one examines conceptualizations of labor disputes on an age continuum starting with first graders, the responses of fifth and seventh graders stand out as relatively abstract. Younger children who had understood that a labor dispute was at issue often attributed it to the anger or recalcitrance of one or both parties. Among older children in our sample, such accounts often centered on the leverage which a work stoppage was intended to exert upon management. There was most definitely an observable age-related trend during the elementary years in the direction of increasingly abstract and sophisticated understanding of labor disputes. Moreover, that age was the most significant variable was attested to by our findings of no significant relationship between conceptions of strikes and the variables of sex, [social class,] and community of residence.

When children were asked to evaluate whether most strikes are right or wrong, two further observations were [made] possible. First, with age children tend to gather enough information to formulate opinions on the matter. Only ten first graders both perceived the situation as a strike and expressed opinions regarding its propriety. The proportion of children at each grade level satisfying both conditions rose steadily thereafter, with the third-to-fifth-grade difference, predictably, shifting the plurality to those with opinions. Second, among children who had such opinions there was a

Table 4. Distribution of Expressed Opinions Regarding Whether Strikes are Right or Wrong by Grade in School

	GRADE IN SCHOOL[12]		
Opinion expressed:	*3rd*	*5th*	*7th*
Strikes are right	41.3%	48.4%	50.4%
	(31)	(74)	(61)
Strikes are wrong	34.7	23.5	22.3
	(26)	(36)	(27)
Conditional answers	24.0	28.1	27.3
	(18)	(43)	(33)
Total	100.0%	100.0%	100.0%
	(75)	(153)	(121)

tendency, as Table 4 shows, to consider strikes right. This did not shift significantly with age. It is of interest to note also that a substantial minority of children in grades three, five, and seven indicated conditional answers, saying "it depends," or "they're right if . . . " or "they're wrong if . . . " [I]n most of these cases, the conditions specified were monetary, i.e., depending upon whether or not wage levels were fair, or the employer's ability to pay.

Haire and Morrison had earlier noted pronounced SES difference in students' evaluations of strikes. They had found that by seventh grade response patterns were already well established: Middle-class youngsters overwhelmingly thought strikes wrong, while working-class youth felt them to be, if not right, at least necessary.[13] Here, we found much more modest differences. At grades three and five, [middle-class] children were more likely than others to have formulated their opinions in conditional terms rather than to have expressed unequivocal opposition to strikes.[14] In fact, strikes were viewed as at least potentially acceptable by the majority of children of both [social-class] groups at all grade levels tested. Surprisingly, no significant differences by [class] were found in the response patterns of seventh graders. Whether the dissimilarities between our findings and those of Haire and Morrison can be accounted for by differences in the composition of the samples, or the sixteen-year time lag, or some other factors cannot be estimated here. It is, however, certain that the opinions of these children were far less organized along predictable ideological lines, by [social-class], than were those of the somewhat older group examined by Haire and Morrison.

While no significant sex difference had emerged in the opinions of third and fifth graders regarding the propriety of strikes, this was a factor in the responses of seventh graders. Boys were significantly more disposed toward viewing strikes as right whereas girls were more tentative, expressing their opinions more frequently in conditional terms.[15]

WELFARE PAYMENTS: Our final effort to explore children's knowledge of work-related phenomena involved the issue of welfare payments. Again, we found very few first graders conversant with the concept. "My father tells me everything," said seven-year-old Gene, "but I've never heard of that one!" Over 90 percent of first graders shared his lack of knowledge. By third grade the distribution had changed little, although there were a smattering of "correct" responses.[16] As Table 5 shows, however, the previous findings of a quantum leap in awareness of strikes from third to fifth grade [were repeated] here with regard to knowledge of welfare. But such knowledge was in general neither as extensive nor as widespread as had been awareness of labor disputes. Among fifth graders, for example, about half could furnish a correct response; among seventh graders, about two-thirds could do so.[17]

It is of interest to note that while the proportion of "Don't know" responses decreased with age, largely in favor of correct information, the proportion of misconceptions also rose steadily. Our interpretation is that this pattern attests to the existence of incremental increases in awareness or, if you will, progressive stages of understanding quite possibly indicative of growing readiness to grasp the concept. A few examples will clarify this. First graders either admit to no recognition of the term, or merely surmise from the context of the question that it has to do with money. Only a very few could specify for whom the money was intended or the rationale for the practice. Among some third graders, welfare was often equated with charity or even with the practice of extending credit. Nine-year-old William identified welfare as: "When people come over and help you when you're poor. They do things for you, like get rid of the rats. [Who does?] The rich people." Eight-year-old Jerry said, "When you're poor, you get money. And after you get a job, you pay them back. [Where does the money come from?] The taxes people pay." Thus, some third graders grasped at least the gist of the matter, even if their conceptions may have been muddled or simplistic.

Many fifth graders evidenced a more complex understanding of the matter. Not only had the "Don't know" responses dropped off greatly, but pupils were typically able to name categories of persons believed eligible as welfare recipients. It was also obvious that many confused welfare with

Table 5. Responses to Question "What is Welfare?" by Grade in School

	GRADE IN SCHOOL			
Response:	1st	3rd	5th	7th
Don't know	91.9%	73.8%	20.6%	4.9%
	(159)	(144)	(41)	(5)
"Correct" responses	5.8	15.9	51.8	65.6
	(10)	(31)	(103)	(67)
Misconceptions	2.3	10.3	27.6	29.4
	(4)	(20)	(55)	(30)
Total	100.0%	100.0%	100.0%	99.9%
	(173)	(195)	(199)	(102)

other programs of social insurance, especially unemployment insurance, social security payments to the retired or disabled, death benefits paid to surviving families either by the government or by private firms, even union strike benefits. The common denominator, that welfare represents financial help for those facing hard times, was relatively well understood, although the details may have been confused. Seventh graders were the most likely to supply such information. In fact, most of them (65 percent) furnished multiple responses regarding imputed categories of eligible welfare recipients including: the poor, the disabled, children in fatherless homes, large families with inadequate means of support, the elderly, the sick, those temporarily out of work, and, finally, those too lazy to work. While many of these answers are technically incorrect, they nonetheless suggest the growth of social awareness of the world of work.

We found no differences in children's knowledge of welfare by sex or community of residence. One would, however, expect differences in such awareness by [social class], if only because middle-class families may be presumed to have less first-hand contact with welfare and are [possibly] less outspoken on the issue within the home. This was found not to be the case, however, until grade seven, at which time [working-class] children display somewhat greater awareness of the concept than did middle-class children.[18]

It should be noted, however, that the [social-class] split in this sample is between middle-class and working-class children, often from the same communities. There are few children from "poverty areas" represented, and to our knowledge only a handful of children from families receiving welfare. That first-hand experience with welfare is an important contributor to knowledge of the concept is eloquently attested to by the following interview with Kevin, a nine-year-old from one of the rural communities:

I: Do you know what welfare is, Kevin?

R: My dad's on welfare. And when we go to school, you get tickets and get free lunches. And sometimes, when you don't have a mother, the welfare . . . [He pauses, losing train of thought.]

I: [Changing the subject] Does everyone get welfare?

R: No, because some people don't like welfare. [He then stresses that his father appreciates it, and that he does not know why others look down upon it.]

I: Do you know why some people get it?

R: No, but my dad gets it and other people do, too.

I: Where does it come from?

R: It's from "The Welfare." Your dad pays half and the Welfare pays half—for the babysitter. So when you need a babysitter [He means day-care service] you don't have to spend all that money. The Welfare pays half.

This last point, illustrative of children's vague allusions to the source of welfare payments, points up another aspect of their general pattern of awareness of the phenomena. Only one first grader could correctly identify the government as the source of such payments. Among third graders who had attempted an explanation, only 29 percent had "correctly" identified the source, citing either the government, the state, the city, or tax revenues in their answers. By fifth grade, this figure had risen to 51 percent of those attempting an explanation; by seventh grade it was 90 percent. The range of misconceptions in this regard was greatest among fifth graders, one of whom, for example, explained that those who could afford to do so purchased policies from Mutual of Omaha, which subsequently made welfare payments if they were needed.

As had been the case with children's opinions regarding strikes, older children proved not only better informed concerning the nature of welfare, but more inclined to evaluate it as well. Children were asked their opinions on whether they were "for" or "against" welfare. Admittedly, since we have already established that children perceived welfare as a benefit to the unfortunate, this was a loaded question. The "pro" responses far outweighed the "cons." But the former diminished somewhat with age in favor, not of negative answers, but conditional responses.

In order to ascertain children's opinions regarding welfare, we posited a hypothetical situation in which two men argued its "pros" and "cons." We then asked children which person they thought was right. Among young children, support of the welfare program tends to be unequivocal, largely because the perceived stakes were so high. "If they don't get enough money," said eight-year-old Jimmy of welfare recipients, "they could die." For ten-year-old Sandra, who claimed several of her neighbors are on welfare, the threat is very real. "The one for welfare [was right]," she said, "because they need to take care of them, so they don't die." For Stanley, age six, the logic of the practice was evident: "Some people don't got enough money to buy things, like food . . . some people would die if they didn't have welfare, 'cause they wouldn't have enough money to buy food." For others, like eleven-year-old Bryan, there is a moral imperative involved: "[the one] for it [was right], because he wants to help people who aren't as well off as themselves." Still others think of the social consequences of doing away with the program. "If there weren't welfare," observed a fifth grade girl, "people would be outside roaming the streets."

The older children, however, tended to qualify their evaluations. "If everyone got it, the world would be a big mess," noted ten-year old Andrea, who nonetheless supported the concept, ". . . because if there was no welfare, we would have beggars, and people living in the middle of the street." Most supported the practice, but "only for the people that need it—that don't have a job and they're poor," to borrow the words of ten-year-old Diane. "If you're not very sick or very hurt," offered a male classmate, then as far as he was concerned, "you don't get it!"

Very few shared the opinion of ten-year-old Eddie, who described welfare as "getting money free," and said he opposed it on grounds that, "People have to work for their money." Such pejorative views of welfare recipients, presumably common among adults, were *not* found to any significant degree among the children sampled.

In conclusion, lest anyone remain tempted to dismiss all elementary children as ill-informed or incapable of understanding the matters discussed in these pages, we offer the thoughts of a remarkably well informed fifth-grade girl:

I: Do you know what welfare is, Laura?

R: Welfare is money given out to people that don't have jobs and can't get jobs.

I: Where does it come from?

R: The government.

I: Which person do you think was right, the one for welfare or the one against it?

R: I think the one for it, because without welfare how would these people be able to live? They wouldn't be able to buy food. The only other thing they could get would be unemployment, and they would need a job for a little while for that.

SUMMARY

Alexander Pope, in his *Essay on Man*, long ago declared that "The child is father to the man." The task of determining at what point the child "gives birth," as it were, to a socialized "product" has largely been left to social scientists. In this chapter we have been concerned in particular with the child's cognitive development with respect to work. We have explored a number of issues under that umbrella question. Do we have a pattern to point to for our efforts? The answer would seem to be a qualified yes. The pattern of age-related growth in awareness of work-related phenomena has been apparent throughout our findings thus far. While we have noted, on the one hand, examples of surprisingly high awareness from very early ages and, on the other, a few instances of genuine "threshold effects," it is nonetheless possible to point to a general pattern of steady cognitive growth throughout the elementary years, with the greatest changes usually coming around grade five.

Such a general observation requires considerable qualification. In the first place, it should be acknowledged that variations by specific items were in some cases quite large. And, there were instances in which other [background factors], particularly sex and socioeconomic status, influenced the results. On the other hand, there were very few cases of no cognitive growth to report despite the great many variables examined here. Moreover, that the pattern is indeed developmental or age-related is attested to by the consistency with which changes in cognition were found to be significantly, and often strongly, related to grade in school, without regard to any existing relationships with other variables. The latter, in any event, were surprisingly few.

NOTES

1. Philippe Aries, *Centuries of Childhood: A Social History of Family Life*, trans. Robert Baldick (New York: Vintage Books, 1965), p. 128.

2. Throughout this report all respondents' names, indeed all proper nouns have been changed to preserve the anonymity of the pupils involved and their families. Also, in some cases, probe questions were inserted by the interviewer in order to get children to elaborate on matters under discussion. For purposes of clarity and simplicity probe questions are omitted wherever this practice does no damage to the substance of the child's answer.

3. Seventh graders answered the same question in writing as did fifth graders, but on the Knowledge of Work Questionnaire, Part II.

4. Eli Ginzberg et al., *Occupational Choice* (New York: Columbia University Press, 1951).

5. The child's idealization of political authority figures prominently in several studies of political socialization. For a review of this literature, see: Fred I. Greenstein, *Children and Politics* (New Haven, Conn.: Yale University Press, 1969), pp. 31–54. See also: Fred I. Greenstein, "The Benevolent Leader: Children's Images of Political Authority," *American Political Science Review* 14 (December 1960), pp. 934–943. For consideration of how such imagery is thought to translate into attachment to a political system, see: Robert D. Hess and Judith V. Torney, *The Development of Political Attitudes*, especially chapters 2 and 3.

6. Edward S. Greenberg, "Orientations of Black and White Children to Political Authority Figures," *Social Science Quarterly* 51 (December 1970), pp. 561–571.

7. Danziger, in his 1958 study of Australian schoolchildren, had noted a similar shift from the purely social to the economic in children's conceptualizations of the role of the boss. He, however, was able to discern this shift by age eight, the oldest level at which he tested. Here the shift comes somewhat later. See Kurt Danziger, "Children's Earliest Concepts."

8. Children in grades one, three, and five were asked to explain the term "boss" to a hypothetical alien. Seventh graders were asked to explain what was involved in being a boss.

9. Kurt Danziger, "Children's Earliest Concepts."

10. Mason Haire and Florence Morrison, "School Children's Perceptions of Labor and Management," *Journal of Social Psychology* 44 (November 1957), pp. 179–197.

11. Mason Haire and Florence Morrison, "School Children's Perceptions," p. 189.

12. First graders are not included in Table 4 since only ten both recognized the strike situation as a labor dispute and had formulated opinions on the matter.

13. Mason Haire and Florence Morrison, "School Children's Perceptions."

14. Specifically, the actual responses of the third and fifth graders were distributed as follows. Thirty percent of respondents from middle-class families as compared to 50 percent of respondents from working-class families thought strikes are right; 28 percent of both groups thought strikes were wrong; and 39 percent of the former and 22 percent of the latter gave conditional responses.

15. Among seventh graders, 58 percent of the boys said strikes were right, compared to 35 percent of the girls. On the other hand, 37 percent of seventh grade girls answered conditionally, versus only 18 percent [of] boys.

16. Here the standard applied in classifying children's responses as correct was rather liberal indeed. Any child who identified welfare as money for the poor or for those *unable* to work, and/or as a situation in which the government pays for the living expenses of the poor, was considered to have at least a functional understanding of the concept.

17. Children in grades one, three, and five were asked to explain the concept of welfare to the alien, who had supposedly overheard two men arguing over whether the practice was right or wrong. Fifth graders answered in writing. Younger children were interviewed. Seventh graders were asked to define welfare in writing, and to evaluate it.

18. Among seventh graders 51 percent of those from middle-class backgrounds correctly identified welfare, compared to 71 percent of those of working-class backgrounds.

Review Questions

1. With respect to which of the following concepts are children socialized *gradually*, or incrementally? Which of the concepts seem to be grasped more *suddenly* at a given stage of intellectual development?
   a. how one gets a job
   b. why pay differentials exist
   c. the role of the boss
   d. the meaning of worker strikes
   e. the meaning of social welfare

2. To what extent were the first graders studied by Goldstein and Oldham aware of the world of work? The older children?

3. What differences were found between working-class and middle-class children with regard to perceptions about work? What factors might account for these differences?

4. What differences were found between girls and boys with regard to perceptions about work? What factors might account for these differences?

THE FATE OF IDEALISM IN MEDICAL SCHOOL

Howard S. Becker and Blanche Geer

IT MAKES SOME DIFFERENCE IN A MAN'S PERFORMANCE OF HIS WORK WHETHER HE BELIEVES wholeheartedly in what he is doing or feels that in important respects it is a fraud, whether he feels convinced that it is a good thing or believes that it is not really of much use after all. The distinction we are making is the one people have in mind when they refer, for example, to their calling as a "noble profession" on the one hand or a "racket" on the other. In the one case they idealistically proclaim that their work is all that it claims on the surface to be; in the other they cynically concede that it is first and foremost a way of making a living and that its surface pretensions are just that and nothing more. Presumably, different modes of behavior are associated with these perspectives when wholeheartedly embraced. The cynic cuts corners with a feeling of inevitability while the idealist goes down fighting. *The Blackboard Jungle* and *Not as a Stranger* are only the most recent in a long tradition of fictional portrayals of the importance of this aspect of a man's adjustment to his work.

Professional schools often receive a major share of the blame for producing this kind of cynicism—and none more than the medical school. The idealistic young freshman changes into a tough, hardened, unfeeling doctor; or so the popular view has it. Teachers of medicine sometimes rephrase the distinction between the clinical and preclinical years into one between the "cynical" and "precynical" years. Psychological research supports this view, presenting attitude surveys which show medical students year by year scoring lower on "idealism" and higher on "cynicism."[1] Typically, this cynicism is seen as developing in response to the shattering of ideals consequent on coming face-to-face with the realities of professional practice.

In this paper, we attempt to describe the kind of idealism that characterizes the medical freshmen and to trace both the development of cynicism and the vicissitudes of that idealism in the course of the four years of medical training. Our main themes are that though they develop cynical feelings in specific situations directly associated with their medical school experience, the medical students never lose their original idealism about the practice of medicine; that the growth of both cynicism and idealism are not simple developments, but are instead complex transformations; and that the

Howard S. Becker and Blanche Geer, "The Fate of Idealism in Medical School," *American Sociological Review*, vol. 23 (1958), pp. 50–56.

very notions "idealism" and "cynicism" need further analysis, and must be seen as situational in their expressions rather than as stable traits possessed by individuals in greater or lesser degree. Finally, we see the greater portion of these feelings as being collective rather than individual phenomena.

Our discussion is based on a study . . . conduct[ed] at a state medical school[2] in which we have carried on participant observation with students of all four years in all of the courses and clinical work to which they are exposed. We joined the students in their activities in school and after school and watched them at work in labs, on the hospital wards, and in the clinic. Often spending as much as a month with a small group of from five to fifteen students assigned to a particular activity, we came to know them well and were able to gather information in informal interviews and by overhearing the ordinary daily conversation of the group.[3] In the course of our observation and interviewing we have gathered much information on the subject of idealism. Of necessity, we shall have to present the very briefest statement of our findings with little or no supporting evidence.[4] The problem of idealism is, of course, many-faceted and complex and we have dealt with it in a simplified way, describing only some of its grosser features.[5]

THE FRESHMEN

The medical students enter school with what we may think of as the idealistic notion, implicit in lay culture, that the practice of medicine is a wonderful thing and that they are going to devote their lives to service to mankind. They believe that medicine is made up of a great body of well-established facts that they will be taught from the first day on and that these facts will be of immediate practical use to them as physicians. They enter school expecting to work industriously and expecting that if they work hard enough they will be able to master this body of fact and thus become good doctors.

In several ways the first year of medical school does not live up to their expectations. They are disillusioned when they find they will not be near patients at all, that the first year will be just like another year of college. In fact, some feel that it is not even as good as college because their work in certain areas is not as thorough as courses in the same fields in undergraduate school. They come to think that their courses (with the exception of anatomy) are not worth much because, in the first place, the faculty (being Ph.D.s) know nothing about the practice of medicine, and, in the second place, the subject matter itself is irrelevant, or as the students say, "ancient history." The freshmen are further disillusioned when the faculty tells them in a variety of ways that there is more to medicine than they can possibly learn. They realize it may be impossible for them to learn all they need to know in order to practice medicine properly. Their disillusionment becomes more profound when they discover that this statement of the faculty is literally true.[6] Experience in trying to master the details of the anatomy of the extremities convinces them that they cannot do so in the time they have.

Their expectation of hard work is not disappointed; they put in an eight-hour day of classes and laboratories, and study four or five hours a night and most of the weekend as well.

Some of the students, the brightest, continue to attempt to learn it all, but succeed only in getting more and more worried about their work. The majority decide that, since they can't learn it all, they must select from among all the facts presented to them those they will attempt to learn. There are two ways of making this selection. On the one hand, the student may decide on the basis of his own uninformed notions about the nature of medical practice that many facts are not important, since they relate to things which seldom come up in the actual practice of medicine; therefore, he reasons, it is useless to learn them. On the other hand, the student can decide that the important thing is to pass his examinations and, therefore, that the important facts are those which are likely to be asked on an examination; he uses this as a basis for selecting both facts to memorize and courses for intensive study. For example, the work in physiology is dismissed on both of these grounds, being considered neither relevant to the facts of medical life nor important in terms of the amount of time the faculty devotes to it and the number of examinations in the subject.

A student may use either or both of these bases of selection at the beginning of the year, before many tests have been given. But after a few tests have been taken, the student makes "what the faculty wants" the chief basis of his selection of what to learn, for he now has a better idea of what this is and also has become aware that it is possible to fail examinations and that he therefore must learn the expectations of the faculty if he wishes to stay in school. The fact that one group of students, that with the highest prestige in the class, took this view early and did well on examinations was decisive in swinging the whole class around to this position. The students were equally influenced to become "test-wise" by the fact that, although they had all been in the upper range in their colleges, the class average on the first examination was frighteningly low.

In becoming test-wise, the students begin to develop systems for discovering the faculty wishes and learning them. These systems are both methods for studying their texts and short-cuts that can be taken in laboratory work. For instance, they begin to select facts for memorization by looking over the files of old examinations maintained in each of the medical fraternity houses. They share tip-offs from the lectures and offhand remarks of the faculty as to what will be on the examinations. In anatomy, they agree not to bother to dissect out subcutaneous nerves, reasoning that it is both difficult and time consuming and the information can be secured from books with less effort. The interaction involved in the development of such systems and short-cuts helps to create a social group of a class which had previously been only an aggregation of smaller and less organized groups.

In this medical school, the students learn in this way to distinguish between the activities of the first year and their original view that everything that happens to them in medical school will be important. Thus, they become cynical about the value of their activities in the first year. They feel that the real thing—learning which will help them to help mankind—has been postponed perhaps until the second year, or perhaps even further, at which time they will be able again to act on idealistic premises. They believe that what they do in their later years in school under supervision will be about the same thing they will do, as physicians, on their own; the first year had disappointed this expectation.

There is one matter, however, about which the students are not disappointed during the first year: the so-called trauma of dealing with the cadaver. But this experience, rather than producing cynicism, reinforces the student's attachment to his idealistic view of medicine by making him feel that he is experiencing at least some of the necessary unpleasantness of the doctor's [life]. Such difficulties, however, do not loom as large for the student as those of solving the problem of just what the faculty wants.

On this and other points, a working consensus develops in the new consolidated group about the interpretation of their experience in medical school and its norms of conduct. This consensus, which we call *student culture,*[7] focuses their attention almost completely on their day-to-day activities in school and obscures or sidetracks their earlier idealistic preoccupations. Cynicism, griping, and minor cheating become endemic, but the cynicism is specific to the educational situation, to the first year, and to only parts of it. Thus the students keep their cynicism separate from their idealistic feelings and by postponement protect their belief that medicine is a wonderful thing, that their school is a fine one, and that they will become good doctors.

LATER YEARS

The sophomore year does not differ greatly from the freshman year. Both the work load and anxiety over examinations probably increase. Though they begin some medical activities, as in their attendance at autopsies and particularly in their introductory course in physical diagnosis, most of what they do continues to repeat the pattern of the college science curriculum. Their attention still centers on the problem of getting through school by doing well in examinations.

During the third and fourth, or clinical years, teaching takes a new form. In place of lectures and laboratories, the students' work now consists of the study of actual patients admitted to the hospital or seen in the clinic. Each patient who enters the hospital is assigned to a student who interviews him about his illnesses, past and present, and performs a physical examination. He writes this up for the patient's chart, and appends the diagnosis and the treatment that he would use were he allowed actually to treat the patient. During conferences with faculty physicians, often held at the patient's bedside, the student is quizzed about items of his report and called upon to defend them or to explain their significance. Most of the teaching in the clinical years is of this order.

Contact with patients brings a new set of circumstances with which the student must deal. He no longer feels the great pressure created by tests, for he is told by the faculty, and this is confirmed by his daily experience, that examinations are now less important. His problems now become those of coping with a steady stream of patients in a way that will please the staff man under whom he is working, and of handling what is sometimes a tremendous load of clinical work so as to allow himself time for studying diseases and treatments that interest him and for play and family life.

The students earlier have expected that once they reach the clinical years they will be able to realize their idealistic ambitions to help people and to learn those things immediately useful in aiding people who are ill. But they find themselves working to understand cases as medical problems rather than working to help the sick and memorizing the relevant available facts so that these can be produced immediately for a questioning staff man. When they make ward rounds with a faculty member they are likely to be quizzed about any of the seemingly countless facts possibly related to the condition of the patient for whom they are "caring."

Observers speak of the cynicism that overtakes the student and the lack of concern for his patients as human beings. This change does take place, but it is not produced solely by "the anxiety brought about by the presence of death and suffering."[8] The student becomes preoccupied with the technical aspects of the cases with which he deals because the faculty requires him to do so. He is questioned about so many technical details that he must spend most of his time learning them.

The frustrations created by his position in the teaching hospital further divert the student from idealistic concerns. He finds himself low man in a hierarchy based on clinical experience, so that he is allowed very little of the medical responsibility he would like to assume. Because of his lack of experience, he cannot write orders, and he receives permission to perform medical and surgical procedures (if at all) at a rate he considers far too slow. He usually must content himself with "mere" vicarious participation in the drama of danger, life, and death that he sees as the core of medical practice. The student culture accents these difficulties so that events (and especially those involving patients) are interpreted and reacted to as they push him toward or hold him back from further participation in this drama. He does not think in terms the layman might use.

As a result of the increasingly technical emphasis of his thinking the student appears cynical to the nonmedical outsider, though from his own point of view he is simply seeing what is "really important." Instead of reacting with the layman's horror and sympathy for the patient to the sight of a cancerous organ that has been surgically removed, the student is more likely to regret that he was not allowed to close the incision at the completion of the operation, and to rue the hours that he must spend searching in the fatty flesh for the lymph nodes that will reveal how far the disease has spread. As in other lines of work, he drops lay attitudes for those more relevant to the way the event affects *someone in his position*.

This is not to say that the students lose their original idealism. When issues of idealism are openly raised in a situation they define as appropriate, they respond as they might have when they were freshmen. But the influence of the student culture is such that questions which might bring forth this idealism are not brought up. Students are often assigned patients for examination and follow-up whose conditions might be expected to provoke idealistic crises. Students discuss such patients, however, with reference to the problems they create for the *student*. Patients with terminal diseases who are a long time dying, and patients with chronic diseases who show little change from week to week, are more likely to be viewed as creating extra work without extra compensation in knowledge or the opportunity to practice new skills than as examples of illness which raise questions about euthanasia. Such cases require the student to spend time every day checking on progress which he feels will probably not take place and to write long "progress" notes in the patient's chart although little progress has occurred.

This apparent cynicism is a collective matter. Group activities are built around this kind of workaday perspective, constraining the students in two ways. First, they do not openly express the lay idealistic notions they may hold, for their culture does not sanction such expression; second, they are less likely to have thoughts of this deviant kind when they are engaged in group activity. The collective nature of this "cynicism" is indicated by the fact that students become more openly idealistic whenever they are removed from the influence of student culture—when they are alone with a sociologist as they near the finish of school and sense the approaching end of student life, for example, or when they are isolated from their classmates and therefore are less influenced by this culture.[9]

They still feel, as advanced students, though much less so than before, that school is irrelevant to actual medical practice. Many of their tasks, like running laboratory tests on patients newly admitted to the hospital or examining surgical specimens in the pathology laboratory, seem to them to have nothing to do with their visions of their future activity as doctors. As in their freshman year, they believe that perhaps they must obtain the knowledge they will need in spite of the school. They still conceive of medicine as a huge body of proven facts but no longer believe that they will ever be able to master it all. They now say that they are going to try to apply the solution of the practicing M.D. to their own dilemma: learn a few things that they are interested in very well and know enough about other things to pass examinations while in school and, later on in practice, to know to which specialist to send difficult patients.

Their original medical idealism reasserts itself as the end of school approaches. Seniors show more interest than students in earlier years in serious ethical dilemmas of the kind they expect to face in practice. They have become aware of ethical problems laymen often see as crucial for the physician—whether it is right to keep patients with fatal diseases alive as long as possible, or what should be done if an influential patient demands an [illegal treatment]—and worry about them. As they near graduation and student culture begins to break down as the soon-to-be doctors are about to go their separate ways, these questions are more and more openly discussed.

While in school, they have added to their earlier idealism a new and peculiarly professional idealism. Even though they know that few doctors live up to the standards they have been taught, they intend always to examine their patients thoroughly and to give treatment based on firm diagnosis rather than merely to relieve symptoms. This expansion and transformation of idealism appear most explicitly in their consideration of alternative careers, concerning both specialization and the kind of arrangements to be made for setting up practice. Many of their hypothetical choices aim at making it possible for them to be the kind of doctors their original idealism pictured. Many seniors consider specialty training so that they will be able to work in a limited field in which it will be more nearly possible to know all there is to know, thus avoiding the necessity of dealing in a more ignorant way with the wider range of problems general practice would present. In the same manner, they think of schemes to establish partnerships or other arrangements making it easier to avoid a work load which would prevent them from giving each patient the thorough examination and care they now see as ideal.

In other words, as school comes to an end, the cynicism specific to the school situation also comes to an end and their original and more general idealism about medicine comes to the fore again, though within a framework of more realistic alternatives. Their idealism is now more informed although no less selfless.

DISCUSSION

We have used the words "idealism" and "cynicism" loosely in our description of the changeable state of mind of the medical student, playing on ambiguities we can now attempt to clear up. Retaining a core of common meaning, the dictionary definition, in our reference to the person's belief in the worth of his activity and the claims made for it, we have seen that this is not a generalized trait of the students we studied but rather an attitude which varies greatly, depending on the particular activity the worth of which is questioned and the situation in which the attitude is expressed.

This variability of the idealistic attitude suggests that in using such an element of personal perspective in sociological analysis one should not treat it as homogeneous but should make a determined search for subtypes which may arise under different conditions and have differing consequences. Such subtypes presumably can be constructed along many dimensions. There might, for instance, be consistent variations in the medical students' idealism through the four years of school that are related to their social backgrounds. We have stressed in this report the subtypes that can be constructed according to variations in the object of the idealistic attitude and variations in the audience the person has in mind when he adopts the attitude. The medical students can be viewed as both idealistic and cynical, depending on whether one has in mind their view of their school activities or the future they envision for themselves as doctors. Further, they might take one or another of these positions depending on whether their implied audience is made up of other students, their instructors, or the lay public.

A final complication arises because cynicism and idealism are not merely attributes of the actor, but are as dependent on the person doing the attributing as they are on the qualities of the individual to whom they are attributed.[10] Though the student may see his own disregard of the unique personal troubles of a particular patient as proper scientific objectivity, the layman may view this objectivity as heartless cynicism.[11]

Having made these analytic distinctions, we can now summarize the transformations of these characteristics as we have seen them occurring among medical students. Some of the students' determined idealism at the outset is reaction against the lay notion, of which they are uncomfortably aware, that doctors are money-hungry cynics; they counter this with an idealism of similar lay origin stressing the doctor's devotion to service. But this idealism soon meets a setback, as students find that it will not be relevant for awhile, since medical school has, it seems, little relation to the practice of medicine, as they see it. As it has not been refuted, but only shown to be temporarily beside the point, the students "agree" to set this idealism aside in favor of a realistic approach to the problem of getting through school. This approach, which we have labeled as the cynicism specific to the school experience, serves as protection for the earlier grandiose feelings about medicine by postponing their exposure to reality to a distant future. As that future approaches near the end of the four years and its possible mistreatment of their ideals moves closer, the students again worry about maintaining their integrity, this time in actual medical practice. They use some of the knowledge they have gained to plan careers which, it is hoped, can best bring their ideals to realization.

We can put this in propositional form by saying that when a man's ideals are challenged by outsiders and then further strained by reality, he may salvage them by postponing their application to a future time when conditions are expected to be more propitious.

NOTES

1. Leonard D. Eron, "Effect of Medical Education on Medical Students," *Journal of Medical Education* 10 (October 1955), pp. 559–566.
2. This study [was] sponsored by Community Studies, Inc., of Kansas City, Missouri, and [was] carried on at the University of Kansas Medical School, to whose dean, staff, and students we are indebted for their wholehearted cooperation. Professor Everett C. Hughes of the University of Chicago is director of the project.
3. The technique of participant observation has not been fully systematized, but

some approaches to this have been made. See, for example, Florence R. Kluckhohn, "The Participant Observer Technique in Small Communities," *American Journal of Sociology*, 45 (November 1940), pp. 331–343; Arthur Vidich, "Participant Observation and the Collection and Interpretation of Data," *ibid.*, 60 (January 1955), pp. 354–360; William Foote Whyte, "Observational Field-Work Methods," in Maria Jahoda, Morton Deutsch, and Stuart W. Cook (editors), *Research Methods in the Social Sciences*, New York: Dryden Press, 1951, 11, pp. 393–514; *Street Corner Society* (Enlarged Edition), Chicago: University of Chicago Press, 1955, pp. 279–358; Rosalie Hankey Wax, "Twelve Years Later: An Analysis of Field Experience," *American Journal of Sociology*, 63 (September 1957), pp. 133–142; Morris S. Schwartz and Charlotte Green Schwartz, "Problems in Participant Observation," *Ibid.*, 60 (January 1955), pp. 343–353; and Howard S. Becker and Blanche Geer, "Participant Observation and Interviewing: A Comparison," *Human Organization* 16 (Fall 1957), pp. 28–32. The last item represents the first of a projected series of papers attempting to make explicit the operations involved in this method. For a short description of some techniques used in this study, see Howard S. Becker, "Interviewing Medical Students," *American Journal of Sociology*, 62 (September 1956), pp. 199–201.

4. A fuller analysis and presentation of evidence [is contained in Howard S. Becker, et. al., *Boys in White*, Chicago: University of Chicago Press, 1961].

5. Renée Fox has shown how complex one aspect of this whole subject is in her analysis of the way medical students at Cornell become aware of and adjust to both their own failure to master all available knowledge and the gaps in current knowledge in many fields. See her "Training for Uncertainty," in Robert K. Merton, George G. Reader, and Patricia L. Kendall, *The Student Physician: Introductory Studies in the Sociology of Medical Education*, Cambridge: Harvard University Press, 1957, pp. 207–241.

6. Compare Fox's description of student reaction to this problem at Cornell.

7. The concept of student culture is analyzed in some detail in Howard S. Becker and Blanche Geer, "Student Culture in Medical School," *Harvard Educational Review*, (forthcoming).

8. Dana L. Farnsworth, "Some Observations on The Attitudes and Motivations of the Harvard Medical Student," *Harvard Medical Alumni Bulletin*, January 1956, p. 34.

9. See the discussion in Howard S. Becker, "Interviewing Medical Students," *op. cit.*

10. See Philip Selznick's related discussion of fanaticism in *TVA and the Grass Roots*, Berkeley: University of California Press, 1953, pp. 205–213.

11. George Orwell gives the layman's side in his essay, "How the Poor Die" in *Shooting an Elephant and Other Essays*, London: Secker and Warburg, 1950, pp. 18–32.

Review Questions

1. Explain how various aspects of the *situation* encountered by medical students in medical school caused them to change the values and attitudes they had learned through early socialization.

2. Prior to medical school, students believed that everything that happened to them there would be important. What evidence is presented to illustrate changes in this early view?

3. Define and discuss the "student culture" of the medical student. How does it come about? What are its consequences?

4. What is the part played by the faculty in socializing the medical student?

5. What factors cause the medical student's "cynicism" to decline and "idealism" to reemerge?

6. Describe cases other than the medical school in which *situational constraints* cause individuals to break from or realign previous values, attitudes, and behavior.

Suggested Readings: Transmission of Culture: Socialization

Becker, Howard S. "Becoming a Marijuana User," *American Journal of Sociology*, vol. 59 (November 1953), 235–242.

Clausen, John A. *Socialization and Society*. Boston: Little, Brown, 1968.

Curtis, Susan. *Genie*. New York: Academic Press, 1977.

Denzin, Norman K. "Play, Games and Interaction: The Contexts of Childhood Socialization." *Sociological Quarterly*, 16 (Autumn 1975), 458–478.

Dornbush, Sanford M. "The Military Academy as an Assimilating Institution," *Social Forces*, vol. 33 (May 1955), 316–321.

Henslin, James M. "On Becoming Male: Reflections of a Sociologist on Childhood and Early Socialization," in James M. Henslin (ed.), *Down to Earth Sociology*, 3rd ed. New York: Free Press, 1981, pp. 53–62.

Nemerowicz, Gloria Morris. *Children's Perceptions of Gender and Work Roles*. New York: Praeger, 1979.

Oleson, Virginia L., and Elvi W. Whittaker. *The Silent Dialogue: A Study in the Social Psychology of Professional Socialization*. San Francisco: Jossey-Bass, 1968.

Spiro, Melford. *Children of the Kibbutz*, rev. ed. Cambridge, Mass.: Harvard University Press, 1975.

Part IV. Interaction in Everyday Life

THE STUDY OF SOCIAL LIFE TAKES US INTO ALL KINDS OF ACTIVITIES AND SETTINGS. Even in situations where one might think that "nothing is happening here," sociologists see important elements and processes of social interaction. For one thing, social interaction is much more complicated than simply learning, through socialization, a set of cultural norms and roles and applying them in all situations with all people. Norms and roles are very often situationally tied, and we must try to determine the nature of the situation we are in, in order to behave more or less appropriately.

People are always, therefore, both *reading* and *giving off* cues from and to each other, communicating symbolically even though they may be unaware that they are doing so. When you walk through a lobby or enter a classroom before the class begins, it may seem that nothing is happening. But the others in that setting will begin to "define" who you are by assessing your clothing, appearance, gestures, props, tone of voice, facial expressions, and so on within the framework of meanings already learned from our culture. You will also pay attention to *their* clothing, appearance, etc. The ways in which they act toward you (even if they decide to ignore you) depend on their perceptions of you, and your actions depend on your perceptions of them. None of us acts or reacts in the same way in all settings or situations; we try to figure out what the nature of the situation is and what behavior it calls for. We can rarely say, therefore, that nothing is happening, because we would be ignoring a great deal of mental work involved in social perception and evaluation, as well as various forms of behavior actually taking place.

Consider how differently you would act if a person with gray hair, carrying a briefcase, and speaking forcefully entered your classroom on the first day of the term than if a younger person in informal attire carrying notebooks and texts entered the same room. In the first instance, you would probably decide that the person was the professor; in the second case, you would think you were in the presence of another student. (You may learn through further interaction that you were wrong, but your initial impression is all you have to guide you for the moment.) How might your own tone of voice, facial expressions, language, and behavior differ?

The process we are describing here is an important one for understanding interaction in everyday life. It was termed the "definition of the situation" by an early influential sociologist, W. I. Thomas. In 1923, Thomas outlined this process, contending that each of the participants in any social interaction must define for him or herself what kind of situation exists and what type of others are present, in order to call forth the culturally appropriate behaviors necessary to mesh with the other "actors" who are present. A situation is defined (as, say, a pleasant, informal encounter; a formal dance; or a no-nonsense workplace) by reading *cues* from the environment, including the other actors. In addition, the individual emits cues as to his or her social statuses, expectations, attitudes, and the like which are read by the others involved. Thus, a process of give-and-take occurs in which a more or less agreed upon definition of the situation is negotiated. This process is critical if interaction is to proceed.

W. I. Thomas is probably best remembered for his idea that one's own perception or definition of the situation—whether it is "accurate" or "inaccurate," shared by others or not—is of prime importance in determining one's own behavior, or line of action, in that situation. Thus, "a situation defined as real, is real in its consequences." Returning to our example of the persons entering your classroom, you would probably act toward the gray-haired person with the briefcase *as if* this person were the professor, even if your definition of the situation were inaccurate.

In this section of the book, we have collected four pieces which bear on one aspect or another of the process of defining situations as it affects ensuing interactions. First is an excerpt from *The Presentation of Self in Everyday Life*, a classic book by Erving Goffman. Goffman analyzes everyday interaction using what he terms the *dramaturgical approach*. This approach focuses on those aspects of the lives of everyday people which are similar to the behavior of stage actors and other dramatic performers. Thus, Goffman views *every* encounter between two or more people as an event which calls for each "actor" to present one or more of his or her social roles to the other(s), much as in a stage performance. Individuals are motivated to present (selected) information about themselves to others, a process called "impression management" by Goffman, in order to have some impact on the common definition of the situation. Sometimes we give honest and *sincere* performances, trying to convey accurate information about ourselves. At other times, we give *cynical* performances which we know to be false. Regardless of whether a performance is cynical or sincere, we may use a number of nonverbal means of communicating information about ourselves, including props (e.g., the physician's white coat), settings (furniture arrangements and the like), gestures (such as a shrug of the shoulders), tone of voice, and so on, in addition to strictly verbal cues. Goffman categorizes and describes these elements of impression management as well as showing the ubiquitous presence of self presentation in everyday interaction.

Goffman's view might be disturbing to some of you. If we are all on stage, manipulating what others see and think about us, then we must wonder when we are our "real selves." Goffman does not answer this question directly but, rather, shows us how social actors may present different aspects of themselves to different groups of people. His point is that we have *many* "real selves." After all, don't you act differently with various groups of people? It is unlikely, for example, that you behave the same way in class as you do in the dorm or at your parents' home. (What would your family think if you raised your hand during dinner to ask a question?) Why does your behavior change as the people around you change? Try to list the numerous ways in which your behavior changes during an average week. The tone of your voice, your language, dress, and posture are only a few aspects of your presentation that vary as you present each of your numerous "selves." Think too of what would happen if you did *not* modify your behavior.

The concepts of the definition of the situation and impression management are also central to the work of Edward Gross and Gregory Stone on "Embarrassment and the Analysis of Role Requirements," the second selection in this section. In order to interact with others in everyday life, they contend, individuals must be able to behave in ways that explain to others which role or roles they expect to perform—that is, to establish an "identity" by "presenting themselves." An identity exists when the individual's claims about who and what he or she is are accepted by the others in the situation. At this point, the individual is "located," and a definition of the situation is possible. The parties to the interaction have a fairly good idea not only of who and what each individual is, but also of what each individual can be expected to do in the "future," that is, as the interaction progresses. To summarize, then, in order to give interactants an idea of what we will be doing in the (very near or not so near) future, we must establish identities. Gross and Stone go on to indicate that "poise," or the maintenance of a unified identity, is also required for interaction to begin and to continue.

The focus of this article is actually on the problems that arise when an individual cannot establish an identity that others agree to or when the individual fails to maintain poise. Various "slips," either within or beyond the control of the individual, may disrupt the definition of the situation and lead to embarrassment for that person and for the other interactants, causing interaction to cease. Indeed, the fact that embarrassment occurs was what led Gross and Stone to infer the necessity for establishing and maintaining identities and poise.

In the third selection, Pepper Schwartz and Janet Lever bring us a slice of the everyday interactions of college students at mixers. The behaviors and thoughts of the students involved in these events illustrate beautifully the process of presentation of self to affect the definition of the situation. We can also find examples here of embarrassment due to loss of identity or poise. Perhaps some of you will recognize yourselves and your friends in this study, too. What you should keep in mind is that, no matter what the situation or how long we have known our co-participants, we are always presenting ourselves and defining situations. We may be more aware of these processes in situations where relative strangers meet with the express purpose of evaluating each other (the mixer, the job interview, and the like), but the processes are nonetheless present in all interactions in our everyday lives.

In the final article, J. Robert Lilly and Richard Ball describe how the owners and customers of the "No-Tell Motel" worked together as a sort of team to convey to outsiders the false impression that what was going on there was typical of any motel. We see several examples of *cynical* role performance, or the conscious attempt to create a false definition of the situation. Should outsiders venture within the confines of the motel, expressions were given and given off which subtly defined the situation as off limits for them. Insiders were provided with "social invisibility" by a number of structures and strategies, thus insuring that their "normal" role performances would not be jeopardized by discrepant information which could prove embarrassing. Not only were clients shielded from the outside world by walls, garages, and private entrances, but the norms for interaction among insiders protected them also from having to deal with each other. In other words, all those connected with the No-Tell Motel were engaged in a coordinated and complex attempt at impression management.

THE PRESENTATION OF SELF IN EVERYDAY LIFE

Erving Goffman

WHEN AN INDIVIDUAL ENTERS THE PRESENCE OF OTHERS, THEY COMMONLY SEEK TO AC-quire information about him or to bring into play information about him already possessed. They will be interested in his general socioeconomic status, his conception of self, his attitude toward them, his competence, his trustworthiness, etc. Although some of this information seems to be sought almost as an end in itself, there are usually quite practical reasons for acquiring it. Information about the individual helps to define the situation, enabling others to know in advance what he will expect of them and what they may expect of him. Informed in these ways, the others will know how best to act in order to call forth a desired response from him.

For those present, many sources of information become accessible and many carriers (or "sign-vehicles") become available for conveying this information. If unacquainted with the individual, observers can glean clues from his conduct and appearance which allow them to apply their previous experience with individuals roughly similar to the one before them or, more important, to apply untested stereotypes to him. They can also assume from past experience that only individuals of a particular kind are likely to be found in a given social setting. They can rely on what the individual says about himself or on documentary evidence he provides as to who and what he is. If they know, or know of, the individual by virtue of experience prior to the interaction, they can rely on assumptions as to the persistence and generality of psychological traits as a means of predicting his present and future behavior.

However, during the period in which the individual is in the immediate presence of the others, few events may occur which directly provide the others with the conclusive information they will need if they are to direct wisely their own activity. Many crucial facts lie beyond the time and place of interaction or lie concealed within it. For example, the "true" or "real" attitudes, beliefs, and emotions of the individual can be ascertained only indirectly, through his avowals or through what appears to be involuntary expressive behavior. Similarly, if the individual offers the others a product or service, they will often find that during the interaction there will be no time and place immediately available for eating the pudding that the proof can

Erving Goffman, *The Presentation of Self in Everyday Life*. Garden City, N.Y.: Anchor Books, 1959, pp. 1–15.

be found in. They will be forced to accept some events as conventional or natural signs of something not directly available to the senses. In Ichheiser's terms,[1] the individual will have to act so that he intentionally or unintentionally *expresses* himself, and the others will in turn have to be *impressed* in some way by him.

The expressiveness of the individual (and therefore his capacity to give impressions) appears to involve two radically different kinds of sign activity: the expression that he *gives*, and the expression that he *gives off*. The first involves verbal symbols or their substitutes which he uses admittedly and solely to convey the information that he and the others are known to attach to these symbols. This is communication in the traditional and narrow sense. The second involves a wide range of action that others can treat as symptomatic of the actor, the expectation being that the action was performed for reasons other than the information conveyed in this way. As we shall have to see, this distinction has an only initial validity. The individual does of course intentionally convey misinformation by means of both of these types of communication, the first involving deceit, the second feigning.

Taking communication in both its narrow and broad sense, one finds that when the individual is in the immediate presence of others, his activity will have a promissory character. The others are likely to find that they must accept the individual on faith, offering him a just return while he is present before them in exchange for something whose true value will not be established until after he has left their presence. (Of course, the others also live by inference in their dealings with the physical world, but it is only in the world of social interaction that the objects about which they make inferences will purposely facilitate and hinder this inferential process.) The security that they justifiably feel in making inferences about the individual will vary, of course, depending on such factors as the amount of information they already possess about him, but no amount of such past evidence can entirely obviate the necessity of acting on the basis of inferences. As William I. Thomas suggested:

> It is also highly important for us to realize that we do not as a matter of fact lead our lives, make our decisions, and reach our goals in everyday life either statistically or scientifically. We live by inference. I am, let us say, your guest. You do not know, you cannot determine scientifically, that I will not steal your money or your spoons. But inferentially I will not, and inferentially you have me as a guest.[2]

Let us now turn from the others to the point of view of the individual who presents himself before them. He may wish them to think highly of him, or to think that he thinks highly of them, or to perceive how in fact he feels toward them, or to obtain no clear-cut impression; he may wish to ensure sufficient harmony so that the interaction can be sustained, or to defraud, get rid of, confuse, mislead, antagonize, or insult them. Regardless of the particular objective which the individual has in mind and of his motive for having this objective, it will be in his interests to control the conduct of the others, especially their responsive treatment of him.³ This control is achieved largely by influencing the definition of the situation which the others come to formulate, and he can influence this definition by expressing himself in such a way as to give them the kind of impression that will lead them to act voluntarily in accordance with his own plan. Thus, when an individual appears in the presence of others, there will usually be some reason for him to mobilize his activity so that it will convey an impression to others which it is in his interests to convey. Since a girl's dormitory mates will glean evidence of her popularity from the calls she receives on the phone, we can suspect that some girls will arrange for calls to be made, and Willard Waller's finding can be anticipated:

> It has been reported by many observers that a girl who is called to the telephone in the dormitories will often allow herself to be called several times, in order to give all the other girls ample opportunity to hear her paged.⁴

Of the two kinds of communication—expressions given and expressions given off—this report will be primarily concerned with the latter, with the more theatrical and contextual kind, the nonverbal, presumably unintentional kind, whether this communication be purposely engineered or not. As an example of what we must try to examine, I would like to cite at length a novelistic incident in which Preedy, a vacationing Englishman, makes his first appearance on the beach of his summer hotel in Spain:

> But in any case he took care to avoid catching anyone's eye. First of all, he had to make it clear to those potential companions of his holiday that they were of no concern to him whatsoever. He stared through them, round them, over them—eyes lost in space. The beach might have been empty. If by chance a ball was thrown his way, he looked surprised; then let a smile of amusement lighten his face (Kindly Preedy), looked around dazed to see that there *were* people on the beach, tossed it back with a smile to himself and not a smile *at* the people, and then resumed carelessly his nonchalant survey of space.
>
> But it was time to institute a little parade, the parade of the Ideal Preedy. By devious handlings he gave any who wanted to look a chance to see the title of his book—a Spanish translation of Homer, classic thus, but not daring, cosmopolitan too—and then gathered together his beachwrap and bag into a neat sand-resistant pile (Methodical and Sensible Preedy), rose slowly to stretch at ease his huge frame (Big-Cat Preedy), and tossed aside his sandals (Carefree Preedy, after all).
>
> The marriage of Preedy and the sea! There were alternate rituals. The first involved the stroll that turns into a run and a dive straight into the water, thereafter smoothing into a strong splashless crawl towards the horizon. But of course not really to the horizon. Quite suddenly he would turn on to his back and thrash great white splashes with his legs, somehow thus showing that he could have swum further had he wanted to, and then would stand up a quarter out of water for all to see who it was.
>
> The alternative course was simpler, it avoided the cold-water shock and it avoided the risk of appearing too high-spirited. The point was to appear to be so used to the sea, the Mediterranean, and this particular beach, that one might as well be in the sea as out of it. It involved a slow stroll down and into the edge of

> the water—not even noticing his toes were wet, land and water all the same to
> *him!*—with his eyes up at the sky gravely surveying portents, invisible to others,
> of the weather (Local Fisherman Preedy).[5]

The novelist means us to see that Preedy is improperly concerned with the extensive impressions he feels his sheer bodily action is giving off to those around him. We can malign Preedy further by assuming that he has acted merely in order to give a particular impression, that this is a false impression, and that the others present receive either no impression at all, or, worse still, the impression that Preedy is affectedly trying to cause them to receive this particular impression. But the important point for us here is that the kind of impression Preedy thinks he is making is in fact the kind of impression that others correctly and incorrectly glean from someone in their midst.

I have said that when an individual appears before others his actions will influence the definition of the situation which they come to have. Sometimes the individual will act in a thoroughly calculating manner, expressing himself in a given way solely in order to give the kind of impression to others that is likely to evoke from them a specific response he is concerned to obtain. Sometimes the individual will be calculating in his activity but he relatively unaware that this is the case. Sometimes he will intentionally and consciously express himself in a particular way, but chiefly because the tradition of his group or social status require this kind of expression and not because of any particular response (other than vague acceptance or approval) that is likely to be evoked from those impressed by the expression. Sometimes the traditions of an individual's role will lead him to give a well-designed impression of a particular kind and yet he may be neither consciously nor unconsciously disposed to create such an impression. The others, in their turn, may be suitably impressed by the individual's efforts to convey something, or may misunderstand the situation and come to conclusions that are warranted neither by the individual's intent nor by the facts. In any case, insofar as the others act *as if* the individual had conveyed a particular impression, we may take a functional or pragmatic view and say that the individual has "effectively" projected a given definition of the situation and "effectively" fostered the understanding that a given state of affairs obtains.

There is one aspect of the others' response that bears special comment here. Knowing that the individual is likely to present himself in a light that is favorable to him, the others may divide what they witness into two parts: a part that is relatively easy for the individual to manipulate at will, being chiefly his verbal assertions, and a part in regard to which he seems to have little concern or control, being chiefly derived from the expressions he gives off. The others may then use what are considered to be the ungovernable aspects of his expressive behavior as a check upon the validity of what is conveyed by the governable aspects. In this a fundamental asymmetry is demonstrated in the communication process, the individual presumably being aware of only one stream of his communication, the witnesses of this stream and one other. For example, in Shetland Isle one crofter's [or farmer's] wife, in serving native dishes to a visitor from the mainland of Britain, would listen with a polite smile to his polite claims of liking what he was eating; at the same time she would take note of the rapidity with which the visitor lifted his fork or spoon to his mouth, the eagerness with which he passed food into his mouth, and the gusto expressed in chewing the food, using these signs as a check on the stated feelings of the eater. The same woman, in order to discover what one acquaintance (A) "actually" thought of another acquaintance (B), would wait until B was in the presence of A but engaged in conversation with still another person (C). She would then covertly examine the facial expressions of A as he regarded B in conversation with C. Not being in conversation with B, and not being directly observed by him, A would sometimes relax usual constraints and tactful deceptions, and freely express what he was "actually" feeling about B. This Shetlander, in short, would observe the unobserved observer.

Now given the fact that others are likely to check up on the more controllable aspects of behavior by means of the less controllable, one can expect that sometimes the individual will try to exploit this very possibility, guiding the impression he makes through behavior felt to be reliably informing.[6] For example, in gaining admission to a tight social circle, the participant observer may not only wear an accepting look while listening to an informant, but may also be careful to wear the same look when observing the informant talking to others; observers of the observer will then not as easily discover where he actually stands. A specific illustration may be cited from Shetland Isle. When a neighbor dropped in to have a cup of tea, he would ordinarily wear at least a hint of an expectant warm smile as he passed through the door into the cottage. Since lack of physical obstructions outside the cottage and lack of light within it usually made it possible to observe the visitor unobserved as he approached the house, islanders sometimes took pleasure in watching the visitor drop whatever expression he was manifesting and replace it with a sociable one just before reaching the door. However, some visitors, in appreciating that this examination was occurring, would blindly adopt a social face a long distance from the house, thus ensuring the projection of a constant image.

This kind of control upon the part of the individual reinstates the symmetry of the communication process, and sets the stage for a kind of information game—a potentially infinite cycle of concealment, discovery, false revelation, and rediscovery. It should be added that since the others are likely to be relatively unsuspicious of the presumably unguided aspect of the individual's conduct, he can gain much by controlling it. The others of course may sense that the individual is manipulating the presumably spontaneous aspects of his behavior, and seek in this very act of manipulation some shading of conduct that the individual has not managed to control. This again provides a check upon the individual's behavior, this time his presumably uncalculated behavior, thus re-establishing the asymmetry of the communication process. Here I would like only to add the suggestion that the arts of piercing an individual's effort at calculated unintentionality seem better developed than our capacity to manipulate our own behavior, so that regardless of how many steps have occurred in the information game, the witness is likely to have the advantage over the actor, and the initial asymmetry of the communication process is likely to be retained.

When we allow that the individual projects a definition of the situation when he appears before others, we must also see that the others, however passive their role may seem to be, will themselves effectively project a definition of the situation by virtue of their response to the individual and by virtue of any lines of action they initiate to him. Ordinarily the definitions of the situation projected by the several different participants are sufficiently attuned to one another so that open contradiction will not occur. I do not mean that there will be the kind of consensus that arises when each individual present candidly expresses what he really feels and honestly agrees with the expressed feeling of the others present. This kind of harmony is an optimistic ideal and in any case not necessary for the smooth working of society. Rather, each participant is expected to suppress his immediate heartfelt feelings, conveying a view of the situation which he feels the others will be able to find at least temporarily acceptable. The maintenance of this surface of agreement, this veneer of consensus, is facilitated by each participant concealing [his] wants behind statements while asserting values to which everyone present feels obliged to give lip service. Further, there is usually a kind of division of definitional labor. Each participant is allowed to establish the tentative official ruling regarding matters which are vital to him but not immediately important to others, e.g., the rationalizations and justifications by which he accounts for his past activity. In exchange for this courtesy he remains silent or non-committal on matters important to others but not immediately important to him. We have then a kind of interactional *modus vivendi*. Together, the participants contribute to a single over-all definition of the situation which involves not so much a real argument as to what exists but rather a real agreement as to whose claims concerning what issues will be temporarily honored. Real agreement will also exist concerning the desirability of avoiding an open conflict of definitions of the situation.[7] I will refer to this level of agreement as a "working consensus." It is to be understood that the working consensus established in one interaction setting will be quite different in content from the working consensus established in a different type of setting. Thus, between two friends at lunch, a reciprocal show of affection, respect, and concern for the other is maintained. In service occupations, on the other hand, the specialist often maintains an image of disinterested involvement in the problem of the client, while the client responds with a show of respect for the competence and integrity of the specialist. Regardless of such differences in content, however, the general form of these working arrangements is the same.

In noting the tendency for a participant to accept the definitional claims made by the others present, we can appreciate the crucial importance of the information that the individual *initially* possesses or acquires concerning his fellow participants, for it is on the basis of this initial information that the individual starts to define the situation and starts to build up lines of responsive action. The individual's initial projection commits him to what he is proposing to be and requires him to drop all pretenses of being other things. As the interaction among the participants progresses, additions and modifications in this initial informational state will of course occur, but it is essential that these later developments be related without contradiction to, and even built up from, the initial positions taken by the several participants. It would seem that an individual can more easily make a choice as to what line of treatment to demand from and extend to the others present at the beginning of an encounter than he can alter the line of treatment that is being pursued once the interaction is underway.

In everyday life, of course, there is a clear understanding that first impressions are important. Thus, the work adjustment of those in service occupations will often hinge upon a capacity to seize and hold the initiative in the service relations, a capacity that will require subtle aggressiveness on the part of the server when he is of lower socioeconomic status than his client. W. F. Whyte suggests the waitress as an example:

> The first point that stands out is that the waitress who bears up under pressure does not simply respond to her customers. She acts with some skill to control her behavior. The first question to ask when we look at the customer relationship is, "Does the waitress get the jump on the customer, or does the customer get the jump on the waitress?" The skilled waitress realizes the crucial nature of this question. . . .
>
> The skilled waitress tackles the customer with confidence and without hesitation. For example, she may find that a new customer has seated himself before she could clear off the dirty dishes and change the cloth. He is now leaning on the table studying the menu. She greets him, says, "May I change the cover, please?" and, without waiting for an answer, takes his menu away from him so that he moves back from the table, and she goes about her work. The relationship is handled politely but firmly, and there is never any question as to who is in charge.[8]

When the interaction that is initiated by "first impressions" is itself merely the initial interaction in an extended series of interactions involving the same participants, we speak of "getting off on the right foot" and feel that it is crucial that we do so. Thus, one learns that some teachers take the following view:

> You can't ever let them get the upper hand on you or you're through. So I start out tough. The first day I get a new class in, I let them know who's boss. . . . You've got to start off tough, then you can ease up as you go along. If you start out easy-going, when you try to be tough, they'll just look at you and laugh.[9]

Similarly, attendants in mental institutions may feel that if the new patient is sharply put in his place the first day on the ward and made to see who is boss, much future difficulty will be prevented.[10]

Given the fact that the individual effectively projects a definition of the situation when he enters the presence of others, we can assume that events may occur within the interaction which contradict, discredit, or otherwise throw doubt upon this projection. When these disruptive events occur, the interaction itself may come to a confused and embarrassed halt. Some of the assumptions upon which the responses of the participants had been predicated become untenable, and the participants find themselves lodged in an interaction for which the situation has been wrongly defined and is now no longer defined. At such moments the individual whose presentation has been discredited may feel ashamed while the others present may feel hostile, and all the participants may come to feel ill at ease, nonplussed, out of countenance, embarrassed, experiencing the kind of anomy that is generated when the minute social system of face-to-face interaction breaks down.

In stressing the fact that the initial definition of the situation projected by an individual tends to provide a plan for the cooperative activity that follows—in stressing this action point of view—we must not overlook the crucial fact that any projected definition of the situation also has a distinctive moral character. It is this moral character of projections that will chiefly concern us in this report. Society is organized on the principle that any individual who possesses certain social characteristics has a moral right to expect that others will value and treat him in an appropriate way. Connected with this principle is a second, namely that an individual who implicitly or explicitly signifies that he has certain social characteristics ought in fact to be what he claims he is. In consequence, when an individual projects a definition of the situation and thereby makes an implicit or explicit claim to be a person of a particular kind, he automatically exerts a moral demand upon the others, obliging them to value and treat him in the manner that persons of his kind have a right to expect. He also implicitly forgoes all claims to be things he does not appear to be[11] and hence forgoes the treatment that would be appropriate for such individuals. The others find, then, that the individual has informed them as to what is and as to what they *ought* to see as the "is."

One cannot judge the importance of definitional disruptions by the frequency with which they occur, for apparently they would occur more frequently were not constant precautions taken. We find that preventive practices are constantly employed to avoid these embarrassments and that corrective practices are constantly employed to compensate for discrediting occurrences that have not been successfully avoided. When the individual employs these strategies and tactics to protect his own projections, we may refer to them as "defensive practices"; when a participant employs them to save the definition of the situation projected by another, we speak of "protective practices" or "tact." Together, defensive and protective practices comprise the techniques employed to safeguard the impression fostered by an individual during his presence before others. It should be added that while we may be ready to see that no fostered impression would survive if defensive practices were not employed, we are less ready perhaps to see that few impressions could survive if those who received the impression did not exert tact in their reception of it.

In addition to the fact that precautions are taken to prevent disruption of projected definitions, we may also note that an intense interest in these disruptions comes to play a significant role in the social life of the group. Practical jokes and social games are played in which embarrassments which are to be taken unseriously are purposely engineered.[12] Fantasies are created in which devastating exposures occur. Anecdotes from the past—real, embroidered, or fictitious—are told and retold, detailing disruptions which occurred, almost occurred, or occurred and were admirably resolved. There seems to be no grouping which does not have a ready supply of these games, reveries, and cautionary tales, to be used as a source of humor, a catharsis for anxieties, and a sanction for inducing individuals to be modest in their claims and reasonable in their projected expectations. The individual may tell himself through dreams of getting into impossible positions. Families tell of the time a guest got his dates mixed and arrived when neither the house nor anyone in it was ready for him. Journalists tell of times when an all-too-meaningful misprint occurred, and the paper's assumption of objectivity or decorum was humorously discredited. Public servants tell of times a client ridiculously misunderstood form instructions, giving answers which implied an unanticipated and bizarre definition of the situation.[13] Seamen, whose home away from home is rigorously he-man, tell stories of coming back home and inadvertently asking mother to "pass the fucking butter."[14] Diplomats tell of the time a near-sighted queen asked a republican ambassador about the health of his king.[15]

To summarize, then, I assume that when an individual appears before others he will have many motives for trying to control the impression they receive of the situation.

NOTES

1. Gustav Ichheiser, "Misunderstandings in Human Relations," Supplement to *The American Journal of Sociology*, 55 (September 1949): 6–7.

2. Quoted in E. H. Volkart, editor, *Social Behavior and Personality*, Contributions of W. I. Thomas to Theory and Social Research (New York: Social Science Research Council, 1951), p. 5.

3. Here I owe much to an unpublished paper by Tom Burns of the University of Edinburgh. He presents the argument that in all interaction a basic underlying theme is the desire of each participant to guide and control the responses made by the others present. A similar argument has been advanced by Jay Haley in a recent unpublished paper, but in regard to a special kind of control, that having to do with the relationship of those involved in the interaction.

4. Willard Waller, "The Rating and Dating Complex," *American Sociological Review*, 2: 730.

5. William Sansom, *A Contest of Ladies* (London: Hogarth, 1956), pp. 230–32.

6. The widely read and rather sound writings of Stephen Potter are concerned in part with signs that can be engineered to give a shrewd observer the apparently incidental cues he needs to discover concealed virtues the gamesman does not in fact possess.

7. An interaction can be purposely set up as a time and place for voicing differences in opinion, but in such cases participants must be careful to agree not to disagree on the proper tone of voice, vocabulary, and degree of seriousness in which all arguments are to be phrased, and upon the mutual respect which disagreeing participants must carefully continue to express toward one another. This debaters' or academic definition of the situation may also be invoked suddenly and judiciously as a way of translating a serious conflict of views into one that can be handled within a framework acceptable to all present.

8. W. F. Whyte, "When Workers and Customers Meet," Chap. VII, *Industry and Society*, ed. W. F. Whyte (New York: McGraw-Hill, 1946), pp. 132–33.

9. Teacher interview quoted by Howard S. Becker, "Social Class Variations in the Teacher-Pupil Relationship" *Journal of Educational Sociology*, 25: 459.

10. Harold Taxel, "Authority Structure in a Mental Hospital Ward" (unpublished Master's thesis, Department of Sociology, University of Chicago, 1953).

11. This role of the witness in limiting what it is the individual can be has been stressed by Existentialists, who see it as a basic threat to individual freedom. See Jean-Paul Sartre, *Being and Nothingness*, trans. by Hazel E. Barnes (New York: Philosophical Library, 1956), p. 365 ff.

12. Goffman, *op. cit.*, pp. 319–27.

13. Peter Blau, *Dynamics of Bureaucracy; A Study of Interpersonal Relationships in Two Government Agencies*, 2nd ed. (Chicago: University of Chicago Press, 1963).

14. Walter M. Beattie, Jr., "The Merchant Seaman" (unpublished M.A. Report, Department of Sociology, University of Chicago, 1950), p. 35.

15. Sir Frederick Ponsonby, *Recollections of Three Reigns* (New York: Dutton, 1952), p. 46.

Review Questions

1. Distinguish between the two types of sign activity discussed by Goffman: "expressions given" and "expressions given off."

2. Give examples of performances which are sincere and honest and performances which are cynical and dishonest. Do our norms require us to give cynical performances in some situations?

3. Using Goffman's dramaturgical approach, analyze the behavior of a person being interviewed for a job.

4. When disruptive events occur in interaction which cast doubt on one participant's definitions, how do other participants react?

EMBARRASSMENT AND THE ANALYSIS OF ROLE REQUIREMENTS

Edward Gross and Gregory P. Stone

. . . EMBARRASSMENT OCCURS WHENEVER SOME *CENTRAL* ASSUMPTION IN A TRANSaction has been *unexpectedly* and unqualifiedly discredited for at least one participant. The result is that he is incapacitated for continued role performance.[1] Moreover, embarrassment is infectious. It may spread out, incapacitating others not previously incapacitated. It is destructive dis-ease. In the wreckage left by embarrassment lie the broken foundations of social transactions. By examining such ruins, the investigator can reconstruct the architecture they represent.

To explore this idea, recollections of embarrassment were expressly solicited from two groups of subjects: (1) approximately 800 students enrolled in introductory sociology courses; and (2) about 80 students enrolled in an evening extension class. Not solicited, but gratefully received, were many examples volunteered by colleagues and friends who had heard of our interest in the subject. Finally we drew upon many recollections of embarrassment we had experienced ourselves. Through these means at least one thousand specimens of embarrassment were secured.

We found that embarrassments frequently occurred in situations requiring continuous and coordinated role performance—speeches, ceremonies, processions, or working concerts. In such situations embarrassment is particularly noticeable because it is so devastating. Forgetting one's lines, forgetting the wedding ring, stumbling in a cafeteria line, or handing a colleague the wrong tool, when these things occur without qualification, bring the performance to an obviously premature and unexpected halt. At the same time, manifestations of the embarrassment—blushing, fumbling, stuttering, sweating[2]—coerce awareness of the social damage and the need for immediate repair. In some instances, the damage may be potentially so great that embarrassment cannot be allowed to spread among the role performers. The incapacity may be qualified, totally ignored, or pretended out of existence.[3] For example, a minister, noting the best man's frantic search for an absent wedding ring, whispers to him to ignore it, and all conspire to continue the drama with an imaginary ring. Such rescues are not always possible. Hence we suggest that every enduring social relation will provide means of preventing embarrassment, so that the entire transaction will not

Edward Gross and Gregory P. Stone, "Embarrassment and the Analysis of Role Requirements," *The American Journal of Sociology*, LXX (July 1964), pp. 1-15.

collapse when embarrassment occurs. A second general observation would take into account that some stages in the life cycle, for example, adolescence in our society, generate more frequent embarrassments than others. These are points to which we shall return.

To get at the content of embarrassment, we classified the instances in categories that remained as close to the specimens as possible. A total of seventy-four such categories were developed, some of which were forced choices between friends, public mistakes, exposure of false front, being caught in a cover story, misnaming, forgetting names, slips of the tongue, body exposure, invasions of others' back regions, uncontrollable laughter, drunkenness in the presence of sobriety (or vice versa), loss of visceral control, and the sudden recognition of wounds or other stigmata. Further inspection of these categories disclosed that most could be included in three general areas: (1) inappropriate identity; (2) loss of poise; (3) disturbance of the assumptions persons make about one another in social transactions.

Since embarrassment always incapacitates persons for role performance (to embarrass is, literally, to bar or stop), a close analysis of the conditions under which it occurs is especially fruitful in the revelation of the requirements *necessary* for role-playing, role-taking, role-making, and role performance in general. These role requirements are thus seen to include the establishment of identity, poise, and valid assumptions about one another among all the parties of a social transaction. We turn now to the analysis of those role requirements.

IDENTITY AND POISE

In every social transaction, selves must be established, defined, and accepted by the parties. Every person in the company of others is, in a sense, obligated to bring his best self forward to meet the selves of others also presumably best fitted to the occasion. When one is "not himself" in the presence of others who expect him to be just that, as in cases where his mood carries him away either by spontaneous seizure (uncontrollable laughter or tears) or by induced seizure (drunkenness), embarrassment ensues. Similarly, when one is "shown up" to other parties to the transaction by the exposure of unacceptable moral qualifications or inappropriate motives, embarrassment sets in all around. However, the concept, self, is a rather gross concept, and we wish to single out two phases that frequently provided focal points for embarrassment—identity and poise.[4]

Identity. Identity is the substantive dimension of the self.[5]

> Almost all writers using the term imply that identity establishes what and where the person is in social terms. It is not a substitute word for "self." Instead, when one has identity, he is *situated*—that is, cast in the shape of a social object by the acknowledgement of his participation or membership in social relations. One's identity is established when others *place* him as a social object by assigning the

same words of identity that he appropriates for himself or *announces*. It is in the coincidence of placements and announcements that identity becomes a meaning of the self.

Moreover, . . . identity stands at the base of role. When inappropriate identities are established or appropriate identities are lost, role performance is impossible.

If identity *locates* the person in social terms, it follows that locations or spaces emerge as symbols of identity, since social relations are spatially distributed. Moreover, as Goffman has remarked,[6] there must be a certain coherence between one's personal appearance and the setting in which he appears. Otherwise embarrassment may ensue with the resulting incapacitation for role performance. Sexual identity is pervasively established by personal appearance, and a frequent source of embarrassment among our subjects was the presence of one sex in a setting reserved for the other. Both men and women reported inadvertent invasions of spaces set aside for the other sex with consequent embarrassment and humiliation. The implication of such inadvertent invasions is, of course, that one literally does not know where one is, that one literally has no identity in the situation, or that the identity one is putting forward is so absurd as to render the proposed role performance totally irrelevant. Everyone is embarrassed, and such manifestations as, for example, cries and screams, heighten the dis-ease. In such situations, laughter cannot be enjoined to reduce the seriousness of the unexpected collapse of the encounter, and only flight can insure that one will not be buried in the wreckage.

To establish *what* he is in social terms, each person assembles a set of apparent[7] symbols which he carries about as he moves from transaction to transaction. Such symbols include the shaping of the hair, painting of the face, clothing, cards of identity, other contents of wallets and purses, and sundry additional marks and ornaments. The items in the set must cohere, and the set must be complete. Taken together, these apparent symbols have been called *identity documents*,[8] in that they enable others to validate announced identities. Embarrassment often resulted when our subjects made personal appearances with either invalid or incomplete identity documents. It was embarrassing for many, for example, to announce their identities as customers at restaurants or stores, perform the customer role and then, when the crucial validation of this identity was requested—the payoff—to discover that the wallet had been left at home.

Because the social participation of men in American society is relatively more frequently caught up in the central structures, for example, the structure of work, than is the social participation of women who are relatively more immersed in interpersonal relations, the identities put forward by men are often *titles;* by women, often *names.* Except for very unusual titles,[9] such identities are shared, and their presentation has the consequence of bringing people together. Names, on the other hand, mark people off from one another. So it is that a frequent source of embarrassment for women in our society occurs when they appear together in precisely the same dress. Their identity documents are invalidated. The embarrassment may be minimized, however, if the space in which they make their personal appearance is large enough. In one instance, both women met the situation by spending an entire evening on different sides of the ballroom in which their embarrassing confrontation occurred, attempting to secure validation from social circles with minimal intersection, or, at least, where intersection was temporally attenuated. Men, on the other hand, will be embarrassed if their clothing does not resemble the dress of the other men present in public and official encounters. Except for "the old school tie" their neckties seem to serve as numbers on a uniform, marking each man off from every other. Out of uniform, their structural membership cannot be visibly established, and role performance is rendered extremely difficult, if not impossible.[10]

Not only are identities undocumented, they are also misplaced, as in misnaming or forgetting, or other incomplete placements. One relatively frequent source of embarrassment we categorized as "damaging someone's personal representation." This included cases of ethnically colored sneers in the presence of one who, in fact, belonged to the deprecated ethnic group but did not put that identity forward, or behind-the-back slurs about a woman who turned out to be the listener's wife. The victim of such misplacement, however inadvertent, will find it difficult to continue the transaction or to present the relevant identity to the perpetrators of the embarrassment in the future. The awkwardness is reflexive. Those who are responsible for the misplacement will experience the same difficulties and dis-ease.

Other sources of embarrassment anchored in identity suggest a basic characteristic of all human transactions, which, as Strauss puts it, are "carried on in thickly peopled and complexly imaged contexts."[11] One always brings to transactions more identities than are necessary for his role performance. As a consequence, two or more roles are usually performed at once by each participant.[12]

If we designate the relevant roles in transactions as *dominant roles*[13] then we may note that *adjunct roles*—a type of side involvement, as Goffman would have it,[14] or better, a type of side *activity*—are usually performed in parallel with dominant role performance. Specifically, a lecturer may smoke cigarettes or a pipe while carrying out the dominant performance, or one may carry on a heated conversation with a passenger while operating a motor vehicle. Moreover, symbols of *reserve identities* are often carried into social transactions. Ordinarily, they are concealed, as when a court judge wears his golfing clothes beneath his robes. Finally, symbols of abandoned or *relict identities* may persist in settings where they have no relevance for dominant role performances.[15] For example, photographs of the performer as an infant may be thrust into a transaction by a doting mother or wife, or one's newly constituted household may still contain the symbols of a previous marriage.

In these respects, the probability of avoiding embarrassment is a function of at least two factors: (1) the extent to which adjunct roles, reserve identities and relict identities are not incongruent with the dominant role performance;[16] and (2) the allocation of prime attention to the dominant role performance so that less attention is directed toward adjunct role performance, reserve identities, and relict identities. Thus the professor risks embarrassment should the performance of his sex role appear to be the main activity in transactions with female students where the professorial role is dominant—for example, if the student pulls her skirt over her knees with clearly more force than necessary. The judge may not enter the courtroom in a golf cap, nor may the husband dwell on the symbols of a past marriage in the presence of a new wife while entertaining guests in his home. Similarly, should adjunct role performance prove inept, as when the smoking lecturer ignites the contents of a wastebasket or the argumentative driver fails to observe the car in front in time to avert a collision, attention is diverted from the dominant role performance. Even without the golf cap, should the judge's robe be caught so that his golfing attire is suddenly revealed in the courtroom, the transactions of the court will be disturbed. Fetishistic devotion to the symbols of relict identities by bereaved persons is embarrassing even to well-meaning visitors.

However, the matter of avoiding incongruence and allocating attention appropriately among the several identities a performer brings to a transaction verges very closely on matters of poise, as we shall see. Matters of poise converge on the necessity of controlling representations of the self, and identity-symbols are important self-representations.

Personal poise. Presentation of the self in social transactions extends considerably beyond making the appropriate personal appearance. It includes the presentation of an entire situation. Components of situations, however, are often representations of self, and in this sense self and situation are two sides of the same coin. Personal poise refers to the performer's control over self and situation, and whatever disturbs that control, depriving the transaction, as we have said before, of any relevant future, is incapacitating and consequently embarrassing. . . .

First, *spaces* must be so arranged and maintained that they are role-enabling. This is sometimes difficult to control, since people appear in spaces that belong to others, over which they exercise no authority and for which they are not responsible. Students, invited to faculty parties where faculty members behave like faculty members, will "tighten up" to the extent that the students' role performance is seriously impeded. To avoid embarrassment, people will go to great lengths to insure their appearance in appropriate places, and to some to be deprived of access to a particular setting is to limit performance drastically. . . .

We have already touched upon problems presented by invasions of spaces, and little more need be said. Persons lose poise when they discover they are in places forbidden to them, for the proscription itself means they have no identity there and hence cannot act. They can do little except with-draw quickly. It is interesting that children are continually invading the ter-ritories of others—who can control the course of a sharply hit baseball?—and part of the process of socialization consists of indications of the importance of boundaries. . . .

Such considerations raise questions concerning both how boundaries are defined and how boundary violations may be prevented. Walls provide physical limits, but do not necessarily prevent communications from pass-ing through.[17] Hence walls work best when there is also tacit agreement to ignore audible communication on the other side of the wall. Embarrassment frequently occurs when persons on one side of the wall learn that intimate matters have been communicated to persons on the other side. A common protective device is for the captive listeners to become very quiet so that their receipt of the communication will not be discovered by the unsuspect-ing intimates. When no physical boundaries are present, a group gathered in one section of a room may have developed a common mood which is bounded by a certain space that defines the limits of their engagement to one another. The entry of someone new may be followed by an embar-rassed hush. It is not necessary that the group should have been talking about that person. Rather, since moods take time to build up, it will take time for the newcomer to "get with it" and it may not be worth the group's trouble to "fill him in." However unintentionally, he has destroyed a mood that took some effort to build up and he will suffer for it, if only by being stared at or by an obvious change of subject. In some cases, when the mood is partially sustained by alcohol, one can prepare the newcomer immedi-ately for the mood by loud shouts that the group is "three drinks ahead" of him and by thrusting a drink into his hand without delay. So, too, a func-tion of foyers, halls, anterooms, and other buffer zones or decompression chambers around settings is to prepare such newcomers and hence reduce the likelihood of their embarrassing both themselves and those inside. . . .

Next, every social transaction requires the manipulation of *equipment*. If props are ordinarily stationary during encounters, equipment is typically moved about, handled, or touched.[18] Equipment can range from *words* to *physical objects*, and a loss of control over such equipment is a frequent source of embarrassment. Here are included slips of the tongue, sudden dumbness when speech is called for, stalling cars in traffic, dropping bowl-ing balls, spilling food, and tool failures. Equipment appearances that cast doubt on the adequacy of control are illustrated by the clanking motor, the match burning down to the fingers, tarnished silverware, or rusty work tools. Equipment sometimes extends beyond what is actually handled in the transaction to include the stage props. Indeed, items of equipment in disuse, reserve equipment, often become props—the Cadillac in the driveway or the silver service on the shelf—and there is a point at which the objects used or scheduled for use in a situation are both equipment and props. At one instant, the items of a table setting lie immobile as props; at the next, they are taken up and transformed into equipment. The close linkage of equipment and props may be responsible for the fact that *embarrassment* at times not only *infects* the participants in the transaction but the *objects* as well. For example, at a formal dinner, a speaker was discovered with his fly zipper undone. On being informed of this embarrassing oversight after he was re-seated, he proceeded to make the requisite adjustment, unknowingly catch-ing the table cloth in his trousers. When obliged to rise again at the close of the proceedings, he took the stage props with him and of course scattered the dinner tools about the setting in such a way that others were forced to doubt his control. His poise was lost in the situation. . . .

[C]*lothing* must also be maintained, controlled, and coherently arranged. Its very appearance must communicate this. Torn clothing, frayed cuffs, stained neckties, and unpolished shoes are felt as embarrassing in situations where they are expected to be untorn, neat, clean, and polished. Clothing is of special importance since, as William James observed,[19] it is as much a part of the self as the body—a part of what he called the "material me." Moreover, since it is so close to the body, it conveys the impression of body maintenance, paradoxically, by concealing body-maintenance activities.[20] Hence, the double wrap—outer clothes and underclothes. Underclothes bear the marks of body maintenance and tonic state, and their unexpected exposure is a frequent source of embarrassment. The broken brassière strap sometimes produces a shift in appearance that few women (or men, for that matter) will fail to perceive as embarrassing.

[T]he *body* must always be in a state of readiness to act, and its appear-ance must make this clear. Hence any evidence of unreadiness or clumsiness is embarrassing. Examples include loss of whole body control (stumbling, trembling, or fainting), loss of visceral control (flatulence, involuntary uri-nation, or drooling), and the communication of other "signs of the animal." The actress who is photographed from her "bad side" loses poise, for it shakes the foundation on which her fame rests. So does the person who is embarrassed about pimples, warts, or missing limbs, as well as those em-barrassed in his presence.

Ordinarily, persons will avoid recognizing such stigmata, turn their eyes away, and pretend them out of existence, but on occasion stigmata will ob-trude upon the situation causing embarrassment all around. A case in point was a minor flirtation reported by one of our students. Seated in a library a short distance from a beautiful girl, the student began the requisite gestural invitation to a more intimate conversation. The girl turned, smiling, to ac-knowledge the bid, revealing an amputated left arm. Our student's gestural line was brought to a crashing halt. Embarrassed, he abandoned the role he was building even before the foundation was laid, pretending that his invit-ing gestures were directed toward some imaginary audience suggested by his reading. Such stigmata publicize body-maintenance activities, and, when they are established in social transactions, interfere with role performances. The pimples on the face of the job applicant cast doubt on his maturity, and, consequently, on his qualifications for any job requiring such maturity. . . .

MAINTENANCE OF CONFIDENCE

When identities have been validated and persons poised, interaction may begin. Its continuation, however, requires that a scaffolding be erected and that attention be given to preventing this scaffolding from collapsing. The scaffold develops as the relationship becomes stabilized. In time persons come to expect that the way they place the other is the way the other announces himself, and that poise will continue to be maintained. Persons now begin to count on these expectations and to have confidence in them. But at any time they may be violated. It was such violations of confidence that made up the greatest single source of embarrassment in our examples. Perhaps this is only an acknowledgment that the parties to every transaction must always maintain themselves *in role* to permit the requisite role-taking, or that identity-switching ought not be accomplished so abruptly that others are left floundering in the encounter as they grope for the new futures that the new identity implies.

This is all the more important in situations where roles are tightly linked together as in situations involving a division of labor. In one instance, a group of social scientists was presenting a progress report of research to a representative of the client subsidizing the research. The principal investigator's presentation was filled out by comments from the other researchers, his professional peers. Negatively critical comments were held to a bare minimum. Suddenly the principal investigator overstepped the bounds. He made a claim that they were well on the road to confirming a hypothesis which, if confirmed, would represent a major contribution. Actually, his colleagues (our informant was one of them) knew that they were very far indeed from confirming the hypothesis. They first sought to catch the leader's eye to look for a hidden message. Receiving none, they lowered their eyes to the table, bit their lips, and fell silent. In the presence of the client's representative, they felt they could not "call" their leader for that would be embarrassing, but they did seek him out immediately afterward for an explanation. The leader agreed that they were right, but said his claim was politic, that new data might well turn up, and that it was clearly too late to remedy the situation.

Careful examination of this case reveals a more basic reason for the researchers' hesitance to embarrass the leader before the client's representative. If their leader were revealed to be the kind of person who goes beyond the data (or to be a plain liar), serious questions could have been raised about the kind of men who willingly work with such a person. Thus they found themselves coerced into unwilling collusion. It was not simply that their jobs depended on continued satisfaction of the client. Rather they were unwilling to say to themselves and to the client's representative that they were the kind of researchers who would be party to a fraud. To embarrass the leader, then, would have meant embarrassing themselves by casting serious question upon their identities as researchers. Indeed, it was their desire to cling to their identities that led, not long afterward (and after several other similar experiences), to the breakup of the research team.

Just as, in time, an identity may be discredited, so too may poise be upset. Should this occur, each must be able to assume that the other will render assistance if he gets into such control trouble, and each must be secure in the knowledge that the assumption is tenable. Persons will be alert for incipient signs of such trouble—irrelevant attitudes—and attempt to avert the consequences. Goffman has provided many examples in his discussion of dramaturgical loyalty, discipline, and circumspection in the presentation of the self, pointing out protective practices that are employed, such as clearing one's throat before interrupting a conversation, knocking on doors before entering an occupied room, or begging the other's pardon before an intrusion.[21]

The danger that one's confidence in the other's continued identity or his ability to maintain his poise may be destroyed leads to the generation of a set of *performance norms*. These are social protections against embarrassment.[22] If persons adhere to them, the probability of embarrassment is reduced. We discovered two major performance norms.

First, *standards of role performance almost always allow for flexibility and tolerance*. One is rarely, if ever, totally in role (an exception might be highly ritualized performances where to acknowledge breaches of expectation is devastatingly embarrassing)[23]. To illustrate, we expect one another to give attention to what is going on in our transactions, but the attention we anticipate is always *optimal*, never total. To lock the other person completely in one's glance and refuse to let go is very embarrassing. A rigid attention is coerced eventuating in a loss of poise. . . . Similarly, never to give one's attention to the other is role-incapacitating. If one focuses his gaze not on the other's eyes, but on his forehead, let us say, the encounter is visibly disturbed.[24] Norms allowing for flexibility and tolerance permit the parties to social transactions ordinarily to assume that they will not be held to rigid standards of conduct and that temporary lapses will be overlooked. . . .

The second performance norm was that of *giving the other fellow the benefit of the doubt*. For the transaction to go on at all, one has at least to give the other fellow a *chance* to play the role he seeks to play. Clearly, if everyone went around watching for chances to embarrass others, so many would be incapacitated for role performance that society would collapse. Such considerate behavior is probably characteristic of all human society, because of the dependence of social relations on role performance. A part of socialization, therefore, must deal with the prevention of embarrassment by the teaching of tact. People must learn not only not to embarrass others, but to ignore the lapses that can be embarrassing whenever they occur. In addition, people must learn to *cope* with embarrassment. Consequently, embarrassment will occasionally be deliberately perpetrated to ready people for role incapacitation when it occurs.

. . .

CONCLUSION

In this paper, we have inquired into the conditions necessary for role performance. Embarrassment has been employed as a sensitive indicator of those conditions, for that which embarrasses incapacitates role performance. Our data have led us to describe the conditions for role performance in terms of identity, poise, and sustained confidence in one another. When these become disturbed and discredited, role performance cannot continue. Consequently, provisions for the avoidance or prevention of embarrassment, or quick recovery from embarrassment when it does occur, are of key importance to any society or social transaction, and devices to insure the avoidance and minimization of embarrassment will be part of every persisting social relationship. . . .

NOTES

1. Not all incapacitated persons are always embarrassed or embarrassing, because others have come to expect their *incapacities* and are consequently prepared for them.

2. Erving Goffman, in "Embarrassment and Social Organization," *American Journal of Sociology*, LXII (November 1956), 264–71, describes these manifestations vividly.

3. A more general discussion of this phenomenon, under the rubric civil inattention, is provided in Erving Goffman, *Behavior in Public Places* (New York: Free Press of Glencoe, 1963), pp. 83–88 and *passim*.

4. Other dimensions of the self—value and mood—will be taken up in subsequent publications.

5. Gregory P. Stone, "Appearance and the Self," in Arnold Rose (ed.), *Human Behavior and Social Processes* (Boston: Houghton Mifflin, 1962), p. 93.

6. Erving Goffman, *The Presentation of Self in Everyday Life* (New York: Doubleday Anchor Books, 1959), p. 25.

7. We use the term "appearance" to designate that dimension of a social transaction given over to identifications of the participants. Apparent symbols are those symbols used to communicate such identifications. They are often non-verbal. Appearance seems, to us, a more useful term than Goffman's "front" (*ibid.*), which in everyday speech connotes misrepresentation.

8. Erving Goffman, *Stigma* (Englewood Cliffs, N.J.: Prentice-Hall, 1963), pp. 59–62. Goffman confines the concept to personal identity, but his own discussion extends it to include matters of social identity.

9. For example, the title, "honorary citizen of the United States," which was conferred on Winston Churchill, served the function of a name, since Churchill was the only living recipient of the title. Compare the titles, "professor," "manager," "punch-press operator," and the like.

10. The implication of the discussion is that structured activities are uniformed, while interpersonal activities emphasize individuation in dress. Erving Goffman suggests, in correspondence, that what may be reflected here is the company people keep in their transactions. The work of men in our society is ordinarily teamwork, and teams are uniformed, but housework performed by a wife is solitary work and does not require a uniformed appearance, though the "housedress" might be so regarded.

11. Anselm L. Strauss, *Mirrors and Masks* (Glencoe, Ill.: Free Press, 1959), p. 57.

12. This observation and the ensuing discussion constitute a contribution to and extension of present perspectives on role conflict. Most discussions conceive of such conflict as internalized contradictory obligations. They do not consider simultaneous multiple-role performances. An exception is Everett C. Hughes' discussion of the Negro physician innocently summoned to attend a prejudiced emergency case in "Dilemmas and Contradictions in Status," *American Journal of Sociology*, L (March 1945), pp. 353–59.

13. We have rewritten this discussion to relate to Goffman's classification which came to our attention after we had prepared an earlier version of this article. Goffman distinguishes between what people do in transactions and what the situation calls for. He recognizes that people do many things at once in their encounters and distinguishes those activities that command most of their attention and energies from those which are less demanding of energy and time. Here, the distinction is made between *main* and *side involvements*. On the other hand, situations often call for multiple activities. Those which are central to the situation, Goffman speaks of as *dominant involvements*; others are called *subordinate involvements*. Dominant roles, therefore, are those that are central to the transactional situation—what the participants have come together to do (see Goffman, *Behavior in Public Places*, pp. 43–59).

14. Adjunct roles are one type of side involvement or activity. We focus on them because we are concerned here with identity difficulties. There are other side *activities* which are *not* necessarily adjunct *roles*, namely, sporadic nosepicking, scratching, coughing, sneezing, or stomach growling, which are relevant to matters of embarrassment, but not to the conceptualization of the problem in these terms. Of course, such activities, insofar as they are consistently proposed and anticipated, may become incorporated in the *personal role* (always an adjunct in official transactions), as in the case of Billy Gilbert, the fabulous sneezer.

15. This phenomenon provides the main theme and source of horror and mystery in Daphne du Maurier's now classic *Rebecca*.

16. Adjunct roles reserve identities, and relict identities need not cohere with the dominant role; they simply must not clash so that the attention of participants in a transaction is not completely diverted from the dominant role performance.

17. See Erving Goffman, *Behavior in Public Places*, pp. 151–52.

18. Whether objects in a situation are meant to be moved, manipulated, or taken up provides an important differentiating dimension between equipment on the one hand and props (as well as clothing, to be discussed shortly) on the other. Equipment is meant to be moved, manipulated, or taken up *during* a social transaction whereas clothing and props are expected to remain unchanged during a social transaction but will be moved, manipulated, or taken up *between* social transactions. To change

props, as in burning the portrait of an old girl friend (or to change clothes, as in taking off a necktie), signals a change in the situation. The special case of the strip-tease dancer is no exception, for her act transforms clothes into equipment. The reference above to the "stickiness" of props may now be seen as another way of describing the fact that they are not moved, manipulated, or taken up during transactions, but remain unchanged for the course of the transaction. Clothing is equally sticky but the object to which it sticks differs. Clothing sticks to the body; props stick to the settings.

19. William James, *Psychology* (New York: Henry Holt & Co., 1892), pp. 177–78.

20. A complete exposition of the body-maintenance function of clothing is set forth in an advertisement for Jockey briefs, entitled: "A Frank Discussion: What Wives Should Know about Male Support," *Good Housekeeping*, May, 1963, p. 237.

21. Goffman, *The Presentation of Self in Everyday Life*, pp. 212–33.

22. Implicit in Georg Simmel, *The Sociology of Georg Simmel*, trans. Kurt H. Wolff (Glencoe, Ill.: Free Press, 1950), p. 308.

23. See the discussion of "role distance" in Erving Goffman, *Encounters* (Indianapolis, Ind.: Bobbs-Merrill Co., 1961), pp. 105–52.

24. Here we are speaking of what Edward T. Hall calls the "gaze line." He points out there are cultural variations in this phenomenon. See his "A System for the Notation of Proxemic Behavior," *American Anthropologist*, LXV (October 1963), 1012–14.

Review Questions

1. Define the terms "identity" and "poise." How do threats to identity and poise disrupt interaction?

2. How are spaces, props, equipment, and clothing used to validate identities and to maintain poise?

3. Distinguish between dominant roles, adjunct roles, reverse identities, and relict identities. How are these related to embarrassment?

4. Discuss the two "performance norms" described by Gross and Stone which protect against embarrassment. Give examples of these norms from your own experiences.

FEAR AND LOATHING AT A COLLEGE MIXER

Pepper Schwartz and Janet Lever

T HE PREDOMINANT VIEW EXPRESSED IN THE SOCIOLOGICAL LITERATURE ON DATING IS that the social events and interactions are "fun" for the participants. An adult observer of adolescents at a social gathering would see them dressed up for the occasion, flirting with one another, dancing to loud music, engaging in light conversation, and generally seeming to be enjoying themselves.

A sociologist might look at this kind of scene and describe it as an example of what Simmel (1950) called "sociability," the formal, superficial expression of human communication. However, we think it would be wrong to confuse adolescent dating with "a play form of sociation" in which form is more important than content. Instead of viewing such interactions as pure fun, we suggest that dating is a serious socialization process with potentially negative consequences for the individual.

Our study of social patterns on a college campus leads us to believe that the moves and countermoves of dating carry great meaning for the individual and for the group and that the process of finding a balance between self-protection and self-exposure is anything but pure play. The participant, while supposedly in a "light" environment of introduction to peers, is at the same time in a situation where his or her desirability as a partner is being tested. The rating and ranking of the individual may be apparent and stressful. As the individual seeks to be both vulnerable (open to meeting an attractive other) and self-protective (invulnerable to rejection), the social world becomes fraught with tension, anxiety, and implications for the individual's sense of self.

Other sociologists have recognized that dating has some serious consequences, but they have underestimated the costs of the painful exchanges inherent in these situations. They acknowledge the following functions of dating: first, as we have mentioned, dating is seen as pleasurable for both members of the couple.[1] For example, Winch (1968: 507) concludes:

> Dating provides an opportunity to explore the personality and values of another human being in a situation of erotically-tinged fun-oriented recreation.

Pepper Schwartz and Janet Lever, "Fear and Loathing at a College Mixer," *Urban Life*, Vol. 4, No. 4 (January 1976), pp. 413–430.

Authors' Note: The authors are grateful to Wendell Bell, Philip Blumstein, Louis Wolf Goodman, R. Stephen Warner, and Stanton Wheeler for their helpful comments on an earlier draft of this paper. We also wish to thank J. A. Gilboy and Erving Goffman for the constructive criticism they offered at the 66th Annual Meeting of the American Sociological Association.

Second, all see dating as providing a status-grading function in the school community of young adults. In his famous article on "the Rating and Dating Complex," Willard Waller (1937: 730) sees dating as a determinant of one's prestige on campus and points out that the students are quite aware of the ranking system and their own position on the social hierarchy. As Bowman (1948: 212) indicates, one's prestige ranking is based on a combination of the frequency of dating and the rating of the persons one dates. And Burgess and Locke (1945: 384) add that the competitive nature of dating makes it a game—an end in itself—the object being to date as many high-ranking persons of the opposite sex as possible. They explain that one's rating depends upon physical attractiveness, personality characteristics, participation in university activities, and membership in prestigious organizations.

Third, these sociologists see important consequences in the dating game for one's self-image. Waller (1937: 731) reminds, "This competitive dating process often inflicts traumas upon individuals who stand low in the scale of courtship desirability." That is, the dating process is seen as a "testing ground," a way to determine one's attractiveness to the opposite sex, and can result in feelings of inferiority if one fails to secure acceptable dates (Winch, 1968: 506; Bowman, 1948: 212).

Fourth, dating is seen as an educational process, an arena in which one learns "proper deportment" and "social graces" (Winch, 1968: 506). Bowman (1948: 212) suggests that one can insure success in this social arena by improving manners, appearance, and by cultivating a variety of interests and the art of conversation.

Fifth, dating is considered important for its role in mate-selection. Through a series of dating encounters, one learns what kind of partner provides the most gratifying relationship (Winch, 1968: 504), and presumably, one such relationship will deepen and pass through the successive stages of courtship toward marriage.

These sociologists state serious consequences but they overlook these important points:

1. Dating continues for many years before courtship goals are introduced. Theorists analytically separate dating and courtship patterns, but neglect to note that modes of dating interaction may continue into the courtship context. This means that Waller's "exploitative" rating and dating syndrome may have farther reaching consequences than he imagined.

2. The process of social interaction must be given greater significance in dating studies. Otherwise, one must assume, as the authors imply, that all kinds of dating have the same outcomes. The subtleties of interaction are ignored, yet we feel that it is these repeated exchanges that have significant impact on the self and on the way an individual learns to treat others.

3. The progression of dating to courtship is seen as an orderly process during which the goal of mate selection is furthered. We believe that some of the stated goals can in fact be subverted by the process itself.

In this essay we will present data on a college mixer that support our competing view of dating processes. The mixer is a dance sponsored for the express purpose of meeting members of the opposite sex. Mixers have always been an integral part of the formal social system in most high schools, colleges, and universities. The ideal-type is represented by the schoolwide dance which ends freshman orientation week each fall. But graduate student "happy hours," sorority-fraternity exchanges, and dorm dances are variations on the same theme.

We have chosen to outline the mixer scenario at a traditionally one-sex campus as we observed it and as it was described to us by its participants. We are focusing on the mixer rather than the dyadic date because it is an environment which allows us to view attraction and rejection, coupling and uncoupling, in a public setting. By observing the mixer we hope to view both personal and ritualized modes of coping with success and failure.

These data were collected as part of a larger study chronicling the first year of coeducation at Yale (Lever and Schwartz, 1971). We conducted 96 in-depth interviews with Yale undergraduates.[2] Sixty-five percent of the women in our sample had transferred to Yale from Eastern women's colleges and had been long acquainted with the mixer system. Ninety percent of the men and the women in the sample had attended at least one mixer during their college career. In addition, the authors were participant observers at five mixer dances during the academic year.

THE MIXER

Heterosexual encounters are universal features of the social world, but their forms vary according to the structural constraints of the environment. The physical location of monosexual schools place severe strains on the natural development of heterosexual relationships.[3] Yale is approximately 80 miles from Vassar, Smith, and Mt. Holyoke—the closest of the prestigious Seven Sister schools. The scheduling of classes forces monosexual institutions to endorse a weekend dating system, encouraging their students to study for five days and play for the remaining two. Even with the beginning of coeducation at Yale, the sex ratio remained weighted with eight men to every woman. Clearly, the men were forced to take steps to increase the recruitment pool of available women if they wanted to participate in heterosexual dating activities.

The mixer has long been the solution to this structural problem. Each of Yale's twelve residential colleges sponsors its own dances several times during the year. The social committees at the women's colleges charter buses for the trip and sell low-cost tickets on a first-come-first-serve basis. The less prestigious schools from the immediate vicinity also send small envoys, but the main purpose of mixers is to attract women of comparable social status and educational attainment, i.e., potential future mates, not just sex partners for an evening. In this sense, mixers perform the same endogamous screening services of the sorority-fraternity system described by Scott (1965: 12).[4] Although the monosexual mixer bears important similarities to institutions on coeducated campuses, it also has special properties that cause strained relations between the sexes that we wish to explore.

Before the women arrive, the men take their positions in the college dining hall where the dance will take place. The dining room, like high school gymnasiums decked out for a prom, is suitably changed. The tables have been cleared away, the lights are low, and a stage has been marked off at one end of the room for the band. A beer table is set up, usually in the common room outside the dancing hall. Here the lights are brighter and groups of men stand around talking. This beer table will serve as a prop for them throughout the dance. Getting a beer gives people something to do when they need to look busy, provides an avenue of escape ("Pardon me, I think I'll go get a beer"), and allows people to get drunk to loosen inhibitions and numb sensitivities for the personal tests that are to come.

The typical mixer at Yale starts around 8:30 p.m., when the buses from surrounding women's colleges begin to arrive. These same buses leave promptly at midnight. So time pressure exists. In fact, the element of time points to one major difference between the mixer and other kinds of formal dating. The mixer is not like a Saturday night dance on a coeducated campus. The girl will not be there throughout the week. Both male and female are aware that they have approximately two hours to find out if they want to get to know each other better.

People must quickly evaluate each other and attempt to make contact with those they have decided are desirable partners for the evening. Some are mutually attracted, but many more get rebuffed or end up with someone they do not really care for. All night long people are being approved or discarded on the basis of one characteristic that is hard, or at least painful, to discount—their appearance.

When persons are asked to dance, their names are exchanged and often some light conversation occurs but the rating and ranking that goes on is still primarily by personal appearance. The music level is deafening. As one woman said, "How can you expect to really meet anyone at 400 decibels?" Since conversation is difficult and people have just met one another, physical appearance is the only criterion of selection. There is little chance to talk, to be clever or interesting or simply flattering. Therefore, if the other person is not interested, that fact cannot be rationalized as a lack of things in common, a fundamental difference in world views, or dissimilar kinds of temperament. Only one criterion exists, so the situation is bound to be more tense. When rejection is obvious and even recurrent within the same four-hour period, it makes inroads on one's self-image. Students reported feelings of "ugliness," "fatness," "clumsiness," and so forth during and after the mixer situation.[5]

Thus, there is a strong approach-avoidance tension in the air. Some women stand slightly apart so that they are more approachable; some stand close together and look indifferent. The general strategy of both sexes seems to be a question of how to achieve the maximum exposure with the least possible risk.[6] That is, one wants to be seen and appreciated and asked for a dance (or be given the cue that someone would like you to ask her for a dance) without being seen as alone and needing someone. Erving Goffman (1967: 43) maintains that social life is orderly because people voluntarily stay away from places where they might be disparaged for going. The monosexual arena is different from the coeducated one precisely because the opportunities to meet others of the opposite sex in "safer" situations where one can protect his or her "face" have been minimized. Defensive maneuvers available in the mixer are few, difficult to manage, and, as we shall see, can be self-defeating.

The men first ask pretty women or those with good figures to dance; women usually prefer handsome men or men with some sort of "cool." Being "cool" is not necessarily based on looks for a man. It means that somebody "puts himself together" well, that he walks or talks with some authority, or that he looks "interesting" or at ease.[7] The participants know that the appearance criterion is inadequate and demeaning, but they use it. People are very conscious about how their partner will reflect on their own desirability. A male junior was very frank about the situation:

> There have been times when I've seen a girl and, you know, I imagined I might not get along too well with her just from talking with her, but she was so good-looking that I just wanted to be seen walking into the dining hall with her or something like that, something prestigious.

Since there is only one "prestigious" criterion, meeting the standard becomes more and more consuming. You try to better your own game. One man put it this way:

> It's such a superficial thing. You judge a girl there strictly by her looks. So you talk to a pretty girl while your eyes scan the floor for another pretty girl. . . . It's like looking at an object in the window. It's probably mutual.

Women *are* under the same sort of pressures. Besides appearance, a man's age influences his overall rating.[8] A sophomore man testified to this fact bitterly:

> Sophomore and freshman girls really have a thing. It's very important to them that they be dating an upperclassman. Like last year when I would be at a dance and it would come out that I was a freshman, that was it.

Even though the women are ranking the same way as men, they are more vocal in their resentment of the emphasis on "superficial beauty." Perhaps their anger is due to the fact that males have the advantage in initiating an encounter, or it may be a reaction to the cultural value that says it is more important for a woman to be beautiful than for a man to be handsome, or that men have more ways to be "cool" other than looks. If a woman objects to what one coed called a "pageant of appearance," it is hard for her to change the pattern of interaction. Some women complained of abortive at-

tempts to try to distinguish themselves as minds as well as bodies. A sophomore transfer from Smith told us about a disturbing conversation she had
with a man at a mixer:

> I hate mixers. I hate the mixer game. I hate the questions. You know, how do you
> like Smith? What are you majoring in? What year are you in? etc. And that was
> the extent of your conversation. I once came to a mixer here, and it was right be-
> fore Nixon got elected and I was very interested in political science. And so I be-
> gan talking about the election and the guy told me that didn't I know that at mix-
> ers you're only supposed to talk about trite things. And I wasn't supposed to get,
> you know, intellectual?

We asked our respondents to describe the kind of person who does like
mixers. The women understood that being "good-looking" was a prerequisite for having a good time at a mixer. A Yale transfer from Bennington described it this way:

> Who would like a mixer? I guess a very pretty girl. A girl who doesn't make her
> conquests intellectually. A girl who likes to be dominated. A girl who likes to be
> "chosen." A girl who likes to dance and knows she's good at it. And somebody
> who has no other alternative.

A transfer from Smith added:

> If you really like asserting yourself and proving to yourself that you're attractive,
> I think a mixer can be a big ego trip.

But none of the women we interviewed, and only one of the men, claimed
personally to like mixers. They referred to mixers as "body exchanges" and
"meat markets." The women reacted most strongly against the mixer system. A junior transfer described her feelings:

> I generally think mixers are grotesque. There you are, a piece of meat lined up
> along a wall in this herd of ugly females. You try to stand casually as guys walk
> back and forth and you know you're on display. You just want to crawl up the
> wall. Then you're asked to dance by these really gross creatures. I'm so revolted
> by the whole thing.

And a transfer from Manhattanville saw mixers as the "ultimate objectify-
ing occasion":

> I stopped by [a mixer] for about twenty minutes and I wondered why the people
> present needed the extreme sensations—the loud music and flashing lights. There
> was so much tension. I guess I wondered why everyone was laughing as hard as
> they were and smiling as hard as they were. Everybody started to look alike to
> me, so I left.

Even the single male who admitted he liked mixers drew a similar picture
of the event:

> Mixers are pretty funny. I sort of enjoy watching the changes in personalities. My
> first impression of a mixer my freshman year reminded me a great deal of cattle

auctions I'd seen. Where huge crowds of inspectors and buyers and such would climb the entryways and dining hall and this group of very frightened creatures would charge through the middle.

Throughout the evening men and women are conscious of being constantly evaluated, desired, or disregarded. But they don't leave the mixer even though they feel uncomfortable there. The women are captive until their buses leave at midnight; the men stay because the mixer is the place to secure names for the year's dating events. Because everyone's ego is threatened, people devise ways to protect themselves. Verbal patter and social maneuvering are used in this instance to avoid being too vulnerable. Fear of ridicule and rejection is so great that methods of ego preservation (be they cruel, clever, even ultimately self-defeating) are seen as essential.

In a sense, the mixer offers people a kind of "freedom."[9] The majority of students we interviewed reported that they did not feel like themselves at a mixer. Certain impolite or barely masked rejections are expected. People who are not ordinarily cruel allow themselves to hurt someone's feelings because they have so little time to find someone for themselves and because they can reasonably expect never to see that person again. The three protective devices we saw and heard about most frequently were "eye messages," the "ritualistic brush-off," and the "offensive-defensive" tactic.

"Eye messages" are part of the more general category of body language.[10] If someone undesirable is approaching, the uninterested party allows her eyes to glaze over; she looks past the individual and concentrates on some other direction. Or the person finds "something to do." A man becomes engrossed in the beer stand; a woman can be totally preoccupied in a hitherto trivial conversation with a friend. The eyes are straight—locked into the diversion—never once glancing in the direction of the person to be avoided. The intent is usually obvious: by denying eye contact, one is refusing to acknowledge the other's presence or claim on one's attentions. If eye contact is achieved, then the individuals are forced to interact, if only to the extent that now they must acknowledge ignoring one another.

On the other hand, eye contact can be used for the opposite effect. If the individual wishes to engage someone in an encounter, eye contact is used to grab attention. A really aggressive person may lock eyes with someone, but many just glance at one another. The meaning is clear, that is "I consider you very attractive. Come over." (Or, "Can I come over?") One senior described the technique which had served him well during his four years at Yale:

> You try to meet eyes with a girl who doesn't look happy with the person she's with, in the hope that she'll say she has to go to the bathroom. Then you pick her up on the return trip. It's a big game, obviously.

The woman who changes partners in the manner described above is employing what we call the "ritualistic brush-off." Excuses and lines that would be embarrassing to use elsewhere are used with great frequency during a mixer to get out of an unpleasant mismatch with the least amount of trauma and embarrassment for all concerned. Unfortunately, because they have become ritualized, they only mute the surface blow. Everyone recognizes them for what they are, and the rejection still hurts. The favorite line used by men, as we have mentioned, is "Pardon me, I think I'll go get a beer." At a mixer the ladies' room is to women what the beer table is to men. Leaving for the bathroom, as indicated in the quotation above, serves as an excuse for the woman to get out of an uncomfortable match and to re-enter the room in a different area and meet new partners. Of course, she is bound to see the man she has "temporarily" left, but they usually avert eyes. It is an effective "good-bye."

Sometimes the rituals are only recognizable to one partner in the interaction. This way of ending further contact is even less benign. One woman related common practices among her friends at Wellesley:

> At Wellesley, I heard stories about how to brush off a guy you don't like. Like one thing you do is give him your phone number and when he calls he gets "Dial-A-Prayer." Or you tell him it's your number and it's really a guy's.

Instead of lines, some people merely say "thank you" with a final-sounding air. After the dance is over there are a couple of seconds of undefined meaning. The girl is undecided whether she is going to be asked to dance again, and the boy may be unsure whether the girl would like to stay with him. A "thank you" and exit often end the suspense—sometimes precipitously. Afraid to be the one who is turned down, people protect themselves by terminating the interaction first. We call this the "offensive-defensive" tactic. No matter what the original likelihood was that the couple would not get along, by "jumping the gun" the individual has made the outcome virtually guaranteed. This protective device often condemns the innocent before any act has been committed and nurtures the type of interaction that the individuals say they are trying to escape.

One can liken this type of interaction dilemma to the "Prisoners' Dilemma" so frequently discussed in game theory.[11] Anatol Rapoport (1965: 9) describes the "Prisoners' Dilemma" as a mixed-motive game:

> Psychologically, most interesting situations arise when the interests of the players are partly coincident and partly opposed, because then one can postulate not only a conflict among the players, but also inner conflicts within the players. Each is torn between a tendency to cooperate, so as to promote the common interests, and a tendency to compete, so as to enhance his own individual interests.

This mixed-motive quality differentiates the mixer from most boy-girl encounters where there is a greater face-saving potential, and explains why the mixer situation is potentially so devastating to one's self-concept and one's relationships to others. In *Interaction Ritual* Erving Goffman (1967: 11) describes the normative order of most encounters.

The combined effect of the rule of self-respect and the rule of considerateness is that the person tends to conduct himself during an encounter so as to maintain both his own face and the face of the other participants. This means that the line taken by each participant is usually allowed to prevail, and each participant is allowed to carry off the role he appears to have chosen for himself.

But let us review the several ways in which the monosexual-school mixer is distinct from ordinary encounters. First, it is our belief that the lines used have become so ritualized that they no longer serve to protect the face of the other participants. Second, the informational character of the encounter—i.e., what one can learn about the other person beyond factors of appearance—is greatly limited due to time and noise constraints at the mixer. Third, the chances of meeting the person again are smaller than on a coeducated campus, so the necessity for the "rule of considerateness" is greatly reduced.

One might argue that the "cost" of being nice is also reduced if these persons never have to see each other again. However, we believe that because of the need to find a desirable partner, the "costs" of niceness may be being "trapped" with an unwanted person for the evening—a cost that seems too high for most participants. Thus, given the fact that individuals can avoid reencountering persons they have maligned, they will more likely act "inconsiderately."

In other words, the mixer is important sociologically precisely because it, like the prisoners' dilemma, can be seen as a noncooperative game. People at a mixer, or in a mixer-like situation, describe members of the opposite sex as the "enemy." They act as though their chosen roles are conflicting, not complementary. They assess the risks of "winning" and "losing," net outcomes, and maintenance of face. Winning means a date, self-enhancement, status in the eyes of others. Losing means letting someone feel superior to you and perhaps accepting their definition of your unworthy status. It means being seen as less attractive than you had previously thought and having that verified in front of your peers. It means for some very vulnerable people, taking on an identity as a social maladept or Unattractive Person. This identity is one that most people will avoid even if avoidance means "cutting off one's nose to spite one's face."

Thus, a situation forces these kinds of choices (see Table 1): if the person terminates the encounter quickly, s/he has saved face, but s/he loses the opportunity to establish a new relationship. On the other hand, if the initiator (always the male) waits and tries to engage his partner for another dance, the woman may terminate the encounter and the man will consequently lose face. Again, the opportunity for a successful relationship—which is one's motive for risking "face" in the first place—is lost. Or if both the man and woman trust each other, there is a possibility that both will win what they are seeking. Unfortunately, since both have been to a mixer or similar event before, or heard about mixer norms, they do not expect that the other person will "cooperate" and openly court their attention; therefore, they mini-

Table 1

| | | MALE | |
		Continues	*Terminates*
FEMALE	*Continues*	opportunity for new relationship	loss of face for female
	Terminates	loss of face for male	no loss of face but loss of opportunity for relationship

mize risk-taking by showing a low level of affect. The individuals have saved face, but in so doing they have undermined their initial goals.

Of course, some do play the game cooperatively, and risk face while allowing the other person to decide whether to continue the relationship or break it off. If the other person takes a similar risk, the couple will most likely remain together for the duration of the evening. Sometimes such unions are immediately romanticized by both persons as part of what we call the "pit or the pedestal" syndrome. That is, the boy then treats the girl as a "one-nighter" or as a "dream girl," and the girl makes a similar judgment. Because the mixer is experienced as unpleasant, both men and women are searching for someone they can date so that they minimize the number of mixers they must attend during the year. Because they live so far apart, there is encouragement for an immediate, intense experience that will justify a weekend together in the future.[12]

For the majority, however, it is clear that the effects of the mixer are seen as personally destructive. To take a symbolic interactionist perspective, one's image of self grows out of interaction with significant others. Repeated failures can cause people to doubt their attractiveness to the opposite sex. A junior transfer reflected back on her three years in the mixer system:

> I always ended up with someone I was very unhappy with. I used to wonder why I attracted that type. Very few people ever found anyone decent. Most people came back from those things feeling negatively about the experience and feeling negatively about themselves.

Mixers had long-term effects on the self-images of the successful as well; many of those individuals had come to see their worth mostly in terms of their surface qualities. For everyone involved, the mixer situation encourages a calculating approach to heterosexual contact that is more starkly visible than in settings which do not limit such encounters to specific times and places.

CONCLUSION

The mixer, as we see it, illustrates the serious consequences that dating can have for the participant. We have described a major socializing process during which the individuals are given continual information about their physical attractiveness and marketability. A set of values emerge that indicate that individuals should not only assess themselves according to these criteria, but that they are appropriate standards to apply to others. One learns to use the opposite sex to establish high rank for oneself.

It must be remembered that the participants get assessed and rejected repeatedly in the course of a single evening. Rather than seeing the event as "pure fun," to the contrary, the participants feel the tension and anxiety associated with a situation where high personal stakes are involved. Interactions with the opposite sex occur in a predominantly conflict-ridden context where mutual satisfaction rarely occurs. Noncooperative strategies to protect face are accepted as rational by nearly everyone, and the "battle of the sexes" becomes more than a metaphor.

Therefore, we feel that it is inappropriate to consider dating as merely a means to the ends of courtship (i.e., finding a suitable long-term mate). First, as we have seen, certain forms of heterosexual contact may, in fact, undermine the goals of courtship. Second, the overall effect of negative encounters on one's self-image has been underestimated. Finally, the self-protective patterns of interaction that are learned are not necessarily unlearned at the end of adolescence, but are most likely carried into the intimate interpersonal relationships of adulthood.

NOTES

1. See Bowman (1948), Burgess and Locke (1945), Waller (1937), and Winch (1968).

2. We drew a stratified sample which included an equal number of males and females, randomly selected from the student body of approximately 4,000 men and 500 women. According to all available indicators, the sample well represented the Yale undergraduate population, except for the deliberate over-representation of females. All grade levels were represented equally, as were all twelve residential colleges. The percentage of students in our sample (1) from public high schools versus private schools, (2) from the Eastern seaboard versus other regions of the country, and (3) from alumni families, mirrored the percentages for the entire student population.

3. We are primarily speaking of those institutions not affiliated with a coordinate college for the opposite sex.

4. Although the singles' bar and the mixer share structural similarities they are functionally distinct in that the former does not perform the endogamous screening services of the latter. The customers in a singles' bar will vary with respect to age, educational attainment and social class background (and often marital status as well).

5. During participant observation at mixers, the authors never grew accustomed to the role of "coeds." Considering that we as "researchers" had little personally at

stake, we found that our egos were, nevertheless, involved. No matter how peripheral one is to this kind of situation, it is never easy to disregard completely someone else's estimation of one's attractiveness.

6. For a more detailed look at risk-taking in interpersonal relationships, see Blau, 1960: 545–556.

7. Berscheid et al. (1971) provide empirical evidence to support the observation that males are less dependent on looks for social success. They found that physical attractiveness (as judged by fellow students) and the number of dates in the past year correlated .61 for females on one college campus; the correlation for males was .25. In an earlier investigation of a "blind-date" dance on a coeducational campus, Walster et al. (1966) found that the physical attractiveness of *both* partners was the sole predictor of a couple's desire to see each other again; intelligence and social skills did not determine success in that social setting.

8. This value placed on the boy's age is not new. Waller (1937: 730) described the student tradition that prohibited freshman men from dating the coeds on a campus with a similarly unbalanced sex ratio.

9. In his essay on "Face-Work: An Analysis of Ritual Elements in Social Interaction," Erving Goffman (1967: 7) describes encounters between relative strangers as situations where the actors are free to use lines or suffer humiliations that would make future interaction embarrassing.

10. The foundation for the broad study of nonverbal communication is found in Birdwhistell (1952) and later in Hall (1966). Within the narrower category of facial expressions, Simmel (1973: 87) attributed special sociological importance to the eye; he said: "The union and interaction of individuals is based upon mutual glances. This is perhaps the most direct and purest reciprocity which exists anywhere." Most recent studies of eye contact stress its positive uses, i.e., in communicating mutual attraction; for empirical research in the area, see Exline and Winters (1965).

11. Anatol Rapoport (1965: 9–25) discusses the following 2×2 game matrix: each prisoner has two choices. He can trust his partner and keep their pact by maintaining silence in the suspicion that the police do not have enough evidence to convict them, with the outcome of their action either being the freedom for both or the incarceration of both, depending upon the strength of evidence against them. Or each prisoner has the option to confess and win his own freedom by breaking his pact with his partner and turning state's evidence against the other. The outcome of this choice is either the freedom for one and incarceration of the other or the incarceration of the two, if they both confess. The risk and uncertainty render the game a genuine dilemma with its mixture of *interpersonal* and *intrapersonal* conflict.

12. Elaine Walster and Ellen Berscheid's (1971: 47–62) article "Adrenaline Makes the Heart Grow Fonder" may provide an alternate explanation for the "pit and the pedestal" syndrome we noted. It is their hypothesis that physical arousal—be it caused by fear, rejection, anger, or sexual interest—makes people predisposed to romance. That is, in a setting that contextually permits them to fall in love, they interpret this barrage on their senses as "true love."

REFERENCES

Berscheid, E., K. Dion, E. Walster, and G. W. Walster
    1971 "Physical attractiveness and dating choice: a test of the matching hypotheses." J. of Experimental Social Psych. 7: 173–189.

Birdwhistell, R. L.
1952 Introduction to Kinesics. Louisville: Univ. of Louisville Press.

Blau, P.
1960 "A theory of social integration." Amer. J. of Sociology 65 (May): 545–556.

Bowman, H.
1948 Marriage for Moderns. New York: McGraw-Hill.

Burgess, E. and H. Locke
1945 The Family: From Institution to Companionship. New York: American Book.

Exline, R. V. and L. C. Winters
1965 "Affective relations and mutual glances in dyads," in S. S. Tomkins and C. E. Izard (eds.) Affect, Cognition and Personality. New York: Springer.

Goffman, E.
1967 Interaction Ritual: Essays on Face-to-Face Behavior. New York: Anchor.

Hall, E. T.
1966 The Hidden Dimension. Garden City: Doubleday.

Lever, J. and P. Schwartz
1971 Women at Yale: Liberating a College Campus. Indianapolis: Bobbs-Merrill.

Rapoport, A. and A. Chammel
1965 Prisoners' Dilemma: A Study in Conflict and Cooperation. Ann Arbor: Univ. of Michigan Press.

Scott, J. R.
1965 "Sororities and husbands." Transaction 2 (Sept./Oct.): 10–14.

Simmel, G.
1973 "Sociology of the senses: visual interaction," in D. E. Linder (ed.) Psychological Dimension of Social Interaction: Readings and Perspectives. Reading, Mass.: Addison-Wesley.
1950 The Sociology of Georg Simmel. Kurt Wolff (ed.) New York: Free Press.

Waller, W.
1937 "The Rating and Dating Complex." Amer. Soc. Rev. 2 (October): 727–734.

Walster, E. and E. Berscheid
1971 "Adrenaline Makes the Heart Grow Fonder." Psych. Today 5 (June): 47–62.

Walster, E., V. Aronson, D. Abrahams, and L. Rottman
1966 "The importance of physical attractiveness in dating behavior." J. of Personality and Social Psych. 4: 508–516.

Winch, R.
1968 "The functions of dating in middle-class America," pp. 505–507 in Robert F. Winch and Louis Wolf Goodman (eds.) Selected Studies in Marriage and the Family. New York: Holt, Rinehart and Winston.

Review Questions

1. Social events are supposed to be "fun" for the participants. What sociological factors determine the likelihood that one will have fun at a college mixer?

2. How do college mixers affect the self conceptions of those who are successful *and* those who are unsuccessful?

3. What factors minimized the chances of men and women getting to know each other at the college mixers studied by Schwartz and Lever?

4. What functions and consequences of dating do Schwartz and Lever suggest may have been overlooked by previous researchers?

NO-TELL MOTEL:
THE MANAGEMENT OF SOCIAL
INVISIBILITY

J. Robert Lilly and Richard A. Ball

Conventional hotels and motels are reported to be settings for a variety of socially interesting activities, including socially disapproved sexual behavior, yet there has been remarkably little research on such establishments.[1] There has been even less research into the "no-tell motel," a facility which specializes in renting rooms by the hour for heterosexual trysts. The paucity of research on such establishments is due not only to the fact that data are extremely difficult to obtain in this "infrarealm of private sex" (Humphreys, 1970: 162) but also to the fact that researchers have generally tended to pay little attention to the issue of social visibility, a situation which is being corrected but very slowly (Ball, 1967).[2] In this study we will address the question of how social invisibility is constructed and maintained by the staff and patrons of an illicit motel operation. We are interested in the interaction and information strategies that operate to admit and regulate the informed patron while identifying and deflecting the naive customer. Special attention will be given to those situations which threaten the everyday routines of the motel by exposing the premises upon which its social invisibility rests.

Central to our concern is the notion of "copresence" as the way in which people are rendered "uniquely accessible, available, and subject to one another" (Goffman, 1963: 22). Humphreys (1970: 157), one of the few researchers to explore this issue, has stressed the extent to which people seem to define what is public and what is private in terms of copresence, attempting to regulate public order by controlling this mutual accessibility. In many cases the most important factor involved is the "social visibility" of the activity to be defined (Reiss, 1960: 319). . . .

METHOD

Access to the confidential motel was obtained through a friend, toward whom casual inquiries were made about the motel, including questions about its age, rates, seasonal variations in occupancy, nature of competition, and forms of record keeping. More than a year elapsed between the

J. Robert Lilly and Richard A. Ball, "No-Tell Motel: The Management of Social Invisibility," *Urban Life*, Vol. 10, No. 2 (July 1981), pp. 179–197.

first casual probes and request for research permission. After several months and repeated assurances of our appreciation for the more delicate aspects of relationships with patrons, permission was granted with the understanding of a quid pro quo. Among other requests, we had asked to see registration records over a period of years so that we could plot occupancy rates against a number of other variables. The owner-manager was interested in this information himself, and we agreed to share it with him.

Records for the past seven years were made available and we were permitted to interview all employees, some of whom had worked at the motel throughout its history. We were allowed to stay at the motel as guests of the owner at any time for any duration, and to work there, either on the grounds as maintenance employees or within the office in some capacity. The only restriction placed on the research was that we were never to speak to any patron. Since our interest lay in the operation of the facility rather than in the lives of its clientele, this posed no problem.

Both authors have observed motel operations over a variety of shifts on different days of the week and under various circumstances. During the past six years, one of the authors has spent many available holidays, weekends, and vacations in observing, interviewing, working, or living at the motel. We have drawn data through different forms of participant observation from every shift, every day of the week, and nearly every month of the year.[3]

We have had the benefit of close association with the owner-manager of the motel, have interviewed him at some length on various occasions, and have spent a great deal of time with him both at the motel and at his other places of business. He explained our presence to the staff, requesting their cooperation and assuring them that we were interested only in understanding daily routines and their methods of dealing with different problems, and not in identifying patrons in any specific way. This was very important clearance since many of our questions were subject to this interpretation. We also learned a great deal about the original owner, who had sold the motel a few years before, and his strategies for construction and operation of the facility. The current owner-manager volunteered a great deal of information of his own, as did staff members with whom we were also able to establish excellent rapport.

THE SETTING

The research site, located in a major city of the Southwest, was specifically constructed and has been operated for its entire 25-year existence as a confidential, heterosexual rendezvous. It has never advertised as such, having relied exclusively upon word-of-mouth to alert potential patrons. The original builder and owner was a successful gambler and nightlife devotee who provided the groundwork for establishing the motel's reputation as "safe."

The first customers were his friends and acquaintances who had frequented the city's red-light district before it was "cleaned up." The original owner was very frank about this:

> My married friends complained there was no place to go for women and no safe place to take 'em after you found one. I decided to build a small motel to see if enough people would use it if they were guaranteed privacy. You see, when I built this place in the 50s, it was hard for a man and woman to rent a room if they weren't married. Besides, getting a room in a local hotel meant you might be seen.

For the original proprietor, nothing was more important than social invisibility. He stressed the need for caution: "I built the motel so it would be hard as hell to see who was here. I figured people would really use the place if we could just hide 'em. It took three years to get the place right." Not only was it important to hide the patrons, it was also necessary to keep the motel itself out of trouble by keeping it out of the sight of moral crusaders and other potential intruders, and the establishment dramatizes certain everyday techniques for insuring privacy through physical construction (Manning, 1972). There are two sets of rooms facing each other across a heavily treed and shrubbed courtyard, which makes it difficult to see most of the entrance doors. The establishment is surrounded by an eight-foot-high stone wall. The lone street entrance offers sole access to the motel and provides the only point from which the facility is visible. Most of the rooms have garages equipped with electronically controlled doors that are operated from within the motel office as well as by the customers once they are in the garage. There are no windows facing the drive that separates the garages from the perimeter wall. Entrance to the typical room is through the garage into a short, connecting hallway with double doors between garage and room. Each room has a door to the courtyard, but these are seldom used by patrons except to gain access to secluded payphones when there is some reason to avoid the motel switchboard.

The office is located on the rear end of the wing to the right as one faces the motel from the street entrance. At the end of the left set of rooms is a laundry that runs nearly 24 hours a day. Immediately next to the laundry but heavily insulated is a special room recently refurbished at cost of nearly $16,000. Furnishings in the remaining 39 rooms are considerably less elaborate, with a bath, one double bed, a table with an attached radio, and two chairs. Three groups of rooms have joining doors for patrons who want to get together for more complicated activities. Ten have television sets which show closed-circuit, pornographic films.[4] The current rental rate is $10 for 4.5 hours, except for the rooms equipped with television, which rent for $15 for the same amount of time.

Anyone entering the office might suspect that this is an unusual motel. The rear of the office is surrounded by a bulletproof glass shield with one small opening suitable for exchanging money. Instead of the usual cluster of pigeonholes for room keys and messages, there is behind the desk a 12-

gauge pump shotgun hung next to a television monitor showing pornographic films. Outside is a sign reading as follows: "Adult Movies Available
Upon Request. Inquire at Office."

· · ·

FICTIONAL COPRESENCE

[T]he motel is a complicated *copresence context* [in which several categories
of people act with awareness of the others in the situation but try not to pay
much attention to each other and to actually pretend that they are unaware
of each other. Hence, the term "fictional copresence." The motel situation
includes] a block of bounded time, a particular partner, and a specific site
with a limited number of rooms available. Desk clerks handle requests for
rooms with a keen eye to renting only to customers who understand the
rules. Patrons are distinguished as "old" or "new." "Old" customers pose no
threat to the operation of the motel. The following is a standard exchange
between a desk clerk and an "old" customer who has come into the office:

Clerk: Hello.
Customer: Hi, I want a room.
Clerk: With or without a T.V.?
Customer: I'll take the T.V.
Clerk: That'll be $15.

While this exchange is taking place, the desk clerk pushes a registration
card through the opening, without asking the customer to fill it out and
without eye contact, a technique which helps the customer to maintain
"face" (Goffman, 1967: 12). The increasing importance of "credentials"
means that most of us have a number of "paper selves" which can be shifted
to fit circumstances (Manning, 1972). The use of fictional paper selves can
contribute significantly to social invisibility, but only if the fiction is accepted. The customer usually fills out the card and passes his money
through the opening, but some merely return the blank card with the rental
fee. Occasionally a patron will ask the clerk to put through to his room any
telephone calls. Never is an "old" customer asked for any form of identification. . . .

In addition to the physical techniques and interactional strategies designed to maintain genuine social invisibility, there is a great deal of effort
devoted to the *symbolism* of secrecy. Thus, for example, the motel staff is
very cautious in making every effort to impress the customer that they are
not being scrutinized, either overtly or covertly. It is important that the fictional copresence context be continuously validated.

· · ·

As Bates (1964: 432) has pointed out, one of the most interesting of all
privacy phenomena is the situation in which the individual *seeks* a loss of

some personal privacy as a means to a desired end, with the privacy surrendered only on the understanding that no one will take advantage of the vulnerability. Certain social roles, such as those of physician, lawyer, or priest, are organized to provide for what we may term *privacy releases*, allowing one to expose certain discreditable aspects of self without fear of publicity. To some extent, the motel staff fill such roles, although in a very special context.

On rare occasions, usually during the vacation season of heaviest demand on conventional motels, naive tourists may enter the office. If after looking around they still want a room, they are asked a series of questions: "How long do you plan to stay?"; "How many are in your party?" and so on. If the person plans to stay all night, he (the individual is almost always male) is informed that he cannot rent a room for that length of time. If he still insists, he is told that all rooms are filled. We have never seen anyone persist beyond this point. Exceptions to the "admission rule" are very rare and occur only when a naive customer asks for a room on nights when business is exceptionally slow and is not expected to improve. Even then, however, no exceptions are made for those with children, who are fended off by additional ploys, such as the information that each room has only one bed. No one at the motel could recall ever renting a room to a family.

Before a room is rented to a naive customer, he is required to provide at least three sources of identification. These are carefully verified. A list of identification sources is recorded on the ledger next to the registration card number, but the names themselves are never recorded. Identification of the companion is verified and recorded in the same way. The clerk is careful to be sure that both are at least 21 years old. During these transactions, the clerk will give additional signals that something is unusual about the motel, so that even the most naive patron, while remaining uninformed about the details of the setting, can hardly fail to see that he is entering a socially questionable environment. These efforts seem extraordinary, but the reasons are simple enough:

> We don't want no one here who don't want to be here. So we make sure they's old enough and know what's goin' on here. That way we can say, "You must of wanted to stay here," case they say they goin' to complain [office employee].

As these remarks indicate, the staff is very concerned about avoiding confrontations with customers who might object to the way the motel is operated. The management wants no one to be upset by what is experienced during a stay. To let such a thing happen would be to run the risk of publicity that could destroy the social invisibility of the establishment. Thus, it is important to control copresence, not only in such a way that patrons will not have their activities disrupted by unwelcome intruders but also in such a way that no patron will be forced to witness anything that might be morally offensive.

Although the motel is not listed in any travel register available to individuals and/or travel agencies, there is a listing in the yellow pages of the telephone directory, so that it is possible for naive callers to telephone the motel for reservations. Since telephone contact by "old" customers is quite common, the desk clerk must employ various information-gathering strategies which serve to maintain the fictional copresence context while screening calls. In a special sense, this motel differs markedly from conventional motels where the customer selects the lodging. Here the desk clerk serves as a patron selector, albeit from a limited pool of callers. For instance, if a caller asks whether a room is available without specifying time of arrival, the desk clerk will ask what time the caller expects to arrive. If the answer is somewhat vague (e.g. "between 5:00 and 6:30 p.m.") and the call is taking place sometime before (e.g., 2:00-3:00 a.m.), the desk clerk does not yet have enough information for a screening decision. Such a caller is typically asked how many people are in the party wanting a room. If the answer is, for example, "Three of us" or "Myself, my wife and child," the caller is told that there are no vacancies. If the answer is "two of us" or "My wife and I," additional information is needed, because all patrons are treated *as if* they are married couples. Next comes what we may call the *closure question*, asking how long the customers plan to stay. If the answer is a general remark such as, "Only a short while" or a more specific, "No more than a couple of hours," the reservation is made. An answer such as, "Until tomorrow morning," will produce, "Sorry, we have no vacancies."

Informed callers will usually specify an exact time of arrival, indicate whether pornographic films are expected and very often request a room by number. In this case, the desk clerk engages in the minimum conversation required to provide the customer with the necessary instrumental information. Those who have not secured a room by phone run the risk that none will be available upon their arrival. Such a caller may end the conversation with a general signal such as "I'll be there shortly, hold that room for me," or some more specific closing such as "I'll be there shortly, please have someone come to the room for my money." In the latter case, the caller is using further options for maximizing the social invisibility. Having one of the staff come to the room for payment allows the patron to avoid any exposure created by getting out of the car, going into the office, returning to the car, and driving to the garage. Since the automobile is itself a source of identification, the practice of driving directly into the garage is even more of a contribution to social invisibility. Finally, the invisibility of partners is also enhanced, since it is not necessary to leave them in an exposed position during rental transactions. Once in their rooms, patrons cannot be seen even during payment, for each door has a hinged peephole suitable for passing through the payment and the registration card.[5]

Thus far we have outlined the . . . strategies employed by the staff and the customers of the motel as they engage in the minimum interaction and exchange the minimum information necessary to accomplish room rental. Implicit here has been the assumption that the members of a given party arrive together, whether the rental was arranged in the office or by telephone. This is not always the case. Frequently, the male arrives alone. His partner appears a little later, usually by taxi after the patron has used one of the payphones to inform her of the room number. This strategy eliminates the possibility the patrons will be seen together even during transit to the motel. As one member of the staff said, "Some of these people are very careful. They don't take no chances at all." Here entrance is accomplished with almost total invisibility.[6]

Although the entry process poses the greatest risk of social visibility, both for the motel and the patrons, problems can also arise during the rental period, and those too must be managed. For example, in the case of an incoming call for someone by name, the desk clerk will put the caller on "hold" and check the registration cards for that name. If a customer has rented a room under the name mentioned by the caller, his room will be rung to ascertain if any calls had been expected. If no calls had been expected, the caller is informed that no such person is registered. The same strategy is employed in the event that a caller asks to speak with the occupants of a specific room except when an unwelcome caller is told that the room is vacant.

If incoming telephone calls hold a considerable potential for disruption of social invisibility, so do outgoing calls. These may be channeled through the office by dialing the office switchboard and giving the number desired. All numbers called are noted next to the room number of the caller, creating a potential violation of the fictional copresence context, but an ad hoc solution to certain problems.

> It's a way to know how many calls are made per renter. We have to charge for more than two calls. Also, it is a way to keep cabs from driving around the motel looking for someone. We had trouble one time when a cabbie came here looking for a fare. He knocked on doors and asked for someone by name. We got complaints about that. So we decided to keep taxis from going to rooms until they stopped by the office first. We call the room the cabbie is supposed to go to, to see if they want one. Then we send it around to the right garage door [owner].

· · ·

As long as both the staff and patrons are "in the situation," we have a "tightly defined occasion" (Goffman, 1963: 22) and things go smoothly except for the possibility of disasters such as fires and floods or external social contingencies such as riots or exposes. On the other hand, the problematic aspects of the situation are highlighted during those occasional disruptions which threaten to upset the normal, everyday operations of the motel. There are, for example, "dirty people"—who occasionally tear drapes, spill liquor on the bed, and [the like]. . . . Theft increased substantially soon after installation of the televisions, a problem that was essentially solved by connecting each television to a warning buzzer that is triggered in the office. "Drunks" sometimes become so intoxicated that they cannot or will not leave at the end of the rental period. The strategies developed to insure social invisibility serve to compound these problems. The rules of the information game make use of the registration cards impractical as a means of tracing troublemakers. Instead of involving the police and disrupting the fictional copresence context even further, the management simply tries to screen out such patrons as best it can.

. . .

The relationship between the motel and the community is also characterized by an elaborate pattern of social fictions. The local police, for example, act as if patrons are using their real names and addresses and as if the motel has no reason to suspect otherwise. This is formal dereliction of duty, since registrations are required to identify patrons in case of illness or perhaps injury or death, either by natural causes, violence, or catastrophy. As some compensation, the police receive a reduced room rate. Indeed, they account for approximately 5% of the daily rentals. The "special" room described above is the only back region about which the owner was less than completely open, but occupants have been described to us in general terms as "politicians" and in slightly more specific terms as "judges, lawyers, police detectives, police captains, and lieutenants." They often secure the room for a particular time by calling the owner at another place of business, maximizing social invisibility by avoiding staff entirely.

Problems in community relations arise occasionally usually because of some "crackdown" brought on by a moral crusade. . . . A local television station produced and aired a "special" on "adult motels," claiming to identify all of them in the area, but confining the report to those which advertised their specialty. The relative *visibility* of those establishments actually directed attention away from the confidential motel we were investigating where business went on as usual.

The simplest management strategy employed by our more invisible motel was to turn off the television monitor showing pornographic films. Telephone inquiries in which the caller asked whether the motel had X-rated movies were always answered in the negative. According to the owner, "All our old customers know we still have movies. Anybody who asks must not be a regular customer." Special precautions were taken to admit only "old" customers during the period. Patrons were checked more closely, and every effort was made to avoid even minor disruptions. The importance of these strategy shifts became obvious almost immediately. Motels publicly identified became the focus of organized attention by some local churches. Pickets appeared, complete with placards such as "Families Ruined Here" and "Sex for Sale Here." Business at these establishments was so curtailed that they were either closed temporarily (from one to four months), were sold under pressure, or were forced to remove all X-rated films.

CONCLUSION

Some years ago Williams (1958: 357–371) described a variety of "patterned evasions" based on "contravening norms" sustained by "cultural fictions." Earlier commentaries had been made by Simmel (1950), who was impressed with the importance of secrecy in human relations. The concept of social visibility helps to clarify those interactional dimensions. The patrons of the clandestine motel . . . conceal their transgressions rather than openly challenging the normative order. The motel succeeds in managing its social invisibility by controlling a copresence context of the sort we have termed "fictional," where each set of participants knows what is going on but pretends that something different is occurring, where each has access to much knowledge but strives to remain ignorant so as to maintain a certain uninvolved posture. The importance of an experienced staff is difficult to overestimate here, for it is the staff that prevents disruptions and contains those that occur in spite of their efforts.

The fictional copresence that provides all this social invisibility is facilitated by certain cultural norms. As Bates (1964: 421–432) has pointed out, we generally recognize the individual's right to privacy with respect to bodily functions, including sexual activities and sleeping arrangements, and one is granted a certain right to withhold information which might be embarrassing or harmful to oneself. Social invisibility is not infrequently the result of a tacit agreement to remain ignorant of circumstances which might introduce dissonance into ongoing human relationships; it can be as much a matter of unwillingness to see as of eagerness to avoid being seen. The respectable members of the community may be somewhat aware that socially disapproved behavior is going on but most are willing to ignore it. If problem patrons can be managed and community relations handled judiciously, a fictional copresence context can be sustained and the socially disapproved behavior can be sufficiently hidden to satisfy conventional morality. Without this tacit bargain, the necessary social invisibility would be impossible to manage, no matter how sophisticated the copresence context.

NOTES

1. The most notable exception is Hayner (1936), but it has become rather dated. Boylan (1971) has only touched on the conventional motel, while Prus and Vassilakopoulos (1979) have offered the only description of hustling in a "shady" hotel of which we are aware.

2. Examples of research on socially disapproved behaviors within protective settings include Ball's (1967) work on the abortion clinic, Bryant and Palmer's (1977) research on massage parlors, Cavan's (1963) study of bar behavior, Humphreys's (1970) study of homosexual activity in public restrooms, Roebuck and Frese's (1976) research on after-hours clubs, and Weinberg and Williams's (1975) investigation of gay baths. With a few exceptions, these studies have not pursued the more complex issues of social visibility.

3. Using two research assistants, we have assembled and analyzed the registration records for the past seven years. Staff members have cooperated by supplying data on such variables as race and sex of patrons, this data being noted at time of registration.

4. There are 30 different films, and they are changed each day. The tapes are a problem, for they tend to become so worn that they are subject to frequent breaks. The heavy usage means that those surviving deteriorate to the point where visual quality is low enough to bring complaints. The solution is to have copies made. When asked about the legality of this (widely used) technique, the owner answered with a shrug, "So what. The man I buy my originals from copies them from the original cuts." This is one minor facet of the socially invisible, *sub rosa* marketplace, a hidden economy into which the motel is linked.

5. Patrons are not given keys. The doors between garage and room as well as those opening onto the courtyard are locked only from within, so that keys are not necessary. If one member of the party wishes to leave and return during the rental period, the person(s) left behind arranges reentry. This policy puts more control in the hands of the staff. Since keys cannot be duplicated, the risk of intrusions is further minimized, and social invisibility is maximized.

6. Of the approximately 150 calls made through the motel switchboard each month, nearly 95% are made by males. We were unable to find any ethical means by which to monitor the number of calls made from the payphones. Our impression, confirmed by the staff, is that at least one half of the patrons arrive alone and then make final arrangements with the partner(s) by telephone.

REFERENCES

Ball, D. W.
1967 "An abortion clinic ethnography." Social Problems 14: 293–301.

Bates, A. P.
1964 "Privacy—a useful concept?" Social Forces 42: 429–434.

Boylan, B. R.
1971 Infidelity. Englewood Cliffs, NJ: Prentice-Hall.

Bryant, C. and C. E. Palmer
1977 "Tense muscles and the tender touch: Massage parlors, 'hand whores,' and the subversion of service," pp. 131–145 in C. D. Bryant (ed.) Sexual Deviancy in Social Context. New York: Watts.

Cavan, S.
1963 Liquor License. Chicago: Aldine.

Goffman, E.
1967 Interaction Ritual. Garden City, NY: Doubleday.
1963 Behavior in Public Places. New York: Free Press.

Hayner, W.
1936 Hotel Life. Englewood Cliffs, NJ: Prentice-Hall.

Humphreys, L.
1970 Tearoom Trade. Chicago: Aldine.

Manning, P.
1972 "Locks and keys: An essay on privacy," pp. 83–94 in J. M. Henslin (ed.) Down to Earth Sociology. New York: Free Press.

Reiss, A. J., Jr.
1960 "Sex offenses: The marginal status of the adolescent." Law and Contemporary Problems 25: 312–319.

Roebuck, J. B. and W. Frese
1976 "After-hours club." Urban Life 5: 131–164.

Schwartz, B.
1968 "The social psychology of privacy." Amer. J. of Sociology 73: 741–752.

Simmel, G.
1950 "The secret and the secret society," pp. 40–52 in K. Wolfe (ed.) The Sociology of Georg Simmel. New York: Free Press.

Weinberg, M. S. and C. J. Williams
1975 "Gay baths and the social organization of impersonal sex." Social Problems 22: 124–136.

Williams, R.
1958 American Society. New York: Knopf.

Review Questions

1. Impression management is a concept usually applied to individuals' actions which are intended to control what others may know about them. How does the concept of impression management apply to a system such as the No-Tell Motel?

2. How does the management of the No-Tell Motel define the situation for outsiders who happen to ask for rooms? Be sure to discuss nonverbal as well as verbal cues.

3. What strategies and structures were devised to create social invisibility for the No-Tell Motel and for those connected with it? How are customers kept invisible from each other, even when they meet by chance?

Suggested Readings: Interaction in Everyday Life

Becker, Howard S. "Becoming a Marijuana User," *American Journal of Sociology* (November 1953), 235–242.

Cooley, Charles Horton. *Human Nature and the Social Order.* New York: Schocken Books, 1964.

Festinger, Leon, Henry W. Riecken, and Stanley Schacter. *When Prophecy Fails*. Minneapolis: University of Minnesota Press, 1956.

Goffman, Erving. *The Presentation of Self in Everyday Life*. Garden City, N.Y.: Anchor Books, 1959.

_____. *Behavior in Public Places*. New York: Free Press, 1963.

Henslin, James M. "What Makes for Trust?" in James M. Henslin, ed., *Down to Earth Sociology*. 3rd ed. New York: Free Press, 1981.

Lemert, Edwin. "Paranoia and the Dynamics of Exclusion," *Sociometry* 25 (1962), 2–20.

Lyman, Stanford M., and Marvin B. Scott. *The Sociology of the Absurd*. New York: Appleton-Century-Crofts, 1970.

Mead, George Herbert, in Charles W. Morris, ed., *Mind, Self and Society: From the Standpoint of a Social Behaviorist*. Chicago: University of Chicago Press, 1934.

Sherif, Muzafer. "Experiments in Group Conflict," *Scientific American* 195 (1956), 54–58.

Stone, Gregory P. "Appearance and the Self," in Arnold Rose, ed., *Human Behavior and Social Processes*. Boston: Houghton Mifflin, 1962, pp. 86–118.

_____, and Harvey A. Farberman, eds., *Social Psychology Through Symbolic Interaction*. 2nd ed. New York: Wiley, 1980.

Part V. Social Organization: From Primary Group to Society

ALTHOUGH A GREATER PROPORTION OF OUR INTERACTIONS OCCURS WITH STRANGERS than was the case in agricultural societies of the past, still most occur within groups. All of the groups of which we are members—from the level of the primary group, to the secondary group, to the formal organization, to the society—are organized. What we mean by this is that each of these types of groups—even the small friendship group—develops a system of beliefs and norms, a division of labor, a method of ranking members, and a system of social-control techniques to ensure conformity to the group's goals and rules. Sociologists have paid attention to a number of elements of group organization: group size (primary groups usually being small, societies large), the ways in which norms are created (informally within primary groups, formally in secondary groups or large-scale organizations), the degree of intimacy among members (greater within the primary group than the secondary group), the method of determining leadership and power positions (informally in the primary group, usually formally in secondary groups and societies), and so on. They have also focused on the internal processes of both small and large groups such as communication, development of group cohesion, boundary maintenance, and facilitation of smooth interaction.

Of course, we are all members of many groups, of all types, simultaneously; and within large groups, smaller ones may be found. The expectations and demands of these groups may conflict at times, causing problems for the individual torn between competing claims. As societies themselves have become larger, more complex, more industrialized, and more interdependent, the number of claims on the individual have increased and, as a result, the very character of everyday life has changed.

The articles and excerpts presented in this part of our reader are intended to illustrate the patterning and constraining aspects of various levels of social organization, as well as the differences between types of groups in the kinds of behavior they call for. The *organization* of the small, intimate groups into which we are born (families); of the associations we join; of the formal organizations in which we work, study, and even play; and of the larger society has important implications for our daily lives.

First, William Foote Whyte, in "Corner Boys," directs our attention to interaction in *primary groups*, which are relatively small, intimate, and informal. Whyte moved into a neighborhood where groups of young men spent much of their free time hanging around on the street. He spent more than three years as a participant observer studying these peer groups, and his research resulted in one of the best known and frequently cited works in sociology, *Street Corner Society*.

In this article by Whyte, he explains his research methods and a few of the research findings pertaining to group processes. He demonstrates, for example, the determinants of leadership among the corner boys. We are also shown how an individual's status within the group affects with whom he or she is likely to spend time. Further, there is the issue of who initiates and who receives more of the interactional flow. At the most general level, Whyte's research shows the powerful influence of the group upon individual behavior.

As you read this article, you may think of similar experiences in the social groups with which you are familiar. To take but one example, most of us have been in the position of being a newcomer in a group. Newcomers must often convince more established and powerful members to introduce or implement their ideas rather than voicing them directly. You should be able to illustrate from your own experience this and many other general principles of primary-group behavior described here.

The college classroom, a setting familiar to us all, is the situation which David Karp and William Yoels have chosen for study. The members of a classroom form a collectivity which is much less intimate and more formal than a primary group (although, to be sure, primary groups may exist *within* the classroom). Role relationships, as in other *secondary groups*, are segmental, which means that teacher and students interact within (usually) fairly narrow boundaries rather than becoming involved with each other in a more total way. The occupants of each of these reciprocal positions have expectations both for their own behavior and for the behavior of those in the reciprocal role. When these expectations differ, a kind of *role strain* may develop. Whose definition of the situation will win out? Can social processes arise to alleviate the strain?

The professor expects the students to be prepared for class—to have read and carefully considered the assigned material and, in class, to ask questions or make comments based on their reading. Ideally, much of the class period will be spent in a stimulating discussion that will involve most of the students.

Many of the students, on the other hand, prefer to take a passive role. They view their professor as an expert who will "feed" them his or her views on the subject at hand. Because they know that the professor expects them to have read the material thoroughly, perhaps with a greater commitment than they actually care to generate, they enter the classroom with a "presentation of self" that indicates a solid knowledge of the material. As long as they are not asked to discuss anything, an uneasy silence is maintained.

How is the issue of participation actually resolved? Fortunately, each class contains a few talkers. These individuals assume the responsibility of carrying on class discussion and thus take the pressure off both the "silent majority" and the professor. When the professor asks a question, it is almost always one of the group of "regulars" who responds. Although a regular talker in one class may not fulfill that role in another, someone will probably do so, easing the strain so that the class may proceed. Rarely will the teacher or the students place one another under such stress that their behavior will deviate from the relatively distant, formal attitude appropriate in secondary groups.

The next selection, "Women and the Structure of Organizations," deals with the highly bureaucratized *formal organization*. Rosabeth Moss Kanter reports on her research dealing with the social organization of corporations as it affects female and male employees differently. Amid the myriad formal rules and roles specifying the corporate structure are those which channel women and men in separate directions.

In the worlds of finance and industry, organizations are supposed to be rational, impersonal, and efficient. Yet cultural norms, assumptions, and stereotypes about the "proper" role of women invade these worlds too. Although they constitute a significant proportion of the labor force in large scale industrial and financial organizations, women are poorly represented in the managerial ranks. In fact, women could be described as a virtual *caste* of clerical workers, carrying out the less prestigious tasks and holding the lowest-paying jobs. Furthermore, women in clerical positions are often treated as "office wives," ruled in patriarchal fashion by a caste of middle-level male managers. Female clerical and secretarial workers are dependent on their male superiors, are subject to arbitrary conditions of work (having to make coffee and shop for their bosses), are poorly paid, and often lack entry to higher-paid and more responsible positions. This last point is important; male workers who begin as messengers or mail clerks may be promoted up the ranks of the company, but secretaries rarely are. The few women who do obtain managerial positions also face serious problems because of their sex. Interaction with male co-workers is often so difficult that women must divert their energies from exercising leadership to insuring survival. Kanter notes that women's behavior may be shaped by their interactions in the work place as much as by childhood socialization.

Kanter is one of the first sociologists to focus on women's roles within business organizations. She finds that theories of management, the structure of the organization, and problems of interaction have combined to perpetuate inequality within financial and industrial corporations. In fact, these same social forces appear to be operating within other large-scale organizations in our society such as government, hospitals, and even universities.

We turn next to a consideration of how characteristics of social organization at the *societal* level come to have their impact on us. We will look at the degree of urbanization and at societal demographic factors in this regard.

Life in cities is necessarily different in many respects from life in rural areas or even small towns or suburbia. Residents of these different areas develop differing patterns of interaction in response to constraints of the situation. The worldwide trend toward urbanization which has occurred over the past several hundred years has meant, among other things, that social interaction takes place in a more crowded context, that coordination of the activities of large numbers of people is accomplished by recourse to time clocks, rules, traffic lights, and the like. Louis Wirth, is an early classic article entitled "Urbanism as a Way of Life," gives us the outlines of some of the consequences of *urbanism* for behavior and interaction. The portion of his work which is presented here focuses on what he saw as the three major characteristics of urban areas—large population size, high density, and heterogeneity. These characteristics have important consequences for the organization of human interaction, many of which Wirth spelled out almost half a century ago.

Furthermore, *demographic trends—changes in rates of birth, death,* and *migration*—limit and are limited by social interaction. For instance, black Americans have a *sex ratio* that "favors" black women (that is, there are more women than men), because of high *death rates* for black men. There are approximately 90 men for every 100 women among this group (thus, the sex ratio is roughly 90/100). For this reason, the opportunities for marriage—an important form of interaction in our society—are limited for black women, and other forms of intimate relationships may be substituted.

Demographers have also shown that the women of the "baby boom" generation (born when *birth rates* increased dramatically after World War II) had a smaller number of available older males to marry than other generations of women had. This "marriage squeeze" for baby-boom women has contributed to a later age at marriage than had existed for women born during the Great Depression and the war years. It has led also to a change in the norms for the appropriate age for husbands. The age gap between spouses, which used to be as great as three to four years at the turn of the century, is now less than two years.

As yet another example of the effects of demographic trends, we note the remarkable change in attitudes toward infants and children that have come about over the past few centuries. When *death rates* were very high, and only about half of all children born survived until their first birthdays, parents were less attached to and paid less attention to children than is now common. That is, changes in infant mortality rates have affected the quality and type of interaction between parents and children.

In the selection by John Weeks in this section, excerpts from his book entitled *Population: An Introduction to Concepts and Issues* have been pulled together so that we can see in detail several examples of societal population trends affecting the ways in which people act and interact. First, he discusses implications of the changing *age structure* of the United States for crime rates. Next, we see how declining *mortality rates*, declining *fertility rates*, and a rise in *urbanization* have set the stage for a change in the status of women, a change which may have far reaching implications for relationships between the sexes. Finally, Weeks takes a look at some additional consequences of our changing *age structure*, namely changes in patterns of interaction between the elderly and other societal members.

CORNER BOYS: A STUDY OF CLIQUE BEHAVIOR

William Foote Whyte

THIS PAPER PRESENTS SOME OF THE RESULTS OF A STUDY OF LEADERSHIP IN INFORMAL groupings or gangs of corner boys in "Cornerville," a slum area of a large eastern city. The aim of the research was to develop methods whereby the position (rank or status) of the individual in his clique might be empirically determined; to study the bases of group cohesion and of the subordination and superordination of its members; and, finally, to work out means for determining the position of corner gangs in the social structure of the community.

. . .

While my subjects called themselves corner boys, they were all grown men, most of them in their twenties, and some in their thirties. . . . While some of the men I observed were engaged in illegal activities, I was not interested in crime as such; instead, I was interested in studying the nature of clique behavior, regardless of whether or not the clique was connected with criminal activity. . . . I made an intensive and detailed study of 5 gangs on the basis of personal observation, intimate acquaintance, and participation in their activities for an extended period of time. Throughout three-and-a-half years of research, I lived in Cornerville, not in a settlement house, but in tenements such as are inhabited by Cornerville people.

The population of the district is almost entirely of Italian extraction. Most of the corner boys belong to the second generation of immigrants. In general, they are men who have had little education beyond grammar school and who are unemployed, irregularly employed, or working steadily for small wages.

Their name arises from the nature of their social life. For them "the corner" is not necessarily at a street intersection. It is any part of the sidewalk which they take for their social headquarters, and it often includes a poolroom, barroom, funeral parlor, barbershop, or clubroom. Here they may be found almost any afternoon or evening, talking and joking about sex, sports, personal relations, or politics in season. Other social activities either take place "on the corner" or are planned there.

William Foote Whyte, "Corner Boys: A Study of Clique Behavior," *American Journal of Sociology*, 46 (March 1941), 647–664.

HIERARCHY OF PERSONAL RELATIONS

The existence of a hierarchy of personal relations in these cliques is seldom explicitly recognized by the corner boys. Asked if they have a leader or boss, they invariably reply, "No, we're all equal." It is only through the observation of actions that the group structure becomes apparent. My problem was to apply methods which would produce an objective and reasonably exact picture of such structures.

In any group containing more than two people there are subdivisions to be observed. No member is equally friendly with all other members. In order to understand the behavior of the individual member it is necessary to place him not only in his group but also in his particular position in the subgroup.

My most complete study of groupings was made from observations in the rooms of the Cornerville Social and Athletic Club. This was a club of corner boys, which had a membership of about fifty and was divided primarily into two cliques, which had been relatively independent of each other before the formation of the club. There were, of course, subdivisions in each clique.

I sought to make a record of the groupings in which I found the members whenever I went into the club. While the men were moving around, I would be unable to retain their movements for my record, but on most occasions they would settle down in certain spatial arrangements. In the accompanying example (Figure 1) two were at a table playing checkers with one watching, four at another table playing whist and three more watching the game, and six talking together toward the back of the room. As I looked around the room, I would count the number of men present so that I should know later how many I should have to account for. Then I would say over to myself the names of the men in each grouping and try to fix in my mind their positions in relation to one another. In the course of an evening there might be a general reshuffling of positions. I would not be able to remember every movement, but I would try to observe with which members the movements began; and, when another spatial arrangement had developed, I would go through the same mental process as I had with the first. As soon as I got home from the club, I would draw a map or maps of the spatial positions I had observed and add any movements between positions which I recalled. The map (Figure 1) indicates the sort of data that came out of these observations.

In this case I have the following notes on movements of the members:

> Eleven walked over to One and pinched his cheek hard, went out of the club rooms, returned and pinched cheek again. One pretended to threaten Eleven with an ash tray. Eleven laughed and returned to seat on couch. I [the observer] asked Eleven about the purpose of the club meeting. He asked Ten and Ten explained. Eleven laughed and shrugged his shoulders. Sixteen, the janitor, served beer for the card players.

Figure 1. The Cornerville S & A Club, February 29, 1940, 8–8:15 P.M.

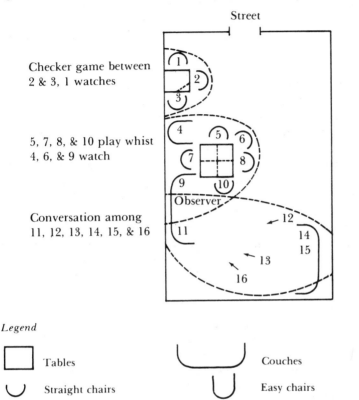

Checker game between
2 & 3, 1 watches

5, 7, 8, & 10 play whist
4, 6, & 9 watch

Conversation among
11, 12, 13, 14, 15, & 16

Legend

☐ Tables   ⌣ Couches

⌣ Straight chairs   ⊔ Easy chairs

Direction in which chairs & couches face indicates direction in which men face.
Arrows indicate direction in which standing men face.
Dotted lines enclose those interacting.

On the basis of a number of maps such as this it is not difficult to place most of the men in the clique and grouping within the clique to which they belong. I did not attempt to place all the men, because the club had a fluctuating membership and some of the men were available for observation for only a short time. There were, throughout the ten months of my observation, some thirty-odd members who were active most of the time. Events in the club could be explained largely in terms of the actions of these men; and, therefore, when I had placed them in relation to one another, I did not need to press further in this direction.

Positional map-making is simply an extension of the techniques of observation and recording which have been used in the past by social anthropologists and sociologists. All these techniques require practice before they can be effectively applied. While my first maps left out a number of men, later I was able to record accurately enough so that on most occasions I could account for every man present at a particular time; and on several occasions I was able to work out two maps giving different positional arrangements during the course of the same period of observation. Beyond two I did not attempt to go, and it was not necessary to do so because there would rarely be more than two positional arrangements in the course of an evening sufficiently different from one another to require additional maps.

While the data from such maps enable one to determine groupings, they do not reveal the position or rank of the men in the groupings. For this purpose other data are needed. In practice they may be gathered at the same time as the positional arrangements are observed.

As I conceive it, position in the informal group means power to influence the actions of the group. I concentrated my attention upon the origination of action, to observe who proposed an action, to whom he made the proposal, and the steps that followed up to the completion of the action. I was dealing with "pair events" and "set events," to use the terminology of Arensberg and Chapple.[1] A "pair event" is an event between two people. A "set event" is an event in which one person originates action for two or more others at the same time. In working out the relations between men in an informal group, this is an important distinction to bear in mind. I found that observations of pair events did not provide a safe guide for the ranking of the members of the pair. At times A would originate action for B, at other times B would originate action for A. In some cases there would be a predominance of originations in one direction; but on the whole the data did not support rankings based upon quantitative comparisons of the rates of origination of action in pair events. Qualitatively one could say that when A originated action for B he used a tone of voice and words which indicated that he held a superior position. To take the extreme case, it is not difficult to tell the difference between an order and a request, although both may originate action. It is not safe, however, to rely upon such qualitative differences. The observer may read into the situation his own impression of the relative positions of the men and thus lose the objective basis for his conclusions.

It is observation of set events which reveals the hierarchical basis of informal group organization. As defined by Arensberg and Chapple,

> a *set* is an aggregate of relations such that every individual related in the set is a member either (a) of a class of individuals who only originate action, or (b) of an intermediate class of individuals who at some time originate action and at another time terminate action, or (c) of a class of individuals who only terminate action.[2]

Study of corner-boy groups reveals that the members may, indeed, be divided and ranked upon this basis. Several examples will illustrate.

At the top of the Cornerville S. and A. Club (see Figure 2), we have Tony, Carlo, and Dom. They were the only ones who could originate action for the entire club. At the bottom were Dodo, Gus, Pop, Babe, Marco, and Bob, who never originated action in a set event involving anyone above their positions. Most of the members fell into the intermediate

Figure 2. Informal Organization of the Cornerville S & A Club, February 1940

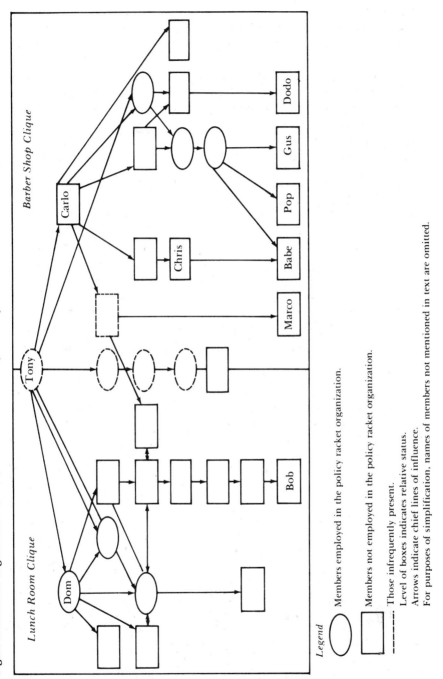

Legend

◯ Members employed in the policy racket organization.

▭ Members not employed in the policy racket organization.

------ Those infrequently present.
Level of boxes indicates relative status.
Arrows indicate chief lines of influence.
For purposes of simplification, names of members not mentioned in text are omitted.

class. They terminated action on the part of the top men and originated action for the bottom men. Observations of the actions of the men of the intermediate class when neither top nor bottom men were present revealed that there were subdivisions or rankings within that class. This does not mean that the intermediate or bottom men never have any ideas as to what the club should do. It means that their ideas must go through the proper channels if they are to go into effect.

In one meeting of the Cornerville S. and A. Club, Dodo proposed that he be allowed to handle the sale of beer in the clubrooms in return for 75 percent of the profits. Tony spoke in favor of Dodo's suggestion but proposed giving him a somewhat smaller percentage. Dodo agreed. Then Carlo proposed to have Dodo handle the beer in quite a different way, and Tony agreed. Tony made the motion, and it was carried unanimously. In this case Dodo's proposal was carried through, after substantial modifications, upon the actions of Tony and Carlo.

In another meeting Dodo said that he had two motions to make: that the club's funds be deposited in a bank and that no officer be allowed to serve two consecutive terms. Tony was not present at this time. Dom, the president, said that only one motion should be made at a time and that, furthermore, Dodo should not make any motions until there had been opportunity for discussion. Dodo agreed. Dom then commented that it would be foolish to deposit the funds when the club had so little to deposit. Carlo expressed his agreement. The meeting passed on to other things without action upon the first motion and without even a word of discussion on the second one. In the same meeting Chris moved that a member must be in the club for a year before being allowed to hold office. Carlo said that it was a good idea, he seconded the motion, and it carried unanimously.

All my observations indicate that the idea for group action which is carried out must originate with the top man or be accepted by him so that he acts upon the group. A follower may originate action for a leader in a pair event, but he does not originate action for the leader and other followers at the same time—that is, he does not originate action in a set event which includes the leader.

One may also observe that, when the leader originates action for the group, he does not act as if his followers were all of equal rank. Implicitly he takes the structure of the group into account. An example taken from the corner gang known as the "Millers" will illustrate this point. The Millers were a group of twenty corner boys, who were divided into two subgroups. Members of both subgroups frequently acted together; but, when two activities occupied the men at the same time, the division generally fell between the subgroups. Sam was the leader of the Millers. Joe was directly below him in one subgroup. Chichi led the other subgroup. Joe as well as Sam was in a position to originate action for Chichi and his subgroup.

It was customary for the Millers to go bowling every Saturday night. On this particular Saturday night Sam had no money, so he set out to persuade the boys to do something else. They followed his suggestion. Later Sam explained to me how he had been able to change the established social routine of the group. He said:

> I had to show the boys that it would be in their own interests to come with me—that each one of them would benefit. But I knew I only had to convince two of the fellows. If they start to do something, the other boys will say to themselves, "If Joe does it—or if Chichi does it—it must be a good thing for us too." I told Joe and Chichi what the idea was, and I got them to come with me. I didn't pay no attention to the others. When Joe and Chichi came, all the other boys came along too.

Another example from the Millers indicates what happens when the leader and the man next to him in rank disagree upon group policy. This is Sam talking again:

> One time we had a raffle to raise money to build a camp on Lake _____ [on property lent them by a local business man]. We had collected $54, and Joe and I were holding the money. . . . That week I knew Joe was playing pool, and he lost three or four dollars gambling. When Saturday came, I says to the boys, "Come on, we go out to Lake _____ . We're gonna build that camp on the hill. . . ." Right away Joe said, "If yuz are gonna build the camp on the hill, I don't come. I want it on the other side. . . ." All the time I knew he had lost the money, and he was only making up excuses so he wouldn't have to let anybody know. . . . Now the hill was really the place to build that camp. On the other side, the ground was swampy. That would have been a stupid place. . . . But I knew that if I tried to make them go through with it now, the group would split up into two cliques. Some would come with me, and some would go with Joe. . . . So I let the whole thing drop for a while. . . . After, I got Joe alone, and I says to him, "Joe, I know you lost some of that money, but that's all right. You can pay up when you have it and nobody will say nothin'. But Joe, you know we shouldn't have the camp on the other side of the hill because the land is no good there. We should build it on the hill. . . ." So he said, "All right," and we got all the boys together, and we went out to build the camp.

Under ordinary circumstances the leader implicitly recognizes and helps to maintain the position of the man or men immediately below him, and the group functions smoothly. In this respect the informal organization is similar to the formal organization. If the executive in a factory attempts to pass over his immediate subordinates and gives orders directly to the men on the assembly line, he creates confusion. The customary channels must be used.

The social structures vary from group to group, but each one may be represented in some form of hierarchy. The members have clearly defined relations of subordination and superordination, and each group has a leader. Since we are concerned with informal organization, the Cornerville S. and A. members must be considered as two groups, with Carlo leading the barbershop boys, and Dom leading the lunchroom boys. Since Tony's position requires special consideration, he will be discussed later.

BASES OF GROUP STRUCTURE

Observation not only serves to provide a description of the group structure.
It also reveals information upon the bases of structure and the factors differentiating between the positions of members. The clique structure arises out
of the habitual association of the members over a long period of time. The
nuclei of most gangs can be traced back to early boyhood years when living
close together provided the first opportunities for social contacts. School
years modified the original pattern somewhat, but I know of no corner
gangs which arose through classroom or school-playground association.
The gangs grew up "on the corner" and have remained there with remarkable persistence. In the course of years some groups have been broken up by
the movement of families away from Cornerville, and the remaining members have merged with gangs on nearby corners; but frequently movement
out of the district does not take the corner boy away from his corner. On
any evening in Cornerville on almost any corner one finds corner boys who
have come in from other parts of the city or from suburbs to be with their
old friends. The residence of the corner boy may also change within the district, but nearly always he retains his allegiance to his original corner.

The leader of one group spoke to me in this way about corner boys:

> Fellows around here don't know what to do except within a radius of about 300
> yards. That's the truth, Bill. . . . They come home from work, hang on the cor-
> ner, go up to eat, back on the corner, up (to) a show, and they come back to hang
> on the corner. If they're not on the corner, it's likely the boys there will know
> where you can find them. . . . Most of them stick to one corner. It's only rarely
> that a fellow will change his corner.

The stable composition of the group over a long period and the lack of social assurance felt by most of the members contribute toward producing a
very high rate of social interaction within the group. *The structure to be observed is a product of past interactions.*

Out of these interactions there arises a system of mutual obligations
which is fundamental to group cohesion. If the men are to carry on their activities as a unit, there are many occasions when they must do favors for
one another. Frequently, one member must spend money to help another
who does not have the money to participate in some of the group activities.
This creates an obligation. If the situation is later reversed, the recipient is
expected to help the man who gave him aid. The code of the corner boy requires him to help his friends when he can and to refrain from doing anything to harm them. When life in the group runs smoothly, the mutual obligations binding members to one another are not explicitly recognized. A
corner boy, asked if he helped a fellow-member because of a sense of obligation, will reply, "No, I didn't have to do it. He's my friend. That's all." It is
only when the relationship breaks down that the underlying obligations are
brought to light. When two members of the group have a falling-out, their

actions form a familiar pattern. One tells a story something like this: "What a heel Blank turned out to be. After all I've done for him, the first time I ask him to do something for me, he won't do it." The other may say: "What does he want from me? I've done plenty for him, but he wants you to do everything." In other words, the actions which were performed explicitly for the sake of friendship are now revealed as being part of a system of mutual obligations.

ROLE OF LEADER

Not all the corner boys live up to their obligations equally well, and this factor partly accounts for the differentiation in status among the men. The man with a low status may violate his obligations without much change in his position. His fellows know that he has failed to discharge certain obligations in the past, and his position reflects his past performances. On the other hand, the leader is depended upon by all the members to meet his personal obligations. He cannot often fail to do so without causing confusion and losing his position. The relationship of status to the system of mutual obligations is most clearly revealed when we consider the use of money. While all the men are expected to be generous, the flow of money between members can be explained only in terms of the group structure.

The Millers provide an illustration of this point. During the time that I knew them, Sam, the leader, was out of work except for an occasional odd job; yet, whenever he had a little money, he spent it on Joe and Chichi, his closest friends, who were next to him in the structure of the group. When Joe or Chichi had money, which was less frequent, they reciprocated. Sam frequently paid for two members who stood close to the bottom of the structure and occasionally for others. The two men who held positions immediately below Joe and Chichi in the subgroups were considered very well off according to Cornerville standards. Sam said that he occasionally borrowed money from them, but never more than fifty cents at a time. Such loans he tried to repay at the earliest possible moment. There were four other members, with positions ranging from intermediate to the bottom, who nearly always had more money than Sam. He did not recall ever having borrowed from them. He said that the only time he had obtained a substantial sum from anyone around his corner was when he borrowed eleven dollars from a friend who was the *leader* of another corner-boy group.

The system is substantially the same for all the groups on which I have information. The leader spends more money on his followers than they on him. The farther down in the structure one looks, the fewer are the financial relations which tend to obligate the leader to a follower. This does not mean that the leader has more money than others or even that he necessarily spends more—though he must always be a free spender. It means that the financial relations must be explained in social terms. Unconsciously, and in some cases consciously, the leader refrains from putting himself under obligations to those with low status in the group.

Relations of rivalry or outright hostility with other groups are an important factor in promoting in-group solidarity, as has been well recognized. . . . Present-day corner gangs grew up in an atmosphere of street fighting against gangs of Irish or of fellow-Italians. While actual fights are now infrequent, the spirit of gang loyalty is maintained in part through athletic contests and political rivalries.

As the structures indicate, members have higher rates of interaction with men close to their own positions in their subgroups than with men who rank much higher or much lower or belong to a different subgroup. That is a significant fact for the explanation of group cohesion.

In the case of the Millers, Sam's best friends were Joe and Chichi. As his remarks have indicated, Sam realized that the solidarity of the Millers depended in the first instance upon the existence of friendly and co-operative relations between himself, Joe, and Chichi. A Cornerville friend, who was aware of the nature of my observations, commented in this manner:

> On any corner, you would find not only a leader but probably a couple of lieutenants. They could be leaders themselves, but they let the man lead them. You would say, they let him lead because they like the way he does things. Sure, but he leans upon them for his authority. . . . Many times you find fellows on a corner that stay in the background until some situation comes up, and then they will take over and call the shots. Things like that can change fast sometimes.

Such changes are the result not of an uprising of the bottom men but of a shift in the relations between men at the top of the structure. When a gang breaks into two parts, the explanation is to be found in a conflict between the leader and one who ranked close to him in the structure of the original gang.

The distinctive functions of the top men in promoting social cohesion are readily observable in the field. Frequently, in the absence of their leader the members of a gang are divided into a number of small groups. There is no common activity or general conversation. When the leader appears, the situation changes strikingly. The small units form into one large group. The conversation becomes general, and unified action frequently follows. The leader becomes the focal point in discussion. One observes a follower start to say something, pause when he notices that the leader is not listening, and begin again when he has the leader's attention. When the leader leaves the group, unity gives way to the divisions that existed before his appearance. To a certain extent the lieutenants can perform this unifying function; but their scope is more limited because they are more closely identified with one particular subgroup than is the leader.

The same Cornerville friend summed up the point in this way:

> If we leave the followers, they'll go find some other leader. They won't know what they're doing, but that's what they'll do, because by themselves they won't

know what to do. They gather around the leader, and it is the leader that keeps them together.

The leader is the man who knows what to do. He is more resourceful than his followers. Past events have shown that his ideas were right. In this sense "right" simply means satisfactory to the members. He is the most independent in judgment. While his followers are undecided as to a course of action or upon the character of a newcomer, the leader makes up his mind. When he gives his word to one of "his boys," he keeps it. The followers look to him for advice and encouragement, and he receives more of the confidences of the members than any other man. Consequently, he knows more about what is going on in the group than anyone else. Whenever there is a quarrel among the boys, he will hear of it almost as soon as it happens. Each party to the quarrel may appeal to him to work out a solution; and, even when the men do not want to compose their differences, each one will take his side of the story to the leader at the first opportunity. A man's standing depends partly upon the leader's belief that he has been conducting himself as he should.

The leader is respected for his fair-mindedness. Whereas there may be hard feelings among some of the followers, the leader cannot bear a grudge against any man in the group. He has close friends (men who stand next to him in position), and he is indifferent to some of the members; but if he is to retain his reputation for impartiality, he cannot allow personal animus to override his judgment.

The leader need not be the best baseball player, bowler, or fighter, but he must have some skill in whatever pursuits are of particular interest to the group. It is natural for him to promote activities in which he excels and to discourage those in which he is not skillful; and, insofar as he is thus able to influence the group, his competent performance is a natural consequence of his position. At the same time his performance supports his position.

It is significant to note that the leader is better known and more respected outside of his group than is any of his followers. His social mobility is greater. One of the most important functions he performs is that of relating his group to other groups in the district. His reputation outside the group tends to support his standing within the group, and his position in the group supports his reputation among outsiders.

It should not be assumed from this discussion that the corner boys compete with one another for the purpose of gaining leadership. Leadership is a product of social interaction. The men who reach the top in informal groups are those who can perform skillfully the actions required by the situation. Most such skills are performed without long premeditation.

What the leader is has been discussed in terms of what he does. I doubt whether an analysis in terms of personality traits will add anything to such an explanation of behavior. One can find a great variety of personality traits among corner-boy leaders, just as one can among business or political leaders. Some are aggressive in social contacts, and others appear almost retiring. Some are talkative, and others have little to say. Few uniformities of this nature are to be found. On the other hand, there are marked uniformities to be observed in the functions performed by men who hold similar positions in society, and the study of them promises to provide the best clues for the understanding of social behavior.

THE GANGS AND THE WIDER COMMUNITY

For a community study, data upon five corner gangs are hardly more than a beginning. Two problems were involved in extending the research. First, I had to discover whether I could safely generalize my conclusions to apply them to all corner gangs in Cornerville. Second, I had to fit the corner gangs into the fabric of Cornerville society.

To accomplish the first end I solicited the aid of a number of corner-boy leaders, who made for me more or less systematic observations of their own groups and of groups about them. The generalizations, presented earlier, upon the functions of leaders, indicate why I found them the best sources of information upon their groups. This procedure could not be relied upon as a substitute for observation, for it is only through observation that the student can discover what his informants are talking about and understand their remarks in terms of group structure. Observation suggests a framework of significant behavior patterns and indicates subjects that are relevant for discussion with informants.

The student should realize that this procedure changes the attitude of the corner boy toward himself and his group. The quotations from Cornerville men presented here all show the effects of prior discussion with me. However, the effort of informants to make explicit statements upon unreflective behavior does not distort the factual picture as long as they are required to tell their stories in terms of observed interactions.

The most thorough study of this kind was made for me by Sam of the Millers upon his own group. The structure of the Millers was worked out by Sam over a period of months on the basis of such material as I have quoted. My function was to discuss Sam's observations with him, to point out gaps in his data, and to check them with some independent observations.

All the generalizations presented here have been checked against the experience and observations of four such informants. In this way I have been able to expand my study far beyond what I should have been able to cover alone.

Accomplishment of the second purpose—fitting corner gangs into the fabric of society—required study of the relations which linked group to group and the group to persons who held superior positions in Cornerville—politicians and racketeers, for example.

The observation that the leader is the person to relate his group to other people provides the most important lead for such a study. We see that the social behavior of groups pivots around the actions of certain men who hold strategic positions in them. This does not mean that the leader can make his followers do anything he desires. It does mean that he customarily leads the group activity and that outsiders, in order to influence the members, must deal with the group through him. This is to be observed particularly at the time of a political campaign when politicians seek to mobilize group support. Similar observations may be made in order to explain the position and influence of the racketeer in relation to corner-boy groups.

Brief reference to the Cornerville S. and A. study will indicate the nature of the results that may be obtained. Tony, the top man in the chart, was a prominent policy racketeer. The chart indicates that certain members were agents who turned their policy slips in to him. While Tony belonged to the club, his interests were so widespread that he had little time to spend with the members. It was recognized that he held a higher status, that he was not a corner boy.

At the time of the formation of the club, Tony knew Dom, his agent, and recognized Dom's position among the lunchroom boys. He knew Carlo only casually and was not aware of his position as leader of the barbershop clique. In the course of a political campaign (November 1939) a conflict arose over the endorsement of a candidate for alderman. By playing off one clique against the other, Tony was able to secure the adoption of his policy, but Carlo opposed him vigorously and lost out in a close vote. Carlo's position was strengthened when his candidate defeated the man supported by Tony. Following the election, there was a marked change in Tony's actions. He began to attend every meeting and to spend more time with the members. For his purposes Carlo was the most important man in the club, and he made every effort to cement his social relations with Carlo and to place Carlo under obligations to him. During this period a basis for co-operation between the two men was established. When Tony turned his attention to other activities, he was able to deal with the club through Carlo as well as through Dom.

This story illustrates a method of study, not a set of conclusions. Through observing the interactions between Tony and Dom, Tony and Carlo, Dom and the members of his clique, and Carlo and the members of his clique, one can establish the position and influence of the racketeer in relation to this particular organization of corner boys. Other observations establish Tony's position in the racket organization, which extends throughout the district and far beyond it. They also point out Tony's relations with certain politicians. Only in the study of such specific situations can one arrive at reliable generalizations upon the positions and influence of men in the community.

CONCLUSION

The methods I have used call for precise and detailed observation of spatial positions and of the origination of action in pair and set events between members of informal groups. Such observations provide data by means of which one may chart structures of social relations and determine the basis of the structures—a system of mutual obligations growing out of the inter-actions of the members over a long period of time. Observations also point out the distinctive functions of the leader, who serves as chief representative of his group and director and co-ordinator of group activity. A knowledge of the structure and of the social processes carried on through it serves to ex-plain the behavior of individual members in a manner which could not be accomplished if one considered the men as an unstructured aggregation.

Such an understanding of clique behavior seems a necessary first step in the development of knowledge of the nature of the larger social organiza-tion into which the cliques fit. Instead of seeking to place each clique mem-ber in relation to the total social organization, the investigator may concen-trate his attention upon the actions of the leader, who relates his corner boys to other groups and to persons holding superior positions. By discov-ering these strategic points for social integration and by extending the net-work of social relations through them, the investigator can place a large number of the inhabitants of his community in their social positions.

This is a painstaking and time-consuming method. While it does not pro-duce statistics which count all the inhabitants in terms of certain character-istics, it does provide the investigator with a close-up view of the social or-ganization in action.

NOTES

1. *Measuring Human Relations: An Introduction to the Study of the Interaction of Individuals* ("Genetic Psychology Monographs" [Provincetown, Mass.: Journal Press, 1940]).

2. *Op. cit.,* p. 54. To terminate an action is to follow the initiative of another person.

Review Questions

1. How are various aspects of the groups studied by Whyte *similar to* and *different from* formal organizations?

2. According to Whyte, how do clique structures arise? How did his methods of research allow him to discover the answer to this question?

3. Explain Whyte's statement, "Leadership is a product of social interac-tion." Give examples from the groups he discussed as well as from your own experience.

4. Explain how providing aid to friends built up a network of obligations among the corner boys. Were they aware that they expected reciprocity from the friends they aided?

THE COLLEGE CLASSROOM: SOME OBSERVATIONS ON THE MEANINGS OF STUDENT PARTICIPATION

David A. Karp and William C. Yoels

A RECENT REPORT ON THE EMPLOYMENT OF SOCIOLOGISTS AND ANTHROPOLOGISTS IN-dicated that 97 percent of the sociologists in the United States were teaching either full-time or part-time in an institution of higher education (NIMH: 1969). While sociologists earn their "daily bread" by teaching, they earn their scholarly reputations by engaging in research studies of almost every conceivable kind of social setting except, it seems, that of the college class-room. The failure to explore the "routine grounds" of our everyday lives as teachers is testimony to the existence of the college classroom as part of what Alfred Schutz (1962) referred to as "the world as taken-for-granted."

.   .   .

Rarely have researchers attempted to consider the processes through which students and teachers formulate definitions of the classroom as a so-cial setting. The problem of how students and teachers assign "meaning" to the classroom situation has been largely neglected in the various studies mentioned. Although writing about primary and secondary school class-rooms, we would suggest that the following statement from Jackson's (1968:vii) *Life in Classrooms* holds true for college classrooms as well. He writes that:

> Classroom life . . . is too complex an affair to be viewed or talked about from any single perspective. Accordingly, as we try to grasp the meaning of what school is like for students and teachers, we must not hesitate to use all the ways of knowing at our disposal. This means we must read and look and listen and count things, and talk to people, and even muse introspectively.

The present study focuses on the meanings of student participation in the college classroom. Our examination of this problem will center on the way in which definitions of classrooms held by students and teachers relate to their actual behavior in the classroom.

METHODS OF STUDY

In an attempt to investigate the issues mentioned above we initiated an ex-ploratory study of classroom behavior in several classes of a private univer-

David A. Karp and William C. Yoels, "The College Classroom: Some Observations on the Meanings of Student Participation," *Sociology and Social Research*, 60, 421–439.

sity located in a large city in the northeastern United States. Our familiarity with the literature on the "words-deeds" problem (Deutscher, 1973; Phillips, 1971) led us to employ a two-fold process of data collection—namely, systematic observation of classroom behavior in selected classes, accompanied by questionnaires administered at the end of the semester in the classes under observation. None of the previously reviewed studies employed this type of research strategy, and it was hoped that such an approach would yield insights not attainable from reliance on a single data gathering procedure. In addition to the foregoing procedures we also drew upon our numerous years of experience as both students and teachers in college classrooms.

Ten classes were selected for observation. The observers were undergraduate and graduate sociology students who were doing the research as part of a Readings and Research arrangement. The classes were not randomly selected but were chosen in terms of observers' time schedules and the possibility of their observing behavior in the classrooms on a regular basis throughout the semester. The observed classes were located in the following departments: sociology, philosophy, English, psychology, economics, theology. While the classes are certainly not a representative sample of all classes taught in this university, questionnaire responses from an additional sample of students in classes selected at random at the end of the semester indicate a remarkable similarity to the questionnaire responses of the students in the ten classes under observation.[1]

At the end of the semester a questionnaire was distributed in class to the students in the ten classes which had been under prior observation. A shortened version of this questionnaire was also given to the teachers of these classes. Questionnaire items centered on factors deemed important in influencing students' decisions on whether to talk or not in class.[2]

FINDINGS

Table 1 presents a summary of selected observational items by class size. Classes with less than 40 students have a higher average number of interactions per session than those with more than 40 students. More important, however, is the fact that in both categories of class size the *average number* of students participating is almost identical. Moreover, a handful of students account for more than 50 percent of the total interactions in both under 40 and over 40 classes. In classes with less than 40 students, between 4 and 5 students account for 75 percent of the total interactions per session; in classes of more than 40 students, between 2 and 3 students account for 51 percent of the total interactions per session. From the limited data presented here it would appear that class size has relatively little effect on the average number of students participating in class. Such a finding is particularly interesting in view of the fact, as indicated in Table 5, that more than 65 percent of both male and female students indicated that the large size of the class was an important factor in why students would choose not to talk in class.

Data also indicate that students have a conception of classroom participation as being concentrated in the hands of a few students. Ninety-three percent of the males and 94 percent of the females strongly agreed or agreed with the item "In most of my classes there are a small number of students who do most of the talking." Such a conception is in congruence with the observations of actual classroom behavior noted in Table 1.

The students' conception that a handful of students do most of the talking is also coupled with annoyance on the part of many students at those who "talk too much." Responses to a questionnaire item indicated that 62 percent of the males and 61 percent of the females strongly agreed or agreed with the item "I sometimes find myself getting annoyed with students who talk too much in class."

Students also believe it possible to make a decision very early in the semester as to whether professors really want class discussion. Ninety-four percent of the males and 96 percent of the females strongly agreed or agreed with the item "students can tell pretty quickly whether a professor really wants discussion in his/her class."

Students were also asked whether the teacher's sex is likely to influence their participation in class. The overwhelming response of both male and female students to this question is that the professor's sex makes *no difference* in their likelihood of participating in class. Over 93 percent of the males and 91 percent of the female students answered "No Difference" to this question. In effect, then, both male and female students tend to define the classroom as a situation in which the sexual component of the professor's identity is completely irrelevant.

The contrast between what students say about the previous item and what they actually do in classroom is highlighted in Table 2. The data indicate a very clearcut relationship between the sex of the teacher and the likelihood of male or female participation in class. In male taught classes men account for 75.4 percent of the interactions, three times the percentage for women—24.6 percent. In female taught classes, men still account for more

Table 1. Summary Table by Class Size of Selected Observational Items(a)

CLASS SIZE	AVERAGE NUMBER OF INTERACTIONS PER CLASS	AVERAGE NUMBER OF STUDENTS PARTICIPATING	AVERAGE % OF STUDENTS PRESENT PARTICIPATING	AVERAGE NUMBER OF STUDENTS MAKING TWO OR MORE COMMENTS	% OF THOSE PRESENT MAKING TWO OR MORE COMMENTS	% OF TOTAL INTERACTIONS ACCOUNTED FOR BY THOSE MAKING TWO OR MORE COMMENTS
Under 40	25.96	9.83	47.84	4.64	25.06	75.61
40 +	19.40	9.88	23.98	2.70	5.74	51.00

(a)THE SMALLEST CLASS CONTAINED 12 STUDENTS; THE LARGEST CLASS CONTAINED 65 STUDENTS.

of the interactions than women—57.8 percent to 42.2 percent—but the percentage of female participation increases almost 75 percent from 24.7 percent in male taught classes to 42.2 percent in female taught classes. Female student participation is maximized under the influence of female professors.

Since the participation of men and women may be a function of their proportion in class, the right-hand side of Table 2 presents data on the composition of the male and female taught classes. In both male and female taught classes the percentage of male and female students is almost equal, therefore eliminating the possibility that the rate of male-female participation is a function of male student overrepresentation in these classes.

Table 3 presents observational data regarding what the students were responding to when they participated in classroom interactions. There was very little student-to-student interaction occurring in the ten classes under observation. Ten percent of the total number of classroom interactions involved cases in which students responded to the questions or comments of other students. Table 3 indicates quite dramatically that the actions of the teacher are indeed most crucial in promoting classroom interaction. Questions posed by the teacher and teacher comments accounted for 88 percent of the classroom interactions. Especially significant is the fact that very few cases occur in which the teacher directly calls on a particular student to answer a question (category labelled "Direct" under TQ). The percentage for the Direct Question category is 9.9 percent, compared to 46.3 percent for the Indirect Question in which the teacher poses a question to the class in general. Indeed, it might be argued that the current norm in college classrooms is for both students and teachers to avoid any type of direct *personal confrontation* with one another. It might be that "amicability" in the classroom is part of the larger process, described by Riesman (1950) in *The Lonely Crowd*, in which the desire to "get ahead" is subordinated to the desire to "get along." In the college classroom "getting along" means students and teachers avoiding any situation that might be potentially embarrassing to one or the other.

Table 2. Observed Classroom Interaction by Sex of Student and Sex of Teacher

SEX OF TEACHER	% OF OBSERVED INTERACTIONS				% OF STUDENTS IN CLASSES(a)			
	Male	*Female*	*Total*	*N*	*Male*	*Female*	*Total*	*N*
Male	75.4	24.6	100.0	565	52.0	48.0	100.0	152
Female	57.8	42.2	100.0	774	51.5	48.5	100.0	163
Total	65.3	34.7	100.0	1339	51.7	48.3	100.0	315

Note: $X^2 = 44.05$, df $= 1$, p $< .001$

(a)REFERS TO THE NUMBER OF STUDENTS ANSWERING THE QUESTIONNAIRE IN CLASS.

Table 3. Source of Interaction by Sex of Student

			SOURCE OF "STIMULUS"					
Sex of Student	Teacher Question Direct	Teacher Question Indirect	Teacher Comment	Student Question	Student Comment	Source Not Specified	Total	N
Male	10.0%	46.5%	31.9%	3.6%	6.3%	1.5%	99.8%	840
Female	9.8%	45.9%	31.3%	1.6%	8.9%	2.2%	99.7%	437
Total	9.9%	46.3%	31.7%	2.9%	7.2%	1.8%	99.8%	1,277(a)

(a)62 CASES WERE EXCLUDED BECAUSE OF INSUFFICIENT INFORMATION.

Table 4 indicates that in male-taught classes male students are more likely than female students to be directly questioned by the instructor (7.1 percent to 3.1 percent). In addition, men are twice as likely as female students (30.3 percent to 15.0 percent) to respond to a comment made by a male teacher. In female-taught classes the percentage of male and female responses are almost identical in each category under observation. Of interest here is the fact that female teachers are equally likely to directly question male and female students (12.8 percent versus 12.5 percent).

Table 5 presents the student responses to a series of items concerning why students would choose not to talk in class. The items are ranked in terms of the percentage of students who indicated that the particular item was important in keeping them from talking. As the rankings indicate, male and female students are virtually identical in their conceptions of what factors inhibit or promote their classroom participation. The items accorded the most importance—not doing the assigned reading, ignorance of the subject mat-

Table 4. Source of Interaction by Sex of Student, Controlling for Sex of Teacher

			SOURCE OF "STIMULUS"					
Sex of Student	Teacher Question Direct	Teacher Question Indirect	Teacher Comment	Student Question	Student Comment	Source Not Specified	Total	N
			Male-Taught Classes					
Male	7.1%	55.3%	30.3%	1.9%	2.6%	2.6%	99.8%	419
Female	3.1%	67.4%	15.0%	3.9%	3.9%	6.3%	99.6%	126
Total	6.2%	58.1%	26.7%	2.3%	2.9%	3.4%	99.6%	545
			Female-Taught Classes					
Male	12.8%	37.7%	33.4%	5.4%	9.9%	.4%	99.6%	421
Female	12.5%	37.2%	37.9%	.6%	10.9%	.6%	99.7%	311
Total	12.7%	37.5%	35.3%	3.4%	10.3%	.5%	99.7%	732

ter, etc.—are in the highest ranks. The lowest ranking items are those dealing with students and teachers not respecting the student's point of view, the
grade being negatively affected by classroom participation, etc.

In comparing the teachers' rankings of these same items with that of the
students, it appears that, with one important exception, the rankings are
very similar. About 42 percent of both male and female students ranked as
important the item concerning the possibility that other students would find
them unintelligent. Eighty percent of the teachers, on the other hand, indicated that this was likely an important factor in keeping students from talking.

**Table 5. Percentage of Students Who Indicated That an Item Was an
Important Factor in Why Students Would Choose Not to Talk in Class,
by Sex of Student (in Rank Order)**

| | MALE | | | FEMALE | |
Rank	Item	%	Rank	Item	%
1.	I had not done the assigned reading	80.9	1.	The feeling that I don't know enough about the subject matter	84.8
2.	The feeling that I don't know enough about the subject matter	79.6	2.	I had not done the assigned reading	76.3
3.	The large size of the class	70.4	3.	The feeling that my ideas are not well enough formulated	71.1
4.	The feeling that my ideas are not well enough formulated	69.8	4.	The large size of the class	68.9
5.	The course simply isn't meaningful to me	67.3	5.	The course simply isn't meaningful to me	65.1
6.	The chance that I would appear unintelligent in the eyes of the teacher	43.2	6.	The chance that I would appear unintelligent in the eyes of other students	45.4
7.	The chance that I would appear unintelligent in the eyes of other students	42.9	7.	The chance that I would appear unintelligent in the eyes of the teacher	41.4
8.	The small size of the class	31.0	8.	The small size of the class	33.6
9.	The possibility that my comments might negatively affect my grade	29.6	9.	The possibility that my comments might negatively affect my grade	24.3
10.	The possibility that other students in the class would not respect my point of view	16.7	10.	The possibility that the teacher would not respect my point of view	21.1
11.	The possibility that the teacher would not respect my point of view	12.3	11.	The possibility that other students in the class would not respect my point of view	12.5

Table 6. Percentage of Teachers Who Indicated That an Item Was an Important Factor in Why Students Would Choose Not to Talk in Class (in Rank Order)

RANK	ITEM	%
1.5	The large size of the class	80
1.5	The chance that I would appear unintelligent in the eyes of other students	80
4.0	The feeling that I don't know enough about the subject matter	70
4.0	The feeling that my ideas are not well enough formulated	70
4.0	The possibility that my comments might negatively affect my grade	70
6.0	The course simply isn't meaningful to me	50
7.5	I had not done the assigned reading	40
7.5	The chance that I would appear unintelligent in the eyes of the teacher	40
9.5	The possibility that the teacher would not respect my point of view	30
9.5	The possibility that other students in the class would not respect my point of view	30
11.0	The small size of the class	10

DISCUSSION

Although we did not begin this study with any explicit hypotheses to be tested, we did begin with some general guiding questions. Most comprehensive among these, and of necessary importance from a symbolic interactionist perspective, was the question, "What is a college classroom?" We wanted to know how both students and teachers were defining the social setting, and how these definitions manifested themselves in the activity that goes on in the college classrooms. More specifically, we wanted to understand what it was about the definition of the situation held by students and teachers that led to, in most instances, rather little classroom interaction.

What knowledge, we might now ask, do students have of college classrooms that makes the decision not to talk a "realistic" decision? There would seem to be two factors of considerable importance as indicated by our data.

First, students believe that they can tell very early in the semester whether or not a professor really wants class discussion. Students are also well aware that there exists in college classrooms a rather distinctive "consolidation of responsibility." In any classroom there seems almost inevitably to be a small group of students who can be counted on to respond to questions asked by the professor or to generally have comments on virtually any issue raised in class. Our observational data (Table 1) indicated that on the average a very small number of students are responsible for the majority of all talk that occurs in class on any given day. The fact that this "consolidation of responsibility" looms large in students' consciousness is indicated by the fact, reported earlier, that more than 90 percent of the students strongly agreed or agreed with the statement "In most of my classes there are a small number of students who do most of the talking."

Once the group of "talkers" gets established and identified in a college classroom the remaining students develop a strong expectation that these "talkers" can be relied upon to answer questions and make comments. In fact, we have often noticed in our own classes that when a question is asked or an issue raised the "silent" students will even begin to orient their bodies towards and look at this coterie of talkers with the expectation, presumably, that they will shortly be speaking.

Our concept of the "consolidation of responsibility" is a modification of the idea put forth by Latane and Darley (1970) in *The Unresponsive Bystander*. In this volume Latane and Darley developed the concept of "the diffusion of responsibility" to explain why strangers are often reluctant to "get involved" in activities where they assist other strangers who may need help. They argue that the delegation of responsibility in such situations is quite unclear and, as a result, responsibility tends to get assigned to no one in particular—the end result being that no assistance at all is forthcoming. In the case of the classroom interaction, however, we are dealing with a situation in which the responsibility for talking gets assigned to a few who can be relied upon to carry the "verbal load"—thus the *consolidation of responsibility*. As a result, the majority of students play a relatively passive role in the classroom and see themselves as recorders of the teacher's information. This expectation is mutually supported by the professor's reluctance to directly call on *specific* students, as indicated in Table 3.

While students expect that only a few students will do most of the talking, and while these talkers are relied upon to respond in class, the situation is a bit more complicated than we have indicated to this point. It would appear that while these talkers are "doing their job" by carrying the discussion for the class as a whole, there is still a strong feeling on the part of many students that they ought not to talk *too much*. As noted earlier, more than 60 percent of the students responding to our questionnaire expressed annoyance with students who "talk too much in class." This is interesting to the extent that even those who talk very regularly in class still account for a very small percentage of total class time. While we have no systematic data on time spent talking in class, the comments of the observers indicate that generally a total of less than five minutes of class time (in a fifty-minute period) is accounted for by student talk in class.

A fine balance must be maintained in college classes. Some students are expected to do most of the talking, thus relieving the remainder of the students from the burdens of having to talk in class. At the same time, these talkers must not be "rate-busters." We are suggesting here that students see "intellectual work" in much the same way that factory workers define "piecework." Talking too much in class, or what might be called "linguistic rate-busting," upsets the normative arrangement of the classroom and, in the students' eyes, increases the probability of raising the professor's expectations vis-à-vis the participation of other students. It may be said, then, that a type of "restriction of verbal output" norm operates in college classrooms, in which those who engage in linguistic rate-busting or exhibit "overinvolvement" in the classroom get defined by other students as "brown-noses" and "apostates" from the student "team." Other students often indicate their annoyance with these "rate-busters" by smiling wryly at their efforts, audibly sighing, rattling their notebooks and, on occasion, openly snickering.

A second factor that insures in students' minds that it will be safe to refrain from talking is their knowledge that only in rare instances will they be directly called upon by teachers in a college classroom. Our data (Table 3) indicate that of all the interaction occurring in the classes under observation only about 10 percent were due to teachers calling directly upon a specific student. The unwillingness of teachers to call upon students would seem to stem from teachers' beliefs that the classroom situation is fraught with anxiety for students. It is important to note that teachers, unlike students themselves, viewed the possibility that "students might appear unintelligent in the eyes of other students" as a very important factor in keeping students from talking (Table 6). Unwilling to exacerbate the sense of risk which teachers believe is a part of student consciousness, they refrain from directly calling upon specific students.

The direct result of these two factors is that students feel no obligation or particular necessity for keeping up with reading assignments so as to be able to participate in class. Such a choice is made easier still by the fact that college students are generally tested infrequently. Unlike high school, where homework is the teacher's "daily insurance" that students are prepared for classroom participation, college is a situation in which the student feels quite safe in coming to class without having done the assigned reading and, not having done it, safe in the secure knowledge that one won't be called upon.[3] It is understandable, then, why such items as "not having done the assigned reading" and "the feeling that one does not know enough about the subject matter" would rank so high (Table 5) in students' minds as factors keeping them from talking in class.

In sum, we have isolated two factors relative to the way that classrooms actually operate that make it "practically" possible for students not to talk in class. These factors make it possible for the student to pragmatically abide by an early decision to be silent in class. We must now broach the somewhat more complicated question: what are the elements of students' definitions of the college classroom situation that prompt them to be silent in class? To answer this question we must examine how students perceive the teacher as well as their conceptions of what constitutes "intellectual work."

By the time that students have finished high school they have been imbued with the enormously strong belief that teachers are "experts" who possess the "truth." They have adopted, as Freire (1970) has noted, a "banking" model of education. The teacher represents the bank, the huge "fund" of "true" knowledge. As a student it is one's job to make weekly "withdrawals" from the fund, never any "deposits." His teachers, one is led to believe, and often led to believe it by the teachers themselves, are possessors of the truth. Teachers are in the classroom to *teach*, not to *learn*.

If the above contains anything like a reasonable description of the way that students are socialized in secondary school, we should not find it strange or shocking that our students find our requests for criticism of ideas a bit alien. College students still cling to the idea that they are knowledge seekers and that faculty members are knowledge dispensers. Their view of intellectual work leaves little room for the notion that ideas themselves are open to negotiation. It is simply not part of their view of the classroom that ideas are generated out of dialogue, out of persons questioning and taking issue with one another, out of persons being *critical* of each other.

It comes as something of a shock to many of our students when we are willing to give them, at best, a "B" on a paper or exam that is "technically" proficient. When they inquire about their grade (and they do this rarely, believing strongly that our judgment is unquestionable), they want to know what they did "wrong." Intellectual work is for them dichotomous. It is either good or bad, correct or incorrect. They are genuinely surprised when we tell them that nothing is wrong, that they simply have not been critical enough and have not shown enough reflection on the ideas. Some even see such an evaluation as unfair. They claim a kind of incompetence at criticism. They often claim that it would be illegitimate for them to disagree with an author.

Students in class respond as uncritically to the thoughts of their professors as they do to the thoughts of those whom they read. Given this general attitude toward intellectual work, based in large part on students' socialization, and hence their definition of what should go on in classrooms, the notion of using the classroom as a place for generating ideas is a foreign one.

Part of students' conceptions of what they can and ought to do in classrooms is, then, a function of their understanding of how ideas are to be communicated. Students have expressed the idea that if they are to speak in class they ought to be able to articulate their point logically, systematically, and above all completely. The importance of this factor in keeping students from talking is borne out by the very high ranking given to the item (Table 5) "the feeling that my ideas are not well enough formulated."

In their view, if their ideas have not been fully formulated in advance, then the idea is not worth relating. They are simply unwilling to talk "off the top of their heads." They feel, particularly in an academic setting such as the college classroom, that there is a high premium placed on being articulate. This feeling is to a large degree prompted by the relative articulateness of the teacher. Students do not, it seems, take into account the fact that the teacher's coherent presentation is typically a function of the time spent preparing his/her ideas. The relative preparedness of the teacher leads to something of paradox vis-à-vis classroom discussion.

We have had students tell us that one of the reasons they find it difficult to respond in class involves the professor's preparedness; that is, students have told us that because the professor's ideas as presented in lectures are (in their view) so well formulated they could not add anything to those ideas. Herein lies something of a paradox. One might suggest that, to some degree at least, the better prepared a professor is for his/her class, the less likely are students to respond to the elements of his lecture.

We have both found that some of our liveliest classes have centered around those occasions when we have talked about research presently in progress. When it is clear to the student that we are ourselves struggling with a particular problem, that we cannot fully make sense of a phenomenon, the greater is the class participation. In most classroom instances, students read the teacher as the "expert,"[4] and once having cast the professor into that role it becomes extremely difficult for students to take issue with or amend his/her ideas.

It must also be noted that students' perceptions about their incapacity to be critical of their own and others' ideas leads to an important source of misunderstanding between college students and their teachers. In an open-ended question we asked students what characteristics they thought made for an "ideal" teacher. An impressionistic reading of these responses indicated that students were overwhelmingly uniform in their answers. They consensually found it important that a teacher "not put them down" and that a teacher "not flaunt his/her superior knowledge." In this regard the college classroom is a setting pregnant with possibilities for mutual misunderstanding. Teachers are working under one set of assumptions about "intellectual work" while students proceed under another. Our experiences as college teachers lead us to believe that teachers tend to value *critical* responses by students and tend to respond critically themselves to the comments and questions of college students. Students tend to perceive these critical comments as in some way an assault on their "selves" and find it difficult to separate a critique of their thoughts from a critique of themselves. Teachers are for the most part unaware of the way in which students interpret their comments.

The result is that when college teachers begin to critically question a student's statement, trying to get the student to be more critical and analytical about his/her assertions, this gets interpreted by students as a "put-down." The overall result is the beginning of a "vicious circle" of sorts. The more that teachers try to instill in students a critical attitude toward one's own ideas, the more students come to see faculty members as condescending, and the greater still becomes their reluctance to make known their "ill formulated" ideas in class. Like any other social situation where persons are defining the situation differently, there is bound to develop a host of interactional misunderstandings.

Before concluding this section, let us turn to a discussion of the differences in classroom participation rates of male versus female students. Given the fact that men and women students responded quite similarly to the *questionnaire items* reported here, much of our previous discussion holds for both male and female students. There are some important differences, however, in their *actual behavior* in the college classroom (as revealed by our observational data) that ought to be considered. Foremost among these differences is the fact that the sex of the teacher affects the likelihood of whether male or female teachers in these classes are "giving off expressions" that are being interpreted very differently by male and female students. Male students play a more active role in all observed classes regardless of the teacher's sex, but with female instructors the percentage of female participation sharply increases. Also of interest, as indicated in Table 4, is the fact that the male instructors are more likely to directly call on male students than on female students (7.1 percent to 3.1 percent), whereas female instructors are just as likely to call on female students as on male students (12.5 percent to 12.8 percent). Possibly female students in female-taught classes interpret the instructor's responses as being more egalitarian than those of male professors and thus more sympathetic to the views of female students. With the growing [awareness] of women faculty and students [of women's issues] it may not be unreasonable to assume that female instructors are more sensitive to the problem of female students both inside and outside the college classroom.

With the small percentage of women faculty currently teaching in American universities it may well be that the college classroom is still defined by both male and female students as a setting "naturally" dominated by men. The presence of female professors, however, as our limited data suggest, may bring about some changes in these definitions of "natural" classroom behavior.

IMPLICATIONS

For the reasons suggested in the last few pages, it may be argued that most students opt for noninvolvement in their college classroom. This being the case, and because organizational features of the college classroom allow for noninvolvement (the consolidation of responsibility, the unwillingness of professors to directly call on specific students, the infrequency of testing), the situation allows for a low commitment on the part of students. The college classroom, then, rather than being a situation where persons must be deeply involved, more closely approximates a situation of "anonymity" where persons' obligations are few.

We can now perceive more clearly the source of the dilemma for college instructors who wish to have extensive classroom dialogues with students. To use the terminology generated by Goffman (1963) in *Behavior in Public Places*, we can suggest that instructors are treating the classroom as an instance of "focused" interaction while students define the classroom more as an "unfocused" gathering. Focused gatherings are those where persons come into one another's audial and visual presence and see it as their obligation to interact. These are to be distinguished from unfocused gatherings where persons are also in a face-to-face situation but either feel that they are not privileged to interact or have no obligation to do so.[5]

It may very well be that students more correctly "read" how professors interpret the situation than vice versa.[6] Knowing that the teacher expects involvement, and having made the decision not to be deeply involved, students reach a compromise. Aware that it would be an impropriety to be on a total "away" from the social situation, students engage in what might be called "civil *attention.*" They must *appear* committed enough to not alienate the teacher without at the same time showing so much involvement that the situation becomes risky for them. Students must carefully create a show of interest while maintaining non-involvement. A show of too great interest might find them more deeply committed to the encounter than they wish to be.

So, students are willing to attend class regularly, and they do not hold private conversations while the teacher is talking; they nod their heads intermittently, and maintain enough attention to laugh at the appropriate junctures during a lecture, and so on. Students have become very adept at maintaining the social situation without becoming too involved in it. Teachers interpret these "shows" of attention as indicative of a real involvement (the students' performances have proved highly successful) and are, therefore, at a loss to explain why their involvement is not even greater—why they don't talk very much in class.

NOTES

1. Some relevant demographic characteristics of the students in the ten classes under observation are as follows: sex: males—52 percent, females—48 percent; year in college: freshmen and sophomores—60 percent, juniors and seniors—40 percent; father's occupation: proprietor—7 percent, management or executive—21 percent, professional—34 percent, clerical and sales—15 percent, skilled worker—16 percent, unskilled worker—7 percent; religious affiliation: Catholic—79 percent, Protestant—7 percent, Other—14 percent. In comparing the students in the observed classes to those students in unobserved classes which were selected at random at the end of the semester, the following differences should be noted: the observed classes contain more women (48 percent) than the unobserved classes (33 percent); there were twice as many freshmen in the observed classes (31 percent) than in the unobserved classes (14 percent); there were twice as many students whose fathers were in clerical and sales occupations in the observed classes (15 percent) than in the unobserved classes (8 percent).

The questionnaire responses of the students in the unobserved classes are not reported here since these were selected only to check on the representativeness of the students in the original ten classes under observation.

2. Spatial limitations preclude a full treatment of the methodology and findings. More complete details are available from the authors.

3. We have no "hard" data concerning student failure to do the assigned reading other than our own observations of countless instances where we posed questions

that went unanswered, when the slightest familiarity with the material would have been sufficient to answer them. We have also employed "pop" quizzes and the student performance on these tests indicated a woefully inadequate acquaintance with the readings assigned for that session. The reader may evaluate our claim by reflecting upon his/her own experience in the college classroom.

4. This attribution of power and authority to the teacher may be particularly exaggerated in the present study due to its setting in a Catholic university with a large number of students entering from Catholic high schools. Whether college students with different religious and socioeconomic characteristics attribute similar degrees of power and authority to professors is a subject worthy of future comparative empirical investigation.

5. If we think of communication patterns in college classrooms as ranging along a continuum from open-discussion formats to lecture arrangements, the classes studied here all fall toward the traditional lecture end of the continuum. Thus, generalizations to other formats, such as the open discussion ones, may not be warranted by the present data.

6. Of interest here is the recent study by Thomas *et al.* (1972) in which support was found for the "theoretical proposition that role-taking ability varies inversely with the degree of power ascribed to social positions" (1972:612).

REFERENCES

Deutscher, I.
  1973 *What We Say/What We Do*. Glenview, Ill.: Scott, Foresman and Company.

Freire, P.
  1970 *Pedagogy of the Oppressed*. New York: Seabury Press.

Goffman, E.
  1963 *Behavior in Public Places*. New York: Free Press.

Jackson, P.
  1968 *Life in Classrooms*. New York: Holt, Rinehart and Winston.

Latane, B. and J. Darley
  1970 *The Unresponsive Bystander: Why Doesn't He Help?* New York: Appleton-Century-Crofts.

National Institute of Mental Health
  1969 *Sociologists and Anthropologists: Supply and Demand in Educational Institutions and Other Settings*. Chevy Chase, Md: U.S. Government Printing Office.

Phillips, D.
  1971 *Knowledge From What?* Chicago: Rand McNally and Co.

Riesman, D.
  1950 *The Lonely Crowd*. New Haven: Yale University Press.

Schutz, A.
  1962 *Collected Papers: I. The Problem of Social Reality*. Edited by Maurice Natanson, The Hague: Martinus Nijhoff.

Thomas, D.L., D. D. Franks, and J.M. Calonico
1972 "Role-Taking and Power in Social Psychology," *American Sociological Review* 37: 605–614.

Review Questions

1. What is the "banking" model of education? What factors cause students to adopt this model? What are some sociological consequences of the model?

2. Summarize Karp and Yoels' findings regarding the number of students who participate in class and the frequency of participation. What factors affected the rate of participation and what factors didn't?

3. What differences exist in the expectations of students and teachers for their own role and for the reciprocal role?

4. What were students' attitudes toward those who participated in class? Why is it ironic that these attitudes were held? Incorporate the concept of "consolidation of responsibility" in your answer.

5. How did teachers and students differ in terms of why they thought students didn't participate in class?

WOMEN AND THE STRUCTURE OF ORGANIZATIONS

Rosabeth Moss Kanter

THIS IS AN "ORGANIZATIONAL" SOCIETY. THE LIVES OF VERY FEW OF US ARE UNTOUCHED by the growth and power of large, complex organizations in the twentieth century. The consequences of decisions made in these organizations, particularly business enterprises, may affect the availability of goods and services, the distribution of wealth and privilege, and the opportunity for meaningful work. The distribution of functions within organizations affects the quality of daily life for a large proportion of working Americans: their opportunities for growth and self-expression, for good or poor health, as well as their daily social contacts. The distribution of power within organizations affects who benefits, and to what degree, from the things organizations make possible, and whose interests are served by the organization's decisions. Despite a prevalent image in social science of modern organizations as universalistic, sex-neutral tools, sex is a very important determinant of who gets what in and out of organizations.

The ways in which women have been connected to organizations and have operated within them, and whether these ways differ from those of men, have been underinvestigated in social research. While there is a relatively large and growing literature that documents the degree to which women are socialized to perform different kinds of activities from men (often activities with less power and monetary reward), there has been less attention paid to the patterned relationships between women and men in organizations.

This chapter is an attempt to define directions for an enlarged understanding of the sociology of organizations as it concerns women, and of the study of women as it contributes to a more comprehensive and accurate sociology of organizations. The focus throughout is solely on the United States and largely on the administrative levels of business organizations. In part, this was an attempt to place limits on an area with a vast amount of literature. But it is also because the administrative issues of business tended to provide the impetus for the early sociology of organizations. Business organizations, additionally, have great power in American society and, because they are successful, are assumed to be successfully managed, so that

Rosabeth Moss Kanter, "Women and the Structure of Organizations," in Marcia Millman and Rosabeth Moss Kanter, eds., *Another Voice: Feminist Perspectives on Social Life and Social Service*. New York: Doubleday, 1975, pp. 34–74.

their organization and management has often served as a model for other systems. It is also in business organizations that women seem most conspicuously absent from positions of prestige and power.

MANAGEMENT: A MALE CATEGORY

Women generally do not hold positions of power and authority in organizations, especially in American industry. Those few women in management tend to be concentrated in lower-paying positions, in selected fields, in staff rather than line positions, and in less powerful, less prestigious organizations. In 1969 U.S. Census figures indicate that women constituted only 3.25 per cent of the managers and administrators earning over $15,000 per year (before taxes), and 2.26 per cent of those earning over $30,000 per year. Women themselves may make the choice not to compete for managerial positions. Educated women, for example, tend not to enter fields that are linked to, and are preparation for, management. A substantially higher proportion of female college graduates than male become "professional, technical, and kindred" workers rather than managers and administrators, for instance (77.4 per cent as opposed to 58.9 per cent—Bureau of the Census, 1973a). Women with doctorates generally do not take them in management-related fields, as figures on earned doctorates in the United States between 1960 and 1969 indicate.[1] At least a portion of the evidence that women earn less than men can be accounted for by the fact that women hold jobs carrying less pay even in well-paid fields like management. Bureau of Labor Statistics figures indicate that in 1970 the median annual earnings of female managers and administrators (excluding farm administration) were around half of that for men, even in fields such as school administration and wholesale/retail trade, where female administrators are clustered. A recent national personnel survey of 163 U.S. companies discovered that the farther up the management ladder, even scarcer are the women. In over half of the companies, women held only 2 per cent or less of the first-level supervisory jobs (including such positions as manager of secretaries); in *three quarters* of the companies, women held 2 per cent or fewer of the middle-management jobs; and in *over three quarters* of the companies, they held *none* of the top-management jobs (*Personnel Policies Forum*, 1971).

The few management women are also clustered in particular kinds of organizations. The *Personnel Policies Forum* survey found that women were proportionately more represented in management in nonbusiness rather than in business organizations, and, within business, in nonmanufacturing rather than in manufacturing enterprises. A 1965 *Harvard Business Review* survey of 1,000 male and 900 female executives (the men were drawn from the *HBR* readership, but there were so few women among top executives that separate lists had to be used to locate them) found women disproportionately represented in the management of retail/wholesale trade (merchandising fields) and advertising, whereas men were disproportionately represented in the management of banking/investment/insurance companies (financial concerns) and industrial goods manufacturing (Bowman, Worthy, and Greyser, 1965). (Calculations based on 1969 U.S. Census figures confirm the clustering of women managers in retail trade and services, including stenographic services, and men in manufacturing.[2]) The *HBR* respondents, further, felt that opportunities for women in management lie only in: education, the arts, social services, retail trade, office management, personnel work, and nonmanagement positions. One third of the respondents felt, as of 1965, that there were *no* opportunities for women in the management of labor unions; construction, mining, and oil companies; industrial goods manufacturing; production; and top management in general (Bowman, Worthy, and Greyser, 1965). The *HBR* survey is also suggestive of the concentration of women in staff positions, where they tend not to have authority over subordinates, or in low-status areas. Women in the *HBR* study were heavily represented in marketing and office management (39 per cent and 10 per cent of the female respondents, respectively, as opposed to 16 per cent and 3 per cent of the males, respectively) and underrepresented in general management (10 per cent of the women, compared with 40 per cent of the men falling into this category). Similarly, the women were disproportionately found in small (and hence less powerful or statusful) organizations.

These data suggest that women are virtually absent from the management of large industrial enterprises and present to only a slightly greater degree in the management of retail or business-support service organizations. Even in areas in which the workers are likely to be female, their managers are likely to be male. The number of male and of female bank tellers in the United States in 1969 was nearly equal, for example (255,549 men and 220,255 women), but "bank officers and financial managers" were largely male (82.48 per cent male and 17.52 per cent female). Office workers are largely female, yet office *managers*, a relatively low-status management position, are still more likely to be male than female (59.64 per cent male, 40.36 per cent female (calculations based on figures of Bureau of the Census, 1973a).

We need to know the barriers to women in organizational leadership and also what difference their presence makes: how culture and behavior are shaped by the sex distribution of managers. The behavior and experiences of the few women in management and leadership positions should be considered as a function of membership in male-dominated settings. (Some of the findings of the few studies done to date are reported later.) The politics and informal networks of management as influenced by its male membership should be further studied—e.g., the degree to which managerial as well as worker behavior and culture is shaped in part by the traditions, emotions, and sentiments of male groups.[3] How the culture and behavior of management is affected by (or reflected in) the sex ratio of managers is also important (e.g., how retail or service organizations differ from manufacturers), as well as the influence of the sex composition of management on its relations with other organizational strata.

OFFICE WORK: FEMALE FUNCTION

Women are to clerical labor as men are to management. According to Census Bureau data, there were over 10 million female "clerical and kindred workers" in the United States in 1969, 73.78 per cent of the total employed workers in this category. Men in the clerical labor force tend to be concentrated in a few, physically oriented occupations where they far outnumber women (computer operators, messengers, mail carriers, shipping and receiving clerks, and stock clerks). The rest of the occupations, the core of office work, are heavily female. Women comprised 82.14 per cent of the bookkeepers, 81.84 per cent of the billing clerks, 68.96 per cent of the payroll and timekeeping clerks, and 82.08 per cent of the file clerks. In secretarial and related functions, men are as underrepresented as women are in management. Women comprised 93.46 per cent of the stenographers in 1969, 94.18 per cent of the typists, 94.65 per cent of the receptionists, and 97.71 per cent of the secretaries. In fact, these four positions account for nearly 40 per cent of the 1969 female "clerical and kindred workers"; secretaries alone account for 25 per cent of the 1969 female clerical labor force (calculations based on Bureau of the Census, 1973a). Labor Bureau statistics for 1970, calculated on a slightly different basis, show even fewer men in such positions: of the category "stenographers, typists, and secretaries," 98.6 per cent are female and only 1.40 per cent are male (Bureau of Labor Statistics, 1971). *Work in America* (1972), a task force report to HEW, has concluded that the job of secretary is symbolic of the status of female employment, both qualitatively and quantitatively. Office jobs for women have low status, little autonomy or opportunity for growth, and generally low pay.

Women did not always dominate the clerical labor force; office work in the nineteenth century was first a male job. The same turn-of-the-century period (1890–1910) that brought large organizations and the growth of the professional manager also witnessed the emergence of the modern office, with its invention of new roles for women. The three-person office of mid-nineteenth-century Dickens novels was socially reorganized into departments and functional areas headed by office managers, and this change—itself a product of bureaucraticization and machine technology—permitted the massive introduction of office machines. Though invented in the 1870s, the typewriter was not widely used until the twentieth century; but from 1900–20, office employment rose dramatically, and typing soon became women's work (Mills, 1951:192–93).

The rise in the employment of women in the office around the turn of the century was dramatic, and it corresponded to a large decrease in "household occupations" (servants, dressmakers and seamstresses outside of factories, and laundresses). In 1870 the "clerical group" (clerks, stenographers, typists, bookkeepers, cashiers, and accountants) accounted for less than 1 per cent of the women employed outside of agriculture; by 1920 it accounted for over 25 per cent of female nonagricultural employment (Hill, 1929:39). In 1880 the proportion of women in the clerical labor force as a whole was 4 per cent; in 1890, 21 per cent (Davies, 1974). By 1910, women were already 83.2 per cent of the stenographers and typists; by 1920, they were 91.8 per cent of the stenographers/typists and 48.8 per cent of the bookkeepers, cashiers, and accountants (Hill, 1929:56–57). Between 1910 and 1920 the number of female clerks (excluding store clerks) quadrupled; female stenographers and typists more than doubled (Hill, 1929:33). Slightly more women were still employed in factory than in clerical jobs in 1920 (about 1.8 million and 1.5 million, respectively), but less than 1 per cent of those in industry could be classified as managers, superintendents, or officials (calculations based on Hill, 1929: Table 115). The growth of modern administration brought women into domination in the office but absent in management. Whereas factory jobs were divided between men and women (though often sex-typed), clerical jobs rapidly became the work almost exclusively of women. . . .

The secretary may be a prototypical and pivotal role to examine; research should consider the place of this job in the clerical hierarchy, its relations to management, and whether its role demands bar women from moving into management positions. Even though private secretaries represent only a small proportion of the female clerical labor force, this position is sometimes the highest to which a women office worker may aspire—the best-paid, most prestigious, and for secretaries of executives, one with "reflected power" derived from the status of the manager. It is also the job in which there are the most clearly defined male-female relations—the private secretary has been called an "office wife" (Mills, 1951; Bernard, 1971).[4] My field work in a large New York-based corporation indicates that the traditional secretary-manager relationship has striking parallels to Weber's definition of "patrimonial rule" (Bendix, 1960:425), even though this relationship occurs within organizations that social scientists have assumed generally fit Weber's "bureaucratic" model. The relationship can be defined as "patrimonial" to the extent that managers make demands at their own discretion and arbitrarily recruit secretaries on the basis of appearance, personality, and other subjective factors rather than on skill, expect personal service, exact loyalty, and make secretaries part of their private retinue (e.g., expecting them to move when they move). Further, secretaries in many large organizations may derive their status from that of their boss, regardless of the work they do; a promotion for a secretary may mean moving on to a higher-status manager, whether or not her work changes or improves.[5] There may be no job descriptions, as there are for managerial positions, that help match the person's skills to the job or insure some uniformity of demands across jobs, so that there are often no safeguards to exploitation, no standards for promotion other than personal relationships, and no way of determining if a secretary can be moved to another job (all barriers to mobility out of the secretarial ranks for women).[6] The relation of the secretarial work force to management may be one of status in addition to function; e.g., secretaries may be chosen for the status they give their bosses in having educated, attractive secretaries, whether or not their skills are utilized, and acquisition of a secretary may be a status symbol in its own right in many organizations, signifying a manager's importance.[7]

. . .

The "sex typing" of occupations and professions is relatively well known—the fact that many occupations are nearly exclusively filled by members of one sex and come to have a "gender," to be described in sex-role-appropriate terms. But to fully describe the position and behavior of women (and men) in organizations, we must understand not only their typical occupations (e.g., manager and secretary) but how these are *related* to one another and to the larger context of the organization as a social structure. Occupations carry with them membership in particular organizational classes. Each class may have its own internal hierarchy, political groupings and allegiances, interactional rules, ways of coming into contact with other classes, promotion rules, culture, and style, including demeanor and dress.[8] In many organizations, managers and clerical workers, for example, constitute two separate organizational classes, with separate hierarchies, rules, and reward structures, and practically no mobility between them. The managerial elite has the power and a group interest in retaining it. The position of clerical workers, on the other hand, is often anomalous: in contact with the organizational elite, dependent on, and in service to it, thus facilitating identification with it, but similar to other workers in subordination, lack of autonomy, and subjugation to routine (Crozier, 1965).

The economic concept of an "internal labor market" (Doeringer and Piore, 1971) is applicable here. When women enter an organization, they are placed not only in jobs but in an opportunity structure. Internal allocation of personnel is governed by hiring, promotion, and layoff rules within each structure, as well as by "suitability," as defined by the customs of each separate workplace. And ability in one workplace is not always transferable to others; what leads to success in one may even be dysfunctional for mobility into another. The rules of the internal labor market, Doeringer and Piore theorize, may vary from rigid and internally focused to highly responsive to external economic forces; rules also vary among organizational strata. They argue, for example, that there is a tendency for managerial markets, in contrast with other internal labor markets, to span more than one part of a company, to carry an implicit employment guarantee, and to reward ability rather than seniority (1971:3). But women participate in a different labor market than men, even within the same organization. Their "typical jobs" in the office carry with them not only sex-role demands but also placement in a class and hierarchy that itself limits mobility into positions of power.

The issue, thus, is not a mere division of labor between women and men but a difference of organizational class, at least on the administrative levels of modern organizations. Simplistically, women are part of a class rewarded for routine service, while men compose a class rewarded for decision-making rationality and visible leadership, and this potential membership affects even those found outside their own sexual class. This phenomenon constitutes the structural backdrop for an understanding of the organizational behavior of women and men.

Even though it is largely ignored in the organizational behavior literature, sex can be seen to be an important variable affecting the lives of groups, given the significant differences in the positions and power of women and men in society and in organizations. The sexual composition of a group appears to have impact on behavior around issues of power and leadership, aspirations, peer relations, and the relative involvement/visibility or isolation/invisibility of members.

SEX AND ORGANIZATIONAL BEHAVIOR: FEMALE AND MALE SINGLE-SEXED GROUPS

Does a group of women behave differently from a group of men? The situations in which women and men find themselves are often so different that common-sense observation indicates a difference in both themes and process. Organizational research, on the other hand, has generally treated all groups of participants or workers alike, for the most part not distinguishing sex as a variable, and therefore implicitly assuming that gender does not make a difference in organizational behavior—reinforcing the mistaken idea that modern organizational life is universalistic* and sex-neutral. Yet, even in the classic study that first discovered the importance of small, primary groups in worker behavior and opened the study of human relations in organizations, the sex of the groups studied varied and may have contributed to the different sets of specific findings. The experiments at the Hawthorne plant of Western Electric in the late 1920s and early 1930s developed the concept of informal organization by indicating how important a role the small group might play in worker productivity (cf. Roethlisberger and Dickson, 1939). These researches have been examined and re-examined for all possible explanations of the findings, including, recently, operant conditioning (Parsons, 1974); sex composition is, to my knowledge, not mentioned among them. Three small groups were studied. In two sets of conditions, the Relay Assembly Test Room and the Mica Splitting Test

*That is, based on ability and talent rather than on ascribed characteristics such as gender or class origin.

Room, workers encouraged each other in raising productivity and believed that their efforts would be rewarded. In the third, the Bank Wiring Observation Room, workers developed an informal system that discouraged "rate busting" and kept productivity at an even keel, partly out of a mistrust in management—the belief that increased productivity would result in higher expectations, not higher rewards. There were differences among the three sets of conditions in size of group (fourteen in the third, vs. five or six in the first and second, depending on how the team is counted), nature of the task (a large number of units processed by individuals in the first two conditions, a small number of units in the third), experimental manipulations (like rest pauses), and "laboratory" vs. "natural" working conditions. But another striking difference is sex. The first two sets of groups, cooperative and trusting of management, were all-female. The third, counterdependent, aggressively controlling, and suspicious, was all-male.

There is also evidence, if we reinterpret other studies not explicitly focused on sex, that women in female groups may be more oriented toward immediate relationships than men in male groups. Several studies of male professionals in organizations found a correlation between professionalism and a "cosmopolitan" rather than a local orientation. The exception was a study of nurses by Warren Bennis and colleagues. In this *female* group, the more professional oriented nurses "did not differ from others in their loyalty to the hospital, and they were *more* apt than others, not less, to express loyalty to the local work group" (Blau and Scott, 1962:69). While Blau and Scott conclude that this is due to the limited visibility of the nurses' professional competence, other evidence indicates that this finding is consistent with a sex-linked interpretation. Constantini and Craik (1972) found, for example, that women politicians in California were oriented intraparty and locally rather than toward higher office, as men were.

Other evidence confirms that women in organizations, especially in the clerical class, limit their ambitions, prefer local and immediate relationships, and orient themselves to satisfying peer relationships. In a study of values of 120 occupational groups, secretaries, the only female group studied, were unique in placing their highest priorities on such values as security, love, happiness, and responsibility (Sikula, 1973). Female game-playing strategy in several laboratory studies was accommodative, including rather than excluding, and oriented toward others rather than toward winning, whereas the male strategy was exploitative and success-oriented (Vinacke, 1959; Uesugi and Vinacke, 1963). All-female group themes (in a comparison of single-sex and mixed laboratory groups) included affiliation, family, and conflicts about competition and leadership, self, and relationships, in contrast to the male themes: competition, aggression, violence, victimization, practical joking, questions of identity, and fear of self-disclosure (Aries, 1973). An earlier study compared all-male with all-female groups and found *no* significant differences in nine different conditions *ex-*

cept persuasibility (higher in female groups) and level of aspiration (higher in male groups) (Cattell and Lawson, 1962).

In additudinal studies distinguishing factors motivating increased performance as opposed to those merely preventing dissatisfaction ("hygiene" factors), attitudes toward interpersonal relations with peers constituted the only variable differentiating men and women. (The women in two studies included those in both high-level and low-level jobs.) For women, peer relationships were a motivational factor, whereas for men they were merely a hygiene factor (Davis, 1967:35–36). Structural factors can explain this. My field research in progress on a large New York-based corporation indicates that peer relations affect a woman's decision not to seek promotion into managerial ranks, where she will no longer be part of a group of women; for men, of course, peer relations are a given throughout managerial ranks, and therefore, perhaps, more easily "taken for granted."

Other differences in male and female behavior in single-sex settings fail to be consistently demonstrated, as the Cattell and Lawson (1962) research, above, indicates. (See also Mann, 1959.) In studies of sex differences in the "risky shift," for example (the tendency for groups to make riskier decisions than individuals), there were *no* significant differences between male and female college students in initial conservatism or in the shift to risky decisions in the single-sex groups (Wallach, Kogan, and Bem, 1968). Organizational comparisons are rare, but Crozier's data on forty groups of French office workers revealed no difference in an atmosphere between male and female work groups; both kinds of groups showed the same wide range (1965:111).

Thus it is reasonable to hypothesize that groups of women differ from groups of men primarily in orientations toward interpersonal relationships and level of aspiration. One might interpret this as consistent with the training of women for family roles and thus label it a sex-linked attribute. But such orientations could also be seen as *realistic responses* to women's structural situation in organizations, of the kinds of opportunities and their limits, of the role demands in the organizational strata occupied by women, and of the dependence of women on relationships for mobility.

MIXED-SEX GROUPS

When men and women are together, in roughly equal numbers, as peers, tensions may emerge, and the behavior of each sex may be influenced. In Aries' laboratory study, people in two cross-sex groups were more tense, serious, self-conscious, and concerned with heterosexual attractiveness than those in the same-sex groups. Women generally spoke less than men (Aries, 1973). The sexual questions and "cross-cultural" issues that can arise in mixed-sex groups are useful explanations for their tensions; William Foote Whyte has hypothesized, extrapolating from studies of the ethnic composition of groups, that "other things being equal, a one-sex work group is likely to be more cohesive" than a mixed-sex group (1961:511). Crozier's Parisian study found male-female conflicts when men and women worked in the same office (1965:110).

In addition to sexual and cultural issues, there are also *status* and *power issues* when men and women interact, a function of the structural positions and organizational class memberships of the sexes. Much social psychological research has indicated the importance of power and status in determining behavior in groups: e.g., those low in power tend to engage in more approval seeking, while those high in power engage in more influence attempts; those in low-status positions tend to communicate upward in a hierarchy, a form of "substitute locomotion" or "vicarious mobility." The differential behavior of the more and less powerful coincides with the observed group behavior of men and women. A field experiment tested more specifically the effects of high and low power on group relations, using thirty-two six-person groups at a one-day professional conference. Participants were labeled high-power or low-power on the basis of the prestige of their occupations, assumed to correlate with ability to influence. While the authors do not report the sex distribution of participants, it is likely from occupational sex-typing that men were found more often in the high-power category (psychiatrists, psychologists) and women in the low-power category (nurses, social workers, teachers). The researchers found that "highs" were liked more than "lows"; "highs" liked "lows" less than they liked other "highs"; "highs" talked more often than "lows"; "lows" communicated more frequently to "highs" than to other "lows"; and the amount of participation by "lows" was consistently overrated, as though people felt the "lows" talked too much (Hurwitz, Zander, and Hymovitch, 1968).

The interpretation is straightforward. In mixed groups of "peers," men and women may not, in fact, be equal, especially if their external statuses and organizational class memberships are discrepant. The resulting behavior, including frequency of participation, leadership, and conformity, may reflect status and power differences more than sex-linked personality traits.

THE EFFECTS OF SKEWED SEX RATIOS: THE LONE WOMAN IN THE MALE GROUP

The dynamic of interaction in settings with highly skewed sex ratios—numerical dominance by members of one sex and a "lone" or nearly alone member of the other sex—also deserves attention; in management and some professions, women are often one of very few women in a group of men. This makes "sex status" as important for interaction as occupational status (Epstein, 1970:152).

Skewed sex ratios lend themselves, first, to cases of "mistaken identity"— to incorrect attributions. Lone women in male settings are sometimes initially misperceived as a result of their statistical rarity. The men with whom they come into contact may make a judgment about what a woman is doing in that particular situation, based on reasoning about the probabilities of various explanations, and may act toward her accordingly. This can be called "statistical discrimination" (Council of Economic Advisers, 1973:106), to distinguish it from prejudice; that is, an unusual woman may be treated as though she resembles women on the average. This may be the case every time someone assumes a female manager answering the telephone or sitting in an office is a secretary (cf. examples in Lynch, 1973; Epstein, 1970:191). Given the current occupational distribution, that person is likely to be correct a high proportion of the time. But the woman in question may still feel unfairly treated, as indeed she is, and there may be awkward exchanges while the woman's true identity is established.[9]

Attributions may also be made about the lone woman's expected informal role. These attributions put the woman in her place without challenging the male culture of the group. Field observations of lone women in male-dominated groups (including business meetings, academic conferences, sales training programs, and postprofessional training groups) have distinguished four kinds of roles attributed to lone women in male groups: "mother"; "sex object" or "seductress"; "pet" (group mascot); and "iron maiden" (militant and unapproachable) (Kanter, 1975). Such attributed roles affect both what the men in the group expect of the woman and how they interpret what she does. For her, the pressure is to confine her behavior to the limits of the role, whether or not it expresses her competence. Indeed, the roles provide a measure of security and uncertainty-reduction for some women, while others may devote time to struggling against the implications of the attributions. In either case, a woman's behavior in a situation like this is less likely to reflect her competencies, and it may take her longer to establish them than at other times, when she is not a statistical rarity.

Several hypotheses are suggested. When a person is a statistical rarity, it may take her/him *more time* to untangle mistaken identities and establish a competence-based working relationship, particularly with members of the numerically dominant category. This may, in turn, generate a preference for minimizing change in work relations with peers, superiors/subordinates, or clients. As Epstein argues, "status discrepancies make continuous role definition necessary during interactions that should be routine" (1970:194). Margaret Cussler's sample of female executives in the 1950s suggests that this hypothesis may have some validity, for the women apparently changed work situations much less often than would be expected of male counterparts. Thus there may be a longer time-span for the establishment of competence-based relationships and a conservatism about changing relationships among "lone" women in male-dominated organizations.

Isolation and invisibility, self- as well as group-imposed, are often consequences of status as a lone woman in an otherwise all-male collectivity. In one study, six small training groups with only one woman each in a group of eight to twelve men were observed: three sensitivity training groups for business school students, and three work groups of psychiatric residents. In each case, the woman was eventually isolated, failed to become a leader or ally herself with the emergent leaders, and was defined by the researchers as a "casualty" of the groups. The researchers felt that the six groups' productivity tended to be low, in part because of the problematic interactions around the solo woman (Wolman and Frank, 1975). While the results of this study should not be taken as definitive,[10] they do suggest directions for further inquiry.

The female executives studied by Margaret Hennig (1970) support the isolation hypothesis. They reported that their most difficult relationships were with male peers when they (the women) were in the early to middle career. The women had little contact or relationship with the men, tried to be unobtrusive or invisible, and practiced strategies of conflict avoidance, as did lone professional women in Cynthia Epstein's research (1970:176). Epstein also suggests that team membership may be harder for the lone woman among male professional peers than for a man, pointing to institutionalized isolation (such as barriers to membership in male clubs or associations) as well as interactional isolation. As a consequence, she proposes that women have been less likely to be successful in fields that require participation on a team of peers as opposed to individual activity (1970:175).

Lone women may reinforce their own isolation by a series of accommodative strategies. The limiting of visibility ("taking a low profile") is one such accommodation to and reinforcement of isolation. Hennig's respondents reported early career strategies of trying to minimize their sexual attributes so as to blend unnoticeably into the predominant male culture:

> You dressed carefully and quietly to avoid attracting attention; you had to remember to swear once in a while, to know a few dirty jokes, and never to cry if you got attacked. You fended off all attempts of men to treat you like a woman; you opened doors before they could hold them, sat down before a chair could be held, and threw on a coat before it could be held for you [Hennig, 1970:vi–21].

In other reports, lone women managers have also participated in the limiting of the visibility of their competence by not taking credit for accomplishments or letting someone else take the credit (Lynch, 1973; Cussler, 1958). Some women, in interviews, even expressed pride that they could influence a group of men without the men recognizing the origin of the idea, or they rejoiced in the secret knowledge that they were responsible for their boss's success. (These reports match the Megaree finding reported below that high-dominance women may let a man assume official leadership while strongly influencing the decision.) Epstein (1970) points out that, in general, on elite levels women have less-visible jobs than men, promote themselves less often, feel the need to make fewer mistakes, and try to be unobtrusive.

With another context in mind, Seymour Sarason (1973) has argued that members of minority groups who have succeeded may try to limit the visibility of that success in fear of reprisals from the majority-dominant group, which might not be aware of the minority's success and might take action against it if known. He has reported a prevalent feeling among Jews that statistics about the high percentage of Jews in elite colleges such as Yale, for example, should not be broadcast. A concern like this, rather than a female sex-linked characteristic, could account for the woman manager's acceptance of the invisibility of her achievements. In the case of lone women, the pressure to adopt this stance must be even greater because of attributes like modesty assigned to the female stereotype.

This analysis suggests a re-examination of the "fear of success" in women hypothesis. Perhaps what has been called fear of success is really fear of visibility. In the original research by Matina Horner (1968) that identified this concept, women responded to a hypothetical situation in which a woman was at the top of her class in medical school—presumably a lone woman in a male peer group. Such a situation is the kind that creates pressure for a woman to make herself and her achievements invisible. When similar research was conducted using settings in which a woman is not a statistical rarity, "fear of success" imagery was greatly reduced (Tresemer, 1973).

WOMEN AND LEADERSHIP

If it's hard to demonstrate competence as a woman among men, it may be even harder to exercise leadership, given the current sex-stratification patterns in organizations. It is still an open question whether there are major sex differences in leadership *style* (Crozier, 1956:126, finds none); but the structural and interactional context is certainly different for women. Taking directives from a woman has been anathema to most men and some women. In a 1965 *Harvard Business Review* survey of 1,000 male and 900 female executives, over two thirds of the men and nearly one fifth of the women reported that they themselves would not feel comfortable working for a woman. Very few of either sex (9 per cent of the men and 15 per cent of the women) felt that *men* feel comfortable working for a woman; and a proportion of the male respondents said that women did not belong in executive positions. A total of 51 per cent of the men responded that women were "temperamentally unfit" for management, writing comments such as, "They scare male executives half to death. . . . As for an efficient woman manager, this is cultural blasphemy. . . ." (Bowman, Worthy, and Greyser, 1965.)

Male resentment of taking orders from a woman influenced the work flow and the interaction between waitresses and countermen in the restaurants studied by William Foote Whyte during World War II, a classic of organizational analysis. There were several devices in one restaurant by which countermen could avoid direct contact with waitresses (and hence direct orders) or could make their own decisions about the order in which to prepare food and drinks, thus taking initiative and forcing the waitresses to wait. Orders were written on slips and placed on a spindle, and a warming compartment imposed a high barrier between the waitresses and the countermen, thus eliminating face-to-face interaction. In a restaurant without these equalizing devices, satisfaction was low, and there was constant wrangling. Whyte's explanation is simple: People of higher status (men) like to do the directing for people of lower status (women) and resent reversals (1961:128).

Even if women have formal authority, then, they may not necessarily be able to exercise it over reluctant subordinates. Margaret Cussler's (1958) study of female executives provides several examples of this. In one case a woman had formal leadership of a group of men, but the men did not accept this, reporting informally to her male superior. The subordinates further met together at lunch to share information, excluding her. More formal meetings then developed, "conceived of by the woman as meetings of her staff, by the men as a mutual protection society for the interchange of ideas" (1958:76–77).

At the same time, women tend to assume visible leadership reluctantly, in keeping with the invisibility of the lone woman mentioned earlier. A creative laboratory study discovered that for women the situational context rather than a dominant personality tended to predict a woman's exercise of visible leadership. Same-sex and cross-sex dyads were paired by scores on a "dominance" measure and given a task in which one member had to lead and one to follow. Assumption of leadership by high-dominance women paired with a low-dominance man was significantly lower than in any other pairing. The greatest assumption of leadership by high-dominance subjects occurred when a high-dominance man was paired with a low-dominance woman; the high- and low-dominance single-sex pairings showed about the same intermediate distribution of leadership. However, in the situation in which a high-dominance woman was paired with a low-dominance man, the *woman* made the final decision of who was to be the leader more often than in any other group, 91 per cent of the time *appointing the man*. The study suggests that men are not necessarily more "dominant" in character than women, but women are more reluctant to assume leadership, particularly when the subordinate is male (Megaree, 1969). The leadership strategies chosen by successful women executives in Hennig's research (1970) tend to confirm this kind of laboratory finding. The women tended to minimize the authoritative exercise of power and maximize subordinate autonomy and learning through delegation.

But a leader's style may be ultimately less important for the impact on his or her subordinates than another resource unequally distributed between the sexes: power outside of the immediate work group. Early theory in organizational behavior assumed a direct relation between leader behavior and group satisfaction and morale. However, Donald Pelz discovered in the early 1950s that perceived external power was an intervening variable. He compared high- and low-morale work groups to test the hypothesis that the supervisor in high-morale groups would be better at communicating, more supportive, and more likely to recommend promotion. Yet, when he analyzed the data, the association seemed to be nonexistent or even reversed. In some cases supervisors who frequently recommended people for promotion and offered sincere praise for a job well done had *lower* morale scores. The differentiating variable was whether or not the leader had power outside and upward: influence on his or her own superiors and how decisions were made in the department. The combination of good human relations *and* power was associated with high morale. Human-relations skills and low power (a likely combination for women leaders) sometimes had negative consequences (Pelz, 1952).

The implications for female leadership in organizations are significant. A woman's generally more limited power (partly a function of her rarity and isolation in management), as well as her similarity to a subordinate clerical class rather than the elite, may interfere with her effective exercise of leadership *regardless* of her own style and competence. This hypothesis also helps explain the greater resistance to working for a woman. It also may account for the evidence of the importance of a male sponsor in the success of women executives (Cussler, 1958; Hennig, 1970). A high-status man bringing the woman up behind him may provide the visible sign that the woman does have influence upward. While sponsors serve multiple functions (e.g., coaching and socialization in the informal routines) and are found in the careers of men, the "reflected power" they provide may be even more pivotal for women.

CONCLUSION: WOMEN AND THE INFRASTRUCTURE OF ORGANIZATIONS

Women's places in organizations have largely had limited visibility and low status; they have been part of the unexamined infrastructure. When men and women interact in organizations, they often do it across barriers like that of social class; women's mobility has largely been restricted to the infrastructure. In this the women within organizations have a kinship with the "women's auxiliary" outside of it—the network of wives of managers and leaders that perform unpaid tasks, play unofficial but normatively expected roles for the organization, and whose behavior can potentially affect relations in the official organization (Kanter, 1974). Just as managers have a group of women behind them in the office, they do at home, for male managers are largely married to women not employed in the paid labor force.[11]

I have suggested a few of the issues surrounding the sexual structure of organizations and groups that deserve further attention—from the problems of token women to the nature of internal labor markets for managers or secretaries. The sexual division of broad administrative classes was solidified very early in the history of large corporations. But the nature of organizational life for these broad groupings and other occupational subgroups, and how their opportunities and interactions vary in different kinds of organizations (e.g., those with fewer barriers to leadership for women), still require investigation. . . .

NOTES

I wish to thank the following people for their critical comments and support: Nancy Chodorow, Susan Eckstein, Joan Huber, Barry Stein, Chris Argyris, Zick Rubin, William Form, William Torbert, Caroline Butterfield, and Joanna Hiss.

1. Data are from HEW, via a University of Minnesota publication, reprinted by the Women's Equity Action League, Washington, D.C., in 1974. M.D.'s and other professional doctorates are not included. Women earned 11.63 per cent of the doctorates reported, but only 2.82 per cent of the doctorates in business and commerce (a total of 86 women in 10 years), 5 per cent of those in hospital administration (1 woman out of 20 doctorates), and none of those in trade or industrial training. Women earned 11.10 per cent of all the social science doctorates but only 4.17 per cent of those in industrial relations and 8.13 per cent of those in public administration.

2. Of the managers and administrators earning over $15,000 per year, 26.1 per cent of the women vs. 17.2 per cent of the men are in retail trade, 25.8 per cent of the women vs. 8.5 per cent of the men are in "professional and related services," and 12.2 per cent of the women vs. 26.7 per cent of the men are in manufacturing. Women represent 9.3 per cent of the total managers in services but only 1.52 per cent of the total in manufacturing. Calculations from Census Bureau (1973b).

3. Several popularized accounts treat management as an expression of the instincts of male hunting bands and make management, indeed, seem charged with masculine culture and traditions. See Tiger (1969) and Jay (1967, 1971).

4. A New York corporation informant, a former executive secretary promoted into management, told me that leaving her boss was like getting a divorce. For the first four months of her new job, she stopped in to see him every morning and hung her coat in her old office.

5. A manager of clerical employees told me that sometimes promotions mean that secretaries have *less* work to do and have trouble justifying their larger salaries to their peers. As with marriage, if a woman has the good fortune to be connected with a high-status male, she gets more money and does less work.

6. The large corporation in my research, beginning to design "upward mobility" programs for women, has discovered secretarial work to be arbitrary and particularistic. The change effort includes generating job descriptions and decoupling a secretary's status from her boss's so that she will no longer derive rank from him or necessarily move with him when he moves.

7. A chatty advice-to-managers book (Burger, 1964) devotes a chapter to "living with your secretary," with whom, the book declares, a man spends more of his waking hours than with his wife. She is a status symbol: "In many companies, a secretary outside your door is the most visible sign that you have become an executive; a secretary is automatically assigned to each executive, whether or not his work load requires one. . . . When you reach vice-presidential level, your secretary may have an office of her own, with her name on the door. At the top, the president may have

two secretaries. . . . 'Miss Amy, please take a letter,' are words which have inwardly thrilled every young executive with a sense of his own importance . . . they symbolize power and status" (Burger, 1964:219, 220).

8. In a discussion of labor women, Patricia Cayo Sexton defines dress and hair style as well as personal appearance as a barrier to upward mobility, since the styles of labor women are very different from those of more elite women (1974:392–93). Informants in a corporation told me that there was a "caste" barrier between secretaries and professional women visible in style differences: e.g., secretaries wore platform shoes while professional women wore pumps.

9. Sometimes the categorical attributions have extreme and negative implications: e.g., a female manager having a drink with her boss and assumed by a neighbor to be his mistress (Lynch, 1973:136). In another example, a woman executive was the only female present at an executive cocktail party at a New York hotel, when a drunk male guest entered, accosted her, and tried to tear her clothes off, assuming she was a call girl (Lynch, 1973: 137).

10. Aside from *post hoc* reasoning, one of the researchers, a woman, was also a group leader in some of the groups and does not discuss the impact of her own presence as another woman in a *powerful* position.

11. A total of 93.19 per cent of the male managers earning $15,000 or more in 1969 were married; 72.25 per cent of their wives were not in the paid labor force (Bureau of Census, 1973b).

REFERENCES

Bendix, Reinhard.
    1960. *Max Weber: An Intellectual Portrait.* Garden City, New York: Anchor Books, 1962.

Blau, Peter M., and Scott, W. Richard.
    1962. *Formal Organizations.* San Francisco: Chandler.

Bowman, G.W.; Worthy, N.B.; and Greyser, S.A.
    1965. "Are Women Executives People?," *Harvard Business Review* 43 July–August: 14–30.

Bureau of the Census, U.S.
    1973a. *Occupational Characteristics.* Washington, D.C.: U.S. Government Printing Office.
    1973b. *Occupations of Persons with Higher Earnings.*

Bureau of Labor Statistics, U.S.
    1971. *Handbook of Labor Statistics.* Washington, D.C.: U.S. Department of Labor.

Burger, Chester.
    1964. *Survival in the Executive Jungle.* New York: Macmillan.

Cattell, Raymond B., and Lawson, Edwin D.
    1962. "Sex Differences in Small Group Performance," *The Journal of Social Psychology* 58:141–45.

Constantini, Edmond, and Craik, Kenneth H.
    1972. "Women as Politicians: The Social Background, Personality, and Political
    Careers of Female Party Leaders," *Journal of Social Issues* 28:217–36.

Council of Economic Advisers.
    1973. *Annual Report of the Council of Economic Advisers*. Washington, D.C.:
    U.S. Government Printing Office.

Crozier, Michel.
    1965. *The World of the Office Worker*, trans. David Landau. Chicago: Univer-
    sity of Chicago Press, 1971.

Cussler, Margaret.
    1958. *The Woman Executive*. New York: Harcourt, Brace.

Davies, Margery.
    1974. "Woman's Place Is at the Typewriter: The Feminization of the Clerical
    Labor Force," Waltham, Mass.: Brandeis University Department of Soci-
    ology.

Davis, Keith.
    1967. *Human Relations at Work*. New York: McGraw-Hill.

Doeringer, Peter B., and Piore, Michael J.
    1971. *Internal Labor Markets and Manpower Analysis*. Lexington, Mass.: D.C.
    Heath.

Epstein, Cynthia Fuchs.
    1970. *Woman's Place: Options and Limits on Professional Careers*. Berkeley:
    University of California Press.

Hennig, Margaret.
    1970. "Career Development for Women Executives," unpublished doctoral dis-
    sertation. Cambridge, Mass.: Harvard University Graduate School of Busi-
    ness Administration.

Hill, Joseph A.
    1929. *Women in Gainful Occupations, 1870–1920*. Census Monographs IX.
    Washington, D.C.: U.S. Government Printing Office. New York: Johnson
    Reprint Corporation, 1972.

Horner, Matina.
    1968. "Sex Differences in Achievement Motivation and Performance in Competi-
    tive and Non-Competitive Situations," unpublished doctoral dissertation.
    Ann Arbor, Mich.: University of Michigan.

Hurwitz, Jacob I.; Zander, Alvin F.; and Hymovitch, Bernard.
    1968. "Some Effects of Power on the Relations Among Group Members," *Group
    Dynamics*, ed. D. Cartwright and A. Zander. New York: Harper & Row,
    pp. 291–97.

Jay, Anthony.
    1967. *Management and Machiavelli: An Inquiry into the Politics of Corporate
    Life*. New York: Holt, Rinehart & Winston.
    1971. *Corporation Man*. New York: Random House.

Kanter, Rosabeth Moss.
   1974. "The Auxiliary Organization." Waltham, Mass.: Brandeis University Department of Sociology.
   1975. "Women in Organizations: Sex Roles, Group Dynamics, and Change Strategies," *Beyond Sex Roles,* ed. A. Sargent. St. Paul, Minn.: West Publishing.

Lynch, Edith M.
   1973. *The Executive Suite: Feminine Style.* New York: AMACOM.

Megaree, Edwin I.
   1969. "Influence of Sex Roles on the Manifestation of Leadership," *Journal of Applied Psychology* 53: 377–82.

Mills, C. Wright.
   1951. *White Collar: The American Middle Classes.* New York: Oxford University Press.

Parsons, H. M.
   1974. "What Happened at Hawthorne?," *Science* 183 March: 922–32.

Pelz, Donald C.
   1952. "Influence: A Key to Effective Leadership in the First-line Supervisor," *Personnel* 29: 3–11.

Report of a Special Task Force to the Secretary of Health, Education, and Welfare.
   1972. *Work in America.* Cambridge, Mass.: MIT Press.

Roethlisberger, F. J., and Dickson, William J.
   1939. *Management and the Worker.* Cambridge, Mass.: Harvard University Press.

Sarason, Seymour B.
   1973. "Jewishness, Blackishness, and the Nature-Nurture Controversy," *American Psychologist* 28 November: 962–71.

Sexton, Patricia Cayo.
   1974. "Workers (Female) Arise!," *Dissent* Summer: 380–95.

Sikula, Andrew F.
   1973. "The Uniqueness of Secretaries as Employees," *Journal of Business Education* 48 Fall: 203–5.

Tiger, Lionel.
   1969. *Men in Groups.* New York: Random House.

Tresemer, David.
   1973. "Fear of Success: Popular but Unproven," *Psychology Today* 7 November.

Uesugi, Thomas K., and Vinacke, W. Edgar.
   1963. "Strategy in a Feminine Game," *Sociometry* 26:35–88.

Vinacke, W. Edgar.
   1959. "Sex Roles in a Three-person Game," *Sociometry* 22 December: 343–60.

Wallach, Michael A.; Kogan, Nathan; and Bem, Daryl J.
1968. "Group Influence on Individual Risk-taking," *Group Dynamics*, ed. D. Cartwright and A. Zander. New York: Harper & Row, pp. 430-43.

Wolman, Carol, and Frank, Harold.
1975. "The Solo Woman in a Professional Peer Group," *American Journal of Orthopsychiatry* 45: February.

Review Questions

1. Discuss *adult sex-role socialization* of women as it is carried out within the corporations described by Kanter.

2. Discuss the differences between the behavior of men and women in mixed-sex work groups.

3. Describe the difficulties and obstacles women may encounter when exercising leadership in the corporations studied by Kanter.

4. Kanter argues that the "lone" woman in a business organization may play down her own competence. Does Kanter feel that this is the result of personality traits or of the development of realistic coping strategies? Explain your answer.

URBANISM AS A WAY OF LIFE

Louis Wirth

For SOCIOLOGICAL PURPOSES A CITY MAY BE DEFINED AS A RELATIVELY *LARGE, DENSE,* and permanent settlement of socially *heterogeneous* individuals. On the basis of the postulates which this minimal definition suggests, a theory of urbanism may be formulated in the light of existing knowledge concerning social groups.

. . .

A THEORY OF URBANISM

In the pages that follow we shall seek to set forth a limited number of identifying characteristics of the city. Given these characteristics we shall then indicate what consequences or further characteristics follow from them in the light of general sociological theory and empirical research. We hope in this manner to arrive at the essential propositions comprising a theory of urbanism. Some of these propositions can be supported by a considerable body of already available research materials; others may be accepted as hypotheses for which a certain amount of presumptive evidence exists, but for which more ample and exact verification would be required. At least such a procedure will, it is hoped, show what in the way of systematic knowledge of the city we now have and what are the crucial and fruitful hypotheses for future research.

The central problem of the sociologist of the city is to discover the forms of social action and organization that typically emerge in relatively permanent, compact settlements of large numbers of heterogeneous individuals. We must also infer that urbanism will resume its most characteristic and extreme form in the measure in which the conditions with which it is congruent are present. Thus the larger, the more densely populated, and the more heterogeneous a community, the more accentuated the characteristics associated with urbanism will be. It should be recognized, however, that in the social world institutions and practices may be accepted and continued for reasons other than those that originally brought them into existence, and

Louis Wirth, "Urbanism as a Way of Life," *American Journal of Sociology,* vol. 44 (July 1938), pp. 1–24.

that accordingly the urban mode of life may be perpetuated under conditions quite foreign to those necessary for its origin.

Some justification may be in order for the choice of the principal terms comprising our definition of the city. The attempt has been made to make it as inclusive and at the same time as denotative as possible without loading it with unnecessary assumptions. To say that large numbers are necessary to constitute a city means, of course, large numbers in relation to a restricted area or high density of settlement. There are, nevertheless, good reasons for treating large numbers and density as separate factors, since each may be connected with significantly different social consequences. Similarly the need for adding heterogeneity to numbers of population as a necessary and distinct criterion of urbanism might be questioned, since we should expect the range of differences to increase with numbers. In defense, it may be said that the city shows a kind and degree of heterogeneity of population which cannot be wholly accounted for by the law of large numbers or adequately represented by means of a normal distribution curve. Since the population of the city does not reproduce itself, it must recruit its migrants from other cities, the countryside, and—in this country until recently—from other countries. The city has thus historically been the melting-pot of races, peoples, and cultures, and a most favorable breeding-ground of new biological and cultural hybrids. It has not only tolerated but rewarded individual differences. It has brought together people from the ends of the earth *because* they are different and thus useful to one another, rather than because they are homogeneous and like-minded.[1]

There are a number of sociological propositions concerning the relationship between (*a*) numbers of population, (*b*) density of settlement, (*c*) heterogeneity of inhabitants and group life, which can be formulated on the basis of observation and research.

Size of the Population Aggregate

Ever since Aristotle's *Politics*,[2] it has been recognized that increasing the number of inhabitants in a settlement beyond a certain limit will affect the relationships between them and the character of the city. Large numbers involve, as has been pointed out, a greater range of individual variation. Furthermore, the greater the number of individuals participating in a process of interaction, the greater is the *potential* differentiation between them. The personal traits, the occupations, the cultural life, and the ideas of the members of an urban community may, therefore, be expected to range between more widely separated poles than those of rural inhabitants.

That such variations should give rise to the spatial segregation of individuals according to color, ethnic heritage, economic and social status, tastes and preferences, may readily be inferred. The bonds of kinship, of neighborliness, and the sentiments arising out of living together for generations under a common folk tradition are likely to be absent or, at best, relatively weak in an aggregate the members of which have such diverse origins and backgrounds. Under such circumstances competition and formal control mechanisms furnish the substitutes for the bonds of solidarity that are relied upon to hold a folk society together.

Increase in the number of inhabitants of a community beyond a few hundred is bound to limit the possibility of each member of the community knowing all the others personally. Max Weber, in recognizing the social significance of this fact, pointed out that from a sociological point of view large numbers of inhabitants and density of settlement mean that the personal mutual acquaintanceship between the inhabitants which ordinarily inheres in a neighborhood is lacking.[3] The increase in numbers thus involves a changed character of the social relationships. As Simmel points out:

> [If] the unceasing external contact of numbers of persons in the city should be met by the same number of inner reactions as in the small town, in which one knows almost every person he meets and to each of whom he has a positive relationship, one would be completely atomized internally and would fall into an unthinkable mental condition.[4]

The multiplication of persons in a state of interaction under conditions which make their contact as full personalities impossible produces that segmentalization of human relationships which has sometimes been seized upon by students of the mental life of the cities as an explanation for the "schizoid" character of urban personality. This is not to say that the urban inhabitants have fewer acquaintances than rural inhabitants, for the reverse may actually be true; it means rather that in relation to the number of people whom they see and with whom they rub elbows in the course of daily life, they know a smaller proportion, and of these they have less intensive knowledge.

Characteristically, urbanites meet one another in highly segmental roles. They are, to be sure, dependent upon more people for the satisfactions of their life-needs than are rural people and thus are associated with a greater number of organized groups, but they are less dependent upon particular persons, and their dependence upon others is confined to a highly fractionalized aspect of the other's round of activity. This is essentially what is meant by saying that the city is characterized by secondary rather than primary contacts. The contacts of the city may indeed be face to face, but they are nevertheless impersonal, superficial, transitory, and segmental. The reserve, the indifference, and the blasé outlook which urbanites manifest in their relationships may thus be regarded as devices for immunizing themselves against the personal claims and expectations of others.

The superficiality, the anonymity, and the transitory character of urban-social relations make intelligible, also, the sophistication and the rationality generally ascribed to city-dwellers. Our acquaintances tend to stand in a relationship of utility to us in the sense that the role which each one plays in our life is overwhelmingly regarded as a means for the achievement of our own ends. Whereas, therefore, the individual gains, on the one hand, a certain degree of emancipation or freedom from the personal and emotional controls of intimate groups, he loses, on the other hand, the spontaneous self-expression, the morale, and the sense of participation that comes with living in an integrated society. This constitutes essentially the state of *anomie* or the social void to which Durkheim alludes in attempting to account for the various forms of social disorganization in technological society.

The segmental character and utilitarian accent of interpersonal relations in the city find their institutional expression in the proliferation of specialized tasks which we see in their most developed form in the professions. The operations of the pecuniary nexus* leads to predatory relationships, which tend to obstruct the efficient functioning of the social order unless checked by professional codes and occupational etiquette. The premium put upon utility and efficiency suggests the adaptability of the corporate device for the organization of enterprises in which individuals can engage only in groups. The advantage that the corporation has over the individual entrepreneur and the partnership in the urban-industrial world derives not only from the possibility it affords of centralizing the resources of thousands of individuals or from the legal privilege of limited liability and perpetual succession, but from the fact that the corporation has no soul.

The specialization of individuals, particularly in their occupations, can proceed only, as Adam Smith pointed out, upon the basis of an enlarged market, which in turn accentuates the division of labor. This enlarged market is only in part supplied by the city's hinterland; in large measure it is found among the large numbers that the city itself contains. The dominance of the city over the surrounding hinterland becomes explicable in terms of the division of labor which urban life occasions and promotes. The extreme degree of interdependence and the unstable equilibrium of urban life are closely associated with the division of labor and the specialization of occupations. This interdependence and instability is increased by the tendency of each city to specialize in those functions in which it has the greatest advantage.

In a community composed of a larger number of individuals than can know one another intimately and can be assembled in one spot, it becomes necessary to communicate through indirect mediums and to articulate individual interests by a process of delegation. Typically in the city, interests are made effective through representation. The individual counts for little, but the voice of the representative is heard with a deference roughly proportional to the numbers for whom he speaks.

While this characterization of urbanism, in so far as it derives from large numbers, does not by any means exhaust the sociological inferences that

*Or monetary linkage.

might be drawn from our knowledge of the relationship of the size of a group to the characteristic behavior of the members, for the sake of brevity the assertions made may serve to exemplify the sort of propositions that might be developed.

Density

As in the case of numbers, so in the case of concentration in limited space, certain consequences of relevance in sociological analysis of the city emerge. Of these only a few can be indicated.

As Darwin pointed out for flora and fauna and as Durkheim[5] noted in the case of human societies, an increase in numbers when area is held constant (i.e., an increase in density) tends to produce differentiation and specialization, since only in this way can the area support increased numbers. Density thus reinforces the effect of numbers in diversifying men and their activities and in increasing the complexity of the social structure.

On the subjective side, as Simmel has suggested, the close physical contact of numerous individuals necessarily produces a shift in the mediums through which we orient ourselves to the urban milieu, especially to our fellow-men. Typically, our physical contacts are close but our social contacts are distant. The urban world puts a premium on visual recognition. We see the uniform which denotes the role of the functionaries and are oblivious to the personal eccentricities that are hidden behind the uniform. We tend to acquire and develop a sensitivity to a world of artefacts and become progressively farther removed from the world of nature.

We are exposed to glaring contrasts between splendor and squalor, between riches and poverty, intelligence and ignorance, order and chaos. The competition for space is great, so that each area generally tends to be put to the use which yields the greatest economic return. Place of work tends to become dissociated from place of residence, for the proximity of industrial and commercial establishments makes an area both economically and socially undesirable for residential purposes.

Density, land values, rentals, accessibility, healthfulness, prestige, aesthetic consideration, absence of nuisances such as noise, smoke, and dirt determine the desirability of various areas of the city as places of settlement for different sections of the population. Place and nature of work, income, racial and ethnic characteristics, social status, custom, habit, taste, preference, and prejudice are among the significant factors in accordance with which the urban population is selected and distributed into more or less distinct settlements. Diverse population elements inhabiting a compact settlement thus tend to become segregated from one another in the degree in which their requirements and modes of life are incompatible with one another and in the measure in which they are antagonistic to one another. Similarly, persons of homogeneous status and needs unwittingly drift into, consciously select, or are forced by circumstances into, the same area. The different parts of the city thus acquire specialized functions. The city consequently tends to resemble a mosaic of social worlds in which the transition from one to the other is abrupt. The juxtaposition of divergent personalities and modes of life tends to produce a relativistic perspective and a sense of toleration of differences which may be regarded as prerequisites for rationality and which lead toward the secularization of life.[6]

The close living together and working together of individuals who have no sentimental and emotional ties foster a spirit of competition, aggrandizement, and mutual exploitation. To counteract irresponsibility and potential disorder, formal controls tend to be resorted to. Without rigid adherence to predictable routines a large compact society would scarcely be able to maintain itself. The clock and the traffic signal are symbolic of the basis of our social order in the urban world. Frequent close physical contact, coupled with great social distance, accentuates the reserve of unattached individuals toward one another and, unless compensated for by other opportunities for response, gives rise to loneliness. The necessary frequent movement of great numbers of individuals in a congested habitat gives occasion to friction and irritation. Nervous tensions which derive from such personal frustrations are accentuated by the rapid tempo and the complicated technology under which life in dense areas must be lived.

Heterogeneity

The social interaction among such a variety of personality types in the urban milieu tends to break down the rigidity of caste lines and to complicate the class structure, and thus induces a more ramified and differentiated framework of social stratification than is found in more integrated societies. The heightened mobility of the individual, which brings him within the range of stimulation by a great number of diverse individuals and subjects him to fluctuating status in the differentiated social groups that compose the social structure of the city, tends toward the acceptance of instability and insecurity in the world at large as a norm. This fact helps to account, too, for the sophistication and cosmopolitanism of the urbanite. No single group has the undivided allegiance of the individual. The groups with which he is affiliated do not lend themselves readily to a simple hierarchical arrangement. By virtue of his different interests arising out of different aspects of social life, the individual acquires membership in widely divergent groups, each of which functions only with reference to a single segment of his personality. Nor do these groups easily permit of a concentric arrangement so that the narrower ones fall within the circumference of the more inclusive ones, as is more likely to be the case in the rural community or in primitive societies. Rather the groups with which the person typically is affiliated are tangential to each other or intersect in highly variable fashion.

Partly as a result of the physical footlooseness of the population and partly as a result of their social mobility, the turnover in group membership generally is rapid. Place of residence, place and character of employment, income and interests fluctuate, and the task of holding organizations together and maintaining and promoting intimate and lasting acquaintanceship between the members is difficult. This applies strikingly to the local areas within the city into which persons become segregated more by virtue of differences in race, language, income, and social status, than through choice or positive attraction to people like themselves. Overwhelmingly the city-dweller is not a home-owner, and since a transitory habitat does not generate binding traditions and sentiments, only rarely is he truly a neighbor. There is little opportunity for the individual to obtain a conception of the city as a whole or to survey his place in the total scheme. Consequently he finds it difficult to determine what is to his own "best interests" and to decide between the issues and leaders presented to him by the agencies of mass suggestion. Individuals who are thus detached from the organized bodies which integrate society comprise the fluid masses that make collective behavior in the urban community so unpredictable and hence so problematical.

Although the city, through the recruitment of variant types to perform its diverse tasks and the accentuation of their uniqueness through competition and the premium upon eccentricity, novelty, efficient performance, and inventiveness, produces a highly differentiated population, it also exercises a leveling influence. Wherever large numbers of differently constituted individuals congregate, the process of depersonalization also enters. This leveling tendency inheres in part in the economic basis of the city. The development of large cities, at least in the modern age, was largely dependent upon the concentrative force of steam. The rise of the factory made possible mass production for an impersonal market. The fullest exploitation of the possibilities of the division of labor and mass production, however, is possible only with standardization of processes and products. A money economy goes hand in hand with such a system of production. Progressively as cities have developed upon a background of this system of production, the pecuniary nexus which implies the purchasability of services and things has displaced personal relations as the basis of association. Individuality under these circumstances must be replaced by categories. When large numbers have to make common use of facilities and institutions, an arrangement must be made to adjust the facilities and institutions to the needs of the average person rather than to those of particular individuals. The services of the public utilities, of the recreational, educational, and cultural institutions must be adjusted to mass requirements. Similarly, the cultural institutions, such as the schools, the movies, the radio, and the newspapers, by virtue of their mass clientele, must necessarily operate as leveling influences. The political process as it appears in urban life could not be understood without taking account of the mass appeals made through modern propaganda techniques. If the individual would participate at all in the social, political, and economic life of the city, he must subordinate some of his individuality to the demands of the larger community and in that measure immerse himself in mass movements. . . .

NOTES

1. The justification for including the term "permanent" in the definition may appear necessary. Our failure to give an extensive justification for this qualifying mark of the urban rests on the obvious fact that unless human settlements take a fairly permanent root in a locality the characteristics of urban life cannot arise, and conversely the living together of large numbers of heterogeneous individuals under dense conditions is not possible without the development of a more or less technological structure.

2. See esp. vii. 4. 4–14. Translated by B. Jowett, from which the following may be quoted:

> To the size of states there is a limit, as there is to other things, plants, animals, implements; for none of these retain their natural power when they are too large or too small, but they either wholly lose their nature, or are spoiled. . . . [A] state when composed of too few is not as a state ought to be, self-sufficing; when of too many, though self-sufficing in all mere necessaries, it is a nation and not a state, being almost incapable of constitutional government. For who can be the general of such a vast multitude, or who the herald, unless he have the voice of a Stentor?
>
> A state then only begins to exist when it has attained a population sufficient for a good life in the political community: it may indeed somewhat exceed this number. But, as I was saying, there must be a limit. What should be the limit will be easily ascertained by experience. For both governors and governed have duties to perform; the special functions of a governor are to command and to judge. But if the citizens of a state are to judge and to distribute offices according to merit, then they must know each other's characters; where they do not possess this knowledge, both the election to offices and the decision of lawsuits will go wrong. When the population is very large they are manifestly settled at haphazard, which clearly ought not to be. Besides, in an overpopulous state foreigners and metics will readily acquire the rights of citizens, for who will find them out? Clearly, then, the best limit of the population of a state is the largest number which suffices for the purposes of life, and can be taken in at a single view. Enough concerning the size of a city.

3. *Op. cit.*, p. 514.

4. Georg Simmel, "Die Grossstädte und das Geistesleben," *Die Grossstadt*, ed. Theodor Petermann (Dresden, 1903), pp. 187–206.

5. E. Durkheim, *De la division du travail social* (Paris, 1932), p. 248.

6. The extent to which the segregation of the population into distinct ecological and cultural areas and the resulting social attitude of tolerance, rationality, and secular mentality are functions of density as distinguished from heterogeneity is difficult to determine. Most likely we are dealing here with phenomena which are consequences of the simultaneous operation of both factors.

Review Questions

1. When Wirth wrote about urbanism in the 1930's, he had in mind a comparison with the agricultural societies of the 1800's and before. What are the characteristics of areas with *small* population size, *low* density, and *little* heterogeneity?

2. What effects does population size have on human interaction, according to Wirth? Density? Heterogeneity?

3. Many Americans feel that urban life has predominantly negative consequences for individuals. What are the *benefits* of urban life that Wirth discusses?

4. Wirth claims that heterogeneity of the population is actually encouraged and rewarded in urban areas. How does this come about? What are some of the consequences of heterogeneity for everyday interactions?

DEMOGRAPHIC FACTORS AND SOCIAL ORGANIZATION

John R. Weeks

CRIME AND THE AGE STRUCTURE

THE NUMBER OF VIOLENT CRIMES COMMITTED BY 16-YEAR-OLDS IN SAN DIEGO INCREASED by 145 percent between 1968 and 1975. Was the city under siege? Had social control completely broken down? No, what had happened was that the number of 16-year-olds had increased dramatically—by 211 percent—so the number of crimes had increased only because there were more people in that age category. The actual likelihood of a 16-year-old committing a violent crime (which includes murder, attempted murder, forcible rape, robbery, and aggravated assault) actually *declined* in San Diego between 1968 and 1975, from 35 to 27 violent crimes per 1,000 16-year-olds. (Data are from unpublished figures provided by the San Diego Police Department.)

The situation in San Diego is similar to what was going on in Florida between 1958 and 1967, when the number of juvenile crimes more than doubled. The state's population was growing during this period, of course, so total population growth was having an impact, and Chilton and Spielberger (1971) found that the growth of the school-age population accounted for 70 percent of the total rise in juvenile crime in Florida during that time. In the state's SMSAs, 85 percent of the rise in juvenile crime could be accounted for simply by the rise in the number of young people.

You might ask if I am unfairly picking on teenagers for this example. The answer is no. In the late teens and early twenties, a young person's fancy turns to love and, more than at other ages, to crime. In most societies crime is the province of the young, and it stands to reason that a youthful age structure will produce higher overall crime rates (that is, crude crime rates) than will an older age structure. Calculating crime rates by age is a bit tricky for large geographic areas such as the United States, because not all areas report crimes, nor do those reporting necessarily use the same criteria. Furthermore, you know the age of the criminal only after you have caught him or her, so areas that are more efficient at catching criminals will have different data than those less efficient. Nonetheless, this has not deterred me from

John R. Weeks, *Population: An Introduction to Concepts and Issues,* 2nd ed. Belmont, Cal.: Wadsworth, 1981, pp. 190–191, 297–300, 335–337.

making some reasonable estimates of age-specific rates of crime in the United States for 1974.

In the accompanying graph you can see the age-specific crime rates that I have calculated on the assumption that the U.S. population distribution by age in 1974 was identical to that for the population represented by the 5,298 agencies reporting crimes to the FBI in 1974. I have focused on violent crimes because that ignores the smaller petty mischief that might dispropor- tionately get teenagers in trouble. Yet even for these "hard-core" crimes, the rates peak quickly in the late teens and decline steadily by age after that. In 1974 almost eight out of every 1,000 American youths (these data are for both sexes) were charged with a violent crime, and if you were to look at all types of offenses, you would find that 140 out of every 1,000 youths were charged with some kind of crime in 1974.

In 1967 the National Crime Commission concluded that 40–50 percent of the increase in U.S. crime between 1960 and 1965 was due to the changing age structure—the early impact of the Baby Boom children. Therefore, if U.S. crime rates by age remain as they were in 1974 for the foreseeable fu- ture, then the overall crime rate will go down simply because there will be successively fewer people moving into those crime-prone ages. Crime rates are, however, unlikely to go unchanged because they are influenced by a

Figure 1. Age-Specific Rates of Violent Crime in the United States (1974)

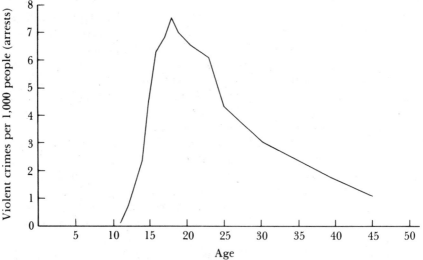

In 1974 in the United States, rates of violent crime (murder, rape, aggravated assault, and robbery) were higher for 18-year-olds than for any other age. *Sources:* FBI Uni- form Crime Reports, 1974, Table 34 (for crime data by age); U.S. Bureau of Census, 1975. Current Population Report, Series P-25, No. 614, Table 1 (for number of peo- ple by age).

wide range of social forces, but the age structure change will almost certainly have an impact.

A less obvious aspect of the age structure's influence on crime is the fact that the age structure of the population of potential victims may also affect the opportunities for crime and thus the crime rate itself. In the United States in the 1970s, the high proportion of the population that was young, at work during the day, and affluent enough to own easily stolen and fenced goods rose dramatically, and thus the opportunity for crime, and the crime rate, rose during the 1970s (Cohen and Felson, 1979).

. . .

DEMOGRAPHIC FACTORS FACILITATING HIGHER STATUS FOR WOMEN

The Influence of Mortality, Fertility, and Urbanization

There are three demographic processes—a decline in mortality, a drop in fertility, and increasing urbanization—that have importantly influenced the ability of women to expand their social roles. A major factor influencing the rise in the status of women has been the more general liberation of humans from early death. In the first part of the nineteenth century, the expectation of life at birth for U.S. females was roughly 40 years, which meant that each girl baby had only about a 30 percent chance of reaching retirement age (age 65); and among every 100 women aged 20, only 45 could expect to be alive at age 65. On the other hand, by 1974 an American female at birth had an 81 percent chance of survival to retirement . . . and of 100 women alive at age 20, 83 will still be around at age 65. Thus, since women and children have much higher probabilities of survival than they used to, lower mortality can reduce the pressure (or at least the need) to initiate childbearing at a young age and to have several children. The decline in mortality does not mean that pressures to have children have evaporated. That is far from the case, . . . but there is a greater chance that the pressures will be less; indeed, remaining single is more acceptable for a woman now than at any time in American history.

Most of a married American woman's lifetime is now spent doing something besides bearing and raising children, since she is having fewer children than in previous generations and she is also living longer. An average American woman bearing two children in her twenties would, at most, spend about 30 years bearing and rearing them. That many years is far fewer, of course, than she will actually have of relative (indeed increasing) independence from child-rearing obligations, since if her two children are spaced 2 years apart and the first child is born when she is 20, then by age 28 her youngest child will be in school all day, and she would still have 50 more years of expected life. Is it any wonder, then, that women have searched for alternatives to family building?

The declines in mortality and fertility that I have been discussing are both associated with economic development, which, in turn, is related to urbanization. Mortality declined in cities before it went down in rural areas . . . and the urban environment is almost always associated with lower levels of fertility than rural areas. . . . In contrast to rural places, cities provide occupational pursuits for both women and men that encourage a delay in marriage (thus potentially lowering fertility) as well as lead to a smaller desired number of children within marriage. Other aspects of the urban environment, particularly the greater difficulty in finding spacious housing, may also help lower the family size in urban areas.

Urbanization initially involved migration from rural to urban areas. This meant that women, as they migrated, were removed from the promarital and pronatalist pressures that may have existed in their parents' homes. Thus, migration may have led to a greater ability to respond independently to the social environment of urban areas, which tends to devalue children. It is also true, from a mother's perspective, that in modern urban, industrial societies, the volume of migration may of itself shorten a mother's active daily involvement with her adult children and grandchildren. . . . [Y]oung adults are especially prone to migration and every adult who moves may well be leaving a mother behind. Of course, that does not mean that she will be less happy (Campbell et al., 1974), but it does mean that she will have more time on her hands to look for alternatives and to question the social norms that prescribe a lower status and fewer out-of-the-home opportunities for women than for men.

It is possible that the process of urbanization in the Western world initially led to an increase in the dependency of women before helping to influence liberation (Nielsen, 1978). The reason for this is that economic development in the West has generally opened up more urban employment opportunities for men than for women. At the same time, life in the city restricts women at home to mainly unpaid domestic activities, in contrast to agrarian women who often have the chance for agricultural work and for the marketing of their produce (Boserup, 1970). Thus, the urban woman who is unemployed may have a smaller economic role in her family than the woman in an agricultural family. Under these circumstances, as the life expectancy of the urban woman has increased and as her childbearing activity has declined, the lack of alternative activities is bound to create pressures for change.

In Figure 2, I have diagrammed the major paths by which mortality, fertility, and urbanization influence the status of women and the breadth of gender roles considered appropriate for women. Again, I emphasize that these demographic conditions are necessary, but not sufficient, to initiate the current rise in the status of women in industrialized societies. What is also required is some change in circumstance to act as a catalyst for the un-

Figure 2. Demographic Components of the Changing Status of Women

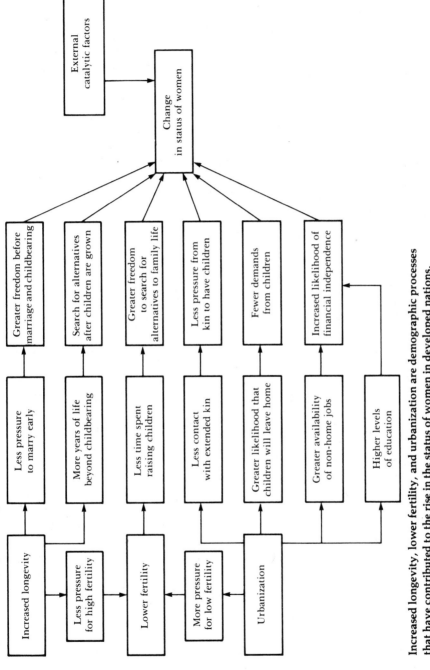

Increased longevity, lower fertility, and urbanization are demographic processes that have contributed to the rise in the status of women in developed nations.

derlying demographic factors. The women's movement has provided that catalytic force.

. . .

AGING AND THE FUTURE OF SOCIETY

What will the future be like for the elderly? How will the growing numbers of older people influence the future of society? Both sides of this coin are of considerable interest since both old age and the future beckon to all of us. Because these questions are so closely interrelated, I will treat them together.

In the United States, the future will include many more people aged 75 and above and many more minority elderly. Adjustments will have to be made to accommodate these increases; adjustments may be in the family system or in public support systems or, more likely, in both. It is possible that the growth of the older population, coupled with the declining fertility of the 1960s and 1970s, will cause the focus of attention within families to shift somewhat away from the young and onto the old. This may lead simultaneously to an increase in the intensity of social interaction between young and old generations and more emphasis on making policy oriented toward the elderly.

One landmark policy decision has already been made by Congress with the passage of legislation in 1978 ending mandatory retirement at age 65 for all but a few professional categories. Thus it is no longer possible for a company to force a person to retire solely on the basis of age (until age 70, that is). Of course, those who continue to work past age 64 face a reduction in social security benefits until age 72, but we may witness a return to the longer work lives characteristic of the pre-Depression years. This could accentuate even more the ability of older people to remain financially independent well into old age. This may be especially true for older women, since they make up a disproportionately large part of the older population (Campbell, 1979). As long as the birth rate remains low and the number of new entrants into the labor force does not greatly exceed the number of jobs available, the intergenerational conflict over access to the labor force should be minimal. However, if new entrants to the labor force (including many younger women) find their job opportunities blocked by the retention of older people in the work force, the possibility of conflict would rise.

A major benefit of this longer potential work life is, of course, that the social security system could find some relief. As the Baby Boom generation moves into old age and becomes eligible for old-age benefits, the ratio of those eligible for benefits to workers will be very large. Thus . . . the financial (tax) burden on the younger generation (people now in childhood or just being born) will be enormous. As a result, there may be considerable pressure on the elderly to be more self-sufficient—not only to work longer but also to become involved in mutual self-help organizations that could relieve some of the burden on the public agencies. It is ironic indeed that the social security system, which was designed in large part to encourage older people to leave the work force, may in the future be bailed out because people can stay in the labor force longer.

The options available to older people are already increasing. These include the ability to work longer, the growth in lifelong learning opportunities—college courses designed for people of all ages, and travel discounts for seniors that may open up opportunities previously closed. These trends are likely to continue almost unabated well into the next century as a result of the previously mentioned cohort flow. For example, the greater participation of women in the labor force and the resulting increase in female financial independence will likely mean a greater sense of personal freedom for these women as they grow older.

Further, the high level of political advocacy of youth in the 1960s will almost certainly be translated into greater political advocacy among the elderly when those people reach old age. Already people aged 55–64 are the most likely to vote in national elections, followed closely by people aged 65–74 (U.S. Bureau of Census, 1979). As the current generation of younger people grows older, we should find the older population becoming more tolerant of a wide range of life-styles and more understanding of the problems and issues facing older people.

It is likely that as a result of the cohort flow in the United States, the original ten objectives of the 1965 Older Americans Act could well be met. Those objectives are:

1. an adequate income
2. the best possible physical and mental health
3. suitable housing
4. full restorative services
5. opportunity for employment without age discrimination
6. retirement in health, honor, and dignity
7. pursuit of meaningful activity
8. efficient community services when needed
9. immediate benefit from proven research knowledge
10. freedom, independence, and the free exercise of individual initiative

The original goal of advocates of the elderly was old-age security, but the goals of the Older Americans Act reveal a shift away from simple security to autonomy. "The idea of old age as a life-stage is yielding to an idea of aging as a life process" (Fischer, 1979:65).

The future of these objectives may be especially rosy when we consider that many of the people who were instrumental in setting the objectives are now moving into the older years themselves.

REFERENCES

Boserup, E.
  1970 Woman's Role in Economic Development. New York: St. Martin's Press.

Campbell, A., P. Converse, and W. Rodgers
  1974 "Measuring the quality of life in America." Institute for Social Research Newsletter.

Campbell, S.
  1979 "Delayed mandatory retirement and the working woman." *The Gerontologist* 19(3):257–63.

Chilton, R., and A. Spielberger
  1971 "Is delinquency increasing? age structure and the crime rate." *Social Forces* 49:487–93.

Cohen, L., and M. Felson
  1979 "Social change and crime rate trends." *American Sociological Review* 44(4):588–607.

Fischer, D. H.
  1979 "The politics of aging in America: a short history." *Journal of the Institute for Socioeconomic Studies* IV(2):51–66.

Nielsen, J.
  1978 *Sex in Society: Perspectives on Stratification.* Belmont, Calif.: Wadsworth Publishing Co.

U.S. Bureau of Census
  1979 "Population Profile of the United States: 1978." Current Population Reports, Series P-20, no. 336.

Review Questions

1. According to the author, how and why did the Baby Boom of the 1940s and 1950s affect the crime rates of the 1960s and 1970s?

2. Many people feel that their choices of life style are based entirely on their own personal preferences. How have demographic trends such as lower mortality and lower fertility affected women's choices of how to spend their time?

3. How are your own expectations regarding how much time mothers should spend on child-care and how much on other activities different from your grandparents' expectations when they were the age you are now?

4. Does the proportion of the population who are elderly appear to have any consequences for the ways in which the elderly and the non-elderly interact? Explain your answer.

Suggested Readings: Social Organization: From Primary Group to Society

Denzin, Norman K. "Notes on the Criminogenic Hypothesis: A Case Study of the American Liquor Industry," *American Sociological Review*, 42, 6 (December 1977), 905–920.

Farberman, Harvey A. "A Criminogenic Market Structure: The Automobile Industry," *Sociological Quarterly*, 16 (Autumn 1975), 438–457.

Freidson, Eliot. *Profession of Medicine: A Study of the Sociology of Applied Knowledge*. New York: Harper & Row, 1970.

Glaser, Barney G., and Anselm M. Strauss. *Time for Dying*. Chicago: Aldine, 1968.

Goffman, Erving. *Asylums: Essays on the Social Situation of Mental Patients and Other Inmates*. Chicago: Aldine, 1961.

Gouldner, Alvin. *Patterns of Industrial Bureaucracy*. Glencoe, Ill.: The Free Press, 1954.

Redfield, Robert. *The Folk Culture of Yucatán*. Chicago: University of Chicago Press, 1941.

Roy, Donald F. "Quota Restriction and Goldbricking in a Machine Shop," *American Journal of Sociology*, 57 (March 1952), 427–442.

Schwartz, Barry. "Notes on the Sociology of Sleep," *Sociological Quarterly*, 11 (Fall 1970), 485–499.

Sudnow, David. *Passing On: The Social Organization of Dying*. Englewood Cliffs, N.J.: Prentice-Hall, 1967.

Tonnies, Ferdinand. *Community and Society*. East Lansing, Mich.: Michigan State University Press, 1957.

Whyte, William Foote. *Street Corner Society: The Social Structure of an Italian Slum*. Chicago: University of Chicago Press, 1943.

Zimbardo, Phillip. "Pathology of Imprisonment," *Society*, 9, 6, 1976.

Part VI. Inequalities

In NEARLY EVERY KNOWN SOCIETY, LIMITED SOCIAL AND MATERIAL REWARDS ARE DIS-
tributed unevenly. Prestige, esteem, honor, and social power as well as
wealth are not granted to each societal member in equal share. Instead, social groupings develop ranking, or *stratification*, systems in which various
"ascribed" (determined at birth) and "achieved" (acquired) attributes—
which may include gender, age, race or ethnicity, family name, occupation,
and even sometimes physique—are weighted. One's attributes, once ranked
in the stratification system, determine those societal rewards which one can
claim and which others are willing to bestow.

The rewards and resources one is able to claim determine to a large extent
one's *life chances*. By life chances we do not mean merely the opportunities
to make a million dollars or to become president of the United States, but
rather the chances of surviving infancy, avoiding malnutrition, obtaining
education, securing a decent-paying and satisfying job, and living in good
health to an advanced age. These life chances are *not* distributed equally in
the United States or in any other modern nation.

Large categories of people who receive similar societal resources—and
who have similar life chances—are termed *social classes*. Social-class ranking is usually applied to families, so that children inherit their parents' positions in the stratification hierarchy. Their inherited positions may adhere to
them long after they have become independent from their parents, since *social mobility*, even in relatively "open" modern industrial societies, is not as
common as we like to think. That is, individuals' rankings in the stratification system tend to be perpetuated.

The coherence and stability of stratification systems is maintained in part
through social interaction. Interaction with people from other classes often
involves "reminders" of one's own class position and actual barriers to upward movement. Interaction with those at one's own class level is, first of
all, much more frequent, since many aspects of our lives, from residence to
religious services, are somewhat segregated on the basis of social class and
even sex, age, race, and the like. It is also more comfortable, because class
members share similar life experiences and develop similar interpretations
of those experiences. Those of you who have grown up in middle-class families may recall uncomfortable instances when you have crossed class
boundaries. Have you ever been invited to a formal affair at an exclusive

restaurant and wondered which of the three spoons to use first, what to do with the four forks? Have you come in contact with a prestigious personage who interrupted your conversation in order to talk to someone "more important"? Have you felt, or been made to feel, "out of place" because of your clothing, income, manners, or ignorance of upper-class customs? Have you been passed over for a job or promotion for these reasons? Have you judged those from a lower social class than your own on similar grounds?

The purpose of this section of our reader is to help you to become aware of the interactional bases of stratification and of the inequalities which result. Our selections place the dynamics of social inequality in an everyday context and illustrate how stratification can be viewed as a *social process* which begins in social interaction and which affects individuals' opportunities, self-conceptions, and even their survival. The "system" of distributing social power, prestige, and wealth is not some far-removed, non-human force. It is comprised of the everyday behavior of us all, as we socialize each other to accept both the cultural rationales for stratification and our own particular positions in the ranking system.

We begin by looking at elites in American society. The writings of G. William Domhoff are part of a tradition or school of thought in sociology called "conflict theory," which stems most directly from the work of C. Wright Mills in the 1950s and 1960s on the U.S. "power elite." Mills argued (along with former Republican President Dwight D. Eisenhower) that major decisions affecting the course of our society and the everyday lives of Americans are *not* made solely by our elected representatives as our traditions tell us they are. Rather, a small cluster of *military, industrial,* and *political* leaders exercise a great deal of both official and behind-the-scenes power.

According to Mills's research, the powerful in these three arenas are likely to come from *privileged backgrounds* and/or to have amassed great wealth in their adult lives. Furthermore, they are likely to *know each other* from prep school, college, and professional contacts; to *circulate* among top positions in the three crucial arenas; and to *overlap* with each other on boards of directors in industry, education, and community organizations.

Eisenhower himself, who actually warned Americans of the increasing power of what he called the "military-industrial complex," was a general and a military hero in World War II, president of the Ivy League's Columbia University, and eventually President of the United States. A close look at the members of President Reagan's Cabinet (or the Cabinet of any President, for that matter) will reveal a number of millionaires with previous corporate leadership positions, former military "top brass," and the like. Military and political leaders often move into private industry after their "public" service. Those who run large (often multi-national) corporations are less visible to the public, but their decisions to manufacture and market their products affect employment rates and patterns, as well as how we eat, dress, drive, keep warm or cool, and entertain ourselves. They are also able to affect lawmakers and laws and questions of peace and war.

Most sociologists agree with the general picture described above: some Americans are simply more powerful than others. They disagree, however, as to how cohesive or competitive the top leaders of our country are. Some sociologists, termed "pluralists," argue that there is a great deal of *diversity*, competition, argument, and divisiveness among those leaders. Decisions made in one issue area, they claim, may be affected by a different set of actors than decisions on other issues. Another group, which includes Domhoff and Mills, contend that the men comprising the "higher circles" of power share a *consensus* over the *major questions* of how the society should operate, only disagreeing over minor issues of how best to implement policies that will achieve their valued goals. They argue further that the interests of the powerful coincide, since the same policies, laws, and customs benefit corporate *and* military *and* political elites.

In the selection from Domhoff's writings presented here, we are offered a glimpse of some of America's major decision makers as they interact, not in the boardroom or the halls of Congress or the White House, but as participants in adult "summer camps" for wealthy and powerful men (no women allowed)—at "The Bohemian Grove and Other Retreats." Sipping martinis under redwood trees or engaging in various forms of "horseplay" on the California ranch lands, the men form and renew bonds of friendship.

As Domhoff notes, his data do not offer conclusive proof that a cohesive national upper-class subculture exists. But, by focusing on the patterns and processes of recreational interaction, he shows us how it could be possible. In this excerpt from his book, we are led to put aside some of our stereotypes of the serious and staid executive or general or statesman, smiling only for press photographers between one high-level meeting and another. We see that the top power- and wealth-holders are not an abstract category of anonymous and isolated individuals, but real human beings whose friendships, networks, contacts, and interactions shape their lives—and ours.

We turn our attention next to the ways in which *status reminders* are manifested in everyday interactions involving waiting. Time is, as we know, an important, scarce resource, and the use or waste of it can gain or deny us access to other valued resources. Since time can be socially used or abused, it entails social costs. And the ability to affect how other people use their time is an indicator of power. In his essay, "Waiting, Exchange, and Power," Barry Schwartz examines the social costs, uses, and abuses of time as a medium of exchange in the interactional relationship of waiting. Waiting, as Schwartz points out, affects the value of the goods, services, and persons one waits for. The social costs that whole categories of people bear in order to obtain some valued thing may be very high.

Waiting is closely related to power, because those who have power can impose waiting upon those who don't. The phrase, "being forced to wait," expresses the coercive power of waiting used as a policy. The power to make others wait is often held by those who have a monopoly on valued things. Our decision to wait expresses "status deference," the willingness to defer to others higher on the pecking order than we are. Yet it is not always the powerful for whom we wait. People low in power may impose waiting upon us because of their access to the powerful.

Schwartz examines the dynamics of waiting in terms of the value we give the objects for which we wait and the distribution of power between servers and their clients. Waiting is thus demonstrated to be not merely an annoyance, as it is often seen, but an indication and a reminder of inequality.

Next we see that judgments about people's class affiliations can have a profound effect on their life chances. In "The Saints and the Roughnecks," William Chambliss traces the interaction between authoritative agents of the community and two white, adolescent youth gangs—the upper-middle-class Saints and the lower-class Roughnecks. His study reveals a pattern of discrimination based on class.

The Saints and the Roughnecks differed little from each other aside from the crucial factors of class background; the visibility of their activities to others; and the biased perceptions of their activities on the part of school-teachers and officials, the police, and the townspeople. Coming from wealthy families and having the mobility that wealth can buy, the Saints were able to carry out what the community, in ignorance, regarded as "pranks" in places beyond the townspeople's visibility. The Saints' low visibility, their polite demeanor before school and police authorities, and the community's bias in their favor combined to keep the gang free of any taint of delinquency. The way remained clear for the Saints to pursue the adult careers to which, in the community's eyes, their class status, school grades, and behavior entitled them.

The Roughnecks, by contrast, had no barriers to the visibility of their behavior to protect them. Both their defiant demeanor and the bias against them assured that their activities would be stamped with a criminal label. (For a discussion of labeling, see the section entitled *Deviance, Conformity, and Social Control.*) The attitudes of the community that produced the label affected the Roughnecks' expectations of their own futures. Thus, when the Roughnecks turned to adult criminal careers, the community's prophecy was fulfilled. Chambliss's study shows us how class labels, imposed in the course of interaction between groups, have an enormous effect on life chances.

Many observers of American society have seen the great differences in the distribution of wealth as resulting from the values and attitudes that prevail in the different social classes. According to this view, middle-class values are different from lower-class values, the latter forming a pattern that has come to be known as the "culture of poverty." The culture-of-poverty theory holds that lower-class values and attitudes form a way of life that keeps poor people from attaining job security and upward mobility. Where middle-class people are seen as future-oriented, lower-class people are seen as present-oriented. The middle class is said to defer its gratifications (they wait to have their desires fulfilled), an attitude favorable to saving; the lower class is said to seek immediate gratification of its needs, an attitude favorable to immediate consumption. The middle class is described as optimistic, and the lower class as fatalistic. These supposed differences between the cultures of the lower class and the middle class are assumed to explain poverty among the lower classes.

Elliot Liebow *challenges* the culture-of-poverty theory in the selection "Men and Jobs." He provides us with a detailed account of his observations of the attitudes and values that lower-class, black, streetcorner men hold toward their jobs, the attitudes that middle-class employers have with respect to those same jobs, and the objective conditions that surround the jobs available to men on the streetcorner.

From a superficial point of view, the men on Tally's Corner might seem to embody every value imparted to them by the culture-of-poverty theory. They appear to be irresponsible and indolent. But, as Liebow points out, most of the men on the corner have jobs—the least prestigious, lowest-paying jobs society has to offer. Both the middle-class employer and the lower-class employee consider the jobs contemptible. Indeed, they are boring, dirty, and monotonous. The wages are insufficient to support a family, and the jobs provide no chance for advancement. Better-paying jobs are usually either physically debilitating, out of reach of the corner men, seasonal, weather-bound, machine-paced, or beyond the training of the corner men.

The system of paying wages for the retail and service jobs available to the streetcorner men provides an excellent illustration of how middle-class employers express their contempt for jobs that lower-class men perform. We see how the power of the employer can be used not only to demean the job but also to threaten whatever marginal security the job might provide.

The men on Tally's corner hold jobs that "are not much to talk about." They are convinced of their own incompetence. They cannot save, and they are reluctant to assume responsibility when responsible jobs are offered. Furthermore, these attitudes and experiences are likely to have been those of their fathers and their fathers' fathers. What is important, indeed critical, to note is that the attitudes that the streetcorner men express are not produced by a culture of poverty but, rather, are the results of objective, valid experience. The culture-of-poverty theory fails to explain why poverty and inequality exist, because it locates the faults in the victims instead of in the system. Liebow's essay demonstrates that the attitudes and values that support inequality are formed not in an isolated subculture but by a process of "self-fulfilling prophecy" in which the beliefs of the more powerful are translated into reality in the course of interaction between groups.

THE BOHEMIAN GROVE AND OTHER RETREATS

G. William Domhoff

THE BOHEMIAN GROVE

Picture yourself comfortably seated in a beautiful open-air dining hall in the midst of twenty-seven hundred acres of giant California redwoods. It is early evening and the clear July air is still pleasantly warm. Dusk has descended, you have finished a sumptuous dinner, and you are sitting quietly with your drink and your cigar, listening to nostalgic welcoming speeches and enjoying the gentle light and the eerie shadows that are cast by the two-stemmed gaslights flickering softly at each of the several hundred outdoor banquet tables.

You are part of an assemblage that has been meeting in this redwood grove sixty-five miles north of San Francisco for nearly a hundred years. It is not just any assemblage, for you are a captain of industry, a well-known television star, a banker, a famous artist, or maybe a member of the President's Cabinet. You are one of fifteen hundred men gathered together from all over the country for the annual encampment of the rich and the famous at the Bohemian Grove.

• • •

["Bohemians" of the 1970s and 1980s include such personages as President Ronald Reagan; Vice President George Bush; Attorney General William French Smith; Secretary of State George P. Shultz; former President Richard Nixon; former President Gerald Ford; Supreme Court Justice Potter Stewart; Herbert Hoover, Jr.; Herbert Hoover III; newspaperman William R. Hearst, Jr.; five members of the Dean Witter family of investment bankers; entertainers Art Linkletter and Edgar Bergen; presidents and chairmen of several oil companies such as Marathon Oil and Standard Oil; the president of Rockefeller University; officers of Anheuser-Busch breweries; the president of Kaiser Industries; bank presidents from California to New York; the president and chairman of Hewlett-Packard Co.; and many other representatives of American industry, finance, government, and entertainment. When these participants arrive for the annual "campout," an elaborate ritual called the Cremation of Care welcomes them and instructs

G. William Domhoff, *The Bohemian Grove and Other Retreats*. New York: Harper & Row, 1974, pp. 1; 7–8; 11; 14–15; 17; 19–21; 31; 72–74; 79–83; 86–96.

them to leave all cares behind while they join together for two weeks of lavish entertainment, fellowship, and "communion with nature."]

The Cremation of Care is the most spectacular event of the midsummer retreat that members and guests of San Francisco's Bohemian Club have taken every year since 1878. However, there are several other entertainments in store. Before the Bohemians return to the everyday world, they will be treated to plays, variety shows, song fests, shooting contests, art exhibits, swimming, boating, and nature rides.

. . .

A cast for a typical Grove play easily runs to seventy-five or one hundred people. Add in the orchestra, the stagehands, the carpenters who make the sets, and other supporting personnel, and over three hundred people are involved in creating the High Jinks each year. Preparations begin a year in advance, with rehearsals occurring two or three times a week in the month before the encampment, and nightly in the week before the play.

Costs are on the order of $20,000 to $30,000 per High Jinks, a large amount of money for a one-night production which does not have to pay a penny for salaries (the highest cost in any commercial production). "And the costs are talked about, too," reports my . . . informant. "'Hey, did you hear the High Jinks will cost $25,000 this year?' one of them will say to another. The expense of the play is one way they can relate to its worth."

. . .

Entertainment is not the only activity at the Bohemian Grove. For a little change of pace, there is intellectual stimulation and political enlightenment every day at 12:30 P.M. Since 1932 the meadow from which people view the Cremation of Care also has been the setting for informal talks and briefings by people as varied as Dwight David Eisenhower (before he was President), Herman Wouk (author of *The Caine Mutiny*), Bobby Kennedy (while he was Attorney General), and Neil Armstrong (after he returned from the moon).

Cabinet officers, politicans, generals, and governmental advisers are the rule rather than the exception for Lakeside Talks, especially on weekends. Equally prominent figures from the worlds of art, literature and science are more likely to make their appearance during the weekdays of the encampment, when Grove attendance may drop to four or five hundred (many of the members only come up for one week or for the weekends because they cannot stay away from their corporations and law firms for the full two weeks).

. . .

[T]he Grove is an ideal off-the-record atmosphere for sizing up politicians. "Well, of course when a politician comes here, we all get to see him, and his stock in trade is his personality and his ideas," a prominent Bohemian told a *New York Times* reporter who was trying to cover Nelson Rockefeller's 1963 visit to the Grove for a Lakeside Talk. The journalist went on to note that the midsummer encampments "have long been a major showcase where leaders of business, industry, education, the arts, and politics can come to examine each other."[1]

• • •

For 1971, [then-] President Nixon was to be the featured Lakeside speaker. However, when newspaper reporters learned that the President planned to disappear into a redwood grove for an off-the-record speech to some of the most powerful men in America, they objected loudly and vowed to make every effort to cover the event. The flap caused the club considerable embarrassment, and after much hemming and hawing back and forth, the club leaders asked the President to cancel his scheduled appearance. A White House press secretary then announced that the President had decided not to appear at the Grove rather than risk the tradition that speeches there are strictly off the public record.[2]

However, the President was not left without a final word to his fellow Bohemians. In a telegram to the president of the club, which now hangs at the entrance to the reading room in the San Francisco clubhouse, he expressed his regrets at not being able to attend. He asked the club president to continue to lead people into the woods, adding that he in turn would redouble his efforts to lead people out of the woods. He also noted that, while anyone could aspire to be President of the United States, only a few could aspire to be president of the Bohemian Club.

• • •

Not all the entertainment at the Bohemian Grove takes place under the auspices of the committee in charge of special events. The Bohemians and their guests are divided into camps which evolved slowly over the years as the number of people on the retreat grew into the hundreds and then the thousands. These camps have become a significant center of enjoyment during the encampment.

At first the camps were merely a place in the woods where a half-dozen to a dozen friends would pitch their tents. Soon they added little amenities like their own special stove or a small permanent structure. Then there developed little camp "traditions" and endearing camp names like Cliff Dwellers, Moonshiners, Silverado Squatters, Woof, Zaca, Toyland, Sundodgers, and Land of Happiness. The next steps were special emblems, a handsome little lodge or specially constructed tepees, a permanent bar, and maybe a grand piano.[3] Today there are 129 camps of varying sizes, structures, and statuses. Most have between 10 and 30 members, but there are one or two with about 125 members and several with less than 10. A majority of the camps are strewn along what is called the River Road, but some are huddled in other areas within five or ten minutes of the center of the Grove.

The entertainment at the camps is mostly informal and impromptu.

Someone will decide to bring together all the jazz musicians in the Grove for a special session. Or maybe all the artists or writers will be invited to a luncheon or a dinner at a camp. Many camps have their own amateur piano players and informal musical and singing groups which perform for the rest of the members.

But the joys of the camps are not primarily in watching or listening to performances. Other pleasures are created within them. Some camps become known for their gastronomical specialties, such as a particular drink or a particular meal. The Jungle Camp features mint juleps, Halcyon has a three-foot-high martini maker constructed out of chemical glassware. At the Owl's Nest [President Reagan's club] it's the gin-fizz breakfast—about a hundred people are invited over one morning during the encampment for eggs Benedict, gin fizzes, and all the trimmings.

· · ·

The men of Bohemia are drawn in large measure from the corporate leadership of the United States. They include in their numbers directors from major corporations in every sector of the American economy. An indication of this fact is that one in every five resident members and one in every three nonresident members is found in Poor's *Register of Corporations, Executives, and Directors*, a huge volume which lists the leadership of tens of thousands of companies from every major business field except investment banking, real estate, and advertising.

Even better evidence for the economic prominence of the men under consideration is that at least one officer or director from 40 of the 50 largest industrial corporations in America was present, as a member or a guest, on the lists at our disposal. Only Ford Motor Company and Western Electric were missing among the top 25! Similarly, we found that officers and directors from 20 of the top 25 commercial banks (including all of the 15 largest) were on our lists. Men from 12 of the first 25 life-insurance companies were in attendance (8 of these 12 were from the top 10). Other business sectors were represented somewhat less: 10 of 25 in transportation, 8 of 25 in utilities, 7 of 25 in conglomerates, and only 5 of 25 in retailing. More generally, of the top-level businesses ranked by *Fortune* for 1969 (the top 500 industrials, the top 50 commercial banks, the top 50 life-insurance companies, the top 50 transportation companies, the top 50 utilities, the top 50 retailers, and the top 47 conglomerates), *29 percent of these 797 corporations were "represented" by at least 1 officer or director*.

· · ·

OTHER WATERING HOLES

[Other camps and retreats were founded by wealthy and powerful men, based on the model provided by the Bohemian Grove. One example is the Rancheros Visitadores (Visiting Ranchers) who meet each May for horseback rides through the California ranch land. These are accompanied by feasts, entertainment, and general merrymaking with a Spanish-ranch motif.]

[Among the Rancheros a] common interest in horses and horseplay provides a social setting in which men with different forms of wealth get to know each other better. *Sociologically speaking, the Rancheros Visitadores is an organization which serves the function (whether the originators planned it that way or not) of helping to integrate ranchers and businessmen from different parts of the country into a cohesive social class.*

* * *

[T]he Rancheros had to divide into camps because of a postwar increase in membership. There are seventeen camps, sporting such Spanish names as Los Amigos, Los Vigilantes, Los Tontos (bums), Los Bandidos, and Los Flojos (lazy ones). They range in size from fifteen to ninety-three, with the majority of them listing between twenty and sixty members. Most camps have members from a variety of geographical locations, although some are slightly specialized in that regard. Los Gringos, the largest camp, has the greatest number of members from out of state. Los Borrachos, Los Picadores, and Los Chingadores, the next largest camps, have a predominance of people from the Los Angeles area. Los Vigilantes, with twenty members, began as a San Francisco group, but now includes riders from Oregon, Washington, New York and southern California.

In 1928 the Bohemian Grove provided John J. Mitchell with the inspiration for his retreat on horseback, the Rancheros Visitadores. Since 1930 the RVs have grown to the point where they are an impressive second best to the Grove in size, entertainment, and stature. Their combination of businessmen and ranchers is as unique as the Bohemian's amalgamation of businessmen and artists. It is hardly surprising that wealthy men from Los Angeles, San Francisco, Honolulu, Spokane, and Chicago would join Mitchell in wanting to be members of both.

* * *

[Another club, the Colorado-based Roundup Riders of the Rockies, imitates the RVs in its emphasis on "roughing it" and socializing.]

The riders do not carry their fine camp with them. Instead, twenty camphands are employed to move the camp in trucks to the next campsite. Thus, when the Roundup Riders arrive at their destination each evening they find fourteen large sleeping tents complete with cots, air mattresses, portable toilets, and showers. Also up and ready for service are a large green dining tent and an entertainment stage. A diesel-powered generator provides the camp with electricity.

Food service is provided by Martin Jetton of Fort Worth, Texas, a caterer advertised in the southwest as "King of the Barbecue." Breakfasts and dinners are said to be veritable banquets. Lunch is not as elaborate, but it does arrive to the riders on the trail in a rather unusual fashion that only those of the higher circles could afford: "lunches in rugged country are often delivered by light plane or helicopter."[4] One year the men almost missed a meal because a wind came up and scattered the lunches which were being parachuted from two Cessna 170s.

In addition to the twenty hired hands who take care of the camp, there are twenty wranglers to look after the horses. The horses on the ride—predominantly such fine breeds as Arabian, Quarter Horse, and Morgan—are estimated to be worth more than $200,000. Horses and riders compete in various contests of skill and horsemanship on a layover day in the middle of the week. Skeet shooting, trap shooting, and horseshoes also are a part of this event.

. . .

The Roundup Riders, who hold their trek at the same time the Bohemians hold their encampment, must be reckoned as a more regional organization. Although there are numerous millionaires and executives among them, the members are not of the national stature of most Bohemians and many Rancheros. They can afford to invest thousands of dollars in their horses and tack, to pay a $300 yearly ride fee, and to have their lunch brought to them by helicopter, but they cannot compete in business connections and prestige with those who assemble at the Bohemian Grove. Building from the Denver branch of the upper class, the Roundup Riders reach out primarily to Nebraska (six), Texas (five), Illinois (five), Nevada (three), California (three), and Arizona (three). There are no members from New York, Boston, Philadelphia, or other large Eastern cities.

Several other regional rides have been inspired by the Rancheros, rides such as the Desert Caballeros in Wickenburg, Arizona, and the Verde Vaqueros in Scottsdale, Arizona. These groups are similar in size and membership to the Roundup Riders of the Rockies. Like the Roundup Riders, they have a few overlapping members with the Rancheros. But none are of the status of the Rancheros Visitadores. They are minor legacies of the Bohemian Grove, unlikely even to be aware of their kinship ties to the retreat in the redwoods.

DO BOHEMIANS, RANCHEROS, AND ROUNDUP RIDERS RULE AMERICA?

The foregoing material on upper-class retreats, which I have presented in as breezy a manner as possible, is relevant to highly emotional questions concerning the distribution of power in modern America. In this final [section] I will switch styles somewhat and discuss these charged questions in a sober, simple, and straightforward way. . . .

It is my hypothesis that there is a ruling social class in the United States. This class is made up of the owners and managers of large corporations, which means the members have many economic and political interests in common, and many conflicts with ordinary working people. Comprising at most 1 percent of the total population, members of this class own 25 to 30 percent of all privately held wealth in America, own 60 to 70 percent of the privately held corporate wealth, receive 20 to 25 percent of the yearly income, direct the large corporations and foundations, and dominate the federal government in Washington.

Most social scientists disagree with this view. Some dismiss it out of hand, others become quite vehement in disputing it. The overwhelming majority of them believe that the United States has a "pluralistic" power structure, in which a wide variety of "veto groups" (e.g., businessmen, farmers, unions, consumers) and "voluntary associations" (e.g., National Association of Manufacturers, Americans for Democratic Action, Common Cause) form shifting coalitions to influence decisions on different issues. These groups and associations are said to have differing amounts of interest and influence on various questions. Contrary to my view, pluralists assert that no one group, not even the owners and managers of large corporations, has the cohesiveness and ability to determine the outcome of a large variety of social, economic, and political issues.

· · ·

As noted, I believe there is a national upper class in the United States. . . . [T]his means that wealthy families from all over the country, and particularly from major cities like New York, San Francisco, Chicago, and Houston, are part of interlocking social circles which perceive each other as equals, belong to the same clubs, interact frequently, and freely intermarry.

Whether we call it a "social class" or a "status group," many pluralistic social scientists would deny that such a social group exists. They assert that there is no social "cohesiveness" among the various rich in different parts of the country. For them, social registers, blue books, and club membership lists are merely collections of names which imply nothing about group interaction.

There is a wealth of journalistic evidence which suggests the existence of a national upper class. It ranges from Cleveland Amory's *The Proper Bostonians* and *Who Killed Society?* to Lucy Kavaler's *The Private World of High Society* and Stephen Birmingham's *The Right People.* But what is the systematic evidence which I can present for my thesis? There is first of all the evidence that has been developed from the study of attendance at private schools. It has been shown that a few dozen prep schools bring together children of the upper class from all over the country. From this evidence it can be argued that young members of the upper class develop lifetime friendship ties with like-status age-mates in every section of the country.[5]

There is second the systematic evidence which comes from studying high-status summer resorts. Two such studies show that these resorts bring together upper-class families from several different large cities.[6] Third, there is the evidence of business interconnections. Several . . . studies have demonstrated that interlocking directorships bring wealthy men from all over the country into face-to-face relationships at the board meetings of banks, insurance companies, and other corporations.[7]

And finally, there is the evidence developed from studying exclusive social clubs. Such studies have been made in the past, but the present investigation of the Bohemian Club, the Rancheros Visitadores, and the Roundup Riders of the Rockies is a more comprehensive effort. *In short, I believe the present [study] to be significant evidence for the existence of a cohesive American upper class.*

The Bohemian Grove, as well as other watering holes and social clubs, are relevant to the problem of class cohesiveness in two ways. First, the very fact that rich men from all over the country gather in such close circumstances as the Bohemian Grove is evidence for the existence of a socially cohesive upper class. It demonstrates that many of these men do know each other, that they have face-to-face communications, and that they are a social network. In this sense, we are looking at the Bohemian Grove and other social retreats as a *result* of social processes that lead to class cohesion. But such institutions also can be viewed as *facilitators* of social ties. Once formed, these groups become another avenue by which the cohesiveness of the upper class is maintained.

In claiming that clubs and retreats like the Bohemians and the Rancheros are evidence for my thesis of a national upper class, I am assuming that cohesion develops within the settings they provide. Perhaps some readers will find that assumption questionable. So let us pause to ask: Are there reasons to believe that the Bohemian Grove and its imitators lead to greater cohesion within the upper class?

For one thing, we have the testimony of members themselves. There are several accounts by leading members of these groups, past and present, which attest to the intimacy that develops among members. John J. Mitchell, El Presidente of Los Rancheros Visitadores from 1930 to 1955, wrote as follows on the twenty-fifth anniversary of the group:

> All the pledges and secret oaths in the universe cannot tie men, our kind of men, together like the mutual appreciation of a beautiful horse, the moon behind a cloud, a song around the campfire or a ride down the Santa Ynez Valley. These are experiences common on our ride, but unknown to most of our daily lives. Our organization, to all appearances, is the most informal imaginable. Yet there are men here who see one another once a year, yet feel a bond closer than between those they have known all their lives.[8]

F. Burr Betts, chairman of the board of Security Life of Denver, says the following about the Roundup Riders:

> I think you find out about the Roundup Riders when you go to a Rider's funeral. Because there you'll find, no matter how many organizations the man belonged to, almost every pallbearer is a Roundup Rider. I always think of the Roundup Riders as the first affiliation. We have the closest knit fraternity in the world.[9]

. . .

A second reason for stressing the importance of retreats and clubs like the Bohemian Grove is a body of research within social psychology which deals with group cohesion. "Group dynamics" suggests the following about cohesiveness. (1) *Physical proximity is likely to lead to group solidarity.* Thus, the mere fact that these men gather together in such intimate physical settings implies that cohesiveness develops. (The same point can be made, of course, about exclusive neighborhoods, private schools, and expensive summer resorts.) (2) *The more people interact, the more they will like each other.* This is hardly a profound discovery, but we can note that the Bohemian Grove and other watering holes maximize personal interactions. (3) *Groups seen as high in status are more cohesive.* The Bohemian Club fits the category of a high-status group. Further, its stringent membership requirements, long waiting lists, and high dues also serve to heighten its valuation in the eyes of its members. Members are likely to think of themselves as "special" people, which would heighten their attractiveness to each other, and increase the likelihood of interaction and cohesiveness. (4) *The best atmosphere for increasing group cohesiveness is one that is relaxed and cooperative.* Again the Bohemian Grove, the Rancheros, and the Roundup Riders are ideal examples of this kind of climate. From a group-dynamics point of view, then, we could argue that one of the reasons for upper-class cohesiveness is the fact that the class is organized into a wide variety of small groups which encourage face-to-face interaction and ensure status and security for members.[10]

In summary, if we take these several common settings together—schools, resorts, corporation directorships, and social clubs—and assume on the basis of members' testimony and the evidence of small-group research that interaction in such settings leads to group cohesiveness, then I think we are justified in saying that wealthy families from all over the United States are linked together in a variety of ways into a national upper class.

Even if the evidence and arguments for the existence of a socially cohesive national upper class are accepted, there is still the question of whether or not this class has the means by which its members can reach policy consensus on issues of importance to them.

A five-year study based upon information obtained from confidential informants, interviews, and questionnaires has shown that social clubs such as the Bohemian Club are an important consensus-forming aspect of the upper class and big-business environment. According to sociologist Reed Powell, "the clubs are a repository of the values held by the upper-level prestige groups in the community and are a means by which these values are transferred to the business environment." Moreover, the clubs are places where problems are discussed:

> On the other hand, the clubs are places in which the beliefs, problems, and values of the industrial organization are discussed and related to other elements in the

larger community. Clubs, therefore, are not only effective vehicles of informal communication, but also valuable centers where views are presented, ideas are modified, and new ideas emerge. Those in the interview sample were appreciative of this asset; in addition, they considered the club as a valuable place to combine social and business contacts.[11]

The revealing interview work of Floyd Hunter, an outstanding pioneer researcher on the American power structure, also provides evidence for the importance of social clubs as informal centers of policy making. Particularly striking for our purposes is a conversation he had with one of the several hundred top leaders that he identified in the 1950s. The person in question was a conservative industrialist who was ranked as a top-level leader by his peers:

> Hall [a pseudonym] spoke very favorably of the Bohemian Grove group that met in California every year. He said that although over the entrance to the Bohemian Club there was a quotation, "Weaving spiders come not here," there was a good deal of informal policy made in this association. He said that he got to know Herbert Hoover in this connection and that he started work with Hoover in the food administration of World War I.[12]

Despite the evidence presented by Powell and Hunter that clubs are a setting for the development of policy consensus, I do not believe that such settings are the only, or even the primary, locus for developing policy on class-related issues. For policy questions, other organizations are far more important, organizations like the Council on Foreign Relations, the Committee for Economic Development, the Business Council, and the National Municipal League. These organizations, along with many others, are the "consensus-seeking" and "policy-planning" organizations of the upper class. Directed by the same men who manage the major corporations, and financed by corporation and foundation monies, these groups sponsor meetings and discussions wherein wealthy men from all over the country gather to iron out differences and formulate policies on pressing problems.

No one discussion group is *the* leadership council within the upper class. While some of the groups tend to specialize in certain issue areas, they overlap and interact to a great extent. Consensus slowly emerges from the interplay of people and ideas within and among the groups.[13] This diversity of groups is made very clear in the following comments by Frazar B. Wilde, chairman emeritus of Connecticut General Life Insurance Company and a member of the Council on Foreign Relations and the Committee for Economic Development. Mr. Wilde was responding to a question about the Bilderbergers, a big-business meeting group which includes Western European leaders as well as American corporation and foundation directors:

> Business has had over the years many different seminars and discussion meetings. They run all the way from large public gatherings like NAM [National Association of Manufacturers] to special sessions such as those held frequently at Arden House. Bilderberg is in many respects one of the most important, if not the

most important, but this is not to deny that other strictly off-the-record meetings and discussion groups such as those held by the Council on Foreign Relations are not in the front rank.[14]

Generally speaking, then, it is in these organizations that leaders within the upper class discuss the means by which to deal with problems of major concern. Here, in off-the-record settings, these leaders try to reach consensus on general issues that have been talked about more casually in corporate boardrooms and social clubs. These organizations, aided by funds from corporations and foundations, also serve several other functions:

1. They are a training ground for new leadership within the class. It is in these organizations, and through the publications of these organizations, that younger lawyers, bankers, and businessmen become acquainted with general issues in the areas of foreign, domestic, and municipal policy.

2. They are the place where leaders within the upper class hear the ideas and findings of their hired experts.

3. They are the setting wherein upper-class leaders "look over" young experts for possible service as corporation or governmental advisers.

4. They provide the framework for expert studies on important issues. Thus, the Council on Foreign Relations undertook a $1 million study of the "China question" in the first half of the 1960s. The Committee for Economic Development created a major study of money and credit about the same time. Most of the money for these studies was provided by the Ford, Rockefeller, and Carnegie foundations.[15]

5. Through such avenues as books, journals, policy statements, discussion groups, press releases, and speakers, the policy-planning organizations greatly influence the "climate of opinion" within which major issues are considered. For example, *Foreign Affairs*, the journal of the Council on Foreign Relations, is considered the most influential journal in its field, and the periodic policy statements of the Committee for Economic Development are carefully attended to by major newspapers and local opinion leaders.

It is my belief, then, that the policy-planning groups are essential in developing policy positions which are satisfactory to the upper class as a whole. As such, I think they are a good part of the answer to any social scientist who denies that members of the upper class have institutions by which they deal with economic and political challenges.

However, the policy-planning groups could not function if there were not some common interests within the upper class in the first place. The most obvious, and most important, of these common interests have to do with the shared desire of the members to maintain the present monopolized and subsidized business system which so generously overrewards them and makes their jet setting, fox hunting, art collecting, and other extravagances possible. But it is not only shared economic and political concerns which make consensus possible. The Bohemian Grove and other upper-class social institutions also contribute to this process: *Group-dynamics research sug-*

gests that members of socially cohesive groups are more open to the opinions of other members, and more likely to change their views to those of fellow members.[16] Social cohesion is a factor in policy consensus because it creates a desire on the part of group members to reconcile differences with other members of the group. It is not enough to say that members of the upper class are bankers, businessmen, and lawyers with a common interest in profit maximization and tax avoidance who meet together at the Council on Foreign Relations, the Committee for Economic Development, and other policy-planning organizations. We must add that they are Bohemians, Rancheros, and Roundup Riders.

NOTES

1. Wallace Turner, "Rockefeller Faces Scrutiny of Top Californians: Governor to Spend Weekend at Bohemian Grove among State's Establishment" (*New York Times*, July 26, 1963), p. 30. In 1964 Senator Barry Goldwater appeared at the Grove as a guest of retired General Albert C. Wedemeyer and Herbert Hoover, Jr. For that story see Wallace Turner, "Goldwater Spending Weekend in Camp at Bohemian Grove" (*New York Times*, July 31, 1964), p. 10.

2. James M. Naughton, "Nixon Drops Plan for Coast Speech" (*New York Times*, July 31, 1971), p. 11.

3. There is a special moisture-proof building at the Grove to hold the dozens of expensive Steinway pianos belonging to the club and various camps.

4. Robert Pattridge, "Closer to Heaven on Horseback" (*Empire Magazine, Denver Post*, July 9, 1972), p. 12. I am grateful to sociologist Ford Cleere for bringing this article to my attention.

5. E. Digby Baltzell, *Philadelphia Gentlemen* (New York: Free Press, 1958), chapter 12. G. William Domhoff, *The Higher Circles* (New York: Random House, 1970), p. 78.

6. Baltzell, *Philadelphia Gentlemen*, pp. 248–51. Domhoff, *The Higher Circles*, pp. 79–82. For recent anecdotal evidence on this point, see Stephen Birmingham, *The Right People* (Boston: Little, Brown, 1968), Part 3.

7. *Interlocks in Corporate Management* (Washington: U.S. Government Printing Office, 1965) summarizes much of this information and presents new evidence as well. See also Peter Dooley, "The Interlocking Directorate" (*American Economic Review*, December, 1969).

8. Neill C. Wilson, *Los Rancheros Visitadores: Twenty-Fifth Anniversary* (Rancheros Visitadores, 1955), p. 2.

9. Robert Pattridge, "Closer to Heaven on Horseback," p. 11.

10. Dorwin Cartwright and Alvin Zander, *Group Dynamics* (New York: Harper & Row, 1960), pp. 74–82; Albert J. Lott and Bernice E. Lott, "Group Cohesiveness as Interpersonal Attraction" (*Psychological Bulletin*, 64, 1965), pp. 259–309; Michael Argyle, *Social Interaction* (Chicago: Aldine Publishing Company, 1969), pp. 220–23. I am grateful to sociologist John Sonquist of the University of California, Santa Barbara, for making me aware of how important the small-groups literature might be for studies of the upper class. Findings on influence processes, communication patterns, and the development of informal leadership also might be applicable to problems in the area of upper-class research.

11. Reed M. Powell, *Race, Religion, and the Promotion of the American Executive* (College of Administrative Science Monograph No. AA-3, Ohio State University, 1969), p. 50.

12. Floyd Hunter, *Top Leadership, U.S.A.* (Chapel Hill: University of North Carolina Press, 1959), p. 109. Hunter also reported (p. 199) that the most favored clubs of his top leaders were the Metropolitan, Links, Century, University (New York), Bohemian, and Pacific Union. He notes (p. 223 n.) that he found clubs to be less important in policy formation on the national level than they are in communities.

13. For a detailed case study of how the process works, see David Eakins, "Business Planners and America's Postwar Expansion," in David Horowitz, editor, *Corporations and the Cold War* (New York: Monthly Review Press, 1969). For other examples and references, see Domhoff, *The Higher Circles*, chapters 5 and 6.

14. Carl Gilbert, personal communication, June 30, 1972. Mr. Gilbert has done extensive research on the Bilderberg group, and I am grateful to him for sharing his detailed information with me. For an excellent discussion of this group, whose role has been greatly distorted and exaggerated by ultra-conservatives, see Eugene Pasymowski and Carl Gilbert, "Bilderberg, Rockefeller, and the CIA" (*Temple Free Press*, No. 6, September 16, 1968). The article is most conveniently located in a slightly revised form in the *Congressional Record*, September 15, 1971, E9615, under the title "Bilderberg: The Cold War Internationale."

15. The recent work of arch-pluralist Nelson Polsby is bringing him dangerously close to this formulation. Through studies of the initiation of a number of new policies, Polsby and his students have tentatively concluded that "innovators are typically professors or interest group experts." Where Polsby goes wrong is in failing to note that the professors are working on Ford Foundation grants and/or Council on Foreign Relations fellowships. If he would put his work in a sociological framework, people would not gain the false impression that professors are independent experts sitting in their ivory towers thinking up innovations for the greater good of humanity. See Nelson Polsby, "Policy Initiation in the American Political System,"in Irving Louis Horowitz, editor, *The Use and Abuse of Social Science* (New Brunswick, N.J.: TransAction Books, 1971), p. 303.

16. Cartwright and Zander, *Group Dynamics*, p. 89; Lott and Lott, "Group Cohesiveness as Interpersonal Attraction," pp. 291–96.

Review Questions

1. The theoretical position on the U.S. class structure taken by Domhoff is called a "conflict" or "elitist" approach. How does this perspective contrast with the "pluralist" approach?

2. *Compare* and *contrast* the Bohemian Club with a club of which you are a member.

3. What does Domhoff argue is the importance of recreational social interaction for the formation of a cohesive national upper class?

4. The members of the Bohemian Club, the Rancheros Visitadores, and to a lesser extent, the Roundup Riders of the Rockies, include top officials of both the Democratic and Republican Parties. Why does this mixing occur? What are its consequences?

5. What is the significance of the fact that many members of the clubs described by Domhoff are industrialists and businessmen?

WAITING, EXCHANGE, AND POWER: THE DISTRIBUTION OF TIME IN SOCIAL SYSTEMS[1]

Barry Schwartz

So far as it limits productive uses of time, waiting generates distinct social and personal costs. The purpose of this paper is to explore the way these costs are distributed throughout a social structure and to identify the principles to which this allocation gives expression. The main proposition of our analysis is that the distribution of waiting time coincides with the distribution of power. . . .The broader implications of this correlation allow us to characterize stratification systems in terms of the apportionment of time as well as the distribution of other kinds of resources.

Delay and congestion are relevant to the analysis of social systems because they undermine the efficiency with which these systems conduct their business. Indeed, one Russian economist (Liberman 1968–69) recently observed that because of its enormous cost in terms of more productive activities foregone, delay in waiting rooms and queues merit the status of a social problem (pp. 12–16). A gross estimate of the dimensions of this problem is furnished by Orlov, who reports that the Soviet population wastes about 30 billion hours a year waiting during their shopping tours alone. This is the equivalent of a year's work for no less than 15 million men (*New York Times*, May 13, 1969, p. 17). Another study shows that monthly queuing for the payment of rent and utilities wastes at least 20 million man-hours a year in Moscow alone (*New York Times*, June 25, 1972, p. 23). If figures like these were aggregated for the entire service sector of the labor force, social inefficiency occasioned by clients waiting would stand out even more dramatically.

The problem of delay may be more acute in some societies than in others; however, no modern society can claim immunity in this respect. Every social system must "decide" not only how much different members are to be given from a collective supply of goods and services; there must also be a decision as to the priority in which their needs are to be satisfied. Queuing for resources is in this sense a fundamental process of social organization, regardless of the specific level of its affluence. Indeed, though the amount of waiting time per unit consumption may be minimal in the richer, consumer-

Barry Schwartz, "Waiting, Exchange, and Power: The Distribution of Time in Social Systems," *American Journal of Sociology*, 79 (1973), 841–870.

oriented societies, a higher volume of consumption leaves open the possibility that more time is lost in waiting under conditions of affluence than under conditions of scarcity.

On the other hand, it may be said that the social costs of waiting, no matter where they are incurred or what their absolute level may be, merely derive from the summation over an entire population of rather negligible individual losses. But this does not seem to be the case. As one American commentator (Bradford 1971) puts it: "None of us would think of throwing away the nickels and quarters and dimes that accumulate in our pockets. But almost all of us do throw away the small-change time—five minutes here, a quarter hour there—that accumulates in any ordinary day. I figure I probably threw away a full working day in the dentist's office this past year, flicking sightlessly through old magazines" (p. 82). Even in the more opulent of modern societies, then, waiting time creates significant deficits for the individual as well as the system. At issue, however, is (1) the way such cost is distributed throughout a social structure and (2) the principles which govern this distribution. These questions are the subject of the present inquiry.

We begin with the assumption that delay is immediately caused by the relations of supply and demand: when the number of arrivals in some time unit is less than the number an organization can accommodate, waiting time will be relatively brief; but if the arrival rate exceeds the service rate, a "bottleneck" is created and a longer waiting period results. Delay is in this sense occasioned by limitations of access to goods and services. However, this model does not explain socially patterned variations in waiting time. We must therefore explore the institutional constraints which sustain observable levels of scarcity and which organize the priorities granted to different groups of clients. These constraints are shown to be the expressions of existing power relations.

. . .

WAITING, SCARCITY, AND POWER

. . .

Stratification of Waiting

Typical relationships obtain between the individual's position within a social system and the extent to which he waits for and is waited for by other members of the system. In general, the more powerful and important a person is, the more others' access to him must be regulated. Thus, the least powerful may almost always be approached at will; the most powerful are seen only "by appointment." Moreover, because of heavy demands on their time, important people are most likely to violate the terms of appointments and keep their clients waiting. It is also true that the powerful tend not to ask for appointments with their own subordinates; rather, the lowly are summoned—which is grounds for them to cancel their own arrangements so as not to "keep the boss waiting."

The lowly must not only wait for their appointments with superiors; they may also be called upon to wait during the appointment itself. This may be confirmed in innumerable ways. For one, consider everyday life in bureaucracies. When, in their offices, superordinates find themselves in the company of a subordinate, they may interrupt the business at hand to, say, take a phone call, causing the inferior to wait until the conversation is finished. Such interruption may be extremely discomforting for the latter, who may wish not to be privy to the content of the conversation but, having no materials with which to express alternative involvement, must wait in this exposed state until his superior is ready to reengage him. The event becomes doubly disturbing when the superior is unable to recover from the distraction, loses his train of thought, and is unable to properly devote himself to the moment's business. Of course, the subordinate is demeaned not only by the objective features of this scene but also by his realization that for more important clients the superior would have placed an embargo on all incoming calls or visitors. He would have made others wait. The assumption that the client correctly makes is that his own worth is not sufficient to permit the superior to renounce other engagements; being unworthy of full engagement, he is seen, so to speak, between the superior's other appointments. In this way, the client is compelled to bear witness to the mortification of his own worthiness for proper social interaction.

While the derogatory implications for self are clear when the person must repeatedly step aside and wait until the superordinate decides that the granting of his time will not be excessively costly, debasement of self may be attenuated by the client's own consideration that his superior is, after all, in a position of responsibility and assailed by demands over which he may not exercise as much control as he would like. But even this comforting account may be unavailable when the server himself initiates the interruption. It is possible for him to make a call, for example, or to continue his work after the client enters, perhaps with the announcement that he will "be through in a minute."

It is especially mortifying when the superior initiates a wait when an engagement is in progress. Thus, a subordinate, while strolling along a corridor in conversation with his superior may find himself utterly alone when the latter encounters a colleague and breaks off the ongoing relationship in his favor. The subordinate (who may not do the same when encountering one of his peers) is compelled to defer by standing aside and waiting until the unanticipated conversation is finished. Nothing less is expected by his superior, who, finding himself gaining less from the engagement than his inferior, assumes the right to delay or interrupt it at will if more profitable opportunities should arise.

THE IMMUNITY OF THE PRIVILEGED: The relationship between rank and accessibility implies that waiting is a process which mediates interchanges between those who stand on different sides of a social boundary. These divisions and the rules of access which correspond to them are found in organizations which are themselves bounded with respect to the outside world. This fact raises the problem of access when outsiders or clients (as well as insiders, that is, employees or co-workers) seek contact with persons situated at different points in a service hierarchy:

> Low down on the scale are the men you can walk right up to. They are usually behind a counter waiting to serve you on the main floor, or at least on the lower floors. As you go up the bureaucracy you find people on the higher floors and in offices: first bull pens, then private offices, then private offices with secretaries—increasing with each step in inaccessibility and therefore the necessity for appointments and the opportunity to keep people waiting. Recently, for example, I had an experience with a credit card company. First, I went to the first floor where I gave my complaint to the girl at the desk. She couldn't help me and sent me to the eighth floor to talk to someone in a bullpen. He came out, after a suitable waiting time, to discuss my problem in the reception room. I thought that if I were to straighten this matter out I was going to have to find a vice-president in charge of something, who would keep me waiting the rest of the day. I didn't have time to wait so I took my chances with said clerk, who, of course, didn't come through. I'm still waiting for the time when I have an afternoon to waste to go back and find that vice-president to get my account straightened out.[2]

The above statement suggests that delaying a typical client may be a prerogative of important servers. However, we must also recognize that powerful clients are relatively immune from waiting. This remark accords with Tawney's (1931) emphasis on the asymmetry of power relations. "Power," he writes, "may be defined as the capacity of an individual, or group of individuals, to modify the conduct of other individuals or groups in the manner which he desires, *and to prevent his own conduct being modified in the manner in which he does not*" (p. 229; emphasis added).

The relative immunity from waiting which the powerful enjoy is guaranteed because they have the resources to refuse to wait; that is, because they can often afford to go elsewhere for faster service or cause others, such as servants or employees, to wait in their places. Thus, while the relationship between privilege and the necessity of waiting cannot be generalized in any deterministic way, there appears nevertheless to be a relationship between the two, with the least-privileged clients compelled to do the most waiting. This general statement is consistent with Mann's (1969) more specific observations regarding the stratification of waiting in lined queues:

> The relationship between cultural equality and public orderliness is attenuated in the area of queuing because waiting in line is not a habit of all social classes in Western society. It is reasonable to suppose that if Mrs. Gottrocks joined a theater or a football line in the United States, Australia, or England, she would not be treated differently than anyone else, but it would be a rare event for someone of Mrs. Gottrock's status to use a line. Ordinarily, in both class-conscious and rela-

tively class-free societies, the privileged class circumvent the line altogether and get their tickets through agents or other contacts.[3] Our point, then, is that queuing is confined largely to the less-privileged groups in society. [p.353]

The privileged also wait less because they are least likely to tolerate its costs; they are more inclined to renege* from as well as balk† at entering congested waiting channels. On the other hand, the less advantaged may wait longer not only because of their lack of resources but also because their willingness to wait exceeds the readiness of those in higher strata. While they might have something else to do besides sitting and waiting, they might not have anything better to do. As a result, the least advantaged may pay less in profitable alternatives foregone and therefore suffer less than even those whose objective wait is shorter.

This relationship may be informed by another consideration, for which health-care delivery systems provide an example. Because of their scarcity, those who are able to pay for medical services are often forced to wait well beyond the time a server agreed to provide them. Yet there is some limit to the server's inconsiderateness, for, in principle at least, the client may decide that he has waited long enough and go elsewhere. On the other hand, those who are unable to pay for medical care may spend the better part of the day in outpatient waiting rooms, for consideration of the value of clients' time is far less imperative when these clients cannot take their business to someone else. In Britain's government-run maternity hospitals, for example, "a major complaint was that women dependent on the health service are treated offhandedly in hospitals and frequently have to wait more than an hour for checkups at antenatal clinics. Women who paid up to $700 for private treatment were dealt with speedily and efficiently" (*Chicago Tribune*, June 12, 1971, p. 10). Thus, while long, agonizing waiting periods may be avoided only if one is willing to settle for more expensive service, the poor may avoid waiting only if they are willing to settle for no service at all. (The frequency with which they do select this option is, of course, unknown—as is the consequence of the selection.)

The above principle may be further illustrated in other, altogether different connections. It is noticeable, for one example, that in the "best" of urban department stores a customer is met by a salesperson as soon as he enters; the customer makes a selection under his guidance and makes payment to him. In establishments which are a grade below the best, customers may have difficulty finding someone to serve them during busy periods but, when they do, are accompanied by him, that is, "waited on," until the transaction is consummated by payment. The lowest-grade stores, however, provide few servers; as a result, customers must for the most part wait on themselves, then line up behind others at a cashier counter in order to make payment.

---

*"Reneging" refers to giving up waiting after initially committing oneself to a line or waiting room.

†"Balking" means refusal to wait at all.

The above patterns are to be observed within as well as among organizations. In the typical department store, customers surveying high-priced goods like furniture and appliances will typically be approached immediately by a salesperson. Those in the process of selecting a handkerchief or pair of socks will not be so quickly attended and, when they finally are, will be dealt with more quickly. Likewise, clients who show interest in very expensive jewelry will be served at once and at length; those who are fascinated with costume jewelry will wait.

In general, it may be said that establishments which cater to a relatively wealthy clientele must serve them quickly (if the clients desire) not only because of the objective or assumed value of clients' time but also because they have the means to take their business elsewhere if it is not respected. Commercial places which service the less wealthy are less constrained in this respect because they tend to deal with a larger and/or less independent clientele. Within organizations, clients who promise to bring the most profit to a server enjoy a competitive advantage; they wait the least, to the disadvantage of their lesser endowed brethren who can find no one to honor the value of their time.[4]

Waiting and the Monopolization of Services

The above rule, however, rests on the assumption that faster alternative services are available to those who want and can pay for them. In fact, the availability of such alternatives is itself variable. Waiting is therefore affected not only by clients' resources and consequent ability to go elsewhere for service but also by the opportunity to do so.

It follows that establishments with many competitors are most likely to be concerned about the amount of time they keep clients waiting. Chicago Loop banks are among such organizations. In the words of one banking consultant, "The industry is too competitive to allow a dozen people waiting in line when they could just as easily take their business across the street where there is a teller at every window, a customer at every teller and waiting time is less than one minute" (*Chicago Tribune*, September 28, 1971, p. 7). However, organizations with few or no competitors are less obliged to reduce the waiting time of clients. (This condition makes waiting a national pastime in the Soviet Union, where most services are rendered by government-run establishments that are not subject to market forces.)

The enormous amounts of waiting time expended in dealings with public people-serving bureaucracies is directly related to monopolization of the various services which they offer or impose. Monopolization accords governmental units the power to maximize their efficiency of operation by minimizing service costs and, in so doing, maximizing client waiting. This "optimum solution" is exemplified by bureaus which distribute welfare benefits to long lines of disadvantaged people:

> The number of Medicaid and public assistance applicants and recipients has become so great that [New York's] Department of Social Services is literally shutting its doors in their faces.

Many of the 45 social service centers close their doors early—12, 1 or 2 o'clock—rather than admit persons the workers realistically know cannot be seen that particular day.

The Medicaid office advises applicants to line up outside the doors before dawn. "You'd better get down here around 6:30 or 7 o'clock," said a person answering the telephone at the Medicaid office. . . . "We can only see 200 persons a day. If you want to be in the first 200 you better get here then—with your application filled out." The Medicaid office does not open until 8:30 A.M. . . .

Last week the department announced it had saved $39 million by employing fewer case workers. [*New York Times*, November 21, 1971, p. 58]

However, the relatively wealthy as well as the poor are put to inconvenience by having to wait in person for licenses, permits, visas, tickets, information and the like. Dealings with government-sponsored transportation facilities can also be cited as an example:

Before Amtrak took over, I would have had to call the Illinois Central to go to Miami. If I wanted to go to New York, I'd call the Penn Central. To go west, the Santa Fe. But now, under the streamlined, tax-supported Amtrak, one number, one central office, makes the reservations. They have computers and other modern devices the old system didn't have.

At 10 minutes after noon, I dialed the new Amtrak reservation number. The line was busy, so I hung up and waited a few minutes and dialed again. It was still busy. Five minutes later, I tried again. It was busy. By 1 o'clock I had tried 10 times, and had heard only busy signals.

Enough was enough. I phoned the Amtrak executive office, to ask what was wrong with their reservation number. A woman there put me on hold. I was on hold for seven minutes. Then when she finally took me off hold, she switched me to somebody's office, and a secretary laughed and said: "Oh, yes, our lines are very busy."

At 2 P.M. it finally happened. Instead of getting a busy signal, it rang. It actually rang. . . . It rang. And it rang. And it rang. For eight minutes it rang. . . . So I hung up, got another cup of coffee and tried again. That was a mistake, because I heard another busy signal.

Then at 2:47 it happened. It rang. And somebody answered. I listened closely to make sure it wasn't a recorded message. No, it was really somebody alive. After that it was easy. In about eight or nine minutes the reservations were made.

The clock said 3 P.M. So I have to congratulate Amtrak. It took me only two hours and 50 minutes to complete a telephone call and make reservations. It would have probably taken me at least 10 minutes more than that to take a cab to O'Hare, board a plane, fly to Miami, and get off the plane. [*Chicago Daily News*, June 9, 1972, p. 3]

This instance is an especially informative one, for it demonstrates that the amount of time clients of an organization are called upon to wait is in large measure determined by the broader competitive structure in which the organization is situated. Longitudinal and cross-sectional means are brought to bear in this assessment. By reference to the temporal barrier to access to rail service after centralization and monopolization, relative ease of access before the transformation is implicitly affirmed. And after documenting the lengthy waiting time required in a noncompetitive service market, we find explicit reference to the ready availability of service offered in highly competitive ones (airlines, in this case). In this double sense, the institutional grounding of waiting time is a conclusion warranted by the facts.

We now turn to public services which by their very nature admit of no alternatives and which at the same time are so organized as to constitute the most radical instance of the principle we are now discussing.

A DAY IN COURT: Discrepancy between demand for and supply of "authoritative judgment" is perhaps the most notorious source of waiting for both rich and poor. In fact, those who look forward to their "day in court," whether civil, criminal, or juvenile, very often find themselves spending their day in the courthouse corridor (many courts do not provide waiting rooms). In some courts, in fact, all parties whose cases are scheduled to be heard on a particular day are instructed to be present at its beginning when the judge arrives.[5] This is a most pronounced manifestation of what we earlier referred to as "overscheduling," which in this case ensures that the judge (whose bench is separated from his office or working area) will not be left with idle time that cannot be put to productive use—a consideration which may help us understand the seemingly irrational practice of assembling together at the beginning of the day those who are to be served during its course. While this tactic guarantees that the judge's valuable time will not be wasted, it also ensures that most parties will be kept waiting for a substantial period of time; some, all day long. Indeed, because they have no means to retaliate against the judge's own tardiness or excessive lunch breaks, some individuals may not be served at all and must return on the next day to wait further. Clients' attorneys, incidentally, keep them company during much of this time—a service for which the former pay dearly.

All of this is not to say that the organization of justice profits. It must, on the contrary, pay a very high price for support of its prima donnas. As one juvenile-court officer puts it: "[W]aiting to be called into court . . . is the most serious problem. Just from an internal point of view this means that a probation counselor usually accomplishes nothing in the hour or more he often has to wait to get his case into court. Usually during this waiting period he sees no people, does no counselling, can't do dictation or other 'desk-work'—his wait is complete, unproductive waste. These same problems apply to other professional people: caseworkers from the Department of Social Services, school principals, lawyers, etc." (Fairfax County [Virginia] Juvenile and Domestic Relations Court, Memorandum, 1971, p.1). While attorneys[6] and other professionals are fortunate enough to claim a fee for doing nothing in a professional way, others are often denied this luxury. Authorities who are mindful of civil security, for example, wisely find it more expedient to dismiss cases (particularly such misdemeanants as traffic violators) for lack of witnesses and evidence than to tie up a large sector of the police force for the better part of the day in a crowded corridor. In this particular sense, the police are too important—their time too valuable—to be kept waiting. On the other hand, it may be claimed that by tying up defendants all day long in these same corridors justice may be served—provided, of course, that the defendants are in fact guilty as charged. However, the situation is quite different in felony cases, where casual dismissals are less probable. Under these circumstances police wait as long as defendants. In the Chicago Gun Court, for example, "40 or 45 police are waiting to testify at 9:30 A.M., when court begins. Cases are not scheduled for specific times, so most of them wait and wait. One recent day 31 were still waiting around at 1 P.M. The next day 20 were there at 1 P.M. And 23 the following day." The same conditions prevail at the Narcotics Court where police waiting time "translates on an annual basis to 13,000 police days lost and $700,000 in expenses" (*Chicago Daily News*, August 21, 1973, p. 14).

Two observations emerge from and transcend the particular content of what has just been said. First, the assertion that clients may pay a high price, in terms of time, in their dealings with public bureaucracies means that a societal cost, expressed in terms of aggregate client time diverted from more productive activities, must be written into the usually implicit but sometimes explicit "optimum solution formulae" by which particular "public service" organizations maximize their own efficiency. Because of this factor, the real cost of governmental services is not to be obviated by budgetary considerations alone.

Second, minimization of a powerful server's idle time may subtract from the productivity of the organization as well as its clients. This observation, which is merely grotesquely evident in court settings, reflects the general principle that increments in efficiency in one part of a social organization often entail malfunction in other sectors. Accordingly, just as high concentration of power in an organization may lend itself to societal inefficiency, indexed by more productive client-time foregone, so concentration of power and honor in an elevated server may render organizations ineffective by maximizing idle time of subordinated servers. The more general import of this statement is that it amends the overly simplistic scarcity theory of waiting, which fixates our attention upon server shortage as a condition of client delay. The present statement shows that the organization of services, as well as their volume, provides occasion for waiting.

An additional point is that some persons and groups are relatively exempt from waiting. If we turn our attention once more to the courtroom, we find that the powerful are most likely to enjoy such advantage. In making up the docket, for example, resources are taken into account. Defendants who are represented by an attorney are very often scheduled before those who are not (in Chicago traffic courts, at least). And cases involving important and powerful contestants, witnesses, and/or lawyers may be scheduled at their convenience and not be delayed for long periods of time. Similarly, attorneys who enjoy favor with the court clerk are also able to avoid long waits because they are allowed to schedule their case early.[7] Thus, while waiting time may be maximized by persons or in organizations which enjoy full or near monopoly on the services they offer, the relationship between the power and waiting time of their clients is probably attenuated rather than negated. For, while the powerful may lack the opportunity to take their business elsewhere, they nevertheless possess the resources to ensure that their needs will be accommodated before the needs of those with fewer means.

· · ·

SOCIAL PSYCHOLOGICAL ASPECTS OF DELAY

Making Others Wait

· · ·

Because the worth of a person is not independent of the amount of time others must wait for him, that person can maintain and dramatize his worth by purposely causing another to wait.

Of course, the imposition of a waiting period does not in itself make a person or his services valuable; it can only magnify existing positive evaluations or transform neutral feelings into positive ones. If these initial feelings are not favorable, or at least neutral, the waiting caused by a server may lower clients' estimations of his worth. Instead of a sought-after and important man, the server becomes an incompetent who cannot perform his job properly; thus is his initial inferiority confirmed. (This is why subordinates who know where they stand do not like to keep their superiors waiting.) Generally, the dramatization of ascendency by keeping another waiting will do a server the most good when his social rank exceeds that of his client or when the difference between their ranks is ambiguous. In the latter case, ascendency accrues to him who can best dramatize it; in the former, ascendency may be dramatized by him to whom it already accrues.

Thus, just as authority is affirmed by the placement of social distance between super and subordinate, so temporal distance subserves the ascendency of the person who imposes it. More precisely, the restriction of access to oneself by forcing another to "cool his heels" is instrumental to the cultivation of social distance.

· · ·

The Imposition of Waiting as an Aggressive Act

If the temporal aspect of relationships between those occupying different social positions may be stated in terms of who waits for whom, then we would expect to find a reversal of the waiting-delaying pattern when persons "switch" positions. Furthermore, this reversal may be accentuated through retaliation by the one who suffered under the initial arrangement. A former president furnishes us with an example:

> Ken Hechler, who was director of research at the White House from 1948 to 1952, recalled the day Mr. Truman kept Winthrop Aldrich, president of the Chase Manhattan Bank, waiting outside the White House office for 30 minutes. Hechler quoted Mr. Truman as saying:
>
> "When I was a United States senator and headed the war investigation committee, I had to go to New York to see this fella Aldrich. Even though I had an appointment he had me cool my heels for an hour and a half. So just relax. He's got a little while to go yet." [*Chicago Daily News*, December 27, 1972, p. 4]

Punitive sanctioning through the imposition of waiting is met in its most extreme forms when a person is not only kept waiting but is also kept ignorant as to how long he must wait, or even of what he is waiting for. One manifestation of the latter form is depicted by Solzhenitsyn (1968a):

> Having met the man (or telephoned him or even specially summoned him), he might say: "Please step into my office tomorrow morning at ten." "Can't I drop in now?" the individual would be sure to ask, since he would be eager to know what he was being summoned for and get it over with. "No, not now," Rusanov would gently, but strictly admonish. He would not say that he was busy at the moment or had to go to a conference. He would on no account offer a clear, simple reason, something that could reassure the man being summoned (for that was the crux of this device). He would pronounce the words "not now" in a tone allowing many interpretations—not all of them favorable. "About what?" the employee might ask, out of boldness or inexperience. "You'll find out tomorrow," Pavel Nikolaevich would answer in a velvet voice, bypassing the tactless question. But what a long time it is until tomorrow. [p. 222]

The underlying technique for the aggressive use of delay involves the withdrawal or withholding of one's presence with a view to forcing another into an interactionally precarious state wherein he might confront, recognize, and flounder in his own vulnerability or unworthiness.[8] By such means, the superordinate not only affirms his ascendency but does so at the direct expense of his inferior's dignity. Russian bureaucrats are masters at invoking this routine in their dealings with waiting clients:

> Casting a disapproving eye at the janitor's wet overshoes, and looking at him severely, Shikin let him stand there while he sat down in an armchair and silently looked over various papers. From time to time, as if he was astonished by what he was reading . . . , he looked up at him in amazement, as one might look at a man-eating beast that has finally been caged. All this was done according to the system and was meant to have an annihilating effect on the prisoner's psyche. A half-hour passed in the locked office in inviolate silence. The lunch bell rang out clearly. Spiridon hoped to receive his letter from home, but Shikin did not even hear the bell; he rifled silently through thick files, he took something out of a box and put it in another box, he leafed, frowning, through various papers and again glanced up briefly in surprise at the dispirited, guilty Spiridon.

All the water from Spiridon's overshoes had dripped on the rubber runner, and they had dried when Shikin finally spoke: "All right, move closer!" [Solzhenitsyn 1968b, pp. 482–83]

This kind of strategy can only be employed by superordinates who have power over a client in the first place. The effect on the client is to further subordinate him, regardless of a server's initial attractiveness or a client's realization that the delay has been deliberately imposed. Furthermore, this practice leaves the client in a psychologically as well as a ritually unsatisfactory state. The two presumably act back on each other in a mutually subversive way, for by causing his client to become tense or nervous the server undermines the self-confidence necessary for him to maintain proper composure. This tendency, incidentally, is routinely applied by skillful police interrogators who deliberately ignore a suspect waiting to be questioned, assuming that a long, uncertain wait will "rattle him" sufficiently to disorganize the kinds of defenses he could use to protect himself (Arthur and Caputo 1959, p. 31).

Ritual Waiting and Autonomy

We have tried to show that while servers may cause others to wait in order to devote their attention to other necessary matters, they may also make people wait for the pure joy of dramatizing their capacity to do so. Such elation, we saw, is understandable, for by effecting a wait the server demonstrates that his presence is not subject to the disposition or whim of another and that access to him is a privilege not to be taken lightly. And, if access is a privilege, then one may sanction another by deliberately holding oneself apart from him. But we must now make explicit a point that was only implied in our previous discussions: that the imposition of waiting expresses and sustains the autonomy as well as the superiority of the self.

While the imposition of delay allows a superordinate to give expression to his authority, waiting may also be imposed in protest against that authority. The latter achievement is valued, naturally, among those of despised status and low rank. Because they lack the wherewithal to do so in most of their other relations, the powerless, in their capacity as servers, delight in keeping their superiors waiting. The deliberately sluggish movements of many store clerks, telephone operators, cashiers, toll collectors, and the like, testify to the ability of the lowly as well as the lofty to dramatize their autonomy. This accords with Meerloo's (1966) assertion that "the strategy of delay is an ambivalent attack on those who command us" (p. 249). This kind of aggression is perhaps most pronounced under sociologically ambivalent conditions: as the legitimacy of the existing distribution of status honor ceases to be taken for granted, prescribed deference patterns give way to institutionalized rudeness, which may be expressed by

appearing late for appointments with a superordinate as well as by dillydal-
lying while he waits for his needs to be serviced.

• • •

SUMMARY

[V]alue foregone through idleness is an extrinsic disadvantage. On the other
hand, the degradational implications of being kept idle are intrinsic to waiting and can arise in no way other than through involuntary delay. The purpose of this paper was to explore the way these costs are distributed
throughout the social structure and to identify the principles to which this
allocation gives expression.

We have introduced the category of power . . . as the ultimate determinant of delay, the main assertion being that the distribution of waiting time
coincides with the distribution of power . . . [R]esourceful persons wait less
within both competitive and monopolistic markets, while delay will be
more pronounced in the latter regardless of personal power.

If waiting is related to a person's position in a power network, then a
server may confirm or enhance his status by deliberately making another
wait for him. In a more general sense, this is to say that the management of
availability itself, regardless of the purpose for which an individual makes
himself available, carries with it distinct psychological implications. Because a person's access to others indexes his scarcity as a social object, that
person's social worth may only be realized by demonstrated inaccessibility.
Openness to social relations may therefore be restricted not only to regulate
interactional demands but also to enhance the self that one brings to an interaction. . . . The initial relationship between waiting and power thus
gives rise to processes which strengthen it. . . .

The broader implication of this essay is that it finds . . . time itself a generalized resource whose distribution affects life chances with regard to the
attainment of other, more specific kinds of rewards. This is true in a number
of respects. Time, like money, is valuable because it is necessary for the
achievement of productive purposes; ends cannot be reached unless an appropriate amount of it is "spent" or "invested" on their behalf. On the other
hand, the power that a time surplus makes possible may be protected and/
or expanded by depriving others of their time. By creating queues to reduce
idle periods, for example, a server exploits clients by converting their time
to his own use. A server does the same by "overcharging" in the sense of deliberately causing a particular client to wait longer than necessary.

The monetary analogies we have used are not without some justification.
Just as money possesses no substantive value independent of its use as a
means of exchange, time can only be of value if put to substantive use in an
exchange relationship. Both time and money may be regarded as generalized means because of the infinity of possibilities for their utilization: both

are possessed in finite quantities; both may be counted, saved, spent, lost, wasted, or invested. . . . Accordingly, while the powerful can allocate monetary means to their own desired ends by controlling the *budget*, they also regulate the distribution of time—rewarding themselves, depriving others—through their control of the *schedule*. What is at stake in the first instance is the *amount* of resources to which different parts of a system are entitled; in the second, it is the *priority* of their entitlements. Far from being a coincidental by-product of power, then, control of time comes into view as one of its essential properties.

NOTES

1. This paper was supported by grant 1-5690-00-4335 from the Ford Foundation and by the Center for Health Administration Studies, University of Chicago. The writer wishes to acknowledge the very useful comments made on this paper by Peter Blau and Morris Janowitz.

2. Personal communication from Florence Levinsohn.

3. Other "contacts" include the radio, over which Saturday and Sunday morning waiting times at many metropolitan golf courses are broadcast. This service, which saves many players many long delays, is performed almost exclusively for the middle and upper-middle classes.

4. Even when circumstances make it necessary for the resourceful to wait, they suffer less than their inferiors. As a general rule, the wealthier the clientele, the more adequate the waiting accommodations. Thus, persons who can afford bail can await their trial (or, far more frequently, attorneys' bargaining on their behalf) in the free community. The poor must wait in jail. The same is true of facilities. In airports, for example, those who can afford it may simultaneously avoid contamination by the masses and engross themselves in a variety of activities, including fabulous eating and drinking, in "VIP lounges." The term "lounge" instead of the vulgar "waiting area" or "gate" is also applied to facilities set aside for those who travel a specified number of miles with (and pay a substantial sum of money to) a particular airline. In this as in many other settings, waiting locales for the poor and less rich lack the elaborate involvement supplies, pleasant decor, and other physical and psychological comforts that diminish the pain of waiting among those who are better off.

5. A functional equivalent is found in the Soviet Union. "Aleksandr Y. Kabalkin and Vadim M. Khinchuk . . . describe what they termed 'classic cases' in everyday life in the Soviet Union, in which customers wait for the television repairman or for a messenger delivering a train or plane ticket that had been ordered by phone. To the question 'About what time can I expect you?' the stereotyped reply is, 'It can be any time during the day.' And people have to excuse themselves from work and wait—there is no other way out" (*New York Times*, November 7, 1971, p. 5).

6. It may not be assumed that all lawyers earn while they wait. For example, the *New York Times* (August 25, 1971, p. 24) recently reported: "A lawyer who specializes in prosecuting landlords' claims against tenants asked permission in Bronx Supreme Court yesterday to bring his cases there rather than in Civil Court because . . . he spent much time 'just sitting and waiting.' And consequently, he said, he was suffering 'financial loss' and felt he could not continue working in Civil Court."

7. This is to say that, as a scarce commodity, time or priority of service routinely becomes the object of struggle. Recognizing this, a court intake officer writes in a memo to his supervisor: "Intake counselors should assume more control over the setting of cases on the docket, with a proportionate decrease in the control now exercised by clerks" (Fairfax County [Virginia] Juvenile and Domestic Relations Court, Memorandum, 1971, p. 1).

8. Of course, the impulse of stationary servers to make others wait for reasons that are independent of the scarcity of time is paralleled by the tactic used by mobile servers, of keeping them waiting for these same reasons. Thus, a person may simultaneously exhibit contempt for a gathering and underscore his own presence (Parkinson 1962, pp. 73–74) by purposely arriving late. This measure is particularly effective when the proceedings require his presence.

REFERENCES

Arthur, R., and R. Caputo
  1959 *Interrogation for Investigators.* New York: Copp.

Bradford, Jean
  1971 "Getting the Most out of Odd Moments." *Reader's Digest* (June), pp. 82–84.

Liberman, E. G.
  1968–69 "The Queue: Anamnesis, Diagnosis, Therapy." *Soviet Review* 9 (Winter): 12–16.

Mann, Leon
  1969 "Queue Culture: The Waiting Line as a Social System." *American Journal of Sociology* 75 (November): 340–54.

Meerloo, Joost
  1966 "The Time Sense in Psychiatry." In *The Voices of Time,* edited by J. T. Fraser. New York: Braziller.

Parkinson, C., Northcote
  1962 *Parkinson's Law.* Boston: Houghton-Mifflin.

Solzhenitsyn, Aleksandr
  1968a *The Cancer Ward.* New York: Dial.
  1968b *The First Circle.* New York: Harper & Row.

Tawney, R. H.
  1931 *Equality.* London: Allen & Unwin.

Review Questions

1. Compare and contrast the positions in the hierarchy of a formal organization such as a factory or school in terms of control over one's own and others' time.

2. Explain how waiting may differ in monopolistic as opposed to competitive types of organizations. In which type of organization will the most waiting on the part of the clients occur? Will powerful clients have an advantage over the lowly in both types of organizations? Explain.

3. Discuss the practice of consciously *forcing* others to wait as it is engaged in by (1) the powerful, and (2) the lowly.

4. When are "reneging" and "balking" likely to occur? Are powerful people or subordinates more likely to renege and balk? Explain your answer.

5. Schwartz contends that waiting is structured (that is, occupants of some positions will usually spend more time waiting than occupants of other positions). Furthermore, waiting entails costs which are both material and psychological. Discuss these contentions, giving evidence from your own experiences.

THE SAINTS AND THE ROUGHNECKS

William J. Chambliss

Eight promising young men—children of good, stable, white upper-middle-class families, active in school affairs, good pre-college students—were some of the most delinquent boys at Hanibal High School. While community residents knew that these boys occasionally sowed a few wild oats, they were totally unaware that sowing wild oats completely occupied the daily routine of these young men. The Saints were constantly occupied with truancy, drinking, wild driving, petty theft and vandalism. Yet no one was officially arrested for any misdeed during the two years I observed them.

This record was particularly surprising in light of my observations during the same two years of another gang of Hanibal High School students, six lower-class white boys known as the Roughnecks. The Roughnecks were constantly in trouble with police and community even though their rate of delinquency was about equal with that of the Saints. What was the cause of this disparity? the result? The following consideration of the activities, social class and community perceptions of both gangs may provide some answers.

THE SAINTS FROM MONDAY TO FRIDAY

The Saints' principal daily concern was with getting out of school as early as possible. The boys managed to get out of school with minimum danger that they would be accused of playing hookey through an elaborate procedure for obtaining "legitimate" release from class. The most common procedure was for one boy to obtain the release of another by fabricating a meeting of some committee, program or recognized club. Charles might raise his hand in his 9:00 chemistry class and ask to be excused—a euphemism for going to the bathroom. Charles would go to Ed's math class and inform the teacher that Ed was needed for a 9:30 rehearsal of the drama club play. The math teacher would recognize Ed and Charles as "good students" involved in numerous school activities and would permit Ed to leave at 9:30. Charles would return to his class, and Ed would go to Tom's English class to obtain his release. Tom would engineer Charles' escape. The strategy would continue until as many of the Saints as possible were freed. After a stealthy trip

William J. Chambliss, "The Saints and the Roughnecks," *Society*, 11 (November–December 1973), 24–31.

to the car (which had been parked in a strategic spot), the boys were off for a day of fun.

Over the two years I observed the Saints, this pattern was repeated nearly every day. There were variations on the theme, but in one form or another, the boys used this procedure for getting out of class and then off the school grounds. Rarely did all eight of the Saints manage to leave school at the same time. The average number avoiding school on the days I observed them was five.

Having escaped from the concrete corridors the boys usually went either to a pool hall on the other (lower-class) side of town or to a cafe in the suburbs. Both places were out of the way of people the boys were likely to know (family or school officials), and both provided a source of entertainment. The pool hall entertainment was the generally rough atmosphere, the occasional hustler, the sometimes drunk proprietor and, of course, the game of pool. The cafe's entertainment was provided by the owner. The boys would "accidentally" knock a glass on the floor or spill cola on the counter—not all the time, but enough to be sporting. They would also bend spoons, put salt in sugar bowls and generally tease whoever was working in the cafe. The owner had opened the cafe recently and was dependent on the boys' business which was, in fact, substantial since between the horsing around and the teasing they bought food and drinks.

THE SAINTS ON WEEKENDS

On weekends the automobile was even more critical than during the week, for on weekends the Saints went to Big Town—a large city with a population of over a million 25 miles from Hanibal. Every Friday and Saturday night most of the Saints would meet between 8:00 and 8:30 and would go into Big Town. Big Town activities included drinking heavily in taverns or nightclubs, driving drunkenly through the streets, and committing acts of vandalism and playing pranks.

By midnight on Fridays and Saturdays the Saints were usually thoroughly high, and one or two of them were often so drunk they had to be carried to the cars. Then the boys drove around town, calling obscenities to women and girls; occasionally trying (unsuccessfully so far as I could tell) to pick girls up; and driving recklessly through red lights and at high speeds with their lights out. Occasionally they played "chicken." One boy would climb out the back window of the car and across the roof to the driver's side of the car while the car was moving at high speed (between 40 and 50 miles an hour); then the driver would move over and the boy who had just crawled across the car roof would take the driver's seat.

Searching for "fair game" for a prank was the boys' principal activity after they left the tavern. The boys would drive alongside a foot patrolman and ask directions to some street. If the policeman leaned on the car in the course of answering the question, the driver would speed away, causing him to lose his balance. The Saints were careful to play this prank only in an area where they were not going to spend much time and where they could quickly disappear around a corner to avoid having their license plate number taken.

Construction sites and road repair areas were the special province of the Saints' mischief. A soon-to-be-repaired hole in the road inevitably invited the Saints to remove lanterns and wooden barricades and put them in the car, leaving the hole unprotected. The boys would find a safe vantage point and wait for an unsuspecting motorist to drive into the hole. Often, though not always, the boys would go up to the motorist and commiserate with him about the dreadful way the city protected its citizenry.

Leaving the scene of the open hole and the motorist, the boys would then go searching for an appropriate place to erect the stolen barricade. An "appropriate place" was often a spot on a highway near a curve in the road where the barricade would not be seen by an on-coming motorist. The boys would wait to watch an unsuspecting motorist attempt to stop and (usually) crash into the wooden barricade. With saintly bearing the boys might offer help and understanding.

A stolen lantern might well find its way onto the back of a police car or hang from a street lamp. Once a lantern served as a prop for a reenactment of the "midnight ride of Paul Revere" until the "play," which was taking place at 2:00 A.M. in the center of a main street of Big Town, was interrupted by a police car several blocks away. The boys ran, leaving the lanterns on the street, and managed to avoid being apprehended.

Abandoned houses, especially if they were located in out-of-the-way places, were fair game for destruction and spontaneous vandalism. The boys would break windows, remove furniture to the yard and tear it apart, urinate on the walls and scrawl obscenities inside.

Through all the pranks, drinking and reckless driving the boys managed miraculously to avoid being stopped by police. Only twice in two years was I aware that they had been stopped by a Big City policeman. Once was for speeding (which they did every time they drove whether they were drunk or sober), and the driver managed to convince the policeman that it was simply an error. The second time they were stopped they had just left a nightclub and were walking through an alley. Aaron stopped to urinate and the boys began making obscene remarks. A foot patrolman came into the alley, lectured the boys and sent them home. Before the boys got to the car one began talking in a loud voice again. The policeman, who had followed them down the alley, arrested this boy for disturbing the peace and took him to the police station where the other Saints gathered. After paying a $5 fine, and with the assurance that there would be no permanent record of the arrest, the boy was released.

The boys had a spirit of frivolity and fun about their escapades. They did not view what they were engaged in as "delinquency," though it surely was by any reasonable definition of that word. They simply viewed themselves as having a little fun and who, they would ask, was really hurt by it? The answer had to be no one, although this fact remains one of the most difficult things to explain about the gang's behavior. Unlikely though it seems, in two years of drinking, driving, carousing and vandalism no one was seriously injured as a result of the Saints' activities.

THE SAINTS IN SCHOOL

The Saints were highly successful in school. The average grade for the group was "B" with two of the boys having close to a straight "A" average. Almost all of the boys were popular and many of them held offices in the school. One of the boys was vice president of the student body one year. Six of the boys played on athletic teams.

At the end of their senior year, the student body selected ten seniors for special recognition as the "school wheels"; four of the ten were Saints. Teachers and school officials saw no problem with any of these boys and anticipated that they would all "make something of themselves."

How the boys managed to maintain this impression is surprising in view of their actual behavior while in school. Their technique for covering truancy was so successful that teachers did not even realize that the boys were absent from school much of the time. Occasionally, of course, the system would backfire and then the boy was on his own. A boy who was caught would be most contrite, would plead guilty and ask for mercy. He inevitably got the mercy he sought.

Cheating on examinations was rampant, even to the point of orally communicating answers to exams as well as looking at one another's papers. Since none of the group studied, and since they were primarily dependent on one another for help, it is surprising that grades were so high. Teachers contributed to the deception in their admitted inclination to give these boys (and presumably others like them) the benefit of the doubt. When asked how the boys did in school, and when pressed on specific examinations, teachers might admit that they were disappointed in John's performance, but would quickly add that they "knew that he was capable of doing better," so John was given a higher grade than he had actually earned. How often this happened is impossible to know. During the time that I observed the group, I never saw any of the boys take homework home. Teachers may have been "understanding" very regularly.

One exception to the gang's generally good performance was Jerry, who had a "C" average in his junior year, experienced disaster the next year and failed to graduate. Jerry had always been a little more nonchalant than the others about the liberties he took in school. Rather than wait for someone to come get him from class, he would offer his own excuse and leave. Although he probably did not miss any more class than most of the others in the group, he did not take the requisite pains to cover his absences. Jerry was the only Saint whom I ever heard talk back to a teacher. Although teachers often called him a "cut up" or a "smart kid," they never referred to him as a troublemaker or as a kid headed for trouble. It seems likely, then, that Jerry's failure his senior year and his mediocre performance his junior year were consequences of his not playing the game the proper way (possibly because he was disturbed by his parents' divorce). His teachers regarded him as "immature" and not quite ready to get out of high school.

THE POLICE AND THE SAINTS

The local police saw the Saints as good boys who were among the leaders of the youth in the community. Rarely, the boys might be stopped in town for speeding or for running a stop sign. When this happened the boys were always polite, contrite and pled for mercy. As in school, they received the mercy they asked for. None ever received a ticket or was taken into the precinct by the local police.

The situation in Big City, where the boys engaged in most of their delinquency, was only slightly different. The police there did not know the boys at all, although occasionally the boys were stopped by a patrolman. Once they were caught taking a lantern from a construction site. Another time they were stopped for running a stop sign, and on several occasions they were stopped for speeding. Their behavior was as before: contrite, polite and penitent. The urban police, like the local police, accepted their demeanor as sincere. More important, the urban police were convinced that these were good boys just out for a lark.

THE ROUGHNECKS

Hanibal townspeople never perceived the Saints' high level of delinquency. The Saints were good boys who just went in for an occasional prank. After all, they were well dressed, well mannered and had nice cars. The Roughnecks were a different story. Although the two gangs of boys were the same age, and both groups engaged in an equal amount of wild-oat sowing, everyone agreed that the not-so-well-dressed, not-so-well-mannered, not-so-rich boys were heading for trouble. Townspeople would say, "You can see the gang members at the drugstore, night after night, leaning against the storefront (sometimes drunk) or slouching around inside buying Cokes, reading magazines, and probably stealing old Mr. Wall blind. When they are outside and girls walk by, even respectable girls, these boys make suggestive remarks. Sometimes their remarks are downright lewd."

From the community's viewpoint, the real indication that these kids were in trouble was that they were constantly involved with the police. Some of them had been picked up for stealing, mostly small stuff, of course, "but still it's stealing small stuff that leads to big time crimes." "Too bad," people said. "Too bad that these boys couldn't behave like the other kids in town; stay out of trouble, be polite to adults, and look to their future."

The community's impression of the degrees to which this group of six boys (ranging in age from 16 to 19) engaged in delinquency was somewhat distorted. In some ways the gang was more delinquent than the community thought; in other ways they were less.

The fighting activities of the group were fairly readily and accurately perceived by almost everyone. At least once a month, the boys would get into some sort of fight, although most fights were scraps between members of the group or involved only one member of the group and some peripheral hanger-on. Only three times in the period of observation did the group fight together: once against a gang from across town, once against two blacks and once against a group of boys from another school. For the first two fights the group went out "looking for trouble"—and they found it both times. The third fight followed a football game and began spontaneously with an argument on the football field between one of the Roughnecks and a member of the opposition's football team.

Jack had a particular propensity for fighting and was involved in most of the brawls. He was a prime mover of the escalation of arguments into fights.

More serious than fighting, had the community been aware of it, was theft. Although almost everyone was aware that the boys occasionally stole things, they did not realize the extent of the activity. Petty stealing was a frequent event for the Roughnecks. Sometimes they stole as a group and coordinated their efforts; other times they stole in pairs. Rarely did they steal alone.

The thefts ranged from very small things like paperback books, comics and ballpoint pens to expensive items like watches. The nature of the thefts varied from time to time. The gangs would go through a period of systematically shoplifting items from automobiles or school lockers. Types of thievery varied with the whim of the gang. Some forms of thievery were more profitable than others, but all thefts were for profit, not just thrills.

Roughnecks siphoned gasoline from cars as often as they had access to an automobile, which was not very often. Unlike the Saints, who owned their own cars, the Roughnecks would have to borrow their parents' cars, an event which occurred only eight or nine times a year. The boys claimed to have stolen cars for joy rides from time to time.

Ron committed the most serious of the group's offenses. With an unidentified associate the boy attempted to burglarize a gasoline station. Although this station had been robbed twice previously in the same month, Ron denied any involvement in either of the other thefts. When Ron and his accomplice approached the station, the owner was hiding in the bushes beside the station. He fired both barrels of a double-barreled shotgun at the boys. Ron was severely injured; the other boy ran away and was never caught. Though he remained in critical condition for several months, Ron finally recovered and served six months of the following year in reform school. Upon release from reform school, Ron was put back a grade in school, and began running around with a different gang of boys. The Roughnecks considered the new gang less delinquent than themselves, and during the following year Ron had no more trouble with the police.

The Roughnecks, then, engaged mainly in three types of delinquency: theft, drinking and fighting. Although community members perceived that this gang of kids was delinquent, they mistakenly believed that their illegal activities were primarily drinking, fighting and being a nuisance to passersby. Drinking was limited among the gang members, although it did occur, and theft was much more prevalent than anyone realized.

Drinking would doubtless have been more prevalent had the boys had ready access to liquor. Since they rarely had automobiles at their disposal, they could not travel very far, and the bars in town would not serve them. Most of the boys had little money, and this, too, inhibited their purchase of alcohol. Their major source of liquor was a local drunk who would buy them a fifth if they would give him enough to buy himself a pint of whiskey or a bottle of wine.

The community's perception of drinking as prevalent stemmed from the fact that it was the most obvious delinquency the boys engaged in. When one of the boys had been drinking, even a casual observer seeing him on the corner would suspect that he was high.

There was a high level of mutual distrust and dislike between the Roughnecks and the police. The boys felt very strongly that the police were unfair and corrupt. Some evidence existed that the boys were correct in their perception.

The main source of the boys' dislike for the police undoubtedly stemmed from the fact that the police would sporadically harass the group. From the standpoint of the boys, these acts of occasional enforcement of the law were whimsical and uncalled for. It made no sense to them, for example, that the police would come to the corner occasionally and threaten them with arrest for loitering when the night before the boys had been out siphoning gasoline from cars and the police had been nowhere in sight. To the boys, the police were stupid on the one hand, for not being where they should have been and catching the boys in a serious offense, and unfair on the other hand, for trumping up "loitering" charges against them.

From the viewpoint of the police, the situation was quite different. They knew, with all the confidence necessary to be a policeman, that these boys were engaged in criminal activities. They knew this partly from occasionally catching them, mostly from circumstantial evidence ("the boys were around when those tires were slashed"), and partly because the police shared the view of the community in general that this was a bad bunch of boys. The best the police could hope to do was to be sensitive to the fact that these boys were engaged in illegal acts and arrest them whenever there was some evidence that they had been involved. Whether or not the boys had in fact committed a particular act in a particular way was not especially important. The police had a broader view; their job was to stamp out these kids' crimes; the tactics were not as important as the end result.

Over the period that the group was under observation, each member was arrested at least once. Several of the boys were arrested a number of times and spent at least one night in jail. While most were never taken to court, two of the boys were sentenced to six months' incarceration in boys' schools.

THE ROUGHNECKS IN SCHOOL

The Roughnecks' behavior in school was not particularly disruptive. During school hours they did not all hang around together, but tended instead to spend most of their time with one or two other members of the gang who were their special buddies. Although every member of the gang attempted to avoid school as much as possible, they were not particularly successful and most of them attended school with surprising regularity. They considered school a burden—something to be gotten through with a minimum of conflict. If they were "bugged" by a particular teacher, it could lead to trouble. One of the boys, Al, once threatened to beat up a teacher and, according to the other boys, the teacher hid under a desk to escape him.

Teachers saw the boys the way the general community did, as heading for trouble, as being uninterested in making something of themselves. Some were also seen as being incapable of meeting the academic standards of the school. Most of the teachers expressed concern for this group of boys and were willing to pass them despite poor performance, in the belief that failing them would only aggravate the problem.

The group of boys had a grade point average just slightly above "C." No one in the group failed either grade, and no one had better than a "C" average. They were very consistent in their perception of the boys' achievement.

Two of the boys were good football players. Herb was acknowledged to be the best player in the school and Jack was almost as good. Both boys were criticized for their failure to abide by training rules, for refusing to come to practice as often as they should, and for not playing their best during practice. What they lacked in sportsmanship they made up for in skill, apparently, and played every game no matter how poorly they had performed in practice or how many practice sessions they had missed.

TWO QUESTIONS

Why did the community, the school and the police react to the Saints as though they were good, upstanding, nondelinquent youths with bright futures but to the Roughnecks as though they were tough, young criminals who were headed for trouble? Why did the Roughnecks and the Saints in fact have quite different careers after high school—careers which, by and large, lived up to the expectations of the community?

The most obvious explanation for the differences in the community's and law enforcement agencies' reactions to the two gangs is that one group of boys was "more delinquent" than the other. Which group *was* more delinquent? The answer to this question will determine in part how we explain the differential responses to these groups by the members of the community and, particularly, by law enforcement and school officials.

In sheer number of illegal acts, the Saints were the more delinquent. They were truant from school for at least part of the day almost every day of the week. In addition, their drinking and vandalism occurred with surprising regularity. The Roughnecks, in contrast, engaged sporadically in delinquent episodes. While these episodes were frequent, they certainly did not occur on a daily or even a weekly basis.

The difference in frequency of offenses was probably caused by the Roughnecks' inability to obtain liquor and to manipulate legitimate excuses from school. Since the Roughnecks had less money than the Saints, and teachers carefully supervised their school activities, the Roughnecks' hearts may have been as black as the Saints', but their misdeeds were not nearly as frequent.

There are really no clear-cut criteria by which to measure qualitative differences in antisocial behavior. The most important dimension is generally referred to as the "seriousness" of the offenses.

If seriousness encompasses the relative economic costs of delinquent acts, then some assessment can be made. The Roughnecks probably stole an average of about $5 worth of goods a week. Some weeks the figure was considerably higher, but these times must be balanced against long periods when almost nothing was stolen.

The Saints were more continuously engaged in delinquency but their acts were not for the most part costly to property. Only their vandalism and occasional theft of gasoline would so qualify. Perhaps once or twice a month they would siphon a tankful of gas. The other costly items were street signs, construction lanterns and the like. All of these acts combined probably did not quite average $5 a week, partly because much of the stolen equipment was abandoned and presumably could be recovered. The difference in cost of stolen property between the two groups was trivial, but the Roughnecks probably had a slightly more expensive set of activities than did the Saints.

Another meaning of seriousness is the potential threat of physical harm to members of the community and to the boys themselves. The Roughnecks were more prone to physical violence; they not only welcomed an opportunity to fight; they went seeking it. In addition, they fought among themselves frequently. Although the fighting never included deadly weapons, it was still a menace, however minor, to the physical safety of those involved.

The Saints never fought. They avoided physical conflict both inside and outside the group. At the same time, though, the Saints frequently endangered their own and other people's lives. They did so almost every time they drove a car, especially if they had been drinking. Sober, their driving was risky; under the influence of alcohol it was horrendous. In addition, the Saints endangered the lives of others with their pranks. Street excavations left unmarked were a very serious hazard.

Evaluating the relative seriousness of the two gangs' activities is difficult. The community reacted as though the behavior of the Roughnecks was a problem, and they reacted as though the behavior of the Saints was not. But the members of the community were ignorant of the array of delinquent acts that characterized the Saints' behavior. Although concerned citizens were unaware of much of the Roughnecks' behavior as well, they were much better informed about the Roughnecks' involvement in delinquency than they were about the Saints'.

VISIBILITY

Differential treatment of the two gangs resulted in part because one gang was infinitely more visible than the other. This differential visibility was a direct function of the economic standing of the families. The Saints had access to automobiles and were able to remove themselves from the sight of the community. In as routine a decision as to where to go to have a milkshake after school, the Saints stayed away from the mainstream of community life. Lacking transportation, the Roughnecks could not make it to the edge of town. The center of town was the only practical place for them to meet since their homes were scattered throughout the town and any noncentral meeting place put an undue hardship on some members. Through necessity the Roughnecks congregated in a crowded area where everyone in the community passed frequently, including teachers and law enforcement officers. They could easily see the Roughnecks hanging around the drugstore.

The Roughnecks, of course, made themselves even more visible by making remarks to passersby and by occasionally getting into fights on the corner. Meanwhile, just as regularly, the Saints were either at the cafe on one edge of town or in the pool hall at the other edge of town. Without any particular realization that they were making themselves inconspicuous, the Saints were able to hide their time-wasting. Not only were they removed from the mainstream of traffic, but they were almost always inside a building.

On their escapades the Saints were also relatively invisible, since they left Hanibal and traveled to Big City. Here, too, they were mobile, roaming the city, rarely going to the same area twice.

DEMEANOR

To the notion of visibility must be added the difference in the responses of group members to outside intervention with their activities. If one of the Saints was confronted with an accusing policeman, even if he felt he was truly innocent of a wrongdoing, his demeanor was apologetic and penitent. A Roughnecks' attitude was almost the polar opposite. When confronted with a threatening adult authority, even one who tried to be pleasant, the Roughneck's hostility and disdain were clearly observable. Sometimes he might attempt to put up a veneer of respect, but it was thin and was not accepted as sincere by the authority.

School was no different from the community at large. The Saints could manipulate the system by feigning compliance with the school norms. The availability of cars at school meant that once free from the immediate sight of the teacher, the boys could disappear rapidly. And this escape was well enough planned that no administrator or teacher was nearby when the boys left. A Roughneck who wished to escape for a few hours was in a bind. If it were possible to get free from class, downtown was still a mile away, and even if he arrived there, he was still very visible. Truancy for the Roughnecks meant almost certain detection, while the Saints enjoyed almost complete immunity from sanctions.

BIAS

Community members were not aware of the transgressions of the Saints. Even if the Saints had been less discreet, their favorite delinquencies would have been perceived as less serious than those of the Roughnecks.

In the eyes of the police and school officials, a boy who drinks in an alley and stands intoxicated on the street corner is committing a more serious offense than is a boy who drinks to inebriation in a nightclub or a tavern and drives around afterwards in a car. Similarly, a boy who steals a wallet from a store will be viewed as having committed a more serious offense than a boy who steals a lantern from a construction site.

Perceptual bias also operates with respect to the demeanor of the boys in the two groups when they are confronted by adults. It is not simply that adults dislike the posture affected by boys of the Roughneck ilk; more important is the conviction that the posture adopted by the Roughnecks is an indication of their devotion and commitment to deviance as a way of life. The posture becomes a cue, just as the type of the offense is a cue, to the degree to which the known transgressions are indicators of the youths' potential for other problems.

Visibility, demeanor and bias are surface variables which explain the day-to-day operations of the police. Why do these surface variables operate as they do? Why did the police choose to disregard the Saints' delinquencies while breathing down the backs of the Roughnecks?

The answer lies in the class structure of American society and the control of legal institutions by those at the top of the class structure. Obviously, no representative of the upper class drew up the operational chart for the police which led them to look in the ghettoes and on street corners—which led them to see the demeanor of lower-class youth as troublesome and that of upper-middle-class youth as tolerable. Rather, the procedures simply developed from experience—experience with irate and influential upper-middle-class parents insisting that their son's vandalism was simply a prank and his drunkenness only a momentary "sowing of wild oats"—experience with co-operative or indifferent, powerless, lower-class parents who acquiesced to the laws' definition of their son's behavior.

ADULT CAREERS OF THE SAINTS AND THE ROUGHNECKS

The community's confidence in the potential of the Saints and the Roughnecks apparently was justified. If anything, the community members underestimated the degree to which these youngsters would turn out "good" or "bad."

Seven of the eight members of the Saints went on to college immediately after high school. Five of the boys graduated from college in four years. The sixth one finished college after two years in the army, and the seventh spent four years in the air force before returning to college and receiving a B.A. degree. Of these seven college graduates, three went on for advanced degrees. One finished law school and is now active in state politics, one finished medical school and is practicing near Hanibal, and one boy is now working for a Ph.D. The other four college graduates entered submanagerial, managerial or executive training positions with large firms.

The only Saint who did not complete college was Jerry. Jerry had failed to graduate from high school with the other Saints. During his second senior year, after the other Saints had gone on to college, Jerry began to hang around with what several teachers described as a "rough crowd"—the gang that was heir apparent to the Roughnecks. At the end of his second senior year, when he did graduate from high school, Jerry took a job as a used-car salesman, got married and quickly had a child. Although he made several abortive attempts to go to college by attending night school, when I last saw him (ten years after high school) Jerry was unemployed and had been living on unemployment for almost a year. His wife worked as a waitress.

Some of the Roughnecks have lived up to community expectations. A number of them were headed for trouble. A few were not.

Jack and Herb were the athletes among the Roughnecks and their athletic prowess paid off handsomely. Both boys received unsolicited athletic scholarships to college. After Herb received his scholarship (near the end of his

296 William J. Chambliss

senior year), he apparently did an about-face. His demeanor became very similar to that of the Saints. Although he remained a member in good standing of the Roughnecks, he stopped participating in most activities and did not hang around on the corner as often.

Jack did not change. If anything, he became more prone to fighting. He even made excuses for accepting the scholarship. He told the other gang members that the school had guaranteed him a "C" average if he would come to play football—an idea that seems far-fetched, even in this day of highly competitive recruiting.

During the summer after graduation from high school, Jack attempted suicide by jumping from a tall building. The jump would certainly have killed most people trying it, but Jack survived. He entered college in the fall and played four years of football. He and Herb graduated in four years, and both are teaching and coaching in high schools. They are married and have stable families. If anything, Jack appears to have a more prestigious position in the community than does Herb, though both are well respected and secure in their positions.

Two of the boys never finished high school. Tommy left at the end of his junior year and went to another state. That summer he was arrested and placed on probation on a manslaughter charge. Three years later he was arrested for murder; he pleaded guilty to second degree murder and is serving a 30-year sentence in the state penitentiary.

Al, the other boy who did not finish high school, also left the state in his senior year. He is serving a life sentence in a state penitentiary for first degree murder.

Wes is a small-time gambler. He finished high school and "bummed around." After several years he made contact with a bookmaker who employed him as a runner. Later he acquired his own area and has been working it ever since. His position among the bookmakers is almost identical to the position he had in the gang; he is always around but no one is really aware of him. He makes no trouble and he does not get into any. Steady, reliable, capable of keeping his mouth closed, he plays the game by the rules, even though the game is an illegal one.

That leaves only Ron. Some of his former friends reported that they had heard he was "driving a truck up north," but no one could provide any concrete information.

REINFORCEMENT

The community responded to the Roughnecks as boys in trouble, and the boys agreed with that perception. Their pattern of deviancy was reinforced, and breaking away from it became increasingly unlikely. Once the boys acquired an image of themselves as deviants, they selected new friends who affirmed that self-image. As that self-conception became more firmly entrenched, they also became willing to try new and more extreme deviances. With their growing alienation came freer expression of disrespect and hostility for representatives of the legitimate society. This disrespect increased the community's negativism, perpetuating the entire process of commitment to deviance. Lack of a commitment to deviance works the same way. In either case, the process will perpetuate itself unless some event (like a scholarship to college or a sudden failure) external to the established relationship intervenes. For two of the Roughnecks (Herb and Jack), receiving college athletic scholarships created new relations and culminated in a break with the established pattern of deviance. In the case of one of the Saints (Jerry), his parents' divorce and his failing to graduate from high school changed some of his other relations. Being held back in school for a year and losing his place among the Saints had sufficient impact on Jerry to alter his self-image and virtually to assure that he would not go on to college as his peers did. Although the experiments of life can rarely be reversed, it seems likely in view of the behavior of the other boys who did not enjoy this special treatment by the school that Jerry, too, would have "become something" had he graduated as anticipated. For Herb and Jack outside intervention worked to their advantage, for Jerry it was his undoing.

Selective perception and labeling—finding, processing and punishing some kinds of criminality and not others—means that visible, poor, non-mobile, outspoken, undiplomatic "tough" kids will be noticed, whether their actions are seriously delinquent or not. Other kids, who have established a reputation for being bright (even though underachieving), disciplined and involved in respectable activities, who are mobile and monied, will be invisible when they deviate from sanctioned activities. They'll sow their wild oats—perhaps even wider and thicker than their lower-class cohorts—but they won't be noticed. When it's time to leave adolescence most will follow the expected path, settling into the ways of the middle class, remembering fondly the delinquent but unnoticed fling of their youth. The Roughnecks and others like them may turn around, too. It is more likely that their noticeable deviance will have been so reinforced by police and community that their lives will be effectively channeled into careers consistent with their adolescent background.

Review Questions

1. What were the typical activities of the Saints? The Roughnecks? Which group committed more illegal acts?

2. Were the community's perceptions of the Saints accurate? Were the community's perceptions of the Roughnecks accurate? What role did the visibility of the two groups play in the community's perceptions of them?

3. How did the social-class backgrounds of the Saints and the Roughnecks affect their visibility to adult members of the community?

4. Why is it important to understand "surface variables"—visibility, demeanor, and bias—to explain the actions of the police?

5. How does Chambliss's research demonstrate the usefulness of looking beyond commonly accepted explanations of social life?

MEN AND JOBS

Elliot Liebow

In SUMMARY OF OBJECTIVE JOB CONSIDERATIONS [OF STREETCORNER MEN], THE MOST important fact is that a man who is able and willing to work cannot earn enough money to support himself, his wife, and one or more children. A man's chances for working regularly are good only if he is willing to work for less than he can live on, and sometimes not even then. On some jobs, the wage rate is deceptively higher than on others, but the higher the wage rate, the more difficult it is to get the job, and the less the job security. Higher-paying construction work tends to be seasonal and, during the season, the amount of work available is highly sensitive to business and weather conditions and to the changing requirements of individual projects.[1] Moreover, high-paying construction jobs are frequently beyond the physical capacity of some of the men, and some of the low-paying jobs are scaled down even lower in accordance with the self-fulfilling assumption that the man will steal part of his wages on the job.[2]

Bernard assesses the objective job situation dispassionately over a cup of coffee, sometimes poking at the coffee with his spoon, sometimes staring at it as if, like a crystal ball, it holds tomorrow's secrets. He is twenty-seven years old. He and the woman with whom he lives have a baby son, and she has another child by another man. Bernard does odd jobs—mostly paint-ing—but here it is the end of January, and his last job was with the Post Of-fice during the Christmas mail rush. It pays well (about $2 an hour) but he has twice failed the Post Office examination (he graduated from a Washing-ton high school) and has given up the idea as an impractical one. He is sup-posed to see a man tonight about a job as a parking attendant for a large apartment house. The man told him to bring his birth certificate and driv-er's license, but his license was suspended because of a backlog of unpaid traffic fines. A friend promised to lend him some money this evening. If he gets it, he will pay the fines tomorrow morning and have his license rein-stated. He hopes the man with the job will wait till tomorrow night.

A "security job" is what he really wants, he said. He would like to save up money for a taxicab. (But having twice failed the postal examination and having a bad driving record as well, it is highly doubtful that he could meet the qualifications or pass the written test.) That would be "a good life." He

Elliot Liebow, "Men and Jobs," in Elliot Liebow, *Tally's Corner: A Study of Negro Street-corner Men.* Boston: Little, Brown, 1967, pp. 50–71.

can always get a job in a restaurant or as a clerk in a drugstore but they don't pay enough, he said. He needs to take home at least $50 to $55 a week. He thinks he can get that much driving a truck somewhere. . . . Sometimes he wishes he had stayed in the army. . . . A security job, that's what he wants most of all, a real security job. . . .

When we look at what the men bring to the job rather than at what the job offers the men, it is essential to keep in mind that we are not looking at men who come to the job fresh, just out of school perhaps, and newly prepared to undertake the task of making a living, or from another job where they earned a living and are prepared to do the same on this job. Each man comes to the job with a long job history characterized by his not being able to support himself and his family. Each man carries this knowledge, born of his experience, with him. He comes to the job flat and stale, wearied by the sameness of it all, convinced of his own incompetence, terrified of responsibility—of being tested still again and found wanting. Possible exceptions are the younger men not yet, or just, married. They suspect all this but have yet to have it confirmed by repeated personal experience over time. But those who are or have been married know it well. It is the experience of the individual and the group; of their fathers and probably their sons. Convinced of their inadequacies, not only do they not seek out those few better-paying jobs which test their resources, but they actively avoid them, gravitating in a mass to the menial, routine jobs which offer no challenge—and therefore pose no threat—to the already diminished images they have of themselves.

Thus Richard does not follow through on [a] real estate agent's offer. He is afraid to do on his own—minor plastering, replacing broken windows, other minor repairs and painting—exactly what he had been doing for months on a piece-work basis under someone else (and which provided him with a solid base from which to derive a cost estimate).

Richard once offered an important clue to what may have gone on in his mind when the job offer was made. We were in the Carry-out, at a time when he was looking for work. He was talking about the kind of jobs available to him.

> I graduated from high school [Baltimore] but I don't know anything. I'm dumb. Most of the time I don't even say I graduated, 'cause then somebody asks me a question and I can't answer it, and they think I was lying about graduating. . . .They graduated me but I didn't know anything. I had lousy grades but I guess they wanted to get rid of me.
>
> I was at Margaret's house the other night and her little sister asked me to help her with her homework. She showed me some fractions and I knew right away I couldn't do them. I was ashamed so I told her I had to go to the bathroom.

And so it must have been, surely, with the real estate agent's offer. Convinced that "I'm dumb. . . I don't know anything," he "knew right away" he couldn't do it, despite the fact that he had been doing just this sort of work all along.

Thus, the man's low self-esteem generates a fear of being tested and prevents him from accepting a job with responsibilities or, once on a job, from staying with it if responsibilities are thrust on him, even if the wages are commensurately higher. Richard refuses such a job, Leroy leaves one, and another man, given more responsibility and more pay, knows he will fail and proceeds to do so, proving he was right about himself all along. The self-fulfilling prophecy is everywhere at work. In a hallway, Stanton, Tonk and Boley are passing a bottle around. Stanton recalls the time he was in the service. Everything was fine until he attained the rank of corporal. He worried about everything he did then. Was he doing the right thing? Was he doing it well? When would they discover their mistake and take his stripes (and extra pay) away? When he finally lost his stripes, everything was all right again.

Lethargy, disinterest and general apathy on the job, so often reported by employers, has its streetcorner counterpart. The men do not ordinarily talk about their jobs or ask one another about them.[3] Although most of the men know who is or is not working at any given time, they may or may not know what particular job an individual man has. There is no overt interest in job specifics as they relate to this or that person, in large part perhaps because the specifics are not especially relevant. To know that a man is working is to know approximately how much he makes and to know as much as one needs or wants to know about how he makes it. After all, how much difference does it make to know whether a man is pushing a mop and pulling trash in an apartment house, a restaurant, or an office building, or delivering groceries, drugs, or liquor, or, if he's a laborer, whether he's pushing a wheelbarrow, mixing mortar, or digging a hole. So much does one job look like every other that there is little to choose between them. In large part, the job market consists of a narrow range of nondescript chores calling for nondistinctive, undifferentiated, unskilled labor. "A job is a job."

A crucial factor in the streetcorner man's lack of job commitment is the overall value he places on the job. *For his part, the streetcorner man puts no lower value on the job than does the larger society around him.* He knows the social value of the job by the amount of money the employer is willing to pay him for doing it. In a real sense, every pay day, he counts in dollars and cents the value placed on the job by society at large. He is no more (and frequently less) ready to quit and look for another job than his employer is ready to fire him and look for another man. Neither the streetcorner man who performs these jobs nor the society which requires him to perform them assesses the job as one "worth doing and worth doing well." Both employee and employer are contemptuous of the job. The employee shows his contempt by his reluctance to accept it or keep it, the employer by paying less than is required to support a family.[4] Nor does the low-wage job offer prestige, respect, interesting work, opportunity for learning or advancement, or any other compensation. With few exceptions, jobs filled by the streetcorner men are at the bottom of the employment ladder in every respect, from wage level to prestige. Typically, they are hard, dirty, uninteresting and underpaid. The rest of society (whatever its ideal values regarding the dignity of labor) holds the job of the dishwasher or janitor or unskilled laborer in low esteem if not outright contempt.[5] So does the streetcorner man. He cannot do otherwise. He cannot draw from a job those social values which other people do not put into it.[6]

Only occasionally does spontaneous conversation touch on these matters directly. Talk about jobs is usually limited to isolated statements of intention, such as "I think I'll get me another gig [job]," "I'm going to look for a construction job when the weather breaks," or "I'm going to quit. I can't take no more of this shit." Job assessments typically consist of nothing more than a noncommittal shrug and "It's O.K." or "It's a job."

One reason for the relative absence of talk about one's job is, as suggested earlier, that the sameness of job experiences does not bear reiteration. Another and more important reason is the emptiness of the job experience itself. The man sees middle-class occupations as a primary source of prestige, pride and self-respect; his own job affords him none of these. To think about his job is to see himself as others see him, to remind him of just where he stands in this society.[7] And because society's criteria for placement are generally the same as his own, to talk about his job can trigger a flush of shame and a deep, almost physical ache to change places with someone, almost anyone, else.[8] The desire to be a person in his own right, to be noticed by the world he lives in, is shared by each of the men on the streetcorner. Whether they articulate this desire (as Tally does below) or not, one can see them position themselves to catch the attention of their fellows in much the same way as plants bend or stretch to catch the sunlight.[9]

Tally and I were in the Carry-out. It was summer, Tally's peak earning season as a cement finisher, a semiskilled job a cut or so above that of the unskilled laborer. His take-home pay during these weeks was well over a hundred dollars—"a lot of bread." But for Tally, who no longer had a family to support, bread was not enough.

"You know that boy came in last night? That Black Moozlem? That's what I ought to be doing. I ought to be in his place."

"What do you mean?"

"Dressed nice, going to [night] school, got a good job."

"He's no better than you, Tally. You make more than he does."

"It's not the money. [Pause] It's position, I guess. He's got position. When he finish school he gonna be a supervisor. People respect him. . . . Thinking about people with position and education gives me a feeling right here [pressing his fingers into the pit of his stomach]."

"You're educated, too. You have a skill, a trade. You're a cement finisher. You can make a building, pour a sidewalk."

"That's different. Look, can anybody do what you're doing? Can anybody just come up and do your job? Well, in one week I can teach you cement finishing. You won't be as good as me 'cause you won't have the experience but you'll be a cement finisher. That's what I mean. Anybody can do what I'm doing and that's what gives me this feeling. [Long pause] Suppose I like this girl. I go over to her house and I meet her father. He starts talking about what he done today. He talks about operating on somebody and sewing them up and about surgery. I knows he's a doctor 'cause of the way he talks. Then she starts talking about what she did. Maybe she's a boss or a supervisor. Maybe she's a lawyer and her father says to me, 'And what do you do, Mr. Jackson?" [Pause] You remember at the courthouse, Lonny's trial? You and the lawyer was talking in the hall? You remember? I just stood there listening. I didn't say a word. You know why? 'Cause I didn't even know what you was talking about. That's happened to me a lot."

"Hell, you're nothing special. That happens to everybody. Nobody knows everything. One man is a doctor, so he talks about surgery. Another man is a teacher, so he talks about books. But doctors and teachers don't know anything about concrete. You're a cement finisher and that's your specialty."

"Maybe so, but when was the last time you saw anybody standing around talking about concrete?"

The streetcorner man wants to be a person in his own right, to be noticed, to be taken account of, but in this respect, as well as in meeting his money needs, his job fails him. The job and the man are even. The job fails the man and the man fails the job.

Furthermore, the man does not have any reasonable expectation that, however bad it is, his job will lead to better things. Menial jobs are not, by and large, the starting point of a track system which leads to even better jobs for those who are able and willing to do them. The busboy or dishwasher in a restaurant is not on a job track which, if negotiated skillfully, leads to chef or manager of the restaurant. The busboy or dishwasher who works hard becomes, simply, a hard-working busboy or dishwasher. Neither hard work nor perseverance can conceivably carry the janitor to a sit-down job in the office building he cleans up. And it is the apprentice who becomes the journeyman electrician, plumber, steam fitter or bricklayer, not the common unskilled Negro laborer.

Thus, the job is not a stepping-stone to something better. It is a dead end. It promises to deliver no more tomorrow, next month or next year than it does today.

Delivering little, and promising no more, the job is "no big thing." The man appears to treat the job in a cavalier fashion, working and not working as the spirit moves him, as if all that matters is the immediate satisfaction of his present appetites, the surrender to present moods, and the indulgence of whims with no thought for the cost, the consequences, the future. To the middle-class observer, this behavior reflects a "present-time orientation"—an "inability to defer gratification." It is this "present-time" orientation—as against the "future orientation" of the middle-class person—that "explains" to the outsider why Leroy chooses to spend the day at the Carry-out rather than report to work; why Richard, who was paid Friday, was drunk Saturday and Sunday and penniless Monday; why Sweets quit his job today because the boss looked at him "funny" yesterday.

But from the inside looking out, what appears as a "present-time" orientation to the outside observer is, to the man experiencing it, as much a future orientation as that of his middle-class counterpart.[10] The difference between the two men lies not so much in their different orientations to time as in their different orientations to future time or, more specifically, to their different futures.[11]

The future orientation of the middle-class person presumes, among other things, a surplus of resources to be invested in the future and a belief that the future will be sufficiently stable both to justify his investment (money in a bank, time and effort in a job, investment of himself in marriage and family, etc.) and to permit the consumption of his investment at a time, place and manner of his own choosing and to his greater satisfaction. But the streetcorner man lives in a sea of want. He does not, as a rule, have a surplus of resources, either economic or psychological. Gratification of hunger and the desire for simple creature comforts cannot be long deferred. Neither can support for one's flagging self-esteem. Living on the edge of both economic and psychological subsistence, the streetcorner man is obliged to expend all his resources on maintaining himself from moment to moment.[12]

As for the future, the young streetcorner man has a fairly good picture of it. In Richard or Sea Cat or Arthur he can see himself in his middle twenties; he can look at Tally to see himself at thirty, at Wee Tom to see himself in his middle thirties, and at Budder and Stanton to see himself in his forties. It is a future in which everything is uncertain except the ultimate destruction of his hopes and the eventual realization of his fears. The most he can reasonably look forward to is that these things do not come too soon. Thus, when Richard squanders a week's pay in two days it is not because, like an animal or a child, he is "present-time oriented," unaware of or unconcerned with his future. He does so precisely because he is aware of the future and the hopelessness of it all.

Sometimes this kind of response appears as a conscious, explicit choice. Richard had had a violent argument with his wife. He said he was going to leave her and the children, that he had had enough of everything and could not take any more, and he chased her out of the house. His chest still heaving, he leaned back against the wall in the hallway of his basement apartment.

> "I've been scuffling for five years," he said. "I've been scuffling for five years from morning till night. And my kids still don't have anything, my wife don't have anything, and I don't have anything.
>
> "There," he said, gesturing down the hall to a bed, a sofa, a couple of chairs and a television set, all shabby, some broken. "There's everything I have and I'm having trouble holding onto that."
>
> Leroy came in, presumably to petition Richard on behalf of Richard's wife, who was sitting outside on the steps, afraid to come in. Leroy started to say something but Richard cut him short.
>
> "Look, Leroy, don't give me any of that action. You and me are entirely different people. Maybe I look like a boy and maybe I act like a boy sometimes but I got

a man's mind. You and me don't want the same things out of life. Maybe some of the same, but you don't care how long you have to wait for yours and *I—want—mine—right—now.*"[13]

Thus, apparent present-time concerns with consumption and indulgences—material and emotional—reflect a future-time orientation. "I want mine right now" is ultimately a cry of despair, a direct response to the future as he sees it.[14]

In many instances, it is precisely the streetcorner man's orientation to the future—but to a future loaded with "trouble"—which not only leads to a greater emphasis on present concerns ("I want mine right now") but also contributes importantly to the instability of employment, family and friend relationships, and to the general transient quality of daily life.

Let me give some concrete examples. One day, after Tally had gotten paid, he gave me four twenty-dollar bills and asked me to keep them for him. Three days later he asked me for the money. I returned it and asked why he did not put his money in a bank. He said that the banks close at two o'clock. I argued that there were four or more banks within a two-block radius of where he was working at the time and that he could easily get to any one of them on his lunch hour. "No, man," he said, "you don't understand. They close at two o'clock and they closed Saturday and Sunday. Suppose I get into trouble and I got to make it [leave]. Me get out of town, and everything I got in the world layin' up in that bank? No good! No good!"

In another instance, Leroy and his girl friend were discussing "trouble." Leroy was trying to decide how best to go about getting his hands on some "long green" (a lot of money), and his girl friend cautioned him about "trouble." Leroy sneered at this, saying he had had "trouble" all his life and wasn't afraid of a little more. "Anyway," he said, "I'm famous for leaving town."[15]

Thus, the constant awareness of a future loaded with "trouble" results in a constant readiness to leave, to "make it," to "get out of town," and discourages the man from sinking roots into the world he lives in.[16] Just as it discourages him from putting money in the bank, so it discourages him from committing himself to a job, especially one whose payoff lies in the promise of future rewards rather than in the present. In the same way, it discourages him from deep and lasting commitments to family and friends or to any other persons, places or things, since such commitments could hold him hostage, limiting his freedom of movement and thereby compromising his security which lies in that freedom.

. . . The streetcorner man is under continuous assault by his job experiences and job fears. His experiences and fears feed on one another. The kind of job he can get—and frequently only after fighting for it, if then—steadily confirms his fears, depresses his self-confidence and self-esteem until finally, terrified of an opportunity even if one presents itself, he stands defeated by his experiences, his belief in his own self-worth destroyed and his fears a confirmed reality.

NOTES

1. The overall result is that, in the long run, a Negro laborer's earnings are not substantially greater—and may be less—than those of the busboy, janitor, or stock clerk. Herman P. Miller, for example, reports that in 1960, 40 percent of all jobs held by Negro men were as laborers or in the service trades. The average annual wage for nonwhite nonfarm laborers was $2,400. The average earning of nonwhite service workers was $2,500 (*Rich Man, Poor Man*, p. 90). Francis Greenfield estimates that in the Washington vicinity, the 1965 earnings of the union laborer who works whenever work is available will be about $3,200. Even this figure is high for the man on the streetcorner. Union men in heavy construction are the aristocrats of the laborers. Casual day labor and jobs with small firms in the building and construction trades, or with firms in other industries, pay considerably less.

2. For an excellent discussion of the self-fulfilling assumption (or prophecy) as a social force, see "The Self-Fulfilling Prophecy," Ch. XI, in Robert K. Merton's *Social Theory and Social Structure* (Glencoe, Ill.: Free Press, 1957).

3. This stands in dramatic contrast to the leisure-time conversation of stable, working-class men. For the coal miners (of Ashton, England), for example, "the topic [of conversation] which surpasses all others in frequency is work—the difficulties which have been encountered in the day's shift, the way in which a particular task was accomplished, and so on." Josephine Klein, *Samples from English Cultures*, Vol. 1 (London: Routledge and Kegan Paul, 1956), p. 88.

4. It is important to remember that the employer is not entirely a free agent. Subject to the constraints of the larger society, he acts for the larger society as well as for himself. Child labor laws, safety and sanitation regulations, minimum wage scales in some employment areas, and other constraints, are already on the books; other control mechanisms, such as a guaranteed annual wage, are to be had for the voting.

5. See, for example, the U.S. Bureau of the Census, *Methodology and Scores of Socioeconomic Status*. The assignment of the lowest SES ratings to men who hold such jobs is not peculiar to our own society. A low SES rating for "the shoeshine boy or garbage man . . . seems to be true for all [industrial] countries." Alex Inkeles, "Industrial Man," *American Journal of Sociology* 66 (July 1960), p. 8.

6. That the streetcorner man downgrades manual labor should occasion no surprise. Merton points out that "the American stigmatization of manual labor . . . *has been found to hold rather uniformly in all social classes*" (emphasis in original; *Social Theory and Social Structure*, p. 145). That he finds no satisfaction in such work should also occasion no surprise: "[There is] a clear positive correlation between the overall status of occupations and the experience of satisfaction in them." Inkeles, "Industrial Man," *American Journal of Sociology* 66 (July 1960), p. 12.

7. "[In our society] a man's work is one of the things by which he is judged, and certainly one of the more significant things by which he judges himself. . . . A man's work is one of the more important parts of his social identity, of his self; indeed, of his fate in the one life he has to live." Everett C. Hughes, *Men and Their Work* (Glencoe, Ill.: Free Press, 1958), pp. 42–43.

8. Noting that lower-class persons "are constantly exposed to evidence of their own irrelevance," Lee Rainwater spells out still another way in which the poor are poor: "The identity problems of lower-class persons make the soul-searching of middle-class adolescents and adults seem rather like a kind of conspicuous consumption of psychic riches," "Work and Identity in the Lower Class," in Sam Bass Warner,

Jr., *Planning for a Nation of Cities* (Cambridge: Cambridge Univ. Press, forthcoming), p. 3.

9. Sea Cat cuts his pants legs off at the calf and puts a fringe on the raggedy edges. Tonk breaks his "shades" and continues to wear the horn-rimmed frames minus the lenses. Richard cultivates a distinctive manner of speech. Lonny gives himself a birthday party. And so on.

10. Taking a somewhat different point of view, S. M. Miller and Frank Riessman suggest that "the entire concept of deferred gratification may be inappropriate to understanding the essence of workers' lives," "The Working Class Subculture: A New View," *Social Problems* 9 (1961), p. 87.

11. This sentence is a paraphrase of a statement made by Marvin Cline at a 1965 colloquium at the Mental Health Study Center, National Institute of Mental Health.

12. And if, for the moment, he does sometimes have more money than he chooses to spend or more food than he wants to eat, he is pressed to spend the money and eat the food anyway since his friends, neighbors, kinsmen, or acquaintances will beg or borrow whatever surplus he has or, failing this, they may steal it. In one extreme case, one of the men admitted taking the last of a woman's surplus food allotment after she had explained that, with four children, she could not spare any food. The prospect that consumer soft goods not consumed by oneself will be consumed by someone else may be related to the way in which portable consumer durable goods, such as watches, radios, television sets or phonographs, are sometimes looked at as a form of savings. When Shirley was on welfare, she regularly took her television set out of pawn when she got her monthly check. Not so much to watch it, she explained, as to have something to fall back on when her money runs out toward the end of the month. For her and others, the television set or phonograph is her savings, the pawnshop is where she banks her savings, and the pawn ticket is her bankbook.

13. This was no simple rationalization for irresponsibility. Richard had indeed "been scuffling for five years" trying to keep his family going. Until shortly after this episode, Richard was known and respected as one of the hardest-working men on the street. Richard had said, only a couple of months earlier, "I figure you got to get out there and try. You got to try before you can get anything." His wife Shirley confirmed that he had always tried. "If things get tough, with me I'll get all worried. But Richard get worried, he don't want to see me worried. . . . He *will* get out there. He's shoveled snow, picked beans, and he's done some of everything. . . . He's not ashamed to get out there and get us something to eat." At the time of the episode reported above, Leroy was just starting marriage and raising a family. He and Richard were not, as Richard thought, "entirely different people." Leroy had just not learned, by personal experience over time, what Richard had learned. But within two years Leroy's marriage had broken up and he was talking and acting like Richard. "He just let go completely," said one of the men on the street.

14. There is no mystically intrinsic connection between "present-time" orientation and lower-class persons. Whenever people of whatever class have been uncertain, skeptical or downright pessimistic about the future, "I want mine right now" has been one of the characteristic responses, although it is usually couched in more delicate terms: e.g., Omar Khayyam's "Take the cash and let the credit go," or Horace's "*Carpe diem.*" In wartime, especially, all classes tend to slough off conventional restraints on sexual and other behavior (i.e., become less able or less willing to defer gratification). And when inflation threatens, darkening the fiscal future, persons who formerly husbanded their resources with commendable restraint almost

stampede one another rushing to spend their money. Similarly, it seems that future-time orientation tends to collapse toward the present when persons are in pain or under stress. The point here is that, the label notwithstanding, (what passes for) present-time orientation appears to be a situation-specific phenomenon rather than a part of the standard psychic equipment of Cognitive Lower Class Man.

15. And proceeded to do just that the following year when "trouble"—in this case, a grand jury indictment, a pile of debts, and a violent separation from his wife and children—appeared again.

16. For a discussion of "trouble" as a focal concern of lower-class culture, see Walter Miller, "Lower Class Culture as a Generating Milieu of Gang Delinquency," *Journal of Social Issues* 14 (1958), pp. 7, 8.

Review Questions

1. According to Liebow, for the streetcorner man, the job fails the man, and the man fails the job. Discuss this statement and give specific examples that support or refute it.

2. Describe Liebow's assessment of the present-time and future-time orientations of streetcorner men. Are there any indications that middle-class people are not always future-time oriented?

3. How do our society's sex roles contribute to the streetcorner men's feelings of failure?

4. Describe the sociological concept of self-fulfilling prophecy and give examples from Liebow's study of streetcorner men.

Suggested Readings: Inequalities

Blau, Peter. *Exchange and Power in Social Life.* New York: Wiley, 1964.

Blumberg, Paul. *Inequality in an Age of Decline.* New York: Oxford, 1980.

Gold, Ray. "Janitors Versus Tenants: A Status Income Dilemma," *American Journal of Sociology*, 57 (1962), 486–493.

Henley, Nancy M. *Body Politics: Power, Sex and Nonverbal Communication.* Englewood Cliffs, N. J.: Prentice-Hall, 1977.

Liebow, Elliot. *Tally's Corner: A Study of Negro Streetcorner Men.* Boston: Little, Brown, 1967.

Schwartz, Barry. *Queuing and Waiting: Studies in the Social Organization of Access and Delay.* Chicago: University of Chicago Press, 1975.

Sennett, Richard, and Jonathan Cobb. *The Hidden Injuries of Class.* New York: Vintage, 1973.

Stone, Gregory P. "The Circumstance and Situation of Social Status," in Gregory P. Stone and Harvey A. Farberman, eds., *Social Psychology Through Symbolic Interaction*. Waltham, Mass.: Ginn-Blaisdell, 1970.

Zetterberg, Hans. "The Secret Ranking," *Journal of Marriage and the Family* (1966), 134–142.

Part VII. Deviance, Conformity, and Social Control

FOR MANY YEARS, MOST SOCIOLOGISTS VIEWED DEVIANCE AND CONFORMITY AS STATES that could be easily distinguished on the basis of whether a norm had been violated or not. A deviant was defined as a person who violated a custom, rule, or law; conformists were those who did not violate norms. In reality, there is often no way to determine validly who has or has not actually violated a norm, and researchers using this approach usually had to rely on the definitions of the courts, the schools, and other authorities to classify criminals and juvenile delinquents. (Such a procedure is of questionable usefulness, of course, since not everyone who violates rules gets caught, and not everyone who is "caught" has violated rules.) What these sociologists then attempted to do was to understand *why some individuals broke the rules and others did not*. They searched for social forces such as poverty, social disruption of neighborhoods, broken homes, or improper socialization which might be associated with rule violation.

More recently, there has emerged widespread recognition of the limitations of the early approach. It was, in a word, too simple to reflect the complexities of deviance and conformity. By asking a limited set of questions, it paid too little attention to the social forces that *produce deviant labels* and *attach them* to some people and not others. A newer approach, called labeling theory or societal-reaction theory, focuses our attention on *social-control agents*—lawmakers, prison guards, parents, the local gossip, and the like—who have varying amounts of power to decide what conditions and behaviors will be considered deviant and/or to decide who should receive negative societal sanctions for alleged deviance. As Edwin Schur explained, in every society labeling processes occur on the levels of (1) *collective rule making*, as when legislatures enact a law or members of a peer group informally arrive at a norm to guide the members' behavior; (2) *interpersonal reactions* such as stares, gossip, "dirty looks," and rule-enforcement techniques including whistle-blowing by sports officials; and (3) *organizational processing*, from detention after school to incarceration in a prison or mental hospital. These are the rule-enforcement processes that students of deviance and conformity are now addressing.

One of the most important assumptions of labeling theory is that almost no behaviors have been automatically considered deviant across all societies. What is "right" and what is "wrong" are decided upon by societal members within their own cultural, or even subcultural, frameworks. The cannibalism of certain native American groups would be considered deviant in our own society, and the relatively free interaction between girls and boys in American society today would be viewed as sinful in many Latin American societies and even by our own ancestors. Walking about a college campus with a brick tied to one's ankle may appear foolish to many, but the individual who engages in this act may be conforming to the norms of the fraternity. What is to be deemed deviant, then, is *relative* to a given culture's or subculture's normative framework. If we accept that behavior is not automatically deviant, it follows that the *creation of rules* for behavior *creates deviants*. Society, not individuals, makes deviance.

Furthermore, as we noted briefly, not everyone who engages in a culturally disapproved behavior comes to be reacted to as a deviant. And, equally important, not all people who conform to the norms come to be seen as conformists. Almost anyone who has grown up with brothers and sisters can remember cases in which two children engaged in exactly the same behavior, yet one was punished and the other was not. Not uncommon also are cases in which a child who is conforming is blamed for deviant acts which she or he did not commit. In the larger society as well, "mistakes" such as these are commonplace. Referring to the table below, we can find many instances which could be classified into cells b and c. What's more, *it may be more important in the long run if a person has been labeled than if a person has actually deviated from a norm.* That is, the consequences of labels for the individual's life chances and future interactions may be of greater weight than the individual's own conforming or deviating behavior. In fact, many sociologists argue that one is not deviant unless defined as deviant by other members of society. Deviance is, thus, a social label.

Finally, any given act is usually sufficiently *ambiguous* that it (and its perpetrator) could be interpreted in a number of ways. Norms are often situationally tied, which means that the context of one's behavior must also be evaluated. Killing someone in an officially declared war is not considered murder, for instance, while killing an adulterous spouse may or may not be so viewed. Contracting arthritis may be considered deviant among the young, but not among the elderly. Just how a condition or act comes to receive meaning within a society of interacting individuals is an important issue for labeling theory.

| | ENGAGED IN A DEVIANT ACT? | |
	Yes	No
RECEIVED A DEVIANT LABEL? Yes	a	b
No	c	d

What factors determine if someone will be labeled as a conformist or a deviant? We know that some types of individuals are more likely to be labeled than others, regardless of their actions. The wealthy person who has several martinis and a bottle of wine with dinner each night is called a "social drinker," while the poor person imbibing an equal amount of (less expensive) liquor is deemed a "drunk" or an "alcoholic." It may be easier for a middle-class person who has political influence or access to lawyers than for a poor person with no "contacts" to escape labeling from police officers, judges, and other agents of the criminal-justice system. Minority-group members may commit no more serious offenses than the WASP, yet because of stereotyping be more readily perceived as deviants (or less readily perceived as conformists). In our society, the poor are often considered less "worthy" in general than are those of greater means. Moreover, once an individual has been successfully labeled by public opinion, by the courts, by parents, or by teachers, other labels may be attached more easily—as with the child who was once caught breaking a family heirloom and who continues to get blamed for all manner of breakage that occurs thereafter, or with the teenager who has a police record and elicits a greater negative reaction from the police officer than the "nice kid." We have seen examples of the latter in Chambliss's article, "The Saints and the Roughnecks," in Part VI.

Another important question is whose interests are served by the laws and rules of society and on whose behalf the agents of social control act when they administer sanctions. The issue of power comes into play here, and there is much evidence to suggest that, in most societies, the rules and rule enforcers function to maintain existing power relations. In the U.S., for instance, the legal system provides more serious punishments for offenses such as burglary and theft committed by individuals than for corporate crimes, from price fixing to the marketing of dangerous products. Deaths resulting from unnecessary surgery are rarely punished as severely as deaths resulting from a barroom brawl. In other words, those with prestige and power may engage in behavior with consequences as serious as those ensuing from the actions of the less powerful and prestigious, but the societal reactions to the former are less severe than reactions to the latter.

Thus, the labeling perspective on deviance and conformity directs our attention *away from* those who have been labeled *toward* those who do the labeling. The questions which researchers are led to ask include: What are the characteristics of the social-control agents who are empowered to make and enforce rules? What systems are developed to define deviance and label deviants? What are the consequences of the labeling process for the individual and for society? Who benefits from the labels and designations of deviance that gain acceptance in a society? How do societal members cope with or attempt to avoid labels?

The articles gathered in this section address a number of these questions. David Sudnow asks how the criminal-justice system and its agents of social control work to label poor people who are accused of committing crimes. In "Normal Crimes: Sociological Features of the Penal Code in a Public Defender Office," he takes us behind the scenes of the court where public defenders process the cases of the accused who are too poor to afford private attorneys. We see how the ideals of justice are suspended in favor of bureaucratic expediency. For the public defender, the goal is to take care of his or her caseload as quickly as possible. To accomplish this goal, the background of the client and the conditions leading to the alleged crime are often stereotyped as "normal" for such crimes, and the client is encouraged to plead guilty to a lesser offense. This act is called plea bargaining, and it often leads to more rapid processing of cases than holding a lengthy trial. Defendants who want to plead not guilty are often considered troublemakers and receive less attention from the public defender than those willing to go along with the proposed "concessions."

As a result of the attitudes and actions of the public defenders, poor defendants receive legally legitimated labels and sanctions (including prison sentences, fines, etc.) which may or may not fit their cases. Reading Sudnow's work should convince us of the folly of focusing on convicts to understand why they committed the crimes for which they were convicted. Among the poor, at least, the crimes committed or not committed may bear little relationship to the court's labels.

Rule enforcers are the subject of the research by Roy Askins, Timothy Carter, and Michael Wood. Rule enforcers are those who are empowered to apply rules to behavior and to mete out sanctions. In "Rule Enforcement in a Public Setting: The Case of Basketball Officiating," they take us to the basketball court for an in-depth view of how social-control agents, referees, link their "calls" of rule violation to the events occurring around them. We see that the successful referee must learn not only to enforce the rules, but also to convince the players, coaches, and the crowd that they are doing the job in a proper manner.

The authors point out the similarities between basketball officials and members of a jury: Both make judgments, justify the judgments to those being judged, and indicate to their audiences the factors which affected their decisions. In many other areas of life, the claims, rationales, and techniques discovered among referees can also be found, be it police officers stopping traffic-law offenders, ministers talking to "sinners," teachers disciplining rowdy children in front of their classes, or even physicians trying to convince their clients to alter their behavior.

Physicians and medical practice provide the focus for Candace Clark's review essay, "Sickness and Social Control." She summarizes a large body of research on the changing conceptions of the causes of deviance and the changing locus of social control in our society. In all human groups, healers have been in charge of controlling those deviant conditions defined as illness. In the Western world, over the past century or so, more and more conditions and behaviors have come to be *interpreted* as illnesses rather than as sin, criminality, or other types of deviance. And as more deviant conditions have come to be viewed as illnesses, medical personnel have been given a larger and larger role in controlling deviance than ever before in history. Surgery, drugs, hospitalization, and other techniques of medical intervention have gained tremendously in recent years, often replacing the old techniques of social control employed by religious leaders, teachers, parents, and the courts.

The ideas in Clark's article challenge the taken-for-granted ways in which most of us think about illness and deviance, medical treatment, and social control. Since Americans have more faith and trust in the expertise and good intentions of physicians than of any other occupational group, it is often difficult for us to stand back and assess the societal functions of medical theories and treatments. Yet just because we are not used to thinking of the social-control aspects of medicine does not mean that they do not exist. If we are to understand life in the U.S. in the late twentieth century, we must come to grips with the expanded role of medicine in defining and enforcing our norms.

From a general discussion of the medical world, we move to the specific case of the mental hospital. Rather than asking what causes mental illness, the psychologist D. L. Rosenhan asks how people come to be labeled as mentally ill, how they are controlled in mental hospitals, and what the consequences of psychiatric labels might be for those who receive them. By having a number of normal, "sane" people approach mental hospitals for help with a (false) complaint, he discovered that the psychiatric branch of medicine was quick to attribute mental illness to his pseudopatients. Furthermore, once an individual received a psychiatric label, the hospital staff reinforced the label by interpreting much of the "normal" behavior that occurred as evidence of insanity. Rosenhan's study shows us how ambiguous conditions and behavior can easily come to be viewed from a deviance perspective. It also shows the constraints of the institutional environment, and especially, of drug treatment, on the behavior of the inmates. We see again, as we did in the cases of the public defender, the basketball official, and the medical practitioner, the many ways in which social control creates deviance.

NORMAL CRIMES: SOCIOLOGICAL FEATURES OF THE PENAL CODE IN A PUBLIC DEFENDER OFFICE

David Sudnow

[The following article is based on a participant-observation study of public defenders in one California county.]

• • •

IN THE COURSE OF ROUTINELY ENCOUNTERING PERSONS CHARGED WITH "petty theft," "burglary," "assault with a deadly weapon," "rape," "possession of marijuana," etc., the P.D. [Public Defender] gains knowledge of the typical manner in which offenses of given classes are committed, the social characteristics of the persons who regularly commit them, the features of the settings in which they occur, the types of victims often involved, and the like. He learns to speak knowledgeably of "burglars," "petty thieves," "drunks," "rapists," "narcos," etc., and to attribute to them personal biographies, modes of usual criminal activity, criminal histories, psychological characteristics, and social backgrounds. The following characterizations are illustrative:

> Most ADWs (assault with deadly weapon) start with fights over some girl.

> These sex fiends (child molestation cases) usually hang around parks or schoolyards. But we often get fathers charged with these crimes. Usually the old man is out of work and stays at home when the wife goes to work and he plays around with his little daughter or something. A lot of these cases start when there is some marital trouble and the woman gets mad.

> I don't know why most of them don't rob the big stores. They usually break into some cheap department store and steal some crummy item like a $9.95 record player, you know.

> Kids who start taking this stuff (narcotics) usually start out when some buddy gives them a cigarette and they smoke it for kicks. For some reason they always get caught in their cars, for speeding or something.

They can anticipate that point when persons are likely to get into trouble:

> Dope addicts do O.K. until they lose a job or something and get back on the streets and, you know, meet the old boys. Someone tells them where to get some and there they are.

David Sudnow, "Normal Crimes: Sociological Features of the Penal Code in a Public Defender Office," *Social Problems*, 12 (Winter 1965), 255–275.

In the springtime, that's when we get all these sex crimes. You know, these kids play out in the schoolyard all day and these old men sit around and watch them jumping up and down. They get their ideas.

The P.D. learns that some kinds of offenders are likely to repeat the same offense while others are not repeat violators or, if they do commit crimes frequently, the crimes vary from occasion to occasion:

You almost never see a check man get caught for anything but checks—only an occasional drunk charge.

Burglars are usually multiple offenders, most times just burglaries or petty thefts.

Petty thefts get started for almost anything—joy riding, drinking, all kinds of little things.

These narcos are usually through after the second violation or so. After the first time some stop, but when they start on the heavy stuff, they've had it.

I shall call *normal crimes* those occurrences whose typical features, e.g., the ways they usually occur and the characteristics of persons who commit them (as well as the typical victims and typical scenes), are known and attended to by the P.D. For any of the series of offense types the P.D. can provide some form of proverbial characterization. For example, *burglary* is seen as involving regular violators, no weapons, low-priced items, little property damage, lower class establishments, largely Negro defendants, independent operators, and a non-professional orientation to the crime. *Child molesting* is seen as typically entailing middle-aged strangers or lower class middle-aged fathers (few women), no actual physical penetration or severe tissue damage, mild fondling, petting, and stimulation, bad marriage circumstances, multiple offenders with the same offense repeatedly committed, a child complainant, via the mother, etc. *Narcotics* defendants are usually Negroes, not syndicated, persons who start by using small stuff, hostile with police officers, caught by some form of entrapment technique, etc. *Petty thefts* are about 50–50 Negro-white, unplanned offenses, generally committed on lower class persons and don't get much money, don't often employ weapons, don't make living from thievery, usually younger defendants with long juvenile assaultive records, etc. *Drunkenness* offenders are lower class white and Negro, get drunk on wine and beer, have long histories of repeated drunkenness, don't hold down jobs, are usually arrested on the streets, seldom violate other penal code sections, etc.

Some general features of the normal crime as a way of attending to a category of persons and events may be mentioned:

1. The focus, in these characterizations, is not on particular individuals but offense types. If asked "What are burglars like?" or "How are burglaries usually committed?", the P.D. does not feel obliged to refer to particular burglars and burglaries as the material for his answer.

2. The features attributed to offenders and offenses are often not of import for the statutory conception. In burglary, it is "irrelevant" for the statutory determination whether or not much damage was done to the premises

(except where, for example, explosives were employed and a new statute could be invoked). Whether a defendant breaks a window or not, destroys property within the house or not, etc., does not affect his statutory classification as a burglar. While for robbery the presence or absence of a weapon sets the degree, whether the weapon is a machine gun or pocket knife is "immaterial." Whether the residence or business establishment in a burglary is located in a higher income area of the city is of no issue for the code requirements. And, generally, the defendant's race, class position, criminal history (in most offenses), personal attributes, and particular style of committing offenses are features specifically not definitive of crimes under the auspices of the penal code. For deciding "Is this a 'burglary' case I have before me," however, the P.D.'s reference to this range of non-statutorily referable personal and social attributes, modes of operation, etc., is crucial for the arrangement of a guilty plea bargain.

3. The features attributed to offenders and offenses are, in their content, specific to the community in which the P.D. works. In other communities and historical periods the lists would presumably differ. Narcotics violators in certain areas, for example, are syndicated in dope rackets or engage in systematic robbery as professional criminals, features which are not commonly encountered (or, at least, evidence for which is not systematically sought) in this community. Burglary in some cities will more often occur at large industrial plants, banking establishments, warehouses, etc. The P.D. refers to the population of defendants in the county as "our defendants" and qualifies his prototypical portrayals and knowledge of the typically operative social structures, "for our county." An older P.D. remembering the "old days," commented:

> We used to have a lot more rapes than we do now, and they used to be much more violent. Things are duller now in. . . .

4. Offenses whose normal features are readily attended to are those which are routinely encountered in the courtroom. This feature is related to the last point. For embezzlement, bank robbery, gambling, prostitution, murder, arson, and some other uncommon offenses, the P.D. cannot readily supply anecdotal and proverbial characterizations. While there is some change in the frequencies of offense-type convictions over time, certain offenses are continually more common and others remain stably infrequent. The troubles created for the P.D. when offenses whose features are not readily known occur, and whose typicality is not easily constructed, will be discussed in some detail below.

5. Offenses are ecologically specified and attended to as normal or not according to the locales within which they are committed. The P.D. learns that burglaries usually occur in such and such areas of the city, petty thefts around this or that park, ADWs in these bars. Ecological patterns are seen as related to socio-economic variables and these in turn to typical modes of criminal and non-criminal activities. Knowing where an offense took place is thus, for the P.D., knowledge of the likely persons involved, the kind of

scene in which the offense occurred, and the pattern of activity characteristic of such a place:

> Almost all of our ADWs are in the same half a dozen bars. These places are Negro bars where laborers come after hanging around the union halls trying to get some work. Nobody has any money and they drink too much. Tempers are high and almost anything can start happening.

6. One further important feature can be noted at this point. Its elaboration will be the task of a later section. As shall be seen, the P.D. office consists of a staff of twelve full time attorneys. Knowledge of the properties of offense types of offenders, i.e., their normal, typical, or familiar attributes, constitutes the mark of any given attorney's competence. A major task in socializing the new P.D. deputy attorney consists in teaching him to recognize these attributes and to come to do so naturally. The achievement of competence as a P.D. is signalled by the gradual acquisition of professional command not simple of local penal code peculiarities and courtroom folklore, but, as importantly, of relevant features of the social structure and criminological wisdom. His grasp of that knowledge over the course of time is a key indication of his expertise. Below, in our brief account of some relevant organizational properties of the P.D. system, we shall have occasion to re-emphasize the competence-attesting aspects of the attorney's proper use of established sociological knowledge. Let us return to the mechanics of the guilty plea procedure as an example of the operation of the notion of normal crimes.

Over the course of their interaction and repeated "bargaining" discussions, the P.D. and D.A. have developed a set of unstated recipes for reducing original charges to lesser offenses. These recipes are specifically appropriate for use in instances of normal crimes and in such instances alone. "Typical" burglaries are reduced to petty theft, "typical" ADWs to simple assault, "typical" child molestation to loitering around a schoolyard, etc. The character of these recipes deserves attention.

The specific content of any reduction, i.e., what particular offense class X offenses will be reduced to, is such that the reduced offense may bear no obvious relation (neither situationally nor necessarily included) to the originally charged offense. The reduction of burglary to petty theft is an example. The important relation between the reduced offense and the original charge is such that the reduction from one to the other is considered "reasonable." At this point we shall only state what seems to be the general principle involved in deciding this reasonableness. The underlying premises cannot be explored at the present time, as that would involve a political analysis beyond the scope of the present report.

Both P.D. and D.A. are concerned to obtain a guilty plea wherever possible and thereby avoid a trial. At the same time, each party is concerned that the defendant "receive his due." The reduction of offense X to Y must be of such a character that the new sentence will depart from the anticipated sentence for the original charge to such a degree that the defendant is likely to plead guilty to the new charge and, at the same time, not so great that the defendant does not "get his due."

PUBLIC "DEFENSE"

Recently, in many communities, the burden of securing counsel has been taken from the defendant.[1] As the accused is, by law, entitled to the aid of counsel, and as his pocketbook is often empty, numerous cities have felt obliged to establish a public defender system. There has been little resistance to this development by private attorneys among whom it is widely felt that the less time they need spend in the criminal courts, where practice is least prestigeful and lucrative, the better.[2]

Whatever the reasons for its development, we now find, in many urban places, a public defender occupying a place alongside judge and prosecutor as a regular court employee. In the county studied, the P.D. mans a daily station, like the public prosecutor, and "defends" all who come before him. He appears in court when court begins and his "clientele," composed without regard for his preferences, consists of that residual category of persons who cannot afford to bring their own spokesmen to court. In this county, the "residual" category approximates 65 per cent of the total number of criminal cases. In a given year, the twelve attorneys who comprise the P.D. Office "represent" about 3,000 defendants in the municipal and superior courts of the county.

While the courtroom encounters of private attorneys are brief, business-like and circumscribed, interactionally and temporally, by the particular cases that bring them there, the P.D. attends to the courtroom as his regular work place and conveys in his demeanor his place as a member of its core personnel.

While private attorneys come and leave court with their clients (who are generally "on bail"), the P.D. arrives in court each morning at nine, takes his station at the defense table, and deposits there the batch of files that he will refer to during the day. When, during morning "calendar,"[3] a private attorney's case is called, the P.D. steps back from the defense table, leaving his belongings in place there, and temporarily relinquishes his station. No private attorney has enough defendants in a given court on a given day to claim a right to make a desk of the defense table. If the P.D. needs some information from his central office, he uses the clerk's telephone, a privilege that few private lawyers feel at home enough to take. In the course of calendar work, a lawyer will often have occasion to request a delay or "continuance" of several days until the next stage of his client's proceedings. The private attorney addresses the prosecutor via the judge to request such an alteration; the P.D. talks directly over to the D.A.:

Private attorney: "If the prosecutor finds it convenient your Honor, my client would prefer to have his preliminary hearing on Monday, the 24th."

Judge: "Is that date suitable to the district attorney?"
Prosecutor: "Yes, your honor."
Private attorney: "Thank you, your Honor."

Public Defender: Bob (D.A.), how about moving Smith's prelim up to the 16th?"
Prosecutor: "Well, Jim, we've got Jones on that afternoon."
Public Defender: "Let's see, how's the 22nd?"
Prosecutor: "That's fine, Jim, the 22nd."

If, during the course of a proceeding, the P.D. has some minor matter to tend to with the D.A., he uses the time when a private attorney is addressing the bench to walk over to the prosecutor's table and whisper his requests, suggestions or questions. The P.D. uses the prosecutor's master calendar to check on an upcoming court date; so does the D.A. with the P.D.'s. The D.A. and P.D. are on a first name basis and throughout the course of a routine day interact as a team of co-workers.

While the central focus of the private attorney's attention is his client, the courtroom and affairs of court constitute the locus of involvements for the P.D. The public defender and public prosecutor, each representatives of their respective offices, jointly handle the greatest bulk of the court's daily activity.

The P.D. office, rather than assign its attorneys to clients, employs the arrangement of stationing attorneys in different courts to "represent" all those who come before that station. As defendants are moved about from courtroom to courtroom throughout the course of their proceedings (both from municipal to superior courtrooms for felony cases, and from one municipal courtroom to another when there is a specialization of courts, e.g., jury, nonjury, arraignment, etc.), the P.D. sees defendants only at those places in their paths when they appear in the court he is manning. A given defendant may be "represented" by one P.D. at arraignment, another at preliminary hearing, a third at trial and a fourth when sentenced.

At the first interview with a client (initial interviews occur in the jail where attorneys go, *en masse*, to "pick up new defendants" in the afternoons) a file is prepared on the defendant. In each file is recorded the charge brought against the defendant and, among other things, his next court date. Each evening attorneys return new files to the central office where secretaries prepare court books for each courtroom that list the defendants due to appear in a given court on a given day. In the mornings, attorneys take the court books from the office and remove from the central file the files of those defendants due to appear in "their court" that day.

There is little communication between P.D. and client. After the first interview, the defendant's encounters with the P.D. are primarily in court. Only under special circumstances (to be discussed below) are there contacts between lawyers and defendants in the jail before and after appearances in court. The bulk of "preparation for court" (either trials or non-trial matters) occurs at the first interview. The attorney on station, the "attending attorney," is thus a stranger to "his client," and vice versa. Over the course of his proceedings, a defendant will have several attorneys (in one instance a man was "represented" by eight P.D.'s on a charge of simple assault). Defendants who come to court find a lawyer they don't know conducting their trials, entering their motions, making their pleas, and the rest. Often there is no introduction of P.D. to defendant; defendants are prepared to expect a strange face:

> Don't be surprised when you see another P.D. in court with you on Tuesday. You just do what he tells you to. He'll know all about your case.

P.D.'s seldom talk about particular defendants among themselves. When they converse about trials, the facts of cases, etc., they do so not so much for briefing, e.g., "This is what I think you should do when you 'get him,' " but rather as small talk, as "What have you got going today." The P.D. does not rely on the information about a case he receives from a previous attending attorney in order to know how to manage his "representation." Rather, the file is relied upon to furnish all the information essential for making an "appearance." These appearances range from morning calendar work (e.g., arraignments, motions, continuances, etc.) to trials on offenses from drunkenness to assault with a deadly weapon. In the course of a routine day, the P.D. will receive his batch of files in the morning and, seeing them for the first time that day, conduct numerous trials, preliminary hearings, calendar appearances, sentencing proceedings, etc. They do not study files overnight. Attorneys will often only look over a file a half hour or so before the jury trial begins.

THE FIRST INTERVIEW

As the first interview is often the only interview and as the file prepared there is central for the continuing "representation" of the defendant by other attorneys, it is important to examine these interviews and the file's contents. From the outset, the P.D. attends to establishing the typical character of the case before him and thereby instituting routinely employed reduction arrangements. The defendant's appearance, e.g., his race, demeanor, age, style of talk, way of attending to the occasion of his incarceration, etc., provides the P.D. with an initial sense of his place in the social structure. Knowing only that the defendant is charged with section 459 (Burglary) of the penal code, the P.D. employs his conception of typical burglars against which the character of the present defendant is assessed.

> . . . he had me fooled for a while. With that accent of his and those Parliaments he was smoking I thought something was strange. It turned out to be just another burglary. You heard him about New York and the way he had a hold on him there

that he was running away from. I just guess N.Y. is a funny place, you can never tell what kinds of people get involved in crimes there.

The initial fact of the defendant's "putting in a request to see the P.D." establishes his lower position in the class structure of the community:

We just never get wealthier people here. They usually don't stay in jail overnight and then they call a private attorney. The P.D. gets everything at the bottom of the pile.

Searching over the criminal history (past convictions and arrests) the defendant provides when preliminary fac[t] sheet data [are] recorded in the file, the P.D. gets a sense of the man's typical pattern of criminal activity. It is not the particular offenses for which he is charged that are crucial, but the constellation of prior offenses and the sequential pattern they take:

I could tell as soon as he told me he had four prior drunk charges that he was just another of these skid row bums. You could look at him and tell.

When you see a whole string of forgery counts in the past you pretty much know what kind of case you're dealing with. You either get those who commit an occasional forgery, or those that do nothing but. . . . With a whole bunch of prior checks (prior forgery convictions) you can bet that he cashes little ones. I didn't even have to ask for the amount you know. I seldom come across one over a hundred bucks.

From the looks of him and the way he said "I wasn't doing anything, just playing with her," you know, it's the usual kind of thing, just a little diddling or something. We can try to get it out on a simple assault.

When a P.D. puts questions to the defendant he is less concerned with recording nuances of the instant event (e.g., how many feet from the bar were you when the cops came in, did you break into the back gate or the front door), than with establishing its similarity with "events of this sort." That similarity is established, not by discovering statutorily relevant events of the present case, but by locating the event in a sociologically constructed class of "such cases." The first questions directed to the defendant are of the character that answers to them either confirm or throw into question the assumed typicality. First questions with ADWs are of the order: "How long had you been drinking before all this started?"; with "child molestation cases": "How long were you hanging around before this began?"; with "forgery" cases: "Was this the second or third check you cashed in the same place?"

We shall present three short excerpts from three first interviews. They all begin with the first question asked after preliminary background data [are] gathered. The first is with a 288 (child molestation), the second with a 459 (burglary) and the last with a 11530 (possession of marijuana). Each interview was conducted by a different Public Defender. In each case the P.D.

had no information about the defendant or this particular crime other than that provided by the penal code number:

288

P.D.: O.K., why don't you start out by telling me how this thing got started.

Def.: Well, I was at the park and all I did was to ask this little girl if she wanted to sit on my lap for awhile and you know, just sit on my lap. Well, about twenty minutes later I'm walkin' down the street about a block away from the park and this cop pulls up and there the same little girl is, you know, sitting in the back seat with some dame. The cop asks me to stick my head in the back seat and he asks the kid if I was the one and she says yes. So he puts me in the car and takes a statement from me and here I am in the joint. All I was doin was playin with her a little. . . .

P.D.: (interrupting) . . . O.K. I get the story, let's see what we can do. If I can get this charge reduced to a misdemeanor then I would advise you to plead guilty, particularly since you have a record and that wouldn't look too well in court with a jury.

([t]he interview proceeded for another two or three minutes and the decision to plead guilty was made)

459

P.D.: Why don't you start by telling me where this place was that you broke into?

Def.: I don't know for sure. . . . I think it was on 13th street or something like that.

P.D.: Had you ever been there before?

Def.: I hang around that neighborhood you know, so I guess I've been in the place before, yeah.

P.D.: What were you going after?

Def.: I don't know, whatever there was so's I could get a little cash. Man, I was pretty broke that night.

P.D.: Was anyone with you?

Def.: No, I was by myself.

P.D.: How much did you break up the place?

Def.: I didn't do nothing. The back window was open a little bit see and I just put my hand in there and opened the door. I was just walking in when I heard police comin' so I turn around and start to run. And, they saw me down the block and that was that.

P.D.: Were you drunk at the time?

Def.: I wasn't drunk, no, I maybe had a drink or two that evening but I wasn't drunk or anything like that.

11530

P.D.: Well, Smith, why don't you tell me where they found it (the marijuana)?

Def.: I was driving home from the drugstore with my friend and this cop car pulls me up to the side. Two guys get out, one of them was wearing a uniform and the other was a plain clothes man. They told us to get out of the car and then they searched me and then my friend. Then this guy without the uniform he looked over into the car and picked up this thing from the back floor and said something to the other one. Then he asked me if I had any more of the stuff and I said I didn't know what he was talking about. So he wrote something down on a piece of paper and made me sign it. Then he told my friend to go home and they took me down here to the station and booked me on possession of marijuana. I swear I didn't have no marijuana.

P.D.: You told me you were convicted of possession in 1959.

Def.: Yeah, but I haven't touched any of the stuff since then. I don't know what it was doing in my car, but I haven't touched the stuff since that last time.

P.D.: You ought to know it doesn't make any difference whether or not they catch you using, just so as they find it on your possession or in a car, or your house, or something.

Def.: Man, I swear I don't know how it got there. Somebody must have planted it there.

P.D.: Look, you know as well as I do that with your prior conviction and this charge now that you could go away from here for five years or so. So just calm down a minute and let's look at this thing reasonably. If you go to trial and lose the trial, you're stuck. You'll be in the joint until you're 28 years old. If you plead to this one charge without the priors then we can get you into jail maybe, or a year or two at the most in the joint. If you wait until the preliminary hearing and then they charge the priors, boy you've had it, it's too late.

Def.: Well how about a trial?

(After ten minutes, the defendant decided to plead guilty to one charge of possession, before the date of the preliminary hearing.)

Let us consider, in light of the previous discussion, some of the features of these interviews.

1. In each case *the information sought is not "data" for organizing the particular facts of the case for deciding proper penal code designations* (or with a view toward undermining the assignment of a designation in an anticipated trial). In the 288 instance, the P.D. interrupted when he had enough information to confirm his sense of the case's typicality and construct a typifying portrayal of the present defendant. The character of the information supplied by the defendant was such that it was specifically lacking detail about the particular occurrences, e.g., the time, place, what was said to the girl, what precisely did the defendant do or not do, his "state of mind," etc. The defendant's appearance and prior record (in this case the defendant was a fifty-five-year-old white, unemployed, unskilled laborer,

with about ten prior drunk arrests, seven convictions, and two prior sex offense violations) was relied upon to provide the sense of the present occasion. The P.D. straightforwardly approached the D.A. and arranged for a "contributing to the delinquency of a minor" reduction. In the burglary case, the question, "Had you ever been there before?", was intended to elicit what was received, e.g., that the place was a familiar one to the defendant. Knowing that the place was in the defendant's neighborhood establishes its character as a skid row area business; that the First Federal Bank was not entered has been confirmed. "What were you going after?", also irrelevant to the 459 section of the penal code, provides him with information that there was no special motive for entering this establishment. The question, "Was anyone with you?", when answered negatively, placed the event in the typical class of "burglaries" as solitary, non-coordinated activities. The remaining questions were directed as well to confirming the typical character of the event, and the adequacy of the defendant's account is not decided by whether or not the P.D. can now decide whether the statutory definition of the contemplated reduction or the original charge is satisfied. Its adequacy is determined by the ability with which the P.D. can detect its normal character. The accounts provided thus may have the character of anecdotes, sketches, phrases, etc. In the first instance, with the 288, the prior record and the defendant's appearance, demeanor and style of talking about the event was enough to warrant his typical treatment.

2. The most important feature of the P.D.'s questioning is the presupposition of guilt that makes his proposed questions legitimate and answerable at the outset. To pose the question, "Why don't you start by telling me where this place was that you broke into?" as a lead question, the P.D. takes it that the defendant is guilty of a crime and that the crime for which he is charged probably describes what essentially occurred.

The P.D.'s activity is seldom geared to securing acquittals for clients. He and the D.A., as co-workers in the same courts, take it for granted that the persons who come before the courts are guilty of crimes and are to be treated accordingly:

> Most of them have records as you can see. Almost all of them have been through our courts before. And the police just don't make mistakes in this town. That's one thing about—, we've got the best police force in the state.

As we shall argue below, the way defendants are "represented," (the station manning rather than assignment of counselors to clients), the way trials are conducted, the way interviews are held and the penal code employed—all of the P.D.'s work is premised on the supposition that people charged with crimes have committed crimes.

This presupposition makes such first questions as "Why don't you start by telling me where this place was . . ." reasonable questions. When the answer comes: "What place? I don't know what you are talking about," the defendant is taken to be a phony, making an "innocent pitch." The conceivable first question: "Did you do it?", is not asked because it is felt that this gives the defendant the notion that he can try an "innocent pitch":

> I never ask them, "did you do it?" because on one hand I know they did and mainly because then they think that they can play games with us. We can always check their records and usually they have a string of offenses. You don't have to, though, because in a day or two they change their story and plead guilty. Except for the stubborn ones.

Of the possible answers to an opening question, bewilderment, the inability to answer or silence are taken to indicate that the defendant is putting the P.D. on. For defendants who refuse to admit anything, the P.D. threatens:

> Look, if you don't want to talk, that's your business. I can't help you. All I can say is that if you go to trial on this beef you're going to spend a long time in the joint. When you get ready to tell me the story straight, then we can see what can be done.

If the puzzlement comes because the wrong question is asked, e.g., "There wasn't any fight—that's not the way it happened," the defendant will start to fill in the story. The P.D. awaits to see if, how far, and in what ways the . . . case is deviant. If the defendant is charged with burglary and a middle class establishment was burglarized, windows shattered, a large payroll sought after and a gun used, then the reduction to petty theft, generally employed for "normal burglaries," would be more difficult to arrange.

Generally, the P.D. doesn't have to discover the atypical kinds of cases through questioning. Rather, the D.A., in writing the original complaint, provides the P.D. with clues that the typical recipe, given the way the event occurred, will not be allowable. Where the way it occurs is such that it does not resemble normal burglaries and the routinely used penalty would reduce it *too far* commensurate with the way the crime occurred, the D.A. frequently charges various situationally included offenses, indicating to the P.D. that the procedure to employ here is to suggest "dropping" some of the charges, leaving the originally charged greatest offense as it stands.

In the general case he doesn't charge all those offenses that he legally might. He might charge "child molesting" and "loitering around a schoolyard" but typically only the greater charge is made. The D.A. does so so as to provide for a later reduction that will appear particularly lenient in that it seemingly involves a *change* in the charge. Were he to charge both molesting and loitering, he would be obliged, moreover, should the case come to trial, to introduce evidence for both offenses. The D.A. is thus always constrained not to set overly high charges or not situationally included multiple offenses by the possibility that the defendant will not plead guilty to a lesser offense and the case will go to trial. Of primary importance is that he doesn't charge multiple offenses so that the P.D. will be in the best position vis-à-vis the defendant. He thus charges the first complaint so as to provide for a "setup."

The alteration of charges must be made in open court. The P.D. requests to have a new plea entered:

P.D.: Your honor, in the interests of justice, my client would like to change his plea of not guilty to the charge of burglary and enter a plea of guilty to the charge of petty theft.
Judge: Is this new plea acceptable to the prosecution?
D.A.: Yes, your honor.

The prosecutor knows beforehand that the request will be made, and has agreed in advance to allow it.

I asked a P.D. how they felt about making such requests in open court, i.e., asking for a reduction from one offense to another when the latter is obviously not necessarily included and often (as is the case in burglary-to-petty theft) not situationally included. He summarized the office's feeling:

> . . . in the old days, ten or so years ago, we didn't like to do it in front of the judge. What we used to do when we made a deal was that the D.A. would dismiss the original charge and write up a new complaint altogether. That took a lot of time. We had to re-arraign him all over again back in the muni court and everything. Besides, in the same courtroom, everyone used to know what was going on anyway. Now, we just ask for a change of plea to the lesser charge regardless of whether it's included or not. Nobody thinks twice about asking for petty theft on burglary, or drunkenness on car theft, or something like that. It's just the way it's done.

Some restrictions are felt. Assaultive crimes (e.g., ADW, simple assault, attempted murder, etc.) will not be reduced to or from "money offenses" (burglary, robbery, theft) unless the latter involve weapons or some violence. Also, victimless crimes (narcotics, drunkenness) are not reduced to or from assaultive or "money offenses," unless there is some factual relation, e.g., drunkenness with a fight might turn out to be simple assault reduced to drunkenness.

For most cases that come before their courts, the P.D. and D.A. are able to employ reductions that are formulated for handling typical cases. While some burglaries, rapes, narcotics violations and petty thefts are instigated in strange ways and involve atypical facts, some manipulation in the way the initial charge is made can be used to set up a procedure to replace the simple charge-alteration form of reducing.

RECALCITRANT DEFENDANTS

Most of the P.D.'s cases that "have to go to trial" are those where the P.D. is not able to sell the defendant on the "bargain." These are cases for which reductions are available, reductions that are constructed on the basis of the typicality of the offense and allowable by the D.A. These are normal crimes committed by "stubborn" defendants.

So-called "stubborn" defendants will be distinguished from a second class of offenders, those who commit *crimes which are atypical in their character (for this community, at this time, etc.) or who commit crimes which while typical (recurrent for this community, this time, etc.) are committed atypically.* The manner in which the P.D. and D.A. must conduct the representation and prosecution of these defendants is radically different. To characterize the special problems the P.D. has with each class of defendants, it is first necessary to point out a general feature of the P.D.'s orientation to the work of the courts that has hitherto not been made explicit. This orientation will be merely sketched here.

As we noticed, the defendant's guilt is not attended to. That is to say, the presupposition of guilt, as a *presupposition,* does not say "You are guilty" with a pointing accusatory finger, but "You are guilty, you know it, I know it, so let's get down to the business of deciding what to do with you." When a defendant agrees to plead guilty, he is not *admitting* his guilt; when asked to plead guilty, he is not being asked, "Come on, admit it, you know you were *wrong,*" but rather, "Why don't you be sensible about this thing?" What is sought is not a *confession,* but reasonableness.

The presupposition of guilt as a way of attending to the treatment of defendants has its counterpart in the way the P.D. attends to the entire court process, prosecuting machinery, law enforcement techniques, and the community.

For P.D. and D.A. it is a routinely encountered phenomenon that persons in the community regularly commit criminal offenses, are regularly brought before the courts, and are regularly transported to the state and county penal institutions. To confront a "criminal" is, for D.A. and P.D., no special experience, nothing to tell their wives about, nothing to record as outstanding in the happenings of the day. Before "their court" scores of "criminals" pass each day.

* * *

In the P.D.'s interviews, the defendant's guilt only becomes a topic when the defendant himself attempts to direct attention to his innocence. Such attempts are never taken seriously by the P.D. but are seen as "innocent pitches," as "being wise," as "not knowing what is good for him." Defendants who make "innocent pitches" often find themselves able to convince the P.D. to have trials. The P.D. is in a professional and organizational bind in that he requires that his "clients" agree with whatever action he takes "on their behalf":

> Can you imagine what might happen if we went straight to the D.A. with a deal to which the client later refused to agree? Can you see him in court screaming how the P.D. sold him out? As it is, we get plenty of letters purporting to show why we don't do our job. Judges are swamped with letters condemning the P.D. Plenty of appeals get started this way.

Some defendants don't buy the offer of less time as constituting sufficient grounds for avoiding a trial. To others, it appears that "copping out" is worse than having a trial regardless of the consequences for the length of sentence. The following remarks, taken from P.D. files, illustrate the terms in which such "stubborn" defendants are conceived:

> Def wants a trial, but he is dead. In lieu of a possible 995, DA agreed to put note in his file recommending a deal. This should be explored and encouraged as big break for Def.

> Chance of successful defense negligible. Def realizes this but says he ain't going to cop to no strong-arm. See if we can set him straight.

> Dead case. Too many witnesses and . . . used in two of the transactions. However, Def is a very squirmy jailhouse lawyer and refuses to face facts.

> Possibly the DA in Sup/Ct could be persuaded into cutting her loose if she took the 211 and one of the narco counts. If not, the Def, who is somewhat recalcitrant and stubborn, will probably demand a JT (jury trial).

The routine trial, generated as it is by the defendant's refusal to make a lesser plea, is the "defendant's fault":

> What the hell are we supposed to do with them. If they can't listen to good reason and take a bargain, then it's their tough luck. If they go to prison, well, they're the ones who are losing the trials, not us.

When the P.D. enters the courtroom, he takes it that he is going to lose, e.g., the defendant is going to prison. When he "prepares" for trial, he doesn't prepare to "win." There is no attention given to "how am I going to construct a defense in order that I can get this defendant free of the charges against him." In fact, he doesn't "prepare for trial" in any "ordinary" sense (I use the term *ordinary* with hesitation; what *preparation for trial* might in fact involve with other than P.D. lawyers has not, to my knowledge, been investigated).

For the P.D., "preparation for trial" involves, essentially, learning what "burglary cases" are like, what "rape cases" are like, what "assaults" are like. The P.D.'s main concern is to conduct his part of the proceedings in accord with complete respect for proper legal procedure. He raises objections to improper testimony; introduces motions whenever they seem called for; demands his "client's rights" to access to the prosecution's evidence before trial (through so-called "discovery proceedings"); cross examines all witnesses; does not introduce evidence that he expects will not be allowable; asks all those questions of all those people that he must in order to have addressed himself to the task of insuring that the *corpus delicti* has been established; carefully summarizes the evidence that has been presented in making a closing argument. Throughout, at every point, he conducts his "defense" in such a manner that no one can say of him "He has been negligent, there are grounds for appeal here." He systematically provides, in accord with the prescriptions of due process and the fourteenth amendment, a completely proper, "adequate legal representation."

At the same time, the district attorney, and the county which employs them both, can rely on the P.D. not to attempt to morally degrade police officers in cross examination; not to impeach the state's witnesses by trickery; not to attempt an exposition of the entrapment methods of narcotics agents; not to condemn the community for the "racial prejudice that produces our criminals" (the phrase of a private attorney during closing argument); not to challenge the prosecution of "these women who are trying to raise a family without a husband" (the statement of another private attorney during closing argument on a welfare fraud case); in sum, not to make an issue of the moral character of the administrative machinery of the local courts, the community or the police. He will not cause any serious trouble for the routine motion of the court conviction process. Laws will not be challenged, cases will not be tried to test the constitutionality of procedures and statutes, judges will not be personally degraded, police will be free from scrutiny to decide the legitimacy of their operations, and the community will not be condemned for its segregative practices against Negroes. The P.D.'s defense is completely proper, in accord with correct legal procedure, and specifically amoral in its import, manner of delivery, and perceived implications for the propriety of the prosecution enterprise.

In "return" for all this, the district attorney treats the defendant's guilt in a matter-of-fact fashion, doesn't get hostile in the course of the proceedings, doesn't insist that the jury or judge "throw the book," but rather "puts on a trial" (in their way of referring to their daily tasks) in order to, with a minimum of strain, properly place the defendant behind bars. Both prosecutor and public defender thus protect the moral character of the other's charges from exposure. Should the P.D. attend to demonstrating the innocence of his client by attempting to undermine the legitimate character of police operations, the prosecutor might feel obliged to return to employ devices to degrade the moral character of the P.D.'s client. Should the D.A. attack defendants in court, by pointing to the specifically immoral character of their activities, the P.D. might feel obligated, in response, to raise into relief the moral texture of the D.A.'s and police's and community's operations. Wherever possible, each holds the other in check. But the "check" need not be continuously held in place, or even attended to self consciously, for both P.D. and D.A. trust one another implicitly. The D.A. knows, with certainty, that the P.D. will not make a closing argument that resembles the following by a private attorney, from which I have paraphrased key excerpts:

If it hadn't been for all the publicity that this case had in our wonderful local newspapers, you wouldn't want to throw the book at these men.

If you'd clear up your problems with the Negro in . . . maybe you wouldn't have cases like this in your courts.

(after sentence was pronounced) Your honor, I just would like to say one thing—that I've never heard or seen such a display of injustice as I've seen here in this court today. It's a sad commentary on the state of our community if people like yourself pay more attention to the local political machines than to the lives of our defendants. I think you are guilty of that, your Honor.

(At this last statement, one of the P.D.s who was in the courtroom turned to me and said, "He sure is looking for a contempt charge").

The P.D. knows how to conduct his trials because he knows how to conduct "assault with deadly weapons" trials, "burglary" trials, "rape" trials, and the rest. The *corpus delicti* here provides him with a basis for asking "proper questions," making the "proper" cross examinations, and pointing out the "proper" things to jurors about "reasonable doubt." He need not extensively gather information about the specific facts of the instant case. Whatever is needed in the way of "facts of the case" arise in the course of the D.A.'s presentation. He employs the "strategy" of directing the same questions to the witness as were put by the D.A. with added emphasis on the question mark, or an inserted "Did you really see . . .?" His "defense" consists of attempting to "bring out" slightly variant aspects of the D.A.'s story by questioning his own witnesses (whom he seldom interviews before beginning trial but who are interviewed by the Office's two "investigators") and the defendant.

With little variation the same questions are put to all defendants charged with the same crimes. The P.D. learns with experience what to expect as the "facts of the case." These facts, in their general structure, portray social circumstances that he can anticipate by virtue of his knowledge of the normal features of offense categories and types of offenders. The "details" of the instant case are "discovered" over the course of hearing them in court. In this regard, the "information" that "comes out" is often as new to him as to the jury.

· · ·

SOME CONCLUSIONS

An examination of the use of the penal code by actually practicing attorneys has revealed that categories of crime, rather than being "unsuited" to sociological analysis, are so employed as to make their analysis crucial to empirical understanding. What categories of crime are, i.e., who is assembled under this one or that, what constitute the behaviors inspected for deciding such matters, what "etiologically significant" matters are incorporated within their scope, is not, the present findings indicate, to be decided on the basis of an *a priori* inspection of their formally available definitions. The sociologist who regards the category "theft" with penal code in hand and proposes necessary, "theoretically relevant" revisions, is constructing an imagined use of the penal code as the basis for his criticism. For in their actual use, categories of crime, as we have reiterated continuously above, are, at least for this legal establishment, the shorthand reference terms for that knowledge of the social structure and its criminal events upon which the task of practically organizing the work of "representation" is premised. That knowledge includes, embodied within what burglary, petty theft, narcotics violations, child molestation and the rest *actually stand for*, knowledge of modes of criminal activity, ecological characteristics of the community, patterns of daily slum life, psychological and social biographies of offenders, criminal histories and futures; in sum, practically tested criminological wisdom. The operations of the Public Defender system, and it is clear that upon comparative analysis with other legal "firms" it would be somewhat distinctive in character, are routinely maintained via the proper use of categories of crime for everyday decision making.

NOTES

1. For general histories of indigent defender systems in the United States, see The Association of the Bar of the City of New York, *Equal Justice for the Accused*, Garden City, New York: 1959; and E. A. Brownell, *Legal Aid in the United States*, Rochester, New York: The Lawyers Cooperative Publishing Company, 1951.

2. The experience of the Public Defender system is distinctly different in this regard from that of the Legal Aid Societies, which, I am told, have continually met very strong opposition to their establishment by local bar associations.

3. "Calendar part" consists of that portion of the court day, typically in the mornings, when all matters other than trials are heard, e.g., arraignments, motions, continuances, sentencing, probation reports, etc.

Review Questions

1. How did the P.D.'s studied by Sudnow come to define a "normal crime"?

2. What were the likely consequences if a defendant refused to accept the label considered appropriate by the P.D.?

3. How did the first interview between the defendant and the P.D. usually proceed? What kind of information did the P.D. seek?

4. Based on Sudnow's research findings, discuss why it would be difficult to try to understand why a convicted criminal committed the offense for which he or she was convicted. Consider the role that plea bargaining plays in the court's labeling process.

RULE ENFORCEMENT IN A PUBLIC SETTING: THE CASE OF BASKETBALL OFFICIATING[1]

Roy L. Askins, Timothy J. Carter, and Michael Wood

RULE ENFORCEMENT DECISIONS MADE IN PUBLIC SETTINGS REQUIRE LEGITIMATION, AN indication about the applicability of a given rule. The decision maker must provide for the audience some logical connection between the unique event and the general rule in order that his/her performance and self both be judged competent and legitimate. Research on enactment and interpretation of formal rules has been conducted in various organizational and bureaucratic settings (e.g., Garfinkel, 1967; Cicourel, 1968; Zimmerman, 1970) but comparatively little work has been carried out in settings for which the rule enforcer's role includes a public and performing aspect.

This study presents an analytic description of the work of basketball officials as they interpret and enact formal rules in the presence of an audience: spectators, coaches, players, and fellow officials. We find that the social work of basketball officials consists of two main lines of action: (1) routine legitimation activities, by which calls and noncalls are justified by reference to four main contexts, and (2) dramaturgical work, by which the official attempts to evoke positive audience evaluations for problematic decisions.

METHODS

The basketball officials we observed came from eighteen different officiating organizations. The sample was composed of a variety of officials, from those working high school games to those officiating professional games. Information about the negotiating and dramaturgical work of the officials was obtained from the observation of one hundred and seventy basketball games, three hundred and fifty conversations with officials at game sites, and participation in the training programs given to both new members and veterans. Training program participation included attendance of weekly meetings and training sessions, the taking of examinations, and general participation in informal discussions concerning the practice of working a game.[2]

Observation began with the attendance of games being worked by officials previously known to us. The number of officials gradually expanded

Roy L. Askins, Timothy J. Carter, and Michael Wood, "Rule Enforcement in a Public Setting: The Case of Basketball Officiating," *Qualitative Sociology*, vol. 4, no. 2 (Summer 1981), 87–101.

through a snowball sampling technique. An unanticipated benefit of becoming known to a large number of officials was the opportunity to sit with non-working officials while others were working the game. This situation afforded the opportunity to observe and record the off-duty officials' evaluations and observations of their colleagues.

Similar benefits were derived from attending weekly meetings. Many informal discussions took place before the meetings, during breaks, and at the conclusion of formal business. These informal discussions were particularly helpful for understanding the interpretations and the situated accounts* produced by officials.

Repetitive contact with the formal and informal activities of officials allowed continual comparison between observer interpretation and the subjects' ongoing actions. Although many of the concepts used in this report are not the concepts of the actors involved, the ideas conveyed in our descriptions were found to be appropriate by the subjects themselves. Each description was submitted to several officials for evaluation and found suitable. . . .

THE DUAL FACETS OF DECISION-MAKING

In juxtaposition with a material world of physical events and objects there is a social world of identification and interpretation. Officiating requires participation in both worlds. For officials, making a good call (i.e., making a connection between a concrete particular event and a formal rule of the game) involves two distinct activities: (1) a veridical [accurate] experience of the event itself, and (2) a public rendition of the experience through the use of verbal and nonverbal display (signals).

Officials approach their task with the firm conviction that the events of a game and the game itself are real and identifiable only if they: (1) have a thorough understanding of the game and how it is to be perceived, (2) practice good techniques, and (3) assume an objective stance that precludes contaminating influences.

The public rendition of one's phenomenological experience†—the social accounting of the objective events of the game—is considered by the officials to be largely unteachable and a true reflection of character strength. Such strength is valued, and the officials consider it an indication of independence and self-sufficiency to occasionally make unpopular decisions in public under stressful conditions.

The ambiguity of the events officials must identify, coupled with the public nature of their work, prevents them from being oblivious to the responses of the audience. Officials are aware of the significance of audience judgments for evaluation of their competency. They believe not only that

---

*An explanation or account which makes reference to unique features of a situation.

†One's own unique view or experience of an event or phenomenon.

other officials take audience reactions as accurate descriptions of their work, but also that audience reactions influence members of the organizations which are responsible for game assignments and promotions.[3] It is a source of considerable irritation to all officials that important evaluations of their work are performed by individuals whom they deem unqualified. According to officials these audiences "just don't understand what is involved in the working of a game" and "never give you credit for having more experience and less bias than they have." Such reactions are particularly acute on those occasions when the official believes he/she has performed particularly well and yet audience reaction does not verify that appraisal. Thus, to work a good game is in some respects self-immolating: a competent official displays a willingness to make decisions contrary to popular sentiment, yet in so doing he/she alienates those audiences which otherwise might legitimate claims of competency.

Generally, officials believe that a good call is one in which the public rendition is determined by the phenomenological experience rather than audience reaction. However, audience reaction sometimes elicits the official's public interpretation. Such an occurrence is expected to happen when an official becomes swept up in the emotions of the game, or when he/she is inexperienced. However, even the most veteran and gutsy official is known to occasionally make calls that are contrary to his/her own experience of the event. The statement "I don't know why, but I saw it one way but called it another" is common. In this event, the apparent contradiction between the experience and the public display is explained by making reference to the overt behavior as involuntary or "reflex action." The control over reflex behaviors is considered a most admirable feature of a good official. Officials, in adopting such accounts, indicate that their physical movements can be independent of, or even contrary to, their mental states.

On several occasions we inquired of officials making what appeared to be anomalous calls what the overt display was in response to. We wanted to know the reason for the physical response, if it differed from the conscious identification. This question was often received with remarks which indicated that a "bad call" needed no explanation, that is, it was to be taken as an acceptable account in itself and not an issue to be pressed by further inquiry. For example, one official became somewhat irate and screamed: "How the hell should I know?" Other officials, however, accounted for anomalous physical responses by adopting a more psychological stance. References were made to unpremeditated balancing tendencies and habitual behavior (stemming from anticipations). In addition, features of the setting such as variable audiences or timing requirements for making calls were cited. Such accountings for apparently incongruous behaviors allow officials to deny intentionally or consciously playing to a crowd.

In sum, our analysis has begun with the discovery that officiating involves both a technical and social character. Technically, officials must have the skill to connect a particular incident with a formal rule. Socially, officials must communicate to the audience, players and coaches that their (the official's) connection between the incident and the rule is appropriate. While the technical character of officiating is [a mere reaction], the social character of officiating involves an active participation by the official in *defining the situation for others*. To insure that others define a call or non-call as appropriate (and, thereby, the official as a competent actor) officials must demonstrate the rationale for their decisions. The rationale for a decision depends as much on the context within which an incident occurs as it does on the incident itself. Officials, then, can legitimate (i.e., justify, explain or excuse) a call or non-call by selecting the appropriate grounds. Our analysis now turns to the identification of contexts (grounds) used by officials to legitimate their decisions to themselves and others.

CONTEXTS OF LEGITIMATION

Selecting the context for which a call or non-call is appropriate is a key component in the social character of officiating and imposes a social reality on the game apart from the physical reality of the events themselves. We were able to identify four different contexts for making a call: (1) bureaucratic appeal; (2) invoking the spirit of the rules; (3) claiming the requirements of consistency; and (4) appeal to order.

1. We use the expression bureaucratic appeal to designate those occasions in which the official explains his/her decisions by reference to a formal rule applicable to the situation. Bureaucratic appeals are considered minimally subjective and therefore the safest means of justifying a call. The bureaucratic appeal not only makes a claim to objectivity but disassociates the official from responsibility for the rule or its enforcement. "It's in the book" is an accounting that renders a decision virtually unchallengeable. In addition, such an appeal has the effect of redirecting criticisms away from the "message carrier" to the "message" itself or to the competency of the critic (e.g.: "He simply doesn't know the rules").

2. Invoking the spirit of the rules is a means of accounting for calls or non-calls which denies the appropriateness of a literal application of the formal rules. "Spirit of the rules" is considered to be more subjective than bureaucratic appeals, but provides the official with strategic role distance from the formal rules. Spirit-of-the-rules groundings are also applied when challenges to an official's consistency are made: they are a means of demonstrating why some rules on some occasions are not applicable. The appeal to the spirit of the rule constitutes a claim by the official of insight into its true meaning. The decision is not made merely because a certain rule is "in the book," but in order to fulfill the general intent of the rule. If an official feels that a player or coach is attempting to use a literal interpretation of a rule to gain an unfair advantage no call is made. Frequently, officials interpret the

physical contact between players as "incidental contact" rather than "charging," "blocking" or an "illegal pick," especially when the contact is away from the ball and unlikely to affect the outcome of the play. In such instances the official is invoking the spirit of the rule rather than the letter.

3. Claiming consistency is a context which points to previous work as a grounds for making present decisions. The appeal here is not to the accuracy of such calls but to their consistency. Statements such as "I didn't call it earlier so I can't call it now" or "I didn't call it against him so I can't call it against the other guy" are examples of accounts which emphasize the consistency requirements of working a game. At times consistency accounts take precedence over other appeals.

4. Appeals to order reveal the existence of other grounds for making decisions than those pertaining to formal rules and contexts. Considerations such as intent of actions, or respect for the game and its officials are taken as grounds for making decisions that would otherwise be unaccountable. "I let him get away with it for a while but I finally had to put a stop to it"[4] and "if we hadn't called it sooner or later we would have had a brawl" are examples. Appeals to order are made with reference to the overall and not individual or particular consequences of the event in question.

No matter how appropriate a call or non-call may be in relation to a particular context, legitimacy depends on the evaluation of others. Thus, officials often employ dramaturgical devices to increase the probability of legitimation. Dramaturgical devices are outward expressions of an official's experience (e.g., facial gestures, body movements, talk, sounds, etc.) strategically displayed to elicit the desired audience response.

DRAMATURGICAL ASPECTS OF OFFICATING

We were able to distinguish three general dramaturgical strategies used by officials in legitimating their work: "footnoting," "mystifying" and "disattending."

FOOTNOTING: Footnoting is used to specify an official's interpretation of an event. The purpose is to explain why a particular event constitutes an example of the call that is signaled. Footnoting not only possesses an adjective character but also provides conjunctive links between the event identified and other calls made by the official. Footnoting clarifies to both the audience and the official himself/herself the nature of the interpretive work being performed. By embellishing upon standard forms of signals, officials indicate to the audience: (1) how the official is seeing events, (2) how events are logically connected in thematic fashion, (3) exactly what boundaries of tolerance are being enforced, and (4) how and why apparently different events (or similar events) are being identified as the same (or different) on that particular occasion.[5]

One of the most prominent methods of footnoting used by officials is talk. Officials vary in the amount and kind of talk they use with players or coaches during the course of a game. Some do not speak directly to players or coaches but carry on a running description of events taking place on the floor in much the same manner as a radio commentator broadcasting the game. Officials utilizing this device believe that it not only helps to insure a common experiencing of events between the official, players, and coaches, but that it also minimizes the possibility of misunderstanding of the meanings of formal signals when they are given. In addition, such talk makes the context in which calls are made available to those audiences at all times. While viewing a player preparing to shoot an official commented: "He double pumps, he's up and down—no shot; that's a travel." Although the player and/or coach may not agree with the official's observation that the player's feet left the floor and came back down before the shot, neither can argue that the official was not "on top of the play," nor that what the official said occurred does not constitute "traveling."

Talk may also be used by officials to legitimize their work when, for all practical purposes, no work is being done. Rather than making specific their interpretive work, as in the case of footnoting, officials may intentionally mystify their identifications.

MYSTIFYING: The activity of producing ambiguous talk or signals calling for audiences to infer their own meaning (thus indirectly legitimating the call) may be termed "mystifying" (cf. Goffman, 1959:67; Scott and Lyman, 1968:60). Officials sometimes deliberately produce ambiguous talk calling for audience interpretation so that they will be appropriate for almost any occasion. One veteran official of both college and professional games reported that he confined his comments to players during a game to one expression: "Okay." "By doing this," he reported, "players will take it to mean something about whatever it is that they are doing or watching." Here, the officials utterance "okay" is taken to mean "watch out," "I'm watching you," "good play," "I won't tolerate much more," "calm down" or whatever else a player might infer depending upon the occasion. . . .

The practice of purposely making ambiguous communications is not restricted to verbal comments to players and coaches. During the course of any game there are events that officials view as confusing enough to allow a call which is virtually unchallengeable. In other words, the situation appears in such disarray that no interpretation is forthcoming. When this is the case the official will not make a signal any more specific than is absolutely necessary. If possible, officials will even avoid identifying when and where an infraction occurred as well as who was responsible. This allows the natural inclination of audiences to assume the official knows what he/she is doing even if the audiences do not. This is a normalizing practice in its own right, an evocation of supportive responses, so to speak.

The decision to footnote or to mystify a signal rests on the official's assumption of how the audience is likely to interpret his/her actions. Whenever an official believes that he/she has experienced an event in a manner unique or at odds with what others have experienced, he/she is inclined to footnote the call. The working assumption used by the official in this case is that he/she, by virtue of proximity or perspective, possesses more valid knowledge than other observers. Footnoting is a claim to privileged knowledge or perception of the event which justifies it being identified in a particular manner. On the other hand, when an official believes that audience interpretations are not crystallized in a negative manner, and due to *situation vagueness* are likely to support the legitimacy of his/her actions, supplemental interpretation is not called for and mystification is believed to produce the best results.[6]

Thus far our descriptions have centered around dramaturgical devices produced by officials in making a particular call. Our attention now turns to accounts produced by officials in avoiding the responsibility of a bad call or inappropriate non-call. We term these dramaturgical devices "disattenders."

DISATTENDING: Disattenders are dramaturgical devices produced by officials to minimize their responsibility for calls or non-calls that might be judged to be the result of incompetence, or even worse, a lack of integrity.

Disattenders are relatively common because of the frequency with which ambiguous events or flukes arise. Disattenders are used by officials to indicate to audiences that negative views they may have toward the official's immediate work are improper, or to deny or ignore the existence of such negative views. Our observations reveal two general types of disattending accounts: spatial and temporal.

Spatial disattending accounts represent a claim to ignorance about the event in question. It is a rule in the common sense reasoning of both officials and audiences alike that an official cannot be held responsible for events he/she cannot see—as long as he/she is attending other "reasonable" activities pertaining to his/her responsibilities. Knowing this, officials occasionally will feign ignorance on the grounds that they were attending something else or were prevented from clearly experiencing the event in question by an occurrence for which they could not be held completely responsible, e.g.: "I tripped" or "I was screened out."[7]

Temporal disattenders deal with audience criticism by establishing action distance between the call in question and present activities. Immediately following a call which the official knows will be challenged, or a call about which he/she feels uncertain, the official may become involved in some other activity which brings closure to the issue of the call's legitimacy. A sudden concern over the welfare of a fallen player, becoming involved in certain janitorial duties (e.g., cleaning the floor of debris, wiping up wet spots, etc.), engaging in a conversation, or attending "official" business at the scorer's table are all means by which officials attempt to shut off further consideration of potentially troublesome calls or non-calls.

The use of disattenders is viewed by officials as a somewhat dishonorable practice because it is an attempt to evade the responsibility of having to make a call or to face up to one that has been made. Therefore, considerable caution is used by officials in disattending. Overuse may be taken as a sign of incompetence, or worse, the disattenders may be recognized for what they are and the official judged as "copping out." The interesting feature of disattenders, however, is that to some extent they are truthful representations of a problematic situation. Thus, a spatial disattender, being a claim to ignorance, is the result of uncertainty as to what a call should be. A temporal disattender is simply a statement that the call is "old business" and that the official will not recognize the legitimacy or appropriateness of further criticism. To members of the community of officials, however, they are attempts to reduce the trial effect of working a game and avoid public criticism of their decisions.

THE OFFICALS' VIEW OF OFFICIATING

Officials do not seriously consider the intentionality of their own work. In fact, the suggestion that they do not see events as they really are, or that events require interpretation and negotiation, is met with some hostility. Officials believe they experience the natural orderliness of events, and that in consequence their decisions are not subjective constructions. However, officials claim considerable importance for two prerequisites of good officiating that seem to undermine a purely objective approach to making decisions. These prerequisites are experience and concentration. The more experience an official has the more competent he/she is believed to be because of his/her ability to identify events readily. As one official noted, "the experienced official simply knows what it is he is seeing because he has seen it before." Thus, experience is assumed to provide a means for understanding the way things are. To look for or expect an event, or a conclusion to an event, to follow in a situational context is not vulgar anticipation but a learned understanding of the causal direction of the natural world.[8]

Officials also place importance on their ability to concentrate on events as they occur. They believe that without such concentration they are likely to be surprised, or not able to recognize events in their immediacy. In either case the competency of the official would be questioned. The exact meaning of "concentration" is never explained in any detail, but is understood by all competent members of the officiating community as a parallelism between the conscious processes of the official, and the development of events in the independent world of physical events. Concentration differs from mere anticipation in the eyes of the official in that the former is quasi-open in its expectations, whereas the latter is relatively closed.

Officials believe that experience and concentration enhance understanding of the game, the development of good officiating techniques, and an objective stance that precludes contaminating influences—all of which reinforces their conviction that the events of a game are real and independent of their identifications and communications of these events to audiences.

DISCUSSION

The game of basketball, like other games, can be defined largely in terms of a particular body of rules which allow and limit action among players. Games vary markedly according to the degree of formality of the rules and of play, and the amount of deviance tolerated. The basketball games we observed were conducted on a more formalized basis than much of what passes for basketball in school yards and backyard courts. The games we observed featured written and codified "official" rules, specified and regulated playing area and materials, and uniforms. More important for our purposes was the presence of specialized personnel charged with keeping time, tabulating score, and with upholding the codified rules of the game.

The role of the official in the games we observed is in many respects similar to that of actors in organizational and bureaucratic settings. The basketball official has formally specified rights and duties vis-à-vis players, coaches, spectators, and other officials working the game. The official is expected to carry out his or her duties in a competent and objective manner. Occupation of the role is based upon the possession of expertise and technical qualifications, and the official is protected from arbitrary dismissal.

Our overall observations of rule interpretation and enforcement by basketball officials are consistent with the findings of research on the routine activities of organizational and bureaucratic agents charged with connecting formal rules with concrete situations (Sudnow, 1965; Garfinkel, 1967; Cicourel, 1968; Zimmerman, 1970). Formal rules have been found to possess an essential component of incompleteness, bearing out Bittner's (1965) observation that the literal interpretation of formal schemes is impossible. . . . [S]tudents of formal organization have not been unaware of the real differences between official rules and policies, and actual operating procedures (see, e.g., Page, 1946; Blau, 1955).

• • •

Legitimation contexts as we have identified them are analogous to the "decision rules" used by the jurors studied by Garfinkel (1967). Jurors and basketball officials share a similar task—to develop an interpretation of what "really" happened. The jurors, like the officials, approached their task with the belief that the events of a case (or game) were real in themselves, and that valid decisions about the applicability of formal rules could be made. As Garfinkel (1967) observed however, formal rules were insufficient to guide action, and were of necessity complemented by the application of interpretive rules to construct the corpus of what "really" happened. Along similar lines, we observed that basketball officials altered the context of on-going events in order to construct the corpus of what "really" happened, thereby legitimating the application of a formal rule.

While the content of the dramaturgical strategies we observed are grounded in a particular setting, the use of verbal and nonverbal actions to restore meaningful interaction in problematic situations can be subsumed under the heading of "aligning actions"[9] (Stokes and Hewitt, 1976). Al-though Stokes and Hewitt (1976:838) restrict their definition of aligning actions to "largely verbal efforts," the distinctive setting of basketball offi-cials and other team sport officials requires a much increased scope for the use of nonverbal efforts (signals and gestures). The necessity for the pre-dominant use of signals over talk is related to the public and performing as-pect of the official's role. The official must observe the game, deliberate, and act mainly as a performer in front of an audience. The setting provides little opportunity for officials to leave the "front region." Furthermore, over the long run it is audience reactions and not organizational formal criteria that determine evaluation of the official's performance. As we discussed above this fact leads to a complex and ambivalent relationship between the official and the audience. . . .

[In sum, t]he definitional and dramaturgical activities of basketball and other sports officials offer excellent opportunities for insight into the generic processes of rule use and construction of social reality.

NOTES

1. An earlier draft of this paper was presented at the annual meeting of the South-ern Sociological Society, Knoxville, Tennessee, March, 1980. We would like to thank Michael Hughes and James Michaels for abetting suggestions and comments. The authors share equal responsibility for the paper, the names have been listed al-phabetically.

2. These data were primarily collected by Dr. Askins.

3. It seems that even though officials themselves may be capable of discrediting the negative responses of audiences they do not believe others are capable of making these discretionary judgments. Indeed, in the conduct of their discussions it would appear that officials are considerably less willing to discredit such audiences when their negative reactions are directed at another official.

4. The "it" in this statement refers to a behavior that may not in itself be sanction-able but in its repetition may be seen as violating the rules of propriety, "taking un-fair advantage," or imperiling the proper conduct of the game.

5. This last feature of "footnoting" is an accounting which supports a claim of consistency.

6. Overspecification of the "obvious" by an official is usually grounds for ques-tioning his/her competency. It presents audiences with an image of a person who is more involved in events than is assumed proper for a competent official.

7. "Disattenders" are also used between officials, much to the chagrin of one of them.

8. The very use of the term anticipation is likely to bring forth an angry response from an official even when the expression is not directed at him/her. It seems to be one of those terms which is not to be applied to any specific official or officiating in general.

9. Aligning actions include *motives* (acceptable justifications for conduct perceived by others as unexpected or alternative; Mills, 1940; Gerth and Mills, 1953, Chapter V), *accounts* (statements made by actors to explain unanticipated or untoward behavior; Scott and Lyman, 1968), *quasi-theories* ("ad hoc explanations brought to problematic situations to give them order and hope . . .;" Hewitt and Hall, 1973:367–368), and *disclaimers* (verbal devices "employed to ward off and defeat in advance doubts and negative typifications which may result from intended conduct," Hewitt and Stokes, 1975:3).

REFERENCES

Blau, Peter
    1955 *The Dynamics of Bureaucracy.* Chicago: University of Chicago Press.

Bittner, Egon
    1965 "The concept of organization." *Social Research* 32:239–258.

Cicourel, Aaron V.
    1968 *The Social Organization of Juvenile Justice.* New York: John Wiley.

Garfinkel, Harold
    1967 *Studies in Ethnomethodology.*Englewood Cliffs: Prentice-Hall.

Gerth, Hans and C. Wright Mills
    1953 *Character and Social Structure: The Psychology of Social Institutions.* New York: Harcourt, Brace & World.

Goffman, Erving
    1959 *The Presentation of Self in Everyday Life.* New York: Doubleday Anchor.

Hewitt, John P. and Peter M. Hall
    1973 "Social problems, problematic situations and quasi-theories" *American Sociological Review* 38:367–374.

Hewitt, John P. and Randall Stokes
    1975 "Disclaimers." *American Sociological Review* 40:1–11.
    1970 "Talking and becoming: A view of organizational socialization." Pp. 239–256 in T. D. Douglas (ed.), *Understanding Everyday Life.* Chicago: Aldine.

Mills, C. Wright
    1940 "Situated actions and vocabularies of motive." *American Sociological Review* 5:904–913.

Page, Charles H.
    1946 "Bureaucracy's other fare." *Social Forces* 25:88–94.

Scott, Marvin and Stanford Lyman
    1968 "Accounts." *American Sociological Review* 33:46–62.

Stokes, Randall and John P. Hewitt
   1976 "Aligning actions." *American Sociological Review* 41:838–849.

Sudnow, David
   1965 "Normal crimes: Sociological features of the penal code in a public de-
       fenders office." *Social Problems* 12:255–272.

Zimmerman, Don H.
   1970 "The practicalities of rule use." Pp. 221–238 in J. D. Douglas (ed.), *Under-
       standing Everyday Life*. Chicago: Aldine.

Review Questions

1. Briefly describe the four types of claims or justifications used by basketball officials to legitimate their calls and decisions. Are there any parallels between these claims used by officials in working a game and the justifications employed by police officers in directing traffic? The justifications
employed by teachers who are monitoring an examination to prevent cheating? The justifications employed by other agents of social control?

2. In order to communicate to the audience why a particular call was
made, basketball officials used footnoting, mystification, and disattenders.
What are these techniques, and how do they make the job of the official easier? What other types of social-control agents use these techniques?

3. Askins, et al., show clearly that events occurring on the basketball
court are often ambiguous—that is, they could be interpreted in a number
of ways. Officals are often unaware that their job is to *interpret* these
events, claiming that they merely call what is "really" happening. Discuss
the officials' view of their job. What other types of social-control agents are
unaware of the interpretive nature of their actions?

SICKNESS AND SOCIAL CONTROL

Candace Clark

INTRODUCTION

JUST AS EVERY SOCIETY HAS DEVELOPED A FAMILY SYSTEM AND AN ECONOMIC SYS-
tem, every society known to social scientists has developed a normative system to define, locate, and control illness (Wellin, 1978; Fábrega, 1974).
What is considered illness in one society may be a mark of health in another—that is, illness categories are devised or constructed differently from
one culture to another—yet every human group recognizes something as
constituting illness and mobilizes resources in response to illness. We hope
to demonstrate in this review essay that *the control of illness and sick people is one form of the more general phenomenon of social control.* Social
control, any behavior or social-structural arrangement which encourages
people to conform to societal norms and values, is an essential feature of all
societies. Medical forms of social control have increased tremendously in
importance in American society over the past century, edging aside religious, legal, educational, and familial forms and techniques of social control. An accurate and comprehensive picture of life and interaction in modern Western societies cannot omit the expanded role of medical models
offering explanations of human experience and of medical means of trans-
forming human behavior.

A first step in presenting this sociological view of the role of medicine is
the clarification of the key terms illness, sickness, and disease, all of which
have distinct and specific meanings here. As the terms are understood
by sociologists today (Twaddle and Hessler, 1977:97), "illness"[1] refers to the
individual's perception or claim of a problematic physiological experience,
state, or change that he or she is feeling which is presumed to have biological causes. By "sickness" we mean the state of being defined and reacted to
by *other societal members*, including relatives, friends, and employers, as
having a problem or condition with presumed biological causes.

While all societies recognize illness and sickness, the concept of disease is
a relatively new product of Western culture. "Disease" is used here to refer
to *whatever medical practitioners define* as a cause of illness (Freidson,
1970:206, passim). This explanation may seem overly general, but it is impossible to be more specific when the phenomena considered as disease in
our society, let alone others, are as varied as bacterial infection, diabetes,

346

alcohol "dependence," and *anorexia nervosa* (an inability or unwillingness to eat). It is commonly believed by the public that a condition seen as a disease has a known biophysiological cause and cure. There is widespread acceptance within Western biomedicine of the theory that certain bacteria produce toxic reactions in human hosts; but the causes and cures of the other conditions mentioned above are not well understood at all. With regard to alcohol dependence, there is at present no single accepted theory as to its cause, nor is there even an adequate definition of "dependence" (Conrad and Schneider, 1980:82–102). And even with the bacterium, it is not necessarily the case that a disease will be recognized.

As Dubos (1959), Freidson (1970), and Dingwall (1976) have argued, diseases do not exist "in nature," but rather are culturally created *meanings* attached to particular conditions by human beings. As Sedgwick put it, "the blight that strikes at corn or potatoes is a *human invention*, for if man wished to cultivate parasites (rather than corn or potatoes) there would be no 'blight.'" And, "the invasion of a human organism by cholera germs carries with it no more the stamp of 'illness' than the souring of milk by other forms of bacteria" (Sedgwick, 1972:211). In order for a condition to come to be seen or interpreted as a disease, *it must first be considered a problem* by many members of a society. In societies in which diarrhea is widespread, for instance, this condition may be seen as normal rather than problematic, although in our own culture it is viewed as a problem to be dealt with by medicine and, therefore, evidence of disease.

If a problematic condition is related in some way to biological functioning, and if no means of control by other than medical techniques (for instance, prayer or legal action) are considered acceptable, medical practitioners may attempt to deal with it. In some cases, a medical treatment is discovered *before* the problem comes to be seen in medical terms. For instance, the discovery that the stimulant Ritalin has a tranquilizing effect on children led to the interpretation of children's disruptive behavior, short attention span, and fidgeting as a disease called hyperkinesis. Previously, such children were simply defined as "bad" and dealt with by teachers and parents as such (Conrad, 1975). In other cases, the medical profession has come to view certain conditions as diseases even though there is little evidence as to biological causes and no medical cure or effective treatment. Such was the case with many of the conditions which have come to be seen as "mental illness" rather than as sinful or illegal behavior (Szasz, 1961, 1970; Conrad and Schneider, 1980).

The process by which a condition comes to be viewed as a disease is in some respects a political one. That is, some groups may lobby for or against a disease interpretation. In our own society, a major lobbying effort by various homosexual organizations led to the removal of homosexuality from the list of mental illnesses in 1974 (Conrad and Schneider, 1980:204–8). Pediatric radiologists lobbied to have Battered Child Syndrome seen as a mental illness of parents who use violent techniques of child-rearing (Conrad and Schneider, 1980:163–66). Such behavior was not even viewed as a "problem" two centuries ago, let alone a "disease."

The final decisions as to whether a condition will be interpreted as a disease are made by those physicians who are in charge of preparing the diagnostic manuals of the profession. The U.S. government's National Institutes of Health and the World Health Organization based in Geneva, Switzerland, are in large part responsible for the listing of diseases. There may be widespread agreement among medical practitioners as to the decisions reached by these groups, or there may be less of a consensus. In some cases, votes have been taken of medical practitioners throughout the country, with the majority view determining whether a condition "is" or "is not" a disease.

It is often difficult for us to accept the position that the diseases recognized by Western biomedicine are socially constructed, because medical models for interpreting conditions have become deeply embedded in our culture's "common stock of knowledge" and are now part of our taken-for-granted reality. In fact, social scientists have sometimes argued that some diseases are "real" while some (such as alcohol use, violence toward children, and *anorexia nervosa*) are "abnormal" *behaviors* which happen to have physiological consequences but which are *not* "real" diseases. In doing so, they are participating in part in our culture's taken-for-granted reality. Rather than arguing what should and should not properly be called a disease, we have adopted the view here that disease is what medical practitioners say it is. This view will allow us to focus on *how practitioners treat* those they define as diseased.

Following these three definitions, we can see that one may *define oneself* as "ill" or claim to have an illness; be *diagnosed* as having a "disease" by a medical practitioner; and/or come to be *seen as* "sick" by parents, teachers, and co-workers. A moment's reflection will illustrate that these three distinct statuses are not necessarily occupied simultaneously. For instance, one may perceive oneself to be healthy, yet be diagnosed as having a disease and come to be viewed by significant others as sick. Or, one may feel ill, but be regarded as healthy (disease free) by medical practitioners and as healthy (not sick) by one's spouse and boss. In societies such as ours where the legitimacy of medical practitioners as experts is great, definitions of disease have a strong influence on the individual's definition of him or herself as ill and the significant others' determination of sickness.

SICKNESS AS DEVIANCE

To understand the conceptual link between the control of sickness and social control in general, it is helpful first to come to view sickness (or impairment) as a special case or form of *deviance*, as medical sociologist Eliot Freidson argued cogently over a decade ago (1970:205–23; see also Mechanic, 1968:44–48; Goffman, 1963; Zola, 1972; Twaddle, 1973).

Deviance as a Label

Deviance is *not* a quality of an act or state which exists outside the confines of culture, but is rather a meaning, designation, or label which is both created by societal members and attached to particular individuals and/or to their behavior in the course of social interaction (Becker, 1973; Lemert, 1962, 1972; Katz, 1975). A behavior itself has no meaning unless societal members assign it one within their cultural framework of norms and within their understanding of situational contexts. Two individuals may engage in precisely the same behavior, yet one will be viewed as normal and the other as a criminal. The labeling process involves locating the individual within a more or less elaborate classification system as, say, a sex pervert or a check forger. In short, as situations are defined (Thomas, 1923), so are individuals—some as deviant, some as normal.

Sickness as a Label

As implied in our introduction above, a similar labeling process occurs regarding illness, sickness, and disease. This labeling process involves the use of the culture's "common stock of knowledge" and its stock of "expert knowledge" to make sense of or interpret a societal member's problematic physiological states and experiences. It must first be determined if the individual is to be seen as healthy or unhealthy. Then the unhealthy individual is classified (by self or others) as suffering from a particular type of ill health. The problematic physiological conditions or states we experience ourselves or recognize in others are almost always *ambiguous*; that is, they could be interpreted in a number of different ways even within one culture. For example, if an individual notices some physiological change, that change may be attributed to illness or it may (1) be seen as a non-problem or (2) be seen as a consequence of tiredness, possession by the devil, laziness, or some other "cause" that is culturally acceptable. ("Is this pain 'normal,' or am I having a heart attack?", "I may be getting the flu, or I may just be working too hard", "I've never thought about it this way before, but maybe his behavior does indicate that he is mentally ill.")

Recent research by David Locker indicates that a general pattern often followed by lay individuals in Western societies is first to define a problematic experience tentatively as "normal" until later evidence or the input of others causes a change in interpretation (1981:87–92; see also Zola, 1973). Medical practitioners, on the other hand, tend to view even the most ambiguous symptoms as evidence of disease (Freidson, 1970:263; Scheff, 1966:105–27; Rosenhan, 1973). Whatever the general tendencies of the parties involved in interpreting states of health, it is clear that the process of definition is a negotiated one. Our own interpretations are "validated" by checking them with others (Berger and Luckmann, 1966; Locker, 1981:62, passim). ("What do you think, Doctor? Is this sore throat serious?" "Do you think these spots are measles, Mom?" A physician says, "It doesn't *look* serious to me, but how do you *feel*?") All stages of the process of interpretation, validation, reinterpretation, and so on are rooted in interaction. The label "unhealthy" is, therefore, a negotiated social product. And the process of defining always involves comparison against a similarly socially constructed definition of "health" or "normality" (Lewis, 1953).

Societal Reaction to Labels

The act of labeling someone as either deviant or unhealthy usually implies that some sorts of responses will be made by societal members which are different from their responses to those labeled as non-deviants or healthy. As Lennard, et al. put it, labels are instructions or messages for treatment, not just descriptive categories (1971). The sick person is considered "not normal," as is the deviant; and the reactions of societal members to the mugger, to the drunk driver, to the genius, or to the sick are not the same as responses to "normal" people. Various attempts, legal or medical, are often made to return deviants and the sick to a relatively normal state of functioning and/or to protect other societal members from interaction with them. In fact, it is by viewing these societal reactions that sociologists determine whether or not deviance or sickness exists. That is, an individual can be said to be deviant or sick *when others respond as if* that person belonged in the category (Becker, 1973; Sudnow, 1967). Moreover, the sick are labeled and reacted to as deviants.

Blame and Discreditation

To be sure, the term deviance usually carries negative connotations (except in the case of the "positive" deviant, e.g., the genius or the hero), while the term sickness may not (Locker, 1981:4–5). It is a general norm in most cultures that people viewed as sick are not to be blamed for their conditions or states (a "right"), if they act in ways that indicate their desire to improve (a "duty") (Parsons, 1951). On the other hand, those recognized as deviants are commonly felt to be able to control their actions and are therefore blamed for them (Locker, 1981:4–5). While the sick are described as "victims of" or "suffering from" diseases which they "contract," deviants presumably choose to act or think in certain ways—and are viewed by some as having more in common with disease than with the sick.

This generalization breaks down, however, when we consider the cases of venereal disease and obesity, both of which are conditions recognized as diseases that evoke blame from many members of society (Cahnman, 1979). Studies of physicians' attitudes toward those labeled as alcoholics show that the majority hold alcoholics personally responsible for drinking (Conrad and Schneider, 1980:98). It is also common for medical practitioners to complain that some of their clients "bring their illness on themselves" by their living habits or by their disregard of medically meaningful symptoms until they reach an advanced state (Millman, 1976; Locker, 1981: 138–39).[2] These practitioners are blaming the sick.

More important, there is a "moral" aspect to sickness; sickness may not evoke blame, but neither does it evoke credit. Many sicknesses call forth severe negative evaluations of the moral worth of the sick, resulting in revulsion or ostracism—as in the cases of Typhoid Mary, those with disfiguring birth defects, the mentally ill, epileptics, and lepers (Goffman, 1963). In fact, medical anthropologist Horacio Fábrega (1974) has concluded from extensive research that, in all known societies, designating an individual as sick *inevitably involves discreditation* of that person. Over and above the fact that the sick person may not be blamed for his or her condition, he or she is not viewed as being as worthy, as creditable, as reliable, or as adequate as the healthy. Thus, the amputee and the flu sufferer, the cancer patient and the mentally ill are seen (to a greater or lesser degree) as less desirable prospective interactants than the healthy—even though the sick can claim a certain amount of sympathy and attention from the healthy. Discreditation in many ways sets up barriers to routine interaction between the sick and the "normal" population in everyday life. It should come as no surprise to find that there is often some reluctance to accept the label of sickness. On the contrary, we should expect an imperfect fit between definitions of disease and sickness, on the one hand, and definitions of illness, on the other.

We now see that sickness, though unique because of its actual or presumed biological causes, has a great deal in common with what is more commonly considered deviance and can, indeed, be seen as one form of deviance. Since the mere fact of defining deviance implies social control, it follows that diagnosing and defining disease and sickness imply social control as well.

CONTROL OF SICKNESS

What do gossip, smiles, frowns, awards, imprisonment, stares, fines, and the prescribing of antibiotics have in common? They are all behaviors or structural arrangements which serve to encourage societal members to conform to social norms—to think, to act, and indeed to look in ways which are within the culture's acceptable limits—or to discourage thinking or acting or looking outside acceptable limits. As such they constitute *social control*. Negative sanctions addressed to the deviant may induce return to normality; positive sanctions reward normality. Furthermore, negative sanctions allow those people seen as normal to view the consequences of their potential deviance, and a better understanding of what the boundaries of normality are considered to be is fostered (Dentler and Erikson, 1959).

Cultural norms, values, and beliefs tend to become manifested in our social organization and social structure. "Specialist" social statuses emerge, and patterned ways of dealing with nonconformity develop. Social-control specialists are charged with more than the ordinary degree of responsibility for exercising control, and are commensurately empowered to punish, reward, and treat. These specialists, in general, are termed *agents of social control*. Examples include teacher, judge, prison guard, child-guidance professional, advice columnist, and medical practitioner.

Practitioners and Social Control

Assume for a moment that we are societal engineers attempting to create a system for organizing and controlling the behavior of societal members so that the group can maintain its existence into the future. One problem we would have to face would be how to insure a reasonable supply of productive members to carry out tasks which are important for societal survival. Our society could not long persist if most of its members were sick most of the time, since sickness is almost universally seen as a legitimate reason for not engaging in one's regular social functions, such as feeding and dressing oneself, going to school, going to work, and caring for others. That is, one of the norms of the sick role is that those recognized as legitimately sick should not be required to carry out their normal responsibilities (Parsons, 1951). One societal problem, then, is to guarantee that not everyone is sick—enters the sick role—at the same time.

Additionally, we may find that continual performance of social functions by our societal members, day in and day out, rain or shine, may prove difficult and stressful. An occasional release from the demands of work, family, and community roles may make it easier for our members to function—and the population easier to control—over the long run. Thus, another problem is to provide "safety valves," occasional releases from constant drudgery, for our societal members.

As societal engineers, we might devise any number of strategies to deal with these problems. One such strategy might be to rely on medical practitioners as our agents of social control. While the process is by no means as conscious and formal as this hypothetical case makes it seem, we submit that practitioners have come to function in just such a manner in all societies.

Treatment as Social Control

Let us take up these problems in order, beginning with supplying productive societal members. The reader will recall that the designation of sickness brings with it discreditation. It might be suggested that this discreditation, coupled with pain and suffering, could be sufficient to motivate people to return to normality or to feel inadequate enough to shun association with normal individuals. Rather than trusting solely to the motivation and abilities of the afflicted individuals to get better, however, all societies have evolved one or more "specialist" positions of medical practitioner (Hughes,

1968). Practitioners—shamans, mechanists, physicians, and the like—are relied upon by their societies to develop models or theories of what illness is, how it is caused, and how it can be eliminated or controlled, thereby contributing to the maintenance of a reasonable supply of productive societal members.

A rather small number of *techniques* of medical treatment have been devised in the course of human history. Drugs, poultices, surgery, bone setting, confinement and isolation, instrumental interventions (such as acupuncture, electric shock, or leeching), talking, ritual, magic, and appeal to the supernatural—all are techniques which have been used by medical practitioners in a wide variety of societies to control sickness and the sick. These techniques have been put to use in several *forms* or *modes* of social control: (1) returning the sick to formal functioning, (2) punishment, (3) isolation, and—occasionally—(4) altering society to prevent or alleviate sickness.

A few words are in order concerning the general implications of the disease concept of Western biomedicine for treatment in our society. Some belief systems, including Christian Science, see the causes of illness in the supernatural rather than in disease. Other systems have pointed to the social conditions of poverty and crowding as the causes of illness (Twaddle and Hessler, 1977:9–11). Our current belief system views illness as a result of foreign organisms attacking a person or an organ of a person or as a result of the malfunctioning of the body itself. In a word, we view disease as the cause of illness and as "person-centered" rather than societally, environmentally, or supernaturally centered. Our searches for cures and treatments for those conditions we interpret as disease-caused are, therefore, likely to focus on the individual level. The great success of germ theory in controlling illness related to microbial infection has probably been responsible for this thrust in Western biomedicine, although germ theory has come to be recognized as not very useful for understanding chronic, degenerative, or mental illnesses (Strauss, 1975; Twaddle and Hessler, 1977:13–15). *As a result of the person-centered disease concept, control and treatment of sickness often means control and treatment of the sick,* as we shall see below.

RETURN TO NORMALITY: First, medical techniques may be used in an effort to return the sick to a level of functioning as close as possible to, or better than, that existing before the onset of sickness. (Of course, the societal expert, the medical practitioner, has a large voice in determining what is "normal.") Thus, the physician prescribes drugs in an attempt to rid the body of toxic microbes or to reduce the effects of stress, sets a broken bone, or removes abnormal tissues. The shaman or *curandero* (curer) administers herbs to try to reduce fever. Early physicians in the U.S. who viewed "Negritude" (the state of being Negro) as a disease used drugs, poultices, and the like to change blacks into whites (Szasz, 1970:153–59). All of these activities have as their goal, at least partially, the return of the sick person to "normality." This form of social control is the one which is most widely recognized as an appropriate goal of medical treatment, since it is usually assumed to be in line with the interests of the individual sufferer as well as the interests of the society.

PUNISHMENT: Second, both treatment itself and certain healers in specific may serve to punish the sick, whether the healers are conscious of this effect or not.[3] Punishment may encourage return to normality among the sick as well as signaling to the normal the consequences of their potential lapses from normality.

Confinement in a hospital is often deemed punishing by the hospital's clients (Roth, 1972:426-28). The restrictions and routines of the bureaucratically organized hospital demand that the client give up claims to privacy, mobility, and liberty in general. Diet and sleeping times are out of the control of the client. Even ambulatory clients are often refused permission to leave the hospital temporarily; those who do so may forfeit the benefits of medical insurance and the right to future care (Roth, 1973).

A more extreme case of this general rule applies in the case of incarceration in a mental hospital (especially involuntary incarceration). Not only are daily activities regimented, conformity to dress regulations enforced, and personal liberty circumscribed, but civil rights are forfeited (Szasz, 1970:65-66). All of these practices lead to a redefinition of self for the client (Goffman, 1961; Scheff, 1966). Additionally, non-ordinary measures are adopted in the mental hospital to ensure conformity to the bureaucratic regimen, such as routine administration of large quantities and dosages of tranquilizing drugs (Rosenhan, 1973), assignment to solitary confinement, and the use of the straitjacket. These techniques may be painful and/or dangerous, as is electroconvulsive shock, still a common form of "treatment" for the depressed which is quite often viewed explicitly as punishment by the clients. Psychiatrist Thomas Szasz has noted the punishing aspects of the treatment of mental patients, stating that "people often prefer a cure that kills to no cure at all" (1982).

Moreover, incarceration in a mental hospital produces stigma so great as to limit the ex-patient's ability to participate in society after his or her release (Goffman, 1961). Ex-convicts may be more readily accepted as neighbors, workers, and friends than ex-mental patients. Phillips (1963) reports that public views of the so-called mentally ill are more negative in cases where hospitalization has occurred than when less formalized treatment has been given or when no treatment at all was administered. Hospitalization, rather than the individual's behavior, elicited stigma.

Outside the realm of the hospital as well, examples of the use of medical techniques as punishment can be found. Barker-Benfield (1976) documents, for instance, the widespread practice during the late 1800s and early 1900s in the United States of performing hysterectomies and clitoroidectomies to eliminate "non-feminine" behavior in women. Sterilization operations performed on the poor and the mentally retarded (usually women) without their informed consent serve to remove the rewards of parenthood from people considered unworthy (Davis, 1974; Vaughan, 1974; Caress, 1975) as the family-planning movement of the 1960s may also have done (Kammeyer, et al., 1975).

Additionally, programs to "help" handicapped or impaired populations are often punitive in their effects (Freidson, 1966; Sussman, 1966; Wiseman, 1979), a point of which many handicapped are painfully aware. Scott (1969) found that the blind, for example, very often attempted to avoid the label of blindness and the services of agencies to aid the blind. They recognized that, by accepting the label, they would be set apart from sighted society both symbolically—as when white canes and guide dogs signal a deviant condition—and physically—as a result of work and leisure activities organized for the blind only. These consequences of defining themselves as blind and accepting "help" were considered punishments by many.

In a less severe form, contacts with medical personnel in our society involve a host of other *degradations* and *inconveniences* related to the unequal distribution of power in the client-practitioner relationship. In most cases these days, the client (the sufferer) must leave his/her own surroundings and travel to receive services from the practitioner on the latter's home "turf." The cost in time and money is added to the *interactional* disadvantage to the client of trying to maintain poise in strange surroundings. As Barry Schwartz points out elsewhere in this book, the expenditure of time in waiting is a cost also borne disproportionately by the client. The use of mystifying terminology and jargon by medical personnel underscores the client's feelings of ignorance and the practitioner's status as an "insider." Outright condescension by the practitioner that challenges the client's competence may also occur (Locker, 1981:155-65).

Although the client is the one who has the problematic condition, it is common in our society to treat the sick as though they cannot be trusted to be "in their right minds" when giving accounts of what they are experiencing. Clients' assessments of their own conditions are, therefore, often ignored or discounted, adding to their feelings of helplessness. The "good patient" is one who asks no questions, turning control over his or her fate to the practitioner (Glogow, 1973).

As if this were not enough, the client may be asked to disrobe. In most settings in our society, nudity or semi-nudity puts one at a severe interactional disadvantage. Members of what other occupational groups are allowed to remain clothed while interacting with clients who sit or lie *sans* apparel? The gynecological exam is an example of one situation fraught with embarrassment and uneasiness, in part for this reason (Emerson, 1970).

If medical treatment can be costly or punishing in terms of loss of liberty, pain, danger, stigmatization, and degradation, it is also costly in monetary terms in our society. The United States is one of the very few industrialized countries in the world today in which the sick person is expected to pay the costs of services as they are rendered—i.e., when he or she is ill (Waitzkin and Waterman, 1974; Navarro, 1976).[4] Other societies finance medical care with public funds, the practitioners receiving salaries or yearly "capitation" payments for each client under their care, rather than collecting a fee from the ill for each service performed (Anderson, 1972). Some segments of our population—the poor and the elderly—receive some aid with medical bills, and medical insurance (itself very costly) eases or diffuses the financial burden for many others. Still, ours is a nation in which high medical costs lead many to delay or forego treatment and in which a catastrophic condition or accident may result in severe financial difficulty for the sick and their family members. Medical costs, then, may be seen as a type of disincentive to seek treatment, or as a punishment similar to a fine levied by a judge or jury.

Closely related to the financing issue is that of "unnecessary" medical procedures. In essence, the practitioner in the U.S. can create a portion of the "demand" for his or her services by recommending that clients be observed and/or treated. The fee-for-service method of paying physicians encourages high rates of service, since procedures ranging from laboratory tests to surgery are financially beneficial to the practitioner. Some examples of commonly overrecommended procedures are hysterectomies, tonsillectomies, routine blood work, and the annual physical checkup (Scully, 1980; Millman, 1976; Freidson, 1970:257–58). The costs to the client of unnecessary procedures can be measured in terms of pain and suffering (occasionally death), money, time, and inconvenience.

Many of us are not used to thinking of medical treatment as having such a wide variety of punishing aspects. Or, we calculate the benefits of medical care as outweighing the costs. Nevertheless, medical treatment does entail costs and punishments. To the extent that these punishments encourage those who are sick to return to "normal" and those who are not sick to remain healthy, society "benefits" from them and they function as social control.

ISOLATION: A third major form of medical social control over sickness involves *protecting the healthy by removal of the sick person* from his or her normal environment. A quarantine approach such as this is based on a *contagion model* of the cause of illness, in which the removal of the "bad apple" is deemed appropriate to prevent the spread of the condition to others. It has been most often applied when evidence exists that a microbe is causing an illness. Room (1975) argues, however, that the contagion-quarantine model is the logic increasingly applied in the case of drug use (a newly recognized disease). The drug user is seen as capable of "infecting" others and thus must be removed from normal society to a special location, for the protection of the larger group. Additionally, the public relies on the staff of the mental hospital to isolate those mental patients believed to be dangerous to others. Thus, we can see that some aspects of incarcerating people in mental hospitals and segregating the handicapped, in addition to punishing them, fit with this model of protection of the healthy.

In a similar vein, medical diagnosis and treatment may serve as a sorting process for other societal institutions. By certifying who is healthy, the physician aids employers, the military, sports teams, and the like to select healthy members and reject others (Daniels, 1969; Illich, 1976:76–77).

ALTERING SOCIETY: Fourth, and more rarely, social organization itself may be altered in order to control sickness. Stressful working conditions may be eliminated, sanitation systems may be put into operation, pollution-producing industrial practices may be controlled, and so on. (See Reverby, 1972, for further discussion of health-promoting measures as distinct from illness-response measures.) Such practices are usually regarded in our society as in the province of public health, a branch of medicine which is distinctly lower in prestige and monetary rewards than those branches which take a more person-centered approach to control. The concern is often voiced that altering societal conditions is more expensive than treating persons; yet, with one of every ten dollars of the total Gross National Product of the United States being spent on medicine ($247 billion, or $1067 per person, in 1980; *New York Times*, 1981), it is difficult to view costs alone as the reason for the limited use of societal alterations. For whatever reasons, we see again that control of sickness is often accomplished by controlling the sick.

Sickness As Social Control

We turn now to the issue of release from the lifelong burden of societal responsibilities. Vacations provide a degree of release (except for mothers who attend to child-care duties whether the family is at home or away). Sleep also, in addition to having physiological benefits, allows the individual to escape temporarily from the pressures of interaction (Schwartz, 1970). Another form of release occurs when one is defined as sick and enters the sick role, as Talcott Parsons noted over thirty years ago (1951). Because most conditions are temporary and self-limiting, and because the sick person is expected (1) to want to improve and (2) to cooperate with the experts in order to do so, the release associated with sickness is usually temporary and controlled. Medical practitioners, as the primary legitimate definers of sickness, serve as *gatekeepers* channeling people into the sick role. They serve as societal agents controlling "release time." The uses of treatment discussed above are then brought into play to channel the sick out of the temporary role. Thus, sickness itself, defined and controlled by medical practitioners, may serve an important social-control function for society.

The importance of the sick role as a safety valve has long been recognized by prison officials who must maintain control over their "societies of inmates." Prisoners in most penal facilities are routinely cycled through sick bay, presenting their claims of illness to practitioners who confirm or deny them (Twaddle, 1976). When prison physicians adopt get-tough policies and refuse to legitimate claims to illness, control of the prisoners often becomes difficult or impossible to accomplish (Waitzkin and Waterman,

1974:46–52).[5] In the prison context—and in the military as well (Waitzkin and Waterman, 1974:56)—allowing people to enter the sick role on a temporary basis facilitates social control in the long run. The medical practitioner may be seen as providing an important social-control service here as in the larger society.

THE MEDICALIZATION OF SOCIAL CONTROL IN THE · UNITED STATES

It should be clear by this point that medical practitioners have a great potential for wielding power to the end of social control. In our own society, that power has increased dramatically over the past half century or so, for several interrelated reasons. First, our own trust and faith in the medical profession has increased, legitimating and reinforcing the power of healers (Krause, 1977). Few question the expertise of the medical profession, the benefits of prescribed treatments, or the size of the medical bill. Medical models of defining problematic experiences and medical techniques of treating them have caught on in the lay public's consciousness and imagination. Whereas medical explanations of events—or definitions of situations—were once regarded with suspicion or hostility or amused tolerance, the medical approach has become not only accepted but also popularized and has entered the common stock of knowledge of our culture. That is, the lay public themselves increasingly invoke medical models to define situations, states, and events. Medical metaphors abound: "There is a cancer growing on the presidency." "We live in a sick world." "If you don't take that offer, you're crazy." "Surgery is required to rid ourselves of the tangle of laws governing this area." Medical diagnoses by lay persons are legion: "That's just a virus." "John has strep throat." "Of course, your headache is due to stress." Furthermore, many occupational groups such as social workers and parole officers are adopting medical and para-medical approaches to their clients, thereby borrowing a degree of prestige from medicine (Chalfant, 1977).

Second, the profession of medicine has achieved a state of professional autonomy of impressive magnitude (Freidson, 1970; Brown, 1979). Physicians, unlike most other occupational groups, control the production of new members by determining the content of medical education and the numbers and types of new recruits. Licensing of physicians also rests solely in the hands of the medical profession. Medical mistakes (deviance among the agents of social control) are dealt with mainly within the medical community, despite what the widespread publicity of some recent legal suits brought against physicians might lead us to believe (Millman, 1976). Fees for medical services are also subject to little outside regulation. The terms, hours, and content of physicians' jobs are dictated by no outside source, except perhaps the clients' willingness and ability to pay for certain types of services. Physicians enjoy a great deal of autonomy and freedom from outside intervention in their own profession, and they also exercise control and influence over other medical groups, such as nursing, pharmacy, and the like (Freidson, 1970:47–70). The trend toward group- and hospital-based practice, and especially the rise of medical "empires" connected with university research-and-teaching hospitals, have contributed to a heightening and consolidation of medical control over their own and other occupational groups (Ehrenreich and Ehrenreich, 1970).

Third, and perhaps most important, more and more conditions have come to be defined as diseases every year by the medical profession. Currently there are more than a thousand categories of disease. A large proportion of the new diseases recognized since World War II are behavioral rather than physiological in origin, and most fall into the general category of "functional" mental illness (Conrad and Schneider, 1980:53). Hundreds of conditions have been added to the medical nosology in recent decades, including obesity, sociopathy, alcoholism, hyperactivity in children, *anorexia nervosa*, minimal brain dysfunction, and drug addiction. These conditions once were interpreted in terms of "sin" or "badness" or "illegality" but are now routinely conceived of as actual diseases. Another candidate for disease status is *hysteroid dysphoria*, a recently coined term to describe "love junkies" who feel a need to be in love. "Limerance" is another recently created term for this love obsession, although some prefer the less mystifying "lovesickness." Drug therapy is offered by some physicians for this condition (Sobel, 1980). Although *hysteroid dysphoria* may not ultimately come to be widely recognized as a disease, many other conditions undoubtedly will. Thus, the domain of medicine is expanding, and the proportion of the population subject to treatment with medical techniques is growing correspondingly. The increase in the number of disease categories explains in part the increased expenditures for medicine in our society, from about five percent of the Gross National Product in 1950 to almost ten percent today (Fenninger and Meeker, 1980:6).

In sum, social control can be said to be increasingly medicalized, because both the power and domain of medicine have expanded, with the blessing of the lay public.

SOCIOLOGICAL IMPLICATIONS

In concluding, we should note a few of the implications of the increased medicalization of social control for American society which are of particular sociological importance. First, social control is achieved over many types of problems without the imposition of extreme degrees of discreditation. Since blame is often not assigned to the sick, they may receive attention and support not available under other systems of social control. Furthermore, much medical treatment is more effective and efficient than previous methods of control. In these cases, employing medical models to define and treat conditions is actually useful to individuals and/or to society. This outcome, which may be more humane than the effects of legal social control, is balanced, however, with others not as sanguine.

Second, medical treatment is less readily recognized as social control than is legal intervention. While the court and the prison are seen as overtly "on society's side," medicine is presumed (as is religion) to act in the interests of the individual. This presumption is particularly dangerous given the great power, prestige, and influence of medical practitioners vis-à-vis their clients. If the social-control functions of medical treatments are not obvious, we are less likely to provide safeguards for individual rights in this arena (Kittrie, 1971; Mechanic, 1973). Social control is not recognized as such and, in a manner of speaking, goes underground. Currently, legal and ethical debates are surfacing over the rights of clients to refuse treatment, to be informed of medical diagnoses and procedures, and to ask questions of medical practitioners regarding their bills. These debates may signal a degree of public awareness of the problems of "hidden" social control.

A third consequence of the medicalization of social control is not unique to medicine, but it is nonetheless important. The person-centered nature of much medical treatment focuses attention away from societal problems and "privatizes" them. That is to say, what *could* be viewed as a failure of societal organization and structure comes to be interpreted as the "failure" of the individual. Conrad (1975) gives a telling example to illustrate this point in his analysis of hyperactivity in children. What could have been seen as a problem of rigidly organized schools has become a disease located in the child. Treatment involves drug therapy for the individual rather than a restructuring of the school environment.

Stress provides yet another example. Stress has increasingly come to be seen as related to any manner of other problematic conditions, from digestive-tract problems to suicide to the susceptibility to influenza. Medical models of stress have tended to focus on the individual and to find solutions in psychoanalysis or tranquilizers or physical exercise. By focusing thus, attention is shifted from societal conditions—time clocks, traffic jams, deadlines, competition, rapid social change, and unemployment—to the person. Taking the opposite, society-centered approach, Brenner has found evidence for increases in suicides and heart problems corresponding to increases in unemployment (1973). Evidence such as this calls into question the usefulness of person-centered approaches to disease. That is, from the standpoint of the individual or from the standpoint of the society, medical models for defining and treating some human problems may not be useful at all, *over the long run*. The society, by not paying attention to social-structural problems, may allow them to grow to the point that they are insoluble.

NOTES

1. Impairment and disability may also be considered as categories similar to illness (Freidson, 1966); but, for the sake of brevity, we will not make continued reference to impairment and disability.

2. Of course, clients may also be criticized for presenting themselves to their physicians with "unimportant" or "nonexistent" symptoms (Locker, 1981:62, passim)—a classic double-bind situation for the client.

3. We are ignoring in this discussion the issue of iatrogenic (treatment- or physician-produced) disease or impairment, since we assume that most cases of this type are accidental. Nonetheless, iatrogenic conditions are a common feature of treatment. It is estimated that about 20 per cent of hospital clients leave the hospital with a problem they did not have when they entered (Roth, 1972). Illich contends that the increased tendency of the population to seek care in modern times has meant that treatment has become a considerable public-health problem (Illich, 1976:26–34, passim). To the extent that clients and potential clients are aware of the dangers involved in medical treatment, that aspect of treatment may be seen as a deterrent or punishment.

4. For a more detailed discussion of the problems inherent in the U.S. system of medical-care financing, see Fuchs (1974) and Carlson (1976).

5. Note that we are not attempting to judge whose claims are more valid, the prisoner's or the physician's. In fact, in most cases it probably makes little difference, since the power to define rests so one-sidedly with the practitioner in the prison setting.

REFERENCES

Anderson, Odin W.
   1972 *Health Care: Can There Be Equity? The United States, Sweden and England.* New York: Wiley.

Barker-Benfield, G. J.
   1976 *The Horrors of the Half-Known Life.* New York: Harper & Row.

Becker, Howard S.
   1973 *Outsiders: Studies in the Sociology of Deviance* (2nd ed.). New York: Free Press.

Berger, Peter, and Thomas Luckmann
   1966 *The Social Construction of Reality: A Treatise in the Sociology of Knowledge.* Garden City, N.Y.: Doubleday.

Brenner, M. Harvey
   1973 *Mental Illness and the Economy.* Cambridge: Harvard University Press.

Brown, E. Richard
   1979 *Rockefeller Medicine Men: Medicine and Capitalism in America.* Berkeley: University of California Press.

Cahnman, Werner
   1979 "The Moral Treatment of Obesity." Pp. 439–54 in Howard Robboy, Sidney L. Greenblatt, and Candace Clark, eds., *Social Interaction* (1st ed.). New York: St. Martin's Press.

Caress, Barbara
   1975 "Sterilization: Fit to Be Tied," *Health/PAC Bulletin* 62:1–6, 10–13.

Carlson, Rick J.
   1976 *The End of Medicine.* New York: Wiley-Interscience.

Chalfant, Paul
   1977 "Professionalization and the Medicalization of Deviance: The Case of Probation Officers," *Offender Rehabilitation* 2:77–85.

Conrad, Peter
  1975 "The Discovery of Hyperkinesis: Notes on the Medicalization of Deviant Behavior," *Social Problems* 23:12–21.

Conrad, Peter and Joseph Schneider
  1980 *Deviance and Medicalization: From Badness to Sickness*. St. Louis: Mosby.

Daniels, Arlene Kaplan
  1969 "The Captive Professional: Bureaucratic Limitation in the Practice of Military Psychiatry," *Journal of Health and Social Behavior* 10:255–65.

Davis, Morris E.
  1974 "Involuntary Sterilization: A History of Social Control," *Journal of Black Perspectives* 1:46.

Dentler, Robert A. and Kai T. Erikson
  1959 "The Functions of Deviance in Groups," *Social Problems* 7:98–107.

Dingwall, Robert
  1976 *Aspects of Illness*. New York: St. Martin's Press.

Dubos, Rene
  1959 *Mirage of Health*. Garden City, N.Y.: Doubleday.

Ehrenreich, Barbara and John E. Ehrenreich
  1970 *The American Health Empire*. New York: Random House.

Emerson, Joan P.
  1970 "Behavior in Private Places: Sustaining Definitions of Reality in Gynecological Examinations." Pp. 74–97 in Hans P. Dreitzel, ed., *Recent Sociology No. 2*. New York: Macmillan.

Fábrega, Horacio, Jr.
  1974 *Disease and Social Behavior*. Cambridge: M.I.T. Press.

Fenninger, Randolph B. and Edward F. Meeker
  1980 "Decade of the 1970's: Window on the 1980's: A Review of Health Care Policy." Pp. 3–21 in Gerald L. Glandon and Roberta Shapiro, eds., *Profile of Medical Practice 1980*. Monroe, Wisc.: American Medical Association.

Freidson, Eliot
  1966 "Disability as Social Deviance." Pp. 71–99 in Marvin Sussman, ed., *Sociology and Rehabilitation*. Washington, D.C.: American Sociological Association.
  1970 *Profession of Medicine*. New York: Dodd, Mead.

Fuchs, Victor
  1974 *Who Shall Live? Health, Economics, and Social Choice*. New York: Basic Books.

Glogow, Eli
  1973 "The Bad Patient Gets Better Quicker," *Social Policy* 4:72–76.

Goffman, Erving
  1961 *Asylums*. Garden City, N.Y.: Doubleday.
  1963 *Stigma: Notes on the Management of a Spoiled Identity*. Englewood Cliffs, N.J.: Prentice-Hall.

Hughes, Charles C.
   1968 "Medical Care: Ethnomedicine." Pp. 87–97 in David Sills, ed., *International Encyclopedia of the Social Sciences*, Vol. 10. New York: Crowell, Collier & Macmillan.

Illich, Ivan
   1976 *Medical Nemesis: The Expropriation of Health*. New York: Pantheon.

Kammeyer, Kenneth C. W., Norman R. Yetman, and McKee J. McClendon
   1975 "Race and Public Policy: Family Planning Services and the Distribution of Black Americans." Pp. 402–21 in Norman R. Yetman and C. Hoy Steele, *Majority and Minority: The Dynamics of Racial and Ethnic Relations*, 2nd ed. Boston: Allyn & Bacon.

Katz, Jack
   1975 "Essences as Moral Identities, *American Journal of Sociology* 80:1369–90.

Kittrie, Nicholas
   1971 *The Right to Be Different: Deviance and Enforced Therapy*. Baltimore: Johns Hopkins University Press.

Krause, Elliott A.
   1977 *Power and Illness: The Political Sociology of Health and Medical Care*. New York: Elsevier.

Lemert, Edwin
   1962 "Paranoia and the Dynamics of Exclusion," *Sociometry* 25:2–20.
   1972 *Human Deviance, Social Problems, and Social Control* (2nd ed.). Englewood Cliffs, N.J.: Prentice-Hall.

Lennard, Henry, et al.
   1971 *Mystification and Drug Misuse*. New York: Perennial Library.

Lewis, Aubrey
   1953 "Health as a Social Concept," *British Journal of Sociology* 4:109–24.

Locker, David
   1981 *Symptoms and Illness: The Cognitive Organization of Disorder*. London: Tavistock.

Mechanic, David
   1968 *Medical Sociology: A Selective View*. New York: Free Press.
   1973 "Health and Illness in Technological Societies," *Hastings Center Studies* 1:7–18.

Millman, Marcia
   1976 *The Unkindest Cut: Life in the Backrooms of Medicine*. New York: Morrow.

Navarro, Vicente
   1976 *Medicine under Capitalism*. New York: Prodist.

New York Times
   1981 "U.S. Report Says Increase in Health Spending is Biggest in 15 Years," October 31, I, 19.

Parsons, Talcott
  1951 *The Social System,* Chapter 10. Glencoe, Ill.: Free Press.

Phillips, Derek L.
  1963 "Rejection: A Possible Consequence of Seeking Help for Mental Disorders,"
  American Sociological Review 28:963–72.

Reverby, Susan
  1972 "A Perspective on the Root Causes of Illness," *American Journal of Public
  Health* 62:1140–42.

Room, Robin
  1975 "The Epidemic Model and Its Assumptions," *Quarterly Journal of Studies in
  Alcohol* 1:16–21.

Rosenhan, David L.
  1973 "On Being Sane in Insane Places," *Science* 179:250–58.

Roth, Julius
  1972 "The Necessity and Control of Hospitalization," *Social Science and Medicine* 6:425–46.
  1973 "The Right to Quit," *Sociological Review* 21:381–96.

Scheff, Thomas
  1966 *Being Mentally Ill.* Chicago: Aldine.

Schwartz, Barry
  1970 "Notes on the Sociology of Sleep," *Sociological Quarterly* 11:485–99.

Scott, Robert A.
  1969 *The Making of Blind Men.* New York: Russell Sage.

Sobel, Dava
  1980 "In Pursuit of Love: Three Current Studies," *New York Times,* Jan. 22,
  III, 1; 5.

Strauss, Anselm L.
  1975 *Chronic Illness and the Quality of Life.* St. Louis: Mosby.

Sudnow, David
  1967 *Passing On: The Social Organization of Dying.* Englewood Cliffs, N.J.:
  Prentice-Hall.

Sussman, Marvin (ed.)
  1966 *Sociology and Rehabilitation.* Washington, D.C.: American Sociological
  Association.

Szasz, Thomas
  1961 *The Myth of Mental Illness.* New York: Hoeber-Harper.
  1970 *The Manufacture of Madness.* New York: Harper-Colophon.
  1982 "The Lady in the Box," editorial, *New York Times,* Feb. 16.

Thomas, W. I.
  1923 *The Unadjusted Girl.* Boston: Little, Brown.

Twaddle, Andrew C.
  1973 "Illness and Deviance," *Social Science and Medicine* 7:751–62.

1976 "Utilization of Medical Services by a Captive Population: Analysis of Sick Call in a State Prison," *Journal of Health and Social Behavior* 17:236–48.

Twaddle, Andrew C. and Richard M. Hessler
1977 *A Sociology of Health.* St. Louis: Mosby.

Vaughan, Denton and Gerald Sparer
1974 "Ethnic Group and Welfare Status of Women Sterilized in Federally Funded Family Planning Programs," *Family Planning Perspectives* 6:224–229.

Waitzkin, Howard B. and Barbara Waterman
1974 *The Exploitation of Illness in Capitalist Society.* Indianapolis: Bobbs-Merrill.

Wellin, Edward
1978 "Theoretical Orientations in Medical Anthropology: Change and Continuity over the Past Half Century." Pp. 23–39 in Michael H. Logan and Edward E. Hunt, Jr., eds., *Health and the Human Condition: Perspectives on Medical Anthropology.* North Scituate, Mass.: Duxbury.

Wiseman, Jacqueline P.
1979 *Stations of the Lost: The Treatment of Skid Row Alcoholics.* Chicago: University of Chicago Press.

Zola, Irving K.
1972 "Medicine as an Institution of Social Control," *Sociological Review* 20:487–504.
1973 "Pathways to the Doctor: From Person to Patient," *Social Science and Medicine* 7:677–88.

Review Questions

1. What are the distinctions among illness, sickness, and disease made by Clark?

2. How can sickness be seen as one form of deviance? Discuss situations from your own experience in which a person considered sick was treated, or reacted to, as "not normal."

3. How does the sick role contribute to social control?

4. How does medical treatment contribute to social control?

5. What are some of the consequences for society and for individuals of the medicalization of social control?

ON BEING SANE IN INSANE PLACES

D. L. Rosenhan

I F SANITY AND INSANITY EXIST, HOW SHALL WE KNOW THEM?
The question is neither capricious nor itself insane. However much we may be personally convinced that we can tell the normal from the abnormal, the evidence is simply not compelling. It is commonplace, for example, to read about murder trials wherein eminent psychiatrists for the defense are contradicted by equally eminent psychiatrists for the prosecution on the matter of the defendant's sanity. More generally, there are a great deal of conflicting data on the reliability, utility, and meaning of such terms as "sanity," "insanity," "mental illness," and "schizophrenia."[1] Finally, as early as 1934, Benedict suggested that normality and abnormality are not universal.[2] What is viewed as normal in one culture may be seen as quite aberrant in another. Thus, notions of normality and abnormality may not be quite as accurate as people believe they are.

To raise questions regarding normality and abnormality is in no way to question the fact that some behaviors are deviant or odd. Murder is deviant. So, too, are hallucinations. Nor does raising such questions deny the existence of the personal anguish that is often associated with "mental illness." Anxiety and depression exist. Psychological suffering exists. But normality and abnormality, sanity and insanity, and the diagnoses that flow from them may be less substantive than many believe them to be.

At its heart, the question of whether the sane can be distinguished from the insane (and whether degrees of insanity can be distinguished from each other) is a simple matter: do the salient characteristics that lead to diagnoses reside in the patients themselves or in the environments and contexts in which observers find them? From Bleuler, through Kretchmer, through the formulators of the recently revised *Diagnostic and Statistical Manual* of the American Psychiatric Association, the belief has been strong that patients present symptoms, that those symptoms can be categorized, and, implicitly, that the sane are distinguishable from the insane. More recently, however, this belief has been questioned. Based in part on theoretical and anthropological considerations, but also on philosophical, legal, and therapeutic ones, the view has grown that psychological categorization of mental illness is useless at best and downright harmful, misleading, and pejorative

D. L. Rosenhan, "On Being Sane in Insane Places," *Science,* vol. 179 (January 1973), 250–258.

at worst. Psychiatric diagnoses, in this view, are in the minds of the observers and are not valid summaries of characteristics displayed by the observed.[3-5]

Gains can be made in deciding which of these is more nearly accurate by getting normal people (that is, people who do not have, and have never suffered, symptoms of serious psychiatric disorders) admitted to psychiatric hospitals and then determining whether they were discovered to be sane and, if so, how. If the sanity of such pseudopatients were always detected, there would be prima facie evidence that a sane individual can be distinguished from the insane context in which he is found. Normality (and presumably abnormality) is distinct enough that it can be recognized wherever it occurs, for it is carried within the person. If, on the other hand, the sanity of the pseudopatients were never discovered, serious difficulties would arise for those who support traditional modes of psychiatric diagnosis. Given that the hospital staff was not incompetent, that the pseudopatient had been behaving as sanely as he had been outside of the hospital, and that it had never been previously suggested that he belonged in a psychiatric hospital, such an unlikely outcome would support the view that psychiatric diagnosis betrays little about the patient but much about the environment in which an observer finds him.

This article describes such an experiment. Eight sane people gained secret admission to 12 different hospitals.[6] Their diagnostic experiences constitute the data of the first part of this article; the remainder is devoted to a description of their experiences in psychiatric institutions. Too few psychiatrists and psychologists, even those who have worked in such hospitals, know what the experience is like. They rarely talk about it with former patients, perhaps because they distrust information coming from the previously insane. Those who have worked in psychiatric hospitals are likely to have adapted so thoroughly to the settings that they are insensitive to the impact of that experience. And while there have been occasional reports of researchers who submitted themselves to psychiatric hospitalization,[7] these researchers have commonly remained in the hospitals for short periods of time, often with the knowledge of the hospital staff. It is difficult to know the extent to which they were treated like patients or like research colleagues. Nevertheless, their reports about the inside of the psychiatric hospital have been valuable. This article extends those efforts.

PSEUDOPATIENTS AND THEIR SETTINGS

The eight pseudopatients were a varied group. One was a psychology graduate student in his 20's. The remaining seven were older and "established." Among them were three psychologists, a pediatrician, a psychiatrist, a painter, and a housewife. Three pseudopatients were women, five were men. All of them employed pseudonyms, lest their alleged diagnoses embarrass them later. Those who were in mental health professions alleged another occupation in order to avoid the special attentions that might be accorded by staff, as a matter of courtesy or caution, to ailing colleagues.[8] With the exception of myself (I was the first pseudopatient and my presence was known to the hospital administrator and chief psychologist and, so far as I can tell, to them alone), the presence of pseudopatients and the nature of the research program w[ere] not known to the hospital staffs.[9]

The settings were similarly varied. In order to generalize the findings, admission into a variety of hospitals was sought. The 12 hospitals in the sample were located in five different states on the East and West coasts. Some were old and shabby, some were quite new. Some were research-oriented, others not. Some had good staff-patient ratios, others were quite understaffed. Only one was a strictly private hospital. All of the others were supported by state or federal funds or, in one instance, by university funds.

After calling the hospital for an appointment, the pseudopatient arrived at the admissions office complaining that he had been hearing voices. Asked what the voices said, he replied that they were often unclear, but as far as he could tell they said "empty," "hollow," and "thud." The voices were unfamiliar and were of the same sex as the pseudopatient. The choice of these symptoms was occasioned by their apparent similarity to existential symptoms. Such symptoms are alleged to arise from painful concerns about the perceived meaninglessness of one's life. It is as if the hallucinating person were saying, "My life is empty and hollow." The choice of these symptoms was also determined by the *absence* of a single report of existential psychoses in the literature.

Beyond alleging the symptoms and falsifying name, vocation, and employment, no further alterations of person, history, or circumstances were made. The significant events of the pseudopatient's life history were presented as they had actually occurred. Relationships with parents and siblings, with spouse and children, with people at work and in school, consistent with the aforementioned exceptions, were described as they were or had been. Frustrations and upsets were described along with joys and satisfactions. These facts are important to remember. If anything, they strongly biased the subsequent results in favor of detecting sanity, since none of their histories or current behaviors were seriously pathological in any way.

Immediately upon admission to the psychiatric ward, the pseudopatient ceased simulating *any* symptoms of abnormality. In some cases, there was a brief period of mild nervousness and anxiety, since none of the pseudopatients really believed that they would be admitted so easily. Indeed, their shared fear was that they would be immediately exposed as frauds and greatly embarrassed. Moreover, many of them had never visited a psychiatric ward; even those who had, nevertheless had some genuine fears about what might happen to them. Their nervousness, then, was quite appropriate to the novelty of the hospital setting, and it abated rapidly.

Apart from that short-lived nervousness, the pseudopatient behaved on the ward as he "normally" behaved. The pseudopatient spoke to patients and staff as he might ordinarily. Because there is uncommonly little to do on a psychiatric ward, he attempted to engage others in conversation. When asked by staff how he was feeling, he indicated that he was fine, that he no longer experienced symptoms. He responded to instructions from attendants, to calls for medication (which was not swallowed), and to dining-hall instructions. Beyond such activities as were available to him on the admissions ward, he spent his time writing down his observations about the ward, its patients, and the staff. Initially these notes were written "secretly," but as it soon became clear that no one much cared, they were subsequently written on standard tablets of paper in such public places as the dayroom. No secret was made of these activities.

The pseudopatient, very much as a true psychiatric patient, entered a hospital with no foreknowledge of when he would be discharged. Each was told that he would have to get out by his own devices, essentially by convincing the staff that he was sane. The psychological stresses associated with hospitalization were considerable, and all but one of the pseudopatients desired to be discharged almost immediately after being admitted. They were, therefore, motivated not only to behave sanely, but to be paragons of cooperation. That their behavior was in no way disruptive is confirmed by nursing reports, which have been obtained on most of the patients. These reports uniformly indicate that the patients were "friendly," "cooperative," and "exhibited no abnormal indications."

THE NORMAL ARE NOT DETECTABLY SANE

Despite their public "show" of sanity, the pseudopatients were never detected. Admitted, except in one case, with a diagnosis of schizophrenia,[10] each was discharged with a diagnosis of schizophrenia "in remission." The label "in remission" should in no way be dismissed as a formality, for at no time during any hospitalization had any question been raised about any pseudopatient's simulation. Nor are there any indications in the hospital records that the pseudopatient's status was suspect. Rather, the evidence is strong that, once labeled schizophrenic, the pseudopatient was stuck with that label. If the pseudopatient was to be discharged, he must naturally be "in remission"; but he was not sane, nor, in the institution's view, had he ever been sane.

The uniform failure to recognize sanity cannot be attributed to the quality of the hospitals, for, although there were considerable variations among them, several are considered excellent. Nor can it be alleged that there was simply not enough time to observe the pseudopatients. Length of hospitalization ranged from 7 to 52 days, with an average of 19 days. The pseudopatients were not, in fact, carefully observed, but this failure clearly speaks more to traditions within psychiatric hospitals than to lack of opportunity.

Finally, it cannot be said that the failure to recognize the pseudopatients' sanity was due to the fact that they were not behaving sanely. While there was clearly some tension present in all of them, their daily visitors could detect no serious behavioral consequences—nor, indeed, could other patients. It was quite common for the patients to "detect" the pseudopatients' sanity. During the first three hospitalizations, when accurate counts were kept, 35 of a total of 118 patients on the admissions ward voiced their suspicions, some vigorously. "You're not crazy. You're a journalist, or a professor [referring to the continual note-taking]. You're checking up on the hospital." While most of the patients were reassured by the pseudopatient's insistence that he had been sick before he came in but was fine now, some continued to believe that the pseudopatient was sane throughout his hospitalization.[11] The fact that the patients often recognized normality when staff did not raises important questions.

Failure to detect sanity during the course of hospitalization may be due to the fact that physicians operate with a strong bias toward what statisticians call the type 2 error.[5] This is to say that physicians are more inclined to call a healthy person sick (a false positive, type 2) than a sick person healthy (a false negative, type 1). The reasons for this are not hard to find: it is clearly more dangerous to misdiagnose illness than health. Better to err on the side of caution, to suspect illness even among the healthy.

But what holds for medicine does not hold equally well for psychiatry. Medical illnesses, while unfortunate, are not commonly pejorative. Psychiatric diagnoses, on the contrary, carry with them personal, legal, and social stigmas.[12] It was therefore important to see whether the tendency toward diagnosing the sane insane could be reversed. The following experiment was arranged at a research and teaching hospital whose staff had heard these findings but doubted that such an error could occur in their hospital. The staff was informed that at some time during the following 3 months, one or more pseudopatients would attempt to be admitted into the psychiatric hospital. Each staff member was asked to rate each patient who presented himself at admissions or on the ward according to the likelihood that the patient was a pseudopatient. A 10-point scale was used, with a 1 and 2 reflecting high confidence that the patient was a pseudopatient.

Judgments were obtained on 193 patients who were admitted for psychiatric treatment. All staff who had had sustained contact with or primary responsibility for the patient—attendants, nurses, psychiatrists, physicians, and psychologists—were asked to make judgments. Forty-one patients were alleged, with high confidence, to be pseudopatients by at least one member of the staff. Twenty-three were considered suspect by at least one psychiatrist. Nineteen were suspected by one psychiatrist *and* one other staff member. Actually, no genuine pseudopatient (at least from my group) presented himself during this period.

The experiment is instructive. It indicates that the tendency to designate sane people as insane can be reversed when the stakes (in this case, prestige and diagnostic acumen) are high. But what can be said of the 19 people who were suspected of being "sane" by one psychiatrist and another staff member? Were these people truly "sane," or was it rather the case that in the course of avoiding the type 2 error the staff tended to make more errors of the first sort—calling the crazy "sane"? There is no way of knowing. But one thing is certain: any diagnostic process that lends itself so readily to massive errors of this sort cannot be a very reliable one.

THE STICKINESS OF PSYCHODIAGNOSTIC LABELS

Beyond the tendency to call the healthy sick—a tendency that accounts better for diagnostic behavior on admission than it does for such behavior after a lengthy period of exposure—the data speak to the massive role of labeling in psychiatric assessment. Having once been labeled schizophrenic, there is nothing the pseudopatient can do to overcome the tag. The tag profoundly colors others' perceptions of him and his behavior.

From one viewpoint, these data are hardly surprising, for it has long been known that elements are given meaning by the context in which they occur. Gestalt psychology made this point vigorously, and Asch[13] demonstrated that there are "central" personality traits (such as "warm" versus "cold") which are so powerful that they markedly color the meaning of other information in forming an impression of a given personality.[14] "Insane," "schizophrenic," "manic-depressive," and "crazy" are probably among the most powerful of such central traits. Once a person is designated abnormal, all of his other behaviors and characteristics are colored by that label. Indeed, that label is so powerful that many of the pseudopatients' normal behaviors were overlooked entirely or profoundly misinterpreted. Some examples may clarify this issue.

Earlier I indicated that there were no changes in the pseudopatient's personal history and current status beyond those of name, employment, and where necessary, vocation. Otherwise, a[n accurate] description of personal history and circumstances was offered. Those circumstances were not psychotic. How were they made consonant with the diagnosis of psychosis? Or were those diagnoses modified in such a way as to bring them into accord with the circumstances of the pseudopatient's life, as described by him?

As far as I can determine, diagnoses were in no way affected by the relative health of the circumstances of a pseudopatient's life. Rather, the reverse occurred: the perception of his circumstances was shaped entirely by the diagnosis. A clear example of such translation is found in the case of a pseudopatient who had had a close relationship with his mother but was rather remote from his father during his early childhood. During adolescence and beyond, however, his father became a close friend, while his relationship with his mother cooled. His present relationship with his wife was characteristically close and warm. Apart from occasional angry exchanges, friction was minimal. The children had rarely been spanked. Surely there is nothing especially pathological about such a history. Indeed, many readers may see a similar pattern in their own experiences, with no markedly delete-rious consequences. Observe, however, how such a history was translated in the psychopathological context, this from the case summary prepared after the patient was discharged.

> This white 39-year-old male . . . manifests a long history of considerable ambiva-lence in close relationships, which begins in early childhood. A warm relationship with his mother cools during his adolescence. A distant relationship to his father is described as becoming very intense. Affective stability is absent. His attempts to control emotionality with his wife and children are punctuated by angry outbursts and, in the case of the children, spankings. And while he says that he has several good friends, one senses considerable ambivalence embedded in those relation-ships also. . . .

The facts of the case were unintentionally distorted by the staff to achieve consistency with a popular theory of the dynamics of a schizophrenic reac-tion.[15] Nothing of an ambivalent nature had been described in relations with parents, spouse, or friends. To the extent that ambivalence could be in-ferred, it was probably not greater than is found in all human relationships. It is true the pseudopatient's relationships with his parents changed over time, but in the ordinary context that would hardly be remarkable—indeed, it might very well be expected. Clearly, the meaning ascribed to his verbal-izations (that is, ambivalence, affective instability) was determined by the diagnosis: schizophrenia. An entirely different meaning would have been ascribed if it were known that the man was "normal."

All pseudopatients took extensive notes publicly. Under ordinary circum-stances, such behavior would have raised questions in the minds of observ-ers, as, in fact, it did among patients. Indeed, it seemed so certain that the notes would elicit suspicion that elaborate precautions were taken to re-move them from the ward each day. But the precautions proved needless. The closest any staff member came to questioning these notes occurred when one pseudopatient asked his physician what kind of medication he was receiving and began to write down the response. "You needn't write it," he was told gently. "If you have trouble remembering, just ask me again."

If no questions were asked of the pseudopatients, how was their writing interpreted? Nursing records for three patients indicate that the writing was seen as an aspect of their pathological behavior. "Patient engages in writing behavior" was the daily nursing comment on one of the pseudopatients who was never questioned about his writing. Given that the patient is in the hos-pital, he must be psychologically disturbed. And given that he is disturbed, continuous writing must be a behavioral manifestation of that disturbance, perhaps a subset of the compulsive behaviors that are sometimes correlated with schizophrenia.

One tacit characteristic of psychiatric diagnosis is that it locates the sources of aberration within the individual and only rarely within the com-plex of stimuli that surrounds him. Consequently, behaviors that are stimu-lated by the environment are commonly misattributed to the patient's disorder. For example, one kindly nurse found a pseudopatient pacing the long hospital corridors. "Nervous, Mr. X?" she asked. "No, bored," he said.

The notes kept by pseudopatients are full of patient behaviors that were misinterpreted by well-intentioned staff. Often enough, a patient would go "berserk" because he had, wittingly or unwittingly, been mistreated by, say, an attendant. A nurse coming upon the scene would rarely inquire even cursorily into the environmental stimuli of the patient's behavior. Rather, she assumed that his upset derived from his pathology, not from his present interactions with other staff members. Occasionally, the staff might assume that the patient's family (especially when they had recently visited) or other patients had stimulated the outburst. But never were the staff found to assume that one of themselves or the structure of the hospital had anything to do with a patient's behavior. One psychiatrist pointed to a group of patients who were sitting outside the cafeteria entrance half an hour before lunchtime. To a group of young residents he indicated that such behavior was characteristic of the oral-acquisitive nature of the syndrome. It seemed not to occur to him that there were very few things to anticipate in a psychiatric hospital besides eating.

A psychiatric label has a life and an influence of its own. Once the impression has been formed that the patient is schizophrenic, the expectation is that he will continue to be schizophrenic. When a sufficient amount of time has passed, during which the patient has done nothing bizarre, he is considered to be in remission and available for discharge. But the label endures beyond discharge, with the unconfirmed expectation that he will behave as a schizophrenic again. Such labels, conferred by mental health professionals, are as influential on the patient as they are on his relatives and friends, and it should not surprise anyone that the diagnosis acts on all of them as a self-fulfilling prophecy. Eventually, the patient himself accepts the diagnosis, with all of its surplus meanings and expectations, and behaves accordingly.[5]

The inferences to be made from these matters are quite simple. Much as Zigler and Phillips have demonstrated that there is enormous overlap in the symptoms presented by patients who have been variously diagnosed,[16] so there is enormous overlap in the behaviors of the sane and the insane. The sane are not "sane" all of the time. We lose our tempers "for no good reason." We are occasionally depressed or anxious, again for no good reason. And we may find it difficult to get along with one or another person—again for no reason that we can specify. Similarly, the insane are not always insane. Indeed, it was the impression of the pseudopatients while living with them that they were sane for long periods of time—that the bizarre behaviors upon which their diagnoses were allegedly predicated constituted only a small fraction of their total behavior. If it makes no sense to label ourselves permanently depressed on the basis of an occasional depression, then it takes better evidence than is presently available to label all patients insane or schizophrenic on the basis of bizarre behaviors or cognitions.

• • •

THE EXPERIENCE OF PSYCHIATRIC HOSPITALIZATION

The term "mental illness" is of recent origin. It was coined by people who were humane in their inclinations and who wanted very much to raise the station of (and the public's sympathies toward) the psychologically disturbed from that of witches and "crazies" to one that was akin to the physically ill. And they were at least partially successful, for the treatment of the mentally ill *has* improved considerably over the years. But while treatment has improved, it is doubtful that people really regard the mentally ill in the same way that they view the physically ill. A broken leg is something one recovers from, but mental illness allegedly endures forever.[17] A broken leg does not threaten the observer, but a crazy schizophrenic? There is by now a host of evidence that attitudes toward the mentally ill are characterized by fear, hostility, aloofness, suspicion, and dread.[18] The mentally ill are society's lepers.

That such attitudes infect the general population is perhaps not surprising, only upsetting. But that they affect the professionals—attendants, nurses, physicians, psychologists, and social workers—who treat and deal with the mentally ill is more disconcerting, both because such attitudes are self-evidently pernicious and because they are unwitting. Most mental health professionals would insist that they are sympathetic toward the mentally ill, that they are neither avoidant nor hostile. But it is more likely that an exquisite ambivalence characterizes their relations with psychiatric patients, such that their avowed impulses are only part of their entire attitude. Negative attitudes are there too and can easily be detected. Such attitudes should not surprise us. They are the natural offspring of the labels patients wear and the places in which they are found.

Consider the structure of the typical psychiatric hospital. Staff and patients are strictly segregated. Staff have their own living space, including their dining facilities, bathrooms, and assembly places. The glassed quarters that contain the professional staff, which the pseudopatients came to call "the cage," sit out on every dayroom. The staff emerge primarily for caretaking purposes—to give medication, to conduct a therapy or group meeting, to instruct or reprimand a patient. Otherwise, staff keep to themselves, almost as if the disorder that afflicts their charges is somehow catching.

So much is patient-staff segregation the rule that, for four public hospitals in which an attempt was made to measure the degree to which staff and patients mingle, it was necessary to use "time out of the staff cage" as the operational measure. While it was not the case that all time spent out of the cage was spent mingling with patients (attendants, for example, would occasionally emerge to watch television in the dayroom), it was the only way in which one could gather reliable data on time for measuring.

The average amount of time spent by attendants outside of the cage was 11.3 percent (range, 3 to 52 percent). This figure does not represent only time spent mingling with patients, but also includes time spent on such chores as folding laundry, supervising patients while they shave, directing ward clean-up, and sending patients to off-ward activities. It was the relatively rare attendant who spent time talking with patients or playing games with them. It proved impossible to obtain a "percent mingling time" for nurses, since the amount of time they spent out of the cage was too brief. Rather, we counted instances of emergence from the cage. On the average, daytime nurses emerged from the cage 11.5 times per shift, including instances when they left the ward entirely (range, 4 to 39 times). Late afternoon and night nurses were even less available, emerging on the average 9.4 times per shift (range, 4 to 41 times). Data on early morning nurses, who arrived usually after midnight and departed at 8 a.m., are not available because patients were asleep during most of this period.

Physicians, especially psychiatrists, were even less available. They were rarely seen on the wards. Quite commonly, they would be seen only when they arrived and departed, with the remaining time being spent in their offices or in the cage. On the average, physicians emerged on the ward 6.7 times per day (range, 1 to 17 times). It proved difficult to make an accurate estimate in this regard, since physicians often maintained hours that allowed them to come and go at different times.

The hierarchical organization of the psychiatric hospital has been commented on before,[19] but the latent meaning of that kind of organization is worth noting again. Those with the most power have least to do with patients, and those with the least power are most involved with them. Recall, however, that the acquisition of role-appropriate behaviors occurs mainly through the observation of others, with the most powerful having the most influence. Consequently, it is understandable that attendants not only spend more time with patients than do any other members of the staff—that is required by their station in the hierarchy—but also, insofar as they learn from their superiors' behavior, spend as little time with patients as they can. Attendants are seen mainly in the cage, which is where the models, the action, and the power are.

I turn now to a different set of studies, these dealing with staff response to patient-initiated contact. It has long been known that the amount of time a person spends with you can be an index of your significance to him. If he initiates and maintains eye contact, there is reason to believe that he is considering your requests and needs. If he pauses to chat or actually stops and talks, there is added reason to infer that he is individuating you. In four hospitals, the pseudopatient approached the staff member with a request which took the following form: "Pardon me, Mr. [or Dr. or Mrs.] X, could you tell me when I will be eligible for grounds privileges?" (or " . . . when I will be presented at the staff meeting?" or ". . . when I am likely to be discharged?"). While the content of the question varied according to the appropriateness of the target and the pseudopatient's (apparent) current needs the form was always a courteous and relevant request for information. Care was taken never to approach a particular member of the staff more than once a day, lest the staff member become suspicious or irritated. In examining these data, remember that the behavior of the pseudopatients was neither bizarre nor disruptive. One could indeed engage in good conversation with them.

The data for these experiments are shown in Table 1, separately for physicians (column 1) and for nurses and attendants (column 2). Minor differences between these four institutions were overwhelmed by the degree to which staff avoided continuing contacts that patients had initiated. By far, their most common response consisted of either a brief response to the question, offered while they were "on the move" and with head averted, or no response at all.

The encounter frequently took the following bizarre form: (pseudopatient) "Pardon me, Dr. X. Could you tell me when I am eligible for grounds privileges?" (physician) "Good morning, Dave. How are you today?" (Moves off without waiting for a response.)

It is instructive to compare these data with data recently obtained at Stanford University. It has been alleged that large and eminent universities are characterized by faculty who are so busy that they have no time for students. For this comparison, a young lady approached individual faculty members who seemed to be walking purposefully to some meeting or teaching engagement and asked them the following six questions.

1. "Pardon me, could you direct me to Encina Hall?" (at the medical school: ". . . to the Clinical Research Center?").

2. "Do you know where Fish Annex is?" (there is no Fish Annex at Stanford).

3. "Do you teach here?"

4. "How does one apply for admission to the college?" (at the medical school: ". . . to the medical school?").

5. "Is it difficult to get in?"

6. "Is there financial aid?"

Without exception, as can be seen in Table 1 (column 3), all of the questions were answered. No matter how rushed they were, all respondents not only maintained eye contact, but stopped to talk. Indeed, many of the respondents went out of their way to direct or take the questioner to the office she was seeking, to try to locate "Fish Annex," or to discuss with her the possibilities of being admitted to the university.

Similar data, also shown in Table 1 (columns 4, 5, and 6), were obtained in the hospital. Here too, the young lady came prepared with six questions. After the first question, however, she remarked to 18 of her respondents (column 4), "I'm looking for a psychiatrist," and to 15 others (column 5), "I'm looking for an internist." Ten other respondents received no inserted comment (column 6). The general degree of cooperative responses is considerably higher for these university groups than it was for pseudopatients in psychiatric hospitals. Even so, differences are apparent within the medical

Table 1. Self-initiated Contact by Pseudopatients with Psychiatrists and Nurses and Attendants, Compared to Contact with Other Groups

| | PSYCHIATRIC HOSPITALS | | UNIVERSITY CAMPUS (NONMEDICAL) | UNIVERSITY MEDICAL CENTER PHYSICIANS | | |
CONTACT	(1) Psychiatrists	(2) Nurses and attendants	(3) Faculty	(4) "Looking for a psychiatrist"	(5) "Looking for an internist"	(6) No additional comment
Responses						
Moves on, head averted (%)	71	88	0	0	0	0
Makes eye contact (%)	23	10	0	11	0	0
Pauses and chats (%)	2	2	0	11	0	10
Stops and talks (%)	4	0.5	100	78	100	90
Mean number of questions answered (out of 6)	*	*	6	3.8	4.8	4.5
Respondents (No.)	13	47	14	18	15	10
Attempts (No.)	185	1283	14	18	15	10

*NOT APPLICABLE.

school setting. Once having indicated that she was looking for a psychiatrist, the degree of cooperation elicited was less than when she sought an internist.

POWERLESSNESS AND DEPERSONALIZATION

Eye contact and verbal contact reflect concern and individuation; their absence, avoidance and depersonalization. The data I have presented do not do justice to the rich daily encounters that grew up around matters of depersonalization and avoidance. I have records of patients who were beaten by staff for the sin of having initiated verbal contact. During my own experience, for example, one patient was beaten in the presence of other patients for having approached an attendant and told him, "I like you." Occasionally, punishment meted out to patients for misdemeanors seemed so excessive that it could not be justified by the most radical interpretations of psychiatric canon. Nevertheless, they appeared to go unquestioned. Tempers were often short. A patient who had not heard a call for medication would be roundly excoriated, and the morning attendants would often wake patients with, "Come on, you m-----f-----s, out of bed!"

Neither anecdotal nor "hard" data can convey the overwhelming sense of powerlessness which invades the individual as he is continually exposed to the depersonalization of the psychiatric hospital. It hardly matters *which* psychiatric hospital—the excellent public ones and the very plush private hospital were better than the rural and shabby ones in this regard, but, again, the features that psychiatric hospitals had in common overwhelmed by far their apparent differences.

Powerlessness was evident everywhere. The patient is deprived of many of his legal rights by dint of his psychiatric commitment.[20] He is shorn of credibility by virtue of his psychiatric label. His freedom of movement is restricted. He cannot initiate contact with the staff, but may only respond to such overtures as they make. Personal privacy is minimal. Patient quarters and possessions can be entered and examined by any staff member, for whatever reason. His personal history and anguish is available to any staff member (often including the "grey lady" and "candy striper" volunteer) who chooses to read his folder, regardless of their therapeutic relationship to him. His personal hygiene and waste evacuation are often monitored. The water closets may have no doors.

At times, depersonalization reached such proportions that pseudopatients had the sense that they were invisible, or at least unworthy of account. Upon being admitted, I and other pseudopatients took the initial physical examinations in a semipublic room, where staff members went about their own business as if we were not there.

On the ward, attendants delivered verbal and occasionally serious physical abuse to patients in the presence of other observing patients, some of whom (the pseudopatients) were writing it all down. Abusive behavior, on the other hand, terminated quite abruptly when other staff members were known to be coming. Staff are credible witnesses. Patients are not.

A nurse unbuttoned her uniform to adjust her brassiere in the presence of an entire ward of viewing men. One did not have the sense that she was being seductive. Rather, she didn't notice us. A group of staff persons might point to a patient in the dayroom and discuss him animatedly, as if he were not there.

One illuminating instance of depersonalization and invisibility occurred with regard to medications. All told, the pseudopatients were administered nearly 2100 pills, including Elavil, Stelazine, Compazine, and Thorazine, to name but a few. (That such a variety of medications should have been administered to patients presenting identical symptoms is itself worthy of note.) Only two were swallowed. The rest were either pocketed or deposited in the toilet. The pseudopatients were not alone in this. Although I have no precise records on how many patients rejected their medications, the pseudopatients frequently found the medications of other patients in the toilet before they deposited their own. As long as they were cooperative, their behavior and the pseudopatients' own in this matter, as in other important matters, went unnoticed throughout.

Reactions to such depersonalization among pseudopatients were intense. Although they had come to the hospital as participant observers and were fully aware that they did not "belong," they nevertheless found themselves caught up in and fighting the process of depersonalization. Some examples: a graduate student in psychology asked his wife to bring his textbooks to the hospital so he could "catch up on his homework"—this despite the elaborate precautions taken to conceal his professional association. The same student, who had trained for quite some time to get into the hospital, and who had looked forward to the experience, "remembered" some drag races that he had wanted to see on the weekend and insisted that he be discharged by that time. Another pseudopatient attempted a romance with a nurse. Subsequently, he informed the staff that he was applying for admission to graduate school in psychology and was very likely to be admitted, since a graduate professor was one of his regular hospital visitors. The same person began to engage in psychotherapy with other patients—all of this as a way of becoming a person in an impersonal environment.

THE SOURCES OF DEPERSONALIZATION

What are the origins of depersonalization? I have already mentioned two. First are attitudes held by all of us toward the mentally ill—including those who treat them—attitudes characterized by fear, distrust, and horrible expectations on the one hand, and benevolent intentions on the other. Our ambivalence leads, in this instance as in others, to avoidance.

Second, and not entirely separate, the hierarchical structure of the psychiatric hospital facilitates depersonalization. Those who are at the top have least to do with patients, and their behavior inspires the rest of the staff. Average daily contact with psychiatrists, psychologists, residents, and physicians combined ranged from 3.9 to 25.1 minutes, with an overall mean of 6.8 (six pseudopatients over a total of 129 days of hospitalization). Included in this average are time spent in the admissions interview, ward meetings in the presence of a senior staff member, group and individual psychotherapy contacts, case presentation conferences, and discharge meetings. Clearly, patients do not spend much time in interpersonal contact with doctoral staff. And doctoral staff serve as models for nurses and attendants.

There are probably other sources. Psychiatric installations are presently in serious financial straits. Staff shortages are pervasive, staff time at a premium. Something has to give, and that something is patient contact. Yet, while financial stresses are realities, too much can be made of them. I have the impression that the psychological forces that result in depersonalization are much stronger than the fiscal ones and that the addition of more staff would not correspondingly improve patient care in this regard. The incidence of staff meetings and the enormous amount of recordkeeping on patients, for example, have not been as substantially reduced as has patient contact. Priorities exist, even during hard times. Patient contact is not a significant priority in the traditional psychiatric hospital, and fiscal pressures do not account for this. Avoidance and depersonalization may.

Heavy reliance upon psychotropic medication tacitly contributes to depersonalization by convincing staff that treatment is indeed being conducted and that further patient contact may not be necessary. Even here, however, caution needs to be exercised in understanding the role of psychotropic drugs. If patients were powerful rather than powerless, if they were viewed as interesting individuals rather than diagnostic entities, if they were socially significant rather than social lepers, if their anguish truly and wholly compelled our sympathies and concerns, would we not *seek* contact with them, despite the availability of medications? Perhaps for the pleasure of it all?

THE CONSEQUENCES OF LABELING AND DEPERSONALIZATION

Whenever the ratio of what is known to what needs to be known approaches zero, we tend to invent "knowledge" and assume that we understand more than we actually do. We seem unable to acknowledge that we simply don't know. The needs for diagnosis and remediation of behavioral and emotional problems are enormous. But rather than acknowledge that we are just embarking on understanding, we continue to label patients "schizophrenic," "manic-depressive," and "insane," as if in those words we had captured the essence of understanding. The facts of the matter are that we have known for a long time that diagnoses are often not useful or reliable, but we have nevertheless continued to use them. We now know that we cannot distinguish insanity from sanity. It is depressing to consider how that information will be used.

Not merely depressing, but frightening. How many people, one wonders, are sane but not recognized as such in our psychiatric institutions? How many have been needlessly stripped of their privileges of citizenship, from the right to vote and drive to that of handling their own accounts? How many have feigned insanity in order to avoid the criminal consequences of their behavior, and, conversely, how many would rather stand trial than live interminably in a psychiatric hospital—but are wrongly thought to be mentally ill? How many have been stigmatized by well-intentioned, but nevertheless erroneous, diagnoses? On the last point, recall again that a "type 2 error" in psychiatric diagnosis does not have the same consequences it does in medical diagnosis. A diagnosis of cancer that has been found to be in error is cause for celebration. But psychiatric diagnoses are rarely found to be in error. The label sticks, a mark of inadequacy forever.

Finally, how many patients might be "sane" outside the psychiatric hospital but seem insane in it—not because craziness resides in them, as it were, but because they are responding to a bizarre setting, one that may be unique to institutions which harbor nether people? Goffman[4] calls the process of socialization to such institutions "mortification"—an apt metaphor that includes the processes of depersonalization that have been described here. And while it is impossible to know whether the pseudopatients' responses to these processes are characteristic of all inmates—they were, after all, not real patients—it is difficult to believe that these processes of socialization to a psychiatric hospital provide useful attitudes or habits of response for living in the "real world." . . .[21]

REFERENCES AND NOTES

1. P. Ash, *J. Abnorm. Soc. Psychol.* 44, 272 (1949); A. T. Beck, *Amer. J. Psychiat.* 119, 210 (1962); A. T. Boisen, *Psychiatry* 2, 233 (1938); N. Kreitman, *J. Ment. Sci.* 107, 876 (1961); N. Kreitman, P. Sainsbury, J. Morrisey, J. Towers, J. Scrivener, *ibid.*, p. 887; H. O. Schmitt and C. P. Fonda, *J. Abnorm. Soc. Psychol.* 52, 262 (1956); W. Seeman, *J. Nerv. Ment. Dis.* 118, 541 (1953). For an analysis of these artifacts and summaries of the disputes, see J. Zubin, *Annu. Rev. Psychol.* 18, 373 (1967); L. Phillips and J. G. Draguns, *ibid.* 22, 447 (1971).

2. R. Benedict, *J. Gen. Psychol.* 10, 59 (1934).

3. See in this regard H. Becker, *Outsiders: Studies in the Sociology of Deviance* (Free Press, New York, 1963); B. M. Braginsky, D. D. Braginsky, K. Ring, *Methods of Madness: The Mental Hospital as a Last Resort* (Holt, Rinehart & Winston, New York, 1969); G. M. Crocetti and P. V. Lemkau, *Amer. Sociol. Rev.* 30, 577 (1965); E. Goffman, *Behavior in Public Places* (Free Press, New York, 1964); R. D. Laing, *The Divided Self: A Study of Sanity and Madness* (Quadrangle, Chicago, 1960);

D. L. Phillips, *Amer. Sociol. Rev.* 28, 963 (1963); T. R. Sarbin, *Psychol. Today* 6, 18 (1972); E. Schur, *Amer. J. Sociol.* 75, 309 (1969); T. Szasz, *Law, Liberty and Psychiatry* (Macmillan, New York, 1963); *The Myth of Mental Illness: Foundations of a Theory of Mental Illness* (Hoeber-Harper, New York, 1963). For a critique of some of these views, see W. R. Gove, *Amer. Sociol. Rev.* 35, 873 (1970).

4. E. Goffman, *Asylums* (Doubleday, Garden City, N.Y., 1961).

5. T. J. Scheff, *Being Mentally Ill: A Sociological Theory* (Aldine, Chicago, 1966).

6. Data from a ninth pseudopatient are not incorporated in this report because, although his sanity went undetected, he falsified aspects of his personal history, including his marital status and parental relationships. His experimental behaviors therefore were not identical to those of the other pseudopatients.

7. A. Barry, *Bellevue Is a State of Mind* (Harcourt Brace Jovanovich, New York, 1971); I. Belknap, *Human Problems of a State Mental Hospital* (McGraw-Hill, New York, 1956); W. Caudill, F. C. Redlich, H. R. Gilmore, E. B. Brody, *Amer. J. Orthopsychiat.* 22, 314 (1952); A. R. Goldman, R. H. Bohr, T. A. Steinberg, *Prof. Psychol.* 1, 427 (1970); unauthored, *Roche Report* 1 (No. 13), 8 (1971).

8. Beyond the personal difficulties that the pseudopatient is likely to experience in the hospital, there are legal and social ones that, combined, require considerable attention before entry. For example, once admitted to a psychiatric institution, it is difficult, if not impossible, to be discharged on short notice, state law to the contrary notwithstanding. I was not sensitive to these difficulties at the outset of the project, nor to the personal and situational emergencies that can arise, but later a writ of habeas corpus was prepared for each of the entering pseudopatients and an attorney was kept "on call" during every hospitalization. I am grateful to John Kaplan and Robert Bartels for legal advice and assistance in these matters.

9. However distasteful such concealment is, it was a necessary first step to examining these questions. Without concealment, there would have been no way to know how valid these experiences were; nor was there any way of knowing whether whatever detections occurred were a tribute to the diagnostic acumen of the staff or to the hospital's rumor network. Obviously, since my concerns are general ones that cut across individual hospitals and staffs, I have respected their anonymity and have eliminated clues that might lead to their identification.

10. Interestingly, of the 12 admissions, 11 were diagnosed as schizophrenic and one, with the identical symptomatology, as manic-depressive psychosis. This diagnosis has a more favorable prognosis, and it was given by the only private hospital in our sample. On the relations between social class and psychiatric diagnosis, see A. deB. Hollingshead and F. C. Redlich, *Social Class and Mental Illness: A Community Study* (Wiley, New York, 1958).

11. It is possible, of course, that patients have quite broad latitudes in diagnosis and therefore are inclined to call many people sane, even those whose behavior is patently aberrant. However, although we have no hard data on this matter, it was our distinct impression that this was not the case. In many instances, patients not only singled us out for attention, but came to imitate our behaviors and styles.

12. J. Cumming and E. Cumming, *Community Ment. Health* 1, 135 (1965); A. Farina and K. Ring, *J. Abnorm. Psychol.* 70, 47 (1965); H. E. Freeman and O. G. Simmons, *The Mental Patient Comes Home* (Wiley, New York, 1963); W. J. Johannsen, *Ment. Hygiene* 53, 218 (1969); A. S. Linsky, *Soc. Psychiat.* 5, 166 (1970).

13. S. E. Asch, *J. Abnorm. Soc. Psychol.* 41, 258 (1946); *Social Psychology* (Prentice-Hall, New York, 1952).

14. See also I. N. Mensh and J. Wishner, *J. Personality* 16, 188 (1947); J. Wishner,

Psychol. Rev. 67, 96 (1960); J. S. Bruner and R. Tagiuri, in *Handbook of Social Psychology*, G. Lindzey, Ed. (Addison-Wesley, Cambridge, Mass., 1954), vol. 2, pp. 634–654; J. S. Bruner, D. Shapiro, R. Tagiuri, in *Person Perception and Interpersonal Behavior*, R. Tagiuri and L. Petrullo, Eds. (Stanford Univ. Press, Stanford, Calif., 1958), pp. 277–288.

15. For an example of a similar self-fulfilling prophecy in this instance dealing with the "central" trait of intelligence, see R. Rosenthal and L. Jacobson, *Pygmalion in the Classroom* (Holt, Rinehart & Winston, New York, 1968).

16. E. Zigler and L. Phillips, *J. Abnorm. Soc. Psychol.* 63, 69 (1961). See also R. K. Freudenberg and J. P. Robertson, *A.M.A. Arch. Neurol. Psychiatr.* 76, 14 (1956).

17. The most recent and unfortunate instance of this tenet is that of Senator Thomas Eagleton.

18. T. R. Sarbin and J. C. Mancuso, *J. Clin. Consult. Psychol.* 35, 159 (1970); T. R. Sarbin, *ibid.* 31, 447 (1967); J. C. Nunnally, Jr., *Popular Conceptions of Mental Health* (Holt, Rinehart & Winston, New York, 1961).

19. A. H. Stanton and M. S. Schwartz, *The Mental Hospital: A Study of Institutional Participation in Psychiatric Illness and Treatment* (Basic, New York, 1954).

20. D. B. Wexler and S. E. Scoville, *Ariz. Law Rev.* 13, 1 (1971).

21. I thank W. Mischel, E. Orne, and M. S. Rosenhan for comments on an earlier draft of this manuscript.

Review Questions

1. According to Rosenhan, how easy is it for mental-health workers to determine who is "really" sane and who is "really" insane?

2. How did the staff members of mental hospitals act to legitimate the labels which psychiatrists gave to the "mental patients"?

3. How does psychiatric labeling in general serve social-control functions for society? What particular social-control techniques were used in the hospitals studied here to make the everyday routine run smoothly?

4. Why did none of the "patients" in Rosenhan's study get turned away from the mental hospitals?

Suggested Readings: Deviance, Conformity, and Social Control

Becker, Howard S. *Outsiders.* New York: Free Press, 1963.

Conrad, Peter and Joseph W. Schneider. *Deviance and Medicalization: From Badness to Sickness.* St. Louis: C.V. Mosby, 1980.

Erikson, Kai T. *Wayward Puritans.* New York: Wiley, 1966.

Goffman, Erving. *Stigma: Notes on the Management of a Spoiled Identity.* Englewood Cliffs, N.J.: Prentice-Hall, 1963.

Schur, Edwin M. *Crimes Without Victims—Deviant Behavior and Public Policy.* Englewood Cliffs, N.J.: Prentice-Hall, 1965.

Szasz, Thomas. *The Manufacture of Madness.* New York: Harper & Row, 1970.

Wiseman, Jacqueline P. *Stations of the Lost: The Treatment of Skid Row Alcoholics.* Chicago: University of Chicago Press, 1979.

Part VIII. Interaction in Institutional Contexts

Individuals may face a host of problems as they attempt to survive in their environments. Societies, too, must develop strategies, plans, or systems to deal with problems that occur *at the collective level*. That is, in order for the *group* to survive—regardless of what happens to any given individual—solutions to group problems must be worked out and agreed upon, formally or informally, by societal members. A complex system of attitudes, norms, beliefs, and roles outlining what *should* occur to solve a societal problem is called an *institution*.

Suppose your sociology class were stranded on a Caribbean island, with no prospect of contact with or aid from any other human society. A number of threats to the survival of your group will sooner or later arise, requiring the interdependent action of societal members. For instance, the society will no longer exist if all of its members die of starvation or exposure, so some coordinated system of producing and distributing food and shelter will have to be worked out. That system—a plan, or set of norms, governing the behavior of your societal members with regard to who engages in what productive functions and what will have to be done to acquire goods once they are produced—is called the *economic institution* of your society. Literally thousands of interrelated norms may be involved in the institution: One should begin work promptly at 7 A.M. and work for ten hours. One should take all goods produced to a central storehouse. All members who need or want any of the goods merely collect them from the storehouse. No private property will be permitted. People who work too hard or not hard enough will receive negative sanctions. Women should do one kind of work, while men do another. People must begin their work activities when they are eight years old. And so on. The specific rules will vary from one culture to another—your sociology class might not develop the same economic institution as ours—but some economic system is sure to emerge.

Your society will face other problems and develop other institutional solutions. Questions of how to create new members to replace those who eventually die will probably be answered with a *family institution* specifying who is allowed to marry whom (marriage seems to be a cultural universal), how the spouses will interact, who will be allowed to have how many children and at what times in their lives, how children are to be cared for and socialized, and so on. To keep your societal members from killing each

other off or being killed by outsiders before they can reproduce enough people to take their places, you will develop a system to control and protect
your members, or a *political institution.* Problems of *health and illness* will
be met by an *institution* which includes rules for defining what should be
seen as health and what as illness and how the latter should be treated.
Transmitting your culture to new members may require the creation of an
institution or system of rules and roles to provide *education.* Questions
about aspects of your world which defy other culturally available explanations may be answered by a *religious institution,* a set of beliefs, rules for religious expression, and roles for religious leaders and followers.

There are several important points regarding social institutions which the
articles in this section address. First, a *society's institutions are taught and
learned in the process of socialization,* once they have been created. Although the general problems societies confront are similar, the emergent institutions which attempt to cope with these problems vary from one society
to another and from one historical period to another. They are not fixed or
immutable, nor are they automatically understood by the society's children.
Institutions must be transmitted from one generation to the next, and of
course they may be changed somewhat in the process.

Second, once these arrangements or systems are incorporated into the
culture, *they constrain the behavior of individuals in many ways.* Institutions are not usually so rigid that people are allowed *no* choice in type of
work, marriage partners, religious beliefs, and the like. At the same time,
the individual does not have total freedom to work, marry, or believe as he
or she chooses without running the risk of receiving negative sanctions from
other societal members.

Moreover, institutions tend to structure one's time and activities. For instance, beliefs about how best to prepare children for adult life have resulted in the school—a social organization of rules and roles which requires
some people to spend long periods of time sitting in small rooms at desks
facing toward an older person who stands or sits in front of the room. The
young people may be separated by age into classes. One result of this arrangement is that the population becomes "age-segregated." Old people
have fewer and fewer structured opportunities to interact with children, and
children themselves are not always allowed free interaction with other children of different ages. As one consequence, children (and all students) are
much better able to distinguish small differences in age than are adults. The
structural constraints produced by age-segregation and age-grading in
schools may entail benefits *and/or* costs for individuals and for societies;
the point here is that the educational institution channels and limits human
activity and interaction.

As another example of the constraining effects of social institutions, consider the norms of the economic institution of the U.S. They specify that
one must use money in order to obtain goods and services and, further, that
this money may be gained by inheritance, by work, or by providing capital

(factories, equipment, and the like) for the production process. Permitting money and other valuable assets to be passed from one generation to the next automatically insures that the children of poor parents will have fewer chances to acquire wealth than the children of affluent parents. In other words, the structural arrangement that allows for inheritance of money, wealth, and capital creates inequality as a feature of social life. Thus, while our society's myths tell us that poverty and wealth are the results of individual efforts, the sociological perspective allows us to see that the way a society is organized, including its institutional systems, actually produces its own effects on the individual's behavior and life chances.

A third important point regarding institutions is that *they tend to be interrelated* so that a change in one area—say a declaration of war to protect a society's interests—will have effects in other institutional areas—the rules about marriage and childbearing may change as young people are removed from their normal activities to perform military duties. Many sociologists contend that the one institution which is most likely to affect all the others is the economic system. The society's economic norms may have a powerful impact on the system of courtship and marriage; the system of educating the young for adult roles; the system of laws, law making, and law enforcement; and so on. The change from an agricultural economy to one based on industry, for example, upsets prior beliefs and norms concerning work itself as well as beliefs and norms about religious observance, family size, and what constitutes a proper education. Furthermore, the *structural changes* in the way society is organized which accompany industrialization have a limiting effect on other institutions, and on individuals as well. Consider the consequences of the change from working on one's own homesite to working in a factory or office.

Try to keep in mind these general characteristics of institutions—they are learned sets of norms which represent collective responses to collective problems, they constrain human activity and interaction, and they are interrelated—as we move to a discussion of the nature and consequences of several specific institutions in the United States.

A. Family

T HE FIRST INSTITUTIONAL CONTEXT FOR HUMAN INTERACTION THAT WE WILL EXAMINE here is the one that first affects our lives—the family system. Everyone knows a great deal about families. After all, most of us grew up in one and were probably socialized to want to form new families as adults. Our own personal family involvements, however, form a very *poor* base of knowledge about family norms and patterns of the larger society. We must step outside our own lives to gain a sociological perspective on the family.

Sociologically, a society's family institution serves several important functions. It provides societal members with ascribed statuses—a position in the social-class structure and racial, ethnic, and sexual identities. The family system also affects sexual behavior and reproduction. It further provides a plan for socializing infants and children and for providing emotional support and stability to family members. It is in interaction with family members that our self-concepts are initially developed.

Within the family circle—whatever members the society defines this as including—intensive interaction takes place. This interaction is not unstructured, however, since a division of labor is usually present, with parents and children, and perhaps men and women, performing different tasks to meet the needs of the group as a whole. Thus learned social roles guide our interaction here.

It is also the case that the norms of our culture specify that a newly-married couple should live in a private household, interacting frequently and intensely with each other. These norms create an isolated setting in which each couple is likely to develop a unique world view, or "nomic order." In "Marriage and the Construction of Reality," Peter Berger and Hansfried Kellner discuss why and how marriage in our society (as well as other long-term relationships) results in new "nomic (normative) orders." In essence, the partners alter their definitions of themselves, of their daily lives, of their past experiences, and of their futures. All of these come to be seen from a perspective different from the one either partner had before marriage.

In general, we arrive at constructions of what is going on in the world around us by using ready-made "typifications" and by "objectivating," or *validating*, these typifications through discussion and interaction with other people. From our culture's common stock of knowledge, we draw typifications, categories or meanings, which seem to be applicable to an event we are trying to "make sense of," thereby *typifying* (or classifying) that event.

In other words, we match the event to what we think are the relevant cultural categories for describing it. Then, because most events are ambiguous and could be interpreted in a number of ways, we turn to others to validate our use of the culture's typifications. If those whose opinions are important to us do not seem to share our matching of the typification to the event, we may redefine the event, drawing on other categories or meanings (other typifications) from our culture to explain it. If others do seem to concur with our application of the typification, it becomes "objectivated," or turned into a validated, agreed-upon "fact." We need no longer wonder what the event means (unless we are philosophers or social scientists); our actions and sentiments toward the event will be aligned with the actions and sentiments of others, and further interaction can proceed smoothly. In this way, reality is constructed.

In marriage, the partners' former interpretations or constructions of reality are reexamined and redefined. The social processes that lead to the construction of a new "nomic order" are subtle, and few people are aware that they are occurring. The key mechanism by which the new "coupled" world view is constructed is *conversation*, itself a normatively encouraged activity for spouses. In discussions, chats, and quarrels, former friends of the husband and wife come to be redefined and reevaluated—reobjectivated. New comparisons are made of one's self with friends and family members, and new self-definitions are formed.

Marriage, then, is much more than an agreement to live with another person. Marriage has consequences for the individual in all spheres of public and private life—even to the extent of determining how one views the world.

The aptness of Berger and Kellner's description of the construction of a coupled identity is perhaps most apparent when we examine those who are *leaving* a marriage, and a "nomic order," because of the death of a spouse or divorce. The formerly married must adjust in a number of obvious ways to their change in marital status. One less obvious problem of adjustment involves creating a new "single" world view. Consider the husband who was uninterested in the theater before his marriage to a theater "buff." Over the years, he has heard his wife discussing the theater a great deal and has himself come to see himself as a "theatergoer," to pay attention to new performers, openings on Broadway, and such. After his divorce, he hears on the radio an announcement of a new play and automatically thinks, "We should get tickets to that." Then he realizes that "we" no longer exist, and he's really not very interested in sitting in some stuffy theater straining to understand the play's existential message anyway. In this hypothetical incident, we see in a small way that the former husband is caught between a coupled identity created in his marriage and a new single identity that reflects his own views (or the views of his new associates) more closely.

Diane Vaughan explores the theme of shifting identities corresponding to shifting marital statuses in "Uncoupling: The Social Construction of Divorce." Previously, "uncoupling" was thought to be a chaotic period in the lives of those involved, characterized by pain, guilt, and anxiety about their uncertain futures. Through intensive interviews with people who have undergone this experience, Vaughan uncovers the order that lies behind the apparent chaos. She finds that the individual usually goes through identifiable stages, gradually shedding his or her marital identity and gaining a new world view and a new self-concept as a single adult, possibly available for future "re-coupling."

Vaughan's work is indeed timely, since divorce has come to be a common and accepted feature of life in the United States over the past half-century. It is estimated that about half of the marriages formed in our society at this time will end in divorce. Of course, remarriage rates are also high, but many more people than ever before are finding that they must rely more on "single" identities—and "single" strategies for survival—for substantial portions of their adult lives.

Other changes in family form and functioning which have come about in recent decades reinforce this trend. The combination of increased divorce rates with postponement of marriage, decreased fertility rates, postponement of childbearing, and longer life expectancies have led to the current situation in which between a fifth and a fourth of all households in our country are comprised of a single individual *living alone* rather than in a family group. Many others find themselves living with their children as single parents. All of these changes, and more, bring about new interaction patterns and strategies and necessitate adaptations of the old institutional system.

Our final selections on the family institution present two cases in which family interaction is seen to be responding to our unstable era. In one, the focus is on extremely poor black women in an urban community. The second treats young part-time and full-time divorced fathers.

"Sex Roles and Survival Strategies in an Urban Black Community," by Carol Stack, views the complicated inner workings of poor black families from their own perspective. Stack spent several years living among the residents of "The Flats," the poorest section of a black community located in a midwestern city, called here "Jackson Harbor." Her observations of the family structure—the roles and norms for behavior and interaction— present us with a type of family quite different from the nuclear family common among the black and white middle-class that we often read about in textbooks. Economic problems are particularly severe in The Flats, and the family ideals of the larger society often cannot be realized. The type of family interaction that has developed is *flexible* and *supportive* of the needs of its members. The form and functioning of these family "support systems" constitute a rational response to a true economic plight.

Although not as limited financially as parents in The Flats, the divorced and separated fathers studied by Kristine Rosenthal and Harry Keshet are operating in what might be called a "role vacuum." As the authors point out in "Child-care Responsibilities of Part-Time and Single Fathers," our conception of the father role increasingly includes duties in addition to economic support, for fathers who are divorced as well as the married. Yet precisely what fathering should involve is currently undergoing negotiation in our society and is not clearly spelled out.

Rosenthal and Keshet provide us with a look at how some young, formerly married fathers are struggling to reshape the father role to include more interaction and intimacy with their children, as well as more direct child-care. Greater involvement has its consequences, especially in the economic sphere. New sexual and marriage partners for the fathers may also complicate matters. We see in addition the active involvement of the children in the reshaping process. Not only are they helping to redefine fatherhood, but they are redefining childhood into the bargain. An interesting question arises as to how the children of families such as these will behave when they themselves become parents.

It is important to point out that the men interviewed by Rosenthal and Keshet are *not typical* of all divorced and separated fathers in our country. In the vast majority of cases of divorce in which children are involved (which occurs in about a third of all divorces), the mother retains primary if not sole custody of and responsibility for the children. In fact, the majority of divorced fathers do not have custody of their children even on a part-time basis, do not see their children often or regularly, and do not even continue to make court-decreed child-care payments after the initial years of the divorce period have passed. It is *because* most of the fathers in Rosenthal and Keshet's study are novel and, we suspect, at the forefront of new institutional patterns of organization that their cases are included here.

In summary, we will be looking at how marriage norms set up a situation in which spouses construct a new, "coupled" world view and how that world view is affected if uncoupling occurs. We will also look at two nontraditional types of responses to family needs emerging out of interaction among family members who find themselves, for a variety of reasons, in circumstances which are not conducive to the older patterns of family organization. It is interesting to note that, even as institutional changes such as these come about, they do not represent radical departures from the previous values and norms, but rather adaptations that preserve a great deal from the past.

MARRIAGE AND THE CONSTRUCTION OF REALITY

Peter L. Berger and Hansfried Kellner

Ever since Durkheim it has been a commonplace of family sociology that marriage serves as a protection against anomie [normlessness] for the individual. Interesting and pragmatically useful though this insight is, it is but the negative side of a phenomenon of much broader significance. If one speaks of *anomic* states, then one ought properly to investigate also the *nomic* processes that, by their absence, lead to the aforementioned states. If, consequently, one finds a negative correlation between marriage and anomie, then one should be led to inquire into the character of marriage as a *nomos*-building instrumentality, that is, of marriage as a social arrangement that creates for the individual the sort of order in which he can experience his life as making sense. It is our intention here to discuss marriage in these terms. While this could evidently be done in a macrosociological perspective, dealing with marriage as a major social institution related to other broad structures of society, our focus will be microsociological, dealing primarily with the social processes affecting the individuals in any specific marriage, although, of course, the larger framework of these processes will have to be understood. In what sense this discussion can be described as microsociology of knowledge will hopefully become clearer in the course of it.[1]

Marriage is obviously only *one* social relationship in which this process of *nomos*-building takes place. It is, therefore, necessary to first look in more general terms at the character of this process. In doing so, we are influenced by three theoretical perspectives—the Weberian perspective on society as a network of meanings, the Meadian perspective on identity as a social phenomenon, and the phenomenological analysis of the social structuring of reality especially as given in the work of Schutz and Merleau-Ponty.[2] Not being convinced, however, that theoretical lucidity is necessarily enhanced by terminological ponderosity, we shall avoid as much as possible the use of the sort of jargon for which both sociologists and phenomenologists have acquired dubious notoriety.

The process that interests us here is the one that constructs, maintains and modifies a consistent reality that can be meaningfully experienced by indi-

Peter L. Berger and Hansfried Kellner, "Marriage and the Construction of Reality," *Diogenes*, 45 (1964), 1–25.

viduals. In its essential forms this process is determined by the society in which it occurs. Every society has its specific way of defining and perceiving reality—its world, its universe, its overarching organization of symbols. This is already given in the language that forms the symbolic base of the society. Erected over this base, and by means of it, is a system of ready-made *typifications* [stereotypical explanations of events in the world], through which the innumerable experiences of reality come to be ordered.[3] These typifications and their order are held in common by the members of society, thus acquiring not only the character of objectivity, but being taken for granted as *the* world *tout court*, the only world that normal men can conceive of.[4] The seemingly objective and taken-for-granted character of the social definitions of reality can be seen most clearly in the case of language itself, but it is important to keep in mind that the latter forms the base and instrumentality of a much larger world-erecting process.

The socially constructed world must be continually mediated to and actualized by the individual, so that it can become and remain indeed *his* world as well. The individual is given by his society certain decisive cornerstones for his everyday experience and conduct. Most importantly, the individual is supplied with specific sets of typifications and criteria of relevance, predefined for him by the society and made available to him for the ordering of his everyday life. This ordering or (in line with our opening considerations) nomic apparatus is biographically cumulative. It begins to be formed in the individual from the earliest stages of socialization on, then keeps on being enlarged and modified by himself throughout his biography.[5] While there are individual biographical differences making for differences in the constitution of this apparatus in specific individuals, there exists in the society an overall consensus on the range of differences deemed to be tolerable. Without such consensus, indeed, society would be impossible as a going concern, since it would then lack the ordering principles by which alone experience can be shared and conduct can be mutually intelligible. This order, by which the individual comes to perceive and define his world, is thus not chosen by him, except perhaps for very small modifications. Rather, it is discovered by him as an external datum, a ready-made world that simply is *there* for him to go ahead and live in, though he modifies it continually in the process of living in it. Nevertheless, this world is in need of *validation*, perhaps precisely because of an ever-present glimmer of suspicion as to its social manufacture and relativity. This validation, while it must be undertaken by the individual himself, requires ongoing interaction with others who co-inhabit this same socially constructed world. In a broad sense, *all* the other co-inhabitants of this world serve a validating function. Every morning the newspaper boy validates the widest coordinates of my world and the mailman bears tangible validation of my own location within these coordinates. However, some validations are more significant than others. Every individual requires the ongoing validation of his world, including crucially the validation of his identity and place in this world, by those few who are his truly significant others.[6] Just as the individual's deprivation of relationship with his significant others will plunge him into anomie, so their continued presence will sustain for him that *nomos* by which he can feel at home in the world at least most of the time. Again in a broad sense, all the actions of the significant others and even their simple presence serve this sustaining function. In everyday life, however, the principal method employed is speech. In this sense, it is proper to view the individual's relationship with his significant others as an ongoing conversation. As the latter occurs, it validates over and over again the fundamental definitions of reality once entered into, not, of course, so much by explicit articulation, but precisely by taking the definitions silently for granted and conversing about all conceivable matters on this taken-for-granted basis. Through the same conversation the individual is also made capable of adjusting to changing and new social contexts in his biography. In a very fundamental sense it can be said that one converses one's way through life.

If one concedes these points, one can now state a general sociological proposition: the plausibility and stability of the world, as socially defined, is dependent upon the strength and continuity of significant relationships in which conversation about this world can be continually carried on. Or, to put it a little differently: *the reality of the world is sustained through conversation with significant others*. This reality, of course, includes not only the imagery by which fellowmen are viewed, but also includes the way in which one views oneself. The reality-bestowing force of social relationships depends on the degree of their nearness,[7] that is, on the degree to which social relationships occur in face-to-face situations and to which they are credited with primary significance by the individual. In any empirical situation, there now emerge obvious sociological questions out of these considerations, namely, questions about the patterns of the world-building relationships, the social forms taken by the conversation with significant others. Sociologically, one must ask how these relationships are *objectively* structured and distributed, and one will also want to understand how they are *subjectively* perceived and experienced.

With these preliminary assumptions stated we can now arrive at our main thesis here. Namely, we would contend that marriage occupies a privileged status among the significant validating relationships for adults in our society. Put slightly differently: marriage is a crucial nomic instrumentality in our society. We would further argue that the essential social functionality of this institution cannot be fully understood if this fact is not perceived.

We can now proceed with an ideal-typical analysis of marriage, that is, seek to abstract the essential features involved. Marriage in our society is a *dramatic* act in which two strangers come together and redefine themselves. The drama of the act is internally anticipated and socially legitimated long before it takes place in the individual's biography, and amplified by means of a pervasive ideology, the dominant themes of which (romantic love, sexual fulfillment, self-discovery and self-realization through love and sexuality, the nuclear family as the social site for these processes) can be found distributed through all strata of the society. The actualization of these ideologically predefined expectations in the life of the individual occurs to the accompaniment of one of the few traditional rites of passage that are still meaningful to almost all members of the society. It should be added that, in using the term "strangers," we do not mean, of course, that the candidates for the marriage come from widely discrepant social backgrounds—indeed, the data indicate that the contrary is the case. The strangeness rather lies in the fact that, unlike marriage candidates in many previous societies, those in ours typically come from different face-to-face contexts—in the terms used above, they come from different areas of conversation. They do not have a shared past, although their pasts have a similar structure. In other words, quite apart from prevailing patterns of ethnic, religious and class endogamy [or marriage within the same group], our society is typically exogamous [involving marriage between those who differ] in terms of nomic relationships. Put concretely, in our mobile society the significant conversation of the two partners previous to the marriage took place in social circles that did not overlap. With the dramatic redefinition of the situation brought about by the marriage, however, all significant conversation for the two new partners is now centered in their relationship with each other—and, in fact, it was precisely with this intention that they entered upon their relationship.

It goes without saying that this character of marriage has its root in much broader structural configurations of our society. The most important of these, for our purposes, is the crystallization of a so-called private sphere of existence, more and more segregated from the immediate controls of the public institutions (especially the economic and political ones), and yet defined and utilized as the main social area for the individual's self-realization.[8] It cannot be our purpose here to inquire into the historical forces that brought forth this phenomenon, beyond making the observation that these are closely connected with the industrial revolution and its institutional consequences. The public institutions now confront the individual as an immensely powerful and alien world, incomprehensible in its inner workings, anonymous in its human character. If only through his work in some nook of the economic machinery, the individual must find a way of living in this alien world, come to terms with its power over him, be satisfied with a few conceptual rules of thumb to guide him through a vast reality that otherwise remains opaque to his understanding, and modify its anonymity by whatever *human relations* he can work out in his involvement with it. It ought to be emphasized, against some critics of "mass society," that this does not inevitably leave the individual with a sense of profound unhappiness and lostness. It would rather seem that large numbers of people in our society are quite content with a situation in which their public involvements have little subjective importance, regarding work as a not too bad necessity and politics as at best a spectator sport. It is usually only intellectuals with ethical and political commitments who assume that such people must be terribly desperate. The point, however, is that the individual in this situation, no matter whether he is happy or not, will turn elsewhere for the experiences of self-realization that do have importance for him. The private sphere, this interstitial area created (we would think) more or less haphazardly as a by-product of the social metamorphosis [or unfolding] of industrialism, is mainly where he will turn. It is here that the individual will seek power, intelligibility and, quite literally, a name—the apparent power to fashion a world, however Lilliputian, that will reflect his own being: a world that, seemingly having been shaped by himself and thus unlike those other worlds that insist on shaping him, is translucently intelligible to him (or so he thinks); a world in which, consequently, he is *somebody*—perhaps even, within its charmed circle, a lord and master. What is more, to a considerable extent these expectations are not unrealistic. The public institutions have no need to control the individual's adventures in the private sphere, as long as they really stay within the latter's circumscribed limits. The private sphere is perceived, not without justification, as an area of individual choice and even autonomy. This fact has important consequences for the shaping of identity in modern society that cannot be pursued here. All that ought to be clear here is the peculiar location of the private sphere within and between the other social structures. In sum, it is above all and, as a rule, only in the private sphere that the individual can take a slice of reality and fashion it into his world. If one is aware of the decisive significance of this capacity and even necessity of men to externalize themselves in reality and to produce for themselves a world in which they can feel at home, then one will hardly be surprised at the great importance which the private sphere has come to have in modern society.[9]

The private sphere includes a variety of social relationships. Among these, however, the relationships of the family occupy a central position and, in fact, serve as a focus for most of the other relationships (such as those with friends, neighbors, fellow-members of religious and other voluntary associations). . . . [T]he central relationship in this whole area is the marital one. It is on the basis of marriage that, for most adults in our society, existence in the private sphere is built up. It will be clear that this is not at all a universal or even a cross culturally wide function of marriage. Rather . . . marriage in our society [has] taken on a very peculiar character and functionality. It has been pointed out that marriage in contemporary society has lost some of its older functions and taken on new ones instead.[10] This is certainly correct, but we would prefer to state the matter a little differently. Marriage and family used to be firmly embedded in a matrix of wider community relationships, serving as extensions and particularizations of the latter's social controls. There were few separating barriers between the world of the individual family and the wider community, a fact even to be seen in the physical conditions under which the family lived before the industrial revolution.[11] The same social life pulsated through the house, the street and the community. In our terms, the family and within it the marital relationship were part and parcel of a considerably larger area of conversation. In our contemporary society, by contrast, each family constitutes its own segregated subworld, with its own controls and its own closed conversation.

This fact requires a much greater effort on the part of the marriage partners. Unlike an earlier situation in which the establishment of the new marriage simply added to the differentiation and complexity of an already existing social world, the marriage partners now are embarked on the often difficult task of constructing for themselves the little world in which they will live. To be sure, the larger society provides them with certain standard instructions as to how they should go about this task, but this does not change the fact that considerable effort of their own is required for its realization. The monogamous character of marriage enforces both the dramatic and the precarious nature of this undertaking. Success or failure hinges on the present idiosyncrasies and the fairly unpredictable future development of these idiosyncrasies of *only two individuals* (who, moreover, do not have a shared past)—as Simmel has shown, the most unstable of all possible social relationships.[12] Not surprisingly, the decision to embark on this undertaking has a critical, even cataclysmic connotation in the popular imagination, which is underlined as well as psychologically assuaged by the ceremonialism that surrounds the event.

Every social relationship requires *objectivation*, that is, requires *a process by which subjectively experienced meanings become objective to the individual and*, in interaction with others, *become common property* and thereby massively objective.[13] The degree of objectivation will depend on the number and the intensity of the social relationships that are its carriers. A relationship that consists of only two individuals called upon to sustain, by their own efforts, an ongoing social world will have to make up in intensity for the numerical poverty of the arrangement. This, in turn, accentuates the drama and the precariousness. The later addition of children will add to the, as it were, density of objectivation taking place within the nuclear family, thus rendering the latter a good deal less precarious. It remains true that the establishment and maintenance of such a social world make extremely high demands on the principal participants.

The attempt can now be made to outline the ideal-typical process that takes place as marriage functions as an instrumentality for the social construction of reality. The chief protagonists of the drama are two individuals, each with a biographically accumulated and available stock of experience.[14] As members of a highly mobile society, these individuals have already internalized a degree of readiness to redefine themselves and to modify their stock of experience, thus bringing with them considerable psychological capacity for entering new relationships with others.[15] Also, coming from broadly similar sectors of the larger society (in terms of region, class, ethnic and religious affiliations), the two individuals will have organized their stock of experience in similar fashion. In other words, *the two individuals have internalized the same overall world, including the general definitions and expectations of the marriage relationship itself.* Their society has provided them with a taken-for-granted image of marriage and has socialized them into an anticipation of stepping into the taken-for-granted roles of marriage. All the same, *these relatively empty projections now have to be actualized, lived through and filled with experiential content* by the protagonists. This will require a dramatic change in their definitions of reality and of themselves.

As of the marriage, most of each partner's actions must now be projected in conjunction with those of the other. Each partner's definitions of reality must be continually correlated with the definitions of the other. The other is present in nearly all horizons of everyday conduct. Furthermore, the identity of each now takes on a new character, having to be constantly matched with that of the other, indeed being typically perceived by the people at large as being symbiotically conjoined with the identity of the other. In each partner's psychological economy of significant others, the marriage partner becomes the other *par excellence*, the nearest and most decisive co-inhabitant of the world. Indeed, all other significant relationships have to be almost automatically reperceived and regrouped in accordance with this drastic shift.

In other words, from the beginning of the marriage each partner has new modes in his meaningful experience of the world in general, of other people and of himself. By definition, then, marriage constitutes a nomic rupture. In terms of each partner's biography, the event of marriage initiates a new nomic process. Now, the full implications of this fact are rarely apprehended by the protagonists with any degree of clarity. There rather is to be found the notion that one's world, one's other-relationships and, above all, oneself have remained what they were before—only, of course, that world, others and self will now be shared with the marriage partner. It should be clear by now that this notion is a grave misapprehension. Just because of this fact, marriage now propels the individual into an unintended and unarticulated development, in the course of which the nomic transformation takes place. What typically *is* apprehended are certain objective and concrete problems arising out of the marriage—such as tensions with in-laws, or with former friends, or religious differences between the partners, as well as immediate tensions between them. These are apprehended as external, situational and practical difficulties. What is *not* apprehended is the subjective side of these difficulties, namely, the transformation of *nomos* and identity that has occurred and that continues to go on, so that all problems and relationships are experienced in a quite new way, that is, experienced within a new and ever-changing reality.

Take a simple and frequent illustration—the male partner's relationships with male friends before and after the marriage. It is a common observation that such relationships, especially if the extramarital partners are single, rarely survive the marriage, or, if they do, are drastically redefined after it. This is typically the result of neither a deliberate decision by the husband nor deliberate sabotage by the wife. What rather happens, very simply, is a slow process in which the husband's image of his friend is transformed as he keeps talking about this friend with his wife. Even if no actual talking goes on, the mere presence of the wife forces him to see his friend differently. This need not mean that he adopts a negative image held by the wife. Regardless of what image she holds or is believed by him to hold, it will be different from that held by the husband. This difference will enter into the joint image that now must needs be fabricated in the course of the ongoing conversation between the marriage partners—and, in due course, must act powerfully on the image previously held by the husband. Again, typically, this process is rarely apprehended with any degree of lucidity. The old friend is more likely to fade out of the picture by slow degrees, as new kinds of friends take his place. The process, if commented upon at all within the marital conversation, can always be explained by socially available formulas about "people changing," "friends disappearing" or oneself "having become more mature." This process of conversational liquidation is especially powerful because it is one-sided—the husband typically talks with his wife about his friend, but *not* with his friend about his wife. Thus the friend is deprived of the defense of, as it were, counterdefining the relationship. *This dominance of the marital conversation over all others is one of its most important characteristics.* It may be mitigated by a certain amount of protective segregation of some non-marital relationships (say "Tuesday night out with the boys," or "Saturday lunch with mother"), but even then there are powerful emotional barriers against the sort of conversation (conversation *about* the marital relationship, that is) that would serve by way of counter-definition.

Marriage thus posits a new reality. The individual's relationship with this new reality, however, is a dialectical one—he acts upon it, in collusion with the marriage partner, and it acts back upon both him and the partner, welding together their reality. Since, as we have argued before, the objectivation that constitutes this reality is precarious, the groups with which the couple associates are called upon to assist in co-defining the new reality. The couple is pushed towards groups that strengthen their new definition of themselves and the world, avoids those that weaken this definition. This in turn releases the commonly known pressures of group association, again acting upon the marriage partners to change their definitions of the world and of themselves. Thus the new reality is not posited once and for all, but goes on being redefined not only in the marital interaction itself but also in the various maritally based group relationships into which the couple enters.

In the individual's biography marriage, then, brings about a decisive phase of socialization that can be compared with the phases of childhood and adolescence. This phase has a rather different structure from the earlier ones. There the individual was in the main socialized into already existing patterns. Here he actively collaborates rather than passively accommodates himself. Also, in the previous phases of socialization, there was an apprehension of entering into a new world and being changed in the course of this. In marriage there is little apprehension of such a process, but rather the notion that the world has remained the same, with only its emotional and pragmatic connotations having changed. This notion, as we have tried to show, is illusionary.

The reconstruction of the world in marriage occurs principally in the course of conversation, as we have suggested. *The implicit problem of this conversation is how to match two individual definitions of reality.* By the very logic of the relationship, a common overall definition must be arrived at—otherwise the conversation will become impossible and, *ipso facto*, the relationship will be endangered. Now, this conversation may be understood as the working away of an ordering and typifying apparatus—if one prefers, an objectivating apparatus. Each partner ongoingly contributes his conceptions of reality, which are then "talked through," usually not once but many times, and in the process become objectivated by the conversational apparatus. The longer this conversation goes on, the more massively real do the objectivations become to the partners. In the marital conversation a world is not only built, but it is also kept in a state of repair and ongoingly refurnished. The subjective reality of this world for the two partners is sustained by the same conversation. The nomic instrumentality of marriage is concretized over and over again, from bed to breakfast table, as the partners carry on the endless conversation that feeds on nearly all they individually or jointly experience. Indeed, it may happen eventually that no experience is fully real unless and until it has been thus "talked through."

This process has a very important result—namely, *a hardening or stabilization of the common objectivated reality*. It should be easy to see now how this comes about. The objectivations ongoingly performed and internalized by the marriage partners become ever more massively real, as they are confirmed and reconfirmed in the marital conversation. The world that is made up of these objectivations at the same time gains in stability. For example, the images of other people, which before or in the earlier stages of the marital conversation may have been rather ambiguous and shifting in the minds of the two partners, now become hardened into definite and stable characterizations. A casual acquaintance, say, may sometimes have appeared as lots of fun and sometimes as quite a bore to the wife before her marriage. Under the influence of the marital conversation, in which this other person is frequently "discussed," she will now come down more firmly on one *or* the other of the two characterizations, or on a reasonable compromise between the two. In any of these three options, though, she will have concocted with her husband a much more stable image of the person in question than she is likely to have had before her marriage, when there may have been no conversational pressure to make a definite option at all. The same process of stabilization may be observed with regard to self-definitions as well. In this way, the wife in our example will not only be pressured to assign stable characterizations to others but also to herself. Previously uninterested politically, she now identifies herself as liberal. Previously alternating between dimly articulated religious positions, she now declares herself an agnostic. Previously confused and uncertain about her sexual emotions, she now understands herself as an unabashed hedonist in this area. And so on and so forth, with the same reality—and identity—stabilizing process at work on the husband. Both world and self thus take on a firmer, more reliable character for both partners.

Furthermore, it is not only the ongoing experience of the two partners that is constantly shared and passed through the conversational apparatus. The same *sharing extends into the past*. The two distinct biographies, as subjectively apprehended by two individuals who have lived through them, are overruled and reinterpreted in the course of their conversation. Sooner or later, they will "tell all"—or, more correctly, they will tell it in such a way that it fits into the self-definitions objectivated in the marital relationship. The couple thus construct not only present reality but reconstruct past reality as well, fabricating a common memory that integrates the recollections of the two individual pasts.[16] The comic fulfillment of this process may be seen in those cases when one partner "remembers" more clearly what happened in the other's past than the other does—and corrects him accordingly. Similarly, there occurs a *sharing of future horizons*, which leads not only to stabilization, but inevitably to a narrowing of the future projections of each partner. Before marriage the individual typically plays with quite discrepant daydreams in which his future self is projected.[17] Having now considerably stabilized his self-image, the married individual will have to project the future in accordance with this maritally defined identity. This narrowing of future horizons begins with the obvious external limitation that marriage entails, as, for example, with regard to vocational and career plans. However, it extends also to the more general possibilities of the individual's biography. To return to a previous illustration, the wife, having "found herself" as a liberal, an agnostic and a "sexually healthy" person, *ipso facto* liquidates the possibilities of becoming an anarchist, a Catholic or a Lesbian. At least until further notice she has decided upon who she is—and, by the same token, upon who she will be. The stabilization brought about by marriage thus affects that total reality in which the partners exist. In the most far-reaching sense of the word, the married individual "settles down"—and *must* do so, if the marriage is to be viable, in accordance with its contemporary institutional definition.

It cannot be sufficiently strongly emphasized that this process is typically unapprehended, almost automatic in character. The protagonists of the marriage drama do *not* set out deliberately to create their world. Each continues to live in a world that is taken for granted—and keeps its taken-for-granted character even as it is metamorphosed. The new world that the married partners, Prometheuslike, have called into being is perceived by them as the normal world in which they have lived before. Reconstructed present and reinterpreted past are perceived as a continuum, extending forward into a commonly projected future. *The dramatic change that has occurred remains in bulk, unapprehended and unarticulated.* And where it forces itself upon the individual's attention, it is retrojected into the past, explained as having always been there, though perhaps in a hidden way. Typically, the reality that has been "invented" within the marital conversation is subjectively perceived as a "discovery." Thus the partners "discover" themselves and the world, "who they really are," "what they really believe," "how they really feel, and always have felt, about so-and-so." This retrojection of the world being produced all the time by themselves serves to enhance the stability of this world and at the same time to assuage the "existential anxiety" that, probably inevitably, accompanies the perception that nothing but one's own narrow shoulders supports the universe in which one has chosen to live. . . .

The use of the term "stabilization" should not detract from the insight into the difficulty and precariousness of this world-building enterprise. Often enough, the new universe collapses *in statu nascendi*. Many more times it continues over a period, swaying perilously back and forth as the two partners try to hold it up, finally to be abandoned as an impossible undertaking. If one conceives of the marital conversation as the principal drama and the two partners as the principal protagonists of the drama, then one can look upon the other individuals involved as the supporting chorus for the central dramatic action. Children, friends, relatives and casual acquaintances all have their part in reinforcing the tenuous structure of the new reality. It goes without saying that the *children form the most important part of this supporting chorus*. Their very existence in predicated on the maritally established world. The marital partners themselves are in charge of their socialization *into* this world, which to them has a pre-existent and self-evident character. They are taught from the beginning to speak precisely those lines that lend themselves to a supporting chorus, from their first invocations of "Daddy" and "Mummy" on to their adoption of the parents' ordering and typifying apparatus that now defines *their* world as well. The marital conversation is now in the process of becoming a family symposium, with the necessary consequence that its objectivations rapidly gain in density, plausibility and durability.

In sum: the process that we have been inquiring into is, ideal-typically, one in which reality is crystallized, narrowed and stabilized. Ambivalences are converted into certainties. Typifications of self and of others become settled. Most generally, possibilities become facticities. What is more, this process of transformation remains, most of the time, unapprehended by those who are both its authors and its objects.[18]

• • •

NOTES

1. The present article has come out of a larger project on which the authors have been engaged in collaboration with three colleagues in sociology and philosophy. The project is to produce a systematic treatise that will integrate a number of now separate theoretical strands in the sociology of knowledge.

2. Cf. especially Max Weber, *Wirtschaft und Gesellschaft* (Tuebingen: Mohr 1956), and *Gesammelte Aufsaetze zur Wissenschaftslehre* (Tuebingen: Mohr 1951);

George H. Mead, *Mind, Self and Society* (University of Chicago Press 1934); Alfred Schutz, *Der sinnhafte Aufbau der sozialen Welt* (Vienna: Springer, 2nd ed. 1960) and *Collected Papers*, 1 (The Hague: Nijhoff 1962); Maurice Merleau-Ponty, *Phénoménologie de la perception* (Paris: Gallimard 1945) and *La structure du comportement* (Paris: Presses universitaires de France 1953).

3. Cf. Schutz, *Aufbau*, 202-20 and *Collected Papers*, I, 3-27, 283-6.

4. Cf. Schutz, *Collected Papers*, I, 207-28.

5. Cf. especially Jean Piaget, *The Child's Construction of Reality* (Routledge & Kegan Paul 1955).

6. Cf. Mead, *op. cit.*, 135-226.

7. Cf. Schutz, *Aufbau*, 181-95.

8. Cf. Arnold Gehlen, *Die Seele im technischen Zeitalter* (Hamburg: Rowohlt 1957), 57-69 and *Anthropologische Forschung* (Hamburg: Rowohlt 1961), 69-77, 127-40; Helmut Schelsky, *Soziologie der Sexualitaet* (Hamburg: Rowohlt 1955), 102-33. Also cf. Thomas Luckmann, "On religion in modern society," *Journal for the Scientific Study of Religion* (Spring 1963), 147-62.

9. In these considerations we have been influenced by certain presuppositions of Marxian anthropology, as well as by the anthropological work of Max Scheler, Helmuth Plessner and Arnold Gehlen. We are indebted to Thomas Luckmann for the clarification of the social-psychological significance of the private sphere.

10. Cf. Talcott Parsons and Robert Bales, *Family: Socialization and Interaction Process* (London: Routledge & Kegan Paul 1956), 3-34, 353-96.

11. Cf. Philippe Aries, *Centuries of Childhood* (New York: Knopf 1962), 339-410.

12. Cf. Georg Simmel (Kurt Wolff ed.), *The Sociology of Georg Simmel* (New York: Collier-Macmillan 1950), 118-44.

13. Cf. Schutz, *Aufbau*, 29-36, 149-53.

14. Cf. Schutz, *Aufbau*, 186-92, 202-10.

15. David Riesman's well-known concept of "other-direction" would also be applicable here.

16. Cf. Maurice Halbwachs, *Les Cadres sociaux de la memoire* (Paris: Presses universitaires de France 1952), especially 146-77; also cf. Peter Berger, *Invitation to Sociology—A Humanistic Perspective* (Garden City, N.Y.: Doubleday-Anchor 1963), 54-65 (available in Penguin).

17. Cf. Schutz, *Collected Papers*, I, 72-3, 79-82.

18. The phenomena here discussed could also be formulated effectively in terms of the Marxian categories of reification and false consciousness. Jean-Paul Sartre's recent work, especially *Critique de la raison dialectique*, seeks to integrate these categories within a phenomenological analysis of human conduct. Also cf. Henri Lefebvre, *Critique de la vie quotidienne* (Paris: l'Arche 1958-61).

Review Questions

1. Berger and Kellner explain that "reality is socially constructed." What do they mean?

2. The process of constructing social reality involves: (a) matching the "typifications," or taken-for-granted cultural explanations, to events or

people in our worlds; and (b) "objectivating," or validating (and redefining if necessary), our typifications of reality through interaction with significant others. Discuss how husbands and wives in the contemporary world validate and redefine ("objectivate") each other's world views, thus engaging in "nomos-building." How do they develop a "common memory"? How do they stabilize their coupled world view?

3. Why do former friends and other family members exert little influence on the redefinition process experienced by the marital pair?

4. How and why do children strengthen the couple's world view?

UNCOUPLING: THE SOCIAL CONSTRUCTION OF DIVORCE

Diane Vaughan

BERGER AND KELLNER (1964) DESCRIBE MARRIAGE AS A DEFINITIONAL PROCESS. TWO AU-
tonomous individuals come together with separate and distinct biographies
and begin to construct for themselves a subworld in which they will live as a
couple. A redefinition of self occurs as the autonomous identity of the two
individuals involved is reconstructed as a mutual identity. This redefinition
is externally anticipated and socially legitimated before it actually occurs in
the individual's biography.

Previously, significant conversation for each partner came from nonoverlapping circles, and self-realization came from other sources. Together, they
begin to construct a private sphere where all significant conversation centers in their relationship with each other. The coupled identity becomes the
main source of their self-realization. Their definitions of reality become correlated, for each partner's actions must be projected in conjunction with the
other. As their worlds come to be defined around a relationship with a significant other who becomes *the* significant other, all other significant relationships have to be reperceived, regrouped. The result is the construction
of a joint biography and a mutually coordinated common memory.

Were this construction of a coupled identity left only to the two participants, the coupling would be precarious indeed. However, the new reality is
reinforced through objectivation, that is, "a process by which subjectively
experienced meanings become objective to the individual, and, in interaction with others, become common property, and thereby massively objective" (Berger and Kellner, 1964:6). Hence, through the use of language in
conversation with significant others, the reality of the coupling is constantly
validated.

Of perhaps greater significance is that this definition of coupledness becomes taken for granted and is validated again and again, not by explicit articulation, but by conversing around the agreed [upon] definition of reality
that has been created. In this way a consistent reality is maintained, ordering the individual's world in such a way that it validates his identity. Marriage, according to Berger and Kellner, is a constructed reality which is "no-
mosbuilding" (1964:1). That is, it is a social arrangement that contributes

This paper was presented at the annual meetings of the American Sociological Association in
1977 and first appeared in print in the first edition of this reader. Another version was later
published in *Alternative Life Styles*.

order to individual lives, and therefore should be considered as a significant validating relationship for adults in our society.

Social relationships, however, are seldom static. Not only do we move in and out of relationships, but the nature of a particular relationship, though enduring, varies over time. Given that the definitions we create become socially validated and hence constraining, *how do individuals move from a mutual identity, as in marriage, to assume separate, autonomous identities again?* What is the process by which new definitions are created and become validated?

The Berger and Kellner analysis describes a number of interrelated yet distinguishable stages that are involved in the social construction of a mutual identity; for example, the regrouping of all other significant relationships. In much the same way, the *demise* of a relationship should involve distinguishable social processes. Since redefinition of self is basic to both movement into and out of relationships, the social construction of a singular identity also should follow the patterns suggested by Berger and Kellner. This paper is a qualitative examination of this process. Hence, the description that follows bears an implicit test of Berger and Kellner's ideas.

The dimensions of sorrow, anger, personal disorganization, fear, loneliness, and ambiguity that intermingle every separation are well known.[1] Their familiarity does not diminish their importance. Though in real life these cannot be ignored, the researcher has the luxury of selectivity. Here, it is not the pain and disorganization that are to be explored, but the existence of an underlying orderliness.

Though the focus is on divorce, the process examined appears to apply to *any* heterosexual relationship in which the participants have come to define themselves and be defined by others as a couple. The work is exploratory and, as such, not concerned with generalizability. However, the process may apply to homosexual couples as well. Therefore, the term "uncoupling" will be used because it is a more general concept than divorce. Uncoupling applies to the redefinition of self that occurs as mutual identity unravels into singularity, regardless of marital status or sex of the participants.

The formal basis from which this paper developed was in-depth, exploratory interviews. The interviews, ranging from two to six hours, were taped and later analyzed. All of the interviewees were at different stages in the uncoupling process. Most were divorced, though some were still in stages of consideration of divorce. Two of the interviews were based on long-term relationships that never resulted in marriage. All of the relationships were heterosexual. The quality of these interviews has added much depth to the understanding of the separation process. The interviewees were of high intellectual and social level, and their sensitivity and insight have led to much valuable material, otherwise unavailable.

A more informal contribution to the paper comes from personal experiences and the experiences of close friends. Further corroboration has come from autobiographical accounts, newspapers, periodicals, and conversations, which have resulted in a large number of cases illustrating certain points. Additional support has come from individuals who have read or heard the paper with the intent of proving or disproving its contentions by reference to their own cases.

Since the declared purpose here is to abstract the essential features of the process of uncoupling, some simplification is necessary. The separation of a relationship can take several forms. To trace all of them is beyond the scope of this study. Therefore, to narrow the focus, we must first consider the possible variations.

Perhaps the coupled identity was not a major mechanism for self-validation from the outset of the union. Or the relationship may have at one time filled that function, but, as time passed, this coupled identity was insufficient to meet individual needs. Occasionally this fact has implications for both partners simultaneously, and the uncoupling process is initiated by both. More frequently, however, one partner still finds the marriage a major source of stability and identity, while the other finds it inadequate. In this form, one participant takes the role of initiator of the uncoupling process. However, this role may not consistently be held by one partner, but instead may alternate between them, due to the difficulty of uncoupling in the face of external constraints, social pressure not to be the one responsible for the demise of the marriage, and the variability in the self-validating function of the union over time. For the purpose of this study, the form of uncoupling under consideration is that which results when one partner, no longer finding the coupled identity self-validating, takes the role of initiator in the uncoupling process. The other partner, the significant other, still finds the marriage a major source of stability and identity.

UNCOUPLING: THE INITIATION OF THE PROCESS

> I was never psychologically married. I always felt strained by attempts that coupled me into a marital unit. I was just never comfortable as "Mrs." I never got used to my last name. I never wanted it. The day after my marriage was probably the most depressed day of my life, because I had lost my singularity. The difference between marriage and a deep relationship, living together, is that you have this ritual, and you achieve a very definite status, and it was *that* that produced my reactions—because I became in the eyes of the world a man's wife. And I was never comfortable and happy with it. It didn't make any difference who the man was.

An early phase in the uncoupling process occurs as one or the other of the partners begins to question the coupled identity. At first internal, the challenging of the created world remains for a time as a doubt within one of the partners in the coupling. Though there is a definition of coupledness, subjectively the coupledness may be experienced differently by each partner. Frequently, these subjective meanings remain internal and unarticulated.

Thus, similarly, the initial recognition of the coupling as problematic may be internal and unarticulated, held as a secret. The subworld that has been constructed, for some reason, doesn't "fit."

A process of definition negotiation is begun, initiated by the one who finds the mutual identity an inadequate definition of self. Attempts to negotiate the definition of the coupledness are likely to result in the subjective meaning becoming articulated for the first time, thus moving the redefinition process toward objectivation. The secret, held by the initiator, is shared with the significant other. When this occurs, it allows both participants to engage in the definitional process.

Though the issue is made "public" in that private sphere shared by the two, the initiator frequently finds that a lack of shared definitions of the coupled identity stalemates the negotiations. While the initiator defines the marriage as a problem, the other does not. The renegotiation of the coupled identity cannot proceed unless both agree that the subworld they have constructed needs to be redefined. Perhaps for the significant other, the marriage as it is still provides important self-validation. If so, the initiator must bring the other to the point of sharing a common definition of the marriage as "troubled."

ACCOMPANYING RECONSTRUCTIONS

Though this shared definition is being sought, the fact remains that, for the initiator, the coupled identity fails to provide self-validation. In order to meet this need, the initiator engages in other attempts at redefining the nature of the relationship. Called "accompanying reconstructions," these *may* or *may not* be shared with the significant other. They may begin long before the "secret" of the troubled marriage is shared with the other, in an effort to make an uncomfortable situation more comfortable without disrupting the relationship. Or they may occur subsequent to sharing the secret with the significant other, as a reaction to the failure to redefine the coupledness satisfactorily. Time order for their occurrence is not easily imposed—thus, "accompanying reconstructions."

The initiator's accompanying reconstructions may be directed toward the redefinition of (1) the coupledness itself, (2) the identity of the significant other, or (3) the identity of the initiator. A change in definition of either of the three implies a change in at least one of the others. Though they are presented here separately, they are interactive rather than mutually exclusive and are not easily separable in real life.

The first form of accompanying reconstruction to be considered is the initiator's redefinition of the coupledness itself. One way of redefining the coupledness is by an unarticulated conversion of the agreed-upon norms of the relationship.

> I had reconceptualized what marriage was. I decided sexual fidelity was not essential for marriage. I never told her that. And I didn't even have anyone I was inter-

ested in having that intimate a relationship with—I just did a philosophical thing. I just decided it was O.K. for me to have whatever of what quality of other relationship I needed to have. Something like that—of that caliber—was something I could never talk to her about. So I did it all by myself. I read things and decided it. I was at peace with me. I knew that we could stay married, whatever that meant. O.K., I can stay legally tied to you, and I can probably live in this house with you, and I can keep working the way I have been. I decided I can have my life and still be in this situation with you, but you need some resources, because I realize now I'm not going to be all for you. I don't want to be all for you, and I did tell her that. But I couldn't tell her this total head trip I'd been through because she wouldn't understand.

Or, the coupledness may be redefined by acceptance of the relationship with certain limitations. Boundaries can be imposed on the impact that the relationship will have on the total life space of the initiator.

I finally came to the point where I realized I was never going to have the kind of marriage I had hoped for, the kind of relationship I had hoped for. I didn't want to end it, because of the children, but I wasn't going to let it hurt me any more. I wasn't going to depend on him any more. The children and I were going to be the main unit, and, if he occasionally wanted to participate, fine—and if not, we would go ahead without him. I was no longer willing to let being with him be the determining factor as to whether I was happy or not. I ceased planning our lives around his presence or absence and began looking out for myself.

A second form of accompanying reconstruction occurs when the initiator attempts to redefine the significant other in a way that is more compatible with his own self-validation needs. The initiator may direct efforts toward specific behaviors, such as drinking habits, temper, sexual incompatibilities, or finance management. Or, the redefinition attempt may be of a broader scope.

I was aware of his dependence on the marriage to provide all his happiness, and it wasn't providing it. I wanted him to go to graduate school, but he postponed it, against my wishes. I wanted him to pursue his own life. I didn't want him to sacrifice for me. I wanted him to become more exciting to me in the process. I was aware that I was trying to persuade him to be a different person.

Redefinition of the significant other may either be directed toward maintaining the coupledness, as above, or moving away from it, as is the case following.

The way I defined being a good wife and the way John defined being a good wife were two different quantities. He wanted the house to look like a hotel and I didn't see it that way. He couldn't see why I couldn't meet his needs. . . . When he first asked for a divorce and I refused, he suggested I go back to school. I remembered a man who worked with John who had sent his wife back to school so she could support herself, so he could divorce her. I asked John if he was trying to get rid of me. He didn't answer that. He insisted I go, and I finally went.

A third form of accompanying reconstruction may be directed toward the redefinition of the initiator. Intermingled with attempts at redefinition of the significant other and redefinition of the coupledness itself is the seeking of self-validation outside the marriage by the initiator. A whole set of other behaviors may evolve that have the ultimate effect of moving the relationship away from the coupledness toward a separation of the joint biography.

SELF-VALIDATION OUTSIDE THE MARRIAGE

What was at first internally experienced and recognized as self-minimizing takes a more concrete form and becomes externally expressed in a search for self-maximization. Through investment of self in career, in a cause requiring commitment, in a relationship with a new significant other, in family, in education, or in activities and hobbies, the initiator develops new sources of self-realization. These alternative sources of self-realization confirm not the coupled identity but the singularity of the initiator.

Furthermore, in the move toward a distinct biography, the initiator finds ideological support that reinforces the uncoupling process. Berger and Kellner (1964:3) note the existence of a supporting ideology which lends credence to marriage as a significant validating relationship in our society. That is, the nuclear family is seen as the site of love, sexual fulfillment, and self-realization. In the move toward uncoupling, the initiator finds confirmation for a belief in *self* as a first priority.

> I now see my break with religion as a part of my developing individuality. At the time I was close friends with priests and nuns, most of whom have since left the church. I felt a bitterness toward the church for its definition of marriage. I felt constrained toward a type of marriage that was not best for me.

Whether this ideology first begins within the individual, who then actively *seeks* sources of self-realization that are ideologically congruent, or whether the initiator's own needs come to be met by a serendipitous "elective affinity" of ideas (Weber:1930), is difficult to say. The interconnections are subtle. The supporting ideology may come from the family of orientation, the women's movement, the peer group, or a new significant other. It may grow directly, as through interaction, or indirectly, as through literature. No matter what the source, the point is that, in turning away from the marriage for self-validation, a separate distinct biography is constructed in interaction with others, and this beginning autonomy is strengthened by a supporting belief system.

The initiator moves toward construction of a separate subworld wherein significant conversation comes from circles which no longer overlap with those of the significant other. And, the significant other is excluded from that separate subworld.

> I shared important things with the children that I didn't share with him. It's almost as if I purposefully punished him by not telling him. Some good thing would happen and I'd come home and tell them and wouldn't tell him.

The initiator's autonomy is further reinforced as the secret of the troubled marriage is shared with others in the separate subworld the initiator is constructing. It may be directly expressed as a confidence exchanged with a close friend, family member, or children, or it may be that the sharing is indirect. Rather than being expressed in significant conversation, the definition of the marriage as troubled is created for others by a variety of mechanisms that relay the message that the initiator is not happily married. The definition of the marriage as problematic becomes further objectivated as the secret, once held only by the initiator, then shared with the significant other, moves to a sphere beyond the couple themselves.

Other moves away occur that deeply threaten the coupled identity for the significant other and at the same time validate the autonomy of the initiator.

> I remember going to a party by myself and feeling comfortable. She never forgot that. I never realized the gravity of that to her.

> Graduate school became a symbolic issue. I was going to be a separate entity. That's probably the one thing I wanted to do that got the biggest negative emotional response from him.

> All that time I was developing more of a sense of being away from her. I didn't depend on her for any emotional feedback, companionship. I went to plays and movies with friends.

The friendship group, rather than focusing on the coupledness, relies on splintered sources that support separate identities. Though this situation can exist in relationships in which the coupled identity is validating for both participants, the distinction is that, in the process of uncoupling, there may not be shared conversation to link the separate subworld of the initiator with that of the significant other.

These movements away by the initiator heighten a sense of exclusion for the significant other. Deep commitment to other than the coupled identity—to a career, to a cause, to education, to a hobby, to another person—reflects a lessened commitment to the marriage. The initiator's search for self-validation outside the marriage even may be demonstrated symbolically to the significant other by the removal of the wedding ring or by the desire, if the initiator is a woman, to revert to her maiden name. If the initiator's lessened commitment to the coupled identity is reflected in a lessened desire for sexual intimacy, the challenge to the identity of the significant other and the coupledness becomes undeniable. As the significant other recognizes the growing autonomy of the initiator, he, too, comes to accept the definition of the marriage as "troubled."

The roles assumed by each participant have implications for the impact of the uncoupling on each. Whereas the initiator has found other sources of self-realization outside the marriage, usually the significant other has not. The marriage still performs the major self-validating function. The significant other is committed to an ideology that supports the coupled identity.

The secret of the "troubled" marriage has not been shared with others as it has by the initiator, meaning for the significant other the relationship in its changed construction remains unobjectivated. The challenge to the identity of the significant other and to the coupledness posed by the initiator may result in increased commitment to the coupled identity for the significant other. With the joint biography already separated in these ways, the couple enters into a period of "trying."

TRYING

Trying is a stage of intense definition negotiation by the partners. Now both share a definition of the marriage as troubled. However, each partner may seek to construct a new reality that is in opposition to that of the other. The significant other tries to negotiate a shared definition of the marriage as savable, whereas the initiator negotiates toward a shared definition that marks the marriage as unsavable.[2]

For the initiator, the uncoupling process is well underway. At some point the partner who originally perceived the coupled identity to be problematic and sought self-validation outside the coupled identity has experienced "psychological divorce." Sociologically, this can be defined as the point at which the individual's newly constructed separate subworld becomes the major nomos-building mechanism in his life space, replacing the nomos-building function of the coupled identity.

The initiator tries subtly to prepare the significant other to live alone. By encouraging the other to make new friends, find a job, get involved in outside activities, or seek additional education, the initiator hopes to decrease the other's commitment to and dependence upon the coupled identity for self-validation and move the other toward autonomy. This stage of preparation is not simply one of cold expediency for the benefit of the initiator, but is based on concern for the significant other and serves to mitigate the pain of the uncoupling process for both the initiator and the other.

For both, there is a hesitancy to sever the ties. In many cases, neither party is fully certain about the termination of the marriage. Mutual uncertainty may be more characteristic of the process. The relationship may weave back and forth between cycles of active trying and passive acceptance of the status quo due to the failure of each to pull the other to a common definition and the inability of either to make the break.

> I didn't want to hurt him. I didn't want to be responsible for the demise of a marriage I no longer wanted. I could have forced him into being the one to achieve the breach, for I realized it was never going to happen by itself.

> I didn't want to be the villain—the one to push her out into the big, bad world. I wanted to make sure she was at the same point I was.

> I kept hoping some alternative would occur so that he would be willing to break. I kept wishing it would happen.

Frequently, in the trying stage, the partners turn to outside help for formal negotiation of the coupled identity. Counseling, though entered into with apparent common purpose, becomes another arena in which the partners attempt to negotiate a shared definition from their separately held definitions of the marriage as savable or unsavable. For the initiator, the counseling may serve as a step in the preparation of the significant other to live alone. Not only does it serve to bring the other to the definition of the marriage as unsavable, but also the counseling provides a resource for the significant other, in the person of the counselor. Often it happens that the other has turned to no one for comfort about the problem marriage. The initiator, sensitive to this need and unable to fill it himself, hopes the counselor will fill this role. The counseling has yet another function. It further objectivates the notion of the coupled identity as problematic.

At some point during this period of trying, the initiator may suggest separation. Yet, separation is not suggested as a formal leave-taking but as a *temporary* separation meant to clarify the relationship for both partners. Again, the concern on the part of the initiator for the significant other appears. Not wanting to hurt, yet recognizing the coupled identity as no longer valid, the temporary separation is encouraged as a further means of bringing the other to accept a definition of the marriage as unsavable, to increase reliance of the other on outside resources of self-realization, and to initiate the physical breach gently.

> Even at that point, at initial separation, I wasn't being honest. I knew fairly certainly that when we separated, it was for good. I let her believe that it was a means for us first finding out what was happening and then eventually possibly getting back together.

Should the initiator be hesitant to suggest a separation, the significant other may finally tire of the ambiguity of the relationship. No longer finding the coupling as it exists self-validating, the significant other may be the one to suggest a separation. The decision to separate may be the result of discussion and planning, or it may occur spontaneously, in a moment of anger. It may be mutually agreed upon, but more often it is not. However it emerges, the decision to separate is a difficult one for both partners.

OBJECTIVATION: RESTRUCTURING OF THE PRIVATE SPHERE

The separation is a transitional state in which everything needs definition, yet very little is capable of being defined. Economic status, friendship networks, personal habits, and sex life are all patterns of the past which need simultaneous reorganization. However, reorganization is hindered by the ambiguity of the relationship. The off-again, on-again wearing of the wedding rings is symbolic of the indecision in this stage. Each of the partners searches for new roles, without yet being free of the old.

For the initiator who has developed outside resources, the impact of this uncertainty is partially mitigated. For the significant other, who has not spent time in preparation for individual existence, the major self-validating function of the marriage is gone and nothing has emerged as a substitute.

> I had lost my identity somewhere along the way. And I kept losing my identity. I kept letting him make all the decisions. I couldn't work. I wasn't able to be myself. I was letting someone else take over. I didn't have any control over it. I didn't know how to stop it. I was unsure that if anything really happened I could actually make it on my own or not.

The separation precipitates a redefinition of self for the significant other. Without other resources for self-validation, and with the coupled identity now publicly challenged, the significant other begins a restructuring of the private sphere.

This restructuring occurs not only in the social realm but also entails a form of restructuring that is physical, tangible, and symbolic of the break in the coupled identity. For instance, if the initiator has been the one to leave, at some point the significant other begins reordering the residence they shared to suit the needs of one adult rather than two. Furniture is rearranged or thrown out. Closets and drawers are reorganized. A thorough house-cleaning may be undertaken. As the initiator has moved to a new location that reinforces his singularity, the significant other transforms the home that validated the coupling into one that likewise objectivates the new definition. Changes in the physical appearance of either or both partners may be a part of the symbolic restructuring of the private sphere. Weight losses, changes of hair style, or changes in clothing preferences further symbolize the yielding of the mutual identity and the move toward autonomy.

Should the significant other be the one to leave, the move into a new location aids in the redefinition of self as an autonomous individual. For example, the necessity of surviving in a new environment, the eventual emergence of a new set of friends that define and relate to the significant other as a separate being instead of as half of a couple, and the creation of a new residence without the other person are all mechanisms which reinforce autonomy and a definition of singularity.

Though the initiator has long been involved in objectivating a separate reality, frequently for the significant other this stage is just beginning. Seldom does the secret of the troubled marriage become shared with others by this partner until it can no longer be deferred. Although the initiator actively has sought objectivation, the significant other has avoided it. Confronted with actual separation, however, the significant other responds by taking the subjectively experienced meanings and moving them to the objective level—by confiding in others, perhaps in writing, in letters or in diaries—any means that helps the other deal with the new reality.

There are some who must be told of the separation—children, parents, best friends. Not only are the two partners reconstructing their own reality, but they now must reconstruct the reality for others. Conversation provides the mechanism for reconstruction, simultaneously creating common definitions and working as a major objectivating apparatus. The longer the conversation goes on, the more massively real do the objectivations become to the partners. The result is a stabilization of the objectivated reality, as the new definition of uncoupledness continues to move outward.

Uncoupling precipitates a reordering of all other significant relationships. As in coupling, where all other relationships are reperceived and regrouped to account for and support the emergence of *the* significant other, in uncoupling the reordering supports the singularity of each partner. Significant relationships are lost, as former friends of the couple now align with one or the other or refuse to choose between the two. Ties with families of orientation, formerly somewhat attenuated because of the coupling, are frequently renewed. For each of the partners, pressure exists to stabilize characterizations of others and of self so that the world and self are brought toward consistency. Each partner approaches groups that strengthen the new definition each has created, and avoids those that weaken it. The groups with which each partner associates help co-define the new reality.

OBJECTIVATION: THE PUBLIC SPHERE

The uncoupling is further objectivated for the participants as the new definition is legitimized in the public sphere. Two separate households demand public identification as separate identities. New telephone listings, changes of mailing address, separate checking accounts, and charge accounts, for example, all are mechanisms by which the new reality becomes publicly reconstructed.

The decision to initiate legal proceedings confirms the uncoupling by the formal negotiation of a heretofore informally negotiated definition. The adversary process supporting separate identities, custody proceedings, the formal separation of the material base, the final removal of the rings all act as means of moving the new definition from the private to the public sphere. The uncoupling now becomes objectivated not only for the participants and their close intimates, but for casual acquaintances and strangers.

Objectivation acts as a constraint upon whatever social identity has been constructed. It can bind a couple together, or hinder their recoupling, once the uncoupling process has begun. Perhaps this can better be understood by considering the tenuous character of the extramarital affair. The very nature of the relationship is private. The coupling remains a secret shared by the two and seldom becomes objectivated in the public realm. Thus, the responsibility for the maintenance of that coupling usually rests solely with the two participants. When the relationship is no longer self-validating for one of the participants, the uncoupling does not involve a reconstruction of reality for others. The constraints imposed by the objectivation of a marital relationship which function to keep a couple in a marriage do not exist to the same extent in an affair. The fragility of the coupling is enhanced by its limited objectivation.

Berger and Kellner (1964:6) note that the "degree of objectivation will depend on the number and intensity of the social relationships that are its carriers." As the uncoupling process has moved from a nonshared secret held within the initiator to the realm of public knowledge, the degree of objectivation has increased. The result is a continuing decline in the precariousness of the newly constructed reality over time.

DIVORCE: A STAGE IN THE PROCESS

Yet a decrease in precariousness is not synonymous with a completion of the uncoupling process. As marriage, or coupling, is a dramatic act of redefinition of self by two strangers as they move from autonomous identities to the construction of a joint biography, so uncoupling involves yet another redefinition of self as the participants move from mutual identity toward autonomy. It is this redefinition of self, for each participant, that completes the uncoupling. Divorce, then, may not be the final stage. In fact, divorce could be viewed as a nonstatus that is at some point on a continuum ranging from marriage (coupling) as an achieved status, to autonomy (uncoupling), likewise an achieved status. In other words, the uncoupling process might be viewed as a status transformation which is complete when the individual defines his salient status as "single" rather than "divorced." When the individual's newly constructed separate subworld becomes nomos-building— when it creates for the individual a sort of order in which he can experience his life as making sense—the uncoupling process is completed.

The completion of uncoupling does not occur at the same moment for each participant. For either or both of the participants, it may not occur until after the other has created a coupled identity with another person. With that step, the tentativeness is gone.

> When I learned of his intention to remarry, I did not realize how devastated I would be. It was just awful. I remember crying and crying. It was really a very bad thing that I did not know or expect. You really aren't divorced while that other person is still free. You still have a lot of your psychological marriage going—in fact, I'm still in that a little bit because I'm still single.

For some, the uncoupling may never be completed. One or both of the participants may never be able to construct a new and separate subworld that becomes self-validating. Witness, for example, the widow who continues to call herself "Mrs. John Doe," who associates with the same circle of friends, who continues to wear her wedding ring and observes wedding anniversaries. For her, the coupled identity is still a major mechanism for self-validation, even though the partner is gone.

In fact, death as a form of uncoupling may be easier for the significant other to handle than divorce. There exist ritual techniques for dealing with it, and there is no ambiguity. The relationship is gone. There will be no further interaction between the partners. With divorce, or any uncoupling that occurs through the volition of one or both of the partners, the interaction may continue long after the relationship has been formally terminated. For the significant other—the one left behind, without resources for self-validation—the continuing interaction between the partners presents obstacles to autonomy.

> There's a point at which it's over. If your wife dies, you're a lot luckier, I think, because it's over. You either live with it, you kill yourself, or you make your own bed of misery. Unlike losing a wife through death, in divorce, she doesn't die. She keep resurrecting it. I can't get over it, she won't die. I mean, she won't go away.

CONTINUITIES

Continuities are linkages between the partners that exist despite the formal termination of the coupled identity. Most important of these is the existence of shared loved ones—children, in-laws, and so on. Though in-laws may of necessity be excluded from the separately constructed subworlds, children can rarely be and, in their very existence, present continued substantiation of the coupled identity.

In many cases continuities are actively constructed by one or both of the participants after the formal termination of the relationship. These manufactured linkages speak to the difficulty of totally separating that common biography, by providing a continued mechanism for interaction. They may be constructed as a temporary bridge between the separated subworlds, or they may come to be a permanent interaction pattern. Symbolically, they seem to indicate caring on the part of either or both of the participants.

> The wife moves out. The husband spends his weekend helping her get settled— hanging pictures, moving furniture.

> The husband moves out, leaving his set of tools behind. Several years later, even after his remarriage, the tools are still there, and he comes to borrow them one at a time. The former wife is planning to move within the same city. The tools are boxed up, ready to be taken with her.

> The wife has moved out, but is slow to change her mailing address. Rather than marking her forwarding address on the envelopes and returning them by mail, the husband either delivers them once a week or the wife picks them up.

> The wife moves out. The husband resists dividing property with her that is obviously hers. The conflict necessitates many phone calls and visits.

> The husband moves out. Once a week he comes to the house to visit with the children on an evening when the wife is away. When she gets home, the two of them occasionally go out to dinner.

A nice part of the marriage was shared shopping trips on Sunday afternoons. After the divorce, they still occasionally go shopping together.

The holidays during the first year of separation were celebrated as they always had been—with the whole family together.

During a particularly difficult divorce, the husband noted that he had finally succeeded in finding his wife a decent lawyer.

Continuities present unmeasurable variables in the uncoupling process. In this paper, uncoupling is defined as a reality socially constructed by the participants. The stages that mark the movement from a coupled identity to separate autonomous identities are characterized, using divorce for an ideal-type analysis. Yet, there is no intent to portray uncoupling as a compelling linear process from which there is no turning back. Such conceptualization would deny the human factor inherent in reality construction. Granted, as the original secret is moved from private to public, becoming increasingly objectivated, reconstructing the coupled identity becomes more and more difficult.

Each stage of objectivation acts as the closing of a door. Yet at any stage the process may be interrupted. The initiator may not find mechanisms of self-validation outside the coupling that reinforce his autonomy. Or the self-validation found outside the coupling may be the very stuff that allows the initiator to stay *in* the relationship. Or continuities may intervene and reconstruction of the coupled identity may occur, despite the degree of objectivation, as in the following case.

Ellen met Jack in college. They fell in love and married. Jack had been blind since birth. He had pursued a college career in education and was also a musician. Both admired the independence of the other. In the marriage, she subordinated her career to his and helped him pursue a masters degree, as well as his musical interests. Her time was consumed by his needs—for transportation and the taping and transcribing of music for the musicians in his group. He was teaching at a school for the blind by day and performing as a musician at night. They had a son, and her life, instead of turning outward, as his, revolved around family responsibilities. She gained weight. Jack, after twelve years of marriage, left Ellen for his high school sweetheart. Ellen grieved for a while, then began patching up her life. She got a job, established her own credit, went back to college, and lost weight. She saw a lawyer, filed for divorce, joined Parents Without Partners, and began searching out singles groups. She dated. Throughout, Jack and Ellen saw each other occasionally and maintained a sexual relationship. The night before the divorce was final, they reconciled.

The uncoupling never was completed, though all stages of the process occurred, including the public objectivation that results from the initiation of the legal process. Ellen, in constructing an autonomous identity, became again the independent person Jack had first loved.[3] This, together with the continuities that existed between the two, created the basis for a common definition of the coupling as savable.

DISCUSSION

Berger and Kellner describe the process by which two individuals create a coupled identity for themselves. Here, we have started from the point of the coupled identity and examined the process by which people move out of such relationships. Using interview data, we have found that, although the renegotiation of separate realities is a complex web of subtle modifications, clear stages emerge which mark the uncoupling process. The emergent stages are like benchmarks which indicate the increasing objectivation of the changing definitions of reality, as these definitions move from the realm of the private to the public.

Beginning within the intimacy of the dyad, the initial objectivation occurs as the secret of the troubled marriage that the initiator has held is shared with the significant other. With this, the meaning has begun to move from the subjective to the objective. Definition negotiation begins. While attempting to negotiate a common definition, the initiator acts to increase the validation of his identity and place in the world by use of accompanying reconstructions of reality. The autonomy of the initiator increases as he finds self-validation outside the marriage and an ideology that supports the uncoupling. The increased autonomy of the initiator brings the significant other to accept a definition of the marriage as troubled, and they enter into the stage of "trying." The process continues, as counseling and separation further move the new definition into the public sphere.

The telling of others, the symbolic physical signs of the uncoupling, and the initiation of formal legal proceedings validate the increasing separation of the partners as they negotiate a new reality which is different from that constructed private sphere which validated their identity as a couple. Eventually, a redefinition of the mutual identity occurs in such a way that the joint biography is separated into two separate autonomous identities. As Berger and Kellner state that marriage is a dramatic act of redefinition of self by two individuals, so uncoupling is characterized by the same phenomenon. Self-realization, rather than coming from the coupledness, again comes from outside sources. Significant conversation again finds its source in nonoverlapping circles. The new definition of the relationship constructed by the participants has, in interaction with others, become common property.

Language is crucial to this process. Socially constructed worlds need validation. As conversation constantly reconfirms a coupled identity, so also does it act as the major validating mechanism for the move to singularity, not by specific articulation, but by the way in which it comes to revolve around the uncoupled identity as taken for granted.

The notion that the stages uncovered do broadly apply needs to be further confirmed. We need to know whether the process is invariant regardless of the heterosexuality, homosexuality, or social class of couples. Does it also apply for close friends? In what ways does the sex of the interviewer bias the data? Additionally, the stages in the process should be confirmed by interviews with both partners in a coupling. Due to the delicacy of the subject matter, this is difficult. In only one instance were both partners available to be interviewed for this study. Notwithstanding these limitations, the findings which emerge deserve consideration.

Most significant of these is the existence of an underlying order in a phenomenon generally regarded as a chaotic and disorderly process. Undoubtedly the discovery of order was encouraged by the methodology of the study. The information was gained by retrospective analysis on the part of the interviewees. Certainly the passage of time allowed events to be reconstructed in an orderly way that made sense. Nonetheless, as was previously noted, the interviewees were all at various stages in the uncoupling process—some at the "secret" stage and some five years hence. Yet, the stages which are discussed here appeared without fail in every case and have been confirmed repeatedly by the other means described earlier.

In addition to this orderliness, the examination of the process of uncoupling discloses two other little-considered aspects of the process that need to be brought forth and questioned.

One is the caring. Generally, uncoupling is thought of as a conflict-ridden experience that ends as a bitter battle between two adversaries intent on doing each other in. Frequently, this is the case. Yet, the interviews for this study showed that in all cases, even the most emotion generating, again and again the concern of each of the participants for the other revealed itself. Apparently, the patterns of caring and responsibility that emerge between the partners in a coupling are not easily dispelled and in many cases persist throughout the uncoupling process and after, as suggested by the concept of continuities.

A second question that emerges from this examination of uncoupling is related to Berger and Kellner's thesis. They state that, for adults in our society, marriage is a significant validating relationship, one that is nomos-building. Marriage is, in fact, described as "a crucial nomic instrumentality" (1964:4). Though Berger and Kellner at the outset do delimit the focus of their analysis to marriage as an ideal type, the question to be answered is, To what degree is this characterization of marriage appropriate today?

Recall, for example, the quote from one interviewee: "I was never psychologically married. I always felt strained by attempts that coupled me into a marital unit. I was just never comfortable as 'Mrs.' " The interviews for this study suggest that the nomos-building quality assumed to derive from marriage to the individual should be taken as problematic rather than as given. Gouldner (1959) suggests that the parts of a unit vary in the degree to which they are interdependent. His concept of functional autonomy may be extended to illuminate the variable forms that marriage, or coupling, may take and the accompanying degree of nomos. A relationship may exist in which the partners are highly interdependent, and the coupled identity does provide the major mechanism for self-validation, as Berger and Kellner suggest. Yet it is equally as likely that the participants are highly independent, or "loosely coupled" (Weick, 1976; Corwin, 1977), wherein mechanisms for self-validation originate *outside* the coupling rather than from the coupling itself. The connection between the form of the coupling, the degree to which it is or is not nomos-building, and the subsequent implications for uncoupling should be examined in future research.

NOTES

1. For a sensitive and thought-provoking examination of these as integral components of divorce, see Willard Waller's beautiful qualitative study, *The Old Love and the New*.

2. This statement must be qualified. There are instances when the partners enter a stage of trying with shared definitions of the marriage as savable. The conditions under which the coupling can be preserved have to be negotiated. If they can arrive at a common definition of the coupling that is agreeable to both, the uncoupling process is terminated. But this analysis is of uncoupling, and there are two alternatives: (1) that they enter with common definitions of the marriage as savable but are not able to negotiate the conditions of the coupling so that the self-validation function is preserved or (2) that they enter the period of trying with opposing definitions, as stated here.

3. Waller interprets this phenomenon by using Jung's conceptualization of the container and the contained, analogous to the roles of initiator and significant other, respectively, in the present discussion. Notes Waller, "Or the contained, complicated by the process of divorcing, may develop those qualities whose lack the container previously deplored" (Waller:163–168).

REFERENCES

Berger, Peter L. and Hansfried Kellner, 1964, "Marriage and the Construction of Reality," *Diogenes*, 46:1–23.

Berger, Peter L. and Thomas Luckmann, 1966, *The Social Construction of Reality*. New York: Doubleday.

Bohanon, Paul, 1971, *Divorce and After*. Garden City, N.Y.: Anchor.

Corwin, Ronald G., 1976, "Organizations as Loosely Coupled Systems: Evolution of a Perspective," Paper presented, Seminar on Educational Organizations as Loosely Coupled Systems. Palo Alto, Calif.

Davis, Murray S., 1973, *Intimate Relations*. New York: Free Press.

Epstein, Joseph E., 1975, *Divorce: The American Experience*. London: Jonathan Cape.

Goode, William J., 1956, *Women in Divorce*. New York: Free Press.

Gouldner, Alvin W., 1959, "Organizational Analysis," in R. K. Merton, L. Bloom, and L. S. Cottrell, Jr., eds. *Sociology Today*. New York: Basic Books, pp. 400–428.

Krantzler, Mel, 1973, *Creative Divorce*. New York: New American Library.

Nichols, Jack, 1975, *Men's Liberation: A New Definition of Masculinity*. New York: Penguin.

Sullivan, Judy, 1974, *Mama Doesn't Live Here Anymore*. New York: Pyramid.

Waller, Willard, 1930, *The Old Love and the New*. Carbondale: Southern Illinois University Press.

Walum, Laurel Richardson, 1977, *The Dynamics of Sex and Gender: A Sociological Perspective*. Chicago: Rand McNally.

Weber, Max, 1930, *The Protestant Ethic and the Spirit of Capitalism*, translated by Talcott Parsons. New York: Charles Scribner's Sons.

Weick, Karl E., 1976, "Educational Organizations as Loosely Coupled Systems," *Administrative Science Quarterly*, 21:1–19.

Weiss, Robert, 1975, *Marital Separation*. New York: Basic Books.

Review Questions

1. Briefly describe the following stages of "uncoupling": (1) initiation, (2) accompanying reconstructions and redefinitions, (3) self-validation outside marriage, (4) trying, (5) objectivation in the private sphere, (6) objectivation in the public sphere, (7) divorce, and (8) continuities.

2. Once a couple moves through several or all of these stages, is uncoupling inevitable? Why, or why not?

3. How do the "initiator" and the "significant other" each work to define the marital situation differently?

4. Vaughan's research shows that divorce is neither the beginning nor the end of the uncoupling process. Why? What part does the coupled world view play in the various stages of the process?

SEX ROLES AND SURVIVAL STRATEGIES IN AN URBAN BLACK COMMUNITY

Carol B. Stack

THE POWER AND AUTHORITY ASCRIBED TO WOMEN IN THE BLACK GHETTOS OF AMERICA, women whose families are locked into lifelong conditions of poverty and welfare, have their roots in the inexorable unemployment of Black males and the ensuing control of economic resources by females. These social-economic conditions have given rise to special features in the organization of family and kin networks in Black communities, features not unlike the patterns of domestic authority that emerge in matrilineal societies, or in cultures where men are away from home in wage labor (Gonzalez, 1969, 1970). The poor in Black urban communities have evolved, as the basic unit of their society, a core of kinsmen and non-kin who cooperate on a daily basis and who live near one another or co-reside. This core, or nucleus, has been characterized as the basis of the consanguineal household (Gonzalez, 1965) and of matrifocality (Tanner, 1975; Abrahams, 1963; Moynihan, 1965; Rainwater, 1966).

The concept of "matrifocality," however, has been criticized as inaccurate and inadequate. Recent studies (Ladner, 1971; Smith, 1970; Stack, 1970; Valentine, 1970) show convincingly that many of the negative features attributed to matrifocal families—that they are fatherless, unstable, and produce offspring that are "illegitimate" in the eyes of the folk culture— are not general characteristics of low-income Black families in urban America. Rather than imposing widely accepted definitions of the family, the nuclear family, or the matrifocal family on the ways in which the urban poor describe and order their world, we must seek a more appropriate theoretical framework. Elsewhere I have proposed an analysis based on the notion of a domestic network (Stack, 1974). In this view, the basis of familial structure and cooperation is not the nuclear family of the middle class, but an extended cluster of kinsmen related chiefly through children but also through marriage and friendship, who align to provide domestic functions. This

Carol B. Stack, "Sex Roles and Survival Strategies in an Urban Black Community," in Michelle Zimbalist Rosaldo and Louise Lamphere, eds., *Women, Culture and Society*: Stanford, Calif.: Stanford University Press, 1975, pp. 113–128. This article is adapted for the most part from Chapter 7 of the book *All Our Kin: Strategies for Survival in a Black Community*, by Carol B. Stack (Harper & Row, 1974). I am grateful to Harper & Row for permission to use most of the material from that chapter. I should like to thank Professors Louise Lamphere, Michelle Rosaldo, Robert Weiss, Nancie Gonzalez, and Eva Hunt for helpful suggestions in the analysis and organization of this paper, and William W. Carver, of Stanford University Press, for his thoughtful editorial advice.

cluster, or domestic network, is diffused over several kin-based households, and fluctuations in individual household composition do not significantly affect cooperative arrangements.

In this paper I shall analyze the domestic network and the relationships within it from a woman's perspective—from the perspective that the women in this study provided and from my own interpretations of the domestic and social scene. Many previous studies of the Black family (e.g. Liebow, 1967 and Hannerz, 1969) have taken a male perspective, emphasizing the street-corner life of Black men and viewing men as peripheral to familial concerns. Though correctly stressing the economic difficulties that Black males face in a racist society, these and other studies (Moynihan, 1965; Bernard, 1966) have fostered a stereotype of Black families as fatherless and subject to a domineering woman's matriarchal rule. From such simplistic accounts it is all too easy to come to blame juvenile delinquency, divorce, illegitimacy, and other social ills on the Black family, while ignoring the oppressive reality of our political and economic system and the adaptive resiliency and strength that Black families have shown.

My analysis will draw on life-history material as well as on personal comments from women in The Flats, the poorest section of a Black community in the Midwestern city of Jackson Harbor.[1] I shall view women as strategists—active agents who use resources to achieve goals and cope with the problems of everyday life. This framework has several advantages. First, because the focus is on women rather than men, women's views of family relations, often ignored or slighted, are given prominence. Second, since households form around women because of their role in child care, ties between women (including paternal aunts, cousins, etc.) often constitute the core of a network; data from women's lives, then, crucially illuminate the continuity in these networks. Finally, the life-history material, taken chiefly from women, also demonstrates the positive role that a man plays in Black family life, both as the father of a woman's children and as a contributor of valuable resources to her network and to the network of his own kin.

I shall begin by analyzing the history of residential arrangements during one woman's life, and the residential arrangements of this woman's kin network at two points in time, demonstrating that although household composition changes, members are selected or self-selected largely from a single network that has continuity over time. Women and men, in response to joblessness, the possibility of welfare payments, the breakup of relationships, or the whims of a landlord, may move often. But the very calamities and crises that contribute to the constant shifts in residence tend to bring men, women, and children back into the households of close kin. Newly formed households are successive recombinations of the same domestic network of adults and children, quite often in the same dwellings. Residence histories, then, are an important reflection of the strategy of relying on and strengthening the domestic kin network, and also reveal the adaptiveness of households with "elastic boundaries." (It may be worth noting that middle-class whites are beginning to perceive certain values, for their own lives, in such households.)

In the remainder of the paper, the importance of maximizing network strength will be reemphasized and additional strategies will be isolated by examining two sets of relationships within kin networks—those between mothers and fathers and those between fathers and children. Women's own accounts of their situations show how they have developed a strong sense of independence from men, evolved social controls against the formation of conjugal relationships, and limited the role of the husband-father within the mother's domestic group. All of these strategies serve to strengthen the domestic network, often at the expense of any particular male-female tie. Kin regard any marriage as a risk to the woman and her children, and the loss of either male or female kin as a threat to the durability of the kin network. These two factors continually augment each other and dictate, as well, the range of socially accepted relationships between fathers and children.

RESIDENCE AND THE DOMESTIC NETWORK

In The Flats, the material and cultural support needed to sustain and socialize community members is provided by cooperating kinsmen. The individual can draw upon a broad domestic web of kin and friends—some who reside together, others who do not. Residents in The Flats characterize household composition according to where people sleep, eat, and spend their time. Those who eat together may be considered part of a domestic unit. But an individual may eat in one household, sleep in another, contribute resources and services to yet another, and consider himself or herself a member of all three households. Children may fall asleep and remain through the night wherever the late-evening visiting patterns of the adult females take them, and they may remain in these households and share meals perhaps a week at a time. As R. T. Smith suggests in an article on Afro-American kinship (1970), it is sometimes difficult "to determine just which household a given individual belongs to at any particular moment." These facts of ghetto life are, of course, often disguised in the statistical reports of census takers, who record simply sleeping arrangements.

Households in The Flats, then, have shifting memberships, but they maintain for the most part a steady state of three generations of kin: males and females beyond child bearing age; a middle generation of mothers raising their own children or children of close kin; and the children. This observation is supported in a recent study by Ladner (1971: 60), who writes, "Many children normally grow up in a three-generation household and they absorb the influences of a grandmother and grandfather as well as a mother and father." A survey of eighty-three residence changes among welfare families, whereby adult females who are heads of their own households merged households with other kin, shows that the majority of moves created three-generation households. Consequently, it is difficult to pinpoint structural beginning or end to household cycles in poor Black urban communities (Buchler and Selby, 1968; Fortes, 1958; Otterbein, 1970). But it is clear that authority patterns within a kin network change with birth and death; with the death of the oldest member in a household, the next generation assumes authority.

Residence changes themselves are brought on by many factors, most related to the economic conditions in which poor families live. Women who have children have access to welfare, and thus more economic security than women who do not, and more than all men. Welfare regulations encourage mothers to set up separate households, and women actively seek independence, privacy, and improvement in their lives. But these ventures do not last long. Life histories of adults show that the attempts by women to set up separate households with their children are short-lived: houses are condemned; landlords evict tenants; and needs for services among kin arise. Household composition also expands or contracts with the loss of a job, the death of a relative, the beginning or end of a sexual partnership, or the end of a friendship. But fluctuations in household composition rarely affect the exchanges and daily dependencies of participants. The chronology of residence changes made by Ruby Banks graphically illuminates these points (see Table 1).

Ruby's residential changes, and the residences of her own children and kin, reveal that the same factors contributing to the high frequency of moving also bring men, women, and children back into the household of close kin. That one can repeatedly do so is a great source of security and dependence for those living in poverty.

A look in detail at the domestic network of Ruby's parents, Magnolia and Calvin Waters, illustrates the complexity of the typical network and also shows kin constructs at work both in the recruitment of individuals to the network and in the changing composition of households within the network, over less than three months (see Table 2).

These examples do indeed indicate the important role of the Black woman in the domestic structure. But the cooperation between male and female siblings who share the same household or live near one another has been underestimated by those who have isolated the female-headed household as the most significant domestic unit among the urban Black poor. The close cooperation of adult siblings arises from the residential patterns typical of young adults (Stack, 1970). Owing to poverty, young women with or without children do not perceive any choice but to remain living at home with their mothers or other adult female relatives. Even when young women are collecting welfare for their children, they say that their resources go further when they share food and exchange goods and services daily. Likewise, the jobless man, or the man working at a part-time or seasonal job, often remains living at home with his mother—or, if she is dead, with his sisters and brothers. This pattern continues long after such a man becomes a father and

Table 1.

AGE	HOUSEHOLD COMPOSITION AND CONTEXT OF HOUSEHOLD FORMATION
Birth	Ruby lived with her mother, Magnolia, and her maternal grandparents.
4	To be eligible for welfare, Ruby and Magnolia were required to move out of Ruby's grandparents' house. They moved into a separate residence two houses away, but ate all meals at the grandparents' house.
5	Ruby and Magnolia returned to the grandparents' house and Magnolia gave birth to a son. Magnolia worked and the grandmother cared for her children.
6	Ruby's maternal grandparents separated. Magnolia remained living with her father and her (now) two sons. Ruby and her grandmother moved up the street and lived with her maternal aunt Augusta and maternal uncle. Ruby's grandmother took care of Ruby and her brothers, and Magnolia worked and cooked and cleaned for her father.
7–16	The household was now composed of Ruby, her grandmother's new husband, Augusta and her boyfriend, and Ruby's maternal uncle. At age sixteen Ruby gave birth to a daughter.
17	Ruby's grandmother died and Ruby had a second child, by Otis, the younger brother of Ruby's best friend, Willa Mae. Ruby remained living with Augusta, Augusta's boyfriend, Ruby's maternal uncle and her daughters.
18	Ruby fought with Augusta and she and Otis moved into an apartment with her two daughters. Ruby's first daughter's father died. Otis stayed with Ruby and her daughters in the apartment.
19	Ruby broke up with Otis. Ruby and her two daughters joined Magnolia, Magnolia's "husband," and her ten half-siblings. Ruby had a miscarriage.
19½	Ruby left town and moved out of state with her new boyfriend, Earl. She left her daughters with Magnolia and remained out of state for a year. Magnolia then insisted she return home and take care of her children.
20½	Ruby and her daughters moved into a large house rented by Augusta and her mother's brother. It was located next door to Magnolia's house, where Ruby and her children ate. Ruby cleaned for her aunt and uncle, and gave birth to another child, by Otis, who had returned to the household.
21	Ruby and Otis broke up once again. She found a house and moved there with her daughters, Augusta, and Augusta's boyfriend. Ruby did the cleaning, and Augusta cooked. Ruby and Magnolia, who now lived across town, shared child care, and Ruby's cousin's daughter stayed with Ruby.
21½	Augusta and her boyfriend have moved out because they were all fighting, and the two of them wanted to get away from the noise of the children. Ruby has a new boyfriend.

Table 2.

HOUSEHOLD	DOMESTIC ARRANGEMENTS, APRIL 1969	DOMESTIC ARRANGEMENTS, JUNE 1969
1	Magnolia, her husband Calvin, their eight children (4–18.)	Unchanged.
2	Magnolia's sister Augusta, Augusta's boyfriend, Ruby, Ruby's children, Ruby's boyfriend Otis.	Augusta and boyfriend have moved to #3 after a quarrel with Ruby. Ruby and Otis remain in #2.
3	Billy (Augusta's closest friend), Billy's children, Lazar (Magnolia's sister Carrie's husband, living in the basement), Carrie (from time to time—she is an alcoholic).	Augusta and boyfriend have moved to a small, one-room apartment upstairs from Billy.
4	Magnolia's sister Lydia, Lydia's daughters Georgia and Lottie, Lydia's boyfriend, Lottie's daughter.	Lottie and her daughter have moved to an apartment down the street, joining Lottie's girl friend and child. Georgia has moved in with her boyfriend. Lydia's son has moved back into Lydia's home #4.
5	Ruby's friend Willa Mae, her husband and son, her sister, and her brother James (father of Ruby's daughter).	James has moved in with his girl friend, who lives with her sister; James keeps most of his clothes in household #5. James's brother has returned from the army and moved into #5.
6	Eloise (Magnolia's first son's father's sister), her husband, their four young children, their daughter and her son, Eloise's friend Jessie's brother's daughter and her child.	Unchanged.
7	Violet (wife of Calvin's closest friend Cecil, now dead several years), her two sons, her daughter Odessa, and Odessa's four children.	Odessa's son Raymond has fathered Clover's baby. Clover and baby have joined household #7.

establishes a series of sexual partnerships with women, who are in turn living with their own kin or friends or are alone with their children. A result of this pattern is the striking fact that households almost always have men around: male relatives, affines, and boyfriends. These men are often intermittent members of the households, boarders, or friends who come and go—men who usually eat, and sometimes sleep, in these households. Children have constant and close contact with these men, and especially in the case of male relatives, these relationships last over the years. The most predictable residential pattern in The Flats is that individuals reside in the households of their natal kin, or the households of those who raised them, long into their adult years.

Welfare workers, researchers, and landlords in Black ghetto communities have long known that the residence patterns of the poor change frequently and that females play a dominant domestic role. What is much less understood is the relationship between household composition and domestic organization in these communities. Household boundaries are elastic, and no one model of a household, such as the nuclear family, extended family, or matrifocal family, is the norm. What is crucial and enduring is the strength of ties within a kin network; the maintenance of a strong network in turn has consequences for the relationships between the members themselves, as demonstrated in the following discussion of relationships between mothers and fathers and between fathers and their children.

MOTHERS AND FATHERS

Notwithstanding the emptiness and hopelessness of the job experience in the Black community, men and women fall in love and wager buoyant new relationships against the inexorable forces of poverty and racism. At the same time, in dealing with everyday life, Black women and men have developed a number of attitudes and strategies that appear to mitigate against the formation of long-term relationships. Even when a man and woman set up temporary housekeeping arrangements, they both maintain primary social ties with their kin. If other members of a kin network view a particular relationship as a drain on the network's resources, they will act in various and subtle ways to break up the relationship. This is what happened in the life of Julia Ambrose, another resident of The Flats.

When I first met Julia, she was living with her baby, her cousin Teresa, and Teresa's "old man." After several fierce battles with Teresa over the bills, and because of Teresa's hostility toward Julia's boyfriends, Julia decided to move out. She told me she was head over heels in love with Elliot, her child's father, and they had decided to live together.

For several months Julia and Elliot shared a small apartment, and their relationship was strong. Elliot was very proud of his baby. On weekends he would spend an entire day carrying the baby around to his sister's home, where he would show it to his friends on the street. Julia, exhilarated by her independence in having her own place, took great care of the house and her baby. She told me, "Before Elliot came home from work I would have his dinner fixed and the house and kid clean. When he came home he would take his shower and then I'd bring his food to the bed. I'd put the kid to sleep and then get into bed with him. It was fine. We would get in a little piece and then go to sleep. In the morning we'd do the same thing."

After five months, Elliot was laid off from his job at a factory that hires seasonal help. He couldn't find another job, except part-time work for a cab company. Elliot began spending more time away from the house with his friends at the local tavern, and less time with Julia and the baby. Julia finally had to get back "on aid" and Elliot put more of his things back in his sister's home so the social worker wouldn't know he was staying with Julia. Julia noticed changes in Elliot. "If you start necking and doing the same thing that you've been doing with your man, and he don't want it, you know for sure that he is messing with someone else, or don't want you anymore. Maybe Elliot didn't want me in the first place, but maybe he did 'cause he chased me a lot. He wanted me and he didn't want me. I really loved him, but I'm not in love with him now. My feelings just changed. I'm not in love with no man, really. Just out for what I can get from them."

Julia and Elliot stayed together, but she began to hear rumors about him. Her cousin, a woman who had often expressed jealousy toward Julia, followed Elliot in a car and told her that Elliot parked late at night outside the apartment house of his previous girl friend. Julia told me that her cousin was "nothing but a gossip, a newspaper who carried news back and forth," and that her cousin was envious of her having an "old man." Nevertheless, Julia believed the gossip.

After hearing other rumors and gossip about Elliot, Julia said, "I still really liked him, but I wasn't going to let him get the upper hand on me. After I found out that he was messing with someone else, I said to myself, I was doing it too, so what's the help in making a fuss. But after that, I made him pay for being with me!

"I was getting a check every month for rent from welfare and I would take the money and buy me clothes. I bought my own wardrobe and I gave my mother money for keeping the baby while I was working. I worked here and there while I was on aid and they were paying my rent. I didn't really need Elliot, but that was extra money for me. When he asked me what happened to my check I told him I got off and couldn't get back on. My mother knew. She didn't care what I did so long as I didn't let Elliot make an ass out of me. The point is a woman has to have her own pride. She can't let a man rule her. You can't let a man kick you in the tail and tell you what to do. Anytime I can make an ass out of a man, I'm going to do it. If he's doing the same to me, then I'll quit him and leave him alone."

After Elliot lost his job, and kin continued to bring gossip to Julia about how he was playing around with other women, Julia became embittered toward Elliot and was anxious to hurt him. There had been a young Black man making deliveries for a local store who would pass her house every day, and flirt with her. Charles would slow down his truck and honk for Julia when he passed the house. Soon she started running out to talk to him in his truck and decided to "go" with him. Charles liked Julia and brought nice things for her child.

"I put Elliot in a trick," Julia told me soon after she stopped going with Charles. "I knew that Elliot didn't care nothing for me, so I made him jealous. He was nice to the kids, both of them, but he didn't do nothing to show me he was still in love with me. Me and Elliot fought a lot. One night Charles and me went to a motel room and stayed there all night. Mama had the babies. She got mad. But I was trying to hurt Elliot. When I got home, me and Elliot got into it. He called me all kinds of names. I said he might as well leave. But Elliot said he wasn't going nowhere. So he stayed and we'd sleep together, but we didn't do nothing. Then one night something happened. I got pregnant again by Elliot. After I got pregnant, me and Charles quit, and I moved in with a girl friend for a while. Elliot chased after me and we started going back together, but we stayed separate. In my sixth month I moved back in my mother's home with her husband and the kids."

Many young women like Julia feel strongly that they cannot let a man make a fool out of them, and they react quickly and boldly to rumor, gossip, and talk that hurts them. The power that gossip and information have in constraining the duration of sexual relationships is an important cultural phenomenon. But the most important single factor affecting interpersonal relationships between men and woman in The Flats is unemployment. The futility of the job experience for street-corner men in a Black community is sensitively portrayed by Elliot Liebow in *Tally's Corner*. As Liebow (1967: 63) writes, "The job fails the man and the man fails the job." Liebow's discussion (p. 142) of men and jobs leads directly to his analysis of the street-corner male's exploitive relationships with women: "Men not only present themselves as economic exploiters of women but they expect other men to do the same." Ghetto-specific male roles that men try to live up to at home and on the street, and their alleged round-the-clock involvement in peer groups, are interpreted in *Soulside* (Hannerz, 1969) as a threat to marital stability.

Losing a job, then, or being unemployed month after month debilitates one's self-importance and independence and, for men, necessitates sacrificing a role in the economic support of their families. Faced with these familiar patterns in the behavior and status of men, women call upon life experiences in The Flats to guide them. When a man loses his job, that is the time he is most likely to begin "messing around."

And so that no man appears to have made a fool of them, women respond with vengeance, out of pride and self-defense. Another young woman in The Flats, Ivy Rodgers, told me about the time she left her two children in The Flats with her mother and took off for Indiana with Jimmy River, a young man she had fallen in love with "the first sight I seen."

Jimmy asked Ivy to go to Gary, Indiana, where his family lived. "I just left the kids with my mama. I didn't even tell her I was going. My checks kept coming so she had food for the kids, but I didn't know he let his people tell him what to do. While he was in Gary, Jimmy started messing with another woman. He said he wasn't, but I caught him. I quit him, but when he told me he wasn't messing, I loved him so much I took him back. Then I got to thinking about it. I had slipped somewhere. I had let myself go. Seems like I forgot that I wasn't going to let Jimmy or any man make an ass out of me. But he sure was doing it. I told Jimmy that if he loved me, he would go and see my people, take them things, and tell them we were getting married. Jimmy didn't want to go back to The Flats, but I tricked him and told him I really wanted to visit. I picked out my ring and Jimmy paid thirty dollars on it and I had him buy my outfit that we was getting married in. He went along with it. What's so funny was when we come here and he said to me, 'You ready to go back?' and I told him, 'No, I'm not going back. I never will marry you.' "

Forms of social control in the larger society also work against successful marriages in The Flats. In fact, couples rarely chance marriage unless a man has a job; often the job is temporary, low-paying, and insecure, and the worker is arbitrarily laid off whenever he is not needed. Women come to realize that welfare benefits and ties within kin networks provide greater security for them and their children. In addition, caretaker agencies such as public welfare are insensitive to individual attempts for social mobility. A woman may be immediately cut off the welfare rolls when a husband returns home from prison or the army, or if she gets married. Unless there is either a significant change in employment opportunities for the urban poor or a livable guaranteed minimum income, it is unlikely that urban low-income Blacks will form lasting conjugal units.

Marriage and its accompanying expectations of a home, a job, and a family built around the husband and wife have come to stand for an individual's desire to break out of poverty. It implies the willingness of an individual to remove himself from the daily obligations of his kin network. People in The Flats recognize that one cannot simultaneously meet kin expectations and the expectations of a spouse. Cooperating kinsmen continually attempt to draw new people into their personal network; but at the same time they fear the loss of a central, resourceful member in the network. The following passages are taken from the detailed residence life history of Ruby Banks. Details of her story were substantiated by discussions with her mother, her aunt, her daughter's father, and her sister.

"Me and Otis could be married, but they all ruined that. Aunt Augusta told Magnolia that he was no good. Magnolia was the fault of it, too. They don't want to see me married! Magnolia knows that it be money getting away from her. I couldn't spend the time with her and the kids and be giving her the money that I do now. I'd have my husband to look after. I couldn't go where she want me to go. I couldn't come every time she call me, like if Calvin took sick or the kids took sick, or if she took sick. That's all the running I do now. I couldn't do that. You think a man would put up with as many times as I go over her house in a cab, giving half my money to her all the time? That's the reason they don't want me married. You think a man would let Aunt Augusta come into the house and take food out of the icebox from his kids? They thought that way ever since I came up.

"They broke me and Otis up. They kept telling me that he didn't want me, and that he didn't want the responsibility. I put him out and I cried all night long. And I really did love him. But Aunt Augusta and others kept fussing and arguing so I went and quit him. I would have got married a long time ago to my first baby's daddy, but Aunt Augusta was the cause of that, telling Magnolia that he was too old for me. She's been jealous of me since the day I was born.

"Three years after Otis I met Earl. Earl said he was going to help pay for the utilities. He was going to get me some curtains and pay on my couch. While Earl was working he was so good to me and my children that Magnolia and them started worrying all over again. They sure don't want me married. The same thing that happened to Otis happened to many of my boyfriends. And I ain't had that many men. I'm tired of them bothering me with their problems when I'm trying to solve my own problems. They tell me that Earl's doing this and that, seeing some girl.

"They look for trouble to tell me every single day. If I ever marry, I ain't listening to what nobody say. I just listen to what he say. You have to get along the best way you know how, and forget about your people. If I got married they would talk, like they are doing now, saying, 'He ain't no good, he's been creeping on you. I told you once not to marry him. You'll end up right back on aid.' If I ever get married, I'm leaving town!"

Ruby's account reveals the strong conflict between kin-based domestic units and lasting ties between husbands and wives. When a mother in The Flats has a relationship with an economically nonproductive man, the relationship saps the resources of others in her domestic network. Participants in the network act to break up such relationships, to maintain kin-based household groupings over the life cycle, in order to maximize potential resources and the services they hope to exchange. Similarly, a man's participation is expected in his kin network, and it is understood that he should not dissipate his services and finances to a sexual or marital relationship. These forms of social control made Ruby afraid to take the risks necessary to break out of the cycle of poverty. Instead, she chose the security and stability of her kin group. Ruby, recognizing that to make a marriage last she would have to move far away from her kin, exclaimed, "If I ever get married, I'm leaving town!" While this study was in progress, Ruby did get married, and she left the state with her husband and her youngest child that very evening.

FATHERS AND CHILDREN

People in The Flats show pride in all their kin, and particularly new babies born into their kinship networks. Mothers encourage sons to have babies, and even more important, men coax their "old ladies" to have their babies. The value placed on children, the love, attention, and affection children receive from women and men, and the web of social relationships spun from the birth of a child are all basic to the high birthrate among the poor.

The pride that kinsmen take in the children of their sons and brothers is seen best in the pleasure that the mothers and sisters of these men express. Such pride was apparent during a visit I made to Alberta Cox's home. She introduced me to her nineteen-year-old son Nate and added immediately, "He's a daddy and his baby is four months old." Then she pointed to her twenty-two-year-old son Mac and said, "He's a daddy three times over." Mac smiled and said, "I'm no daddy," and his friend in the kitchen said, "Maybe going on four times, Mac." Alberta said, "Yes you are. Admit it, boy!" At that point Mac's grandmother rolled back in her rocker and said, "I'm a grandmother many times over, and it make me proud." A friend of Alberta's told me later that Alberta wants her sons to have babies because she thinks it will make them more responsible. Although she usually dislikes the women her sons go with, claiming they are "no-good trash," Alberta accepts the babies and asks to care for them whenever she has a chance.

Although Blacks, like most Americans, acquire kin through their mothers and fathers, the economic insecurity of the Black male and the availability of welfare to the mother-child unit make it very difficult for an unemployed Black husband-father to compete with a woman's kin for authority and control over her children. As we have seen, women seek to be independent, but also, in order to meet everyday needs, they act to strengthen their ties with their kin and within their domestic network. Though these two strategies, especially in the context of male joblessness, may lead to the breakup of a young couple, a father will maintain his ties with his children. The husband-father role may be limited, but, contrary to the stereotype of Black family life, it is not only viable but culturally significant.

Very few young couples enter into a legal marriage in The Flats, but a father and his kin can sustain a continuing relationship with the father's children if the father has acknowledged paternity, if his kin have activated their claims on the child, and if the mother has drawn these people into her personal network. Widely popularized and highly misleading statistics on female-headed households have contributed to the assumption that Black children derive nothing of sociological importance from their fathers. To the contrary, in my recent study of domestic life among the poor in a Black community in the Midwest (Stack, 1972), I found that 70 percent of the fathers of 1,000 children on welfare recognized their children and provided them with kinship affiliations. But because many of these men have little or no access to steady and productive employment, out of the 699 who acknowledged paternity, only 84 (12 percent) gave any substantial financial support to their children. People in The Flats believe a father should help his child, but they know that the mother cannot count on his help. Community expectations of fathers do not generally include the father's *duties* in relation to a child; they do, however, assume the responsibilities of the father's kin. Kinship through males in The Flats is reckoned through a chain of acknowledged genitors, but social fatherhood is shared by the genitor with his kin, and with the mother's husband or with her boyfriends.

Although the authority of a father over his genealogical children or his wife's other children is limited, neither the father's interest in his child nor the desire of his kin to help raise the child strains the stability of the domestic network. Otis's kin were drawn into Ruby's personal network through his claims on her children, and through the long, close friendship between Ruby and Otis's sister, Willa Mae. Like many fathers in The Flats, Otis maintained close contact with his children, and provided goods and care for them even when he and Ruby were not on speaking terms. One time when Otis and Ruby separated, Otis stayed in a room in Ruby's uncle's house next door to Ruby's mother's house. At that time Ruby's children were being kept by Magnolia each day while Ruby went to school to finish working toward her high school diploma. Otis was out of work, and he stayed with Ruby's uncle over six months helping Magnolia care for his children. Otis's kin were proud of the daddy he was, and at times suggested they should take over the raising of Otis and Ruby's children. Ruby and other mothers know well that those people you count on to share in the care and nurturing of your children are also those who are rightfully in a position to judge and check upon how you carry out the duties of a mother. Shared responsibilities of motherhood in The Flats imply both a help and a check on how one assumes the parental role.

Fathers like Otis, dedicated to maintaining ties with their children, learn that the relationship they create with their child's mother largely determines the role they may assume in their child's life. Jealousy between men makes it extremely difficult for fathers to spend time with their children if the mother has a boyfriend, but as Otis said to me, "When Ruby doesn't have any old man then she starts calling on me, asking for help, and telling me to do something for my kids." Between such times, when a man or a woman does not have an ongoing sexual relationship, some mothers call upon the fathers of their children and temporarily "choke" these men with their personal needs and the needs of the children. At these times, men and women reinforce their fragile but continuing relationship, and find themselves empathetic friends who can be helpful to one another.

A mother generally regards her children's father as a friend of the family whom she can recruit for help, rather than as a father failing his parental duties. Although fathers voluntarily help out with their children, many fathers cannot be depended upon as a steady source of help. Claudia Williams talked to me about Harold, the father of her two children. "Some days he be coming over at night saying, 'I'll see to the babies and you can lay down and rest, honey,' treating me real nice. Then maybe I don't even see him for two or three months. There's no sense nagging Harold. I just treat him as some kind of friend even if he is the father of my babies." Since Claudia gave birth to Harold's children, both of them have been involved in other relationships. When either of them is involved with someone else, this effectively cuts Harold off from his children. Claudia says, "My kids don't need their daddy's help, but if he helps out then I help him out, too. My kids are well behaved, and I know they make Harold's kinfolk proud."

CONCLUSIONS

The view of Black women as represented in their own words and life histories coincides with that presented by Joyce Ladner: "One of the chief characteristics defining the Black woman is her [realistic approach] to her [own] resources. Instead of becoming resigned to her fate, she has always sought creative solutions to her problems. The ability to utilize her existing resources and yet maintain a forthright determination to struggle against the racist society in whatever overt and subtle ways necessary is one of her major attributes" (Ladner, 1971: 276–77).

I have particularly emphasized those strategies that women can employ to maximize their independence, acquire and maintain domestic authority, limit (but positively evaluate) the role of husband and father, and strengthen ties with kin. The last of these—maximizing relationships in the domestic network—helps to account for patterns of Black family life among the urban poor more adequately than the concepts of nuclear or matrifocal family. When economic resources are greatly limited, people need help from as many others as possible. This requires expanding their kin networks—increasing the number of people they hope to be able to count on. On the one hand, female members of a network may act to break up a relationship that has become a drain on their resources. On the other, a man is expected to contribute to his own kin network, and it is assumed that he should not dissipate his services and finances to a marital relationship. At the same time, a woman will continue to seek aid from the man who has fathered her children, thus building up her own network's resources. She also expects something of his kin, especially his mother and sisters. Women continually activate these lines to bring kin and friends into the network of exchange and obligation. Most often, the biological father's female relatives are poor and also try to expand their network and increase the number of people they can depend on.

Clearly, economic pressures among cooperating kinsmen in the Black community work against the loss of either males or females—through marriage or other long-term relationships—from the kin network. The kin-based cooperative network represents the collective adaptations to poverty of the men, women, and children within the Black community. Loyalties and dependencies toward kinsmen offset the ordeal of unemployment and racism. To cope with the everyday demands of ghetto life, these networks have evolved patterns of co-residence; elastic household boundaries; life-long, if intermittent, bonds to three-generation households; social constraints on the role of the husband-father within the mother's domestic group; and the domestic authority of women.

NOTES

1. This work is based on a recent urban anthropological study of poverty and domestic life of urban-born Black Americans who were raised on public welfare and whose parents had migrated from the South to a single community in the Urban North (Stack, 1972). Now adults in their twenties to forties, they are raising their own children on welfare in The Flats. All personal and place names in this paper are fictitious.

Review Questions

1. While place of residence and family may coincide for many people in our society, for the poor community described by Stack they do not. What can we say about the meaning of the term "family" in light of this fact?

2. What is the importance of economic factors in shaping both the residence patterns and family interactions of residents of The Flats?

3. What are the roles played by men in the family system of this poor neighborhood? What features of our society affect which family roles men occupy and how they are performed?

4. Despite the fact that the poor families described here have developed flexible household boundaries and extensive networks of kin support and obligations not characteristic of the nuclear family, family life in The Flats can be seen as embodying and responding to many of the central values and norms of the family institution of the larger culture. Give examples of conformity to cultural norms and values.

CHILDCARE RESPONSIBILITIES OF PART-TIME AND SINGLE FATHERS

Kristine M. Rosenthal and Harry F. Keshet

· · ·

For a long time fathers were little encouraged to participate in the life of their children, and the effects of this participation were little understood. The 1960s produced a great deal of literature focused on the detrimental effects of father absence, but it has been difficult to distinguish these from the effects of the severely reduced economic circumstances of mother-headed families. In several studies which controlled for socioeconomic variables, the absence of the father appeared to have no detrimental effect on the children's development (Nye, 1957; Parry and Phufl, 1963; Crain and Stamn, 1965).

A decade later, the rapidly increasing rate of divorce, the changing ideology about sex-role stereotypes, the new economic and social independence of women, and the attendant pressures for sex-role equality all have contributed to a developing redefinition of the fathering role. There has been new interest in the importance of fathers for children (Biller and Meredith, 1974; Lynn, 1974) and a new consciousness about males participating in the nurturant tasks of family life. "Parenting has become a desirable male role for many, and fathers are accepting major parenting responsibility within the two parent family context and the single parent context" (Warren, 1976).

For many men this new involvement in the fathering role is a direct consequence of marital separation. Faced with the choice of seeing the relationship with their children erased through lack of contact and intimacy, some fathers are opting for the still difficult and strange role of daily caretaker. The number of children who live with a divorced father has tripled in the past ten years, although that still represents only one-tenth of the number of children who live with their divorced mother. Joint custody and informal sharing of childcare are becoming more common among young divorced couples with children. Unlike the once-or-twice-a-month visiting fathers whose parenting role diminishes over time, involved fathers, like single mothers, find themselves with a role overload. They must learn to coordinate work obligations, social life needs, and attempts to create a new family for themselves with the continuing daily responsibilities of childcare (Keshet and Rosenthal, 1978).

Kristine M. Rosenthal and Harry F. Keshet, "Childcare Responsibilities of Part-Time and Single Fathers," *Alternative Life Styles*, 1 (November 1978), 465–91.

The present study was designed to determine the effects of childcare involvement on the lifestyles of young fathers. One hundred and twenty-seven separated or divorced fathers were interviewed about their childcare responsibilities. Each man had at least one child aged three to seven. Twenty-eight of the fathers saw their children at least every other weekend, for a total of six or less days each month—these we have called the "occasional" fathers; 21 of the fathers spent no less then seven days a month, and no more than 13 days with their children—they are the "quartertime" fathers. Twenty-nine of the fathers in the sample spent half of each month with their children, and the remaining 49 are full-time fathers. All respondents live in the Greater Boston Area. They represent a highly educated urban population, close to half of the sample having completed, or about to complete, graduate or professional training. The majority are in professional or semiprofessional occupations (40 percent and 16 percent), another 20 percent are in business, and 16 percent have blue-collar jobs or work in crafts.

The joint-care fathers in the sample had the highest concentration of professional men. This group, as distinct from the full-time fathers, can be assumed to have taken on their childcare voluntarily and to have some flexibility in their work schedules. Eighty-three percent of the fathers worked full-time or more. With increased childcare time the work hours tended to decrease. Income also fluctuated with childcare time. The fact that full-time and half-time fathers average considerably less income gives us some indication of the effect of childcare on the work lives of actively parenting men.

The conflicts between work and childcare experienced by these fathers are similar to those reported frequently by single mothers. Men who during their married lives expected their family to adjust to the demands of their work suddenly find themselves having to coordinate and juggle the schedules of work and childcare. Here accepted standards of nine-to-five duties begin to seem unreasonable. As one father employed by a large engineering firm told us:

> My boss is old-fashioned, he does not care what work I actually do, but he must see me there from nine to five. It is very inconvenient for me, and I knew I could get as much or more work done on a more flexible schedule, but he would not hear of it.

Other fathers who had more work independence found that it was their own expectations they had to overcome:

> I had to give up this image of being a scholar, sitting in the library till all hours of the night. Others in my department did that and they were family men too. But pretty soon I only came in to teach and did some extra work when [son] was not with me. I started to enjoy being at home. After all he would grow up and I might have missed all that, the library would always be there.

The fathers report passing up promotions that might mean a move away from the children, reducing their work hours, and choosing work for its compatibility with the demands of childcare. We must not underestimate the importance of this change for highly achieving professional men. Socialization for career performance is one of the outstanding features of male identity (Pleck, 1975). Much has been written about the general importance of work as a source of well-being for men—work as a source of life purpose (Morse & Weiss, 1955), as a prized self-image (Wilensky, 1966), and as a validating experience (Rainwater, 1974).

The reduction of work involvement has two sources. On one hand, it is a practical response to the overload of demands on the father's time. Even with daycare services, babysitters, and the help of the extended family, although the last is rare for middle-class men, much time and energy are absorbed by the child's needs. On the other hand, as indicated later, eventually childcare becomes defined as another job for which the father has contracted. When this happens the rewards of doing that job well and feeling competent in it begin to compete with work satisfaction, thus reducing the salience of occupational role for the men.

·   ·   ·

[T]he initial feelings of inadequacy which many fathers experience when doing "women's work" can be more easily overcome when the childcare tasks are seen as a legitimate new assignment to be "worked on." New definitions of fathering have to be developed. "Getting a divorce really made me pause and think what is my role as a father; am I any good at raising the children? I often found myself lacking." But only at first. With additional experience comes competence and self-assurance.

For men, the issue of parenting by themselves is the issue of competence and the ways in which they understand competent performance in caring for and relating to children. Women evaluate parenting more often through their feeling relationship with the child.

The issue of competence and efficacy dominates the self-image of males. The cultural image of competence is cold and impersonal, but it also can be a way to think about feelings and to begin to learn how to function interpersonally. A man who begins to parent and who can meet the purely practical needs of children—bathing, feeding, getting them to school on time—begins to feel more effective. This sense of effectiveness translates into good feelings about the children and good feelings which he learns that the children have about him. The crisis often comes when the needs to be satisfied are purely emotional—the temper tantrum is the most trying event for a newly independent father.

> It's when she cried and I didn't know what to do for her, I didn't understand it. So I would try to figure it out by trial and error. Did I do something bad? I go through a series of hypotheses. It took a while but I finally learned how to figure out what's bothering her. I feel a lot better now. I can get an idea what's upsetting her now. I also can get her to tell me what's wrong and I can generally do something about it.

. . .

Once the feelings of competence begin to be introduced into the area of dealing with children's emotions, reinforced by the child's well-being, the whole area of emotions becomes less threatening for men. Each father can develop his own criteria for doing a good job as a father in the way he relates to the children.

For men socialized to believe that feelings must be kept hidden and are a barrier to effective functioning, experiencing competency in this area can be a source of positive self-regard.

> Suddenly I found I could really do it. I saw that I could take care of the girls and respond to their emotional needs as well as run the house.

Bringing the perimeters and criteria of work performance, familiar to men, to the parenting role appears to make men at ease with their new obligations. It also gives the parenting role an external legitimacy and internal satisfaction which undermines the impact of work socialization for men, and frees them to develop a more individually determined balance of work and family commitment.

What remains to be seen is whether these individual adjustments can be maintained over time against the pressures of employees' expectations, especially when new relationships with women may reduce the father's family obligations.

THE CHANGING PATTERNS OF INTIMACY

Freud has been widely quoted as having said the two components of mental health are the ability to work and the ability to love. Both these functions are disrupted by marital breakup. At the time of separation it is difficult for many men to imagine that they could ever again feel closeness with a woman and plan a future with her. Even men who are involved with another sexual partner at the time of separation are wary of commitment. In the case of men who did not desire or initiate the divorce proceedings the process of psychological separation is even slower. These men often have hopes and expectations of reconciliation which to an objective observer appear clearly unrealistic. While the legal separation or divorce decree entitles a man to take up his single life, many are unaware that the psychological divorce may take much longer. Bohannan (1970), in describing the "six stations" of divorce, places psychic divorce at the very last, defining it as a slow process of regaining individual autonomy. Waller (1967) also describes final estrangement between the ex-spouses as complete only some time after the partners have entered new social worlds.

The divorced men themselves describe this time as one of depression or apathy. They may be tired or rushed, transient in their living arrangements, or burdened with childcare. All these become reasons to defend against an immediate involvement with a new partner. Somehow, however, new relationships do get established. We know that approximately 50 percent of the people who get divorced remarry within three years (Glick and Norton, 1977), so that not long after the separation—needing to reassert themselves as attractive males—men begin "dating." The term "dating" is used self-consciously and evokes all the insecurities, hesitations, and posturing that are part of its adolescent origins. It is a time of "trying out" a new self, even though most divorced people do not really enter the world of single people, but that of the formerly married (Hunt, 1966; Cox, 1978).

The relationships retain the status for as long as the dating couple avoids the formation of any mutual ties or obligations, even though at any given moment in time the date might fulfill all the functions of a temporary marriage mate. It is important to the partners that they maintain separate residences and have separate friends and activities. The purpose of the separateness is to underlie the "casual" nature of the relationship. The man is reestablishing his *independence*, which might be easily threatened. It is understood that the relationship could be easily terminated if either party so desired. There should be no mutual property, no need to explain to the children why "she" is not there on Sundays anymore—in other words, as little as possible which might be reminiscent of the marital breakup.

It is difficult if not impossible to adhere to such a definition of dating for a long time with one person. Deliberately or not, communalities develop, friends and children begin to expect the presence of the date, comfortable habits set in. Men who explicitly and determinably wish to prevent such a development, find themselves in the peculiar, and often hard to explain, situation of wanting to break off a relationship precisely because it feels comfortable, and because they are beginning to depend on it for both emotional sustenance and real help around the house. The experience leaves the woman bewildered and bitter. "What went wrong?"

> He wants to break off just when everything is going so well, the children have finally gotten to like me, and we've been so comfortable together, why just last week he said he does not know how he would have managed without me.

It is not often that she can get a satisfactory explanation. "I am just not ready," the man is likely to say obliquely, or else he disagrees over some small matter to create an opportunity to divest himself of the encroaching commitment.

· · ·

[F]athers after divorce often give a great deal of power to their children and become dependent on them emotionally. Following the natural status position of father and child, this situation can be gradually adjusted in accord with the strengthening self-image of the father. The situation is different vis-à-vis an emotional involvement with a new lover. The father's newly emerged independence is threatened because he recognizes aspects of real dependency in his parental responsibilities. Furthermore, to accept and recognize this dependency may undermine his still-vulnerable masculinity. Thus the father who is in fact engaged in the process of personal growth through his childcare adjustments is wary of being interfered with through a new relationship with a woman. . . . Given this configuration, divorce may, in part, serve the need for autonomy in the area of emotional and parental coping, allowing necessary competence to emerge. Once a man feels good about himself, and secure in his familial capabilities, he may be much more available for a new love relationship.

DATING PATTERNS

Relationships of short duration, or multiple dating, serve to enforce the barriers between new potential partners. All the men interviewed had, shortly after separation, dated more than one woman at a time. The pattern, which appears to repeat, begins with a fairly intense involvement immediately after separation which has the quality of a "port in a storm." The woman in question is often more a confidante than a lover: she listens to complaints against the ex-spouse, the legal system, and whatever other forces seem to conspire against the newly divorced man. She is a witness to his insecurities and a focus in gropings for a new identity. When that first stage is past, however, and some sort of emotional equilibrium is reached, this is rarely the relationship that lasts. For men anxious to try out new powers, the woman who has witnessed his setbacks is not the ideal partner. The time of quiet recuperation with one sympathetic and supportive woman is often followed by frequent and varied dating. After the first year, relationships become more exclusive and of longer duration and may lead to a more serious partnership or cohabitation.

•   •   •

It is also likely that men use their prerogative of seeking out new partners less out of real sexual interest, and more as a reminder to both themselves and their primary partner that they are not in fact married. Such a reminder provides the safety margin that at an earlier stage required the actual breaking off of the dating relationship.

CHARACTERISTICS OF NEW PARTNERS

It was common for the men we interviewed to date women with certain social characteristics. They were frequently considerably younger than the men, of similar social class, and, whether single, divorced, or separated, were unlikely to have children of their own. Only a third of the respondents reported forming "serious relationships" with women who had children. Although such relationships were more common for men in the early stages of

separation and seem to represent a desire to reconstruct the marriage configuration, they generally did not last. Whatever the attraction of the ready-
made family—the woman whose life is set up for childcare, who can usually
include the children of the separated father in the weekly activities, and who
has a child-equipped house—it does not last. In the long run, such relationships presented difficulties in coordination and planning for the two partners.

· · ·

Dating women of similar social class characteristics, often of similar work
interests or professional concerns, increases the opportunity to separate a
sense of oneself as a single adult from that of a part-time parent. This is true
both emotionally and in terms of time flexibility. Many of the fathers
needed the support of this love relationship immediately after delivering the
children to the ex-spouse—a time of more than ordinary stress.

Dating women who did not have children of their own allowed for more
time flexibility. Since most fathers take their children on the weekend, dating a woman without children of her own made it easier to plan the time
alone on the weekdays when neither had other obligations. It also made it
possible for the woman to be of company and assistance to the father when
the children were with him and to sleep over on the nights when the children
were not there. Divorced women with similar childcare arrangements were
likely to resent having to spend time with someone else's children on the
weekends when they themselves were free from childcare. One father complained that he had stopped dating a woman with children partly because it
was so difficult to have time alone together.

REFAMILYING

Eighty percent of all divorced people eventually remarry. Remarriage often
follows a period of cohabitation. By the end of the second year of separation many men are seriously considering living with a woman.

· · ·

The newly separated man, anxious to make his quarters feel like home for
himself and his children, is . . . [not] likely to make himself a part-time in-
habitant of his lover's house. It is she, therefore, who must come to his
house—a situation that she may be unused to but one that many women do
in fact find intriguing or different. She is likely to find there a much more
domesticated man, one who is aware of whether or not the dishes are
washed, one who does not automatically assume that she will take on the
homemaking (in its true sense) responsibilities, one who may in fact be
somewhat possessive of his newly acquired housekeeping skills. Many fathers are still proving to their ex-spouse and children that they are competent parents; still proving to themselves that they can maintain control over

their domestic and parental lives; their unwillingness to return to the division of roles which characterized their marriage may present a very different possibility of coexistence to a new female lover.

•   •   •

The case of men and their children cohabiting with a new sexual partner provides us with an opportunity to view a family situation which is almost the reverse of the traditional marriage. The children are first and foremost the responsibility of the father. The female partner is usually economically independent, having work of her own which existed prior to the family situation and which continues to have priority. Not only are the house and children a major responsibility of the father, but he also views it as his function to coordinate the members of the household and make sure that they feel good about each other. This is the "expressive" leadership function described by Parsons and Bales (1955) as the very core of the wife's role in the family. He retains his dominant status, however, both in the family as head of the household and in the larger society. The woman's socialization may lead her to expect to take on the mother and wife role, but the structural conditions of the particular circumstance force her to deal with these expectations in a new and innovative way. We have here, then, within the family a microcosm of an experimental situation in which the roles are reversed without a corresponding major change in the wider social structures.

•   •   •

Younger, childless women, who are more likely to have grown up with expectations of independence and self-assertion, are better equipped emotionally to function within this configuration. It is not unlikely that divorced men who have this mode of coping with their new state gravitate toward this type of women. Men who, on the other hand, are anxious to replicate their previous marital arrangements may be more likely to marry more traditional women or ones who have children of their own from a previous marriage.

ADJUSTMENTS TO COHABITATION

The transition from a dating relationship—in which the woman has her own home to retreat to and functions more like a guest in the father's house—to cohabitation is a major transition because it puts a strain on the equilibrium that has been worked out. Women who have learned to be sensitive to the autonomy needs of the man in and out of the house, and to their own secondary position within the new family, may find that their natural inclination or expectation to take over family responsibilities becomes very strong when the cues for separateness are diminished. In other words, once moved in, can the not-quite stepmother maintain her nontraditional role within the household configuration? And can the man in turn respect her autonomy and maintain his own functioning as the responsible parent despite the clear temptation to increase the reliance on the new partner to a degree which might naturally slip into a relationship reminiscent of the discarded marriage? The couple must evidence a great deal of self-awareness and commitment to the new lifestyle in order to defend themselves against these changes.

• • •

There are many aspects of role reversal entailed in sharing parenting with a divorced father. The tone of the relationship is generally set by the fact that the new woman moves into a house already occupied by the father. The house was chosen for its suitability for his childcare obligations, distance from the children's mother or school, and space for their visits, and has been tested by his developing and routinizing his parenting tasks there. If a move is made it is usually for the same reasons as the above; that is, the father's parenting obligations set the perimeters of their decisions.

• • •

Fathers are especially conscious of needing to reassure the children, and perhaps their ex-spouses as well, that the new partner will not usurp the father's time and attention or even the physical space in the house. Many men admitted favoring the children when their lover first moved in. It was difficult to distinguish how much such behavior was meant to reassure the children and how much it was due to their own insecurity in the new situation. The children provided an excuse for creating some real and emotional barriers against the increasing intimacy.

Men who have only recently gained control over their children and a sense of competence in their parenting roles are generally happy to share housekeeping tasks, but are much less eager to relinquish their direct relationship with the children. "I would consult with [her] about helping me with childcare, but basically I was still the parent and they were still my responsibility." There was, in fact, often a special effort on the part of the father to let the children know that he, the father, would continue to be the "real" parent and was not abdicating his rights and responsibilities vis-à-vis the children. At the same time the cohabiting partner had lost the status of a guest in the house which might have given her special privileges and instead had assumed the more modest role of a helper. This is the new family socialization which takes place and further reinforces the role reversal we have described. The new woman is *not*, strictly speaking, a mother substitute, because in most cases the children have a perfectly adequate mother. Instead, *she shares the fathering role*, emulates his behavior, relies on his approval. As the husband once babysat for his wife, she now "babysits" for him. The traditional fatherly functions of driving children to school or picking them up are often taken over by the new partner.

*   *   *

It was difficult for many of the fathers clearly to define a role for their partner that did not in some way seem to displace either themselves or their ex-spouse. In many cases there was a great fear of engendering even the slightest conflict between the partner and the ex-spouse, and possibly threatening the often informal childcare agreement.

In the majority of the cases, the respondents definitely defined their partners as helpers but not as parents or even parent substitutes, thus explicitly limiting their emotional involvement with the child and reemphasizing their own importance as a biological parent.

> I am not looking for a mother substitute for [daughter]. She already has a mother that she is very close to.

> We are struggling about the extent to which she [partner] wants to be involved [with the children] and can be psychologically involved given her position [here the father emphasized the insecurity and possible transience of the new relationship].

The children themselves participated in many of these struggles. They, too, were wary of forming new dependencies on people whose permanence and status in their lives was not to be trusted. They were often reluctant to allow the partner to care for them even after having known them for years. They competed for the father's attention and protected their special relationship. They often rejected the attempts of the new parent surrogate for emotional closeness, affection, or direction. All respondents reported such experiences of rejection of their partners. Fathers of male children reported this more frequently than fathers of female children.

Despite the resistance, despite the caution and the jealousies, somehow during the first year of living together emotional closeness does become possible between the new woman and the children. Affection becomes openly shared; children freely express their concern for and interest in the newly accepted family member. The relationship appears more mutual and independent of the father and his mediation. The women are able to relate directly to the children and view them as their friends. In many cases, the fathers, having overcome their initial possessiveness, are able to encourage the developing bonds with the children and can now appreciate, unthreatened, the contribution that their partners make to the childcare.

*   *   *

The acknowledgment of an independent relationship between the lover and the children indicates a definite shift in the woman's role in the household and indicates the growth of new family-like relationships.

At this point the partner becomes much more active in the parenting. Fathers become freer in discussing problems of child-rearing with their partners and consulting them on issues of discipline and authority. Discussion of styles of parenting and standards for children's behavior is also more frequent, indicating the greater participation on the part of the lovers in the direct dealing with the children. The women in turn feel freer to voice their own opinions. As the living situation continues the sharing becomes more total, and the ties of family member to family member become more balanced.

It remains to be seen whether within this reconstituted family the redesigned roles of parental involvement and responsibility, based on the new emotional growth of the fathers and the consciousness of women as independent individuals with their own rights and priorities, can be maintained even when they run counter to the expected family functioning. It may be that the drastic reduction of the responsibilities on the part of the woman for the maintenance of the family unit and the increased involvement of the father are necessary preconditions for the development of a truly egalitarian or symmetrical marriage. It will also be interesting to see whether these innovative roles are maintained when the couple begins to have children of their own, in addition to the father's previous offspring.

•   •   •

REFERENCES

Biller, H., and D. Meredith (1974) *Father Power*, New York: David McKay.

Bohannan, P. (1970) *Divorce and After*. Garden City, NY: Doubleday.

Cox, F. D. (1978) *Human Intimacy: Marriage, the Family and its Meaning*. St. Paul, MN: West.

Crain, A. J., and C. S. Stamn (1965) "Intermittent absence of fathers and children's perceptions of parents." *J. of Marriage and the Family* 27: 344–347.

Glick, P. C., and A. Norton (1977) "Marrying, divorcing and living together in the U.S. today." *Population Bull.* 32 (October).

Hunt, M. (1966) *The World of the Formerly Married*. New York: McGraw-Hill.

Keshet, H., and K. Rosenthal (1978) "Fathering after marital separation." *Social Work* 23 (January): 11–18.

Lynn, D. (1974) *The Father: His Role in Child Development*. Monterey, CA: Brooks-Cole.

Morse, N. C., and R. S. Weiss (1955) "The function and meaning of work and the job." *Amer. Soc. Rev.* 20: 191–198.

Nye, F. I. (1957) "Child adjustment in broken and in unhappy broken homes." *Marriage and Family Living* 19: 356–361.

O'Neill, N., and G. O'Neill (1972) *Open Marriage*. New York: Avon.

Parry, J. B., and E. M. Phufl (1963) "Adjustment of children in 'sole' and 'remarriage' homes." *Marriage and Family Living* 25: 221–223.

Parsons T., and R. Bales (1955) *Family, Socialization and Interaction Process*. New York: Free Press.

Pleck, J. (1975) "Work and family roles: from sex-patterned segregation to integration." Paper presented at the annual American Sociological Association meetings. San Francisco, August.

Rainwater, L. (1974) "Work, well-being and family life," in J. O'Toole (ed.) *Work and the Quality of Life*. Cambridge, MA: MIT Press.

Roy, R., and D. Roy (1970) *Honest Sex*. New York: New American Library.

Waller, W. (1967) *The Old Love and the New*. Carbondale, IL: Southern Illinois University Press.

Warren, R. L. (1976) *Family Maintenance in Father Only Families*. Study Project, Brandeis University.

Wilensky, H. L. (1966) "Work as a social problem," in H. S. Becker (ed.) *Social Problems: a Modern Approach*. New York: John Wiley.

Review Questions

1. Many of the fathers in Rosenthal and Keshet's study had difficulty dealing with intimacy with their children as well as some of the mundane aspects of child-care until they viewed them as assignments to be "worked on." Why might we have expected such a response?

2. What impact did parenting have on the work roles of the fathers?

3. What part did parenting play in the fathers' establishment of new dating and love relationships?

4. Were new partners for the fathers likely to be mother substitutes? Why, or why not?

5. In what ways did father-child interaction both affect and come to be affected by the emergent father role?

Suggested Readings: Interaction in Institutional Contexts: Family

Goode, William. *After Divorce*. New York: Free Press, 1956.

————, "The Theoretical Importance of Love," *American Sociological Review*, 24 (February 1959), 38–47.

Gutman, Herbert G. *The Black Family in Slavery and Freedom, 1750–1925*. New York: Pantheon, 1976.

Lopata, Helena Z. *Occupation Housewife*. New York: Oxford University Press, 1971.

Motz, Annabelle B. "The Family as a Company of Players," *Transaction*, 2 (March–April 1965), 27–30.

Rubin, Lillian Breslow. *Worlds of Pain: Life in the Working-Class Family*. New York: Basic Books, 1976.

Scanzoni, John. *Sexual Bargaining: Power Politics in the American Marriage*, 2nd ed. Englewood Cliffs, N.J.: Prentice-Hall, 1982.

Stack, Carol B. *All Our Kin: Strategies for Survival in a Black Community*. New York: Harper & Row, 1974.

Staples, Robert, ed. *The Black Family: Essays and Studies*. Belmont, Calif.: Wadsworth, 1971.

Stein, Peter, ed. *Single Life: Unmarried Adults in Social Context*. New York: St. Martin's Press, 1981.

Waller, Willard, "The Rating and Dating Complex," *The American Sociological Review*, 2 (1937), 727–734.

B. Education

THE CONCEPT OF EDUCATION AS A SET OF ACTIVITIES SEPARATE FROM WHAT TRANspires in the course of everyday interactions is relatively new. Although all societies throughout human history have developed family systems, it is only in the past two or three centuries that the roles of teacher and student have occupied more than a tiny fraction of the population. Schooling has become so widespread and highly valued today that we can scarcely imagine that it was not always so. We begin dividing our time and attention between the family and the school at about the same age that generation after generation of people living in pre-industrial societies were beginning to move directly into work and apprenticeship roles.

How did we come from the point where schooling was a luxury for those (of any age) who had sufficient money and leisure time to the point where schooling is compulsory for many years of one's life and intimately tied to other institutions of our culture? The most obvious answer is that the skills required of individuals by an industrial, technological society are more *diverse* and more *specialized* than the skills needed to survive in an agricultural age. Parents today simply cannot give their children enough information to carry them through their adult lives, while earlier generations of parents usually could. Furthermore, factories and corporations benefit from having skills taught in schools, rather than having to train and educate workers themselves. Thus, one explanation for the rise of a separate educational institution is that it is functional in economic terms, both for soon-to-be workers and for employers.

Other less obvious factors have also contributed to the growth and spread of schooling in the United States. Legislation removing children from factory work in the late 1800s, often seen as a humanitarian movement to protect children from dreadful working conditions, was actually passed in order to keep children from competing with adults for employment opportunities in the urban centers. Once large numbers of children were "freed" from employment by this legislation, the question became what to do with them. The answer was often schooling, and in time education came to be seen as a duty of the young.

But schooling was not made *compulsory* until the early 1900s, when vast waves of Southern- and Eastern-European immigrants arrived in our country. These groups were less likely to speak English or to have economically valued skills than previous immigrants, and "Americanizing" their children was attempted by enacting compulsory-education laws. Schooling thus came to be seen as a vehicle for socialization and education as a prime factor in upward social mobility.

As a result of the growing number of students, more and more jobs were created in the educational field and in allied industries—from teacher to administrator, from text-book publisher to cap-and-gown manufacturer. It is, you will agree, unlikely that individuals who earn a living from these activities would favor decreasing the role of schooling in society. In fact, these categories of people have worked consistently throughout this century to protect their own employment by expanding the educational sector.

As for post-secondary education, many of the same forces (except for compulsory legislation) have been operating to increase its importance. In addition, the G.I. Bill (providing tuition and living expenses for former military personnel) and the availability of federally financed college loans led to a virtual explosion of college enrollments in the post-World War II period. That explosion continues to the present day in terms of the *proportion* of "college-age" people who are enrolled (rather than the actual number, which is declining because of lower birth rates after the post-war baby boom). Currently, over half of those graduating from high school are attending college. Only about half of these will complete a four-year course, but the trend is sufficient to lead many observers to speak of the U.S. as a mass-educated society, especially when we consider that many adults are entering or returning to college and that graduate education is also being pursued at unprecedented rates. The "pull" of the learning environment is only part of the story; a "push" is also provided by employers who rely on the college or graduate degree as a criterion for employment. The meaning and value of these degrees has changed substantially in recent decades, because of the increasing number of college graduates. A college diploma may be the required ticket to board the economic train, but it no longer guarantees one a seat.

The institutionalization of schooling has had a number of important consequences for the ways in which we form our self-concepts and interact with others. The reader will recall our earlier discussion of the effects of age-segregation and age-grading on social interaction among the old and the young. We can further note that the age-segregation associated with mass schooling has, in conjunction with other societal trends, shaped new social roles—childhood, adolescence, and youth. Childhood was little different from adulthood until industrialization, urbanization, schooling, and a new religious view of the very young as needing moral molding were underway. Adolescence was not seen as a stage of life until around 1900 when educators began arguing that teenagers (the age of high-school students) had special needs. Of course, teenagers probably did *not* have special needs before this time, since their lives were essentially undistinguishable from the lives of their elders. Since the Second World War, another stage of movement toward adulthood has been created—youth—corresponding to the ages of college (and perhaps graduate-school) attendance. Each of these stages now has a special role specifying rights and obligations of those occupying the age-status. In sum, as entry into work roles is postponed for longer and longer periods, and as new stages of schooling emerge to occupy the time and energy of the postponers, our conceptions of what it means to be a certain age change and new social roles are added.

These processes have also meant that the young person today interacts with new types of significant others within new organizational arrangements. The *teacher* and the *peer group* of age-mates have become sources of socialization to be reckoned with. Both may have a significant impact on the values, self-concept, aspirations, and behavior of the young in their roles as student, child, adolescent, and youth, as well as in their future roles as adults. The *bureaucratic* style of organizing the activities of large numbers of students and educators is a rather rigid system for keeping order and processing people. Some of the key features of educational bureaucracies, such as the grading system of evaluating student performance, have often been cited as producing competition and frustration among students. The informal systems emerging to cope with bureaucratic rules and regulations—often termed the *student culture*—are also modern developments that could not have arisen without schools.

The articles in this section cannot, of course, detail all the consequences of the rise of schooling or of educational systems for social interaction. In the first selection, entitled "Meaninglessness at Utopia High," Ralph Larkin describes the high-school culture of an affluent, Northeastern suburban community in the mid-1970s. These adolescents reported feeling a sense of frustration and boredom with their lives both in and out of school. Many had come to expect and at the same time to resent dependence on parents and teachers. Yet interaction with peers was often stifled because of competition. Larkin attributes these feelings of frustration, boredom, and resentment to the legal and social requirement that one spend one's adolescence obtaining schooling which has few perceived short-term payoffs and which will only be followed by more schooling. Even in what seems to be the distant future after college or graduate school, the students cannot be assured of the meaningful family and work roles for which they have been socialized to strive, because of changing family norms and an economy glutted with college graduates in competition with each other for jobs. Thus we are shown some of the unforeseen results of a prolonged period of dependency before productive adult life begins. Schooling comes to be viewed by many of the young, not as a privilege from which one can gain important skills and knowledge, but as an almost interminable holding area or corral, primarily serving babysitting functions.

The college campus was the focus of research by Howard Becker, Blanche Geer, and Everett C. Hughes. Over twenty years ago, they examined in detail the workings of a midwestern state university. What struck them most forcibly was the degree to which students' and professors' academic roles were structured around grades, as we see in "Making the Grade." Faculty members often deplored the students' emphasis on grades, and students themselves often felt that grades interfered with learning. Both groups, however, found that their actions and interactions centered on the giving and receiving of grades.

Dissension, upheaval, and even revolution have shaken college and university campuses in the decades since this last piece of research was undertaken. As we noted previously, economic and social changes have also affected the importance and value of a college education. One enduring structural feature of most colleges, however, is the grading system. Although college students now face a different set of contingencies after college than the students whom Becker, Geer, and Hughes observed, we submit that much still hinges on grades and that, therefore, this research can tell us much about the formal and informal structuring of the school experience today, as it did in that earlier generation.

Both of the articles in this section present pictures that are at odds with the official version of what is, and what is supposed to be, taking place in the educational process. By looking behind the scenes at the lives of the actors involved in the school, and by listening to those who are actually being "processed" by the bureaucracies, the authors are able to document some of the ways in which the educational institution can shape the lives of the young.

MEANINGLESSNESS AT UTOPIA HIGH

Ralph W. Larkin

[Editors' Note: The following analysis is an excerpt from *Surburban Youth in Cultural Crisis*. It presents the results of a participant-observation study in a progressive and modern high school ("Utopia High") in an affluent Northeastern suburban community ("Pleasant Valley"). Observations and interviews with students, teachers, administrators, and parents were conducted in 1976 and 1977.

Larkin identified three major elite subcultural groups within the student body: the "jock/rah-rah crowd," the "freaks," and the "politicoes." He was able to classify two lower prestige groups, "blacks" and "greasers." The "silent majority" of students were not tied to any particular groups.

In Pleasant Valley, the American dream has come closest to being realized, yet the children who are the products of their parents' struggles to give them every advantage—including an excellent education—are troubled.]

W HEN ADULTS DISCUSS YOUTH OF THE 1970s, IT SEEMS INEVITABLE THAT SOMEONE WILL state, usually with a great deal of assurance and support, that youth culture has returned to the era of the 1950s. Such generalizations tend to be made with a certain amount of relief and self-satisfaction, as if such superficial comparisons negate the intense generational conflict of the 1960s. Of course, there are parallels to the 1950s: the privatization of youth interests, ritualization of drug use, resurgence of alcohol abuse, and, most of all, the disappearance of collective disobedience. Yet the youth of the 1970s is *fundamentally different* from 1950s' youth, which was caught up in sex, dating, cars, fun, rock 'n' roll, football, and drive-in movies. They were activity-oriented. They were not particularly introspective. That was left to the intellectuals or the misfits. With a blithe optimism, 1950s' youth could charge full force into the future showing little concern for the reasons they were doing so. Even as they entered college and came to grips with "ultimate questions," 1950s' youth did not seem to be seriously affected by such issues as whether or not God existed. There were goals and means to achieve them. One merely applied the recipe. If the procedure didn't make sense, one

Excerpted from Ralph W. Larkin, *Suburban Youth in Cultural Crisis*. New York: Oxford University Press, 1979.

didn't ask too many questions and one tolerated absurdity for the purposes of achieving the goal.

For the young, the 1960s wiped away the naive assurance that one could become employed in an occupation that would afford both a comfortable living and add to the social good. The evils that were attacked by youth in the 1960s still exist (with the exception of the Vietnam War) in exacerbated form. With no movement to articulate discontent, the contradiction is experienced as a cultural crisis, which, at the individual level, encompasses the problem of making meaning out of one's life. . . .

Introspection has been absorbed by the youth of the 1970s. They are *serious* about themselves: they are concerned about what kind of people they are and will be. They are suspicious of social labels. They struggle against overwhelming odds to be themselves: authentic, real persons. Yet the larger society works against such authenticity, since it would upset existing social relationships. The young are forced to play the game and put on false fronts. The problem becomes fiendishly difficult for them, because many have already slipped into their personas without really being aware of the fact that they are inauthentic. This constitutes one of the most serious problems for these young people.

•   •   •

BOREDOM

Boredom is the universal element that transcends all social divisions at Utopia High. Throughout the study, the theme of boredom recurred. For the active students, engrossing themselves in projects and events provided a bulwark against it. For the more passive, it has become a way of life. Boredom hung over Utopia like a thick fog. It was something everyone had to cope with: a fact of life even for those who chose to avoid it. Several students led frenetic lives in which they ran from one activity to the next so they would not succumb to boredom. However, most gave in to it.

•   •   •

LARKIN. . . . I'm a sociologist.

STUDENT. Well, what do you want us to say?

L. Well, I don't have anything for you to say, I am interested in what your lives are like. Really.

S. Boring!

OTHERS. That's right! All the way. [They all start talking at once and the tape becomes unintelligible.] (Recorded March 22, 1976.)

In another instance, some students were hanging around in "greaser's alley." We were talking with the tape recorder on. The subject was baby-sitting rates ($1.25 per hour), when all of a sudden a female student said, "I'm a sophomore. We lead humdrum lives." Another said, "It's boring," and still another said, "There's nothing to do around here." Nearly a half hour later in the same interview, some males decided to have the last word on the subject:

LARKIN. I seem to get the same story from everybody, that this place [Pleasant Valley] is boring, that people really have nothing to do.

STUDENT. It's not boring, it's dead. This town is dead. There's nothin' to do. (Recorded March 31, 1976.)

A great many students harbor fantasies or desires to escape the deadening non-existence offered to them in Pleasant Valley. One young man, who was raised in an urban environment retreats to the city every weekend. A young woman was awaiting the summer so she could escape the unidimensionality of Pleasant Valley to become a camp counselor. Still another saw his visit to his sister's farm in New Hampshire as a blessed escape from suburban miasma. Only a small minority of students saw their home town as one in which they would wish to settle themselves. Most felt restless. Since the study was conducted in the spring, many were looking forward to the summer, when they would head for the shore or the mountains. Many students felt like captives of their environment and told me of their desire to "bust out." Yet, they continued to play the waiting game.

Now that the boredom and its manifestations have been described, we must ask of what is it indicative? For Utopia High School students, *boredom is the result of the repression of the impulse to rebel.* They are dissatisfied with their lives. Yet there is no movement to give that dissatisfaction a collective articulation. Acts of defiance or "busting out" are meaningless and accomplish nothing but a ripple in the existing order and they play into the hands of the forces of oppression. For example, some students threw a Coke machine down a stairwell, creating a furor in the school for a day or two. The perpetrators of the act were suspended (or at least, the alleged perpetrators—those who said they were in the know claimed the wrong ones were punished). Most of the students were upset by it, since it could be used for legitimating increased surveillance of the students by the administration. The day after the incident, teachers were pressed into patrolling the halls, a task they detested and the students disliked. A show of force was made, and things returned to normalcy. Yet the increasing vandalism works against the interests of not only the vandals themselves, but also the majority of students, since community leaders use such incidents to justify their claim that the young should be more closely supervised. Collective dissidence is no longer a viable tactic in asserting student interests. When the Student Rights Committee attempted to shut down the school and march on the board of education in protest over budgetary cutbacks, their efforts turned into a miserable failure. Student politics are no longer considered seriously by students or adults. Students are not usually consulted on school board policy which concerns them. When they are, it is usually after the decision has been made and a token presentation is allowed on behalf of the students.

. . .

On several occasions, students compared Utopia High to a prison. I was inclined to regard such statements with a high degree of suspicion; when I pointed out to the students that they were a privileged lot, they agreed. Yet upon analysis, the prison analogy may supply more than what meets the eye. These students are not imprisoned by the school officials, nor by the community residents themselves. They are imprisoned by the lack of alternatives to what they are doing. What else could they be doing? Life in the street is mean and brutal. Full-time decent jobs for high school dropouts are extremely rare. The students are the recipients of a social policy of containment. They are being "contained" in schools until such time as they can assume adult roles. In the schools, administrations are attempting to contain potentially antisocial behavior by limiting it in such a way as to make it controllable by administrative means. An example is the smoking regulations at Utopia High:

STUDENT 1. You know, this school is really mixed up. . . . Seraph [the principal] is more concerned about administration that he is about us. [We're only allowed to smoke] on the basketball courts. In the winter they want us to go outside. They won't even let us on the stairs. We gotta go out to the blacktop.

STUDENT 2. Last year, they had smokin' in the cafeteria. The year before that, they had it in the boys' bathrooms.

S. 1. So now we smoke in the stairways, and they say, "This is no good." And he comes around and says, "You can't smoke here. We're working on a . . ."

OTHERS. (*Interrupting*) They've been working on a plan for twenty years!

. . .

STUDENT POLITICS: AN EXERCISE IN ABSURDITY

In the 1960s, Bob Dylan counseled youth, "Don't follow leaders, Watch the parking meters." Students at Utopia High seem to have pretty much taken his advice to heart. Few students aspire to leadership posts and those who do are distrusted by the rest. Recruitment for student leadership is extremely difficult. Those who do fill the posts are continually frustrated by the fact that they receive no support from the student body and when called upon to lead, there are usually very few persons willing to follow. Becky, a house president, made the following statement:

I have the trouble where if I could find the leader, I could have the people [to move politically.] I can't find the leaders. No one wants to lead anything! What can you do? That's . . . the problem. (Recorded March 29, 1976.)

· · ·

THE GREAT REFUSAL

Students claim they are bored and there is nothing to do. Yet extracurricular activities are withering away because of lack of student participation. Student leaders are often found begging other students for participation in club or committee events. Gordon (1957), in his study of Wabash High in the 1950s found that the extracurricular activities (called the semicurriculum by him) were a device used by the school to maintain the allegiance of the students and co-opt them into school participation through appeals to their interests. It is clear that in the 1970s at Utopia High, the students are not being co-opted in this manner.

Over the past several years, but especially in 1976, there has been a precipitous decline in student participation in school-related clubs. It was estimated that in the past school year, one-third of the student clubs had stopped functioning because of declining enrollments. Gary, the editor of the school yearbook, described the situation:

GARY. Well, all I know is our activities editor went to supposedly all the clubs that existed and it seems that none of them exist any more. No one cares or—

JENNY. They've become obsolete.

G. Yeah, they just didn't exist this year.

· · ·

L. What clubs have gone by the wayside?

ACTIVITIES EDITOR. The tutorial committee. That's not a club, but it's . . . a committee that took students during their free time and other students and they would help them in, like, say one student, let's say I was having trouble with math and May was good in math, then she would help me in it. We'd take my commons and her commons [periods] and, you know, get me up to the rest of my class.

L. Do you know why that went down the tubes?

A. E. It sort of went down when we started having commons periods, because no one wanted to give up their commons. The reason being that during formal study hall students didn't mind giving up their formal studies to be helped in a subject. Once they had commons periods, kids didn't want to give up their free time. So it wasn't that they couldn't find kids to tutor, they couldn't find kids who wanted to be tutored.

L. Oh. Because the commons time is used for hanging out?

A. E. Yeah. Pretty much. . . . I have just found in my involvement as the activities' editor with the students . . . and the teachers . . . that there is a huge amount of—and Gary will back me up on this—of just, I can't think of a word—apathy? They just don't care. I would send out three notices and a teacher wouldn't answer. And then I would call them up and they would say, "Okay, come take a picture of the club. I'll call a meeting." I'd get there with a photographer and there would be one kid there.

• • •

The prom committee, the Black Students' Union (BSU), the skiing and cycling clubs were all cited by the editor as being successful clubs. The BSU caters, of course, to the black students, most of whom are outside the cultural mainstream of Utopia High. It has been a stable group over the past several years. The cycling and skiing clubs both sponsor activities beyond school participation. . . . I found the prom committee hard at work a week and a half before the prom was to be held. Three students were working on prom bids. One was the senior class president and the other two were her close friends and most dedicated workers. Although sixty-eight young women showed up for the first meeting of the prom committee, the number of people actually working had dwindled to about twenty, half the estimate of that of the yearbook editor. The sale of prom bids (tickets) was going slowly. The prom committee workers feared that they might have to cancel the prom due to lack of interest. The prom was held, although only 135 of the 175 bids were sold.

Why has club structure fallen apart? Why is the prom, once the highlight of the social calendar, no longer an important event? Why do students cut classes at ever-increasing rates? We might term this phenomenon "the Great Refusal." When given the alternative of voluntary participation in school activities without coercion, students would rather not participate. The Great Refusal is the negation of the liberal assumption: If students are given greater freedom to choose within a formal structure, they will be thankful for the opportunity to select from administratively determined alternatives. This underestimates the alienation of students and misinterprets the predominant student view of schooling. Most students view school as *inherently* coercive. Therefore, any participation in school activities is participation in one's own oppression. Students would rather hang out and tolerate the boredom and meaninglessness of their own existence than participate in an activity presented in the context of an authority structure. Students tend to view schooling as *unpaid labor*. Therefore, their response to it is to minimize their commitment as much as possible and to try to get away with as little work as possible, given the constraints of grades.

• • •

Equating schooling with class attendance, students are questioning the necessity of remaining on campus when they do not have a class. It is seen as a waste of time, because that time could possibly be used for working at a job and earning money. The relaxation of coercive means does not necessarily co-opt the student population into believing that things are better than they were in the past, but, rather, helps to convince them that all the time spent in school is not necessary. This argument was presented to me in the following conversation:

LARKIN. Are you in a commons period right now?

LOUISE. Yeah. It's one of the things I don't like, 'cause all you can do is walk around and talk to people. You don't feel like doing your homework all the time. I have at least two free periods.

LARKIN. So what do you do during those free periods?

LOUISE. I either go to the library and do my homework or read a magazine. Or I walk around—I usually walk around or go out to eat.

VINNIE. You weren't supposed to say that. [Indicating that it is illegal to leave campus during school hours.]

LOUISE. I know.

LARKIN. What would you do during your commons periods if you had unlimited resources? I mean, what would you really want to do during your commons periods? Would you want to eliminate them or what?

LOUISE. I think they should be eliminated.

V. I don't.

LOUISE. (*To Vinnie*) Because school isn't the place to come and play.

LARKIN. You'd just as soon come in here, get your work done and go home?

LOUISE. I mean, split session. I'd come in [at] eight o'clock and leave at twelve. That's enough time. That's about as much time as I spend in class anyway.

LARKIN. So you feel that you are confined to school longer than is necessary.

LOUISE. Yes. It's like they are baby sittin'. (Recorded May 2, 1976.)

Thus, school is viewed by Louise in terms of its instrumental function only. It is a place to attend classes and do schoolwork. Beyond that, there is no reason to hang around. One's time can be used to one's own purposes better if one were not legally required to be in school. This view is a popular one held on campus. Louise, although alienated from school, is the president of one of the school's more successful clubs, the Black Students' Union, and received a scholarship from Duke University. Similar views were held by members of the "freak" and "greaser" subcultures.

· · ·

AN OPTIMISTIC FEAR OF THE FUTURE

As the students turn inward for meaning and purpose rather than looking for them in a predominantly arbitrary and meaningless institutional life, it is indeed surprising that they view the future with optimism. Although their optimism is guarded and often stems from the belief that "things have got to get better," the students are, nevertheless, optimistic. However, the optimism of Utopia High students in tinged with fear. They realize that sooner or later, they will have to work for a living. They hope that good jobs will be available. Many look forward to settling down to conventional existences, raising a family, and living a stable life. But such plans tend to be thought of as occurring "someday." Most Utopia High students see the process of settling down as a manifestation of a vague and distant future.

For the students from working-class backgrounds, the future is somewhat more immediate. Upon graduation, they plan to get a job or go to technical school to learn a trade. It is through this training that they hope one day they will open up their own businesses. This desire adheres closely to the great American dream. In discussing the future with several working-class students, the following conversation transpired:

LARKIN. What do you see yourselves doing in, say, ten years?
MARGE. Working.
L. Working? Do you plan to get married?
ROGER. [In response to the prior question.] Owning my own shop.
M. Oh, yeah, I want to have my own kids.
R. (*To Marge*) You want to work for somebody all your life? . . .
M. What else? What else am I going to do?
R. Open up your own place.
M. So? I'm still workin'.
JOE. . . . I'm startin' a business selling TVs. I do all right now. I make money.
L. You are actually in business now?
J. Well, not quite. I don't have a license for it yet. (Recorded April 13, 1976.)

For the college-bound students, the future takes on a more nebulous character and they are much less sure what direction their lives will take. However, they tend to be quite optimistic about the possibilities. Jed, who is not college-bound, shares the uncertainties voiced by those who are going to college:

LARKIN. What do you see as the most important issues, problems, or concerns you have?
JED. Getting out of school. (*Laughs*) What are you going to do for the rest of your life.
L. Do you have any answers?
J. Well, I have some things I want to do—that I think I want do do, but I don't know if I want to do them. I'm not sure, you know? (Recorded April 26, 1976.)

Many students were unsure of what direction their lives were going to take beyond high school, but they were not overly concerned. They figured that they would find something to do and that the future would take care of itself. When asked how they viewed their future, a group of students (some college-bound, some not) responded:

JAN. With optimism.
JED. Optimism, definitely.
LARKIN. Do you think things are going to improve?
ROZ. I figure by next year, there's going to be enough unemployed people and dissatisfied people in this country, that if something big doesn't happen it will be amazing. That's what I think. I think that there is no way it can keep getting [worse] without people fighting it. (Recorded April 26, 1976.)

When asked what they saw themselves doing in ten years, they were very unsure of themselves, but figured that, for the most part, life would present them with the opportunities to provide themselves with what they wanted:

LARKIN. What do you see yourselves doing in ten or fifteen years?
ROZ. Not much. (*Laughs*)
JED: Work. That's what I think about.
L. Do you think about having a family, getting married?
J. Oh, no. It's going to be hard enough supporting yourself.
CHUCK. Yeah. There's a lot before that.
L. You're going to put that off for quite awhile?
J. Yeah. We'll put that aside for now.
L. (*Indicating Mary*) How about you? Do you see yourself as getting married right away, putting if off, or never—
MARY. I don't know, really. . . . I know I'm not going to be a secretary taking steno fifteen years from now.
L. What are the alternatives?
M. I can get married—be married and have a family.
L. Does that appeal to you?
M. Eventually. I don't know. . . .
L. How about the rest of you?
R. I guess I've always been taught, directly or indirectly, that if I want to do something, I can do it. And so I kind of—I don't want to be one thing. You know, you ask people, "What are you?" "I'm a lawyer." or "I'm a—a—." I don't want to do that. I don't want to be a professional. I think I want to—I don't know. I want to live on a farm. I want to live in the city and take shitty jobs and do other things on the side. I want to travel. I want to start a school. I want to start an artists' thing. I don't know. I just kind of assume that the whole world is open to me and I can just get and take from it what I want. I don't think I am going to continue in the life-style of my parents. (Recorded April 26, 1976.)

• • •

The views of the future presented by the students of Utopia High are centered around the contradiction between desire and necessity. They all realize the necessity of earning a living, but they would like to pursue the kinds of labor that have intrinsic rewards—work that is meaningful, contributes to the social good, and provides a measure of autonomy. We are reminded of Roger's question, "Do you want to work for someone else the rest of your life?" The overwhelming answer is "no," but only Mary admits that for her, there is no alternative. Sarah's critique of future opportunities seems to summarize the problem well, so she will have the last word on the future:

LARKIN. Do you want to pursue a career, or be a housewife?

SARAH. I would *love* to pursue a career. It's just that right now all the hassle of getting good grades and so on are driving me up a wall and I don't think I will make it into any college that will give me what I really want. I'm very interested in philosophy. I'd love to be a lawyer, I really would, but you need a lot of money. We don't have a lot of money. And I am incredibly lazy. I happen to be a very lazy person. I don't think I could do all the work. It would probably be worth it, but I don't even know, then, because what are you going to do? Get a job as a philosopher? There's no such thing. I mean if you're interested in philosophy, you have to do something to make money. Everything, no matter how you circle around it or beat around the bush about it, it comes down to money. How much money are you going to make in a year? How are you going to support yourself? And I don't like that system at all. (Recorded May 3, 1976.)

CONCLUSION: WHO GIVES A DAMN?

. . . [O]ur main concern has been the subjective experiences of the students at Utopia High. They experience "institutional reality" as unreal. Their lives are pervaded by a lack of purpose and meaning. They have difficulty in making sense of what they do, and feel themselves coerced and "hemmed in." Yet this subjective awareness occurs in a setting that is far more liberal than that in other schools and in other communities around the nation and is certainly more liberal than the educational context that was experienced by high school students of the 1950s and 1960s. This means that the students of the 1970s have sensitized themselves to the repression of their behavior to a much higher degree than students prior to the youth movement of the 1960s.

Since they are acutely aware of the arbitrariness of their lives, much of their behavior is a reaction to this pervasive sense of oppressiveness. Most choose the line of least resistance: they withdraw emotionally from the school experience, accept it as a necessary part of existence, and live for "free time," in which they can indulge in pleasures and experience themselves as "authentic" beings. Most "free time" is spent on the weekends or during vacations. Their lives are pervaded by a sense of boredom and they yearn to participate in non-coerced activities. They look forward to "getting blasted" or "getting wasted" on the weekends and to partying; however, such events merely function as release valves so they can get through another week. The high they obtain on the weekends is only high in comparison to the grayness of the rest of the week. . . . [T]he highs generated through pot and sex tend to be merely physical and emotional releases from otherwise humdrum lives. They are primarily attempts at warding off the abyss of everyday life.

This sense of absurdity is heightened by virtue of the fact that the administration has instituted "student input" channels in the decision-making process, but when push comes to shove, the mechanism is exposed as a sham and student powerlessness is laid bare. Since there is no student movement and since the acts against the system, such as vandalism, work against the students, political activism is seen as futile. Even though student politics is incorporated into the structure of the system, the students have learned to take what is given to them and realize that there is little that can be done about what is taken away.

Because of their powerlessness, students find that "purposive action" in the institutional world is not worth the effort. Instead, they withdraw into themselves as the refuge of last resort. The self is the one thing that is their own. They have power over their own thoughts and feelings. The self is the last bastion of autonomy and is cherished by many students at Utopia High as that which is truly "theirs" and which supplies meaning to their lives. Friends—intimates with whom they can share essentially private experiences—are another source of meaning. The affinity group of like-minded peers provides a bulwark against the formalized world of adults. Yet, friendships are often subject to change and the ephemerality of life at Utopia High serves to undermine the cohesiveness of friends and the meaningfulness of their relationships.

Because their lives are subject to social forces over which they have no control, Utopia High students view the future with uncertainty. They are optimistic, in that they feel that somehow things will get better. They all realize that sooner or later, they will have to encounter the "real world" out there and begin supporting themselves. Nobody particularly wants to work in a hierarchical structure: the working-class students want to operate their own businesses (usually automotive repair shops), while students from a middle-class background want to become artists or free professionals. There is a sense among them that seems to question the necessity of routinized labor, and few are willing to admit that they will probably have to work in a highly bureaucratized structure.

School life is, for the most part, boring and unrewarding. The students are putting in time, hoping that the next phase of their lives will be happier. They participate in social structures in which they don't really give a damn, and they suspect that the teachers and administration don't either, beyond doing what is necessary and collecting their paychecks. School has changed from a pasture to a corral. No longer is its main function to nurture the young and prepare them for community life. It has become a holding pen for superfluous people who are segregated from significant community participation. Because of this shift, the community of the school has been divested of life and spirit. It is just another hurdle in a long line of hurdles to get over in the progression of existence. As such, the school contains little to enrich the lives of Pleasant Valley youth.

REFERENCE

Gordon, C. Wayne. *The Social System of the High School*. Glencoe, Ill.: Free Press, 1957.

Review Questions

1. How, in Larkin's view, have *economic factors* affected high-school students differently in the 1950s than in the 1970s?

2. Students at Utopia High experienced a great deal of boredom and apathy, despite the fact that their family situations were comfortable and their school was lenient and progressive. To what does Larkin attribute the boredom and apathy?

3. On the one hand, students were bored and had "nothing to do"; on the other hand, clubs and activities at Utopia High were not well attended. Discuss Larkin's explanation of this "great refusal."

4. Unlike previous generations of adolescents in the U.S., the students at Utopia High had what Larkin termed an "optimistic fear of the future." In what ways were they optimistic? In what ways were they fearful? Why?

MAKING THE GRADE

Howard S. Becker, Blanche Geer, and Everett C. Hughes

IN OUR STUDY, THREE OBSERVERS ([INCLUDING] BECKER [AND] GEER . . .) SPENT MORE than two years working with students at the University of Kansas. We went to classes with them, spent time with them in their residential units, attended formal and informal meetings of all kinds of campus organizations, and participated in many aspects of informal campus social life. We did not pretend to be students, nor did we assume any of the formal obligations of students; though we went to class with them, we did not do homework or take examinations. The nature of our fieldwork will become clear in the quotations from our field notes that appear throughout the [article].

A fourth observer (Hughes) spent two semesters at the University as a visiting professor and in that capacity gathered data on the perspectives of faculty and administration. The other observers occasionally gathered similar material and, in addition, made extensive use of documents prepared by the administration and by other organizations, largely to characterize the environment in which students act.

. . .

GENERALIZED GOALS

[P]erspectives are modes of collective action groups develop under the conditions set by the situations in which they have to act. The thrust of our analysis is largely situational, emphasizing the constraints and opportunities of the [college] situation and minimizing the influence of ideas and perspectives that students bring with them to college. Yet students do bring with them some notions about college and what they are going to do there, and these have bearing on what actually happens, even though they are transformed in the student's later experience.

Students have, in a rudimentary way when they enter college and in more elaborated form afterward, a *generalized goal*,[1] a point of view about why they have come to college and what they may reasonably expect to get out of their stay there. Generalized goals are, when the student first enters, a

Excerpted from Howard S. Becker, Blanche Geer, and Everett C. Hughes, *Making the Grade: The Academic Side of College Life*. New York: Wiley, 1968.

mixture of vague generalities and fragmentary specific desires, between which the student dimly apprehends some kind of connection. As he goes through school, he will probably (though not necessarily) come to a more precise definition of the general goal and will discern more complicated and precise relations between it and the specific goals he develops in particular areas of college life.

. . .

The chief characteristic of students' generalized goal, in its fully developed form, is an emphasis on college as a place in which one grows up and achieves the status of a mature adult. To manage one's college life properly (whatever meaning is attributed to that vague statement) shows that one has what it takes to be a mature adult, for the problems of college life are seen as much more like those of the adult world than anything that has come before. To do well in college, one must have the qualities students attribute to adults: the ability to manage time and effort efficiently and wisely, to meet responsibilities to other people and to the organizations one belongs to, and to cope successfully with the work one is assigned.

. . .

The generalized goal students have on entering [college] may be no more than an idea that they are going to take their academic work seriously, work hard, and do well. That goal, broadened and its connections to other areas of college life made specific, exerts an influence on the perspective students develop on their academic work. It does not tell the student how to act while he is in college; it only points the direction in which an answer must be sought and specifies a criterion against which any solution to the problems of college life will have to be measured. The generalized goal does not tell students the precise perspective they should adopt toward their academic work; many perspectives might satisfy its requirements. But the generalized goal does stand ready to tell students when a potential perspective is not in keeping with their long-range aims.

THE GRADE POINT AVERAGE PERSPECTIVE

The student's generalized goal enjoins him to be serious about college: to recognize it as a serious place where important things happen and to try to do well in all areas of college life as a sign of having achieved maturity. His perspective on academic work develops as he interacts with other students in an environment in which, as we shall see, grades are the chief form of institutionalized value and the institutional basis of punishment and reward in academic pursuits.

The perspective students develop on their academic work—we can call it the *grade point average perspective*[2]—reflects the environmental emphasis on grades. It describes the situation in which students see themselves working, the rewards they should expect from their academic work, the appropriate actions to take in various circumstances, the criteria by which people should be judged, and relevant conflicts in goals. In general, the perspective specifies the grade point average as the criterion of academic success and directs students to undertake those actions that will earn "good" or adequate grades.[3]

The main elements of the grade point average perspective are these:

Definition of the situation

1. The college is so organized that one can neither remain as a student nor graduate without receiving adequate grades. Furthermore, a number of other rewards that students desire cannot be achieved without sufficiently high grades.

2. A successful student, one who is achieving maturity in college, will "do well" in his academic work, however "doing well" is measured, thus demonstrating that he is capable of meeting the demands of the environment and also opening the way to success in other areas of campus life.

3. Doing well in academic work can be measured by the formal institutional rewards one wins. Since the major academic rewards are grades, success consists of getting a "good" grade point average.

4. Intellectual or other interests may suggest other rewards than grades to be sought in academic experience. Where the actions necessitated by the pursuit of grades conflict with other interests, the latter must be sacrificed.

Actions

5. To be successful a student should do whatever is necessary to get "good" grades, not expending effort on any other goal in the academic area until that has been achieved.

Criteria of judgment

6. Since any student who wants to can achieve adequate grades, failure to do so is a sign of immaturity. Grades can, therefore, be used as a basis of judging the personal worth of other students and of oneself.

7. Faculty members may be judged, among other ways, according to how difficult they make it to achieve adequate or "good" grades.

To say that student perspectives emphasize grades does not mean that there is a unitary standard for all students. What is considered "good" may vary considerably among various groups on the campus. An average of B may be considered adequate in one fraternity house but substandard in another. The grade point average that will satisfy an engineering student may not satisfy a business student or vice versa. The definition of "good" grades depends, as well, on the student's aspirations in other spheres of campus life. Failing grades are satisfactory to no one, but any other set of grades may be acceptable to some student. Although the acceptable level of grades varies from group to group and person to person, the perspective directs students to orient their activities toward getting "good" grades.

.   .   .

An analogy with a money economy . . . is instructive. Anyone participating in such an economy will want to make what might variously be described as "enough money," "good money," or "a decent living." But the conception of "enough" or "decent" will vary widely among social classes, occupations, regions—and between individuals as well. Some will be satisfied only if they are millionaires; some will settle for a bare subsistence; most are in between. Almost everyone recognizes that "money isn't everything," that one must balance the need for money against other needs which are equally important.

Similarly, students vary in the degree to which they personally accept and live according to the rules suggested by the perspective. To some it seems completely normal: "How else could things be?" Others recognize that things might, in some other institutional setting, be quite different, but find the perspective acceptable. And some are irked by it, find it constraining and uncongenial. But it has two features that cause most students to accept it, however they feel about it, as a reasonable way to view the campus world and act in it. First, it is a *realistic way to orient oneself toward the academic aspects of campus life.* To be sure, it may not be the only realistic orientation; but it takes account of what are objectively discernible features of the campus environment. For this reason, it works; a student who adopts it as a standard of action will probably not have academic troubles. Thus, even though other perspectives might produce equally acceptable results, students will probably use this one, because it has worked in the past.

Second, the grade point average perspective is *widely accepted and thus has the force of being "what everyone knows."* Most people the students come in contact with talk and act in ways congruent with it; it embodies the accepted commonsense of his world. To question it or act in ways that deny it requires the student to violate the commonsense assumptions his fellows share; it is easier and more natural to accept them.

.   .   .

Whatever the student's private reservations—and, indeed, no matter how many students may have such private reservations—the terms and assumptions of conventional discourse are those contained in the perspective. To recur to the analogy with money, an adult may feel that money is not very important and privately decide that he will ignore it; but as long as he lives in a money economy, surrounded by people and institutions that assume the importance of money, he will be constrained to accept that assumption in his dealings with them. Just so with students and grades; however the student feels privately, campus life is organized around the terms and assumptions of the grade point average perspective.

• • •

THE FACULTY VIEWPOINT: AN ALTERNATIVE DEFINITION

We have described the university social structure, as students define its effects in the area of academic work, as one that emphasizes grades, grades being the chief and most important valuable. Because this is a matter on which students and faculty have widely differing viewpoints, and because we tend to give more weight to the student viewpoint than academicians commonly do, we want here to indicate what seems to us the typical faculty viewpoint and to criticize it for failing to give sufficient weight to the structural imperatives we have described.

• • •

Some faculty members, no doubt, believe that the grades they give accurately reflect the amount of knowledge the student has acquired and are perfectly content that students should work for grades; in doing so they will learn what they are supposed to know. Other faculty members despise grades and would like to do away with them and all the associated paraphernalia of grade point averages, cumulative averages, and the like. Still others feel great ambivalence. They find it necessary, whether out of inner conviction or because of bureaucratic rules, to give grades and try to do it in a serious and responsible way. But they do not believe that the grades they give adequately reflect student ability; there are always some students who do well on tests although their classroom performance casts doubt on their grasp of the material presented, and others who know the material but get poor grades, perhaps because of poor test-taking skill. The faculty want to reward true achievement rather than the cunning of the accomplished grade-getter.

Faculty in the last two categories probably feel that students should be concerned about grades, but not *that* concerned. In particular, they object to what they see as the student tendency to reduce everything to grades, to raise interminable questions about "what we are responsible for," about the grading system and the criteria that will be used in assigning grades, about the number of questions on the exam—all the common questions that seem to them at best extraneous to the true business of learning and at the worst a deliberate mockery of it.[4]

Faculty are usually at a loss to explain student interest in grades and see no rational basis for it. They may attribute it to misguided competitiveness or to other kinds of irrationality. They do not see its basis in the structure of campus life, do not understand that the student definition of the situation is largely based on the realities of college life.

Faculty members, in complaining about student concern with grades instead of scholarship, complain, we may argue, because they feel that student concern with "beating" the system of tests and assignments designed to test achievement interferes with the true assessment of student ability. Students have a different view. They take tests and grades at face value and see a connection between doing their academic work properly—in such a fashion as to get adequate grades—and the emphasis on maturity contained in their generalized goal. They believe that when they achieve a satisfactory GPA they have demonstrated their ability to do their work and meet their obligations to themselves . . . and their college—in short, their ability to act as responsible adults.

THE CONFLICT BETWEEN GRADES AND LEARNING

Despite what we have just said, some students share the faculty viewpoint in part. They incorporate it into their definition of the situation as one horn of a dilemma they see the college as posing for them. They feel that the workaday world of academic requirements, which forms the basis of the GPA perspective, causes them to miss something they might otherwise get from their courses, that they must meet the requirements before they can attempt to "learn for themselves." Insofar as the dilemma reflects a persisting definition of grades as important, it does not indicate the existence of a different and alternative perspective.

We do not mean to imply that students feel the conflict most of the time or that most students do at one time or another; the implication is not necessary to our argument, which is only that where the conflict is felt it reflects the belief that grades are important. For the most part, indeed, students believe that their courses are "good"; what they are required to do to pass the course is just what they ought to do anyhow to learn the substance of that course. Even when they fail to become excited by the content they are learning, they reason that the teacher knows the subject and that what he is teaching them must be what is important to know. If one gets a good grade, one has therefore necessarily learned something worth knowing. Where students do not accept the rationale, and feel a conflict between grades and learning, we have counted the incident as evidence of the existence of the GPA perspective.

Here is an extended statement of the problem by a successful student leader who himself had very high grades:

> There's an awful lot of work being done up here for the wrong reason. I don't exactly know how to put it, but people are going through here and not learning anything at all. Of course, there are a lot of your classes where you can't really learn anything at all. . . . There's a terrific pressure on everybody here to get good

grades. It's very important. They tell you that when you come in, we tell our own pledges that. We have to, because it's true. And yet there are a lot of courses where you can learn what's necessary to get the grade and when you come out of the class you don't know anything at all. You haven't learned a damn thing, really.

In fact, if you try to really learn something, it would handicap you as far as getting a grade goes. And grades are important. . . .

And, you see, it says in the catalog, if you read it, that C is a satisfactory grade. Well, do they mean that or don't they. Actually it's the minimum grade here. But it's supposed to be a satisfactory grade. OK. Supposing you wanted to work on something in your own way and didn't mind if you got a C. Well, if C was really a satisfactory grade it wouldn't hurt you any. But that's not the truth. C is just barely passing. The most satisfactory thing is an A, and next is a B.

The grading systems are so cockeyed around here you can't tell what's going on. One guy does it this way and another guy does it that way and, as I say, in a lot of these courses the only thing you can do is get in there and memorize a lot of facts. I've done that myself. I've gone into classes where that's all you could do is memorize . . . memorize and memorize. And then you go in to take the final and you put it all down on the paper, everything you've memorized, and then you forget it. You walk out of the class and your mind is purged. Perfectly clean. There's nothing in it. Someone asks you the next week what you learned in the class and you couldn't tell them anything because you didn't learn anything.

There are a lot of guys around here who are very expert at doing that. They can take any course and learn what has to be learned and get through the course with an A. And yet, I don't think those guys are really that smart, not to me anyway. In my opinion there are plenty of people around here who have much greater potential and they just haven't found the classes where you can use it . . . We've got these kids coming in and I don't know what it is, they're not interested themselves in accumulating knowledge for its own sake or because it will be of any use to them. All they want to do is get a grade. Now, of course, grades are important. We tell them [pledges] to go out and get that grade. What else can you tell them? It's very important for the house and it's important for them to get the grade. They want to be offered those good jobs when they graduate. I don't blame them. I would myself. I've always tried to get high grades and I've done pretty well.

—fraternity senior

This articulate student has presented most of the major themes of this aspect of the perspective, themes that recur more briefly in statements by others: Grades are important, for many reasons; one can get good grades without learning; indeed, trying to learn may interfere with grade-getting; the point of view is passed on in his fraternity.

• • •

INDIVIDUAL ACTIONS

Having sized up their situation by discovering what needs to be done in each of their classes and projecting their semester GPA, students take action based on their definition of the importance of grades. Specifically, they express the GPA perspective when they take actions that have as their object getting a "good" grade, a grade sufficient for them in the light of their other grades, the total GPA they desire, and their other responsibilities and desires; in short, when they set their level and direction of effort with an eye to its effect on their GPA.

Student actions designed to get desired grades can take two forms. First, students may attempt to meet the requirements presented to them: they study and try to master the materials and skills they are supposed to acquire. But they may fail in that attempt or decide that they will fail if that is all they do. Then they undertake other actions which, rather than being designed to meet the requirements, try to achieve the reward of grades through other, less legitimate means such as arguing with the instructor, "getting next to" him, or cheating. If they can do the job, they do it, putting their major efforts into academic work; if they cannot, they try to influence their grade in some other way.

Under some circumstances, students making use of the GPA perspective will, instead of raising their effort to meet requirements or looking for alternative forms of action, actually lower their level of effort substantially, leading (as we shall see) to the paradoxical result that an emphasis on grades leads to decreased effort to achieve them.

DOING THE JOB: Students study; they are supposed to. But they study harder at some times than at others, and the variation in effort is not a function of anything in the material they study itself, but rather of whether or not a term paper is due or an examination looms ahead. They study harder, too, when their GPA is lower than they would like it to be.

This may seem overly obvious and not necessarily connected with the perspective we are describing. After all, what do students come to college for if not to study? Why do we think it necessary to explain that they do so? Even if we were to grant this (ignoring the possibility that students might come to college for other reasons and have no intention of studying at all), it is still not obvious why a student should study in any particular rhythm, with peaks of effort at one time and periods of relaxation at another.

Consider the following example. A student says that his work is "piling up" on him, that he is "getting behind." Does he say this because he has come to college to study and learn and feels that he is not learning fast enough? On the contrary, he feels his work is "piling up" because he has a given amount of work to do in a specified amount of time; if he does not keep to a daily schedule, getting so much done every day, he will fall behind and have more to do on the following days.[5] He did not choose those amounts of work and time; because of the relationship of subjection in the academic area, they are set for him by the faculty. He must meet faculty demands because his grades will be based on how well he does just that.

We frequently found students who were not doing well working extremely hard. The poorer student probably studies longest; he has so much difficulty that he must devote all his time to his work. Here is an example, from a conversation with a freshman girl on the verge of flunking out:

Well, I start studying after dinner and I study all night until midnight and sometimes until one o'clock. And sometimes I start at six o'clock and just keep going right through. And I've been getting awfully tired, I think that's why I got that cold. Last weekend I went home and I slept thirteen hours until three o'clock in the afternoon.

—*freshman girl*

Most instances are less dramatic. The student indicates that he has a great deal of work to do because of previous low grades and that he is doing what he thinks will be needed to improve them:

I said to Harry, "How are things going with you?" He immediately replied, "Oh, I got a down slip [a midterm notice that one is likely to fail a course] in one of my courses and that's what I'm studying for now. I have a test in it tomorrow. . . ." I said, "How are your other courses going?" Harry replied, "They're OK, C's and B's. I'm doing all right in those and I think if I can work a little harder on this I can get it up to at least a C by the final. . . . Of course, I have no social life this semester and about all I'm doing is studying."

—*freshman independent man*

Students need not be failing to behave this way; they may simply find it necessary to devote all their time to finishing required work in time to meet a deadline. Thus a student who had previously been quite prepared to engage in long conversations with the observer said: "Gee, you've caught me at a kind of bad time. I'm just trying to finish up a paper for Soc." (*senior man, scholarship hall.*) (Most of the few occasions when students were unwilling to talk to us involved similar situations; the student had too much work to do to allow him to take the time off.)

When devoting more time and effort to study does not work, students who want higher grades seek help. They may, for instance, take advantage of services organized by the faculty, such as tutorial instruction, the Reading Clinic or the University Counseling Center.

More commonly, however, students get help from other students or from files, maintained by their living group, of old examinations, term papers, and the like. During dinner at a fraternity house, an observer overheard the following:

You know how to study for Professor Jones, now, do you? Did you follow the file? Well, if you follow that file the way the course is outlined, then you can't go wrong, because he's been giving that course in the same way for the past ten years. Just be sure that you memorize all of those definitions, just the way that they are set up in the files, and you can't go wrong, you'll be sure of an A if you do.

—*junior fraternity man*

Files of old examinations and papers are a tradition on many campuses. But students rely on fellow members of their living group for more than access to already accumulated files. They also ask for help in completing current assignments:

> The observer was lounging around in a student's room in the dormitory. . . . Long said, "[Bracket is] really busy in there. He's got a theme to turn in tomorrow and I don't think he's done anything on it yet." A little later Bracket arrived saying, "Does anybody know anything about Karl Marx? I've just run out of ideas. That's all there is to it. Where is Tucker? . . . He promised to give me an old term paper of his on Karl Marx that I could use." I said, "Johnny Bracket! Don't tell me that you would turn in somebody else's term paper?" He looked around quite seriously and said, "Oh, no. I didn't mean that. I just wanted to get some ideas out of it for the last two pages of my paper. I need about two more pages." Albright said, "I see. You would just copy the last two pages, is that it?" Bracket said, "Well, I wouldn't exactly copy them."
>
> —*sophomore independent man*

The pressure of assignments and the need to get grades thus push students to do the academic work assigned them. But, if pressure supplies a motive for work, its absence makes work less necessary. If the material need not be mastered now, but can be put off until later, the student may decide to work only as much as is required and no more. If he were sincerely interested in learning for its own sake, he would presumably continue to work on a topic until he lost interest in it or felt that he had learned enough to suit his purpose. But many students do only what is required of them:

> A student described having led a very extensive social life during the last semester. I said, "Did you get pretty good grades with all that?" He said, "I can't complain, I did just about as well as I expected." I said, "What was your grade point average?" He said, "2.6" [B plus]. I said, "Wow, that's pretty good, isn't it?" He said, "Yes, it is pretty good, it really could have been higher if I had applied myself more in English, but I didn't. I think 2.6 is plenty high enough. There's no harm in that. But I didn't have to apply myself to get it. And I didn't have any intention of applying myself. . . .
>
> "I don't mean to say that it was all a breeze. I had to put myself out occasionally. I had to get all those English themes in and so on. But frankly, with the exception of English, I didn't do any work at all the whole last month of school. I was caught up on all my other courses. I had done all the work for the rest of the semester. And the only reason that I hadn't done it in English is that you couldn't tell ahead of time what kind of themes he would assign. Otherwise I would have done all of that too. I really had all the whole last month perfectly free to do whatever I wanted."
>
> I said, "You might have gone out and read some things that weren't assigned. Did you do that?" He smiled very broadly and said, "No, sir, you don't catch me doing that. I'll do just as much as I have to to get the grades and that's all."
>
> —*sophomore fraternity man*

Students who take this point of view make it their business to discover just what is required so that they can do the minimum necessary for the GPA they want. As soon as they discover that some action that seems necessary for a grade in fact is not, they dispense with it, even giving up going to class when that can be managed without running afoul of rules about "cuts":

> I don't know about these classes. I've got one class where the fellow lectured about one set of things and then gave us an exam on a completely different set of things out of the book. I really don't think I'm going to go to that class any more. I mean, what's the sense of sitting there and taking notes if he's going to ask questions straight out of the book? I might as well just read the book and let it go at that.
> —*independent man, year in school unknown*

The emphasis on what is required is reflected even in the interior decoration of student rooms. We repeatedly noticed that many students' bookshelves contained nothing but textbooks. Many other students, of course, had sizable collections of books that were only distantly related, if at all, to their course work. But a substantial number of students apparently had no use for books that would not be helpful in attempting to meet requirements.[6]

ILLEGITIMATE ACTIONS: Some of the actions that students take in pursuit of grades would be regarded as illegitimate by most faculty members. Faculty believe that students should work as well as they are able, and that they will do so if the faculty member can find a way to interest them. If called on to do so, faculty tend to justify the use of grades by defining them as some kind of combined measure of ability and interest. But some student actions make a mockery of that definition, being designed to produce the end product—grades—without an appropriate input of ability, interest, and effort.

Actions designed to circumvent the ability-effort equation, then, may be regarded as illegitimate. We have already noted that students attempt to get information on instructors' prejudices and idiosyncrasies. They act on that information, and even act when they have no information and must rely on guesswork. They want to affect the instructor's judgment of their work and thus raise their grade, either by catering to his prejudices or by getting to know him personally and taking advantage of the personal acquaintance in some way.

The conception underlying such actions is embodied in the commonly used phrase "brownie points." The vulgar origins of the expression are quite lost on campus; innocent young girls use it freely. One gains brownie points, of course, by "brown-nosing," by doing things that will gain the instructor's favor other than simply doing the assigned classwork. The phrase is commonly used in a half-joking way, but its import is perfectly serious. One student explained the technique in detail (though he used a more refined term):

> What I do is apple-polishing, but it's not so obvious as that. It all depends on the teacher. Mainly, I just get to know them. I go up to their offices and talk with

them. [What do you talk about?] Anything, anything they feel like talking about. I might figure out a good question to ask them. That'll show them that I'm really thinking about the course. And sometimes I just go up and say hello and we sit down and start talking about things. Maybe we'll talk about new cars. I'll say I don't like the new Ford this year, what do you think of it? And he'll tell me what he thinks of it.

Just different problems like that. You know, these teachers don't like to talk about their subject all the time, they get tired of it, day in, day out, the same thing. I just size them up and see what I think they will go for. Now my English teacher last year, he was a tough one to figure out the second semester. It took me almost a whole semester to figure out what to do about him. Finally, I figured it out. I praised him, that's what he liked. It paid off, too. I got my mark raised a whole grade.

—sophomore fraternity man

One can get negative brownie points as well—lose points by doing something formally extraneous to the course work which irritates or annoys the instructor; he is thought to retaliate by lowering one's grade:

Prentice said, "Boy, I've got minus brownie points in my speech class. I'm about 200 in the hole to her." His friend said, "What do you mean?" Prentice said, "Well, she just doesn't like me. She's got some reasons too. I mean, they're pretty good reasons." The observer said, "For instance?" Prentice said, "Well, for one thing, I didn't show up for an appointment with her, you know, it was supposed to be for my benefit. She was going to help me out. I just didn't show up, so that doesn't go over too good. And I haven't been to class in a long time."

—freshman independent men

Students fear, particularly, that disagreeing with the instructor, in class or in a paper, will have bad results:

You can write a very good theme on some subject—I mean, the grammar can be perfect and the spelling and the punctuation and everything—and they'll flunk you, if you write something they don't agree with. I've seen it happen. They don't like for you to have a different interpretation than the one they think is right. You take a piece of poetry, for instance. They'll pretty much tell you what you should get out of it, how it should impress you. They'll ask you to write a theme about it. Well, you'd better get the same impressions from it that they told you you should have, or you're going to be in trouble. . . . It just doesn't pay to disagree with them, there's no point in it. The thing to do is find out what they want you to say and tell them that.

—junior fraternity man

• • •

Students also act illegitimately when they attempt to improve their grade by disputing the instructor's interpretation of a term paper or an examination question. As every faculty member knows, returning papers or exams often provokes spirited debate designed to demonstrate that the answer the teacher thought incorrect was really correct, that the paper he thought inadequate actually measured up to the requirements he had set. And, as every teacher also knows, a student can often raise his grade by such tactics; students are ingenious in discovering hidden ambiguities in examination questions and term paper assignments. Here is an example:

> I had to wring a C out of the psychology man [the instructor]. I had to argue with him, you should have seen me. The thing was, on that essay question he took off because I didn't give a name [a heading] for each point. There were eight points and I got each one in the discussion but I thought I would be different and just describe it and not give the name, so he counted off two points for each one, but I made him put some back and that gives me a C.
>
> —*junior independent girl*

Arguments over the interpretation of an answer or assignment seem illegitimate to faculty because, again, they are ways of circumventing the equation of ability and effort with grades. They turn the grade into something that can be achieved by using the academically extraneous skills of a "Philadelphia lawyer."

Some students engage in the ultimate illegitimate act—cheating. A national survey of academic dishonesty among college students suggests, however, that students and faculty differ with respect to the definition of cheating.[7] Students seldom consider that they have cheated when they consult one another about an assignment. But faculty members, who see the teacher-student relationship as a one-to-one relationship between themselves and each individual student (a dyadic model of learning), sometimes feel that if the student consults anyone else he has acted dishonestly. By doing so, he has made his grade depend in some part on the ability and effort of others. (In view of the common scholarly practice of circulating work before publication for collegial comment and criticism, this faculty notion seems unduly rigorous.)

Some acts are on the borderline. A good many students might agree with faculty members that the following chemistry "shortcut" is illegitimate:

> They give you a sample of something and you're supposed to figure out what's in it. They only give you so much of it. The idea is if you use it all up making the wrong tests then you're just out of luck, you fail on that experiment. But guys are getting another sample out of them. You know, they say that their partner knocked the jar over or that they tripped while they are carrying it and spilled it or something like that. I've seen two fellows get away with it. So I don't think it'll be all that tough, if you can get around things like that.
>
> —*sophomore fraternity man*

· · ·

The same national survey reveals that grosser forms of cheating are quite widespread. Fifty per cent of the students questioned admitted that they had, at least once during their college careers, copied during an examination, used crib notes, plagiarized published materials for a term paper, or turned in someone else's paper. We saw very little obvious cheating, although we saw many borderline actions. One case of copying on an examination came to our attention, and one theft of an examination from a departmental office occurred during the time we were in the field. Nevertheless, some cheating must have occurred that we did not see; the nature of the act and students' shame at engaging in it (also documented in the survey referred to) make it hard to detect.

The most important point about illegitimate actions is *that they are a consequence of the existence of a system of examinations, grades, and grade point averages*. If the faculty uses examinations and other assignments to evaluate the student's abilities or progress, some students will attempt to influence the outcome of the evaluation "illegally," by "brown-nosing," arguing, or cheating. Illegitimate actions would be foolish if nothing important could be gained from them. It is because they may be rewarded by a raised grade that students engage in them.

THE GPA AND LOWERED STUDENT EFFORT: The grade point average perspective does not always intensify student academic effort. In fact, it can depress the level of effort a student puts forth, if he feels that he is already in such serious trouble that no conceivable amount of effort will get him out; when he sees his situation this way, he may stop working altogether. If we compare students to the industrial workers studied by Donald Roy, the analogy to a monetary system is again revealing. The workers Roy studied felt that they were "entitled" to a certain hourly average when they worked on piecework. If piecework rates were set so tightly that workers could not achieve the specified amount, they then worked at well below their capacity.[8] Since they could not "make out," they might as well simply collect their hourly wage and be done with it. They saw no sense in expending effort when nothing could be gained.

College students act much the same way. When they know they cannot possibly win, they resign themselves to losing and do not throw good money after bad. Failing students refuse even to calculate their grade point average; they know that they are going to fail and are not interested in the exact degree of failure:

> Brown said, "I sure am going to have to work and pull my grade average up if I want to stay here." The observer said, "What is it now?" He laughed and said, "I haven't even figured it out. It's too awful to think about." Carlson said, "I haven't either. I don't know what I'm going to get in some of these courses, but I know it's going to be pretty bad and I don't really want to bother figuring what my average is. What good would it do? I know I've got to bring everything up."
> —*two independent men, freshman and sophomore*

Likewise, students who are so far behind that it seems impossible to catch up do not bother to do assigned work anymore and sometimes stop doing all schoolwork completely; they report (to the observers and to each other) that they are unable to muster the energy or spirit to do the work:

> Tucker said, "Well, you're a damn fool. You just don't even try." Long said, "Buddy, I just can't get my spirit up. I don't know what's the matter with me." Tucker said, "I know how you feel. I feel the same way. There just doesn't seem to be any point to studying. I mean, I don't feel that I can learn anything and if I did it wouldn't be worth it so the hell with it."
> —*three independent men, a freshman, and two juniors*

The importance students attach to grades is thus exhibited in reverse. If one has already done so poorly that nothing can be salvaged, there is no point in studying or working.

•   •   •

CONCLUSION

Grades are universally defined as important because they are institutionalized; scholarship need not be recognized as important by everyone because its status as a valuable is not ratified by a set of rules and embodied in the organization and daily routine of the college. In the same way, participants in our society may consider beauty or truth more important than money. But one can ignore beauty and truth in one's life because they are not institutionalized; no one can ignore money, no matter how unimportant he thinks it. Not to have money has consequences one must reckon with. To have grades of the wrong kind likewise has consequences one cannot ignore.

Nevertheless, just as economic achievement is not the only important thing in a man's life, so academic achievement is not the only important thing in a student's life. A certain minimum is essential in each case, because of the way the valuable is institutionalized, with other kinds of rewards contingent on reaching that minimum. But beyond the minimum, which represents the level necessary in order to have the privilege of choosing where to put one's remaining time and effort, choice becomes possible, and the person finds that he must balance the various rewards available against one another in making that choice. One may decide to sacrifice the higher grade that would come with more work in a course, choosing to devote that time instead to a political career or a girl friend.

It is at this point that both economic man and the grade-getting student achieve some measure of autonomy. To be sure, they are both captives of a system of performance and reward imposed on them by others; the student is still in a relation of subjection to faculty and administration. But, having achieved the minimum without which participation is impossible, they can then choose to go no farther, to pursue instead other valuables in other areas of life. They become, thus, men in a community, fully alive to all the possibilities available to them in that communal life. . . . [S]tudents make use of that autonomy, though not in the ways that faculty members often hope they will.

NOTES

1. The concept of generalized goal is related to, but not the same as, the concept of long-range perspective used in Howard S. Becker, Blanche Geer, Everett C. Hughes, and Anselm L. Strauss, *Boys in White: Student Culture in Medical School* (Chicago: University of Chicago Press, 1961), pp. 35–36, 68–79. They are alike in pointing to very general definitions of the meaning of one's participation in an organization. They differ in that long-range perspective refers the meaning to some state of affairs that lies beyond the end of the period of participation, while generalized goal refers the meaning to changes that take place during participation.

For further discussion of the relation between the understanding people bring with them to a situation and those they acquire in it, see Howard S. Becker and Blanche Geer, "Latent Culture: A Note on the Theory of Latent Social Roles," *Administrative Science Quarterly*, 5 (September 1960), pp. 304–313. The question has been pursued in studies of prison culture; see, especially, John Irwin and Donald R. Cressey, "Thieves, Convicts and the Inmate Culture," *Social Problems*, 10 (Fall 1962), pp. 142–155, and David A. Ward and Gene G. Kassebaum, *Women's Prison: Sex and Social Structure* (Chicago: Aldine, 1965), pp. 56–79.

2. We occasionally shorten this, in what follows, and refer to the GPA perspective.

3. We will use the expression "good grades" to refer to the level of grades that a student finds satisfactory, given the standards that he, his living group, and his other associates have developed. Those standards will take into account the various other obligations and opportunities relevant to the achievement of a mature balancing of effort and activity. "Good grades" will thus vary among students, living groups, and possibly along other dimensions as well. In contrast, we will use the expression "adequate grades" when we wish to refer to grades that are sufficient to meet some formal requirement; unless otherwise specified, "adequate grades" will refer to the GPA necessary to remain in school. Adequate grades, of course, do not vary, except as the requirement to which they refer varies.

4. See the discussion of medical faculty views in Howard S. Becker, Blanche Geer, Everett C. Hughes, and Anselm L. Strauss, *Boys in White, op. cit.*, pp. 110 and 132–134. Several essays in Nevitt Sanford, ed., *The American College* (New York: John Wiley and Sons, 1962), give evidence of the viewpoint of college faculty members.

5. *Ibid.*, pp. 92–106.

6. We made a practice of describing in detail the student rooms we visited and were thus able to check this point in our field notes.

7. William Bowers, *Student Dishonesty and Its Control in College* (New York: Bureau of Applied Social Research, Columbia University, 1964).

8. Donald Roy, "Quota Restriction and Goldbricking in a Machine Shop," *American Journal of Sociology*, 57 (March 1952), pp. 427–442.

Review Questions

1. Becker, Geer, and Hughes draw a parallel between "making the grade" in college and being financially successful in the larger society. What is this parallel?

2. Students come to college with generalized goals of working hard and doing well. Faculty come to class to impart knowledge and to promote critical thinking. Why and how are these two definitions of the situation subverted?

3. What techniques do students employ to "make the grade"?

4. How does the grading system of evaluating student performance sometimes boomerang, leading to a lack of motivation?

5. The students observed and interviewed by Becker, Geer, and Hughes attended college twenty years ago. Are the processes and systems which affected those students still affecting orientations for success in college in your generation? Could you devise another system for motivating and evaluating students which would promote learning rather than "making the grade"?

Suggested Readings: Interaction in Institutional Contexts: Education

Collins, Randall. *The Credential Society: An Historical Sociology of Education and Stratification.* New York: Academic Press, 1979.

Illich, Ivan. *Deschooling Society.* New York: Harper & Row, 1971.

Rosenthal, Robert, and Lenore Jacobson. *Pygmalion in the Classroom.* New York: Holt, Rinehart and Winston, 1968.

Waller, Willard. *The Sociology of Teaching.* New York: John Wiley, 1967.

C. Work and Economics

W̲E̲ HAVE NOTED REPEATEDLY THAT THE ECONOMIC INSTITUTION OF A SOCIETY—THAT cluster of norms and values that guides the production and distribution of food, shelter, clothing, and the host of other services and material goods we require and want—has major consequences for all other institutions. The rules we must follow in order to survive have changed drastically over the past century, as agriculture gave way to industry. For one thing, we have become in large part a nation of employees, dependent not on the seasons and the climate but on the corporation, the company, the agency, or the factory. A greater *variety* of skills are required in an industrial society, and the systems for interrelating workers with different job descriptions are much more complicated. In a great many instances, the organizations that hire us have adopted bureaucratic methods to coordinate work and workers.

Sociologists take a great interest in work, because it has symbolic meaning both on a social and a personal level. Not all jobs are viewed with equal esteem, and occupational prestige affects both one's position in the class structure and one's self-esteem. The kind of work we do defines us to other members of society by indicating, in many cases, our sex, the income we are likely to earn, the amount of education we are likely to have, and the life-styles we are likely to pursue. Being an attorney, for example, conveys a social meaning different from being a factory worker or a housewife, meanings that are likely to affect how people interact with us in a variety of situations and how we see ourselves. The importance of the work identity is driven home at an early age to most children, who are repeatedly asked, "And what are you going to be when you grow up?"

The workplace itself has also received much attention from sociologists. How do various types of formal organization affect the workers? What informal norms and patterns of behavior emerge among workers in the factory, the university, the corporation? What, in short, are the social processes that surround a job?

One type of work that is done by large numbers of people in our society, but which is nevertheless often seen as "nonwork," is housework. Housewives perform boring, repetitive work that has low prestige and is often taken for granted by the rest of the family—and by the society. Housewives are assumed to engage in these duties out of love; housework, it is presumed, can't be "real" work, because the motivation for work is money. The value of services performed by housewives, while quite substantial if reckoned in terms of salaries in the marketplace, is not even included in the Gross National Product, the economists' measure of the total worth of all goods and services in our society.

But what sociological sense can we make of the role of the housewife if we view it *as an occupation* and compare it to other lines of work? Lewis Coser and Rose Laub Coser do just that in "The Housewife and 'Her Greedy Family.'" They point out that the housewife, because she works alone, is removed from the social rewards that come from interacting with co-workers. Furthermore, because she receives no direct compensation for the tasks she performs, the housewife does not become a source of power in the family and, instead, depends upon the generosity of her spouse for both necessities and luxuries. In a society in which one's worth is often measured in terms of money, her self-esteem may be impaired. No matter how well she does her job, her income—and her worth—are tied to another person.

Our understanding of the dissatisfaction with housewifery displayed by many women today is enhanced by this sociological view. What difference would it make if the occupation of housewife were similar to other occupations, in which the workers are paid for their efforts and receive pensions, vacations, and sick leave? How might our society bring about such a change, thereby making the family less of a "greedy institution"? Would the occupation be any different if men assumed it?

The next article in this section shifts our focus to the factory, but the group processes and social interaction described by Donald Roy are apparent in many other work settings as well. The situation analyzed in "Banana Time" is one in which routine, repetitive tasks are assigned to the workers, who search for ways to pass the time from clock-in to clock-out.

It was Roy's conviction that one cannot understand jobs, workers, or interaction in the workplace without being a true participant in the situation. During his career, Roy followed his conviction. He worked at many types of jobs in several factories, including the one described here. He discovered that both he and the other employees devised private psychological "games" to get them through the boredom, such as quickly completing work on the white materials in order to get to the blue materials. The minimal rewards of "getting to the blues" were, however, meager and were overshadowed by the rewards which came from patterned interaction with co-workers when it was "banana time," "peach time," or "coke time."

Our final selection dealing with work looks at another group of factory workers, but again the processes occurring here can be recognized in other work environments, such as hospitals, prisons, and the like. Howard Robboy, in "At Work with the Night Worker," looks at that small but significant portion of the labor force who think of the night as a time for work rather than sleep. It would be easy to think of night workers merely as deviants, but to do so would give us no clues as to why they have broken from the usual workaday pattern. Robboy shows that the incentives which motivate the night worker are both economic and social. Night workers receive a pay differential (a slightly higher hourly wage) and are free to operate businesses of their own during the day. There is, moreover, a strong sense of solidarity that is not found in the factory at other times. And because night workers do not have the multitude of bosses hovering over them that day workers do, they can claim both greater personal freedom and more control over their duties.

This section of the book can by no means be said to have detailed all of the norms, systems, and behavior patterns pertaining to work in our society. It is our hope that the reader has begun to see how work activities can be viewed sociologically and will apply this vantage point in looking at other occupations and settings. We have tried to show here that work is not motivated *solely* by the promise of economic reward and that, in fact, people will often work very hard for little return or even forego income. The informal social nature of the workplace *combines* with formal structures, rules, and economic incentives to set its tone and character. We have also tried to indicate the variety of meanings that can be attached to economic activities and to those who perform them.

THE HOUSEWIFE AND HER "GREEDY FAMILY"

Lewis A. Coser and Rose Laub Coser

THE MODERN FAMILY, JUST LIKE ITS TRADITIONAL PREDECESSORS, IS A "GREEDY" institution. It is normally headed by a fully employed male. Not he, however, but his wife is expected to devote most of her time, as well as her emotional energies, to their family. Husband and wife, to be sure, are expected to exchange services, sexual and otherwise, with each other, and they are bound by reciprocal obligations that are supposed to result in mutual benefits. But this reciprocity is skewed in the male direction; i.e., it is asymmetrical in the sense that benefits flow unequally to these two role partners.

As Alvin Gouldner has argued,[1] where power relations are unequally distributed between two parties, the weaker party may be constrained to continue services even with minimal reciprocity on the part of the more powerful. Consequently, the continued provision of benefits by one party, the wife, for another party, the husband, depends not only upon the benefits which she receives from him, but also on the power which he possesses over her, and on "the alternative sources of services accessible to each, beyond those provided by the other."

The relative power of husband and wife in the family depends largely on their respective anchorage in the occupational system, since that system is the main determinant of status and privilege. Men mainly derive status from their position in the occupational order, but the status placement of women is determined by their husbands. If her status depends on his, but his status does not depend on hers, an asymmetry of power is built into their relationship, and this asymmetry is a barrier to the operation of the principle of reciprocity which is based on equal exchange. The higher the occupational status the husband achieves, the more asymmetry arises, unless, of course, compensatory mechanisms are at work. Thus, in the upper class, the wife may have high status conferred to her by her own family of orientation, or she may be independently wealthy.[2]

The exclusion or near-exclusion of women from most high-status positions in the occupational system is often justified by reference to her higher emotional investment in the family. In fact, we deal here with a prime instance of the self-fulfilling prophecy.[3] Women are judged to be unfit for

Lewis A. Coser and Rose Laub Coser, "The Housewife and Her 'Greedy Family,' " in Coser and Coser, *Greedy Institutions: Patterns of Undivided Commitment.* New York: Free Press, 1974, pp. 89–100.

high occupational status and they are hence excluded from such positions. If they then turn to the greedy family in search of emotional fulfillment, this is adduced as "proof" of the fact that they indeed do not fit into the occupational world.

Their exclusive attachment to the family, moreover, and the sacrifices they make in its service, binds them more securely to it. They invest considerably more in the family than do their husbands, who find alternative sources of gratification in their occupations. And the more wives sacrifice for the family, the more they are bound to it. The principle of cognitive dissonance operates here: Since it is very difficult to repudiate objects in which one has invested so much, the more one invests in an object, the greater the hold that object has on the person. Thus, not only are women taught and expected to invest their emotions in the family, this very investment once more strengthens their attachment. And this attachment makes them even more vulnerable to the husband's higher-status claims. As E. A. Ross put it a long time ago in advancing a "Law of Personal Exploitation," "In any sentimental relation the one who cares less can exploit the one who cares more."[4]

The small representation of women in the professions and in high-status positions in contemporary America is by no means due to happenstance, but is the logical consequence of women's cultural mandate which prescribes that their primary allegiance be to the family and that men provide the family with economic means and social status. Once the premise of this mandate is granted, *women* who have or wish to have careers are said to have a "conflict," and this is seen as a source of disruption in the occupational as well as in the familial order.[5]

Conflicts experienced by professional women who have a family do not simply result from participation in two different activity systems whose claims on time allocations are incompatible. They derive from the fact that the values underlying these claims are contradictory: Professional women are expected to be committed to their work "just like men" at the same time as they are normatively required to give priority to their family.

The conflict is one of allegiance, and it does not stem from the mere fact of involvement in more than one social system. Such conflicts do not typically arise in the case of husbands. Men can be fully engaged in their occupations without fear of being accused of lack of devotion to their families. It is only when there is a normative expectation that the family will be allocated resources of time, energy, and affect that cannot be shared with other social institutions that conflict arises. And this typically occurs only in the case of women who have the cultural mandate to give primary allegiance to their families. Hence, this mandate sharply limits the access of women to high-status positions and skews the distribution of power in the family in the direction of the male head of the household. This is why the notion of equal access of women to high-status positions in American society is presently discussed with such great affect. What is at stake is not so much equal access to job opportunities as such, but equal power within the family. Power depends on resources, and women who do not have occupational resources are in a very poor position to share it equally with their husbands.[6]

If men are providers and women are provided for, the latter suffer from so large a built-in handicap that the resulting power differential between them and their husbands can be compensated only by special advantages. One such advantage is sexual attractiveness. Such attractiveness, however, is likely to decline over time while the husband's status, to the contrary, is likely to increase over time, especially in the middle class, so that, even if the terms of the marital bargain are relatively more equal in the first stages of marriage, they are likely to become less so in later stages.

Moreover, in the modern family, the wife's decline in sexual attractiveness is likely to coincide with the time in which the children are growing up, so that her motherly responsibilities tend to cease at the same time as her sexual appeals begin to wane. She no longer is a mother, nor is she a playmate. Under these circumstances, the marital dyad becomes especially vulnerable. At this point, the successful husband may attempt to console and compensate his wife by buying her expensive dresses and jewelry. Yet, alas . . . she will but too often feel that by adorning her, he in fact only signifies his own success.

Both husband and wife are normatively expected to work hard in the service of their family. But if her work is confined to the household while his is "at the office," these two types of work are not evaluated in the same way either within the society at large or within the family. Housewives, no matter how hard they work, are not considered to be in the labor force, which means that they are not regarded as contributing to the national product. The old joke that, if the parson marries his housekeeper, this results in a net decline in the national product, is not merely a joke. In achievement and instrumentally oriented societies, those who do household work are led to consider it demeaning since it is symbolically downgraded as not being "real work." The provider-husband receives symbolical reinforcement for his hard work by means of his monetary returns; and these returns typically increase over time as he moves up the ladder of advancement. But the wife's work receives no monetary compensation. And its recompense in terms of symbolic expressions of gratitude on the part of the husband is likely to decrease over time. What seems to be at work here is a law of diminishing returns. Services which may initially have been compensated for by expressions of esteem and gratitude are likely, in the long run, to be expected as a matter of routine and, hence, no longer call forth expressions of appreciation.

In contrast to modern occupations, housework is rooted in an earlier traditional order. It is diffuse and unspecialized rather than functionally specific, and requires involvement of the whole personality. The mother-wife, even more than the domestic servant of earlier times, must always be available. Yet unlike traditional work, housework today demands only a modicum of skill since household needs are provided for in the form of processed consumer goods and labor-saving devices, and this is a society in which achievement based on skill is most highly valued. Helena Lopata was probably mistaken to give to her otherwise very interesting book the title *Occupation: Housewife.*[7] Only when it is realized that this is precisely *not* an occupation in the modern sense of the word, will the specifically modern dissatisfactions that are built into the housewifely role become analytically understandable.

This chapter is limited to the discussion of the marital dyad, since one of the authors has dealt extensively elsewhere with the middle-class mother-children interactive system.[8] It is nevertheless important to point out that the housewife's tasks in the home are not only downgraded by the world at large as well as by her husband, but that such negative appraisals are likely to be shared by growing children. While young children may depend on, and appreciate, the mother's nurturance, older children will soon learn from their significant environment that "real work" is done outside the home, and by males at that, while mother's work, though necessary, is "dirty work." Far from enhancing her in the children's eyes, this work diminishes her stature and downgrades her status relative to the father's work "downtown."

In spite of these compounded drawbacks of the housewifely role, women generally accept it, even if often only grudgingly. They do not flock to educational institutions, even if they have the opportunity to do so, to prepare for more rewarding occupational roles. They do not press for admission to medical schools and law schools nor to the academy generally even where they could crash the gates. By and large, they accept the cultural mandate to give priority to their commitment to the greedy family.

There is a negative connotation to the term "career woman." No such derogatory term exists for men, since their careers are taken for granted. It is acceptable, however, even commendable, if middle-class women take jobs to help their husbands advance their careers while going to school, or to help children go to college. Their caring in this way for members of their family is seen as part of their cultural mandate, and hence, is normatively approved. Their occasional working is even approved if it is to buy some extras for themselves, or for presents, just as children from well-to-do families are encouraged to engage in character-building by occasionally earning their own money.

The mandate, which women accept, that enjoins them to devote their major energies to their family does *not* exclude outside employment. It only serves as a bar to outside occupational involvements which confer status and prestige and, hence, may alter the power constellations within the confines of the greedy family. It is normatively approved and structurally desirable that women are readily available to pick up the slack at times and places where an occupational system gets to be overloaded, and when it does not want to allocate resources that are considered too costly for an activity that nevertheless has to be carried out. Women's availability for such jobs stems, of course, from the fact that the home and family to which they owe primary allegiance, do not need all the time at their disposal. They can fill in as saleswomen (typically called *salesgirls* no matter what their age because of the low status of the activity); be invited on the spur of the moment to teach introductory courses when an unusually high number of freshmen enter a class; or be volunteers in understaffed hospitals where they are supposed to make up for the lack of nurturing services. Paradoxically enough, women's time is considered cheap just because they live up to the highly prized cultural mandate to give priority to their family. "Real work" for women—but emphatically not for men—is considered to detract from the requisite emotional investment in the family so that career and family life are presented as mutually exclusive alternatives for women. Those women who have opted for permanent careers tend to be expected to remain celibate, like Catholic priests.

While part-time non-career jobs for housewives are generally approved by the community at large, other activities that benefit the career of the husband are even more highly valued. As Hanna Papanek has argued,[9] many organizations that employ the husband proceed on the assumption that his wife's time is neither productive nor important, economically speaking, and that her "opportunity costs" are therefore low. They feel free to call on her if the occasion so requires, and their husbands are likely to feel honored and gratified if their wives' services are called for. Volunteer work, entertaining important customers or guests, holding children's parties, or pouring tea are nominally optional activities but are in fact normatively expected. A wife who refuses to participate risks injuring her husband's career. "The high degree of ambivalence which accompanies the induction of women into the institutional orbits of their husbands is based on the need to enlist the women's participation . . . without letting their actual contributions decrease the importance which the institution places on the husbands' work."[10] What is more, while husbands highly approve and desire their wives' services in the enhancement of their own careers, they are likely to look with jaundiced eyes at any occasion which would call for even minimal sacrifices in the service of the wife's career. Husbands are almost always more equal than wives.

The high degree of mobility, both social and geographical, in the careers of middle-class Americans is predicated to a large extent on the readiness of the wife to assume the responsibilities and inconveniences involved in such moves. It is she who bears the major burdens of residential uprooting and social dislocation. Without her contributions as shock absorber, tension manager, and general superintendent, and without her readiness not to be career-bound herself, the mobility chances of her husband would be sharply reduced. The functionalist argument that chances for achievement and upward mobility in American society are well served by the fact that the extended family has been replaced by the nuclear family is indeed correct; but it fails to spell out that the nuclear family is functional for mobility only as long as wives are willingly submitting to its greedy demands. How many moves in academia, for example, have come about because husbands accept appointments at other universities, and how many moves have resulted from the wife's desire to enhance *her* career chances? The question answers itself.

All that has been said so far seems apparently called into question if it is realized that in the early 1970s, working women constituted nearly 40 percent of the entire labor force. Yet a closer look at labor force statistics shows that these figures by no means controvert, and in fact support, the idea that women have the cultural mandate to devote themselves primarily to their "greedy" family. By far the largest proportion of women are found in lower-status occupations. They comprise only eight percent of the nation's physicians and four percent of its lawyers but are predominantly employed in relatively low status "female occupations" such as primary school teaching, nursing, social work and, of course, various low-level white-collar occupations. Women are disproportionately employed in occupations where they are easily replaceable and that do not as a rule command a high degree of commitment and loyalty.

The difference between occupations in which women are well represented and those in which their participation is conspicuously rare can be accounted for in terms of the status of these occupations. High-status positions require high commitment. In these positions, people are likely to have a great deal of control over their own work and, hence, this work is meaningful to the jobholder. But when jobs are meaningful, they are likely to detract attention and commitment from the family which alone is supposed to give meaning to the lives of women. Those women who engage in "unalienated" work are seen as potentially or actually subverting their cultural mandate, as disrupting the role expectations of the family system. The fact that women who have families are not as likely as single women to be found in high-status positions—even though single women are also subject to sex-typed judgments—is easily accounted for if it is kept in mind that "greedy" institutions such as the family are hard task masters. This is not so much due to the fact that a woman's career may cause neglect of the family as to the fact that it implies subversion. Not giving in to the family's "greediness" undermines the very nature of the institution.

Societies always provide cultural definitions of desirable life goals. In modern American society, men are "out to get" occupational status and women are "out to get" men who will get such status. Achieved rather than ascribed status is salient in American life and tends to determine position in the stratification system. Hence, while men are in charge of placing their families in that system, women's status remains vicarious. They tend to be deprived of the opportunity of achieving status for themselves, for they are kept in bondage to the "greedy" male-headed family.

Equal education for women on the high school and college level helps them compete with one another to attract the most valued men and later makes them capable of helping their husbands in their careers. Modern

American society, as distinct from many others, values equality of opportunity for its members, yet women can hardly avail themselves of opportunities as long as they accept the cultural mandate that their major loyalty should be to their family. What is offered them formally is withdrawn normatively. Such contradictory patterns are likely to be highly anxiety-producing for many women and to evoke ambivalence and *ressentiment*.

As long as "greedy" families could rely in the main on housewives who accepted with equanimity their unequal position of power, it could operate with a minimum of friction, even though it seems often to have exerted a high toll in psychic stress and emotional disturbance. But once women began to realize that there existed realistic chances of achieving more nearly equal status with their husbands if and when they involved themselves in the upper reaches of the occupational and professional world and so acquired new resources, the "greedy" family was in trouble. Once women were no longer as ready as they had once been to support the careers of their husbands by offering auxiliary services, once they were no longer as ready to serve as tension relievers, recharging the emotional batteries of husbands come home to find repose from competitive battles, the terms on which the marital dyad was built began to change.

The desires of social actors are never enough if structural conditions are not conducive to their realization. However, the structure of the occupational order as well as of the household order is rapidly changing—largely through the impact of technological advances. The modern office and the modern factory allow the development of flexible work schedules which were hard to institute when technological requirements enforced a more rigid scheduling of labor inputs. At the same time, a variety of labor-saving devices, the availability of packaged and pre-processed foods, easy shopping in supermarkets, and refrigerated storage of foods have made many household tasks obsolescent, and have considerably simplified the management of the home. That is why, at this point in time, one can begin dimly to foresee a new family constellation in which both he and she are the family's providers, co-managers of the household and true partners in the care of the children so that their respective resources of power are more nearly equal. When that day comes, genuine reciprocity will have replaced asymmetrical power.

As Alice Rossi puts it in her pioneering article, "Equality Between the Sexes: An Immodest Proposal."[11]

Marriage [for the woman of the future] will not mark a withdrawal from the life and work pattern that she has established, just as there will be no sharp discontinuity between her early childhood and youthful adult years. Marriage will be an enlargement of her life experiences, the addition of a new dimension to an already established pattern, rather than an abrupt withdrawal to the home and a turning in upon the marital relationship. Marriage will be a 'looking outward in the same direction' for both the woman and her husband.

And that will be the death of the "greedy" family.

NOTES

1. Alvin W. Gouldner, "The Norm of Reciprocity: A Preliminary Statement," *American Sociological Review* 25, 2 (April 1960), pp. 161–78.

2. In the working class, in contrast, where the husband does not typically achieve much prestige at work, conditions for more equalitarian relations seem more propitious. Yet, in fact, in the working class, sex roles in the family remain considerably more segregated than in the middle class, with "her" sphere and "his" sphere of interests and responsibility more sharply defined. It would seem that working-class husbands find it even more threatening to give up male prerogative than middle-class men precisely because they lack compensation in the occupational order. Cf: Mirra Komarovsky, *Blue Collar Marriage*, New York: Vintage Books, 1967.

3. Robert K. Merton, *Social Theory and Social Structure*, enlarged ed., New York: The Free Press, 1968, Chapter 8.

4. E. A. Ross, *Principles of Sociology*, New York: Century, 1921, p. 136.

5. In this paragraph, as well as throughout this chapter, we have freely drawn on a previous paper, "Women in the Occupational World: Social Disruption and Conflict," by Rose Laub Coser and Gerald Rokoff, *Social Problems* 18, 4 (Spring 1971), pp. 536–54.

6. In working-class families, in which both husbands and working wives may typically have quite similar educational statuses, inequality of pay at work and unequal job assignments assure the maintenance of differentials in the resources available to husbands and wives. Cf. William H. Chafe, *The American Woman: Her Changing Social, Economic, and Political Roles, 1920–1970*, New York: Oxford University Press, 1972.

7. Helena Z. Lopata, *Occupation: Housewife*, New York: Oxford University Press, 1971.

8. Rose Laub Coser, "Authority and Structural Ambivalence in the Middle-Class Family," in Rose Laub Coser (Ed.), *The Family: Its Structure and Functions*, New York: St. Martin's Press, 1964, pp. 370–83.

9. Hanna Papanek, "Men, Women, and Work: Reflections on the Two-Person Career," *American Journal of Sociology* 78, No. 4 (January 1973), pp. 852–72.

10. Ibid, p. 860.

11. Alice S. Rossi, "Equality Between the Sexes: An Immodest Proposal," *Daedalus* (Spring 1964).

Review Questions

1. Why is the work in which the housewife engages not seen as "real work" in our society?

2. Discuss the housewife role from an occupational perspective. What are the major duties, working conditions, reward systems? How are new members recruited and trained? Compare and contrast housewifery with other occupations.

3. The "greedy family" demands time, commitment, and sacrifice from the housewife. The "greedy corporation" or the "greedy profession" demand the same from their professional employees. How have these sets of competing demands affected the family and work lives of men and women in our society?

4. What are the consequences of the woman's "greedy family" for her power within the family? For her involvement in the work world?

"BANANA TIME"

Donald F. Roy

My ACCOUNT OF HOW ONE GROUP OF MACHINE OPERATORS KEPT FROM "GOING NUTS" in a situation of monotonous work activity attempts to lay bare the tissues of interaction which made up the content of their adjustment, the talking, fun, and fooling which provided [a] solution to the elemental problem of "psychological survival." . . .

My fellow operatives and I spent our long days of simple repetitive work in relative isolation from other employees of the factory. Our line of machines was sealed off from other work areas of the plant by the four walls of the clicking room. The one door of this room was usually closed. Even when it was kept open, during periods of hot weather, the consequences were not social; it opened on an uninhabited storage room of the shipping department. Not even the sounds of work activity going on elsewhere in the factory carried to this isolated work place. There were occasional contacts with "outside" employees, usually on matters connected with the work; but, with the exception of the daily calls of one fellow who came to pick up finished materials for the next step in processing, such visits were sporadic and infrequent.

Moreover, face-to-face contact with members of the managerial hierarchy were few and far between. No one bearing the title of foreman ever came around. The only company official who showed himself more than once during the two-month observation period was the plant superintendent. Evidently overloaded with supervisory duties and production problems which kept him busy elsewhere, he managed to pay his respects every week or two. His visits were in the nature of short, businesslike, but friendly exchanges. Otherwise he confined his observable communications with the group to occasional utilization of a public address system. During the two-month period, the company president and the chief chemist paid one friendly call apiece. One man, who may or may not have been of managerial status, was seen on various occasions lurking about in a manner which excited suspicion. Although no observable consequences accrued from the peculiar visitations of this silent fellow, it was assumed that he was some sort of efficiency expert, and he was referred to as "The Snooper."

As far as our work group was concerned, this was truly a situation of laissez-faire management. There was no interference from staff experts, no

Donald F. Roy," 'Banana Time': Job Satisfaction and Informal Interaction," *Human Organization* 18 (1959) 158–168.

hounding by time-study engineers or personnel men hot on the scent of efficiency or good human relations. Nor were there any signs of industrial de-
mocracy in the form of safety, recreational, or production committees.
There was an international union, and there was a highly publicized union-
management cooperation program; but actual interactional processes of cooperation were carried on somewhere beyond my range of observation and
without participation of members of my work group. Furthermore, these
union-management get-togethers had no determinable connection with the
problem of "toughing out" a twelve-hour day of monotonous work.

Our work group was thus not only abandoned to its own sources for creating job satisfaction, but left without that basic reservoir of ill-will toward
management which can sometimes be counted on to stimulate the development of interesting activities to occupy hand and brain. Lacking was the
challenge of intergroup conflict, that perennial source of creative experience
to fill the otherwise empty hours of meaningless work routine.

The clicking machines were housed in a room approximately thirty by
twenty-four feet. They were four in number, set in a row, and so arranged
along one wall that the busy operator could, merely by raising his head
from his work, freshen his reveries with a glance through one of the three
large barred windows. To the rear of one of the end machines sat a long cutting table; here the operators cut up rolls of plastic materials into small
sheets manageable for further processing at the clickers. Behind the machine
at the opposite end of the line sat another table which was intermittently the
work station of a female employee who performed sundry scissors operations of a more intricate nature on raincoat parts. Boxed in on all sides by
shelves and stocks of materials, this latter locus of work appeared a cell
within a cell. . . .

Introduction to the new job, with its relatively simple machine skills and
work routines, was accomplished with what proved to be, in my experience, an all-time minimum of job training. The clicking machine assigned to
me was situated at one end of the row. Here the superintendent and one of
the operators gave a few brief demonstrations, accompanied by bits of advice which included a warning to keep hands clear of the descending hammer. After a short practice period, at the end of which the superintendent
expressed satisfaction with progress and potentialities, I was left to develop
my learning curve with no other supervision than that afforded by members
of the work group. Further advice and assistance did come, from time to
time, from my fellow operatives, sometimes upon request, sometimes unsolicited.

THE WORK GROUP

Absorbed at first in three related goals of improving my clicking skill, increasing my rate of output, and keeping my left hand unclicked, I paid little
attention to my fellow operatives save to observe that they were friendly,

middle-aged, foreign-born, full of advice, and very talkative. Their names, according to the way they addressed each other, were George, Ike, and Sammy. George, a stocky fellow in his late fifties, operated the machine at the opposite end of the line; he, I later discovered, had emigrated in early youth from a country in Southeastern Europe. Ike, stationed at George's left, was tall, slender, in his early fifties, and Jewish; he had come from Eastern Europe in his youth. Sammy, number three man in the line, and my neighbor, was heavy set, in his late fifties, and Jewish; he had escaped from a country in Eastern Europe just before Hitler's legions had moved in. All three men had been downwardly mobile as to occupation in recent years. George and Sammy had been proprietors of small businesses; the former had been "wiped out" when his uninsured establishment burned down; the latter had been entrepreneuring on a small scale before he left all behind him to flee the Germans. According to his account, Ike had left a highly skilled trade which he had practiced for years in Chicago.

I discovered also that the clicker line represented a ranking system in descending order from George to myself. George not only had top seniority for the group, but functioned as a sort of leadman. His superior status was marked in the fact that he received five cents more per hour than the other clickermen, put in the longest workday, made daily contact, outside the workroom, with the superintendent on work matters which concerned the entire line, and communicated to the rest of us the directives which he received. The narrow margin of superordination was seen in the fact that directives were always relayed in the superintendent's name; they were on the order of, "You'd better let that go now, and get on the green. Joe says they're running low on the fifth floor," or, "Joe says he wants two boxes of the 3-die today." The narrow margin was also seen in the fact that the superintendent would communicate directly with his operatives over the public address system; and, on occasion, Ike or Sammy would leave the workroom to confer with him for decisions or advice in regard to work orders.

Ike was next to George in seniority, then Sammy. I was, of course, low man on the totem pole. Other indices to status differentiation lay in informal interaction, to be described later.

With one exception, job status tended to be matched by length of workday. George worked a thirteen-hour day, from 7 A.M. to 8:30 P.M. Ike worked eleven hours, from 7 A.M. to 6:30 P.M.; occasionally he worked until 7 or 7:30 for an eleven and a half- or a twelve-hour day. Sammy put in a nine-hour day, from 8 A.M. to 5:30 P.M. My twelve hours spanned from 8 A.M. to 8:30 P.M. We had a half hour for lunch, from 12 to 12:30.

The female who worked at the secluded table behind George's machine put in a regular plantwide eight-hour shift from 8 to 4:30. Two women held this job during the period of my employment; Mable was succeeded by Baby. Both were Negroes, and in their late twenties.

A fifth clicker operator, an Arabian *emigré* called Boo, worked a night shift by himself. He usually arrived about 7 P.M. to take over Ike's machine.

THE WORK

It was evident to me, before my first workday drew to a weary close, that my clicking career was going to be a grim process of fighting the clock, the particular timepiece in this situation being an old-fashioned alarm clock which ticked away on a shelf near George's machine. I had struggled through many dreary rounds with the minutes and hours during the various phases of my industrial experience, but never had I been confronted with such a dismal combination of working conditions as the extra-long workday, the infinitesimal cerebral excitation, and the extreme limitation of physical movement. The contrast with a recent stint in the California oil fields was striking. This was no eight-hour day of racing hither and yon over desert and foothills with a rollicking crew of "roustabouts" on a variety of repair missions at oil wells, pipe lines, and storage tanks. Here there were no afternoon dallyings to search the sands for horned toads, tarantulas, and rattlesnakes, or to climb old wooden derricks for raven's nests, with an eye out, of course, for the telltale streak of dust in the distance which gave ample warning of the approach of the boss. This was standing all day in one spot beside three old codgers in a dingy room looking out through barred windows at the bare walls of a brick warehouse, leg movements largely restricted to the shifting of body weight from one foot to the other, hand and arm movements confined, for the most part, to a simple repetitive sequence of place the die,_____ punch the clicker,_____ place the die,_____ punch the clicker, and intellectual activity reduced to computing the hours to quitting time. It is true that from time to time a fresh stack of sheets would have to be substituted for the clicked-out old one; but the stack would have been prepared by someone else, and the exchange would be only a minute or two in the making. Now and then a box of finished work would have to be moved back out of the way, and an empty box brought up; but the moving back and the bringing up involved only a step or two. And there was the half hour for lunch, and occasional trips to the lavatory or the drinking fountain to break up the day into digestible parts. But after each momentary respite, hammer and die were moving again: click,_____ move die,_____ click,_____ move die.,. . .

The next day was the same: the monotony of the work, the tired legs and sore feet and thoughts of quitting.

THE GAME OF WORK

In discussing the factory operative's struggle to "cling to the remnants of joy in work," Henri de Man makes the general observations that "it is psychologically impossible to deprive any kind of work of all its positive emotional elements," that the worker will find *some* meaning in any activity assigned to him, a "certain scope for initiative which can satisfy after a fashion the instinct for play and the creative impulse." . . . De Man cites the case of one worker who wrapped 13,000 incandescent bulbs a day; she found her outlet for creative impulse, her self-determination, her meaning in work by varying her wrapping movements a little from time to time.

So did I search for *some* meaning in my continuous mincing of plastic sheets into small ovals, fingers, and trapezoids. The richness of possibility for creative expression previously discovered in my experience with the "Taylor system" did not reveal itself here. There was no piecework, so no piecework game. There was no conflict with management, so no war game. But, like the light bulb wrapper, I did find a "certain scope for initiative," and out of this slight freedom to vary activity, I developed a game of work, [which] might be described as a continuous sequence of short-range production goals with achievement rewards in the form of activity change. . . .

But a hasty conclusion that I was having lots of fun playing my clicking game should be avoided. These games were not as interesting in the experiencing as they might seem to be from the telling. Emotional tone of the activity was low, and intellectual currents weak. Such rewards as scraping the block or "getting to do the blue ones" were not very exciting, and the stretches of repetitive movement involved in achieving them were long enough to permit lapses into obsessive reverie. Henri de Man speaks of "clinging to the remnants of joy in work," and this situation represented just that. How tenacious the clinging was, how long I could have "stuck it out" with my remnants, was never determined. Before the first week was out this adjustment to the work situation was complicated by other developments. The game of work continued, but in a different context. Its influence became decidedly subordinated to, if not completely overshadowed by, another source of job satisfaction.

INFORMAL SOCIAL ACTIVITY OF THE WORK GROUP: TIMES AND THEMES

The change came about when I began to take serious note of the social activity going on around me; my attentiveness to this activity came with growing involvement in it. What I heard at first, before I started to listen, was a stream of disconnected bits of communication which did not make much sense. Foreign accents were strong and referents were not joined to coherent contexts of meaning. It was just "jabbering." What I saw at first, before I began to observe, was occasional flurries of horseplay so simple and unvarying in pattern and so childish in quality that they made no strong bid for attention. For example, Ike would regularly switch off the power at Sammy's machine whenever Sammy made a trip to the lavatory or the drinking fountain. Correlatively, Sammy invariably fell victim to the plot by making an attempt to operate his clicking hammer after returning to the shop. And, as the simple pattern went, this blind stumbling into the trap was always followed by indignation and reproach from Sammy, smirking satisfaction from Ike, and mild paternal scolding from George. My interest in this procedure was at first confined to wondering when Ike would weary of his tedious joke or when Sammy would learn to check his power switch before trying the hammer.

But, as I began to pay closer attention, as I began to develop familiarity with the communication system, the disconnected became connected, the nonsense made sense, the obscure became clear, and the silly actually funny. . . .

This emerging awareness of structure and meaning included recognition that the long day's grind was broken by interruptions of a kind other than the formally instituted or idiosyncratically developed disjunctions in work routine previously described. These additional interruptions appeared in daily repetition in an ordered series of informal interactions. They were, in part, but only in part and in very rough comparison, similar to those common fractures of the production process known as the coffee break, the coke break, and the cigarette break. Their distinction lay in frequency of occurrence and in brevity. As phases of the daily series, they occurred almost hourly, and so short were they in duration that they disrupted work activity only slightly. Their significance lay not so much in their function as rest pauses, although it cannot be denied that physical refreshment was involved. Nor did their chief importance lie in the accentuation of progress points in the passage of time, although they could perform that function far more strikingly than the hour hand on the dull face of George's alarm clock. If the daily series of interruptions be likened to a clock, then the comparison might best be made with a special kind of cuckoo clock, one with a cuckoo which can provide variation in its announcements and can create such an interest in them that the intervening minutes become filled with intellectual content. The major significance of the interactional interruptions lay in such a carryover of interest. The physical interplay which momentarily halted work activity would initiate verbal exchanges and thought processes to occupy group members until the next interruption. The group interactions thus not only marked off the time; they gave it content and hurried it along.

Most of the breaks in the daily series were designated as "times" in the parlance of the clicker operators, and they featured the consumption of food or drink of one sort or another. There was coffee time, peach time, banana time, fish time, coke time, and, of course, lunch time. Other interruptions, which formed part of the series but were not verbally recognized as times, were window time, pickup time, and the staggered quitting times of Sammy and Ike. These latter unnamed times did not involve the partaking of refreshments.

My attention was first drawn to this times business during my first week of employment when I was encouraged to join in the sharing of two peaches. It was Sammy who provided the peaches; he drew them from his lunch box after making the announcement, "Peach time!" On this first occasion I refused the proffered fruit, but thereafter regularly consumed my half peach. . . .

Banana time followed peach time by approximately an hour. Sammy again provided the refreshments, namely, one banana. There was, however, no four-way sharing of Sammy's banana. Ike would gulp it down by himself after surreptitiously extracting it from Sammy's lunch box, kept on a shelf behind Sammy's work station. Each morning, after making the snatch, Ike would call out, "Banana time!" and proceed to down his prize while Sammy made futile protests and denunciations. George would join in with mild remonstrances, sometimes scolding Sammy for making so much fuss. The banana was one which Sammy brought for his own consumption at lunch time; he never did get to eat his banana, but kept bringing one for his lunch. At first this daily theft startled and amazed me. Then I grew to look forward to the daily seizure and the verbal interaction which followed.

Window time came next. It followed banana time as a regular consequence of Ike's castigation by the indignant Sammy. After "taking" repeated references to himself as a person badly lacking in morality and character, Ike would "finally" retaliate by opening the window which faced Sammy's machine, to let the "cold air" blow in on Sammy. The slandering which would, in its echolalic repetition, wear down Ike's patience and forbearance usually took the form of the invidious comparison: "George is a good daddy! Ike is a bad man! A very bad man!"

•   •   •

Following window time came lunch time, a formally designated half-hour for the midday repast and rest break. At this time, informal interaction would feature exchanges between Ike and George. The former would start eating his lunch a few minutes before noon, and the latter, in his role as straw boss, would censure him for malobservance of the rules. Ike's off-beat luncheon usually involved a previous tampering with George's alarm clock. Ike would set the clock ahead a few minutes in order to maintain his eating schedule without detection. . . .

Pickup time, fish time, and coke time came in the afternoon. I name it pickup time to represent the official visit of the man who made daily calls to cart away boxes of clicked materials. The arrival of the pickup man, a Negro, was always a noisy one, like the arrival of a daily passenger train in an isolated small town. Interaction attained a quick peak of intensity to crowd into a few minutes all communications, necessary and otherwise. Exchanges invariably included loud depreciations by the pickup man of the amount of work accomplished in the clicking department during the preceding twenty-four hours. Such scoffing would be on the order of "Is that all you've got done? What do the boys do all day?" These devaluations would be countered with allusions to the "soft job" enjoyed by the pickup man. During the course of the exchanges news items would be dropped, some of serious import, such as reports of accomplished or impending layoffs in the various plants of the company, or of gains or losses in orders for company prod-ucts. Most of the news items, however, involved bits of information on plant employees told in a light vein. . . .

About mid-afternoon came fish time. George and Ike would stop work for a few minutes to consume some sort of pickled fish which Ike provided. Neither Sammy nor I partook of this nourishment, nor were we invited. For this omission I was grateful; the fish, brought in a newspaper and with head and tail intact, produced a reverse effect on my appetite. . . .

Coke time came late in the afternoon, and was an occasion for total par-ticipation. The four of us took turns in buying the drinks and in making the trip for them to a fourth floor vending machine. . . .

Themes

To put flesh, so to speak, on this interactional frame of "times," my work group had developed various "themes" of verbal interplay which had be-come standardized in their repetition. These topics of conversation ranged in quality from an extreme of nonsensical chatter to another extreme of seri-ous discourse. Unlike the times, these themes flowed one into the other in no particular sequence of predictability. Serious conversation could sud-denly melt into horseplay, and vice versa. In the middle of a serious discus-sion on the high cost of living, Ike might drop a weight behind the easily startled Sammy, or hit him over the head with a dusty paper sack. Interac-tion would immediately drop to a low comedy exchange of slaps, threats, guffaws, and disapprobations which would invariably include a ten-minute echolalia of "Ike is a bad man, a bad man! George is a good daddy, a very fine man!" Or, on the other hand, a stream of such invidious comparisons as followed a surreptitious switching-off of Sammy's machine by the playful Ike might merge suddenly into a discussion of the pros and cons of saving for one's funeral. "Kidding themes" were usually started by George or Ike, and Sammy was usually the butt of the joke. . . .

The "poom poom" theme was one that caused no sting. It would come up several times a day to be enjoyed as unbarbed fun by the three older clicker operators. Ike was usually the one to raise the question, "How many times you go poom poom last night?" The person questioned usually replied with claims of being "too old for poom poom." If this theme did develop a goat, it was I. When it was pointed out that I was a younger man, this provided further grist for the poom poom mill. I soon grew weary of this poom poom business, so dear to the hearts of the three old satyrs, and, knowing where the conversation would inevitably lead, winced whenever Ike brought up the subject. . . .

Another kidding theme which developed out of serious discussion could be labelled "helping Danelly find a cheaper apartment." It became known to the group that Danelly had a pending housing problem, that he would need new quarters for his family when the permanent resident of his temporary summer dwelling returned from a vacation. This information engendered at first a great deal of sympathetic concern and, of course, advice on apartment hunting. Development into a kidding theme was immediately related to previous exchanges between Ike and George on the quality of their respective dwelling areas. Ike lived in "Lawndale," and George dwelt in the "Woodlawn" area. The new pattern featured the reading aloud of bogus "apartment for rent" ads in newspapers which were brought into the shop. Studying his paper at lunchtime, George would call out, "Here's an apartment for you, Danelly! Five rooms, stove heat, $20 a month, Lawndale Avenue!" Later, Ike would read from his paper, "Here's one! Six rooms, stove heat, dirt floor, $18.50 a month! At 55th and Woodlawn." Bantering would then go on in regard to the quality of housing or population in the two areas. The search for an apartment for Dannelly was not successful.

Serious themes included the relating of major misfortunes suffered in the past by group members. George referred again and again to the loss, by fire, of his business establishment. Ike's chief complaints centered around a chronically ill wife who had undergone various operations and periods of hospital care. Ike spoke with discouragement of the expenses attendant upon hiring a housekeeper for himself and his children; he referred with disappointment and disgust to a teen-age son, an inept lad who "couldn't even fix his own lunch. He couldn't even make himself a sandwich!" Sammy's reminiscences centered on the loss of a flourishing business when he had to flee Europe ahead of Nazi invasion.

But all serious topics were not tales of woe. One favorite serious theme which was optimistic in tone could be called either "Danelly's future" or "getting Danelly a better job." It was known that I had been attending "college," the magic door to opportunity, although my specific course of study remained somewhat obscure. Suggestions poured forth on good lines of work to get into, and these suggestions were backed with accounts of friends, and friends of friends, who had made good via the academic route. My answer to the expected question, "Why are you working here?" always stressed the "lots of overtime" feature, and this explanation seemed to suffice for short-range goals. . . .

The "professor theme" was the cream of verbal interaction. It involved George's connection with higher learning. His daughter had married the son of a professor who instructed in one of the local colleges. This professor theme was not in the strictest sense a conversation piece; when the subject came up, George did all the talking. The two Jewish operatives remained silent as they listened with deep respect, if not actual awe, to George's accounts of the Big Wedding which, including the wedding pictures, entailed an expense of $1,000. It was monologue, but there was listening, there was communication, the sacred communication of a temple, when George told of going for Sunday afternoon walks on the Midway with the professor, or of joining the professor for a Sunday dinner. Whenever he spoke of the professor, his daughter, the wedding, or even of the new son-in-law, who remained for the most part in the background, a sort of incidental like the wedding cake, George was complete master of the interaction. His manner, in speaking to the rank-and-file of clicker operators, was indeed that of master deigning to notice his underlings. I came to the conclusion that it was the professor connection, not the strawboss-ship or the extra nickel an hour, which provided the fount of George's superior status in the group. . . .

So initial discouragement with the meagerness of social interaction I now recognized as due to lack of observation. The interaction was there, in constant flow. It captured attention and held interest to make the long day pass. The twelve hours of "click,_____ move die,_____ click,_____ move die" became as easy to endure as eight hours of varied activity in the oil fields or eight hours of playing the piecework game in a machine shop. The "beast of boredom" was gentled to the harmlessness of a kitten.

. . .

Review Questions

1. In what types of jobs other than factory work could we expect the workers to devise psychological "games" such as "getting to the blues"?

2. Describe what occurred at "banana time," "peach time," etc., and discuss the functions they served for the workers.

3. Roy describes several conversational themes which recurred often in his work group. Why were these particular topics taken up time and time again? That is, what purposes did they serve for the workers?

4. Why was Roy initially unaware of patterns of social interaction in the work group? How did his awareness of them come about?

AT WORK WITH THE NIGHT WORKER

Howard Robboy

AT 11 P.M. OR MIDNIGHT EACH NIGHT, AS MOST AMERICANS ARE EITHER ASLEEP OR thinking about going to sleep, a small but significant number of people are just beginning their night's work.

Working nights means that one's entire daily schedule is thrown out of line from the temporal flow of society. Eating, sleeping, having sexual intercourse, socializing, visiting family members, and seeing one's children must be carefully scheduled by those who work the night shift. In a sense, these people become loners. The entire family must endure the strain of living in and between two time worlds.

In this study, the focus is on married male factory workers who reside and work in central and northern New Jersey and who work at night. The question explored in this article is why these workers agree to work the night shift despite the limitations on their social, family, and personal lives.

The period defined as night—perhaps from 11 P.M. to the breaking of the dawn—exists as a unique time zone in the course of social life (Melbin, 1978). It is here that we find fewer rules governing behavior than at any other time during the twenty-four hour cycle. For example, at this time we find blinking traffic lights and no time-specific norms pertaining to dress or food preferences.

The freer atmosphere of the night is not restrained by the walls of a factory and thus permeates the work experience of those employed on the night shift. Generally, night workers speak of less pressure, less tension, and a more congenial atmosphere than exist for their counterparts on the day shift in the same organization. The more amiable atmosphere manifests itself in many subtle ways during the night workers' time on the job.

THE FREER WORKING ATMOSPHERE ON THE NIGHT SHIFT

When a worker begins to work nights, his work experience is different from that of his counterpart on the day shift. For one thing, he finds that many of the regulations enforced on the day shift are ignored by supervision at night. In most cases, the workers have to report only to their foremen.[1]

Howard Robboy, "At Work With the Night Worker," is drawn from "They Work by Night: Temporal Adaptations in an Industrial Society," unpublished doctoral dissertation, Department of Sociology, Rutgers University, 1976.

The foremen are usually the only ones in charge at night and thus are themselves freed from the scrutiny of superiors. As long as the required amount of work is accomplished, they allow certain things to slide by. After all, they are working nights too.

Case 10

There are fewer supervisors around. The foremen are likely to overlook shop rules like going for extra coffee or goofing off. On this shift you can read or do crossword puzzles to keep your mind from getting tired. You can't do this on days.

Case 34

You don't have to wear safety plugs in your ears. On this job it is dangerous to wear earplugs. There is less pressure on third shift. There are no bigwigs from New York walking around. Also the supervisors don't bug you as much. There are no big shots putting pressure on them.

Having fewer supervisors gives the night worker greater control over his work. This is important for several reasons.[2] First, it means that the worker can move at his own pace while running the machines, controlling the speed at which he works, rather than following the dictum of management. It can be argued, in fact, that reports of alienated workers are less likely to come out of the night shift. It is not that night workers do less work but, rather, that they have some say about how much work will be done, and when, during their eight hours on the job.

Case 24

No one ever bothers me. My boss hardly ever comes to see me. As long as I do my work, things are OK.

A further consequence of working at one's own pace is that on third shift the workers don't have to "dog their job"—go through the motions of working when in fact they are not—as night-shift workers claim day shift workers do to avoid the omnipresent eye of supervision. Not having to "look busy" also lessens the night worker's role distance—there is greater correspondence between what is expected of him and what he accomplishes than is true of day workers.

Case 12

On third shift you don't have to dog your job because you have someone standing over you. You might do in six hours what someone else on day shift drags out to eight. If you have decent supervision they won't mind if you lie down. This is where the other shifts complain.

Third-shift workers often have the opportunity to use their own methods of operation rather than depend on procedures set by management. In my own experience as a bull-block operator in a copper-tubing factory, I was taught that when the machines were "running good" and the copper we were using was of high quality, we were allowed to run the machines faster than permitted by management—and so achieve production bonuses.

Rarely did our foreman check up on us, as we were told was done on the first shift.[3]

Case 26

I have to carry seventy pounds of material between these two machines. It was really hard on my wrists, so I devised a little cart so I could wheel the material between the two machines. On first shift they have to carry the stuff back and forth like horses. . . . We used to have two guys who worked out a system where one of them would run two machines for an hour while the other guy took a break. They showed this to others and soon it was done on the second and third shifts. Meanwhile, on first shift they have two guys doing the job dragging their feet.

Another feature of the third shift is that workers are frequently permitted to stretch their breaks. This adds to their feeling of having greater control over their lives while on the job.

Case 14

We get a little more wash-up time. The shifts overlap in our favor. So if we finish early we can disappear. We don't have all the snoopers around, the white shirts who are always watching over you. . . . They are more lenient about breaks. They are also this lenient on second shift, but not on first.[4]

Case 18

We can stretch our breaks where you can't on days. We can take a walk through the locker room and talk to the guys on breaks. On first shift, if you are not at your machine, you will get caught and get yelled at.

From the literature in industrial sociology, the data reported here, and my own experiences at the copper-tubing factory, it is the bargaining–conflict model of social relationships that most clearly depicts labor–management relationships (see Shelling, 1960; Handelman, 1976). The opportunities for rule breaking by a third-shift worker, seen through this perspective, are important for several reasons. On one level, they provide outlets for worker resentment against management. By breaking the rules, the worker feels that he is getting away with something or getting back at management. When the worker is supervised closely, as he is on the day shift, few opportunities exist for the channeling of resentments. My hunch is that, if the problem of industrial sabotage were to be thoroughly investigated, one would find that it occurs more frequently on the day shift (with adjustment made, of course, for the number of the workers on each of the shifts). For if there are few outlets for a worker's resentments, one of the options remaining when conditions become intolerable is to stop the machines.

On another level, the opportunity to break the rules can be viewed as a way to humanize the workplace. The authoritarian rule of management generates the expectation that the worker is supposed to work during his eight hours on the job (except for his coffee and lunch breaks) and do nothing else. The question then raised is, how often can people realistically do only one thing for such a prolonged period of time? Night workers, because they are able to manage their own time, can, to some extent, create a more humane atmosphere in which to work.

Working nights also provides the worker with the chance to "goof off" occasionally. A colleague, Noel Byrne, relates his experiences while working nights in a mill in Northern California:

> During the night, production would stop as the workers began waging bets on forklift truck races. The forklift trucks, normally used to transport the materials used in production, would be raced against one another. One night the brakes failed on one of the trucks as it went out the door, over a ten-foot embankment and finally stopped as it went head on into a creek which ran alongside the factory. It got so bad that the vice president of the company had to come into the plant one night to stop this practice. The foremen, who normally were the only ones in charge at this time, were the ones who drove the trucks during the races.[5]

In my own experience at the copper-tubing factory, workers were constantly throwing things at the drivers of cranes that rode on monorails attached to the roof of the building. The noise level in the plant was very high, and most of the workers wore their required earplugs. Unless one looked up from his work and saw the crane approaching, it would pass unnoticed. The crane operator, however, seeing the workers below busy at their work, would throw various articles at them. This folly would continue throughout the night.

The opportunity to smoke or drink coffee while working, to control both the pace of work and the production routines, to stretch their breaks, and occasionally to "goof off" on the job becomes an important feature of work on the night shift. Such advantages, along with a quantitative and qualitative difference in supervision, greatly affect the working atmosphere.

The working conditions often give rise to a greater sense of solidarity among third shift workers than among those on other shifts. Solidarity develops not only from the looser atmosphere, which makes greater interaction among the workers possible, but from the stigma of being labeled night workers by the workers on the first and second shifts.

Although working at night doesn't lead to the formation of a deviant identity off the job, there is evidence that a deviant identity does emerge during the hours of work. Such an identity is temporally situated at the workplace and reinforced as the night workers are compared with those on the other shifts.[6] In the nonwork world night workers identify themselves, and are identified by others, as being just working men, but at work they pick up the stigmatized identity of being night workers.[7] And, as the deviance literature suggests, a deviant or stigmatized identity acts as a strong bonding mechanism.

Case 21

People on the third shift are much closer. They confide in each other. They help one another. There is a much closer relationship on this shift.[8]

Case 30

When I go on vacation, I leave the key to my toolbox in case anyone needs anything. At work we share our tools. This is not done on day shift. We share information about the different machines. On days, everyone keeps to themselves and they don't help one another. There is a rivalry between them. . . . The workers are friendlier on night shift. There is more camaraderie. If you are on days the men bitch more. On third, if you are in trouble, someone will come over. There are only eight guys on this shift and they will give you a hand. We are a close-knit group. There are more soreheads on days. On nights the guys are easygoing.

In addition to the issues already discussed, other advantages of working at night emerged during the course of the interviews.

In the summer the night worker is spared from working under the heat of the day, which, along with the heat generated from the work itself, can be oppressive. In my own work experience, bull-block operators on the day shift were issued salt tablets by the plant nurse. These were a necessity to make it through the hot, humid days of New Jersey; on the night shift, these tablets were required only occasionally.

In some cases a night worker has a greater chance of working overtime than he would if he worked days. Usually the third shift is smaller in size than the other shifts, and so the probability is increased that any one worker will get overtime work when it is available.

Case 29

There are fewer people on our shift, so there is a greater probability of getting overtime. I get $2,000 to $3,000 a year in overtime. There is less supervision and we can work at our own speed. We are more united, closer together than they are on the day shift.

Having a smaller number of men working at night can also result in a reduction of the overall noise level in the factory. This is cited as an advantage of the night shift.

Case 15

It is also quieter on nights. The noise is incredible on days if I have to stay over. At my age, more things anger you. There is less aggravation on this shift.

Case 25

There is no hubbub like on second or days. There are fewer bosses and fewer employees. You are closer toward your fellow employees. You don't have the cutthroat attitude like on days and second.

SHIFT DIFFERENTIAL

All the workers interviewed in this study receive a nightshift differential in pay for working the third shift. The shift differential ranges from 12 to 71 cents an hour. Most of the workers view this as a compensation for having to work nights. A minority of the workers, those who like working nights, see the shift differential as a bonus. In any event, the shift differential allows the worker to earn an additional $5 to $28 a week and enables him to feel that he is doing better than his day-shift neighbors. Certainly such an awareness can add to his feelings of competence as a breadwinner of the family. Thus the shift differential provides a second major explanation of why workers agree to work the night shift—it can mean the difference between staying afloat financially or sinking. It can also be the difference between their being forced to work a second or third job and/or their wives being forced to seek employment.

Case 27

I was on day shift for two years until a few months ago. I went back on third because we needed the ten percent. The doctor told me not to work a part-time job any more. Whenever I work two jobs I wind up in the hospital. I have bronchitis, asthma, and emphysema. I got off third shift last time because my wife wanted me to. The kids were getting older and she wanted me to spend more time with them. When I was on days, she worked part-time. Then she stopped working and we needed the ten percent so I went back on third.

MOONLIGHTING

Having the daytime hours to himself gives the night worker the opportunity to obtain a part-time job or start his own business. In his study of moonlighters, Wilensky (1964) found that 6 percent of the male labor force moonlighted.[9] In this sample of night workers, sixteen men, or 40 percent of the forty workers interviewed, either had second jobs or owned small businesses to supplement the earnings from their night-shift positions. Of the sixteen night workers reporting second sources of income, ten operated their own businesses.

Case 16

I work third by choice. The kids were young then and we needed the money. I always worked two jobs. I am a carpenter and a fencer. Working third gave me my days free for a second job. You only work this shift for the money.

Case 28

I chose to work this shift as it gives me time to do other things. I have a part-time job as a handyman as well as a catering business.

Chinoy (1955), in his study of automobile workers, reports that some of the workers considered leaving the assembly line to start their own businesses. Although they are part of the American Dream and the Horatio Alger mystique, small businesses—the kind typically started by blue-collar workers—have a high failure rate. The night shift provides a safety valve for workers who want to set up a business of their own. They can work their night jobs and still run the business. If the business fails or doesn't produce sufficient income to support a family, they still have their jobs. Thus the night shift provides them with a trial period to get their businesses going. This is an option open to few day shift workers.

For workers with businesses of their own, the night shift can be important in other ways. Consider the following night worker who is self-employed during the day as a fence builder.

Case 16

I have a fence business. When someone wants a fence put around their house they want it done right away. Maybe their dog almost got run over, their kid ran out into the street, or they just had a big fight with one of their neighbors. In any case, they want you there the next day. If I was on the day shift I would have to do it on weekends or after five o'clock during the week if it is summer. If you do this, they figure they are getting a half-assed job because you are trying to moonlight. It means that you are not a regular contractor. They are paying a good buck for the work, and they want to get workman's quality. They figure that you can't do quality work at five o'clock. And on weekends they don't want to be bothered by you being there. By working nights I can be there by 9 A.M. They feel that they are getting a real contractor. This way I can charge full price and do a first-rate job. If you come in the afternoon or on a weekend, they want to pay you less because you are not a real fencer.

THE NIGHT-WORK TRAP

A night worker can become a blue-collar entrepreneur. He can work in a factory yet be free of many of the disagreeable features of the workplace that day shift workers encounter. He can earn the shift differential and have the opportunity to hold down a second job or manage a business of his own. But it is not for these reasons that most night workers choose the third shift. More often, little choice is available when they begin employment.

One of the initial reasons why workers agree to work on the night shift is that they have little or no seniority to qualify for the preferred position on the day shift. If a young worker, newly married, wants a job at a factory, he may have to choose between the second and third shifts. He may make the selection with the idea that, once he gains sufficient seniority, he will be able to go onto the day shift. In some cases the wait can be from five to ten years.

The second shift (beginning between 3 P.M. and 4 P.M. and ending between 11 P.M. and midnight) seems to be almost as disagreeable as the night shift. A second-shift worker with a working wife may see his wife and children only on weekends. He can sleep with his wife at night, but "night" often begins at two or three in the morning—because many workers find that they need a few hours to unwind before they are tired enough to go to bed. Many of the workers in this study had had some work experience on the second shift and, because of the scheduling difficulties, chose to transfer to the third shift.[10]

Case 30

I hate second shift. All you do is eat, sleep, and work. You come home at 12:45 A.M. wide awake. When you work nine to five, you have at least four hours free before you go to bed. What do you do at 12:45 A.M.? There is no one to talk to. You watch television until six in the morning, sleep until one-thirty, and then go to work. I call second shift the get-rich shift. All you can do is work and save.

Case 41

I would prefer nights to the afternoon shift. You start work at 2:30 before the kids come home from school. You come home after they are in bed and wake up after they've left for school. I would like to work days. But I prefer nights to the afternoons.

Choosing to work nights with the hope of eventually accumulating enough seniority to go on the day shift is a common strategy among night-shift workers. Consider the plight of a young worker, with a wife and family, who agrees to work nights. When he gains enough seniority to bid successfully for a job on the day shift, he may be faced with a financial dilemma. To go on days would require him to forfeit not only his shift differential but his second job or small business as well. To get off the night shift would entail, then, a substantial loss in income and a corresponding drop in his family's standard of living. For the blue-collar family, whose life style is already far from extravagant, this might prove quite difficult. Thus the night-shift differential and the opportunities for moonlighting, although they are economically seductive at the outset, can prove to be a trap that makes it difficult for a worker to leave the shift.

Case 47

I would much prefer working days. It would be the ultimate to have a straight nine-to-five job. I could work days, but my other involvements stop it. Eventually I will go over to days. This will be when the kids are older and can take care of themselves.

ADDITIONAL REASONS FOR WORKING THE NIGHT SHIFT

For some workers, going on nights means an advancement to a higher-paying position.

Case 1

I want to qualify for a foreman's job. The foreman's job includes a salary increase and job on the day shift. That is why I took this job as a mechanic. I know that if I wanted to advance, I couldn't just be an operator. A mechanic is a step to a foreman. If I knew that I would have to remain a mechanic, I would have stayed an operator and worked days.

Case 18

I have another five years on third in my department before I can go on days. If I switched to another department I could go on days tomorrow. Another job would mean a lower paying job, 13 cents an hour less plus the 10 percent shift differential.

During the course of the interviews, incidents were related of factories suddenly closing and workers finding themselves unemployed. With a family to support, working nights becomes attractive if it means a steady job with a secure future.

Case 12 (Wife)

Bud used to work at G.E. All of a sudden they moved to Texas and left us with nothing.

Case 21

I worked at Studebaker for two years until they closed up. So I went looking for work and I got a job in construction—building homes. This lasted for about a year, but then I got laid off when the weather got bad. I wound up in _____on the second shift. I worked there for two years but wanted a job on days, so I went to the Mack in Plainfield to work the day shift. I was at the Mack exactly five years, because I got a five-year pin. Then Mack moved out in '61, and I went to _____again on the third shift. (*Wife*) When Mack moved out it was really hard to get a job. All those men were thrown out of work. In fact, we used up most of our savings and it was rough. We were just glad that he had a job. (*Husband*) I needed a job and I was glad to work there. When you look for a job, you try to get the most for the least. Some of the places I went to paid so little that it wouldn't cover my mortgage payments. I am very grateful for the job I do have. No one around here pays the money_____does. We also get great benefits. The hospitalization and the other benefits can't be matched. At first I didn't like the third shift. I couldn't get used to it. But I made up my mind, and I got used to it.

If a night worker doesn't have a second job or a business on the side, having the day free provides time to pursue hobbies, care for preschool children, and clean the house.

Case 14

I work nights for the money and to be able to babysit during the day while she is working. I am on third shift now primarily because of our youngest child. . . . I would like to go on days in a few years when my youngest child is older and can take care of herself after school. Right now our lives are set up for me on the third shift. Everything is going so well. I don't know whether I would want to go on days now. Things are going well.

Case 41

I have more time with my family, especially in the winter. I get up when the kids get home from school, and I am with them until they go to bed at night and I go to work.

The third shift is also advantageous for activities like shopping. The worker can leisurely shop away from the evening and weekend crowds.

Case 4

The biggest advantage of the shift is that you can shop with no crowds. If you need a doctor's appointment, shopping, and things done around the house, it is good. You don't have to fight crowds on weekends.

Another advantage of the shift is that if the worker is not tied down by a second job, he can use some of his nonwork time for recreation and avoid the crowded periods which day shift workers utilize for leisure.

Case 37

I love to fish and hunt. On this shift I can come home, change my clothes, and be hunting and fishing in fifteen minutes.

Case 10

It is a perfect shift for camping. I work the Sunday to Thursday schedule and can come home Friday morning and sleep for a few hours. Then I can leave and not return until Sunday night. If I was on the regular third shift, I would have to leave Saturday morning and be back Sunday night for my wife to get to work on Monday morning.

Case 19

During the summer, I can go to the beach during the day and not fight traffic. I can sleep on the beach, and I don't have to fight the weekend crowds.

The night shift can also provide the worker with ample time to pursue his hobbies.

Case 17

If I could take you downstairs and show you my hobby, you would understand why I like this shift so much. I raise show parakeets, and working nights allows me time to take care of them. We also go to bird shows in New York, Boston, and Washington. If we have to go into New York for the day, I don't have to take a day off from work. I also have a greenhouse outside where I raise azaleas. On day shift you can have your evening activities, but you don't have time for a hobby.

Another feature of the night shift is that the workers save time driving to and from work because they do not have to fight rush-hour traffic. This adds to their amount of daily nonwork time.

Case 30

I can go from here to the plant in seventeen minutes. On days it would take thirty-five to forty minutes. I save an hour this way.

One worker used his nonwork time to build a new house for himself and his family.

Case 16

I built this house three years ago. I saved the money from working the two jobs and from my wife working part-time. (*Wife*) We worked six hours a day on this house and in ten months we built it. He came home from work, had breakfast, and worked on the house for six hours. Then he went home and went to sleep. We now rent our old house, and that pays for the mortgage on this house. We pay the smaller mortgage on that house, and we own land in Florida. Now we don't need the money from the third shift. (*Husband*) If I had worked days, I wouldn't have been able to accomplish as much. No one helped us with this. We did it ourselves. We could not have built this house if I wasn't on third shift. I was home when the materials were delivered and could check to make sure there were no shortages or that the wrong materials weren't sent.

It should be noted that all of the "features" of the night shift cited by the workers demonstrate a degree of social isolation. Their nonwork activities act as "side bets" in embellishing their careers as loners. An element common to their remarks is that they are able to avoid crowds.

NEGATIVE ASPECTS OF WORKING THE NIGHT SHIFT

Although the advantages of the night shift are significantly greater than the limitations, still, in the course of the interviews, the workers speak of the negative features.

One of the slang terms used for the third shift is the "dead-man's shift." The phrase symbolizes the feelings on the part of workers that management doesn't care about them or even notice their existence. The feelings manifest themselves in several ways. First, decisions about production and product development are made by management officials who work the day shift. The night workers claim that decisions are made on the basis of day-shift operations, with no consideration given to night-shift needs.

Case 4

You are always left out of new information or new projects being developed. Management decisions are made on the basis of the first shift and not the third. You are never noticed by anyone, so it's hard to advance. You don't get the exposure.

Case 20

If you get a new machine, the person on day shift will know more about the machine. If there is a question about the machine, there is no one to go to.

Night workers are also unknown to management except on paper. This factor may be significant if the worker hopes to advance to a higher position.

Case 12

I know a lot of young guys who are strapped and need the 10 percent. They can't get into training programs or foremanships. No one knows them. You can apply, but when they get into the office, they say, "Who is that guy?"

The night workers complain that fewer plant facilities are open at night. I experienced these difficulties. One night we were working hard trying to make production bonuses, and a 270-pound coil of hot copper tubing began falling off the conveyor belt as it approached my section of the bull block. As I grabbed the coil with my insulated gloves, a section of the tubing hit my arm. The burn wasn't serious enough to require emergency treatment in a local hospital, but a Band-Aid proved to be insufficient. Since there was no nurse on duty on the night shift, I had to wait until 7 A.M. to see the nurse, who came on duty with the day shift.

Case 26

On third shift you can't buy safety shoes or glasses when you want. The foreman has to do it for me. There is no nurse on duty either.

Case 30

On first shift they have a full cafeteria. On third they have a lunch wagon. If I have a problem, I have to see the personnel man on my own time. No one is there at 7 A.M.

SUMMARY AND CONCLUSIONS

This research provides numerous explanations as to why married male factory workers agree to work the night shift despite serious limitations in their family, social, and private lives.

The desires for a good job, easier working conditions, control over one's work, less supervision, and a small bonus becomes immediately apparent as explanations for working this shift. As one looks at the night shift in terms of a career, however, one discovers social and economic factors that serve as traps and consequently make it difficult for a night worker to return to a normal day-shift routine if an opportunity arose.

NOTES

1. Of all the advantages of working nights cited by the workers interviewed, having less supervision was mentioned most often. Twenty-six of the forty workers interviewed raised this issue.

2. For a further discussion of the issue of worker's control, see Gerry Hunnius, G. David Garson, and John Case, eds., *Worker's Control: A Reader on Labor and Social Change*. New York: Vintage, 1973.

3. Donald Roy, in "Efficiency and the Fix: Informal Intergroup Relations in a Piecework Machine Shop," *American Journal of Sociology*, 60, 255–266, reports a similar finding.

4. A colleague, Noel Byrne, reports the following account from his night-work job in a mill in northern California.

One of the advantages of night work was that you didn't have to hide when you finished your work. One night it was almost time to quit when the owner of the plant who lived in Chicago made a tour. He was unknown to us as we had never seen him before. One guy was just standing around, killing time before he could punch out. The owner came up to him and said, "What are you doing?" The worker replied, "Just fucking the dog." The owner, startled, retorted with, "You're fired, because I'm the dog you are fucking."

5. Another colleague, Howard Finkelstein, verifies Byrne's experience in his account of a night shift job he held in a swimming pool factory in New Jersey.

I worked at a place where they manufactured prefab swimming pools. We used to bust our asses getting our work done by lunch time (3:30 A.M.) so that we could goof off the rest of the night. We used to bring in gallon containers of pink lemonade and gin. Following their consumption, we used to have fork-lift truck races on the loading platforms. This practice ended one night when the brakes on one of the trucks failed, and the truck went off the loading platform into a pile of wood.

6. For a discussion of situated identities in relationship to the self, see Edward Gross and Gregory P. Stone, "Embarrassment and the Analysis of Role Requirements, "The American Journal of Sociology", 70 (July 1964), 1–15.

7. Although Pigors and Pigors (1944:3) and Sergean (1971:165) claim that there is a social stigma attached to night work, I found no evidence for this in the course of the interviews.

8. Sergean (1971), Davis (1973), and Kozak (1974) report similar findings in their studies of night workers.

9. According to Michelotti (1975:56–62), the latest statistics show that men between the ages of 25 and 54 have the highest percentage of moonlighting (between 6 and 7 percent). As expected, there is no available national data on the percentage of night workers who moonlight.

10. To complete the "picture" of the American labor force, ethnographies are needed on second and rotating shift workers. For example, the second shift has a reputation among night workers for being a haven for bad marriages. If the couple schedules it "correctly," they can see each other only on weekends, thus minimizing the friction periods when they are together. Meanwhile they can appear married to the outside world.

REFERENCES

Becker, Howard S.
   1953–1954 "Some Contingencies of the Professional Dance Musician's Career," *Human Organization*, 12 (Spring), 22–26.
   1960 "Notes on the Concept of Commitment," *American Journal of Sociology*, 65 (July), 32–40.

Chinoy, Ely
   1955 *The Automobile Worker and the American Dream*. Garden City, N.Y.: Doubleday.

Davis, Murray
  1973 *Intimate Relations*. New York: Free Press.

Goffman, Erving
  1961 *Encounters*. Indianapolis: Bobbs-Merrill.

Gross, Edward and Gregory P. Stone
  1964 "Embarrassment and the Analysis of Role Relationships," *American Journal of Sociology*, 70 (July), 1–15.

Handleman, Don
  1976 "Rethinking Banana Time," *Urban Life*, 4 (January), 433–448.

Hunnius, G., David Garson, and John Case, eds.
  1973 *Workers Control*. New York: Vintage.

Kozak, Lola Jean
  1974 "Night People: A Study of the Social Experiences of Night Workers," *Summation*, 4 (Spring/Fall), 40–61.

Melbin, Murry
  1978 "Night as Frontier," *American Sociological Review*, 43 (February), 1–22.

Michelatti, Kopp
  1975 "Multiple Jobholders in May, 1975," *Monthly Labor Review* (November), 56–62.

Pigors, Paul and Faith Pigors
  1944 *Human Aspects of Multiple Shift Work*. Cambridge: Department of Economics and Social Science, Massachusetts Institute of Technology.

Roy, Donald F.
  1952 "Quota Restriction and Goldbricking in a Machine Shop," *American Journal of Sociology*, 57 (March), 427–442.
  1955 "Efficiency and 'The Fix': Informal Intergroup Relations in a Piecework Machine Shop," *American Journal of Sociology*, 60, 255–266.
  1959–60 "Banana Time," *Human Organization*, 18 (Winter), 158–168.

Sergean, Robert
  1971 *Managing Shiftwork*. London: Gower Press-Industrial Society.

Shelling, Thomas
  1960 *The Strategy of Conflict*. Cambridge, Mass.: Harvard University Press.

Shostak, Arthur
  1969 *Blue Collar Life*. New York: Random House.

Slater, Philip
  1969 *On the Pursuit of Loneliness: American Culture at the Breaking Point*. Boston: Beacon Press.

Stone, Gregory P.
  1971 "*American Sports: Play and Display*," in Eric Dunning, ed., *The Sociology of Sport*. London: Frank Cass, pp. 46–65.

1974 "Remarks," at *The Minnesota Symposium on Symbolic Interaction*. Hudson, Wis., June.

Wilensky, Harold L.
1964 "The Moonlighter: A Product of Relative Deprivation," *Institute of Industrial Relations* (Reprint No. 219). Berkeley: University of California, pp. 105–124.

Review Questions

1. A young married worker in need of a job accepts a position on the night shift. He or she hopes to earn enough seniority to switch to the day shift eventually. According to Robboy's study of night-shift workers, what social and economic traps might prevent an eventual switch to the day shift?

2. Robboy's research indicates that there are numerous advantages and disadvantages to working the night shift. What are they, and why do they exist on the night shift rather than on other shifts?

3. How do you explain the fact that there is less worker alienation and industrial sabotage on the night shift than on the day shift?

Suggested Readings: Interaction in Institutional Contexts: Work and Economics

Bigus, Odis E. "The Milkman and His Customer," *Urban Life and Culture*, 1 (July 1972), 131–165.

Miller, Gale. *It's a Living: Work in Modern Society*. New York: St. Martin's Press, 1981.

Roy, Donald F. "Quota Restriction and Goldbricking in a Machine Shop," *American Journal of Sociology*, 57 (1952), 427–442.

Schrank, Robert. *Ten Thousand Working Days*. Cambridge, Mass.: The M.I.T. Press, 1979.

Spradley, James P. and Brenda J. Mann. *The Cocktail Waitress: Woman's Work in a Man's World*. New York: John Wiley, 1979.

Terkel, Studs. *Working*. New York: Random House, 1974.

D. Religion

M<small>ANY SOCIOLOGICAL PROCESSES, FUNCTIONS, STRUCTURES, AND ROLES ARE ASSOCI-</small>ated with religions, over and above their belief systems. The early sociologist Emile Durkheim noted a century ago that religion serves societal functions by bringing its members together and providing a common element around which group solidarity may form. Religious rituals such as weddings, baptisms, and funerals give some structure to possibly disruptive events and changes. In a country such as ours where religious diversity is a long-standing fact of life, different kinds of issues arise. How do various ethnic groups develop styles of religious practice that are uniquely their own? How does one's religious status affect opportunities for interacting with other people, for marrying, for making employment contacts, and for experiencing discrimination? What is the importance of competing religious world views? How does one decide to change one's religious affiliation, to enter a religious career, or even to become an atheist? How does social interaction shape the individual's religious affiliations and beliefs?

The articles presented in this section deal with two aspects of the impact of religion on individuals' social worlds—religious conversion and relinquishing a religious career. Both place strong emphasis on the *processes* involved in changing one's religious identification and on the consequences of such changes for the *self-concepts* of those involved. Both also make clear the *interactional roots* (and consequences) of changing identities and statuses.

John Lofland and Rodney Stark, in "Becoming a World-Saver: A Theory of Conversion to a Deviant Perspective," describe the adoption of a new world view by converts to the "Divine Precepts" of the "Lord of the Second Advent." The authors are interested first in the characteristics of individuals that "push" them toward conversion to the perspective of the "deviant" subgroup. These conditions are not, however, sufficient to explain conversion. Lofland and Stark look more closely at the patterns of interaction ("predisposing conditions," and "situational contingencies") that serve to "pull" potential recruits into commitment to the beliefs of the subgroup. Conversion to the new group's beliefs is thus seen as a process, a set of sequential steps including both "push" and "pull" factors, no one of which is sufficient to produce total conversion.

Even though we usually think of "conversion" as a religious experience exclusively, the process described by Lofland and Stark may occur in other, nonreligious passages from one status to another. The importance of this article, therefore, goes beyond an understanding of the impact of religion.

What happens when one decides to leave a religious life and enter the secular world? As Lucinda SanGiovanni reports, in "Rediscovering Gender: The Emergent Role Passage of Ex-Nuns," many of the same "push" and "pull" factors described by Lofland and Stark are at work. Rather than focusing on why nuns began leaving their convents in the mid-1960s, however, this article asks how they became reintegrated into the larger society. Since an important aspect of being a nun is a disavowal of and disattention to one's gender, reintegration requires relearning gender roles. From the accounts of ex-nuns in their in-depth interviews, we can see both the impact of their previous convent life on their modes of interaction and self-images and the impact of secular claims and social scripts in shaping new identities.

BECOMING A WORLD-SAVER: A THEORY OF CONVERSION TO A DEVIANT PERSPECTIVE

John Lofland and Rodney Stark

ALL MEN AND ALL HUMAN GROUPS HAVE ULTIMATE VALUES, A WORLD VIEW, OR A PER-spective furnishing them a more or less orderly and comprehensible picture of the world. Clyde Kluckhohn remarked that no matter how primitive and crude it may be, there is a "philosophy behind the way of life of every individual and of every relatively homogeneous group at any given point in their histories."[1] When a person gives up one such perspective or ordered view of the world for another we refer to this process as *conversion*.[2]

Frequently such conversions are between popular and widely held perspectives—from Catholicism to Communism, or from the world view of an underdeveloped or primitive culture to that of a technically more advanced society, as from the Peyote Cult of the Southwest Indians to Christianity. The continual emergence of tiny cults and sects in western industrial nations makes it clear, however, that sometimes persons relinquish a more widely held perspective for an unknown, obscure and often, socially devalued one.

In this paper we shall outline a model of the conversion process through which a group of people came to see the world in terms set by the doctrines of one such obscure and devalued perspective—a small millenarian religious cult. Although it is based on only a single group, we think the model suggests some rudiments of a general account of conversion to deviant perspectives. But the degree to which this scheme applies to shifts between widely held perspectives must, for now, remain problematic.

BACKGROUND

Our discussion is based on observation of a small, millenarian cult headquartered in Bay City,[3] a major urban center on the West Coast. This "movement" constitutes the American following of a self-proclaimed "Lord of the Second Advent," a Mr. Chang, who has attracted more than 5,000 converts in Korea since 1954. The "Divine Precepts," the doctrine Chang claims was revealed to him by God, concerns a complete "Restoration of the World" to the conditions of the Garden of Eden by 1967. The message was

John Lofland and Rodney Stark, "Becoming a World-Saver: A Theory of Conversion to a Deviant Perspective," *American Sociological Review*, 30 (December 1965), 862–874.

brought to this country by Miss Yoon-Sook Lee, a graduate of Methodist seminaries, and a former professor of social welfare at a large, church-supported, women's college in Seoul.

In 1959 Miss Lee arrived in a university town (here called Northwest Town) in the Pacific Northwest, and in two years gained five totally committed converts to the Divine Precepts (hereafter referred to as the D.P.). In December 1960, after difficulties with local clergymen and public opinion, largely touched off when two female converts deserted their husbands and children, the group moved to Bay City.

By mid-1963, 15 more converts had been gained and by the end of 1964 the cult numbered more than 150 adherents. Converts were expected to devote their lives to spreading "God's New Revelation" and preparing for the New Age theocracy which God and a host of active spirits were expected to create on earth shortly. Typically the converts lived communally in a series of houses and flats, contributed their salaries from menial jobs to the common treasury, thus supporting Miss Lee as a full-time leader, and gave all their spare time to witnessing and otherwise proselytizing [or seeking converts].

In this brief report, analysis will be limited to the single problem of conversion.[4] Under what conditions and through what mechanisms did persons come to share the D.P. view of the world, and, conversely, who rejected this perspective?

The logical and methodological structure of the analysis is based on a "value-added"[5] conception. That is, we shall offer a series of seven (more or less) successively accumulating factors, which in their total combination seem to account for conversion to the D.P. All seven factors seem necessary for conversion, and together they appear to be sufficient conditions.

The sequential arrangement of the seven conditions may be conceived in the imagery of a funnel; that is, as a structure that systematically reduces the number of persons who can be considered available for recruitment, and also increasingly specifies who is available. At least theoretically, since the mission of the cult was to "convert America," all Americans are potential recruits. Each condition narrows the range of clientele: ultimately, only a handful of persons responded to the D.P. call.

· · ·

Data were gathered through participant observation in the cult from early 1962 to mid-1963. Further information was obtained from interviews with converts, their acquaintances, families, and workmates; with persons who tooks some interest in the D.P. but were not converts; and with a variety of clergymen, officials, neighbors, employers and others in contact with the adherents. Less intensive observation was conducted through mid-1964.

Although complete data pertinent to all seven steps of the conversion model were not obtainable for all 21 persons who were classified as converts by mid-1963, full information on all seven factors was available for 15 converts. All the available data conform to the model. In presenting biographical information to explicate and document the model, we shall focus on the most central of the early converts, drawing on material from less central and later converts for illustrations. The converts were primarily white, Protestant, and young (typically below 35); some had college training, and most were Americans of lower-middle-class and small-town origins.

CONVERSION OPERATIONALLY DEFINED

How does one determine when a person has "really" taken up a different perspective? The most obvious evidence, of course, is his own declaration that he has done so. This frequently takes the form of a tale of regeneration, about how terrible life was before and how wonderful it is now.[6] But verbal claims are easily made and simple to falsify. Indeed, several persons who professed belief in the D.P. were regarded as insincere by all core members. A display of loyalty and commitment, such as giving time, energy, and money to the D.P. enterprise, invariably brought ratification of the conversion from all core members, but to require such a display as evidence of "actual" conversion overlooks four persons who made only verbal professions but were universally regarded as converts by core members. To avoid this difficulty two classes or degrees of conversion may be distinguished: *verbal converts*, or fellow-travelers and followers who professed belief and were accepted by core members as sincere, but took no active role in the D.P. enterprise; and *total converts*, who exhibited their commitment through deeds as well as words.

Up to a point, the same factors that account for total conversion also account for verbal conversion and initially we shall discuss the two groups together. Later we shall attempt to show that verbal conversion is transformed into total conversion only when the *last stage* in the conversion sequence develops.

A MODEL OF CONVERSION

To account for the process by which persons came to be world-savers for the D.P., we shall investigate two genres [or types] of conditions or factors. The first, which might be called *predisposing conditions*, comprises attributes of persons *prior* to their contact with the cult. These are background factors, the conjunction of which forms a pool of potential D.P. converts. Unfortunately, it has become conventional in sociology to treat demographic characteristics, structural or personal frustrations, and the like, as completely responsible for "pushing" persons into collectivities dedicated to protest against the prevailing social order. These factors are not unimportant, but a model composed entirely of them is woefully incomplete. The character of their incompleteness is expressed by a Meadian paraphrase of T. S. Eliot: "Between the impulse and the act falls the shadow." The second genre of conditions is this shadowed area, the situational contingencies.

Situational contingencies are conditions that lead to the successful recruitment of persons predisposed to the D.P. enterprise. These conditions arise from confrontation and interaction between the potential convert and D.P. members. Many persons who qualified for conversion on the basis of predisposing factors entered interpersonal relations with D.P. members, but because the proper situational conditions were not met, they did not become converts.

With these two classes of factors in mind, we may turn to a discussion of the first and most general of predisposing conditions.

1. Tension. No model of human conduct entirely lacks a conception of tension, strain, frustration, deprivation, or other versions of the hedonic calculus. And, not surprisingly, even the most cursory examination of the life situations of converts before they embraced the D.P. reveals what they at least *perceived* as considerable tension.[7]

This tension is best characterized as a felt discrepancy between some imaginary, ideal state of affairs and the circumstances in which these people saw themselves caught up. We suggest that acutely felt tension is a necessary, but far from sufficient condition for conversion. That is, it creates some disposition to act. But tension may be resolved in a number of ways (or remain unresolved); hence, that these people are in a tension situation does not indicate *what* action they may take.

Just as tension can have myriad consequences, its sources can also be exceedingly disparate. Some concrete varieties we discovered were: longing for unrealized wealth, knowledge, fame, and prestige; hallucinatory activity for which the person lacked any successful definition; frustrated sexual and marital relations; homosexual guilt; acute fear of face-to-face interaction; disabling and disfiguring physical conditions; and—perhaps of a slightly different order—a frustrated desire for a significant, even heroic, religious status, to "know the mind of God intimately," and to be a famous agent for his divine purposes.[8]

Brief life histories of a few central believers will indicate concretely what bothered them as pre-converts. The case of *Miss Lee*, the "Messiah's" emissary in America, illustrates the aspiration to be an important religious figure.

Miss Lee was born and raised in Korea and converted to Chang's cult in 1954 when she was 39. During her early teens she was subject to fits of depression and used to sit on a secluded hilltop and seek spirit contacts. Shortly she began receiving visions and hearing voices—a hallucinatory pattern she was to maintain thereafter. Her adolescent mystical experience convinced her she had a special mission to perform for God and at the age of 19 she entered a Methodist seminary in Japan. She was immediately disenchanted by the "worldly concern" of the seminarians and the training she received, although she stuck out the five-year course. Prior to entering the seminary she had become engrossed in the Spiritualistic writings of Emmanuel Swedenborg, who soon began to appear to her in visions. Her estrangement from conventional religious roles was so great that upon graduating from seminary she, alone among her classmates, refused ordination. She returned to Korea at the start of World War II, and by 1945 was professor of social welfare at a denominational university in Seoul. In 1949 the Methodist Board of Missions sent her to a Canadian university for further theological training. There she wrote her thesis on Swedenborg, who continued to visit her in spirit form. In Canada, as in Japan, she was bitterly disappointed by the "neglect of things of the spirit," caused concern among the faculty by constantly hiding to pray and seek visions, and occasionally stole away to Swedenborgian services. Her spirits continued to tell her that she was a religious figure of great importance. Returning to her academic life in Korea she fell ill with chronic diarrhea and eventually nephritis, both of which resisted all medical treatment. After two years of this, her health was broken and she was completely bedridden. At this time her servant took her to see Chang.

Thus is summarized a portrait of a desperately estranged maiden lady, with secret convictions of grandeur, frequent "heterodox" hallucinations, and failing health, who felt herself badly entangled in the mundane affairs of modern religious bureaucracy.

Although the cultural context is rather different, the case of *Bertha* . . . follows lines rather similar to Miss Lee's, but includes an important sexual theme.

Bertha, 29 at conversion, was the daughter of German immigrants and was raised in a suburban town. After high school she attended a modeling school, the kind operated in large cities for naive, fame-hungry girls, regardless of suitability. She returned to marry a local boy who was employed as a stereotyper in a printing plant. On her wedding night she spent two hours locked in their hotel bathroom, and subsequently did not improve her evaluation of sexual intercourse. Later the couple separated briefly, reunited, and after five years of marriage had their first child (1955). The second came in 1957, and they moved to the West Coast. There Bertha began having private religious hallucinations, including "sanctification"— being made holy and free of all sin. She went to various ministers to tell of her marvelous experiences, but was not warmly received; indeed, most advised psychiatric help. She began, then, to tell her husband that one day she would be very important in the service of the Lord. Following a homosexual episode with a neighbor woman, Bertha demanded to be taken elsewhere and the family went to Northwest Town in April 1959. There they settled in rural Elm Knoll, a collection of half a dozen houses about seven miles from town. This was soon to be the scene of the initial formation of the cult group, and here she came to know two neighbors, Minnie Mae and Alice. These young housewives drew the attention of other neighbors by spending many hours hanging around the nearby general store, sometimes drinking beer and often complaining a good deal about their husbands. During this period, Bertha attended churches of various denominations and continued to have frequent ecstatic religious experiences, mostly while sitting alone in a clump of bushes near her house, where she was also reported to have spent a good deal of time crying and moaning.

•   •   •

Bertha's friend, *Minnie Mae*, did not aspire to significant status, religious or otherwise. She pined, rather, for the more modest goal of marital satisfaction.

Minnie Mae (27 at conversion) was born in Possum Trot, Arkansas, of hillbilly farmers. She was one of 11 children, began dating at 12, and married at 15, having completed only rural elementary school. She and her young husband left Arkansas for lack of jobs and settled in Northwest Town. Her husband took a job as a laborer in a plywood factory. Although the young couple did not join a church, they came from a religious background (Minnie Mae's mother was a Pentecostal lay preacher), and they began attending tent meetings near Northwest Town. During one of these, Minnie Mae began speaking in "tongues" and fell into a several-hour trance. After this her husband discouraged church activities. The couple had three children at roughly two year intervals, and until 1960 Minnie Mae seems to have spent most of her time caring for these children and watching television. She reported tuning in a local channel when she got up in the morning and keeping it on until sign-off at night. In 1958 the couple built a small house in Elm Knoll. Here, in her behavior and conversations with neighbors, she began to reveal severe dissatisfactions in her marriage. She repeatedly complained that her husband only had intercourse with her about once a month, but she also reported being very afraid of getting pregnant again. Furthermore, she wanted to get out and have some fun, go dancing, etc., but her husband only wanted to watch TV and to fish. She wondered if she had let life pass her by because she had been married too young. And, often, she complained about her husband's opposition to fundamentalist religious activities.

Merwin and *Alice* followed quite a different pattern. Theirs was not an intensely religious concern, indeed their grandiose ambitions were for fortune.

Merwin (29 at conversion) was raised in a Kansas hamlet where his father was the railroad depot agent. After high school he tried a small Kansas junior college for a year, did poorly, and joined the Marines. Discharged in 1952, he spent one year at the University of Kansas majoring in architecture, and did well, so he transferred to what he felt was a better school in Northwest Town. Here he didn't do well and adopted a pattern of frequently dropping out, then going back. Estranged and alone, he bought a few acres in Elm Knoll with a small ramshackle cottage and took up a recluse's existence—he rarely shaved or washed, brewed his own beer, and dabbled in health foods, left-wing political writings, and occult publications, while supporting himself by working in a plywood plant. Next door, about 20 yards away, lived Alice, her two children and her husband, also a plywood plant worker. Alice's husband, however, worked a swing shift, while Merwin worked days. The result was that Alice filed for divorce and moved over to Merwin's. The husband departed without undue resistance. After their marriage, Merwin began to put his plans for financial empires into action. He considered a housing development, a junkyard, and finally bought a large frame house in Northwest Town to convert into a boarding house for students. After he had bought furniture and made other investments in the property, the city condemned it. Merwin filed bankruptcy and returned to Elm Knoll to lick his wounds and contemplate his next business venture. Merwin had long been disaffected with the established religions, had considered himself an agnostic, but was also interested in the occult. These interests were developed by his work partner, Elmer, whom we shall meet in a moment.

Alice, also a small-town girl, had traded for what she felt was a better man, one who was "going places," but these hopes seemed to be fading after the bankruptcy. She still bragged to Minnie Mae and Bertha that Merwin would be a big man someday, but there was little evidence to support her.

Elmer's case illustrates yet another kind of frustrated ambition, that of attaining status as a man of knowledge and invention.

Elmer was born on a farm in North Dakota but his parents fled the drought and depression for the West Coast during the late thirties and settled on a farm near Northwest Town. Elmer, 26 at the time of his conversion, was slightly built with something of a vacant stare. After high school, he flunked out of the university after one semester and spent the next two years in the army where he flunked medical technician school. After the army he enrolled in a nearby state college and again lasted only one semester. He then returned to his parents' farm and took a job in the plywood factory. Elmer conceived of himself as an intellectual and aspired to be a learned man. He undertook to educate himself, and collected a large library toward this end. Unfortunately, he was virtually illiterate. In addition to more conventional books (including much of the Random House Modern Library), he subscribed to occult periodicals such as *Fate, Flying Saucers, Search,* etc. He also viewed himself as a practical man of invention, a young Thomas Edison, and dreamed of constructing revolutionary gadgets. . . . On top of all this, Elmer was unable to speak to others above a whisper and looked constantly at his feet while talking. Furthermore, he had great difficulty sustaining a conversation, often appearing to forget what he was talking about. But despite his "objective" failures at intellectual accomplishment, Elmer clung to a belief in his own potential. The consequences of failure were largely to make him withdraw, to protect this self-image from his inability to demonstrate it.

These case histories provide a concrete notion of the kinds of things that bothered pre-converts. These problems apparently are not qualitatively different from the problems presumably experienced by a significant, albeit unknown, proportion of the general population. Their peculiarity, if any, appears to be that pre-converts felt their problems were quite acute, and they experienced high levels of tension concerning them over rather long periods.

· · ·

Explanation cannot rest here, for such tensions could have resulted in any number of other resolutions, and in fact they usually do. Thus, these unresolved problems in living are part of the necessary scenery for the stage, but the rest of the props, the stage itself, and the drama of conversion remain to be constructed.

2. Type of Problem-Solving Perspective. Since conversion to the D.P. is hardly the only thing people can do about their problems, it becomes important to ask what else these particular people could have done, and why they didn't. Because people have a number of conventional and readily available alternative definitions for, and means of coping with, their problems, there were, in the end, very few converts to the D.P. An alternative solution is a perspective or rhetoric defining the nature and sources of problems in living and offering some program for their resolution. Many such alternative solutions exist in modern society. Briefly, three particular genres of solution are relevant here: *the psychiatric, the political* and *the religious.* In the first, the *origin of problems is typically traced to the psyche,* and manipulation of the self is advocated as a solution. Political solutions, mainly radical, locate the *sources of problems in the social structure* and advocate reorganization of the system as a solution. The religious perspective tends to see both *sources and solutions as emanating from an unseen and, in principle, unseeable realm.*

The first two secular rhetorics [or lines of reasoning] bear the major weight of usage in contemporary society. No longer is it considered appropriate to regard recalcitrant and aberrant actors as possessed of devils. Indeed, modern religious institutions tend to offer a secular, frequently psychiatric, rhetoric concerning problems in living. The prevalence of secular definitions of tension is a major reason for the scarcity of D.P. converts. Several persons, whose circumstances met other conditions of the model, had adopted a psychiatric definition of their tensions and failed to become converts. In one exaggerated instance, an ex-GI literally alternated residence between the D.P. headquarters and the psychiatric ward of the veterans' hospital, never able to make a final decision as to which rhetoric he should adopt.

All pre-converts were surprisingly uninformed about conventional psychiatric and political perspectives for defining their problems. Perhaps those from small towns and rural communities in particular had long been accustomed to define the world in religious terms. Although all pre-converts had discarded conventional religious outlooks as inadequate, "spiritless," "dead," etc., prior to contact with the D.P., they retained a *general propensity to impose religious meaning on events.*

Even with these restrictions on the solutions available for acutely felt problems, a number of alternative responses still remain. First, people can persist in stressful situations with little or no relief. Second, persons often take specifically problem-directed action to change troublesome portions of their lives, without adopting a different world view to interpret them. Bertha and Minnie Mae might have simply divorced their husbands, for instance. . . . Clearly many preconverts attempted such action (Merwin *did* start a boardinghouse. Elmer *did* attend college, etc.) but none found a successful direct solution to his difficulties.

Third, a number of maneuvers exist to "put the problem out of mind." In general these are compensations for or distractions from problems in living: e.g., addictive consumption of the mass media, preoccupation with childrearing, or immersion in work. More spectacular examples include alcoholism, suicide, promiscuity, and so on. Recall, for example, that Minnie Mae, Alice and Bertha "hung around" the general store during the day getting high on beer during the summer of 1959. Had they done this in a more urban setting, in bars with strange men available, their subsequent lives might have been different.

In any event, we may assume that many persons with tensions not only explore these possible strategies, but succeed in some cases in "making it," and hence, are no longer potential D.P. recruits.[9]

3. *Seekership.* Whatever the reasons, pre-converts failed to find a way out of their difficulties through any of the strategies outlined above. Their need for solutions persisted, and their problem-solving perspective was restricted to a religious outlook, but all pre-converts found conventional religious institutions inadequate as a source of solutions. Subsequently, each came to define himself as a religious seeker, a person searching for some satisfactory system of religious meaning to interpret and resolve his discontent, and each had taken some action to achieve this end.

Some hopped from church to church and prayer group to prayer group, pursuing their religious search through relatively conventional institutions. . . . Others began to explore the occult milieu, reading the voluminous literature of the strange, the mystical and the spiritual and tentatively trying a series of such occult groups as Rosicrucians, Spiritualists and the various divine sciences.

> In April, 1960, my wife and I . . . [began] to seek a church connection. [We] began an association with Yokefellow, a spiritual growth organization in our local church. . . . I grew emotionally and spiritually during the next two-and-one-half years.
>
> However, as I grew, many spiritual things remained unanswered and new questions came up demanding answers which Yokefellow and the Church seemed not to even begin to touch upon. . . . My wife and I became interested in the revelation of Edgar Cayce and the idea of reincarnation which seemed to answer so much, we read searchingly about the Dead Sea Scrolls, we decided to pursue Rosicrucianism, we read books on the secret disclosures to be gained from Yogi-type meditation. The more we searched the more questions seemed to come up. Through Emmet Fox's writings I thought I had discovered a path through Metaphysics which through study would give me the breakthrough I longed for.

Or, the seeker might display some amalgam of conventional and unusual religious conceptions, as illustrated by a male convert's sad tale:

> I was reared in a Pentecostal church and as a child was a very ardent follower of Christianity. Because of family situations, I began to fall away and search for other meanings in life. This began . . . when I was about 12 years old. From that time on, my life was most of the time an odious existence, with a great deal of mental anguish. These last two years have brought me from church to church trying to find some fusion among them. I ended up going to Religious Science in the morning and fundamentalist in the evening.

Floundering about among religions was accompanied by two fundamental postulates that define more specifically the ideological components of the religious-seeker pattern. Although concrete pre-convert beliefs varied a good deal, all of them espoused these postulates about the nature of ultimate reality.

First, they believed that *spirits* of some variety came from an active supernatural realm to intervene in the "material world." Such entities could, at least sometimes, "break through" from the beyond and impart information, cause "experiences" or take a hand in the course of events.

Second, their conception of the universe was *teleological*, in the sense that beyond all appearances in the "sensate world" exists a purpose for which every object or event is created and exists. The earth is as it is to meet the needs of man, for example, and man manifests the physical structure he does to do the things he does. More important, man himself as a phenomenon must "be on earth" because, somewhere, sometime, somehow, it was decided that *homo sapiens* should "fulfill" a purpose or purposes. Accordingly, each person must have been "put on earth" for some reason, with some sort of "job" to perform.

Beliefs were typically no more specific than this. The religious seeking itself was in terms of finding some more detailed formulation of these problematically vague existential axes.

A few words on the general question of the importance of prior beliefs in effecting conversion are necessary at this point. A number of discussions of conversion have emphasized congruence between previous ideology and a given group's "appeal,"[10] while others treat the degree of congruence as unimportant so long as the ideology is seen as embodied in what appears to be a successful movement.[11] Both views seem extreme.[12]

Our data suggest that only the two gross kinds of congruence that make up the ideology of religious seekership are necessary for conversion to the D.P. Presumptively important items, such as fundamentalist Christianity, millenarian expectations, and hallucinatory experience were far from universal among pre-converts. Most pre-converts believed in a vaguely defined "New Age" that would appear gradually, but they *became* apocalyptic premillenarian only upon conversion.

The role of these gross points of congruence is suggested in the substantive D.P. appeals to pre-converts. Active spirits were rampant in their view of reality. Converts lived with an immediate sense of unseen forces operating on the physical order (e.g., the weather) and intervening in human affairs—in relations among nations, in the latest national disaster, and in their own moment-to-moment lives. Nothing occurred that was not related to the intentions of God's or Satan's spirits. For persons holding a teleological conception of reality, the D.P. doctrine had the virtue of offering a minute and lawful explanation of the whole of human history. It systematically defined and revealed the hidden meaning of individual lives that had lacked coherence and purpose, and of course, it explained all hallucinatory behavior in terms of spirit manifestations. These spirits had been preparing the pre-convert to see the truth of the D.P.

. . .

Converts were assured of being virtual demi-gods for all eternity, beginning with a rule over the restored and reformed earth in the immediate future. By 1967 God was to impose the millennium upon earth, and those who converted early, before the truth of this message became self-evident, would occupy the most favored positions in the divine hegemony. Converts particularly stressed this advantage of conversion in their proselytization: "those who get in early," as one member often put it, "will be in on the ground floor of something big."

Religious seekership emerges, then, as another part of the path through the maze of life contingencies leading to D.P. conversion. It is a floundering among religious alternatives, an openness to a variety of religious views, frequently esoteric, combined with failure to embrace the specific ideology and fellowship of some set of believers.[13] Seekership provided the minimal points of ideological congruence to make these people available for D.P. conversion.

4. The Turning Point. The necessary attributes of pre-converts stated thus far had all persisted for some time before the pre-converts encountered the D.P.; they can be considered "background" factors, or predispositions. Although they apparently arose and were active in the order specified, they are important here as accumulated and simultaneously active factors during the development of succeeding conditions.

We now turn to situational factors in which timing becomes much more significant. The first of these is the rather striking circumstance that *shortly* before, and *concurrently* with their encounter with the D.P., all pre-converts had reached or were about to reach what they perceived as a "turning point" in their lives. That is, each had come to a moment when old lines of action were complete, had failed or been disrupted, or were about to be so, and when they faced the opportunity (or necessity), and possibly the burden, of doing something different with their lives.[14] Thus, Miss Lee's academic career had been disrupted by long illness from which she recovered upon meeting Chang; Bertha was newly arrived in a strange town; . . . Minnie Mae no longer had a pre-school child at home to care for; Merwin had just failed in business after dropping out of school; and Elmer had returned to his parents' farm after failing in college for the second time.

. . .

The significance of these various turning points is that they increased the pre-convert's awareness of and desire to take some action about his problems, *at the same time giving him a new opportunity to do so.* Turning points were situations in which old obligations and lines of action were diminished, and new involvements became desirable and possible.

5. Cult Affective Bonds. We come now to the contact between a potential recruit and the D.P. If persons who go through all four of the previous steps are to be further drawn down the road to full conversion, an affective bond [or positive emotional tie] must develop, if it does not already exist, between the potential recruit and one or more of the D.P. members. . . . That is, persons developed affective ties with the group or some of its members while they still regarded the D.P. perspective as problematic, or even "way out." In a manner of speaking, *final conversion was coming to accept the opinions of one's friends.*[15]

Miss Lee's recollections of her conversion provide a graphic illustration:

> In addition to this change [her recovery from illness] I felt very good spiritually. I felt as if I had come to life from a numb state and there was spiritual *liveliness and vitality within me by being among this group.* As one feels when he comes from a closed stuffy room into the fresh air, or the goodness and warmth after freezing coldness was how my spirit witnessed its happiness. *Although I could not agree with the message intellectually I found myself one with it spiritually.* I reserved my conclusions and waited for guidance from God. [Italics added.]

Miss Lee further revealed she was particularly attracted to Mr. Chang and resided in his dwelling to enjoy the pleasure of his company, until, finally, she decided his message was true. Her statement that she "could not agree with the message intellectually" is particularly significant. Other converts reported and were observed to experience similar reservations as they nevertheless developed strong bonds with members of the group.

· · ·

It is particularly important to note that conversions frequently moved through *preexisting* friendship pairs or nets. In the formation of the original core group, an affective bond first developed between Miss Lee and Bertha (the first to meet Miss Lee and begin to espouse her views). Once that had happened, the rest of the original conversions were supported by prior friendships. Bertha was part of the housewife trio of Minnie Mae and Alice; Merwin was Alice's husband, and Elmer was Merwin's friend and workmate. Subsequent conversions also followed friendship paths, or friendships developed between the pre-convert and the converts, prior to conversion.

Bonds that were unsupported by previous friendships with a new convert often took the form of a sense of instant and powerful rapport with a believer. Consider, for example, a young housewife's account of her first view of Lester while attending an Edgar Cayce Foundation retreat:[16]

> I went to [one of the] Bible class[es] and saw [Lester] in our class—I had seen him for the first time the night before and had felt such love for him—he was my brother, yet I had not met him. He looked as if he were luminous! After the class I wanted to talk to him—but our project group had a discipline that day—complete silence—I did not want to break it, yet I felt such a need to talk to him. I prayed

and asked God what He would have me do—I received such a positive feeling—I took this as an answer and sought out [Lester]. When I found him, I did not have anything to say—I just mumbled something—But he seemed to understand and took me to the beach where he told me "He is on earth!" Oh, what joy I felt! My whole body was filled with electricity.

The less-than-latent sexual overtones of this encounter appeared in a number of other heterosexual attachments that led to conversion (and quite a few that did not). Even after four years of cult membership Elmer could hardly hide his feelings in his testimonial:

Early in 1960, after a desperate prayer, which was nothing more than the words, "Father if there is any truth in this world, please reveal it to me," I met [Miss Lee]. This day I desire to never forget. Although I didn't fully understand yet, I desired to unite with her. . . .

Although a potential convert might have some initial difficulty in taking up the D.P. perspective, given the four previous conditions *and* an affective tie, he began seriously to consider the D.P. and to accept it as his personal construction of reality.

6. Extra-Cult Affective Bonds. One might suppose that non-D.P. associates of a convert-in-process would not be entirely neutral to the now immediate possibility that he would join the D.P. group. We must inquire, then, into the conditions under which extracult controls are activated through emotional attachments, and how they restrain or fail to restrain persons from D.P. conversion.

Recent migration, disaffection with geographically distant families and spouses and very few nearby acquaintances made a few converts "social atoms"; for them extra-cult attachments were irrelevant. More typically, converts were acquainted with nearby persons, but none was intimate enough to be aware that a conversion was in progress or to feel that the mutual attachment was sufficient to justify intervention. . . .

In many cases, positive attachments outside the cult were to other religious seekers, who, even though not yet budding converts themselves, encouraged continued "investigation" or entertainment of the D.P. rather than exercising a countervailing force. Indeed, such an extra-cult person might be only slightly behind his friend in his own conversion process.

In the relatively few cases where positive attachments existed between conventional extra-cult persons and a convert-in-process, control was minimal or absent, because of geographical distance or intentional avoidance of communication about the topic while the convert was solidifying his faith. Thus, for example, a German immigrant in his early thirties failed to inform his mother in Germany, to whom he was strongly attached, during his period of entertainment and only wrote her about the D.P. months after his firm acceptance. (She disowned him.)

During the period of tentative acceptance, and afterwards, converts, of course, possessed a rhetoric that helped to neutralize affective conflicts. An account by a newly converted soldier in Oklahoma conveys the powerful (and classic) content of this facilitating and justifying rhetoric:

> I wrote my family a very long detailed but yet very plain letter about our movement and exactly what I received in spiritual ways plus the fact that Jesus had come to me himself. The weeks passed and I heard nothing but I waited with deep trust in God.
>
> This morning I received a letter from my mother. She . . . surmised that I was working with a group other than those with the "stamp of approval by man." She . . . called me a fanatic. . . .
>
> At first it was the deepest hurt I had ever experienced. But, I remember what others in [the D.P.] family have given up and how they too experienced a similar rejection. But so truly, I can now know a little of the rejection that our beloved Master experienced. I can now begin to understand his deep grief for the Father as he sat peering out of a window singing love songs to Him because he knew that the Father would feel such grief. I can now begin to feel the pain that our Father in heaven felt for 6,000 years. I can now begin to see that to come into the Kingdom of heaven is not as easy as formerly thought.
>
> •   •   •
>
> [In the words of Miss Lee:] "As we get close to the Father the road shall become more difficult"; "Only by truly suffering, can we know the Leader and the heart of the Father"; "You shall be tested." "He will come with a double-edge blade." Only now am I beginning to realize the deep significance of these words. Only now am I beginning to know the heart of the Father and the great suffering of our Lord.

When there were emotional attachments to outsiders who were physically present and cognizant of the incipient transformation, conversion became a "nip-and-tuck" affair. Pulled about by competing emotional loyalties and discordant versions of reality, such persons were subjected to intense emotional strain. A particularly poignant instance of this involved a newlywed senior at the local state university. He began tentatively to espouse the D.P. as he developed strong ties with Lester and Miss Lee. His young wife struggled to accept, but she did not meet a number of the conditions leading to conversion, and in the end, seemed nervous, embarrassed, and even ashamed to be at D.P. gatherings. One night, just before the group began a prayer meeting, he rushed in and tearfully announced that he would have nothing further to do with the D.P., though he still thought the message was probably true. Torn between affective bonds, he opted for his young bride, but it was only months later that he finally lost all belief in the D.P.

When extracult bonds withstood the strain of affective and ideological flirtation with the D.P., conversion was not consummated. Most converts, however, lacked external affiliations close enough to permit informal control over belief. Affectively, they were so "unintegrated" that they could, for the most part, simply fall out of relatively conventional society unnoticed, taking their co-seeker friends, if any, with them.

7. *Intensive Interaction.* In combination, the six previous factors suffice to bring a person to *verbal conversion* to the D.P. but one more contin-

gency must be met if he is to become a "deployable agent,"[17] or what we have termed a *total convert*. Most, but not all, verbal converts ultimately put their lives at the disposal of the cult. Such transformations in commitment took place, we suggest, as a result of intensive interaction with D.P. members, and failed to result when such interaction was absent.

Intensive interaction means concrete, daily, and even hourly accessibility to D.P. members, which implies physical proximity to total converts. Intensive exposure offers an opportunity to reinforce and elaborate an initial, tentative assent to the D.P. world view, and in prolonged association the perspective "comes alive" as a device for interpreting the moment-to-moment events in the convert's life.

The D.P. doctrine has a variety of resources for explicating the most minor everyday events in terms of a cosmic battle between good and evil spirits, in a way that placed the convert at the center of this war. Since all D.P. interpretations pointed to the imminence of the end, to participate in these explications of daily life was to come more and more to see the necessity of one's personal participation as a totally committed agent in this cosmic struggle.[18]

Reminders and discussion of the need to make other converts, and the necessity of supporting the cause in every way, were the main themes of verbal exchanges among the tentatively accepting and the total converts and, indeed, among the total converts themselves. Away from this close association with those already totally committed, one failed to "appreciate" the need for one's transformation into a total convert.

In recognition of this fact, the D.P. members gave highest priority to attempts to persuade verbal converts (even the merely interested) to move into the cult's communal dwellings. During her early efforts in Northwest Town, Miss Lee gained verbal conversions from Bertha, Minnie Mae, Alice, Merwin, and Elmer, many months before she was able to turn them into total converts. This transformation did not occur, in fact, until Miss Lee moved into Alice and Merwin's home (along with Elmer), placing her within a few dozen yards of the homes of Minnie Mae and Bertha. The resulting daily exposure of the verbal converts to Miss Lee's total conversion increasingly engrossed them in D.P. activities, until they came to give it all their personal and material resources.[19] Recalling this period, Minnie Mae reported a process that occurred during other verbal converts' periods of intensive interaction. When one of them began to waver in his faith, unwavering believers were fortunately present to carry him through this "attack of Satan."

· · ·

Thus, verbal conversion and even a resolution to reorganize one's life for the D.P. is not automatically translated into total conversion. One must be intensively exposed to the group supporting these new standards of conduct. D.P. members did not find proselytizing, the primary task of total converts, very easy, but in the presence of persons who reciprocally supported each other, such a transformation of one's life became possible. Persons who accepted the truth of the doctrine, but lacked intensive interaction with the core group, remained partisan spectators, who played no active part in the battle to usher in God's kingdom.

SUMMARY

We have presented a model of the accumulating conditions that appear to describe and account for conversion to an obscure millenarian perspective. These necessary and constellationally-sufficient conditions may be summarized as follows:

For conversion a person must:

1. Experience enduring, acutely felt tensions
2. Within a religious problem-solving perspective,
3. Which leads him to define himself as a religious seeker;
4. Encountering the D.P. at a turning point in his life,
5. Wherein an affective bond is formed (or pre-exists) with one or more converts;
6. Where extra-cult attachments are absent or neutralized;
7. And, where, if he is to become a deployable agent, he is exposed to intensive interaction.

Because this model was developed from the study of a small set of converts to a minor millenarian doctrine, it may possess few generalizable features. We suggest, however, that its terms are general enough, and its elements articulated in such a way as to provide a reasonable starting point for the study of conversion to other types of groups and perspectives.

NOTES

1. Clyde Kluckhohn, "Values and Value-Orientations in the Theory of Action: An Exploration in Definition and Classification," in Talcott Parsons and Edward Shils (eds.), *Toward A General Theory of Action*, New York: Harper Torchbooks, 1962, p. 409.

2. The meaning of this term has been muddied by the inconsistent usage of Christian religious writers. Often they have used "conversion" to refer to an aroused concern among persons who already accept the essential truth of the ideological system. Yet, in keeping with the earliest Christian examples of conversion, such as that of St. Paul, they have also used the word to describe changes from one such system to another. These are very different events and ought to be indicated by different words.

3. All names that might compromise converts' anonymity have been changed.

4. Other aspects of the cult's formation, development, maintenance and proselytization procedures are analyzed in John Lofland, *Doomsday Cult*, Englewood Cliffs, N.J.: Prentice-Hall, 1966.

5. Neil J. Smelser, *Theory of Collective Behavior*, New York: The Free Press of Glencoe, 1963, pp. 12–21. See also Ralph Turner, "The Quest for Universals in Sociological Research," *American Sociological Review*, 18 (1953), pp. 604–611.

6. Peter Berger has given us a delightful characterization of the reconstructive functions of such tales. See his *Invitation to Sociology*, New York: Doubleday Anchor, 1953, Ch. 3.

7. We conceive this tension as subjective to avoid judgments about how tension-producing the "objective" circumstances actually were, attending instead to the way these circumstances were experienced.

8. It is currently fashionable to reduce this last to more mundane "real" causes, but it is not necessary here to pre-judge the phenomenology.

9. Our analysis is confined to isolating the elements of the conversion sequence. Extended analysis would refer to the factors that *in turn* bring each conversion condition into existence. That is, it would be necessary to develop a theory for each of the seven elements, specifying the conditions under which each appears. On the form such theory would probably take, see Ralph Turner's discussion of "the intrusive factor," *op. cit.*, pp. 609–611.

10. E.g., H.G. Brown, "The Appeal of Communist Ideology," *American Journal of Economics and Sociology*, 2 (1943), pp. 161–174; Gabriel Almond, *The Appeals of Communism*, Princeton: Princeton University Press, 1954.

11. E.g., Eric Hoffer, *The True Believer*, New York: Mentor, 1958 (copyright 1951), p. 10.

12. Cf. Herbert Blumer, "Collective Behavior" in Joseph B. Gittler (ed.), *Review of Sociology*, New York: Wiley, 1957, pp. 147–148.

13. For further suggestive materials on seekers and seeking, see H.T. Dohrman, *California Cult*, Boston: Beacon, 1958; Leon Festinger, Henry Riecken and Stanley Schacter, *When Prophecy Fails*, Minneapolis: University of Minnesota Press, 1956; Sanctus De Santis, *Religious Conversion*, London: Routledge and Kegan Paul, 1927, esp. pp. 260–261; H. Taylor Buckner, "Deviant-Group Organizations," Unpublished M.A. thesis, University of California, Berkeley, 1964, Ch. 2. For discussion of a generically similar phenomenon in a different context, see Edgar H. Schein, *Coercive Persuasion*, New York: Norton, 1961, pp. 120–136, 270–277.

14. Everett C. Hughes, *Men and Their Work*, Glencoe: Free Press, 1958, Ch. 1; Anselm Strauss "Transformations of Identity," in Arnold Rose (ed.), *Human Behavior and Social Processes*, Boston: Houghton Mifflin, 1962, pp. 67–71. Cf. the often-noted "cultural dislocation" and migration pattern found in the background of converts to many groups, especially cults.

15. Cf. Tamatsu Shibutani, *Society and Personality*, Englewood Cliffs, N.J.: Prentice-Hall, 1961, pp. 523–532, 588–592. Schein (*op. cit.*, p. 277) reports that "the most potent source of influence in coercive persuasion was the identification which arose between a prisoner and his more reformed cellmate." See also Alan Kerckhoff, Kurt Back and Norman Miller, "Sociometric Patterns in Hysterical Contagion," *Sociometry*, 28 (1965), pp. 2–15.

16. Lester was at this retreat precisely for the purpose of meeting potential converts. Attendance at religious gatherings in the masquerade of a religious seeker was the primary D.P. mode of recruiting.

17. On the concept of the "deployable agent" or "deployable personnel" in social movements see Philip Selznick, *The Organizational Weapon*, New York: Free Press, 1960 (copyright 1952), pp. 18–29.

18. Cf. Schein, *op. cit.*, pp. 136–139, 280–282.

19. Although a number of our illustrative cases are drawn from the period of the group's formation, the process of cult formation itself should not be confused with the analytically distinct process of conversion. The two are merely empirically com-

pounded. Cult formation occurs when a network of friends who meet the first four conditions develop affective bonds with a world-view carrier and collectively develop the last two conditions, except that condition seven, intensive interaction, requires exposure *to each other* in addition to the world-view carrier. (For a different conception of "subculture" formation, see Albert K. Cohen, *Delinquent Boys*, Glencoe, Ill.: The Free Press, 1955, Ch. 3.)

Review Questions

1. Lofland and Stark speak of the Divine Precepts as a "construction of reality." What are some of the key features of this construction which are at odds with more widely accepted constructions of reality in our society today?

2. The authors maintain that the second step toward conversion is the requirement that the individual have a *religious*, rather than a *psychiatric* or *political*, rhetoric, or line of reasoning, to explain the sources of and solutions to life's problems. Explain these three rhetorics. Why would a psychiatric or a political rhetoric lead one away from conversion?

3. The fourth step in the conversion process is called "the turning point." How does the turning point affect prior patterns of social interaction, thereby setting the stage for increased interaction with D.P. members?

4. Distinguish between "verbal converts" and "total converts." What factors led verbal converts to total conversion?

5. Would the steps to conversion described by Lofland and Stark apply to cases in which individuals are converted to Methodism, Catholicism, Judaism, or any other major religion in our society? Why, or why not?

REDISCOVERING GENDER: THE EMERGENT ROLE PASSAGE OF EX-NUNS

Lucinda SanGiovanni

INTRODUCTION

OVER THE COURSE OF OUR LIVES AS SOCIAL BEINGS WE PASS THROUGH MANY ROLES. Some of these personal journeys are quite familiar to us—we pass from child to teenager, from single to married, from civilian to soldier, from employed to retired. These types of *role passages* are fairly institutionalized in our society, guided by those accepted schedules, rituals, rules and meanings that facilitate our movement from certain social locations into different ones.

The aim of the present article is to explore selected dimensions of the *non-institutionalized*, or *emergent*, role passage experienced by former Roman Catholic nuns making the transition from a convent community into the secular society. One of the most astonishing events to occur in the history of American religious orders has been the large exodus of nuns from the convent during the past fifteen years. Membership began to drop dramatically in 1967 and continued to decline through the early seventies. Between 1966 and 1976, the number of nuns in the U.S. dropped from approximately 181,000 to 131,000 (Ebaugh, 1977:67–68).

The decade of the sixties was a time of crisis and change in the Roman Catholic Church and in religious orders (Kavanagh, 1967; Westhues, 1968). Nuns were questioning the authority of superiors and the hierarchical structures of religious communities. New forms of service to lay people were being suggested. The meaning of religious life and its relation to the secular society were under review. New modes of dress, new relationships, and new living arrangements were tried out.

These and a host of other improvisations in religious life were generated and sustained from two sources. One came from within the Roman Catholic Church itself. Vatican Council II, the writings and lectures of theologians and religious leaders, and the grass-roots activities of priests and nuns all came together to dramatically change the structure of religious life and the role of the nun in the modern world. A second source of change came from the larger society itself. The sixties was a decade of movement away from authority, hierarchy, regulation, and rationality. Criticism of conventional

This is an original article prepared for this volume, based in part on Lucinda SanGiovanni, *Ex-Nuns: A Study in Emergent Role Passage*, Norwood, N.J.: Ablex, 1978.

morality, traditional life-styles, modes of interpersonal relations, and the distribution of power gave rise to a variety of social movements that lent ideological support to the efforts at renewal within religious life.

Of course, the impact of these changes on nuns was considerable, and great numbers opted for the alternatives that were emerging in the secular society. The decision to leave the convent was a decision to leave a way of life to which one had once been committed. Being a nun was a vocation or calling to a life very different from that of most other people. It entailed rigorous training, demanded total involvement, and exerted a profound influence on identity. Thus, the decision would involve cutting oneself off from experiences, routines, relations, and self-images that were valued and comfortable while at the same time exposing the individual to new situations for which she was not accustomed or which she did not completely embrace.

Like any other major decision, this one was a consequence of both individual and social forces interacting with one another. It is not enough to *want* to leave a role or way of life. Persons must also be *aware* of alternative structural opportunities as well as coming to define themselves as *able* to make use of these opportunities. The data collected in this study reveal that these three conditions—motivation, knowledge of alternatives, and perceptions of abilities—appeared in approximately this order as the process of relinquishment unraveled itself.

EX-NUNS: A CASE STUDY OF EMERGENT ROLE PASSAGE

This particular passage from religious to secular life presents an ideal opportunity to examine the complex processes involved in role change, because it possesses a generic character that involves a multiple transition of major roles and a fundamental transformation of personal identity. This passage entails accommodation to the basic role sequences of lay life—aging, family, work, marriage and friendship. These are, in turn, the social locations that shape the meanings and qualities in which our very self-images are grounded. In this light, then, it typifies the broad transformation of identities, behaviors and social memberships that individuals normally experience over the entire life cycle.

The choice of this passage, beyond its generic attributes, provides a chance to investigate several dimensions of role passage that have yet to receive much systematic attention in sociology. First, this passage is an *emergent* one (Glaser and Strauss, 1971:85–86) which is created, discovered and shaped by the former nuns as they go along. Few guidelines, precedents, or models are available to facilitate their transfer between roles. Although this type of role passage is seldom explored by sociologists (Clausen, 1968:189), it is becoming more and more significant as our society undergoes continuing transformations. Second, the movement from nun to lay person involves a passage through *multiple* roles. In fact, only a few transitions ever

occur which entail single or isolated transfers from one to another social location. In the case of former nuns, they must simultaneously negotiate transitions to such roles as family members, workers, consumers, lovers,
spouses and women. Third, this passage was a *self-initiated* one and draws
attention to the often-neglected fact that individuals are active agents who
make assessments of their personal and social situations and who are interested in, and capable of, exerting control over various stages of their lives.
A fourth advantage of studying this particular passage derives from the fact
that, by virtue of having been in religious life for some time period, former
nuns do not move with their age-peers through the "typical" sequences of
major roles over the life cycle. They lag behind members of their age cohort
in many institutional spheres of life. Thus, this enables us to study what
Glaser and Strauss (1971:31) term an *arrested passage*. Finally, as we follow
women from their lives as nuns through passages to other lives, our focus is
kept on the *processual* nature of role occupancy. At each phase of the former nun's passage, her problems, meanings, choices and strategies are
somewhat different from earlier and subsequent phases. To grasp these essential differences it is necessary that we pan over the entire passage to underscore the fluidity of structural movement.

During the spring and summer of 1972, I conducted intensive interviews
with a sample of twenty former nuns who had been members of a religious
order located in a major metropolitan area on the East Coast of the United
States. In order to obtain the greatest base of information, the sample included women who differed substantially from one another along the following dimensions: (1) the number of years they had spent in religious life
(from 5 to 15 years or more), (2) their age at the time of leaving (from 25 to
40 years and over), (3) the type of vows they had taken (final vs. temporary
vows), (4) the length of time they spent in secular life after leaving (less than
1 year to over 4 years), (5) their marital status (single vs. engaged or married), and (6) their type of occupation (academic, non-academic or unemployed).[1]

Although the in-depth interviews covered a wide range of topics, we will
examine in the next section one specific passage that was negotiated by these
women. This transition centers on the full resumption by former nuns of
their sex role as women.

SEX ROLES

A person's sex role as female or male is assigned by others at birth and generally is understood to be an ascribed characteristic. While sex refers to biological attributes, sex roles refer to the cluster of social expectations deemed
appropriate for how women and men should behave (Chafetz, 1974:1–5).
The roles of women and men and the gender definitions of their behavior as
feminine and masculine are social constructions rather than biological

givens. These roles and definitions are established by society and learned by individuals, beginning in infancy.

It is a basic sociological truth that all roles, including sex roles, are never static; they continue to be revised to meet changing societal and individual needs (Banton, 1965, pp. 42–67). The role of woman (and indirectly that of man) has, since the mid-sixties, been undergoing exactly such change. There is no longer any doubt that there is presently moving through our society a vigorous, determined, and ideologically informed assault on traditional sex roles (David and Brannon, 1976; Kelly and Boutilier, 1978). This changing role of woman elicits the following question in the context of our study of former nuns: What happens to people when the role that they are trying to learn, and to play with conviction, is itself undergoing profound alteration in the society at large?

All of us reading this article are, to varying degrees, grappling with the same question. But women who once were nuns are in a unique position. During much of their lives as nuns, these women subordinated their sex role to the more generalized and pervasive demands of the *religious role*. Being a nun meant being a celibate woman for whom the ordinary experiences and roles of lay women were either forbidden or unimportant.[2] Paradoxically, while a nun was discouraged—through convent laws, ideology, vows, and routines—from defining herself and acting in terms of her role as a woman, traditional feminine values and behavior were reinforced.

Over the past few years a considerable amount of literature has appeared which criticizes religion and religious organizations as sexist in consequence, if not intent (Bullough, 1973; Doely, 1970; Hageman, 1974). Theologians such as Rosemary Ruether (1974), Mary Daly (1975), and Carol P. Christ and Judith Plaskow (1979) have become well known for their feminist analyses of such questions as the ordination of women, the patriarchal underpinnings of religious traditions, the cult of Mary, and the subordinate position of women in the church. While more has been written about the Christian religions, the position of women in Judaism is also undergoing scrutiny (Koltun, 1976) as a religion grounded in patriarchal beliefs, laws, and traditions.

I believe this feminist framework is essential to understanding the paradoxical nature of the nun as woman and the consequences of the paradox for the former nun's resumption of her role as a secular woman. The culture and social organization of the Roman Catholic Church, and religious orders in particular, are permeated with sexism. The sexist imagery, symbols, language, roles and structure of authority become evident, for example, when we compare the roles of priest and nun.[3] "Father" is superior to "Sister" in authority; his major functions are "sacred" and grounded in the Sacraments, while hers are not; he can own property and have private monies, she cannot; he can drink and smoke and go out alone, she cannot; he can exercise independence, freedom of choice, and individuality, while she must always be a part of the larger "community" and subordinate herself to her order.

The process by which a woman is socialized to become a nun provides us with an unequivocal instance of conditioning women to traditional "female" attributes, virtues, skills and orientations. She is taught to be passive, subordinate, submissive, collectivity-oriented, nurturant, quiet, childlike, pure, hard-working and obedient. She is publicly a paragon of virtue—the "good Sister" who teaches the children and cares for the poor and sick; she is to be unassuming, restrained, innocent; she is to go beyond the sexuality and materialism that flaw the secular individual. She embodies, or is taught and thought to embody, the essential female complex of values, attitudes and behavior.

Thus, the nun, although living outside the mainstream of secular female culture, was nonetheless socialized to a religious role and participated in an organization that closely approximated the society's patriarchal themes. This is a crucial observation because it sheds light on the issue before us; namely, as nuns left the convent and assumed their roles as secular women they had a choice as to what kind of woman they could be. They could resume the society's more traditional female role or could opt for the emerging role of woman that was being created through the feminist movement.

In doing my research during the early seventies, the peak years of the emergent feminist consciousness, I had hypothesized that former nuns would be more likely to embrace the newer vision of women than the more traditional one. Why? My prediction was based on a certain way of looking at religious life. A religious order can be viewed as one of the rare social organizations where women freely choose to organize, staff, coordinate and play out their lives without men and motherhood—those two major coordinates that socially locate the woman in every society. Here is a genuinely radical feminist experiment: women working, eating, sleeping, creating, producing, deciding, defining, playing, praying—in sum, living by themselves with other women. If this is one's conception, and to some extent it contains much empirical validity, then one might expect former nuns to enter the secular world ready to assume the newer configuration of the role of woman. I expected them to respond favorably to this role that stressed independence, self-assertion, achievement and nonfamilistic life-style choices. The findings failed to support my hypothesized prediction. As will soon be evident, the respondents' resumption of their sex role was carried out according to the more traditional vision of women's role. Upon examining the above model of religious life, I came to see several errors in this conceptualization which help explain its failure to correctly predict the respondents' behavior.

First, as I mentioned earlier, the culture and social organization of convent life were shaped along the same patriarchal lines as those of secular institutions of the larger society. These structures, and the process of socializing women to them, were of great importance in sustaining traditional feminine behavior and values. Second, the ability to define oneself in feminist terms and to interpret one's situation within a feminist framework requires at least that one *be aware of oneself as a woman*. Regarding respondents' self-conceptions, their awareness of themselves as women was by and large suppressed under the "master status" (Hughes, 1945) of being a nun. Third, I had erroneously assumed that nuns *chose* a single, celibate, single-sexed community life-style. The fact of the matter is, however, that respondents *chose to become nuns*, and this life-style was the required condition for being officially accepted as a nun. Finally, and perhaps most important for understanding their subsequent adherence to a more traditional model of woman, I had not considered the possibility that these respondents were looking forward to the "benefits" or being women, to which they had been socialized early in their lives and which had been so long denied them while in religious life. Insofar as their goal was to become women again—in the sense in which sex role is a basic axis of self-identity and social membership—assuming the stance of a "liberated woman" could jeopardize this goal. Put bluntly, one's acceptance as a woman by others is not gained by being autonomous, competitive, rational, achieving, assertive, and the like. In most parts of society, even today, the "women's libber," as she is termed, has her credibility *as a woman* cast into doubt.[4] For former nuns, who desired acceptance as women and whose ability to make transitions to other roles was dependent on this acceptance, their choice of the traditional female role became clearly understandable.

We are now prepared to explore the process by which former nuns resumed active roles as women in secular society. One of the first strategies they employed could be called "body work"—a set of activities designed to bring the body, appearance, and overall physical impression in line with the female role. They experimented with different hairstyles, bought clothes, practiced putting on makeup, had their ears pierced, went on diets, and in various ways sought to present public images of themselves as everyday women. As Scott and Lyman (1963:33) observe, "since individuals are aware that appearances may serve to credit or discredit accounts, efforts are understandably made to control their appearances through a vast repertoire of impression management activities." One area over which my respondents had total control was precisely the area of physical impression, and much effort went into it. But even such a simple matter as this was problematic at first, as these comments reveal:

> I started to lose weight, learned how to put on makeup, which was really funny, practicing in front of a mirror; I'd dab it on and look like a clown. I also learned to set my hair, and sometimes I looked pretty awful. I worked on my clothes—a friend helped me buy shoes, clothes, jewelry. I really don't know if I could have done without that kind of help in the beginning. I really didn't know much at first.

> It was really funny now when I look at it, but not then, when we had to go into the stores and of course we didn't have much money to spend and we'd go into the stores where everybody dressed in front of everybody else. (How did you feel

about that?) That was a traumatic experience. I remember going into the dressing room with three or four pairs of slacks because I really didn't know what size I wore. It was pretty bad.

There were so many things I had to learn, like which styles fit me for my build and my age and which colors were flattering. My sister would go shopping with me in the beginning to help pick things out.

Ironically, at a time when many secular women were taking off their makeup, letting their hair return to natural colors and easy-to-keep styles, gaining control of their bodies through sport and other "nonfeminine" activities, these women were reverting to physical activities that were targeted as "objectifications of the female" (Millum, 1975) by the feminist movement.[5] Through trial and error, observation of others, and assistance from friends and family, respondents began to shape their appearance in accord with their traditional image of themselves as women. An interesting observation made by two women suggests that some measure of their movement through transitional stages is reflected in changes in personal attire and attitudes toward one's body:

I wasn't really in tune with my body and I think it took a while. It was a very gradual thing. Like, that first summer out I got a one-piece bathing suit, last summer I had a regular two-piece bathing suit, and this summer I have a bikini, and in my own mind I see that and feel that this is my transition and I often laugh.

When I compare the type of clothes I bought when I first left and those I buy now, there's such a difference that I think it must say something about where I've come from. (Could you explain this?) Well my earlier clothes were too big for me, they were drab and in dark colors—very subdued, conservative. My style has changed, I now know what I like and I'm willing to experiment.

As a result of participating in a secular environment where being a woman is a salient feature of everyday life, respondents began to increasingly refer to *other women* for standards of evaluation. Their involvement in roles and activities which contain norms for sex-role participation made them increasingly attentive to sources for assessing their own performances as women. A respondent captures this more concentrated attention by remarking, "I'm now more likely to look at other women—how they're dressed, how they carry themselves, what they say—and compare myself to them. There was little need to do that in the convent." As time goes by, women, precisely as women, become more significant as reference points for the respondent, which helps to underscore her attachment to the female role and bring her behavior and sentiment in closer alignment with the role. A former nun who had been out for about two years compares herself now as a woman with when she was a nun and observes, "I'm not ashamed to express my emotions now. I am learning to respond more like a woman." Another suggests that, "I have become more interested in womanly things—

cooking, shopping, clothes, sex—and to read and discuss these things with other women." Still another comments that "even my thinking has changed in the sense that as a nun I used to be more logical, more rational; I believe I thought like a man, and now I feel I am looking at things in more than just rational terms."

Even in the management of their other role transitions, respondents worked to integrate them into support of their role as women. Specifically, success in one role may bring confidence in playing others. Just as all roles receive social confirmation and are activated when they elicit appropriate responses from others, a major validation of being a woman in our society is to have men react in anticipated ways (Safilios-Rothschild, 1977). To be whistled at, to be told one is pretty, to be asked for a date are unequivocal signals that men see you as a woman which function to increase one's confidence in that role. Part of the motivation to date (and part of the anxiety over not dating that comes across in many interviews) is tied to this issue of wanting to validate one's claim to being a woman. This is succinctly stated by a former nun who expressed much concern with the initial absence of dating activity during the first year she was out: "I also wanted to date because it helped me know I was attractive to men—that I was a woman." Success in dating and sexual intimacy served to increase the respondent's confidence in herself as a woman and thus facilitated the resumption of her sex role.

Other respondents were also aware that what was happening in other areas of their transition—where they resided, who their friends were, where they worked—had consequences for their successful resumption of the female role:

> I wanted to get a job very badly because I knew that without it I couldn't buy clothes and things that would help me be attractive as a woman and not look like an ex-nun.

> I deliberately began to cultivate women friends who were not ex-nuns because they knew the woman's world and could help me discover it. My friends were ex-nuns; we were all in the same boat and really couldn't help each other out that much.

These activities can be seen as somewhat conscious efforts by respondents to engage in behavior that is supportive of their roles as women. By deliberately manipulating other parts of her passage—work, dating, friendship—she could strengthen her sex-role presentation.

The interview materials we have presented to illustrate ideas about sex-role accommodations can be reread to shed light on the respondents' conception of the female role. Most respondents generally accepted a traditional image of women with its emphasis on the primacy of marriage and children; the existence of "natural differences" between the sexes in terms of sentiment, modes of thinking and biological drives; and the belief that the sexes do, and should continue to, inhabit somewhat distinct spheres of existence regarding work, leisure, community participation, child-rearing, governing, and the like. Only one respondent held to a model of woman that can be called feminist, and she apparently had formulated her conception of being a woman as a result of early family socialization long before entering religious life. With the exception of agreeing to "equal work for equal pay," the majority of respondents were fairly uncritical of the content of institutionalized sex roles.

In examining the interview data I did find a few respondents who had left religious life with traditional images of the female role and had begun to *reevaluate* these ideas in the light of their immediate experiences in the secular community. These respondents were approximately thirty years old, they were single, they had been out of the convent for two to three years, they had relatively active social lives, and they expressed satisfaction with their jobs. Once these women discovered that they could, in fact, build for themselves an independent and satisfying life-style, the pressure they had felt earlier to follow the path of traditional women began to decrease and to be replaced by a wish to leave their present plans open-ended. These women, like the other respondents, had been very concerned about what would happen to them after leaving religious life. They keenly felt the absence of any permanent ties or plans that give most people a feeling of security for the years that stretch before them. Many of them echoed this theme by noting that "at least in the convent you knew what the rest of your life was going to be like; you had that security." It is still true today that for many, many women the life plan that is available in the female role points to marriage, children and noncareer employment. Once some of these women begin to experience success and rewards in pursuing alternate styles of existence, however, they are able to question their attachment to the ideas of what women can and should be. This reevaluation is described in dynamic terms by a very observant respondent:

> It's hard to say what factors began to influence my thinking about women's role in society. When I first left I felt I just had to find a man, get married, settle down. Maybe this was a reaction against not having the security of convent life. But really, I didn't think of any options and was pretty desperate for awhile. As I began to do things on my own and to do them—my finances, the job, new friends, and dating men—well, maybe I became more confident in myself, and more willing to think that there are options for women besides the ones we're taught by society. You come to realize that you, as a person and as a woman, can make your own way, even if it's hard at times.

These changing conceptions of woman's role seem to me to be more of a result of altered social experiences than of solely an intellectual or ideological conversion to feminism as a belief system. This implies that, for ideological shifts to occur in how women respond to roles, they must be backed up by *personal experience* that is valued and effective. Women must continue to be encouraged to play new roles, have new experiences, and join new groups so that they can test for themselves the degree of satisfaction and effectiveness possible in moving beyond the present boundaries of woman's role. Exposure to feminist ideology, either in the form of intellectual analysis or political rhetoric, is not sufficient for producing sustained change in one's personal and social life as a woman.

NOTES

1. For a detailed discussion of the methodology used in this study see San-Giovanni (1978:13–24).

2. In a perceptive observation, Ebaugh (1977:24) interprets the fact that the novice frequently received a male name, such as Sister Mark or Sister Mary Robert, as a formal indication that "sexual differences were no longer emphasized."

3. Although recent changes in religious life have lessened some of these differences between priest and nun the general comparison remains valid even today.

4. This fact may help to explain such intriguing phenomena as the frequent denial by achieving women (in politics, business, the military, etc.) that they are feminist or are concerned with larger feminist issues, or the exaggerated use of "feminine" accoutrements (makeup, ribbons, jewelry, style of uniforms) by successful women athletes.

5. I am indebted to Mary Boutilier for this observation.

REFERENCES

Banton, Michael. *Roles: An Introduction to the Study of Social Relations*. New York: Basic Books, 1965.

Bullough, Vern L. *The Subordinate Sex*. Champaign, Ill.: University of Illinois Press, 1973.

Chafetz, Janet S. *Masculine/feminine or human?* Itasca, Ill.: Peacock, 1974.

Christ, Carol P., and Judith Plaskow (eds.). *Womanspirit Rising*. New York: Harper & Row, 1979.

Clausen, John (ed.), *Socialization and Society*. Boston: Little, Brown, 1968.

Daly, Mary. *The Church and the Second Sex*. New York: Harper & Row, 1975.

David, Deborah S., and Robert Brannon (eds.). *The Forty-Nine Percent Majority: The Male Sex Role*. Reading, Mass.: Addison-Wesley, 1976.

Doely, Sarah B. (ed.). *Women's Liberation in the Church*. New York: Association Press, 1970.

Ebaugh, Helen R. F. *Out of the Cloister: A Study of Organizational Dilemmas.* Austin: University of Texas Press, 1977.

Glaser, Barney, and Anselm Strauss. *Status Passage.* Chicago: Aldine, 1971.

Hageman, Alice L. (ed.). *Sexist Religion and Women in the Church: No More Silence.* New York: Association Press, 1974.

Hughes, Everett C. "Dilemmas and Contradictions of Status," *American Journal of Sociology.* 50 (1945):353–59.

Kavanagh, J. *A Modern Priest Looks at His Outdated Church.* New York: Trident Press, 1967.

Kelly, Rita M., and Mary Boutilier. *The Making of Political Women.* Chicago: Nelson-Hall, 1978.

Koltun, Elizabeth (ed.). *The Jewish Woman: New Perspectives.* New York: Schocken Books, 1976.

Millum, Teresa. *Images of Women: Advertising in Women's Magazines.* London: Chatto and Windus, 1975.

Reuther, Rosemary. *Religion and Sexism: Images of Women in the Jewish and Christian Traditions.* New York: Simon and Schuster, 1974.

Safilios-Rothschild, Constantine. *Love, Sex, and Sex Roles.* Englewood Cliffs, N.J.: Prentice-Hall, 1977.

SanGiovanni, Lucinda. *Ex-Nuns: A Study of Emergent Role Passage.* Norwood, N.J.: Ablex, 1978.

Scott, Marvin B., and Stanford M. Lyman. "Accounts," *American Sociological Review.* 33 (1963), 46–62.

Westhues, K. *The Religious Community and the Secular State.* New York: Lippincott, 1968.

Review Questions

1. How did SanGiovanni expect ex-nuns to differ from other women as a result of their experiences in the convent? Were her expectations confirmed?

2. What does the interview material in her article indicate were the typical effects of convent life on the gender-identities of nuns who are still in the convent?

3. To whom did ex-nuns look for role models and socialization agents as they adjusted to secular life?

4. How might the *seclusion* of nuns in convents reinforce their religious beliefs? Their religious identities?

Suggested Readings: Interaction in Institutional Contexts: Religion

Dodd, David J. "The Sweet Man of Jonestown," *New Society*, 49 (September 1979), 607–610.

Slater, Philip. *The Wayward Gate: Science and the Supernatural.* Boston: Beacon Press, 1977.

Ward, David A. "Toward a Normative Explanation of 'Old Fashioned Revivals,' " *Qualitative Sociology*, 3 (1) (Spring 1980), 3–22.

Part IX. Social and Cultural Change

SOCIAL CHANGE IS A COMPLEX, ONGOING PROCESS. ANY OR ALL OF THE ELEMENTS OF A culture may change—objects, ideas, beliefs, norms, values, patterns of interaction. Change may be dramatic and sudden, as in the wake of a disaster or war. Or it can occur subtly and gradually over many years.

Change may occur as the result of *formal* enactments, when those who are empowered to make laws for a nation, a state, or a company require new ways of doing things. Civil rights legislation, for example, led not only to changes in the procedures and policies of schools, businesses, hospitals, and unions, but to shifts in opinions and beliefs—some favorable to minorities and some which could be called "backlash." As the Food and Drug Administration determines which substances are dangerous to our health, even our eating habits may be altered by formal procedures.

More often, social change is not legislated or dictated but occurs at the *informal* level. Examples of such change can be found in styles of dress, technological innovations, and the declining importance of religion in everyday life. The invention of the automobile has transformed our cities, our economy, and even our courtship practices.

Informal change can also lead to formal change. This process can be seen with the gradual acceptance of marijuana smoking by middle-class society. When the authors of this book were attending college in the mid-1960s, few students were smoking marijuana at Temple University or Oklahoma State University. As marijuana smoking became part of the college experience, more and more young adults became users. Smoking soon spread to the high schools and then to the professions. As marijuana use became more extensive, the laws in many states were revised to focus on the major distributors rather than on individual smokers. Police, too, began looking the other way when college students and other adults were peacefully smoking in public.

Rarely does the alteration of one element in a culture leave the rest of the culture intact. Because social elements are intricately connected, change in one area usually affects many other areas. As women have gained equality in legal terms, for example, the rules for appropriate behavior between men and women are affected too. One pattern of coping with changed definitions and rules regarding what women can expect in male-female relationships is the subject of the first article in this section. Lynn Atwater reports here on interviews with a number of women who were having extramarital relationships (EMRs). Traditionally in our society, men "benefited" from the double standard. They were much more likely than women to have sexual encounters outside marriage. Now we see changes occurring.

As Atwater makes clear, the women in her study were seeking in relationships of kind of intimacy and acceptance that seemed to be lacking in their traditional marriages. They acquired new perceptions, of which their husbands were often unaware, of what to expect from male-female relationships. One way to have these expectations met would be to confront their husbands directly. This approach would require the renegotiation of an ongoing, taken-for-granted relationship stabilized by years of precedent. No doubt many women do this, but others may leave the relationship altogether or may maintain their traditional marriages while engaging in EMRs as well.

Some of Atwater's respondents used their EMR experiences to resocialize their husbands into becoming more satisfying spouses. In such instances, the EMR served as a rehearsal for the primary, or marital, relationship. For women who were less successful in their resocialization attempts, the EMR allowed them to continue their marriages while receiving affection and caring attention elsewhere.

A note about Atwater's methodology is in order. Because of the sensitive nature of her subject matter, acquiring a random sample was out of the question. Atwater decided that some information was better than no information, and she set about obtaining a sample from the readership of Ms. magazine. An innovative approach to interviewing was adopted for some of the subjects: self-administered questionnaires, the responses to which were tape-recorded. Thus, information was collected from women whose stories otherwise would not have been told. The reader should keep in mind, however, that we do not know what proportion of married women in the United States are involved in EMRs.

In part at least, we can trace the roots of a great many social and cultural changes, including alterations in women's roles, to technological changes which have affected the type of work required in our society. Put another way, the introduction of technological innovations can have much greater consequences for social change than anyone had intended or foreseen. The next article illustrates the importance of one type of technological "advancement" for the single-industry town of "Caliente." In "Death by Dieselization," W. F. Cottrell discusses the drastic consequences of the introduction of new train engines, consequences which proved to be dire for the economy and for the personal lives of the town's inhabitants.

Technological innovations, however, do not invariably bring about social change, as the final selection by Gary Albrecht demonstrates. In fact, when the introduction of a computerized information system designed to control the work of probation officers in a court was proposed, it served to mobilize the probation officers to resist the change, thereby maintaining their autonomy. Albrecht does not suggest that computerization or other technological innovations can or will be resisted in all facets of American life. He merely documents conditions under which social stability, rather than social change, has occurred. He shows that the protection of a group's vested interests in the *status quo* and the interdependence of professional groups may both play important parts in change or resistance to it.

WOMEN AND MARRIAGE: ADDING AN EXTRAMARITAL ROLE

Lynn Atwater

EVER LARGER NUMBERS OF WOMEN ARE BECOMING INVOLVED IN AN EXTRAMARITAL RE-lationship (EMR) at some point in their married lives. The best available evidence (Bell et al., 1975; Levin, 1975) shows an increase in every age group as compared to baseline data (Kinsey et al., 1953). The change is highest for younger married women, so that the data suggest an incidence of 40–50 percent will occur as the youngest-age cohort of married women move through the life cycle. It appears that the rate for women's EMRs will approximate the rate for men's and become another area in the trend toward convergence of gender role behavior.

Much of the existing literature on women's EMR behavior was collected during an era of more traditional gender roles and tends to emphasize such reasons for involvement as unhappy marriages, falling in love with another man, or the need to compensate for loss of attractiveness due to aging (Bell, 1971; Gagnon and Simon, 1973; Hunt, 1969). Furthermore, because past studies also reflected the general cultural bias against EMRs, involvements were often seen as "sick" or "abnormal" (see Ellis, 1968, for a discussion of this point) with only negative effects on marriage and the family. Only relatively rarely did research suggest reasons as the desire for new emotional satisfaction or individual growth (Bell and Lobsenz, 1974; Hunt, 1969; Neubeck, 1969).

Because women's experience with EMRs is increasing at the same time as their gender role is undergoing much modification, it was decided to conduct a qualitative study to elicit hypotheses about the current nature of women's extramarital involvement and its integration with family life. For this purpose, exploratory research was carried out with women who were considered receptive to personal and social change.

A sample of women (N = 40) was interviewed in depth about their extramarital experiences. The sample was drawn from a larger group of approximately 300 respondents to an ad in *Ms.* magazine requesting women who were involved now/recently in extramarital relationships to write the researcher. Only two women who were asked refused interviews, and no payment was made to any respondent.

This is an original article especially prepared for the first edition of this volume, based on "Women in Extra-Marital Relationships: A Case Study in Sociosexuality," Ph.D. dissertation, Department of Sociology, Rutgers University, January 1978.

All data were gathered by this researcher during 1974–1975. Interviews followed a nine-page interview guide prepared on the basis of previous test interviews. Questions were primarily open-ended to ensure emphasis on the women's subjective understanding. Women were further encouraged to discuss anything they felt important that was not already the focus of a question. All interviews were tape-recorded with the consent of the respondent.

Analytical considerations guided the selection of the sample, which represented a range of background variables. This variation generates the maximum number of empirical and conceptual possibilities for analysis (Glaser and Strauss, 1967). Although the use of an analytical sample means that the findings are limited in their generalizability, the sample fits the goals of the research in that it probably (1) reveals emergent changes in women's EMRs, (2) suggests factors unique to the understanding of women's sexual behavior, which has consistently been different from men's (Ehrmann, 1964), and (3) uncovers possible explanatory hypotheses to be tested in research on representative samples.

Women who were interviewed lived primarily in urban/suburban areas in twenty-three states. They varied in age from twenty-three to fifty-nine years and in education from high school to graduate work. The sample somewhat overrepresents the more highly educated, middle- to upper-middle-class woman, but these are the women more likely to be in the vanguard of social change.

Occupationally, 30 percent of the women identified themselves as homemakers with one-half of these working or attending school part-time. About one-third held full-time clerical or secretarial jobs, one-third were engaged in full-time managerial-professional employment, and the remaining (3) were full-time students. Seventy percent (28) had children, varying in age from infants to adults; 65 percent (26) of the marriages were still intact at the time of the interviews; the remainder had ended in separation, divorce, or death of the husband at some point after the first EMR involvement.

MEANINGS

The first observation to be made about the meanings of women's extramarital involvements is that the overwhelming majority of answers fell into two categories, those pertaining to the characteristics of the relationship itself or those pertaining to the women's personal needs and desires. It will be noticed that there was relatively infrequent mention of "traditional" reasons or of sex as a dominant concern, as might be expected.

It was very important. It started off just being sexual, but changed to a more encompassing relationship.

It makes me feel so completely a woman.

• • •

It meant learning about another person.

It was a very long-term closeness with another person. I wanted to—and it seemed very natural to—to extend that closeness to include sex.

· · ·

It was like being with a soul brother. It was nice to be able to share intellectually, sexually, emotionally.

It made me happy at a time when there wasn't a lot to be happy about.

This relationship means a great deal to me, as we explore our many differences and similarities, discuss a variety of issues, and express ourselves physically. It is a total trip, taken very slowly since we have as much time as we need to really get to know each other.

It meant I was a person, not an appendage of my husband.

It meant having another friend.

It's made me a happy person because I'm doing what I feel without worrying about someone's rules. I'm the last person that people would think would break a rule. . . . I don't believe in waking up at 65 years old and regretting the chances that you never took.

These responses reflect a distinctly modern vocabulary of meanings. Some center on the pleasures of relating interpersonally and reflect contemporary attitudes toward adding greater expressiveness to our private lives through additional primary interactions. Whether it is done in an organized fashion through encounter groups or individually through EMRs (Berger, 1966:74), it is an empirical difference of degree, not kind.

Other meanings related to self-fulfillment also embody particularly modern values, that of knowing, developing, or rewarding the self through interaction with others (Lyman and Scott, 1970:123; Berger et al., 1973:77). This is in contrast to the traditional female gender role, which emphasizes the *giving* of emotional rewards to others. The majority of these women see EMRs as an opportunity to *receive* and, therefore, to modify the definitions of the usual woman's role.

The opportunity to talk about "getting" rather than "giving" was more directly presented in the question, "What do you get from the relationship?," and the answers allow some refinement of our first observations. Here about one-half of the women talked about the pleasures of interaction as a mutual experience, but the emphasis was still on the enjoyment of communicating and relating.

I guess essentially what I get is the companionship, the closeness and the ability to communicate with a male.

The feeling of being treated as an equal; poems from him, all kinds of communication.

Mostly I get the enjoyment of really getting to know another human being, and working out the differences into a meaningful relationship. That means just knowing that he cares, without needing him to remind me often, regardless of whether he calls or not.

Essentially it was the pleasure of knowing completely a beautiful person who thought of me as being equally beautiful.

Approximately another one-quarter of the women responded to the question of "what do you get" with emphasis on the receipt of expressive rewards, for they make no reference to the relationship itself. There was, however, a distinct flavor of autonomy in the experience of getting.

I get variety. Other than that it was a real stroke, an ego boost, and one that I really needed right then, because I was doing a whole lot to hold other people together and had no support for myself—and this guy was really neat about that. Plus I knew how turned on he was to me, to my head.

It made me feel really cared for; it made me feel I was special.

I got self-confidence, a feeling of individuality, a self-reliance that I didn't have before, and understanding that I have resources and abilities, too, to meet my needs.

• • •

He was very supportive; everything I did was good—uh—and I needed it—a lot. Along with being supportive he also encouraged me to be my own person. He tried to develop that (independence) in me and he was highly successful. I was successful, but he helped me an awful lot in bringing out the independence.

The final one-quarter of cases gave answers that added the dimensions of sex, variety, and thrills that one might more typically expect although there also occurs some overlap with the previously mentioned items. It is surprising that sex was mentioned so rarely, in fact, in responses to questions about what is commonly defined as a sexual activity.

It's a thrill; it's really a thrill. Also, it's a way of knowing a serious, incredibly worthwhile person. And if I hadn't gotten involved with him, I wouldn't have known him as well. My life would be less if I had not met him and gotten to know him so well.

• • •

Well, I get a kick out of the relationship. It's a thrill for me . . . what I get out of the relationship is mostly the thrill of being with a man who wants me as a woman, in a sexy way.

Excitement, being with another man sexually.

When questioned about their feelings toward their EMR partners, approximately three-quarters of the women defined the person as a "friend" or someone they "liked." Less than one-quarter reported feelings of "love" but qualified this to mean a "human" or "person-to-person" kind of love. There was difficulty in finding the proper vocabulary to describe their feelings, suggesting a cultural lag in the development of language to express changing emotions. Only three women described themselves as being "in love" in a romantic sense.

Thus, there are a variety of subjective meanings reported to be a part of the experience of EMRs, with the major emphasis on the EMR as a social experience and the expressive pleasures of relating intimately (but not romantically) with another person. In one sense, this could be labeled a traditional meaning for women, as both sociological (Parsons and Bales, 1955) and psychological (Baken, 1966) theorists have described the female role as oriented toward expressiveness, affectivity, and concern for others. But, as we have already pointed out, these reported meanings emphasize the *mutuality* of the expressiveness or, in some cases, the *getting* instead of *giving* of emotional support, which is a significant variation on the usual female role. These women are not rejecting their interest in expressiveness but are clearly stating through their behavior and words a preference for reciprocity in the expressive dimension and, in some cases, a need, situationally or temporarily at least, for a unilateral expressiveness in which they are the recipients, rather than the donors.

These findings may be coupled with other aspects of this research in which women were questioned about their marriages and what they found particularly dissatisfying about them. The responses of thirty-eight of the forty women to this open-ended question may all be categorized as perceived deficiencies in the area of communication and expressiveness in their husbands. One solution for women with this complaint about their marital relationships is apparently found in EMRs with men who are more accomplished or egalitarian in socioemotional areas. These EMRs do not become a replacement for marriage, however, for in only one case did a woman leave her husband for her EMR partner. The important hypothesis in these data is that a strong motivation for participation in EMRs is a social one, the desire to modify the expressive dimension of the traditional female gender role from a unilateral to a mutual one. If a husband is unable or unwilling to accept such change, women may reach outside the marital framework to accomplish it.

BEHAVIORAL CHANGE TOWARD HUSBANDS

As women's role complex has always been centered in family interaction, several queries explored how women's EMRs affect their playing of family roles. Nearly all the women (85 percent) thought that being involved with someone else had changed their behavior toward their husbands. Of this group, more than one-half characterized it as a change for the better.

> Yes, I'm not as afraid to say what I want to say, I don't think I kowtow to my husband as much as I used to, I don't let him hurt my feelings as easily as I used to 'cause I silently think that somebody else loves me. And if this man, my husband, is getting mad and raging at me, ridiculing me, then I don't bow and paw as much as I used to.

> I think my EMRs have changed my behavior toward my husband. With my husband—obviously before I started these relationships I still had a dependency to meet my needs and however meager his meeting of my psychological, social and physical needs were, or how inadequate I thought they were, he still was the only

one I had to meet them. So, since having the relationships and being involved in them—uh—I have no need for my husband to meet any needs of mine.

Yes, it did change my behavior toward my husband. Initially I was nicer to him because I think I was getting more than I needed and wasn't even conscious that I did need . . . I used to always, even during the first few years of my relationship with Paul, I would always give in to my husband. If he would argue with me I would always sort of in the end let him have the last word. I felt on easier ground that way. I don't do that so much anymore. I never could walk away angry but now I can. I never could go to sleep without resolving something and kissing and making up. I can do that better now and I think that's good.

Oh, yes, my behavior really did change. I bloomed. I became more interested in everything around me. I was on top of the world, and my family found me to be a much happier person, with much, much more to give to them. My God, I was alive!

Now I think I'm much nicer to my husband because I know not many husbands will accept it (her revelation of the EMR) like he did. I love my husband more because of it.

I would be divorced if it hadn't been for somebody else. I would have divorced him a hundred times over. The only thing that keeps us married is the fact that I can find sexual release outside my marriage. . . . Since I have had this second EMR ongoing, I have been able to draw my husband out more and get him to talk more and more and to be more open in expressing my feelings with him on a very gradual basis. I am slowly but surely trying to bring our relationship up to a level that meets more of my needs.

Reported improvements lie in a variety of areas. Most salient to the issue of change in gender roles is an explicit sense of an increase in wifely power and sense of autonomy in the marriage because she has an alternate source of rewards. On the other hand, some wives found that the additional rewards from outside the marriage enabled them to increase either sexual or expressive rewards to their husbands or to be more willing to try to change the marriage relationship to better meet their own needs. In one case, the husband's increase of rewards to the wife because of his acceptance of the EMR situation raised his value in her eyes (as compared to her perception of other husbands), and the woman in turn increased her rewards to him. All these situations seem to add to marital stability, at least during the time period covered by these interviews.

Of the remaining women who felt that the EMR had affected their behavior toward their husbands, ten saw it as a negative consequence and five thought there were both positive and negative effects.

The way that it did affect my behavior was to make me more hostile to him. Having to sit there and read a book or something under his watchful eyes when I knew I could have been out with someone else . . . made it even more attractive to be with the other person and made me more resentful of my husband.

Yes, I was a little strained toward him at times, but I was also mixed up about a lot of other things beside the outside relationship.

I became less tolerant of my husband. I would rather have been with Bill than at home. It did affect my relationship with my husband. I was irritable and tired.

I ignored my marriage. I let it deteriorate while I had an outside diversion.

• • •

Six women said their behavior toward their husbands did not change. Three possibilities suggest themselves: (1) they changed but are not conscious of it, (2) their marriages may either have been "passive-congenial" or "devitalized" (Cuber and Harroff, 1965), in which case the low frequency and intensity of marital interaction may indeed not have been affected by the EMRs, or (3) they were experts at role compartmentalization, as the following excerpt suggests.

No, it didn't, because my husband's relationship to me is in one compartment, my writing is in another, and so on and so on. My private life is in a different one completely from all else and I move within it and then come back to the house. I shut the door on it. I can do that. It works well.

EFFECT OF EMR SEX ON MARITAL SEX

One question specifically asked was, Did the EMR sex have any effect on marital sex? Slightly over one-half (58 percent) of the women reported that it did affect their marital sex, 40 percent replied that it did not, and one woman said she did not know. Of those women who reported an effect on marital sex, only fourteen responses could be characterized as a negative impact. A few women stopped sex completely, but most reduced the frequency of or their emotional involvement in marital sexual activity.

I stopped it completely, but it had been on the wane anyway.

I probably have less sex with my husband since getting involved in an EMR. He has always wanted very little. . . . So, uhmm, you know, quite often I would be the initiator of sex, and since I'm getting all I want—well, maybe sometimes not all I want—so I don't approach him at all now.

I don't know whether it's more or less sex with him. I stopped counting. I guess it's probably pretty much the same. And—uh—I can't say that having an affair with somebody has turned me on to my husband. I think in some ways it's kind of turned me off because I know I can get it somewhere else.

Yes, it does, and as I said, I don't try to lay any trip on him anymore. And it's freed me a lot more. If I am not totally satisfied in a relationship with my husband, I have learned the masturbation in a bathtub trick. We have an old-fashioned bathtub and I can drape my legs over the end, and if he hasn't been able to finish the job, I can take care of it just very nicely in the tub.

I probably started looking for my sexual satisfaction outside the marriage. When I wasn't satisfied with my husband, I didn't even care because I knew the next night I'd be with Ed, and get satisfied.

In addition to the fact that these responses denote a basically negative impact on marital sex, a peripheral theme present was that of a decrease in some women's sexual dependence on their husbands. This finding reiterates the increased sense of autonomy women gain from perceived positive changes in the social area of marital interaction. These consequences tend to occur in situations in which women feel thwarted in making desired changes in their marriages.

The remaining nine of the twenty-three women who reported an effect in marital sex described mostly increases in sexual activity with their husbands or more enjoyment of it.

> Now that the truth is out and he knows I like these things and I wouldn't be horrified, it's amazing. The whole picture's changed.

> Yes, we had much more sex while I was having the relationship.

> It certainly affected my sexual relationship with my husband. I became more interested in sex with him, something I really couldn't understand at the time. I was riding high, returning from a visit with my lover. All those feelings needed an outlet. At times I felt this was terribly unfair to my husband, but it was always so good between us when this happened.

One interpretation of the increase in sexual activity is that it is inspired by guilt, but this does not usually seem to be the case. Rather, it appears more frequently to be the result of an increased libido and suggests one way in which EMRs can positively affect marriage.

One curious comparison to be made in conjunction with the previous observation is that, whereas 85 percent of the sample said that their EMR affected their behavior toward their husbands, only 58 percent said that their EMR affected their sexual activity toward their husbands. Thus, the socioemotional activity in an EMR seems to have a greater impact on the woman and her treatment of her husband than the sexual activity does. Or, alternatively, women are able to compartmentalize the consequences of the sexual activity more than they can the expressive, which emphasizes the previous data that the socioemotional aspects of EMRs mean more in general to these women than the strictly sexual.

BEHAVIORAL CHANGE TOWARD CHILDREN

Of the twenty-eight women in the sample with children, 64 percent stated that their EMR involvement affected their behavior toward their children. Two-thirds of those believing it changed their behavior saw it as a change for the better.

> With my needs being met by a man outside the home, I don't have the same dependency toward my children. And it's a good feeling, in a way. I'm reacting to the children more as people now, just for what they are. I don't have to use them any more. I am also happy to be doing things with them because I have this all

freed up psychic energy and I feel good about myself; and I want to do things and I hopefully do things with my children. I think they've benefited that way.

(2 children, ages 4 and 8)

Yes, very much so, because it's put me in contact with myself in a way that was not possible with just one other person. I have opened up my feelings, in terms of my not being shocked at my own children if they should become involved premaritally, if my children decide not to marry, or decide on a lifestyle that was other than a heterosexual one. It has very much changed my whole attitude. . . . And I think if I hadn't lived the life I'm living, I think my kids would still be dependent on me; I'd be smothering them to death. And I don't think that's enhancing.

(2 children, ages 18 and 13)

With the children—you know—I had more patience with the children because I was happy and having an adult relationship and I just had—you know—a more carefree attitude.

(2 children, ages 5 and 7)

•   •   •

All these comments concerning changed behavior toward children reflect the normal strains of the intensity and isolation of the maternal role in a nuclear family system. It appears that the mother's having another adult relationship helps to offset the overinvolvement and self-sacrifice that are part of the structure and ideology of American motherhood. Not that it is being suggested that women have EMRs to make themselves better mothers, but that the inherent strain in the maternal role as it is conceptualized in America (Skolnick, 1973:290–312) will have a tendency to be relieved by *any* fulfilling activity the mother pursues.

The six women who thought their treatment of their children was negatively affected seemed to focus on their absence from their children.

Yes, but I had been irritable after my second unwanted child was born. My children would cry when I would leave for school or to go out. It used to hurt like hell. I think it's done harm. It's definitely hurt all of us.

(2 children, ages 6 and 5)

Once or twice I felt bad because I put her into bed a little earlier, an hour earlier, because he was coming over. Or if I go out in the evening, sometimes, I feel bad. I don't know if it's rationalization or what, but when I go out in the evening to go to school, it doesn't bother me.

(1 child, age 3)

Again, these remarks evoke a belief in traditional role ideology that mothers belong constantly with their children as well as, perhaps, guilt over the EMR activity. In all these six cases, further questioning by the interviewer elicited information that all the children had been in the care of their fathers or a competent baby-sitter in the mother's absence. Additionally, a number of these research interviews were conducted in the women's houses, and there was an opportunity to do several hours' observation. In no case was there any evidence of anything other than the kind of mother-child interaction that one can observe normally in the course of everyday living. It is a warranted conclusion, from the evidence in this sample, that participation in EMRs does not have any more deleterious effects on mothering than does any other activity external to family life. In other words, the maternal aspect of the female gender role complex, if it is affected at all, is more likely to be affected positively rather than negatively by EMR activity.

CONCLUSION

The predominant meaning of extramarital relationships for this group of change-oriented women lies in the opportunity to change their traditional expressive roles to be reciprocal and to become more autonomous individuals while maintaining the marriage relationship. To the degree that these women's experiences are representative of other women's lives now and in the future, several conclusions are implied.

One is that the probability of maintaining a monogamous relationship may be enhanced by fostering concurrent changes in gender roles within marriage. The recent emphasis on modification in women's roles has resulted in a lack of integration with men's roles. Supportive methods for achieving comparable changes in men's roles may be in the form of self-help groups and marital counseling. Anticipatory and remedial socialization for emerging roles could also be accomplished through various agents such as parents, peers, schools, and the mass media. Changes in other institutional areas to support expressiveness in men and autonomy in women may also be necessary.

An alternative implication concerns the increasing number of persons who will experience extramaritality at some point in their married lives. The evidence suggests that many extramarital relationships do not destroy or even undermine the quality of family life. Because most EMRs in this study did not involve the arousal of traditional romantic feelings, this is congruent with women's characterizations that EMRs mostly affect their behavior positively toward their husbands and children. The absence of conventional "in love" type of "affairs" would predictably generate a less negative impact on family life. The dissemination of information on new styles of EMRs, as well as knowledge of compartmentalization techniques, coping mechanisms, and other strategies for integrating EMRs with marriage, can only prove useful to those married persons whose lives will be touched by this phenomenon.

Finally, as has been noted in this study, variations in the numbers of persons involved in EMR behavior, their reasons for doing it, and the way in which their behavior is interpreted are constantly occurring and are a reflection of other cultural and social changes. Not only is the reality of the behavior being transformed, but the unrealistic public attitudes fostered by the low visibility of EMRs in the past may be modifying. A recent study (Bukstel et al., 1978) indicates that persons with premarital experiences project that they expect to have extramarital experiences in the future. This is an indication of a dramatic attitudinal change that could alter our perception and consciousness of what marriage is all about. For the facts are that extramarital relationships are, always have been, and will continue to be a part of the American institution of marriage.

REFERENCES

Bakan, David, 1966, *The Duality of Human Existence*. Chicago: Rand-McNally.

Bell, Robert R., 1971a, *Social Deviance*. Homewood, Ill.: Dorsey. 1971b, *Marriage and Family Interaction*. Homewood, Ill: Dorsey.

Bell, Robert R., and Norman M. Lobsenz, 1974, "Married Sex: How Uninhibited Can a Woman Dare to Be?," *Redbook*, 143 (September), 75, 176–181.

Bell, Robert R., Stanley Turner, and Lawrence Rosen, 1975, "A Multivariate Analysis of Female Extramarital Coitus," *Journal of Marriage and the Family*, 37 (May), 375–384

Berger, Peter, Brigitte Berger, and Hansfried Kellner, 1973, *The Homeless Mind*. New York: Vintage.

Bukstel, Lee H., Gregory D. Roeder, Peter R. Kilmann, and James Laughlin, 1978, "Projected Extramarital Sexual Involvement in Unmarried College Students," *Journal of Marriage and the Family*, (May), 337–340.

Cuber, John F., and Peggy B. Harroff, 1965, *The Significant Americans*. New York: Appleton-Century-Crofts.

Edwards, John N., and Alan Booth, 1976, "Sexual Behavior in and out of Marriage: An Assessment of Correlates," *Journal of Marriage and the Family*, 38, 73–81.

Ehrmann, W. W., 1964, "Marital and Nonmarital Sexual Behavior," in H. T. Christensen, ed., *Handbook of Marriage and the Family*. Chicago: Rand McNally, pp. 585–622.

Ellis, A., 1968, "Healthy and Disturbed Reasons for Having Extramarital Relations," *Journal of Human Relations*, 16, 490–501.

Gagnon, John H., and William Simon, 1973, *Sexual Conduct: The Social Sources of Human Sexuality*. Chicago: Aldine.

Glaser, Barney G., and Anselm L. Strauss, 1967, *The Discovery of Grounded Theory*. Chicago: Aldine.

Hunt, Morton M., 1969, *The Affair*. New York: New American Library. 1974, "Sexual Behavior in the 1970's. Part IV: Extramarital and Postmarital Sex," *Playboy*, 21, 60–61, 286–287.

Kinsey, Alfred C., Wardell B. Pomeroy, Clyde E. Martin, and Paul H. Gebhard, 1953, *Sexual Behavior in the Human Female*. Philadelphia: Saunders.

Levin, Robert J., 1975, "The Redbook Report on Premarital and Extramarital Sex: The End of the Double Standard?," *Redbook*, (October), 38–44, 190–192.

Lyman, Stanford M., and Marvin B. Scott, 1970, *A Sociology of the Absurd*. New York: Appleton-Century-Crofts.

Neubeck, Gerhard, ed., 1969, *Extra-Marital Relations*. Englewood Cliffs, N.J.: Prentice-Hall.

Parsons, T., and R. F. Bales, 1955, *Family, Socialization and Interaction Process*. New York: Free Press.

Skolnick, Arlene, 1973, *The Intimate Environment*. Boston: Little, Brown.

Review Questions

1. How did women's EMRs affect their relationships with their spouses? Their children?

2. What did the women in Atwater's study gain from their EMRs that they did not have in their marriages?

3. How have changes in the norms regarding male-female relationships contributed to the rise of EMRs among women?

4. What might be the implications of changes in women's involvement in EMRs for other aspects of American life?

5. Why can't Atwater's research findings be generalized to all women in the United States? How could you design a study with a more representative sample? What problems would you encounter?

DEATH BY DIESELIZATION: A CASE STUDY IN THE REACTION TO TECHNOLOGICAL CHANGE

W. F. Cottrell

IN THE FOLLOWING INSTANCE IT IS PROPOSED THAT WE EXAMINE A COMMUNITY CON-
fronted with radical change in its basic economic institution and to trace the
effects of this change throughout the social structure. From these facts it
may be possible in some degree to anticipate the resultant changing attitudes and values of the people in the community, particularly as they reveal
whether or not there is a demand for modification of the social structure or
a shift in function from one institution to another. Some of the implications
of the facts discovered may be valuable in anticipating future social change.

The community chosen for examination has been disrupted by the dieselization of the railroads. Since the railroad is among the oldest of those industries organized around steam, and since therefore the social structure of railroad communities is a product of long-continued processes of adaptation to
the technology of steam, the sharp contrast between the technological requirements of the steam engine and those of the diesel should clearly reveal
the changes in social structure required. Any one of a great many railroad
towns might have been chosen for examination. However, many railroad
towns are only partly dependent upon the railroad for their existence. In
them many of the effects which take place are blurred and not easily distinguishable by the observer. Thus, the "normal" railroad town may not be the
best place to see the consequences of dieselization. For this reason a one-industry town was chosen for examination.

In a sense it is an "ideal type" railroad town, and hence not complicated
by other extraneous economic factors. It lies in the desert and is here given
the name "Caliente" which is the Spanish adjective for "hot." Caliente was
built in a break in an eighty-mile canyon traversing the desert. Its reason for
existence was to service the steam locomotive. There are few resources in
the area to support it on any other basis, and such as they are they would
contribute more to the growth and maintenance of other little settlements in
the vicinity than to that of Caliente. So long as the steam locomotive was in
use, Caliente was a necessity. With the adoption of the diesel it became obsolescent.

This stark fact was not, however, part of the expectations of the residents
of Caliente. Based upon the "certainty" of the railroad's need for Caliente,

W. F. Cottrell, "Death by Dieselization: A Case Study in the Reaction to Technological
Change," *American Sociological Review*, 16 (1951), 358–365.

men built their homes there, frequently of concrete and brick, at the cost, in many cases, of their life savings. The water system was laid in cast iron which will last for centuries. Business men erected substantial buildings which could be paid for only by profits gained through many years of business. Four churches evidence the faith of Caliente people in the future of their community. A twenty-seven bed hospital serves the town. Those who built it thought that their investment was as well warranted as the fact of birth, sickness, accident and death. They believed in education. Their school buildings represent the investment of savings guaranteed by bonds and future taxes. There is a combined park and play field which, together with a recently modernized theatre, has been serving recreational needs. All these physical structures are material evidence of the expectations, morally and legally sanctioned and financially funded, of the people of Caliente. This is a normal and rational aspect of the culture of all "solid" and "sound" communities.

Similarly normal are the social organizations. These include Rotary, Chamber of Commerce, Masons, Odd Fellows, American Legion and the Veterans of Foreign Wars. There are the usual unions, churches, and myriad . . . clubs. . . . In short, here is the average American community with normal social life, subscribing to normal American codes. Nothing its members had been taught would indicate that the whole pattern of this normal existence depended completely upon a few elements of technology which were themselves in flux. For them the continued use of the steam engine was as "natural" a phenomenon as any other element in their physical environment. Yet suddenly their life pattern was destroyed by the announcement that the railroad was moving its division point, and with it destroying the economic basis of Caliente's existence.

Turning from this specific community for a moment, let us examine the technical changes which took place and the reasons for the change. Division points on a railroad are established by the frequency with which the rolling stock must be serviced and the operating crews changed. At the turn of the century when this particular road was built, the engines produced wet steam at low temperatures. The steel in the boilers was of comparatively low tensile strength and could not withstand the high temperatures and pressures required for the efficient use of coal and water. At intervals of roughly a hundred miles the engine had to be disconnected from the train for service. At these points the cars also were inspected and if they were found to be defective they were either removed from the train or repaired while it was standing and the new engine being coupled on. Thus the location of Caliente, as far as the railroad was concerned, was a function of boiler temperature and pressure and the resultant service requirements of the locomotive.

Following World War II, the high tensile steels developed to create superior artillery and armor were used for locomotives. As a consequence it was possible to utilize steam at higher temperatures and pressure. Speed, power, and efficiency were increased and the distance between service intervals was increased.

The "ideal distance" between freight divisions became approximately 150 to 200 miles whereas it had formerly been 100 to 150. Wherever possible, freight divisions were increased in length to that formerly used by passenger trains, and passenger divisions were lengthened from two old freight divisions to three. Thus towns located at 100 miles from a terminal became obsolescent, those at 200 became freight points only, and those at three hundred miles became passenger division points.

The increase in speed permitted the train crews to make the greater distance in the time previously required for the lesser trip, and roughly a third of the train and engine crews, car inspectors, boilermakers and machinists and other service men were dropped. The towns thus abandoned were crossed off the social record of the nation in the adjustment to these technological changes in the use of the steam locomotive. Caliente, located midway between terminals about six hundred miles apart, survived. In fact it gained, since the less frequent stops caused an increase in the service required of the maintenance crews at those points where it took place. However, the introduction of the change to diesel engines projected a very different future.

In its demands for service the diesel engine differs almost completely from a steam locomotive. It requires infrequent, highly skilled service, carried on within very close limits, in contrast to the frequent, crude adjustments required by the steam locomotive. Diesels operate at about 35 per cent efficiency, in contrast to the approximately 4 per cent efficiency of the steam locomotives in use after World War II in the United States. Hence diesels require much less frequent stops for fuel and water. These facts reduce their operating costs sufficiently to compensate for their much higher initial cost.

In spite of these reductions in operating costs the introduction of diesels ordinarily would have taken a good deal of time. The changeover would have been slowed by the high capital costs of retooling the locomotive works, the long period required to recapture the costs of existing steam locomotives, and the effective resistance of the workers. World War II altered each of these factors. The locomotive works were required to make the change in order to provide marine engines, and the costs of the change were assumed by the government. Steam engines were used up by the tremendous demand placed upon the railroads by war traffic. The costs were recaptured by shipping charges. Labor shortages were such that labor resistance was less formidable and much less acceptable to the public than it would have been in peace time. Hence the shift to diesels was greatly facilitated by the war. In consequence, every third and sometimes every second division point suddenly became technologically obsolescent.

Caliente, like all other towns in similar plight, is supposed to accept its fate in the name of "progress." The general public, as shippers and consumers of shipped goods, reaps the harvest in better, faster service and eventually perhaps in lower charges. A few of the workers in Caliente will also share the gains, as they move to other division points, through higher wages. They will share in the higher pay, though whether this will be adequate to compensate for the costs of moving no one can say. Certain it is that their pay will not be adjusted to compensate for their specific losses. They will gain only as their seniority gives them the opportunity to work. These are those who gain. What are the losses, and who bears them?

The railroad company can figure its losses at Caliente fairly accurately. It owns 39 private dwellings, a modern clubhouse with 116 single rooms, and a twelve-room hotel with dining-room and lunch-counter facilities. These now become useless, as does much of the fixed physical equipment used for servicing trains. Some of the machinery can be used elsewhere. Some part of the roundhouse can be used to store unused locomotives and standby equipment. The rest will be torn down to save taxes. All of these costs can be entered as capital losses on the statement which the company draws up for its stockholders and for the government. Presumably they will be recovered by the use of the more efficient engines.

What are the losses that may not be entered on the company books? The total tax assessment in Caliente was $9,946.80 for the year 1948, of which $6,103.39 represented taxes assessed on the railroad. Thus the railroad valuation was about three-fifths that of the town. This does not take into account tax-free property belonging to the churches, the schools, the hospital, or the municipality itself which included all the public utilities. Some ideas of the losses sustained by the railroad in comparison with the losses of others can be surmised by reflecting on these figures for real estate alone. The story is an old one and often repeated in the economic history of America. It represents the "loss" side of a profit-and-loss system of adjusting to technological change. Perhaps for sociological purposes we need an answer to the question "just who pays?"

Probably the greatest losses are suffered by the older "non-operating" employees. Seniority among these men extends only within the local shop and craft. A man with twenty-five years' seniority at Caliente has no claim on the job of a similar craftsman at another point who has only twenty-five days' seniority. Moreover, some of the skills formerly valuable are no longer needed. The boilermaker, for example, knows that jobs for his kind are disappearing and he must enter the ranks of the unskilled. The protection and status offered by the union while he was employed have become meaningless now that he is no longer needed. The cost of this is high both in loss of income and in personal demoralization.

Operating employees also pay. Their seniority extends over a division, which in this case includes three division points. The older members can move from Caliente and claim another job at another point, but in many cases they move leaving a good portion of their life savings behind. The younger men must abandon their stake in railroad employment. The loss may mean a new apprenticeship in another occupation, at a time in life when apprenticeship wages are not adequate to meet the obligations of mature men with families. A steam engine hauled 2,000 tons up the hill out of

Caliente with the aid of two helpers. The four-unit diesel in command of one crew handles a train of 5,000 tons alone. Thus, to handle the same amount of tonnage required only about a fourth the manpower it formerly took. Three out of four men must start out anew at something else.

The local merchants pay. The boarded windows, half-empty shelves, and abandoned store buildings bear mute evidence of these costs. The older merchants stay, and pay; the younger ones, and those with no stake in the community will move; but the value of their property will in both cases largely be gone. . . .

The church will pay. The smaller congregations cannot support services as in the past. As the churchmen leave, the buildings will be abandoned.

Homeowners will pay. A hundred and thirty-five men owned homes in Caliente. They must accept the available means of support or rent to those who do. In either case the income available will be far less than that on which the houses were built. The least desirable homes will stand unoccupied, their value completely lost. The others must be revalued at a figure far below that at which they were formerly held.

In a word, those pay who are, by traditional American standards, *most moral*. Those who have raised children see friendships broken and neighborhoods disintegrated. The childless more freely shake the dust of Caliente from their feet. Those who built their personalities into the structure of the community watch their work destroyed. Those too wise or too selfish to have entangled themselves in community affairs suffer no such qualms. The chain store can pull down its sign, move its equipment and charge the costs off against more profitable and better located units, and against taxes. The local owner has no such alternatives. In short, "good citizens" who assumed family and community responsibility are the greatest losers. Nomads suffer least.

The people of Caliente are asked to accept as "normal" this strange inversion of their expectations. It is assumed that they will, without protest or change in sentiment, accept the dictum of the "law of supply and demand." Certainly they must comply in part with this dictum. While their behavior in part reflects this compliance, there are also other changes perhaps equally important in their attitudes and values.

The first reaction took the form of an effort at community self-preservation. Caliente became visible to its inhabitants as a real entity, as meaningful as the individual personalities which they had hitherto been taught to see as atomistic or nomadic elements. Community survival was seen as prerequisite to many of the individual values that had been given precedence in the past. The organized community made a search of new industry, citing elements of community organization themselves as reasons why industry should move to Caliente. But the conditions that led the railroad to abandon the point made the place even less attractive to new industry than it had hitherto been. Yet the effort to keep the community a going concern persisted.

There was also a change in sentiment. In the past the glib assertion that progress spelled sacrifice could be offered when some distant group was a victim of technological change. There was no such reaction when the event struck home. . . .

The people of Caliente continually profess their belief in "The American Way," but . . . they criticize decisions made solely in pursuit of profit, even though these decisions grow out of a clear-cut case of technological "progress." They feel that the company should have based its decision upon consideration for loyalty, citizenship, and community morale. They assume that the company should regard the seniority rights of workers as important considerations, and that it should consider significant the effect of permanent unemployment upon old and faithful employees. They look upon community integrity as an important community asset. Caught between the support of a "rational" system of "economic" forces and laws, and sentiments which they accept as significant values, they seek a solution to their dilemma which will at once permit them to retain their expected rewards for continued adherence to past norms and to defend the social system which they have been taught to revere but which now offers them a stone instead of bread.

IMPLICATIONS

We have shown that those in Caliente whose behavior most nearly approached the ideal taught are hardest hit by change. On the other hand, those seemingly farthest removed in conduct from that ideal are either rewarded or pay less of the costs of change than do those who follow the ideal more closely. Absentee owners, completely anonymous, and consumers who are not expected to cooperate to make the gains possible are rewarded most highly, while the local people who must cooperate to raise productivity pay dearly for having contributed.

In a society run through sacred mysteries whose rationale it is not man's privilege to criticize, such incongruities may be explained away. Such a society may even provide some "explanation" which makes them seem rational. In a secular society, supposedly defended rationally upon scientific facts, in which the pragmatic test "Does it work?" is continually applied, such discrepancy between expectation and realization is difficult to reconcile.

Defense of our traditional system of assessing the costs of technological change is made on the theory that the costs of such change are more than offset by the benefits to "society as a whole." However, it is difficult to show the people of Caliente just why *they* should pay for advances made to benefit others whom they have never known and who, in their judgment, have done nothing to justify such rewards. Any action that will permit the people of Caliente to levy the costs of change upon those who will benefit from them will be morally justifiable to the people of Caliente. Appeals to the general welfare leave them cold and the compulsions of the price system are not felt to be self-justifying "natural laws" but are regarded as being the specific consequence of specific bookkeeping decisions as to what should be included in the costs of change. They seek to change these decisions through social action. They do not consider that the "American Way" consists primarily of acceptance of the market as the final arbiter of their destiny. Rather they conceive that the system as a whole exists to render "justice," and if the consequences of the price system are such as to produce what they consider to be "injustice" they proceed to use some other institution as a means to reverse or offset the effects of the price system. Like other groups faced with the same situation, those in Caliente seize upon the means available to them. The operating employees had in their unions a device to secure what they consider to be their rights. Union practices developed over the years make it possible for the organized workers to avoid some of the costs of change which they would otherwise have had to bear. Featherbed rules, make-work practices, restricted work weeks, train length legislation and other similar devices were designed to permit union members to continue work even when "efficiency" dictated that they be disemployed. Members of the "Big Four" in Caliente joined with their fellows in demanding not only the retention of previously existing rules, but the imposition of new ones such as that requiring the presence of a third man in the diesel cab. For other groups there was available only the appeal to the company that it establish some other facility at Caliente, or alternatively a demand that "government" do something. One such demand took the form of a request to the Interstate Commerce Commission that it require inspection of rolling stock at Caliente. This request was denied.

It rapidly became apparent to the people of Caliente that they could not gain their objectives by organized community action nor individual endeavor but there was hope that by adding their voices to those of others similarly injured there might be hope of solution. They began to look to the activities of the whole labor movement for succor. Union strategy which forced the transfer of control from the market to government mediation or to legislation and operation was widely approved on all sides. This was not confined to those only who were currently seeking rule changes but was equally approved by the great bulk of those in the community who had been hit by the change. Cries of public outrage at their demands for make-work rules were looked upon as coming from those at best ignorant, ill-informed or stupid, and at worst as being the hypocritical efforts of others to gain at the workers' expense. When the union threat of a national strike for rule changes was met by government seizure, Caliente workers like most of their compatriots across the country welcomed this shift in control, secure in their belief that if "justice" were done they could only be gainers by government intervention. These attitudes are not "class" phenomena purely nor are they merely occupational sentiments. They result from the fact that modern life, with the interdependence that it creates, particularly in one-industry communities, imposes penalties far beyond the membership of the groups presumably involved in industry. When make-work rules contributed to the livelihood of the community, the support of the churches, and the taxes which maintain the schools; when featherbed practices determine the standard of living, the profits of the businessman and the circulation of the press; when they contribute to the salary of the teacher and the preacher they can no longer be treated as accidental, immoral, deviant or temporary. Rather they are elevated into the position of emergent morality and law. Such practices generate a morality which serves them just as the practices in turn nourish those who participate in and preserve them. They are as firmly a part of what one "has a right to expect" from industry as are parity payments to the farmer, bonuses and pensions to the veterans, assistance to the aged, tariffs to the industrialist, or the sanctity of property to those who inherit. On the other hand, all these practices conceivably help create a structure that is particularly vulnerable to changes such as that described here.

Practices which force the company to spend in Caliente part of what has been saved through technological change, or failing that, to reward those who are forced to move by increased income for the same service, are not, by the people of Caliente, considered to be unjustifiable. Confronted by a choice between the old means and resultant "injustice" which their use entails, and the acceptance of new means which they believe will secure them the "justice" they hold to be their right, they are willing to abandon (in so far as this particular area is concerned) the liberal state and the omnicompetent market in favor of something that works to provide "justice."

The study of the politics of pressure groups will show how widely the reactions of Caliente people are paralleled by those of other groups. Amongst them it is in politics that the decisions as to who will pay and who will profit are made. Through organized political force railroaders maintain the continuance of rules which operate to their benefit rather than for "the public good" or "the general welfare." Their defense of these practices is found in the argument that only so can their rights be protected against the power of other groups who hope to gain at their expense by functioning through the corporation and the market.

We should expect that where there are other groups similarly affected by technological change, there will be similar efforts to change the operation of our institutions. The case cited is not unique. Not only is it duplicated in hundreds of railroad division points but also in other towns abandoned by management for similar reasons. Changes in the location of markets or in the method of calculating transportation costs, changes in technology making necessary the use of new materials, changes due to the exhaustion of old sources of materials, changes to avoid labor costs such as the shift of the textile industry from New England to the South, changes to expedite decentralization to avoid the consequences of bombing, or those of congested living, all give rise to the question, "Who benefits, and at whose expense?"

The accounting practices of the corporation permit the entry only of those costs which have become "legitimate" claims upon the company. But the tremendous risks borne by the workers and frequently all the members of the community in an era of technological change are real phenomena. Rapid shifts in technology which destroy the "legitimate" expectations derived from past experience force the recognition of new obligations. Such recognition may be made voluntarily as management foresees the necessity, or it may be thrust upon it by political or other action. Rigidity of property concepts, the legal structure controlling directors in what they may admit to be costs, and the stereotyped nature of the "economics" used by management make rapid change within the corporation itself difficult even in a "free democratic society." Hence while management is likely to be permitted or required to initiate technological change in the interest of profits, it may and probably will be barred from compensating for the social consequences certain to arise from those changes. Management thus shuts out the rising flood of demands in its cost accounting only to have them reappear in its tax accounts, in legal regulations or in new insistent union demands. If economics fails to provide an answer to social demands then politics will be tried.

It is clear that while traditional morality provides a means of protecting some groups from the consequences of technological change, or some method of meliorating the effects of change upon them, other large segments of the population are left unprotected. It should be equally clear that rather than a quiet acquiescence in the finality and justice of such arrangements, there is an active effort to force new devices into being which will extend protection to those hitherto expected to bear the brunt of these costs. A good proportion of these inventions increasingly call for the intervention of the state. To call such arrangements immoral, unpatriotic, socialistic or to hurl other epithets at them is not to deal effectively with them. They are as "natural" as are the "normal" reactions for which we have "rational" explanations based upon some pre-scientific generalization about human nature such as "the law of supply and demand" or "the inevitability of progress." To be dealt with effectively they will have to be understood and treated as such.

Review Questions

1. How did World War II facilitate the shift from steam to diesel locomotives?

2. Did the people of Caliente anticipate the consequences that were to occur after the shift?

3. What groups of workers and what types of citizens suffered the most as Caliente succumbed to "progress"?

4. How did Caliente residents' attitudes toward progress and sacrifice change after the introduction of the diesel locomotive?

5. Trace the implications of the new technology for the major social institutions of Caliente.

DEFUSING TECHNOLOGICAL CHANGE IN JUVENILE COURTS: THE PROBATION OFFICER'S STRUGGLE FOR PROFESSIONAL AUTONOMY[1]

Gary L. Albrecht

THE DEVELOPMENT, USE, AND POTENTIAL OF COMPUTER TECHNOLOGY REPRESENTS ONE of the most dramatic influences in twentieth century America. Given the continuing public concern over crime, computer applications in the criminal justice system have been frequent. In the juvenile justice area alone, there are over 100 juvenile courts in the United States which use computerized systems to store information, monitor case flow, and produce statistical reports (U.S. Department of Justice, 1972; IBM, 1977). This diffusion of computer technology has been viewed as a mixed blessing. Lawyers, social scientists, administrators, and citizens are concerned about the potential use of these computerized information systems to control behavior inappropriately, to infringe upon citizens' rights, and to serve the needs of those who manage the records rather than the needs of society. For example, Gordon et al. (1973) point out that employees of Cook County (Chicago) agencies actively manage the information that they collect and release this information primarily to suit their own needs. Lemert (1969) also indicates how dossiers in California juvenile courts, which by law are confidential, are in fact not confidential nor can they be erased entirely. These dossiers can be used inappropriately to control the behavior of so-called delinquents and court personnel and to give false impressions of what takes place in the judicial system. For such reasons, Garfinkle (1967) states that there are "good reasons for keeping bad records."

Technological innovation does not occur in a vacuum. This paper is concerned with the manner in which professional groups attempt to gain control of a computerized information system so that they can preserve their professional autonomy, maintain control over their work, and give the appearance of a job well done. Based on five years of participant observation in a large metropolitan court system, this paper focuses on the behavior of juvenile court professionals, judges, lawyers, and probation officers who use records in their work.

Gary L. Albrecht, "Defusing Technological Change in Juvenile Courts: The Probation Officer's Struggle for Professional Autonomy," *Sociology of Work and Occupations*, Vol. 6, No. 3, August 1979, 259–263, 267, 270–278, 282. ·

• • •

Two theories of social control bear upon the work of juvenile court staff. The first is the theory of professional dominance which focuses on the relationships of groups within the court. The second is a theory of resource dependence which focuses on the relationship between an organization and its environment.

The theory of professional dominance is represented by the work of Goode (1960), Wilensky (1964), and Freidson (1970, 1976, 1977). Freidson justifies this position by arguing that "a fruitful way of developing theoretical coherence in the field of sociology of occupations lies in adopting as one's central problem the analysis of the organization of control over work, and its consequences for work, workers, organizations and society" (1977: 35). Control of work in modern industrial society generally follows a bureaucratic model in which the essential method of control lies in the creation of an administrative or managerial hierarchy and the direct supervision of workers. In contrast, the locus of control in a professional model resides primarily with the persons who perform the work. Professionals are characterized by extended formal education, a systematic body of knowledge, codes of ethics, and licensing and certification procedures. Proponents of the professional dominance perspective assert that autonomy and control over one's work is the key difference between professionals and other workers. Professionals exercise a self-regulated occupational monopoly over their work which is manifested in the control that they have over the quality, term, conditions, and context of their work. Johnson (1973) and Freidson (1976) refer to this as the collegial control of work by professionals. The professional collegium sets the norms and regulates the work.

While the theory of professional dominance is powerful, it does not adequately represent the complexity of professional work in industrial society, for professionals operate in an environment of variable resources, conflicting pressures, and competing interest groups that influence their work. Advocates of the professional dominance perspective frequently ignore or do not pay sufficient attention to the effect of the work environment on professional activity. Recent literature in organizational behavior points to the symbiotic relationship between organizations and their environments. While authors agree that organizations and environments interact (Campbell, 1965; Hannan and Freeman, 1977), they give differential emphasis to the importance of environmental selection in this process. The resource dependence level advocated by Pfeffer (1972) and his colleagues (Aldrich and Pfeffer, 1976; Pfeffer and Salancik, 1978) stresses that while organizations are dependent on other organizations for necessary resources, they can exercise power and manage their resources to adapt strategically to their environments. Those who control a computerized information system are in a particularly strategic position to exercise power because they can reorganize problems, best allocate resources, and reduce organizational uncertainty.

They possess a special resource, that is, access to important information which others do not share (Pfeffer, 1978; 69–79). At present, this model has been most often applied to bureaucratic organizations and their environments in such areas as mergers (Pfeffer, 1972), the movement of personnel among organizations (Pfeffer and Leblebici, 1973), tacit collusion (Scherer, 1970), and legal contracts (Macaulay, 1963). Yet it can be applied as well to the relationships of professionals to their environments.

This paper analyzes the power struggle between probation officers and legal professionals in a juvenile court largely in terms of the professional dominance model. However, the analysis also considers the struggle for control over work and its effects in the context of the resource dependence model. There are two levels of analysis. The professional dominance model is most applicable to the study of the interrelationship of professional groups within a bureaucracy. The resource dependence model moves the analysis to a more inclusive level to show how the struggle for professional autonomy is a function of the relative statuses of the professional groups in the organization and the relation of these groups to their broader environment. In the particular court studied, the probation staff sabotaged the information system so that the legal professionals could not use the system to control probation officer work. The probation officers effectively defused a technological innovation. In this fashion the probation officers maintained their professional identities by preserving their autonomy and control over their work domain. This fight for professional survival can only be adequately understood in the context of the juvenile court bureaucracy, the internal and external court environments, and the probation officers' struggle for professional survival.

· · ·

THE JUVENILE COURT RESEARCH SITE

The following description of a specific intracourt conflict is based on five years of participant observation in a juvenile court in a southern city.[2] The court has a workload of over 10,000 cases a year of which about 4,000 are delinquency cases. To handle this case volume, there are two judges, three referees, one clerk of the court, two prosecutors, 43 probation officers, and fully staffed intake and detention departments.[3] The legal professionals have offices on the first floor of the juvenile court building near the courtrooms. Since the court record room is adjacent to the judges' chambers, the legal professionals have easy access to, and control of, information. The senior court managers also have offices next to the judges' chambers and report directly to them. Other managers are dispersed throughout the court. The probation and intake departments are physically separated from the legal staff in a daylight basement of the main building. Detention is in a separate but continuous building. Therefore, the legal professionals have the best court space, immediate access to and control over the court records, and close proximity to the top court management, while probation officers are physically separated from the rest of the court.

．　．　．

INSTALLATION OF A COMPUTERIZED INFORMATION SYSTEM IN THE JUVENILE COURT

After attending conferences, visiting computer facilities, and engaging in lengthy discussions, the judges, with the support of the other legal professionals, encouraged the court managers to apply for Law Enforcement Assistance Administration funds to computerize the court record system. The probation staff and other court staff were not participants in these deliberations. Moreover, when the juvenile court computerized information system was funded in early 1971, a computer system staff was formed which reported directly to the judges and top court management.

Immediately after funding, primary attention was given to designing the system and ordering the equipment, a large computer with eight attached cathode ray tubes and a medium-speed printer. The initial system, designed by the judges, legal professionals, top management, and computer information staff, went on line in November 1971. In accord with the needs of the legal professionals, first priority was given to keeping accurate legal records and facilitating speedy case processing. For example, the information system staff was instructed to design systems to produce dockets; schedules; court calendars; petitions; summonses; daily detention lists; and summaries of the basic arrest, legal, and demographic information for each case. However, as the legal professionals became involved in the design of the system, they became increasingly interested in its potential to monitor and control the activities of the rest of the court. With these goals in mind, the judges encouraged the development of family history, probation, detention, case history, medical, and psychological subfiles that could serve as the basis of management reports to monitor the work of the other court staff.

STRUGGLE FOR CONTROL OF WORK IN THE JUVENILE COURT

At this point in the implementation of the computerized information system, probation officers and other staff were brought into the discussions. When the probation officers were told that they would be able to participate in the design of the information system, they became suspicious that the judges were going to use the information to control them. These initial suspicions were confirmed when the judges began to talk about using the information system to evaluate the probation officers' performance. Probation officers were asked to design forms and develop evaluation instruments that could be used for this purpose.

While the probation officers gave public deference to the judges in open meetings, they reacted to this control attempt with outrage. The chief probation officer stormed into her probation staff meeting and announced:

> The judges want the computer to evaluate our work. They want to count numbers and put our work in boxes. The more cases we handle, the better. They don't want trouble or bad press. They just want to push through cases and lock up bad kids so that they look good. We don't work with pieces of paper [cases], we work with kids who need help. What do the judges know about street-wise kids? Hell, I knew more about kids when I was running numbers at 14 than they'll ever know. Let's show them that our work is different and can't be judged by numbers.

The sentiments expressed by the chief probation officer were widely shared when the probation officers realized that the judges were attempting to exercise direct control over their work through the use of a computerized information system. They viewed the plan as a direct threat to their professional autonomy, judgment, and skills. Responding to this situation, a young probation officer argued:

> All judges and lawyers talk about is admissible evidence, laws, due process, and a system that must keep cases moving through the court. Like plea bargaining is just a tool to make the judges and lawyers look good. That's why they lock up anybody with a serious rap. They don't want to look bad by having a recidivist. What do they know about kids or human behavior? Yet they want to tell us what to do. It's crazy.

This probation officer views legal professionals as delivering the appearance of justice and preventing recidivism of serious offenders to protect their public image. Probation officers, he goes on to assert, are more interested in changing the behavior of troubled youth.

These two occupational groups therefore have quite different definitions of the situation. The judges see their mission as both legal and rehabilitative. Yet, probation officers view judges as legal processing agents whose interests in some instances are opposed to the welfare of the juveniles. Consequently, probation officers feel that they must look out for the good of the child. It is this rehabilitative function that forms the ideological justification for their existence as professionals and supports their claim to specialized knowledge.

In addition to these differences, judges and probation officers experience divergent environmental constraints. Judges are elected or appointed and must be conscious of their public image. Probation officers are hired civil servants of the county or state. They have considerable job security after a probationary period and only have to worry about pleasing the judges and court managers.

Probation officers are for the most part social workers specifically trained to deal with troubled youth. Many have a strong professional identification achieved through education, certification, work experience, and demonstrated performance. They are trained to use the methods of case work, group work, and community organization to prevent delinquent behavior, make experienced decisions at intake on whether to detain a youth, gather information, give advice to the legal professionals regarding disposition decisions, and rehabilitate youthful offenders during the probationary period. The probation officers felt that the legal professionals did not understand this work and should *not* be allowed to control it.

While there is little doubt that judges are the seat of power in the juvenile court, there is an unstable equilibrium between the legal professionals and probation officers. Both groups have power and are dependent on each other to reach the goals of the court. While judges can order probation officers to act, probation officers cannot give orders to judges. However, probation officers do control their own work. If judges were to intervene strongly in probation work, they would be accused of overstepping their expertise. Moreover, their impartiality as decision makers could be questioned because they would possess information prior to hearings that they were not supposed to have seen.

Given these dynamics of the situation and the legal professionals' attempts to control probation officer work, the probation officers developed a set of informal strategies to prevent loss of work autonomy. Because of the power dynamic and bureaucratic structure of the court, the probation officers felt compelled to cooperate with the legal professionals and computer design staff. Initially, they responded sequentially to each successive control attempt. Later, as they coordinated these strategies, they became very effective in protecting their autonomy.

At first, the judges asked the probation officers to design forms for the computerized information system. The probation officers responded by spending many hours discussing the weaknesses of the forms currently used by the court; the difficulties in collecting accurate data; the necessity of tracking case flow for the legal professionals; and methods of evaluating judge, referee, clerk, and prosecutor effectiveness. The probation staff redesigned intake and hearing forms to include demographic, arrest, detention, and hearing data. They showed how these data could be entered easily into the computerized information system and used to produce daily management reports monitoring case flow and the consistency and appropriateness of legal decisions. They emphasized such variables as length of time a youth is detained before a hearing; length of time between arrest, adjudicatory and disposition hearings; judge, prosecutor, and public defender case load; and recidivism rates by judge, prosecutor, and disposition choice. They sent this work to the judges and the computerized information systems design team.

Given an ambiguous mandate and a control threat by the judges, the probation staff consumed large quantities of time raising issues about the legal processing of cases and designing a system that would place visible controls on the work of the legal professionals. At the same time, the probation staff included little behavioral data in the forms and did not suggest any forms to evaluate probation officer performance. Thus, the probation staff turned the tables on the legal professionals.

Not surprisingly, the legal professionals and court managers were upset by these tactics. At the next information system team meeting a judge said:

> These forms are a good first step but where are the forms that will be used to summarize the work of the probation staff? . . . Also, the management reports based on these forms seem to me to be potentially misleading. There might be good reasons for considerable length of time between hearings or to explain a recidivism statistic. These reasons do not show up on the proposed management reports. Put in the wrong hands these reports could be used to make us look bad when in fact we're doing a good job.

A probation supervisor responded:

> Exactly. You've put your finger on some of the problems in designing these forms. Management reports can be very misleading and, unless a judge or probation officer were to explain their work, others might be misled by the raw numbers.

Thus, the probation department forcefully pointed out why professionals should have autonomy and control over their own work. Professionals must evaluate their own work because they alone fully understand the goals and the complex work tasks required to achieve them. Self-regulation, therefore, has considerable merit. The judges and other legal professionals agreed that the new forms should be used in the information system for bookkeeping purposes, but they insisted that further study be given to the concept of management reports before implementation. They also tried to refocus attention on control of the probation officers by asking them to design new forms to describe and evaluate probation officer work. The probation representatives did not object and the meeting was adjourned.

After writing to many juvenile courts and governmental agencies for examples of such forms, the probation group constructed case investigation and probation work forms that enumerated over 400 variables, including almost every conceivable demographic, school, family, neighborhood, and work factor. They also recorded home and office visits and probation officers' assessments of the juveniles and their environments. The forms concluded with room for 1,500 words of free-form written comments, impressions, and suggestions. Since all the information was oriented toward the juvenile, his environment, and legal decisions, these forms included very few items describing the work of the probation officer. These new forms were then submitted to the judges and information system design team.

This strategy was carefully planned to preserve probation officers' control over their work. First, while the information on the forms could be used to evaluate the juvenile, the school, the home, the family, the neighborhood, and the court, it only indirectly reflected probation officer performance. Probation officers thus emphasized evaluation of the client, not the professional. If delinquents are recidivists, it is due to *their* failure to use the resources of the court, school, and community. If the youth is not a recidivist, success is attributed to the probation officer and the system. Second, the forms were too long to be useful. The court could not afford to collect and store all the information. Moreover, since much of the information to be obtained is generally unavailable and inaccurate, management reports based on these data would not be comparable across individuals and would be of questionable accuracy. Still, probation officers argued that every piece of information was important because it had been used in other courts and in delinquency research. Third, the probation officers placed themselves in the information control position. They designed the forms, gathered the data, and structured the evaluative techniques.

If the legal professionals agreed that the forms were too long and unwieldy, the probation officers could revert back to their former control strategies of providing the legal professionals with some abbreviated facts and a case summary based on their professional expertise. Recognition of professional work and control over work would thus be returned to the probation officer. Ruzek (1973) and Daniels (1975) show that human service delivery professionals, such as social workers and psychiatrists, exercise control by following their written presentation of facts and case summaries with treatment recommendations for the legal professionals. The probation officers reinforced this advice-control function on the computerized information system by leaving space for a case summary and recommendations. They knew that harried legal professionals gave most attention to this part of the report. In this way probation officers planned to maintain and reinforce their control function.

The next information system design meeting progressed according to the plan of the probation officers. The presiding judge declared:

> This is too much information to put on the computer. Until we can decide what is absolutely necessary and important, let's just go with the other forms and add the probation form to the system later. Right now, all we really need is the case summary and recommendation.

The judges and court managers also decided that they would not produce management reports because they might be "misused." This compromise allowed the computerized information system to be brought on line without threat to legal professionals or to the probation officers.

At this time, the physical equipment was installed and staffed. One terminal was installed in intake, one in detention, one in the record room, one in the systems design team office, and four in the probation department. The probation staff argued that four terminals were needed in their department for information input and access. This configuration of equipment also kept the terminals away from the legal professionals. Actually, all four terminals in probation proved to be necessary for data entry and none was available for inquiry. Although the staff could not make routine use of the system, they did not request additional terminals. With the limited number of terminals and their location, the probation department controlled data entry and inquiry, prevented the system from full management use, and in effect maintained strict control over their work.

THE FATE OF THE COMPUTERIZED INFORMATION SYSTEM

Probation officers were able to prevent legal professionals from gaining control over their work by implementing a multifaceted strategy. The probation department achieved its goals by taking responsibility for designing forms, controlling input of information, limiting the use of information in the system, and suggesting to judges the dangers of public evaluation of court work. As a result, the computerized information system was used for four years as a sophisticated recordkeeping system, but rarely as a basis for management decisions. When the County Manager and Board of Commissioners questioned the operating costs of this online system, the judges and probation officers agreed that a manual system might work just as well. Consequently, the County Manager ordered the discontinuance of the computerized information system and conversion back to a manual system in 1976. The probation professionals had won their struggle for control over their work by effectively defusing a technological innovation.

SUMMARY AND CONCLUSION

The use of technology in a service organization is determined by the organization's goals and structure as well as by the intent of the professionals who use it. If a new technology does not support the goals of an established professional group, it will be either blunted or sabotaged entirely. In this instance, legal professionals in the juvenile court attempted to assert professional dominance over probation officers and other court staff through the use of a computerized information system. This attempt at social control over court work failed because probation officers, when threatened, acted collectively to maintain their professional autonomy by developing a coordinated five-part strategy to: (1) use the computerized information system to threaten the autonomy of legal professions; (2) divert attention away from evaluation of probation officer work to case processing and evaluation of client performance; (3) gain control over information input and access; (4) emphasize the importance of probation officer case summaries and recommendations; and (5) show the system to be inaccurate, inefficient, and costly to operate. Ultimately, the computerized system was even physically removed from the court.

The result of this struggle reflects an uneven balance of power in which both professions maintain autonomy and control over the work directly in their domain, but recognize that their interdependence is necessary both for achieving the goals of the court and for professional survival. While the legal professionals retained dominance in the court, the outcome of the conflict demonstrated that their power is limited. Legal professionals learned the extent of their power when they tried to gain control over the work of the probation officers. The probation officers, on the other hand, did not lose any professional autonomy and even established themselves as a force with which to be reckoned.

In this study of the use of a computerized information system in a juvenile court, the importance of the technological innovation was found to be secondary to the struggle for professional dominance. It is apparent that while computerized information systems have far-reaching behavioral implications, they are not reified objects that act on their own. An analysis of technological innovation therefore must consider its use by professionals to achieve their own goals, which may be compatible with, contradictory to, or independent of the goals of the larger organization.

In this juvenile court, the employees successfully resisted a technological innovation. In other organizations, such as the National Crime Information Center, the innovation has been more readily accepted. The acceptance or rejection of a computerized information system is a complex issue that depends on reasons for the change, the tasks being automated, the jobs being affected, the individuals who control the system, and the type of organization in which the innovation occurs. This juvenile court can function adequately in the immediate future without a computerized information system. However, large banks and airlines would be unable to operate in today's world economy if they did not have computerized accounting and reservation capacities. In addition, there are other reasons for accepting or rejecting new technologies. Tellers and reservation clerks do not perceive themselves as professionals, whereas probation officers do. In banks and airlines, computerized information systems save the tellers and clerks manual work but do not take away their freedom to respond or make decisions. In the court, probation officers perceived that they would lose their professional autonomy. The different responses to the innovation can, then, vary by organizational context and type of situation.

NOTES

1. Author's Note: This research was supported in part by Law Enforcement Assistance Administration Grant 71-EF-658. I would like to thank Edward J. McCabe, Ronald E. Anderson, Arlene Kaplan Daniels, Paul C. Higgins, and Jeylan Mortimer for helpful comments on earlier drafts of this manuscript.

2. During this time I was collecting data for a delinquency study and serving as a consultant to the court. In this capacity I attended many meetings and spent considerable time observing all aspects of court functioning.

3. Referees are lawyers or experienced court personnel permanently appointed by the juvenile court to hear most of the traffic, status offense, and preliminary hearing cases. In some courts they are called masters. They process most of the routine cases and leave the judges free to hear the more serious ones. While referees and masters are common today, there is a national move toward all-judge juvenile courts.

REFERENCES

Aldrich, H. E. and J. Pfeffer
   1976 "Environments of organizations." *Annual Rev. of Sociology* 2: 79–105.

Campbell, D.
   1965 "Variation and selective retention in socio-cultural evolution," pp. 19–48 in
      H. R. Barringer et al. (eds.) *Social Change in Developing Areas: A Reinterpretation of Evolutionary Theory.* Cambridge, MA: Schenkman.

Daniels, A. K.
   1975 "Advisory and coercive functions in psychiatry." *Sociology of Work and Occupations* 2: 55–78.

Freidson, E.
   1977 "The futures of professionalism." Presented at the meeting of the British Sociological Association, Manchester, England.
   1976 *Doctoring Together: A Study of Professional Social Control.* New York: Elsevier.
   1970 *Profession of Medicine.* New York: Dodd, Mead.

Garfinkle, H.
   1967 *Studies in Ethnomethodology.* Englewood Cliffs, NJ: Prentice-Hall.

Goode, W. J.
   1960 "Encroachment, charlatanism, and the emerging profession: psychology, medicine and sociology." *Amer. Soc. Rev.* 25: 902–914.

Hannan, M. T. and J. H. Freeman
   1977 "The population ecology of organizations." *Amer. J. of Sociology* 82: 929–964.

IBM
   1977 Unified Juvenile Court System, State of Utah. White Plains, NY: Author.

Johnson, T. J.
1973 "Imperialism and the professions." *Soc. Rev.* Monograph 20: 281–309.

Lemert, E. M.
1970 *Social Action and Legal Change.* Chicago: Aldine.

1969 "Records in the juvenile court," pp. 355–387 in S. Wheeler (ed.) *On Record: Files and Dossiers in American Life.* New York: Russell Sage.

Macaulay, S.
1963 "Non-contractual relations in business: a preliminary study." *Amer. Soc. Rev.* 28: 55–67.

Pfeffer, J.
1978 *Organizational Design.* Arlington Heights, IL: AHM Publishing Co.
1972 "Merger as a response to organizational interdependence." *Administrative Sci. Q.* 17: 382–394.

_____ and H. Leblebici
1973 "Executive recruitment and the development of interfirm organizations." *Administrative Sci. Q.* 18: 445–461.

_____ and G. R. Salancik
1978 *The External Control of Organizations.* New York: Harper & Row.

Ruzek, S. K.
1973 "Making social work accountable," pp. 217–243 in E. Freidson (ed.), *The Professions and Their Prospects.* Beverly Hills, CA: Sage.

Scherer, F. M.
1970 *Industrial Market Structure and Economic Performance.* Chicago: Rand-McNally.

U.S. Department of Justice, Law Enforcement Assistance Administration
1972 Directory of Automated Criminal Justice Information Systems. Washington, DC: U.S. Government Printing Office.

Wilensky, H. L.
1964 "The professionalism of everyone?" *Amer. J. of Sociology* 70: 137–158.

Review Questions

1. How was the issue of "professional dominance" related to the introduction of the computer into the juvenile court system?

2. How did the threatened group, the probation officers, respond to the introduction of the computer?

3. How did the judges react to the probation officers' response?

4. Do the findings of Albrecht's study suggest under what conditions technological innovations will be adopted or resisted?

Suggested Readings: Social and Cultural Change

Atwater, Lynn. *The Extramarital Connection: Sex, Intimacy, and Identity.* New York: Irvington, 1982.

Berger, Peter, Brigitte Berger, and Hansfried Kellner. *The Homeless Mind.* New York: Vintage Books, 1974.

Cohen, Yehudi A. " 'You're O.K., How Am I?' Loneliness and Its Institutional Frames." In Joseph Hartog, J. Ralph Audy and Yehudi A. Cohen, eds., *The Anatomy of Loneliness.* New York: International Universities Press, 1980.

Erikson, Kai T. *Everything in Its Path.* New York: Simon & Schuster, 1976.

Lerner, David. *The Passing of Traditional Society.* New York: Free Press, 1958.

Spicer, Edward H., ed. *Human Problems in Technological Change.* New York: John Wiley, 1952.

Acknowledgments (continued from p. iv)

Howard S. Becker, Blanche Geer, and Everett Hughes: Excerpt from *Making the Grade: The Academic Side of College Life*, 1968, John Wiley & Sons. Copyright © 1968 by Howard S. Becker. Reprinted by permission of the authors.

Sandra L. Bem and Daryl J. Bem: "Case Study of a Nonconscious Ideology: Trianing the Woman to Know Her Place" from D.J. Bem, *Beliefs, Attitudes and Human Affairs*. Belmont, California: Brooks/Cole, 1970. Reprinted by permission of the authors.

Peter L. Berger: Excerpt from *Invitation to Sociology*. Copyright © 1963 by Peter L. Berger. Reprinted by permission of Doubleday & Company, Inc.

Peter L. Berger and Hansfried Kellner: "Marriage and the Construction of Reality," *Diogenes*, No. 46 (Summer 1964), pp. 1-24 (with deletions). Reprinted by permission of the publisher.

William Chambliss: "The Saints and the Roughnecks," *Society*, Vol. 11, No. 1 (November/December 1973), pp. 24-31. Copyright © 1973 by Transaction, Inc. Reprinted by permission of Transaction, Inc.

Candace Clark: "Sickness and Social Control" was written for this edition of *Social Interaction*.

Lewis A. Coser and Rose Laub Coser: "The Housewife and Her 'Greedy Family'" from *Greedy Institutions*. Copyright © 1974 by The Free Press, A Division of Macmillan Publishing Co., Inc. Reprinted by permission of the publisher.

W. F. Cottrell: "Death by Dieselization: A Case Study in the Reaction to Technological Change," *American Sociological Review*, Vol. 16 (1951), pp. 358-365. Reprinted by permission of the American Sociological Association.

G. William Domhoff: Excerpts from *The Bohemian Grove and Other Retreats*. Copyright © 1974 by G. William Domhoff. Reprinted by permission of Harper and Row Publishers, Inc.

Edwin Eames and Howard Robboy: "The Socio-Cultural Context of an Italian-American Dietary Item," *Cornell Journal of Social Relations*, 2 (Fall 1967), pp. 63-75. Reprinted by permission. © 1967 Cornell Journal of Social Relations.

Erving Goffman: Excerpts from *The Presentation of Self in Everyday Life*. Copyright © 1959 by Erving Goffman. Reprinted by permission of Doubleday & Company, Inc.

Bernard Goldstein and Jack Oldham: Excerpts from *Children and Work*. Copyright © 1979 by Transaction Books. Reprinted by permission of Transaction, Inc.

Edward Gross and Gregory P. Stone: "Embarrassment and the Analysis of Role Requirements," *American Journal of Sociology*, 70 (July 1964), pp. 1-15 (with deletions). Copyright © 1964 by the University of Chicago Press. Reprinted by permission of the University of Chicago Press and the authors.

Rosabeth Moss Kanter: "Women and the Structure of Organizations," excerpted from *Another Voice* by Rosabeth Moss Kanter and Marcia Millman. Copyright © 1975 by *Sociological Inquiry*. Reprinted by permission of Doubleday & Company, Inc.

David Karp and William C. Yoels: "The College Classroom: Some Observations on the Meanings of Student Participation," *Sociology and Social Research*, Vol. 60, No. 4, pp. 421-439. Reprinted by permission.

Ralph W. Larkin: Excerpts from *Suburban Youth in Cultural Crisis*. Copyright © 1979 by Oxford University Press. Reprinted by permission of the publisher and the author.

Elliot Liebow: Excerpts from *Tally's Corner*. Copyright © 1967 by Little, Brown and Company. Reprinted by permission of Little, Brown and Company.

592   Acknowledgments

J. Robert Lilly and Richard A. Ball, "No-Tell Motel: The Management of Social Invisibility," *Urban Life*, Vol. 10, No. 2 (1982), pp. 179–197 (with deletions). Copyright © 1982 by Sage Publications, Inc. Reprinted by permission of Sage Publications, Inc. and the authors.

John Lofland and Rodney Stark: "Becoming a World Saver: A Theory of Conversion to a Deviant Perspective," *American Sociological Review*, Vol. 30 (December 1965), pp. 862–875 (some material deleted). Reprinted by permission of the American Sociological Association and the authors.

Horace Miner: "Body Ritual Among the Nacirema." Reproduced by permission of the American Anthropological Association and the author from the *American Anthropologist*, 58 (1956), pp. 503–507.

Martin T. Orne: "On the Social Psychology of the Psychological Experiment: With Special Reference to Demand Characteristics and Their Implications," *American Psychologist*, 17 (October 1962), pp. 776–783. Copyright 1962 by the American Psychological Association. Reprinted by permission of the American Psychological Association and the author.

D. L. Rosenhan: "On Being Sane in Insane Places," *Science*, Vol. 179, No. 19 (January 1973), pp. 250–258 (with deletions). Copyright © 1973 by the American Association for the Advancement of Science. Reprinted by permission of the American Association for the Advancement of Science and the author.

Kristine M. Rosenthal and Harry F. Keshet: "Childcare Responsibilities of Part-Time and Single Fathers," *Alternative Life Styles*, Vol. 1, No. 4 (November 1978), pp. 465–471 (with deletions). Copyright © 1978 by Human Sciences Press, 72 Fifth Avenue, New York, N.Y. 10011. Reprinted by permission of the publisher and the authors.

Howard Robboy: "At Work with the Night Worker" is taken from the author's doctoral dissertation and was published in the first edition of *Social Interaction*.

Julius A. Roth: "Hired Hand Research," *The American Sociologist*, Vol. 1, (August 1966), pp. 190–196 (with deletions). Reprinted by permission of the American Sociological Association and the author.

Donald F. Roy: "Banana Time—Job Satisfaction and Informal Interaction." Excerpted from *Human Organization*, Vol. 18, No. 4 (Winter 1959–60). Copyright © 1959 by the Society for Applied Anthropology. Reprinted by permission of the publisher and the author.

Lucinda SanGiovanni: "Rediscovering Gender: The Emergent Role Passage of Ex-Nuns" was written for this edition of *Social Interaction*.

Barry Schwartz: "Waiting, Exchange, and Power," *American Journal of Sociology*, Vol. 79, No. 4 (January 1974), pp. 841–870 (with deletions). Copyright © 1974 by the University of Chicago Press. Reprinted by permission of the University of Chicago Press and the author.

Pepper Schwartz and Janet Lever: "Fear and Loathing at a College Mixer," *Urban Life*, Vol. 4, No. 4 (January 1976), pp. 413–432. Copyright © 1976 by Sage Publications, Inc. Reprinted by permission of Sage Publications, Inc. and the authors.

Carol B. Stack: "Sex Roles and Survival Strategies in an Urban Black Community," from Michelle Z. Rosaldo and Louise Lamphere, *Women, Culture and Society*, Stanford University Press, 1975. Reprinted by permission of Carol B. Stack.

David Sudnow: "Normal Crimes: Sociological Features of the Penal Code in a Public Defender Office," *Social Problems*, Vol. 12, No. 3 (Winter 1965), pp. 255–275 (with deletions). Copyright © 1965 by the Society for the Study of Social Problems. Reprinted by permission.

Diane Vaughn: "Uncoupling: The Social Construction of Divorce" was written for the first edition of *Social Interaction*.

ABOUT THE CONTRIBUTORS

Gary L. Albrecht received his Ph.D. in sociology from Emory University and is presently Professor of Health Resources Management at the School of Public Health of the University of Illinois Medical Center in Chicago. He is the co-editor of *Health, Illness, and Medicine* (with Paul C. Higgins) and editor of *The Sociology of Physical Disability and Rehabilitation*.

Roy L. Askins was awarded his Ph.D. at Virginia Tech University. At present, he is Assistant Professor of Sociology at Western Missouri State College.

Lynn Atwater received her Ph.D. from Rutgers University. She is currently Associate Professor at Seton Hall University. She has written *The Extramarital Connection: Sex, Intimacy, and Identity*, a fuller discussion of the subject presented in her article here.

Richard A. Ball was awarded his Ph.D. at Ohio State University. He is currently Professor of Sociology at the University of West Virginia.

Howard S. Becker was awarded his Ph.D. at the University of Chicago and is currently Professor of Sociology at Northwestern University. His published works are numerous, including *The Outsiders: The Other Side* (which he edited), *Sociological Work: Method and Substance*, *Making the Grade: The Academic Side of College Life* (with Blanche Geer and Everett C. Hughes), from which one of our selections was taken, and *Boys in White: Student Culture in Medical School* (with Blanche Geer and others), the source of another of our selections.

Daryl J. Bem earned his Ph.D. in social psychology at the University of Michigan. He is Professor of Psychology at Cornell University and author of *Beliefs, Attitudes and Human Affairs*.

Sandra L. Bem received her Ph.D. in developmental psychology at the University of Michigan and is presently Associate Professor of Psychology at Cornell University.

Peter L. Berger received his Ph.D. from the New School for Social Research and taught at several universities, including Rutgers University and Boston College, before becoming University Professor and Professor of the Sociology of Religion at Boston University in 1981. He has authored and co-authored a great number of books, including *The Social Construction of Reality* (with Thomas Luckmann), *Ru-*

mour of Angels, The Sacred Canopy, and *Invitation to Sociology,* from which the first article in this volume was taken.

Timothy J. Carter, who received his Ph.D. from the University of Tennessee, is now Assistant Professor of Sociology at Virginia Tech University.

William J. Chambliss, who was awarded his doctorate degree from the University of Indiana, is Professor of Sociology at the University of Delaware. His many books include *On the Take, Crime and the Legal Process,* and *Whose Law? What Order?*

Candace Clark received her graduate training at the University of Chicago and Columbia University, where she was awarded the Ph.D. in sociomedical sciences. She is Assistant Professor of Sociology at Fairleigh Dickinson University. Candace Clark is one of the editors of *Social Interaction.*

Lewis A. Coser, who received his Ph.D. from Columbia University, is Distinguished Professor of Sociology at the State University of New York at Stony Brook. A prolific writer, he is the author of *The Functions of Social Conflict, Masters of Sociological Thought, Men of Ideas: A Sociologist's View,* and *Greedy Institutions: Patterns of Undivided Commitment* (with Rose Laub Coser). Our selection was taken from *Greedy Institutions.* Lewis A. Coser is a past president of the American Sociological Association.

Rose Laub Coser was awarded her Ph.D. from Columbia University. She is currently Professor of Sociology and Health Sciences at the State University of New York at Stony Brook. She has written *Training in Ambiguity: Learning through Doing in a Mental Hospital, Life in the Ward,* and *Greedy Institutions: Patterns of Undivided Commitment* (with Lewis A. Coser), the source of our selection. She has also edited *The Family: Its Structure and Functions.*

W. F. Cottrell was Professor of Sociology at Miami University of Ohio and was associated with the Scripps Foundation at the time of his death.

G. William Domhoff received his Ph.D. from the University of Miami. He is Professor of Psychology and Sociology at the University of California at Santa Cruz and is the author of many books about elites, including *The Higher Circles, Fat Cats and Democrats,* and *The Bohemian Grove and Other Retreats,* the latter of which is excerpted here.

Edwin Eames received his Ph.D. from Cornell University. He is presently Professor of Anthropology at Bernard Baruch College of the City University of New York. He has co-authored *Cultural Anthropology* (with Eugene Cohen), *Anthropology* (with Judith Granich Goode), and *Urban Poverty in a Cross-Cultural Context* (also with Goode). He also co-edited *The New Ethnics: Asian Indians in the U.S.* (with Parmatma Saran).

Blanche Geer earned her Ph.D. at Johns Hopkins University and is Professor Emeritus at Northeastern University. Her long term collaboration with Howard S. Becker and Everett C. Hughes has resulted in, among other publications, the co-authored books *Making the Grade: The Academic Side of College Life* and *Boys in White: Student Culture in Medical School.*

Erving Goffman received his Ph.D. from the University of Chicago. At the time of his recent death in 1982, he was Benjamin Franklin Professor at the University of Pennsylvania. His many books include *Behavior in Public Places, Stigma, Asylums, Interaction Ritual, Frame Analysis,* and the early *Presentation of Self in Everyday Life,* from which our selection is taken. Goffman also had served as president of the American Sociological Association.

Bernard Goldstein received his Ph.D. from the University of Chicago and is now Professor of Sociology at Rutgers University. One of his books, *Children and Work* (co-authored with Jack Oldham), is the source of the selection chosen for this volume.

Edward Gross received his Ph.D. from the University of Chicago and is now Professor of Sociology at the University of Washington. His books include *Industry and Social Life, Work and Society,* and *University Goals and Academic Power* (co-authored with Paul Grambsch).

Everett C. Hughes earned a Ph.D. in social anthropology at the University of Chicago. He is now Professor Emeritus of Sociology at Boston College. His many books include *Men and Their Work, The Sociological Eye, French Canada in Transition, Where People Meet: Racial and Ethnic Frontiers* (co-authored with Helen McGill Hughes), and *Making the Grade: The Academic Side of College Life* (co-authored with Howard S. Becker and Blanche Geer), which is the source of our selection. He has also served as president of the American Sociological Association.

Rosabeth Moss Kanter earned her Ph.D. at the University of Michigan. She is Professor of Sociology and of Organization and Management at Yale University, as well as a consultant to industry. Her writings include *Commitment and Community* and *Men and Women of the Corporation.*

David A. Karp, who earned his Ph.D. from New York University, is now Associate Professor of Sociology at Boston College. He is a co-author of *Being Urban: A Social Psychological View of City Life* (with Gregory P. Stone and William C. Yoels), *The Research Craft* (with John B. Williamson, John R. Dalphin, and others), *Symbols, Selves, and Society: Understanding Interaction* (with Yoels), and *Experiencing the Life Cycle* (with Yoels).

Hansfried Kellner is Professor of Sociology at the University of Darmstadt in West Germany. He is a co-author of *The Homeless Mind: Modernization and Consciousness* (with Peter L. Berger and Brigitte Berger) and *Sociology Reinterpreted: An Essay on Method and Vocation* (with Peter L. Berger).

Harry F. Keshet was awarded his Ph.D. in social psychology and social work at the University of Michigan. He is director of Riverside Family Counselling Center in

Newton, Massachusetts, and co-author of *Fathers without Partners: A Study of Fathers and the Family after Marital Separation* (with Kristine M. Rosenthal), an expanded study of the issues on which their article here focuses.

Ralph W. Larkin received his Ph.D. from the University of California at Los Angeles. At present he is operating his own research-consultant business and is at work on a book about social movements. His book *Suburban Youth in Cultural Crisis* is the source of our selection.

Janet Lever received her Ph.D. from Yale University. She is currently Assistant Professor of Sociology at Northwestern University. She is a co-author of *Women at Yale: Liberating a College Campus* (with Pepper Schwartz). She has a new book, *Soccer Madness*.

Elliot Liebow earned his Ph.D. in anthropology at Catholic University of America. His dissertation research resulted in the now-classic book *Tally's Corner*, from which our selection was drawn. Currently he is a social anthropologist at the National Institute of Mental Health of the federal government.

J. Robert Lilly received his Ph.D. from the University of Tennessee. Presently, he is Associate Professor of Sociology at Northern Kentucky University.

John Lofland, who received his Ph.D. at the University of California at San Francisco, is Professor of Sociology at the University of California at Davis. He has written *Analyzing Social Settings, Deviance and Identity* (with Lyn Lofland), *Doomsday Cult*, and several other books.

Horace Miner received his Ph.D. from the University of Chicago. He has long been Professor of Sociology and Anthropology at the University of Michigan.

Jack Oldham earned his doctorate degree in sociology at Rutgers University. Currently, he is Development Officer at Massachusetts Institute of Technology. His dissertation research provided the substance of *Children and Work* (with Bernard Goldstein), from which the current selection was excerpted.

Martin T. Orne, who holds both M.D. and Ph.D. degrees, is Director of the Unit for Experimental Psychiatry at the University of Pennsylvania. He is widely known for his pioneering work in research methodology and has also co-edited *The Nature of Hypnosis: Selected Basic Readings* (with R. E. Shor).

Howard Robboy received his Ph.D. from Rutgers University and is currently Assistant Professor of Sociology at Trenton State College. He is one of the editors of *Social Interaction*, and has written several articles on the sociology of work.

D. L. Rosenhan was awarded his Ph.D. in clinical psychology at Columbia University. Currently at Stanford University, he is Professor of Psychology and Law. He is the co-editor (with Perry London) of two books, *Foundations of Abnormal Psychology* and *Theory and Research in Abnormal Psychology*.

Kristine M. Rosenthal was awarded her Ph.D. in education from Harvard University. She has taught sociology at Northeastern University and Brandeis University and is now a freelance researcher and writer. Her book, *Fathers without Partners: A Study of Fathers and the Family after Marital Separation* (co-authored with Harry F. Keshet), is a more detailed examination of the data presented in the article that is printed here.

Julius A. Roth received his graduate training from the University of Chicago and is now Professor of Sociology at the University of California at Davis. He has written many articles in the field of medical sociology and is currently editor of a series of volumes in this field. He is also the author of *Timetables*.

Donald F. Roy earned his Ph.D. at the University of Chicago. At the time of his death in 1980, he was Professor Emeritus at Duke University. His articles on the industrial workplace are considered classics.

Lucinda SanGiovanni received her Ph.D. from Rutgers University and is presently Associate Professor of Sociology at Seton Hall University. In her book, *Ex-Nuns: A Study in Emergent Role Passage*, she explores in more detail the ideas presented in the selection that is included here.

Barry Schwartz received his Ph.D. at the University of Pennsylvania. He is currently Professor of Sociology at the University of Georgia. His many articles include sociological analyses of sleep and gift giving. He is the editor of *The Changing Face of the Suburbs* and the author of *Queuing and Waiting: Studies in the Social Organization of Access and Delay* and *Vertical Classification: A Study in Structuralism and the Sociology of Knowledge*.

Pepper Schwartz, who earned her Ph.D. at Yale University, is Associate Professor of Sociology at the University of Washington. She has co-authored *Women at Yale: Liberating a College Campus* (with Janet Lever) and *Sexual Scripts: The Social Construction of Female Sexuality* (with Judith Long Laws).

Carol B. Stack received her Ph.D. in anthropology from the University of Illinois. She is Associate Professor in the Institute for Policy Sciences and Public Affairs at Duke University. Her book, *All Our Kin: Strategies for Survival in a Black Community*, is a more detailed exposition of the article included here.

Rodney Stark received his Ph.D. from the University of California at Berkeley and is now Professor of Sociology at the University of Washington. He has written *Police Riots: Collective Violence and Law Enforcement* and has co-authored a number of books with Charles Y. Glock, including *Patterns of Religious Commitment* and *American Piety: The Nature of Religious Commitment*.

Gregory P. Stone completed his Ph.D. at the University of Chicago. Until the time of his death in Costa Rica in 1981, he was Professor of Sociology at the University of Minnesota. He was a co-author of *Being Urban: A Social Psychological View of City Life* (with David A. Karp and William C. Yoels), co-editor and translator of *Herman*

Schmalenback on Society and Experience (with Gunther Luschen), and co-editor of *Social Psychology through Symbolic Interaction* (with Harvey A. Farberman).

David Sudnow received his Ph.D. from the University of California at Berkeley. Jazz musician and sociologist, he is the author of *Passing On: The Social Organization of Dying* and *Ways of the Hand*.

Diane Vaughan received her Ph.D. from Ohio State University and is currently a sociologist at the Center for Research on Women at Wellesley College. She is the author of *On the Social Control of Organizations*.

John R. Weeks was awarded his Ph.D. at the University of California at Berkeley. Now Professor of Sociology at San Diego State University, he is the author of *Population: An Introduction to Concepts and Issues* and *Teenage Marriage: A Demographic Analysis*.

William Foote Whyte received his Ph.D. at the University of Chicago. Now Professor of Sociology at Cornell University, he has served as President of the American Sociological Association. His books include *Men at Work, Industry and Society*, and the classic *Street Corner Society*.

Louis Wirth received his Ph.D. from the University of Chicago, where he became Professor of Sociology. He is the author of *The Ghetto*, and has served as president of the American Sociological Association.

Michael R. Wood was awarded his Ph.D. at the University of Texas at Austin. He is currently Assistant Professor of Sociology at Virginia Tech University.

William C. Yoels received his Ph.D. from the University of Minnesota. He is now Professor of Sociology at the University of Alabama at Birmingham. He has co-authored *Being Urban: A Social Psychological View of City Life* (with Gregory P. Stone and David A. Karp), *Symbols, Selves, and Society: Understanding Interaction* (with Karp), and *Experiencing the Life Cycle* (with Karp).

Mark Zborowski was educated in France and is currently a medical anthropologist at the Pain Center of Mount Zion Hospital and Medical Center in San Francisco. He is also the author of *Life Is with People*.